KNOWLEDGE ENGINEERING
Building Cognitive Assistants for Evidence-Based Reasoning

This book presents a significant advancement in the theory and practice of knowledge engineering, the discipline concerned with the development of intelligent agents that use knowledge and reasoning to perform problem-solving and decision-making tasks. It covers the main stages in the development of a knowledge-based agent: understanding the application domain, modeling problem solving in that domain, developing the ontology, learning the reasoning rules, and testing the agent. The book focuses on a special class of agents: cognitive assistants for evidence-based reasoning that learn complex problem-solving expertise directly from human experts, support experts, and nonexperts in problem solving and decision making, and teach their problem-solving expertise to students.

A powerful learning agent shell, Disciple-EBR, is included with the book, enabling students, practitioners, and researchers to develop cognitive assistants rapidly in a wide variety of domains that require evidence-based reasoning, including intelligence analysis, cybersecurity, law, forensics, medicine, and education.

Gheorghe Tecuci (PhD, University of Paris-South, July 1988, and Polytechnic Institute of Bucharest, December 1988) is Professor of Computer Science and Director of the Learning Agents Center in the Volgenau School of Engineering of George Mason University, Member of the Romanian Academy, and former Chair of Artificial Intelligence in the Center for Strategic Leadership of the U.S. Army War College.

Dorin Marcu (PhD, George Mason University, 2009) is Research Assistant Professor, as well as Senior Software and Knowledge Engineer, in the Learning Agents Center, Volgenau School of Engineering, George Mason University.

Mihai Boicu (PhD, George Mason University, 2003) is Associate Professor of Information Sciences and Technology, and Associate Director of the Learning Agents Center, Volgenau School of Engineering, George Mason University.

David A. Schum (PhD, Ohio State University, 1964) is Emeritus Professor of Systems Engineering, Operations Research, and Law, as well as Chief Scientist of the Learning Agents Center at George Mason University. He is also Honorary Professor of Evidence Science at University College London.

Knowledge Engineering

Building Cognitive Assistants for Evidence-Based Reasoning

GHEORGHE TECUCI

George Mason University

DORIN MARCU

George Mason University

MIHAI BOICU

George Mason University

DAVID A. SCHUM

George Mason University

CAMBRIDGE
UNIVERSITY PRESS

Shaftesbury Road, Cambridge CB2 8EA, United Kingdom

One Liberty Plaza, 20th Floor, New York, NY 10006, USA

477 Williamstown Road, Port Melbourne, VIC 3207, Australia

314–321, 3rd Floor, Plot 3, Splendor Forum, Jasola District Centre, New Delhi – 110025, India

103 Penang Road, #05–06/07, Visioncrest Commercial, Singapore 238467

Cambridge University Press is part of Cambridge University Press & Assessment,
a department of the University of Cambridge.

We share the University's mission to contribute to society through the pursuit of
education, learning and research at the highest international levels of excellence.

www.cambridge.org
Information on this title: www.cambridge.org/9781107122567

First published 2016

A catalogue record for this publication is available from the British Library

Library of Congress Cataloging-in-Publication data
Names: Tecuci, Gheorghe, author. | Marcu, Dorin, author. | Boicu, Mihai, author. |
Schum, David A., author.
Title: Knowledge engineering: building cognitive assistants for evidence-based reasoning /
Gheorghe Tecuci, George Mason University, Dorin Marcu, George Mason University,
Mihai Boicu, George Mason University, David A. Schum, George Mason University.
Description: New York NY : Cambridge University Press, 2016. | Includes bibliographical references and index.
Identifiers: LCCN 2015042941 | ISBN 9781107122567 (Hardback : alk. paper)
Subjects: LCSH: Expert systems (Computer science) | Intelligent agents (Computer software) | Machine learning |
Artificial intelligence | Knowledge, Theory of–Data processing.
Classification: LCC QA76.76.E95 T435 2016 | DDC 006.3/3–dc23 LC record available at
http://lccn.loc.gov/2015042941

ISBN   978-1-107-12256-7   Hardback

Contents

Preface

BOOK PURPOSE

This is a book on knowledge engineering, the discipline concerned with the development of intelligent agents that use knowledge and reasoning to perform problem-solving and decision-making tasks. The book covers the theory and practice of the main stages in the development of a knowledge-based agent: understanding the application domain, modeling problem solving in that domain, developing the ontology, learning the reasoning rules, and testing the agent. However, it does this by focusing on a special class of agents: cognitive assistants that learn complex problem-solving expertise directly from human experts, support experts, and nonexperts in problem solving and decision making and teach their problem-solving expertise to students. These are learning agents that are taught by their users in ways that are similar to how a student, an apprentice, or a new collaborator is taught, through problem-solving examples and explanations and by supervising and correcting their behavior. Because such agents learn to replicate the problem-solving behavior of their users, we have called them Disciple agents.

This book presents a significant advancement in the theory and practice of knowledge engineering, where many tasks are performed by a typical computer user and a learning agent, with only limited support from a knowledge engineer. To simplify further the development of the cognitive assistants by typical users, we have focused on the development of cognitive assistants for evidence-based reasoning. Evidence-based reasoning is at the core of many problem-solving and decision-making tasks in a wide variety of domains, including intelligence analysis, cybersecurity, law, forensics, medicine, physics, chemistry, history, archaeology, education, and many others. Nevertheless, the last part of the book presents Disciple agents for applications that did not involve evidence-based reasoning.

Because knowledge engineering is a practical activity, it is best learned by doing. Therefore, this book presents the theory and methodology of developing cognitive assistants in conjunction with a practical tool, Disciple-EBR, a learning agent shell for evidence-based reasoning (EBR). Consequently, each chapter typically contains a theoretical part presenting general concepts and methods, a methodological part with guidelines on the application of the methods, and a practical part on the actual employment of these methods with Disciple-EBR. It also includes project assignments and review questions.

This book addresses issues of interest to a large spectrum of readers from academia, research, and industry. We have used drafts of this book in our computer science courses on knowledge engineering, expert systems, and knowledge-based agents, at both undergraduate and graduate levels, because it covers the theory and practice of the main stages in the development of knowledge-based agents. We have also used some parts of the book in introductory courses on artificial intelligence, and other parts in the courses on knowledge acquisition and machine learning. These are all examples of courses where this book could be used.

Researchers in knowledge engineering will find in this book an integrated approach that advances the theory and practice in the field. We believe that further research and development of this approach will enable typical computer users to develop their own cognitive assistants without any knowledge engineering assistance. Thus, non–computer scientists will no longer be only users of generic programs developed by others (such as word processors or Internet browsers), as they are today, but also agent developers themselves. They will be able to train their personal assistants to help them with their increasingly complex tasks in the knowledge society, which should have a significant beneficial impact on their work and life.

Practitioners that develop various types of knowledge-based systems will find in this book a detailed, yet intuitive, presentation of an agent development methodology and tool, as well as several case studies of developing intelligent agents that illustrate different types of agents that are relevant to a wide variety of application domains. In fact, a complementary book, *Intelligence Analysis as Discovery of Evidence, Hypotheses, and Arguments: Connecting the Dots* (Tecuci et al., 2016), presents the practical application of Disciple-CD, an agent developed with Disciple-EBR for intelligence analysis problems.

BOOK CONTENTS

Here is a route or map we will follow in the learning venture you will have with the assistance of Disciple-EBR. Chapter 1 is a general introduction to the topics that form the basis of this book. It starts with the problem of understanding the world through evidence-based reasoning. It then presents abductive reasoning, five different conceptions of probability (enumerative, subjective Bayesian, Belief Functions, Baconian, and Fuzzy), and how deductive, abductive, and inductive (probabilistic) reasoning are used in evidence-based reasoning. After that, it introduces artificial intelligence and intelligent agents, and the challenges of developing such agents through conventional knowledge engineering. Afterward, it introduces the development of agents through teaching and learning, which is the approach presented in this book.

Chapter 2 is an overview of evidence-based reasoning, which is a focus of this book. It starts with a discussion of the elements that make evidence-based reasoning an astonishingly complex task. It then introduces a systematic approach that integrates abduction, deduction, and induction to solve a typical evidence-based reasoning task, using intelligence analysis as an example. Finally, it shows the application of the same approach to other evidence-based reasoning tasks in cybersecurity, geospatial intelligence, and critical thinking education.

Chapter 3 is an overview of the main methodologies and tools for the design and development of knowledge-based agents. It first presents the conventional approach of developing such agents by a knowledge engineer working with a subject matter expert. It then introduces different types of agent shells, which are the typical tools for building agents, and discusses the use of foundational and utility ontologies. The more advanced of these tools, the learning agent shells, are at the basis of a new and more powerful approach to agent design and development, an overview of which is presented in the second part of Chapter 3. This learning-based approach is illustrated with the development of a cognitive assistant for assessing a potential PhD advisor for a student, an example that is used in the following chapters to present in detail each of the main agent development stages.

Chapter 4 presents the modeling of the problem-solving process through analysis and synthesis, which is the most challenging task in the development of a knowledge-based agent. This chapter starts with a more general version of this process for any type of problems, which is used in the Disciple agents presented in Chapter 12. After that, the chapter presents an easier, customized version for evidence-based hypothesis analysis, which is used in the chapters that follow. Chapter 4 also introduces an ontology of evidence and presents the modeling of the believability assessment for different types of evidence.

Chapters 5 and 6 present the representation of knowledge through ontologies, as well as their design and development. They discuss the representation of the objects from the agent's application domain and their relationships. These chapters also discuss the basic reasoning operations of transitivity, inheritance, and matching. They cover several approaches to concept elicitation, as well as a systematic approach to modeling-based ontology specification. The chapters also address the complexity of ontology maintenance.

Chapter 7 presents the agent's reasoning based on ontologies and rules, in the context of a production system architecture. It starts with defining the representation of complex ontology-based concepts and the use of these concepts in the reasoning rules. It defines the reduction and syntheses rules in general, and the special case of these rules for evidence-based reasoning. It then presents the process of problem solving through analysis and synthesis, which is accomplished through rule and ontology matching. This chapter also introduces the representation of and reasoning with partially learned concepts, features, hypotheses, and rules.

Chapter 8 starts with a general introduction to machine learning and to several learning strategies that are most relevant for knowledge engineering. It continues with the definition of the generalization and specializations of concepts through the use of inductive rules. After that, the chapter defines the basic operations of minimal and maximal generalizations and specialization of concepts, which are at the basis of rule learning and refinement discussed in Chapters 9 and 10. The chapter ends with the presentation of a formal definition of generalization.

Chapter 9 presents the mixed-initiative rule learning method that enables an agent to learn a general rule from a specific example of a reasoning step. It starts with an overview of the integration of modeling, learning, and problem solving and an illustration of this process. The chapter then introduces the rule learning problem and method. After that, it presents in detail the phases of rule learning, such as the mixed-initiative understanding of the example, and its analogy-based generalizations, which result in a minimal and a maximal generalization forming the plausible version space of the rule. This chapter also discusses the learning of rules involving functions and relational operators.

The refinement of a partially learned rule is presented in Chapter 10. After introducing the incremental rule refinement problem, this chapter presents the refinement of the rule based on positive examples, and then the refinement based on negative examples. This may result in a very complex rule characterized by a main applicability condition and several "except-when" conditions, which capture the reasoning of a subject matter expert. There are various refinement strategies, depending on the position of the examples with respect to the bounds of the rule's conditions and also on the possible explanations of these examples, but in all cases, they involve simple interactions with the subject matter expert. Changes in the ontology require the learned rules to be updated, the corresponding method being presented and illustrated in the second part of this chapter. The chapter ends with a characterization of rule learning and refinement, which enable a non–computer scientist to teach an agent.

The chapters dedicated to the individual phases of agent development end with Chapter 11, which discusses the abstractions of individual hypotheses and of the reasoning tree to facilitate its browsing, understanding, and further development by the end-user.

As previously indicated, this book focuses on the development of agents for evidence-based reasoning tasks. However, the presented theory and methodology are also applicable to other types of agents. These agents have been developed with learning agent shells representing previous implementations of the Disciple theory and methodology. Four of these agents are presented in Chapter 12. Disciple-WA is an agent that uses expert knowledge from military engineering manuals to develop alternative plans of actions that a military unit can use to work around (WA) damages to a transportation infrastructure, such as a damaged, destroyed, or mined bridge, road, or tunnel. The goal is to find the quickest way for the military unit to bypass the encountered obstacle. There were several cases where the Disciple-WA agent generated better solutions than those of the human expert who evaluated the developed systems, as well as cases where the agent generated new solutions that this expert did not consider.

Disciple-COA is an agent trained by a military expert to critique courses of action (COA) with respect to the principles of war and the tenets of Army operations. It receives as input the description of a course of action and returns a list of strengths and weaknesses of various levels, together with their justifications. A remarkable feature of this agent is that it was judged to exceed the performance of the subject matter experts that defined the problems for its evaluation.

Disciple-COG is an agent that was trained to identify and assess the center of gravity (COG) candidates of the opposing forces in a military scenario. Correctly identifying the centers of gravity of the opposing forces is of highest importance in any conflict, and Disciple-COG has been used for many years in courses at the U.S. Army War College, as well as at other military institutions, to teach students how to perform a strategic center-of-gravity analysis of a scenario of interest.

The last agent described in Chapter 12 is Disciple-VPT (Virtual Planning Team). Disciple-VPT consists of virtual planning experts that collaborate to develop plans of actions requiring expertise from multiple domains. They are assembled from an extensible library of such agents. The basic component of Disciple-VPT is the Disciple-VE learning agent shell that can be taught how to plan directly by a subject matter expert. Copies of the Disciple-VE shells can be used by experts in different domains to rapidly populate the library of virtual experts (VEs) of Disciple-VPT.

The learning-based approach to knowledge engineering presented in this book illustrates the application of several design principles that are useful in the development of cognitive assistants in general. Therefore, as a conclusion, Chapter 13 summarizes these principles, which are illustrated throughout this book.

The book also includes several appendices that summarize important aspects from the chapters: the list of the knowledge-engineering guidelines for each of the main stages of agent development, the list of operations of Disciple-EBR, and the list of the hands-on exercises. Answers to selected questions from each chapter are made available to the instructors.

BACKGROUND

The learning-based knowledge-engineering theory, methodology, and tools presented in this book are the result of many years of research and experimentation that produced increasingly more general and powerful versions. During this evolution, one may identify four main stages. The first stage corresponds to the PhD work of Gheorghe Tecuci presented in his thesis "Disciple: A Theory, Methodology and System for Learning Expert Knowledge" (Thèse de Docteur en Science, Université de Paris-Sud, July 1988). The main emphasis of that work was on rule learning. The developed methods are among the first multistrategy approaches to learning that later grew into the subfield of multistrategy machine learning (Tecuci, 1993; Michalski and Tecuci, 1994). They also are among the first attempts to integrate machine learning and knowledge acquisition (Tecuci et al., 1994; Tecuci and Kodratoff, 1995). This work benefited from the collaboration of Yves Kodratoff and the support of Mihai Drăgănescu. It was done with the support of the Romanian Research Institute for Informatics, the Romanian Academy, and the French National Center for Scientific Research.

The second stage in the evolution of the Disciple approach is presented in the book *Building Intelligent Agents: An Apprenticeship Multistrategy Learning Theory, Methodology, Tool and Case Studies*, published by Academic Press in 1998. It includes an improvement of Disciple's multistrategy learning methods and their extension with guided knowledge-elicitation methods. It also includes ontology development tools and illustrations of the application of the Disciple rule-learning approach to a variety of domains, such as teaching of higher-order thinking skills in history and statistics, engineering design, and military simulation. This work benefited from the collaboration of several of Tecuci's PhD students, particularly Thomas Dybala, Michael Hieb, Harry Keeling, and Kathryn Wright, and it was partially supported by George Mason University, the National Science Foundation, and the Defense Advanced Research Projects Agency.

The third stage in the evolution of the Disciple approach is represented by the Disciple agents described in Chapter 12 of this book. This represents a significant extension of the Disciple approach, with methods for problem solving through analysis and synthesis, modeling of the problem solving process, ontology development, and scenario elicitation. At this stage, Disciple has become a complete, end-to-end agent development methodology that has been applied to develop powerful agents, such as Disciple-COG, used for a period of ten years in courses at the U.S. Army War College and at other institutions. This work also benefited from the collaboration of Tecuci's students, first of all Mihai Boicu and Dorin Marcu, and also Michael Bowman, Vu Le, Cristina Boicu, Bogdan Stanescu, and Marcel Barbulescu. This work was partially supported by George Mason University, the Air Force Office of Scientific Research, the Air Force Research Laboratory, the Defense Advanced Research Projects Agency, the National Science Foundation, and others.

Finally, the latest stage in the evolution of the Disciple approach is represented by the rest of this book. A main conceptual advancement over the previous stage consists in its extension with a theory of evidence-based reasoning, greatly facilitated by the collaboration of David A. Schum. This resulted in a very powerful theory, methodology, and tool for the development of agents for complex evidence-based reasoning applications, such as intelligence analysis. Two of such agents are TIACRITIS (Teaching Intelligence Analysts Critical Thinking Skills) and Disciple-CD (Disciple cognitive assistant for Connecting the Dots). This work was partially supported by George Mason University and by several agencies of the U.S. government, including the Department of Defense.

Acknowledgments

We are very grateful to the many individuals who, in various ways, supported our research, including Kelcy Allwein, Cindy Ayers, Murray Burke, Douglas Campbell, William Cleckner, Jerry Comello, John Donelan, Jim Donlon, Susan Durham, Keri Eustis, Michael Fletcher, Erin Gibbens, Lloyd Griffiths, David Gunning, Ben Hamilton, Sharon Hamilton, Robert Herklotz, Phillip Hwang, Eric Jones, Alex Kilpatrick, David Luginbuhl, Joan McIntyre, Jean-Michel Pomrade, Michelle Quirk, Peter Rocci, William Rzepka, Kimberly Urban, Joan Vallancewhitacre, and Ben Wible.

We also want to thank Heather Bergman, who invited us to write this book for the Cambridge University Press, as well as to senior editor Lauren Cowles, who is a great professional to work with.

About the Authors

Gheorghe Tecuci (PhD, Université de Paris-Sud, July 1988, and Polytechnic Institute of Bucharest, December 1988) is Professor of Computer Science and Director of the Learning Agents Center in the Volgenau School of Engineering of George Mason University, Member of the Romanian Academy, and former Chair of Artificial Intelligence in the Center for Strategic Leadership of the U.S. Army War College. He has published around two hundred papers, including eleven books, with contributions to artificial intelligence, knowledge engineering, cognitive assistants, machine learning, evidence-based reasoning, and intelligence analysis. He has received the U.S. Army Outstanding Civilian Service Medal (for "groundbreaking contributions to the application of artificial intelligence to center of gravity determination") and the Innovative Application Award from the American Association for Artificial Intelligence.

Dorin Marcu (PhD, George Mason University, 2009) is Research Assistant Professor, as well as Senior Software and Knowledge Engineer, in the Learning Agents Center, Volgenau School of Engineering, George Mason University. He has published more than forty papers, including five books, with contributions to adaptive user interfaces, mixed-initiative human–computer interaction, and cognitive assistants. He has received the Innovative Application Award from the American Association for Artificial Intelligence.

Mihai Boicu (PhD, George Mason University, 2002) is Associate Professor of Information Sciences and Technology and Associate Director of the Learning Agents Center, in the Volgenau School of Engineering of George Mason University. He has published over ninety papers, including five books, with contributions to problem solving and multistrategy learning in dynamic and evolving representation spaces, mixed-initiative interaction, multi-agent systems architecture, collaboration and coordination, abstraction-based reasoning, knowledge representation, and knowledge acquisition. He has received the Innovative Application Award from the American Association for Artificial Intelligence.

David A. Schum (PhD, Ohio State University, 1964) is Emeritus Professor of Systems Engineering, Operations Research, and Law, as well as Chief Scientist of the Learning Agents Center at George Mason University, and Honorary Professor of Evidence Science at University College London.

He has followed a career-long interest in the study of the properties, uses, discovery, and marshaling of evidence in probabilistic reasoning. Dr. Schum has published more than one hundred papers in a variety of journals and eight books, including *The Evidential Foundations of Probabilistic Reasoning, Analysis of Evidence, Evidence and Inference for the Intelligence Analyst,* and *Probabilistic Analysis of the Sacco and Vanzetti Evidence,* being recognized as one of the founding fathers of the Science of Evidence.

1 Introduction

1.1 UNDERSTANDING THE WORLD THROUGH EVIDENCE-BASED REASONING

We can try to understand the world in various ways, an obvious one being the employment of empirical methods for gathering and analyzing various forms of evidence about phenomena, events, and situations of interest to us. This will include work in all of the sciences, medicine, law, intelligence analysis, history, political affairs, current events, and a variety of other contexts too numerous to mention. In the sciences, this empirical work will involve both experimental and nonexperimental methods. In some of these contexts, notably in the sciences, we are able to devise mathematical and logical models that allow us to make inferences and predictions about complex matters of interest to us. But in every case, our understanding rests on our knowledge of the properties, uses, discovery, and marshaling of evidence. This is why we begin this book with a careful consideration of reasoning based on evidence.

1.1.1 What Is Evidence?

You might think this question is unnecessary since everyone knows what evidence is. However, matters are not quite that simple, since the term *evidence* is not so easy to define and its use often arouses controversy. One problem with the definition of evidence is that several other terms are often used synonymously with it, when in fact there are distinctions to be made among these terms that are not always apparent. Quite unnecessary controversy occurs since some believe that the term *evidence* arises and has meaning only in the field of law.

Consulting a dictionary actually does not assist us much in defining the term. For example, look at the *Oxford English Dictionary* under the term *evidence* and you will be led in a circle; *evidence* is ultimately defined as being evidence.

A variety of terms are often used as synonyms for the term *evidence*: *data, items of information, facts,* and *knowledge*. When examined carefully, there are some valid and important distinctions to be made among these terms, as we will now discuss.

1.1.2 Evidence, Data, and Information

Consider the terms *data* and *items of information*.

Data are uninterpreted signals, raw observations, measurements, such as the number 6, the color "red," or the sequence of dots and lines "...–...".

Information is data equipped with meaning provided by a certain context, such as "6 AM," "red traffic light," "red tomato," or the "S O S" emergency alert.

Untold trillions of data and items of information exist that will almost certainly never become evidence in most inferences. Here's an item of information for you: Professor Schum has a long and steep driveway in front of his house that makes shoveling snow off of it very difficult in the winter. Can you think of any situation in which this item of information could become evidence? About the only matter in which this information could become interesting evidence involves the question: Why did Schum and his wife, Anne, ever purchase this house in the first place? As we will discuss, *items of information become evidence only when their relevance is established regarding some matter to be proved or disproved.*

1.1.3   Evidence and Fact

Now consider the term *fact*; there are some real troubles here as far as its relation to the term *evidence* is concerned. How many times have you heard someone say, "I want all the facts before I draw a conclusion or make a decision," or, "I want to know the facts in this matter"? The first question is easily answered: We will never have all the facts in any matter of inferential interest. Answers to the second question require a bit of careful thought. Here is an example of what is involved:

Suppose we are police investigators interviewing Bob, who is a witness of a car accident that just happened at a particular intersection. Bob tells us that the Ford car did not stop at the red light signal. Now we regard it as fact that Bob gave us this information: We all just heard him give it to us. But whether the Ford car did not stop at the red light *is only an inference and is not a fact.* This is precisely why we need to distinguish carefully between an *event* and *evidence* for this event.

Here is what we have: Bob has given us evidence E*, saying that event E occurred, where E is the event that the Ford car did not stop at the red light signal. Whether this event E did occur or not is open to question and depends on Bob's competence and credibility. If we take it as *fact* that event E did occur, just because Bob said it did, we would be overlooking the *believability* foundation for any inference we might make from his evidence E*. Unfortunately, it so often happens that people regard the events reported in evidence as being facts when they are not. Doing this suppresses all uncertainties we may have about the source's credibility and competence if the evidence is testimonial in nature. We have exactly the same concerns about the credibility of tangible evidence. For example, we have been given a tangible object or an image as evidence E* that we believe reveals the occurrence of event E. But we must consider whether this object or image is authentic and it is what we believe it to be. In any case, the events recorded in evidence can be regarded as facts only if provided by perfectly credible sources, something we almost never have. As another example, any information we find on the Internet should be considered as only a claim by its source rather than as fact, that is, as *evidence* about a potential fact rather than a *fact*.

1.1.4   Evidence and Knowledge

Now consider the term *knowledge* and its relation with evidence. Here is where things get interesting and difficult. As you know, *the field of epistemology is the study of knowledge, what we believe it may be, and how we obtain it.* Two questions we would normally ask regarding what Bob just told us are as follows:

- Does Bob really *know* what he just told us, that the Ford car did not stop at the red light signal?
- Do we ourselves then also *know*, based on Bob's testimony, that the Ford car did not stop at the red light signal?

Let's consider the first question. For more than two millennia, some very learned people have troubled over the question: What do we mean when we say that person A *knows* that event B occurred? To apply this question to our source Bob, let's make an assumption that will simplify our answering this question. Let's assume that Bob is a *competent* observer in this matter. Suppose we have evidence that Bob was actually himself at the intersection when the accident happened. This is a major element of Bob's competence. Bob's credibility depends on different matters, as we will see.

Here is what a standard or conventional account says about whether Bob knows that the car did not stop at the red light signal. First, here is a general statement of the standard account of knowledge: *Knowledge is justified true belief.* Person $\mathcal{A}$ knows that event B occurred if:

- Event B did occur [True];
- $\mathcal{A}$ got nondefective evidence that B occurred [Justified]; and
- $\mathcal{A}$ believed this evidence [Belief].

This standard analysis first says that event B must have occurred for $\mathcal{A}$ to have knowledge of its occurrence. This is what makes $\mathcal{A}$'s belief true. If B did not occur, then $\mathcal{A}$ could not know that it occurred. Second, $\mathcal{A}$'s getting nondefective evidence that B occurred is actually where $\mathcal{A}$'s competence arises. $\mathcal{A}$ could not have gotten any evidence, defective or nondefective, if $\mathcal{A}$ was not where B could have occurred. Then, $\mathcal{A}$ believed the evidence $\mathcal{A}$ received about the occurrence of event B, and $\mathcal{A}$ was justified in having this belief by obtaining nondefective evidence of B's occurrence.

So, in the case involving Bob's evidence, Bob knows that the Ford car did not stop at the red light signal if:

- The car did not stop at the red light signal,
- Bob got nondefective evidence that the car did not stop at the red signal, and
- Bob believed this evidence.

If all of these three things are true, we can state on this standard analysis that Bob knows that the Ford car did not stop at the red light signal.

Before we proceed, we must acknowledge that this standard analysis has been very controversial in fairly recent years and some philosophers claim to have found alleged paradoxes and counterexamples associated with it. Other philosophers dispute these claims. Most of the controversy here concerns the justification condition: What does it mean to say that A is justified in believing that B occurred? In any case, we have found this standard analysis very useful as a heuristic in our analyses of the credibility of testimonial evidence.

But now we have several matters to consider in answering the second question: Do we ourselves also *know*, based on Bob's testimony, that the Ford car did not stop at the red light signal? The first and most obvious fact is that we do not know the extent to which any of the three events just described in the standard analysis are true. We cannot get inside

Bob's head to obtain necessary answers about these events. Starting at the bottom, we do not know for sure that Bob believes what he just told us about the Ford car not stopping at the red light signal. This is a matter of Bob's *veracity* or *truthfulness*. We would not say that Bob is being truthful if he told us something he did not believe.

Second, we do not know what sensory evidence Bob obtained on which to base his belief and whether he based his belief at all on this evidence. Bob might have believed that the Ford car did not stop at the red light signal either because he expected or desired this to be true. This involves Bob's *objectivity* as an observer. We would not say that Bob was objective in this observation if he did not base his belief on the sensory evidence he obtained in his observation.

Finally, even if we believe that Bob was an objective observer who based his belief about the accident on sensory evidence, we do not know how good this evidence was. Here we are obliged to consider Bob's sensory *sensitivities or accuracy in the conditions under which Bob made his observations*. Here we consider such obvious things as Bob's visual acuity. But there are many other considerations, such as, "Did Bob only get a fleeting look at the accident when it happened?" "Is Bob color-blind?" "Did he make this observation during a storm?" and, "What time of day did he make this observation?" For a variety of such reasons, Bob might simply have been mistaken in his observation: The light signal was not red when the Ford car entered the intersection.

So, what it comes down to is that the extent of our knowledge about whether the Ford car did not stop at the red light signal, based on Bob's evidence, depends on these three attributes of Bob's credibility: his veracity, objectivity, and observational sensitivity. We will have much more to say about assessing the credibility of sources of evidence, and how Disciple-EBR can assist you in this difficult process, in Section 4.7 of this book.

Now, we return to our role as police investigators. Based on evidence we have about Bob's competence and credibility, suppose we believe that the event he reports did occur; we believe that "E: The Ford car did not stop at the red light signal," did occur. Now we face the question: So what? Why is knowledge of event E of importance to us? Stated more precisely: How is event E relevant in further inferences we must make? In our investigation so far, we have other evidence besides Bob's testimony. In particular, we observe a Toyota car that has smashed into a light pole at this intersection, injuring the driver of the Toyota, who was immediately taken to a hospital. In our minds, we form the tentative chain of reasoning from Figure 1.1.

This sequence of events, E → F → G → H, is a relevance argument or chain of reasoning whose links represent sources of doubt interposed between the evidence E* and the hypothesis H. An important thing to note is that some or all of these events may not be true. Reducing our doubts or uncertainties regarding any of these events requires a variety

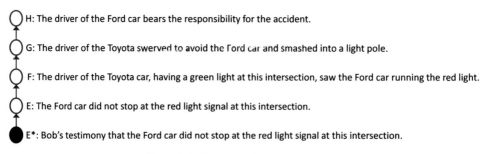

H: The driver of the Ford car bears the responsibility for the accident.

G: The driver of the Toyota swerved to avoid the Ford car and smashed into a light pole.

F: The driver of the Toyota car, having a green light at this intersection, saw the Ford car running the red light.

E: The Ford car did not stop at the red light signal at this intersection.

E*: Bob's testimony that the Ford car did not stop at the red light signal at this intersection.

Figure 1.1. Tentative chain of reasoning.

of additional evidence. The extent of our knowledge about the relative probabilities of our final hypothesis depends on the believability of our evidence and on the defensibility and strength of our relevance arguments, as discussed in Section 2.2. The whole point here is that the relation between evidence and knowledge is not a simple one at all.

1.1.5 Ubiquity of Evidence

Finally, we must consider the controversy over the use of the term *evidence* instead of the other terms we just examined. The mistake made by some people is to consider that evidence concerns only objects, testimony, or other items introduced in a court trial. This controversy and confusion has been recognized by eminent evidence scholars in the field of law. For example, in his marvelous book *Evidence, Proof, and Facts: A Book of Sources*, Professor Peter Murphy (2003, p. 1) notes the curious fact that the term evidence is so commonly associated only with the field of law:

> The word "evidence" is associated more often with lawyers and judicial trials than with any other cross-section of society or form of activity. ... In its simplest sense, evidence may be defined as any factual datum which in some manner assists in drawing conclusions, either favorable or unfavorable, to some hypothesis whose proof or refutation is being attempted.

Murphy notes that this term is appropriate in any field in which conclusions are reached from any relevant datum. Thus, physicians, scientists of any ilk, historians, and persons of any other conceivable discipline, as well as ordinary persons, use evidence every day in order to draw conclusions about matters of interest to them.

We believe there is a very good reason why many persons are so often tempted to associate the term *evidence* only with the field of law. It happens that the Anglo-American system of laws has provided us with by far the richest legacy of experience and scholarship on evidence of any field known to us. This legacy has arisen as a result of the development of the adversarial system for settling disputes and the gradual emergence of the jury system, in which members of the jury deliberate on evidence provided by external witnesses. This legacy has now been accumulating over at least the past six hundred years (Anderson et al., 2005).

Evidence-based reasoning involves abductive, deductive, and inductive (probabilistic) reasoning. The following sections briefly introduce them.

1.2 ABDUCTIVE REASONING

1.2.1 From Aristotle to Peirce

Throughout history, some of the greatest minds have tried to understand the world through a process of discovery and testing of hypotheses based on evidence. We have found the metaphor of an *arch of knowledge* to be very useful in summarizing the many ideas expressed over the centuries concerning the generation of new thoughts and new evidence. This metaphor comes from the work of the philosopher David Oldroyd in a valuable work having this metaphor as its title (Oldroyd, 1986). Figure 1.2 shows this metaphor applied in the context of science. Based upon existing records, it seems that

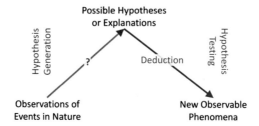

Figure 1.2. The "arch of knowledge" in science.

Aristotle (384 BC–322 BC) was the first to puzzle about the generation or discovery of new ideas in science. From sensory observations, we generate possible explanations, in the form of hypotheses, for these observations. It was never clear from Aristotle's work what label should be placed on the upward, or discovery-related, arm of the arch in Figure 1.2. By some accounts, Aristotle's description of this act of generating hypotheses is called "intuitive induction" (Cohen and Nagel, 1934; Kneale, 1949). The question mark on the upward arm of the arch in Figure 1.2 simply indicates that there is still argument about what this discovery-related arm should be called. By most accounts, the downward arm of the arch concerns the deduction of new observable phenomena, assuming the truth of a generated hypothesis (Schum, 2001b).

Over the millennia since Aristotle, many people have tried to give an account of the process of discovering hypotheses and how this process differs from ones in which existing hypotheses are justified. Galileo Galilei (1564–1642) thought that we "reason backward" inductively to imagine causes (hypotheses) from observed events, and we reason deductively to test the hypotheses. A similar view was held by Isaac Newton (1642–1727), John Locke (1632–1704), and William Whewell (1794–1866). Charles S. Peirce (1839–1914) was the first to suggest that new ideas or hypotheses are generated through a different form of reasoning, which he called *abduction* and associated with imaginative reasoning (Peirce, 1898; 1901). His views are very similar to those of Sherlock Holmes, the famous fictional character of Conan Doyle (Schum, 1999).

1.2.2   Peirce and Sherlock Holmes on Abductive Reasoning

Until the time of Peirce, most persons interested in discovery and investigation supposed that the discovery-related arms of the arch in Figure 1.2 involved some form of inductive reasoning that proceeds from particulars, in the form of observations, to generalities, in the form of hypotheses. But inductive reasoning is commonly associated with the process of justifying or trying to prove existing hypotheses based on evidence. The question remains: Where did these hypotheses come from? Pondering such matters, Peirce relied on a figure of reasoning he found in the works of Aristotle. The reasoning proceeds as follows:

- If H were true, then E, F, and G would follow as a matter of course.
- But E, F, and G have been observed.
- Therefore, we have reason to believe that H *might possibly* be true.

As an illustration, let us assume that we observe E*: "Smoke in the East building" (E* being evidence that event E occurred).

Based on our prior knowledge of contexts in which things like E: "Smoke in a building" have occurred, we say: "Whenever something like H: 'There is fire in a building' has occurred, then something like E: 'Smoke in the building' has also occurred." Thus, there is reason to suspect that H: "There is fire in the East building" may explain the occurrence of the clue E*: "Smoke in the East building." In other words, the clue E* points to H as a possible explanation for its occurrence.

To summarize:

- We observe smoke in the East building.
- Fire causes smoke.
- We hypothesize that there is a fire in the East building.

Peirce was unsure about what to call this form of reasoning. At various points in his work, he called it "abduction," "retroduction," and even just "hypothesis" (Pierce, 1898; 1901).

The essential interpretation Peirce placed on the concept of abduction is illustrated in Figure 1.3. He often used as a basis for his discussions of abduction the observation of an anomaly in science. Let us suppose that we already have a collection of prior evidence in some investigation and an existing collection of hypotheses H_1, H_2, ... , H_n. To varying degrees, these n hypotheses explain the evidence we have so far. But now we make an observation E* that is embarrassing in the following way: We take E* seriously, but we cannot explain it by any of the hypotheses we have generated so far. In other words, E* is an anomaly. Vexed by this anomaly, we try to find an explanation for it. In some cases, often much later when we are occupied by other things, we experience a "flash of insight" in which it occurs to us that a new hypothesis H_{n+1} could explain this anomaly E*. It is these "flashes of insight" that Peirce associated with abduction. Asked at this moment to say exactly how H_{n+1} explains E*, we may be unable to do so. However, further thought may produce a chain of reasoning that plausibly connects H_{n+1} and E*. The reasoning might go as follows:

- I have evidence E* that event E happened.
- If E did happen, then F might be true.
- If F happened, then G might be true.
- And if G happened, then H_{n+1} might be true.

It is possible, of course, that the chain of reasoning might have started at the top with H_{n+1} and ended at E*. This is why we have shown no direction on the links between E* and H_{n+1} in Figure 1.3.

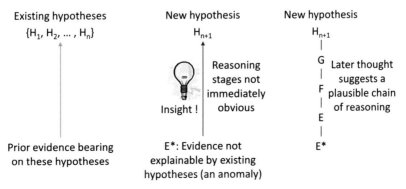

Figure 1.3. Peirce's interpretation of abductive reasoning.

But our discovery-related activities are hardly over just because we have explained this anomaly. Our new hypothesis H_{n+1} would not be very appealing if it explained only anomaly E*. Figure 1.4 shows the next steps in our use of this new hypothesis. We first inquire about the extent to which it explains the prior evidence we collected before we observed E*. An important test of the suitability of the new hypothesis H_{n+1} involves asking how well this new hypothesis explains other observations we have taken seriously. This new hypothesis would be especially valuable if it explains our prior evidence better than any of our previously generated hypotheses. But there is one other most important test of the adequacy of a new hypothesis H_{n+1}: How well does this new hypothesis suggest new potentially observable evidence that our previous hypotheses did not suggest? If H_{n+1} would be true, then B, I, and K would also be true; and if B would be true, then C would be true. Now if C would be true, then we would need to observe D.

In the illustrations Peirce used, which are shown in Figures 1.3 and 1.4, we entered the process of discovery at an intermediate point when we already had existing hypotheses and evidence. In other contexts, we must of course consider abductive reasoning from the beginning of an episode of fact investigation when we have no hypotheses and no evidence bearing on them. Based on our initial observations, by this process of abductive or insightful reasoning, we may generate initial guesses or hypotheses to explain even the very first observations we make. Such hypotheses may of course be vague, imprecise, or undifferentiated. Further observations and evidence we collect may allow us to make an initial hypothesis more precise and may of course suggest entirely new hypotheses.

It happens that at the very same time Peirce was writing about abductive reasoning, insight, and discovery, across the Atlantic, Arthur Conan Doyle was exercising his fictional character Sherlock Holmes in many mystery stories. At several points in the Sherlock Holmes stories, Holmes describes to his colleague, Dr. Watson, his inferential strategies during investigation. These strategies seem almost identical to the concept of abductive reasoning described by Peirce. Holmes did not, of course, describe his investigative reasoning as abductive. Instead, he said his reasoning was "backward," moving from his observations to possible explanations for them. A very informative and enjoyable collection of papers on the connection between Peirce and Sherlock Holmes appears in the work of Umberto Eco and Thomas Sebeok (1983). In spite of the similarity of Peirce's and Holmes's (Conan Doyle's) views of discovery-related reasoning, there is no evidence that Peirce and Conan Doyle ever shared ideas on the subject.

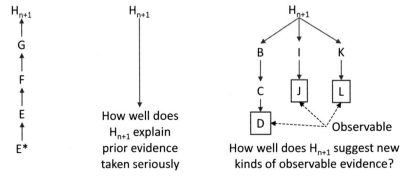

Figure 1.4. Putting an abduced hypothesis to work.

1.3   PROBABILISTIC REASONING

A major trouble we all face in thinking about probability and uncertainty concerns the fact that the necessity for probability calculations, estimations, or judgments arises in different situations. In addition, there are many different attributes of our judgments that we would like to capture in assessments of uncertainty we are obliged to make. There are situations in which you can estimate probabilities of interest by counting things. But there are many other situations in which we have uncertainty but will have nothing to count. These situations involve events that are singular, unique, or one of a kind. In the following, we will briefly discuss several alternative views of probability, starting with two views of probability that involve processes in which we can obtain probabilities or estimates of them by enumerative or counting processes.

1.3.1   Enumerative Probabilities: Obtained by Counting

1.3.1.1 Aleatory Probability

According to Laplace (1814, p. cv), "probability theory is nothing but common sense reduced to calculation." There are two conceptions of probability that involve counting operations. The first is termed *aleatory probability*. This term has its roots in the Latin term *alea,* meaning chance, game of chance, or devices such as dice involved in games of chance. Games of chance have two important ground rules:

- There is a finite number $n(S)$ of possible outcomes
- All outcomes in S are assumed to have equal probability

For example, in a game involving a pair of fair six-sided dice, where we roll and add the two numbers showing up, there are thirty-six ways in which the numbers showing up will have sums between two and twelve, inclusive. So, in this case, $n(S) = 36$. Suppose you wish to determine the probability that you will roll a seven on a single throw of these dice. There are exactly six ways in which this can happen. If E = "the sum of the numbers is seven," then $n(E) = 6$. The probability of E, $P(E)$, is simply determined by dividing $n(E)$ by $n(S)$, which in this example is $P(E) = 6/36 = 1/6$. So, aleatory probabilities are always determined by dividing $n(E)$ by $n(S)$, whatever E and S are, as long as E is a subset of S.

1.3.1.2 Relative Frequency and Statistics

Another way of assessing probabilities involves the many situations in which aleatory ground rules will not apply, but empirical methods are at hand to estimate probabilities. These situations arise when we have *replicable* or *repeatable* processes in which we can count the number of times events have occurred in the past. Suppose that, employing a defensible method for gathering information about the number of times event E has occurred, we determine the *relative frequency* of an occurrence of E by counting the number of times E has occurred, $n(E)$, and then dividing this number by N, where N is the number of observations we have made, or the sample size we have taken. In this case, the relative frequency of E, $f(E)$, equals $n(E)/N$. You recognize that this is a *statistical process* that can be performed in many situations, provided that we assume processes that are replicable or repeatable. It is true, of course, that a relative frequency $f(E)$ is just an estimate of the true probability of E, P(E). The reason, of course, is that the number N of observations we have made is always less than the total number of observations that could be made. In some cases, there may be an infinite number of possible observations. If you have had a course in probability theory, you will remember that there are several formal statements, called the *laws of large numbers*, for showing how f(E) approaches P(E) when N is made larger and larger.

Probability theory presents an interesting paradox. It has a very long history but a very short past. There is abundant evidence that people as far back as Paleolithic times used objects resembling dice either for gambling or, more likely, to foretell the future (David, 1962). But attempts to calculate probabilities date back only to the 1600s, and the first attempt to develop a theory of mathematical probability dates back only to 1933 in the work of A. N. Kolmogorov (1933). Kolmogorov was the first to put probability on an axiomatic basis. The three basic axioms he proposed are the following ones:

Axiom 1: *For any event E, P(E) ≥ 0.*
Axiom 2: *If an event is sure or certain to occur, which we label S, P(S) = 1.0.*
Axiom 3: *If two events, E and F, cannot occur together, or are mutually exclusive, the probability that one or the other of these events occurring is the sum of their separate probabilities. In symbols, P(E or F) = P(E) + P(F).*

All Axiom 1 says is that probabilities are never negative. Axioms 1 and 2, taken together, mean that probabilities are numbers between 0 and 1. An event having 0 probability is commonly called an "impossible event." Axiom 3 is called the *additivity* axiom, and it holds for any number of mutually exclusive events.

Certain transformations of Kolmogorov's probabilities are entirely permissible and are often used. One common form involves *odds*. The odds of event E occurring to its not occurring, which we label Odds(E, ¬E), is determined by Odds(E, ¬E) = P(E)/(1 − P(E)). For any two mutually exclusive events E and F, the odds of E to F, Odds(E, F), are given by Odds (E, F) = P(E)/P(F). Numerical odds scales range from zero to an unlimited upper value.

What is very interesting, but not always recognized, is that Kolmogorov had only enumerative probability in mind when he settled on the preceding three axioms. He makes this clear in his 1933 book and in his later writings (Kolmogorov, 1969). It is easily shown that both aleatory probabilities and relative frequencies obey these three axioms. But Kolmogorov went an important step further in defining conditional probabilities that are necessary to show how the probability of an event may change as we learn new information. He defined the probability of event E, given or conditional upon some other event F, as P(E given F) = P(E and F)/P(F), assuming that P(F) is not zero. P(E given F) is also written as P(E|F). He chose this particular definition since conditional probabilities, so defined, will also obey the three axioms just mentioned. In other words, we do not need any new axioms for conditional probabilities.

Now comes a very important concept you may have heard about. It is called *Bayes' rule* and results directly from applying the definition of the conditional probability. From P(E* and H) = P(H and E*), you obtain P(E*|H) P(H) = P(H|E*)P(E*). This can then be written as shown in Figure 1.5.

This rule is named after the English clergyman, the Reverend Thomas Bayes (1702–1761), who first saw the essentials of a rule for revising probabilities of hypotheses, based on new evidence (Dale, 2003). He had written a paper describing his derivation and use of this rule but he never published it; this paper was found in his desk after he died in 1761 by Richard

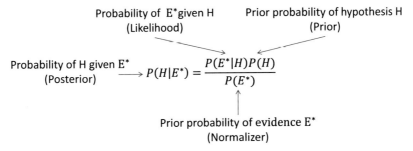

Figure 1.5. The Bayes' rule.

Price, the executor of Bayes' will. Price realized the importance of Bayes' paper and recommended it for publication in the *Transactions of the Royal Society*, in which it appeared in 1763. He rightly viewed Bayes' rule as the first canon or rule for inductive or probabilistic reasoning. Bayes' rule follows directly from Kolmogorov's three axioms and his definition of a conditional probability, and is entirely uncontroversial as far as its derivation is concerned. But this rule has always been a source of controversy on other grounds. The reason is that it requires us to say how probable a hypothesis is before we have gathered evidence that will possibly allow us to revise this probability. In short, we need *prior probabilities* on hypotheses in order to revise them, when they become *posterior probabilities*. Persons wedded to enumerative conceptions of probability say we can never have prior probabilities of hypotheses, since in advance of data collection we have nothing to count. Statisticians are still divided today about whether it makes sense to use Bayes' rule in statistical inferences. Some statisticians argue that initial prior probabilities could be assessed only subjectively and that any subjective assessments have no place in any area that calls itself scientific. Bayes' rule says that if we are to talk about probability *revisions* in our beliefs, based on evidence, we have to say where these beliefs were *before* we obtained the evidence.

The Bayes' rule is useful in practice because there are many cases where we have good probability estimates for three of the four probabilities involved, and we can therefore compute the fourth one (see, e.g., Question 1.9).

It is time for us to consider views of probability in situations where we will have nothing to count, either a priori or anywhere else: the *Subjective Bayesian* view, *Belief Functions*, *Baconian probabilities*, and *Fuzzy probabilities*. We provide a look at only the essentials of these four views, focusing on what each one has to tell us about what the force or weight of evidence on some hypothesis means. More extensive comparisons of these four views appear in (Schum, 1994 [2001a], pp. 200–269).

1.3.2 Subjective Bayesian View of Probability

We refer to our first nonenumerative view as an *epistemic view*, since it assumes that probabilities in any case are based on some kind of knowledge, *whatever form it may take*. In short, probabilities are the result of informed judgments. Many statisticians now favor the use of Bayes' rule for combining subjective assessments of all the prior and likelihood ingredients of Bayes' rule. *But what these persons require is that these assessments be entirely consistent with Kolmogorov's three axioms and his definition of conditional probabilities we previously noted.* Since Bayes' rule rests on these axioms and definition, we must adhere to them in order to say that our assessment process is coherent or consistent.

As we will show, the likelihoods and their ratios are the ingredients of Bayes' rule that concern the inferential force of evidence. Suppose we have two hypotheses, H and $\neg H$, and a single item of evidence, E^*, saying that event E occurred. What we are interested in determining are the posterior probabilities: $P(H|E^*)$ and $P(\neg H|E^*)$. Using the Bayes' rule from Figure 1.5, we can express these posterior probabilities as:

$$P(H|E^*) = \frac{P(E^*|H)P(H)}{P(E^*)}$$

$$P(\neg H|E^*) = \frac{P(E^*|\neg H)P(\neg H)}{P(E^*)}$$

The next step is to divide $P(H|E^*)$ by $P(\neg H|E^*)$, which will produce three ratios; in the process the term $P(E^*)$ will drop out. Here are the three ratios that result:

$$\frac{P(H|E^*)}{P(\neg H|E^*)} = \frac{P(H)}{P(\neg H)} \frac{P(E^*|H)}{P(E^*|\neg H)}$$

The left-hand ratio $\frac{P(H|E^*)}{P(\neg H|E^*)}$ is called the *posterior odds* of H to $\neg H$, given evidence E^*. In symbols, we can express this ratio as $Odds(H : \neg H|E^*)$. The first ratio on the right, $\frac{P(H)}{P(\neg H)}$, is called the *prior odds* of H to $\neg H$. In symbols, we can express this ratio as $Odds(H : \neg H)$. The remaining ratio on the right, $\frac{P(E^*|H)}{P(E^*|\neg H)}$, is called the *likelihood ratio* for evidence E^*; we give this ratio the symbol L_{E^*}. In terms of these three ratios, Bayes' rule applied to this situation can be written simply as follows:

$$Odds(H : \neg H|E^*) = Odds(H : \neg H)L_{E^*}$$

This simple version of Bayes' rule is called the *odds-likelihood ratio* form. It is also called, somewhat unkindly, "idiot's Bayes." If we divide both sides of this equation by the prior odds, $Odds(H : \neg H)$, we observe that the likelihood ratio L_{E^*} is simply the ratio of posterior odds to prior odds of H to $\neg H$. This likelihood ratio shows us how much, and in what direction (toward H or $\neg H$), our evidence E^* has caused us to change our beliefs from what they were before we obtained evidence E^*. In short, likelihood ratios grade the force of evidence in Bayesian analyses.

Here is an example of how likelihoods and their ratios provide a method for grading the force of an item of evidence on some hypothesis. This is an example of a situation involving a singular evidence item where we have nothing to count. Suppose we are interested in determining whether or not the Green state is supplying parts necessary for the construction of shaped explosive devices to a certain insurgent militia group in the neighboring Orange state. Thus we are considering two hypotheses:

- H: "The Greens are supplying parts necessary for the construction of shaped explosive devices."
- ¬H: "The Greens are not supplying parts necessary for the construction of shaped explosive devices."

Suppose we believe, before we have any evidence, that the prior probability of H is $P(H) = 0.20$. Because we must obey the rules for enumerative probabilities, we must also say that $P(\neg H) = 0.80$. This follows from the third axiom we discussed in Section 1.3.1. So, our prior odds on H relative to $\neg H$ have a value $Odds(H : \neg H) = \frac{P(H)}{P(\neg H)} = \frac{0.20}{0.80} = \frac{1}{4}$.

Suppose now that we receive the item of evidence E^* : A member of the Green's military was captured less than one kilometer away from a location in Orange at which parts necessary for the construction of these shaped explosives were found.

We ask ourselves how likely is this evidence E^* if H were true, and how likely is this evidence E^* if H were not true. Suppose we say that $P(E^*|H) = 0.80$ and $P(E^*|\neg H) = 0.10$. We are saying that this evidence is eight times more likely if H were true than if H were not true. So, our likelihood ratio for evidence E^* is $L_{E^*} = \frac{P(E^*|H)}{P(E^*|\neg H)} = \frac{0.8}{0.1} = 8$.

We now have all the ingredients necessary in Bayes' rule to determine the posterior odds and posterior probability of hypothesis H:

$$Odds(H : \neg H|E^*) = Odds(H : \neg H)L_{E^*} = \frac{1}{4} \times 8 = 2.$$

This means that we now believe the posterior odds favoring H over $\neg H$ are two to one. But we started by believing that the prior odds of H to $\neg H$ were one in four, so the evidence E^* changed our belief by a factor of 8.

We could just as easily express this inference in terms of probabilities. Our prior probability of H was $P(H) = 0.20$. But our posterior probability $P(H|E^*) = \frac{2}{1+2} = \frac{2}{3} = 0.67$. So, in terms of probabilities, evidence E^* caused us to increase the probability of H by 0.47.

So, using this subjective Bayesian approach, we would be entitled to express the extent of our uncertainty in an analysis *using numerical probability assessments* provided only that they conform to Kolmogorov's axioms.

1.3.3   Belief Functions

Both the enumerative and the subjective Bayesian interpretations of probability conform to Kolmogorov's three axioms. We asserted that these axioms rest on the investigation of replicable or repeatable processes such as statistical analysis of the results obtained in a sample of observations. But there are many reasons for wondering whether these three axioms remain self-evident concerning subjective probability judgments we all make from time to time involving unique events for which no enumerative process can be involved. In a very influential work, the probabilist Professor Glenn Shafer pointed to an array of difficulties associated with Axiom 3 concerning the additivity of enumerative probabilities for mutually exclusive events (Shafer, 1976). In particular, Shafer asserts that this axiom places various constraints on our judgments or beliefs about uncertainty that we may not be willing to accept. Here it is only necessary to mention two of the difficulties Shafer mentions:

- Indecisions we routinely face concerning ambiguities in our evidence
- Instances in which we encounter what historically has been called "pure" evidence

In so many instances, we may not be sure what evidence is telling us, and so we wish to be able to *withhold* a portion of our beliefs and not commit it to any particular hypothesis or possible conclusion. A very important element in what Shafer terms *Belief Functions* is that the *weight of evidence means the degree of support* evidence provides to hypotheses we are considering. Shafer allows that we can grade the degree of support **s** on a 0 to 1 scale similar to the scale for Kolmogorov probabilities; but we can do things with support assignment **s** that the Kolmogorov additivity Axiom 3 does not allow.

To illustrate, suppose we revisit the issue discussed in the previous section about whether or not the Green state is supplying parts necessary for the construction of shaped explosive devices to a certain insurgent militia group in the neighboring Orange state. At some stage, we are required to state our beliefs about the extent to which the evidence supports H or $\neg H$. Here is our assessment:

	{H}	{¬H}	{H or ¬H}
s	0.5	0.3	0.2

What does this support assignment mean? We are saying that we believe the evidence supports H exactly to degree **s** = 0.5, and that this evidence also supports $\neg H$ exactly to degree **s** = 0.3. But there is something about this evidence that makes us unsure about whether it supports H or $\neg H$. So, we have left the balance of our **s** assignment, **s** = 0.2, *uncommitted among H or ¬H*. In other words, we have withheld a portion of our beliefs because we are not sure what some element of our evidence is telling us.

If we were required to obey Kolmogorov Axiom 3, we would not be allowed to be indecisive in any way in stating our beliefs. Here is what our support assignment would have to look like:

	{H}	{¬H}
s	a	1−a

In this case, we would be required to say that the evidence supports H to degree **s** = a, and supports $\neg H$ to degree **s** = (1 – a) in agreement with Axiom 3 since H and $\neg H$ are mutually exclusive and exhaustive. In short, Kolmogorov Axiom 3 does not permit us any indecision in stating our beliefs; we must commit all of it to H and to $\neg H$. This, we believe, would not be a faithful or accurate account of our beliefs.

But Shafer's Belief Function approach allows us to cope with another difficulty associated with Kolmogorov's axioms. For centuries, it has been recognized that a distinction is necessary between what has been termed *mixed evidence* and *pure evidence. Mixed evidence has some degree of probability under every hypothesis we are considering.* But *pure evidence may support one hypothesis but say nothing at all about other hypotheses.* In other words, we may encounter evidence that we believe offers zero support for some hypothesis. Here is another example involving our Green-Orange situation. Suppose we encounter an item of evidence we believe supports H to a degree, but we believe offers no support at all for $\neg H$. Here is our support assignment **s** for this evidence:

	{H}	{¬H}	{H or ¬H}
s	0.5	0	0.5

In this situation, we are saying that the evidence supports H to degree **s** = 0.5, but offers no support at all to $\neg H$. The rest of our support we leave uncommitted between H and $\neg H$. But now we have to examine what **s** = 0 for $\neg H$ means; does it mean that $\neg H$ could not be supported by further evidence? The answer is *no*, and the reason why it is no allows us to compare what ordinary probabilities mean in comparison with what support **s** means. This comparison is shown in Figure 1.6.

The (a) scale in Figure 1.6, for conventional or Kolmogorov probabilities, has a lower boundary with a meaning quite different from the meaning of this lower boundary on Shafer's support scale shown in (b). The value 0 in conventional probability refers to an event judged to be impossible and one you completely disbelieve. But all 0 means on Shafer's **s** scale is *lack of belief*, not disbelief. This is very important, since we can go from lack of belief to some belief as we gather more evidence. But we cannot go from disbelief to some belief. On a conventional probability scale, a hypothesis once assigned the probability value 0 can never be resuscitated by further evidence, regardless of how strong it may be. But some hypothesis, assigned the value **s** = 0, can be revised upward since we can go from lack of belief to some belief in this hypothesis when and if we have some further evidence to support it. Thus, **s** allows us to account for pure evidence in ways that ordinary probabilities cannot do. We will refer to this scale again in Section 1.3.4 when discussing Baconian probability.

Consider the evidence in the dirty bomb example which will be discussed in Section 2.2. We begin by listing the hypotheses we are considering at this moment:

> H_1: A dirty bomb will be set off somewhere in the Washington, D.C., area.
> $\neg H_1$: A dirty bomb will not be set off in the Washington, D.C., area (it might be set off somewhere else or not at all).

In the Belief Functions approach, we have just specified what is called a *frame of discernment*, in shorthand a *frame F*. What this frame $F = \{H_1, \neg H_1\}$ shows is how we are viewing our hypotheses right now. We might, on further evidence, wish to revise our frame in any one of a variety of ways. For example, we might have evidence suggesting other specific places where a dirty bomb might be set off, such as in Annapolis, Maryland, or in Tysons Corner, Virginia. So our frame F in this case might be:

> H_1: A dirty bomb will be set off in Washington, D.C.
> H_2: A dirty bomb will be set off in Annapolis, Maryland.
> H_3: A dirty bomb will be set off in Tysons Corner, Virginia.

All that is required in the Belief Functions approach is that the hypotheses in a frame be mutually exclusive; they might or might not be exhaustive. The hypotheses are required to be exhaustive in the Bayesian approach. So this revised frame $F' = \{H_1, H_2, H_3\}$, as stated, is not exhaustive. But we are assuming, for the moment at least, that these three

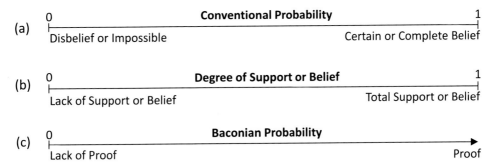

Figure 1.6. Different probability scales.

hypotheses are mutually exclusive: The dirty bomb will be set off at exactly one of these three locations. But, on further evidence, we might come to believe that dirty bombs will be set off in both Washington, D.C., and in Tysons Corner, Virginia. We know that the terrorists we are facing have a preference for simultaneous and coordinated attacks. So, our revised frame F'' might be:

H_1: A dirty bomb will be set off in Washington, D.C., and in Tysons Corner, Virginia.
H_2: A dirty bomb will be set off in Annapolis, Maryland.

The point of all this so far is that the Belief Functions approach allows for the fact that our hypotheses may mutate or change as a result of new evidence we obtain. This is a major virtue of this approach to evidential reasoning.

The next thing we have to consider is the *power set* of the hypotheses in a frame. This power set is simply the list of all possible combinations of the hypotheses in this frame. When we have **n** hypotheses in F, there are 2^n possible combinations of our hypotheses, including all of them and none of them. For example, when $F = \{H_1, \neg H_1\}$, the power set consists of $\{H_1\}$, $\{\neg H_1\}$, $\{H_1, \neg H_1\}$, and $\varnothing$, where $\varnothing$ = the empty set (i.e., none of the hypotheses). For $F' = \{H_1, H_2, H_3\}$, as just defined, there are $2^3 = 8$ possible combinations: $\{H_1\}$, $\{H_2\}$, $\{H_3\}$, $\{H_1, H_2\}$, $\{H_1, H_3\}$, $\{H_2, H_3\}$, $\{H_1, H_2, H_3\}$ and $\varnothing$. Now, here comes an important point about support function **s**: The assigned values of **s** for any item or body of evidence must sum to 1.0 across the power set of hypotheses in a frame. The only restriction is that we must set $\mathbf{s}\{\varnothing\} = 0$. We cannot give any support to the set of none of the hypotheses we are considering.

More details about the Belief Functions approach are provided in Schum (1994 [2001a], pp. 222–243).

1.3.4   Baconian Probability

1.3.4.1 Variative and Eliminative Inferences

Here is a view of probabilistic reasoning that puts particular emphasis on a very important matter not specifically addressed in any other view of probability. In this view, the probability of a hypothesis depends on *how much* relevant and believable evidence we have and on *how complete* is our coverage of existing evidence on matters we ourselves have recognized as being relevant in the analysis at hand.

This Baconian view of probability rests on the work of Professor L. Jonathan Cohen (1977, 1989). The label "Baconian" on this system of probability acknowledges the work of Sir Francis Bacon (1561–1626), who revolutionized the process of inference in science. Bacon argued that attempting to prove some hypothesis by gathering instances favorable to it is mistaken, since all it would take to refute the generality of this hypothesis was one unfavorable instance of it. What Bacon argued was that we ought to design research with the objective of *eliminating* hypotheses. The hypothesis that best resists our eliminative efforts is the one in which we should have the greatest confidence. As this eliminative process proceeds, it is obvious that we should not keep performing the same test over and over again. What we need is an array of *different* tests of our hypotheses. The hypothesis that holds up under the most varied set of tests is the one having the greatest probability of being correct. So, Baconian inferences are *eliminative and variative* in nature.

Baconian probabilities have only ordinal properties and cannot be combined algebraically in any way. The Baconian probability scale is shown as (c) in Figure 1.6, to be compared with the conventional probability scale shown as (a) in Figure 1.6. On the conventional probability scale, 0 means *disproof*; but on the Baconian scale, 0 simply means *lack of proof*. A hypothesis now having zero Baconian probability can be revised upward in probability as soon as we have some evidence for it. As noted, we cannot revise upward in probability any hypothesis disproved, or having zero conventional probability.

1.3.4.2 Importance of Evidential Completeness

Figure 1.7 illustrates a major point of interest in the Baconian system. Professor Cohen (1977, 1989) argued that in any evidential reasoning situation, we are always out on an inferential limb that might be longer and weaker than we may believe it to be. Suppose you have generated three hypotheses {H_1, H_2, and H_3}. You have examined a body of evidence and have used Bayes' rule to combine the likelihoods for this evidence together with stated prior probabilities. The result is that Bayes' rule shows the posterior probability of H_3, in light of the evidence, to be 0.998, very close to certainty on the Kolmogorov probability scale. Therefore, you confidently report your conclusion that H_3 is true, together with its very large posterior probability you have determined. A short time passes, and you hear the depressing news that H_3 is not true. What could have gone wrong? After all, you performed an analysis that is highly respected by many persons.

A person having knowledge of Cohen's Baconian probability (1977, 1989) arrives on the scene of your distress and makes the following comments:

> You gathered some evidence, fair enough, quite a bit of it, in fact. But, how many relevant questions you can think of were not answered by the evidence you had? Depending upon the number of these unanswered questions, you were out on an inferential limb that was longer and weaker than you imagined it to be (see Figure 1.7). If you believed that these unanswered questions would supply evidence that also favored H_3, you were misleading

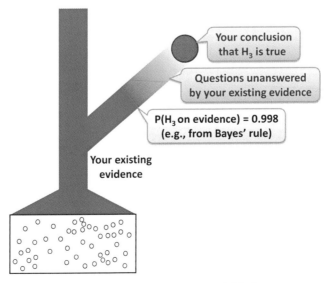

Figure 1.7. A Baconian inferential limb.

yourself since you did not obtain any answers to them. The posterior probability you determined by itself is not a good indicator of the weight of evidence. What makes better sense is to say the weight of evidence depends on the amount of favorable evidence you have and how completely it covers matters you said were relevant. In your analysis, you completely overlooked the inferential importance of questions your existing evidence did not answer.

Apart from the Baconian system, no other probability view focuses on evidential completeness and the importance of taking into account questions recognized as being relevant that remain unanswered by the evidence we do have. This is why Jonathan Cohen's Baconian system is so important (Cohen, 1977; 1989). What we do not take into account in our analyses can hurt us very badly.

In many instances, such as reasoning in intelligence analysis, we frequently have to make inferences about matters for which we have scant evidence, or no evidence at all. In other instances in which there may be available evidence, we may have no time to search for it or consider it carefully. In such cases, we are forced to make *assumptions* or *generalizations* that license inferential steps. But this amounts to giving an assumption or a generalization the *benefit of the doubt* (without supporting it in any way), to believing *as if* some conclusion were true (absent any evidential support for it), or to *taking something for granted* without testing it in any way. All of these situations involve the suppression of uncertainties.

It happens that only the Baconian probability system provides any guidance about how to proceed when we must give benefit of doubt, believe as if, or take things for granted. The major reason is that it acknowledges what almost every logician says about the necessity for asserting generalizations and supplying tests of them in evidential reasoning. Search the Bayesian or Belief Functions literature, and you will find almost no discussion of generalizations (assumptions) and ancillary tests of them. Suppose we are interested in inferring F from E, that is, $P(F|E)$. Bayes' rule grinds to a halt when we have no basis for assessing the likelihoods $P(E|F)$ and $P(E|\neg F)$. Bayesians counter by saying that we will always have some evidence on which to base these judgments. But they never say what this evidence is in particular cases and how credible it might or might not be. The Belief Functions approach comes closer by saying that we can assess the evidential support for a *body* of evidence that may include both directly relevant and at least some ancillary evidence (i.e., evidence about other evidence). Following is an account of the Baconian license for giving an assumption or generalization benefit of doubt, believing as if it were true, or taking it for granted, provided that we are willing to mention all of the uncertainties we are suppressing when we do so. Stated another way, we must try to account for all of the questions we can think of that remain unanswered by the absence, or very scant amount, of evidence.

Here are the essentials of Cohen's Baconian approach to reasoning based on little or no ancillary evidence to either support or undermine a generalization (Cohen 1977; 1989). The first step, of course, is to make sure the generalization is not a non sequitur, that is, that it makes logical sense. In the simplest possible case, suppose we are interested in inferring proposition or event F from proposition or event E. The generalization G in doing so might read, "If E has occurred, then probably F has occurred." We recognize this if-then statement as an *inductive generalization* since it is hedged. Second, we consider various tests of this generalization using relevant ancillary evidence. Third, we consider how many evidential tests of this generalization there might be. Suppose we identify N such tests. The best case would be when we perform all N of these tests and they all produce results favorable to generalization G. But we must not overlook generalization G itself; we do so by assigning it the value 1; so we have N + 1 things to consider. Now we are in a position to show what happens in any possible case.

First, suppose we perform *none* of these N evidential tests. We could still proceed by giving generalization G the *benefit of the doubt* and detach a belief that F occurred (or will occur) just by invoking this generalization G regarding the linkage between events E and F. So, when no evidential tests are performed, we are saying: "Let's believe *as if* F occurred based on E and generalization G." This would amount to saying that the Baconian probability of event F is B(F) = 1/(N + 1). This expression is never a ratio; all it says is that we considered just one thing in our inference about F from E, namely just the generalization G. We could also say, "Let's take event F *for granted* and believe that F occurred (or will occur) because E occurred, as our generalization G asserts." However, note that in doing so, we have left all N ancillary evidential questions unanswered. This we represent by saying that our inference of F from E has involved only one of the N + 1 considerations and so we have (N + 1 – 1) = N, the number of questions we have left unanswered. As far as evidential completeness is concerned, this is when the evidence we have is totally incomplete. But the Baconian system allows us to proceed anyway based on giving a generalization the benefit of doubt. But our confidence in this result should be very low.

Now suppose we have performed some number k of the N possible ancillary evidential tests of generalization G, as asserted previously, and they were all passed. The Baconian probability of F in this situation is given by B(F) = (k + 1)/(N +1). The difference between the numerator and denominator in such an expression will always equal the number of unanswered questions as far as the testing of G is concerned. In this case, we have (N + 1) – (k + 1) = N – k questions that were unanswered in a test of generalization G. How high our confidence is that F is true depends on how high k + 1 is as compared to N + 1.

But now suppose that not all answers to these k questions are favorable to generalization G. Under what conditions are we entitled to detach a belief that event F occurred, based on evidence E, generalization G, and the k tests of G? The answer requires a subjective judgment by the analyst about whether the tests, *on balance*, favor or disfavor G. When the number of the k tests disfavoring G exceeds the number of tests favoring G, we might suppose that we would always detach a belief that event F did not occur, since G has failed more tests than it survived. But this will not always be such an easy judgment if the number of tests G passed were judged to be more important than the tests it failed to pass. In any case, there are N – k tests that remain unanswered. Suppose that k is quite large, but the number of tests favorable to G is only slightly larger than the number of tests unfavorable to G. In such cases, the analyst might still give event F the *benefit of the doubt*, or believe, at least tentatively, *as if* F occurred pending the possible acquisition of further favorable tests of G. And in this case, the confidence of the analyst in this conclusion should also be very low.

Whatever the basis for an assumption or a benefit of doubt judgment there is, one of the most important things about the Baconian approach is that the analyst must be prepared to give an account of the questions that remain unanswered in evidential tests of possible conclusions. This will be especially important when analysts make assumptions, or more appropriately, give generalizations the benefit of doubt, draw as if conclusions, or take certain events for granted. These are situations in which analysts are most vulnerable and in which Baconian ideas are most helpful.

1.3.4.3 Baconian Probability of Boolean Expressions

Some of the most important properties of Baconian probabilities concern their application to Boolean combinations of propositions, such as hypotheses. Because the probabilities in the Baconian system have only *ordinal properties*, we can say only that hypothesis H_1 is more likely than H_2, but we cannot say how much more likely H_1 is than H_2. Also, in the Baconian system, it is never necessary to assess subjective probabilities. In our saying that H_1 is more probable than H_2, all we are saying is that there is more favorably relevant evidence on H_1 than there is on H_2. What counts most in the Baconian system is the *completeness of our evidence* and the extent to which we have questions that remain unanswered by the evidence we have. Here are the three most important Baconian properties of interest to us concerning intersections, unions, and negation.

Baconian Intersection: Suppose we have some events of interest such as events F, G, and H. Suppose we have some favorably relevant evidence about each one of these events and have also considered how complete the evidence is for these events. So we determine that the Baconian probabilities (B) for these three events are $B(F) \geq B(G) \geq B(H)$. Here's what these probabilities say: We have more favorably relevant and complete evidence for event F than we do for event G, and more favorably relevant and complete evidence for event G than we have for event H. So, asked what the Baconian probability is for their intersection (F and G and H), we must say that B(F and G and H) = B(H). What this says is that *the Baconian probability of the intersection of these three events is equal to the Baconian probability of the event with the least favorably relevant and complete evidence.* This is an example of the *MIN rule for Baconian intersections*. We might compare this with the conventional probability of the intersection of these three events. Suppose that events F, G, and H are independent events where $P(F) = 0.8$, $P(G) = 0.6$ and $P(H) = 0.4$. In this case, P(F and G and H) = 0.8*0.6*0.4 = 0.192 < P(H) = 0.4. In the Baconian system, the probability of a conjunction of events or propositions can never be less than that of the event having the smallest Baconian probability.

Baconian Union: Now consider the same case involving events F, G, and H. Again, suppose that $B(F) \geq B(G) \geq B(H)$. Now what we wish to determine is the Baconian probability B(F or G or H). In this case, $B(F \text{ or } G \text{ or } H) \geq B(F)$, where B(F) is the largest of the Baconian probability for the events we are considering. This is the *MAX rule for Baconian probability*, and what it says is that *the probability of a disjunction of events is at least as large as the largest Baconian probability of any of the individual events.*

Baconian Negation: Baconian negation is not complementary. The Baconian rule is quite complex; here's what it says: If we have A and ¬A, if B(A) > 0, then B(¬A) = 0. What this means essentially is that *we cannot commit beliefs simultaneously to two events that cannot both occur.*

What is quite interesting is that the Baconian treatment of conjunctions and disjunctions is the same as in Zadeh's Fuzzy probability system; namely, they both make use of min-max rules for these connectives.

More details about Baconian probabilities are provided in Schum (1994 [2001a], pp. 243–261).

1.3.5   Fuzzy Probability

1.3.5.1 Fuzzy Force of Evidence

One can also express the uncertainty about a conclusion reached by using words, such as "likely," "almost certain," or "much less certain," rather than numbers, as illustrated by the following fragment from the letter sent by Albert Einstein to the United States President Franklin D. Roosevelt, on the possibility of constructing nuclear bombs (Einstein, 1939):

> ... In the course of the last four months it has been made probable – through the work of Joliot in France as well as Fermi and Szilárd in America – that it may become possible to set up a nuclear chain reaction in a large mass of uranium, by which vast amounts of power and large quantities of new radium-like elements would be generated. Now it appears almost certain that this could be achieved in the immediate future.
>
> This new phenomenon would also lead to the construction of bombs, and it is conceivable – though much less certain – that extremely powerful bombs of a new type may thus be constructed. ...

Verbal expressions of uncertainty are common in many areas. In the field of law, for example, forensic standards of proof are always employed using words instead of numbers. We all know about standards such as "beyond reasonable doubt" (in criminal cases); "preponderance of evidence" (in civil cases); "clear and convincing evidence" (in many Senate and congressional hearings); and "probable cause" (employed by magistrates to determine whether a person should be held in custody pending further hearings).

All the verbal examples just cited have a current name: They can be called *Fuzzy probabilities*. Words are less precise than numbers. There is now extensive study of fuzzy inference involving what has been termed *approximate reasoning*, which involves verbal statements about things that are imprecisely stated. Here is an example of approximate reasoning: "Since John believes he is *overworked* and *underpaid*, then he is *probably not very satisfied* with his job." We are indebted to Professor Lofti Zadeh (University of California, Berkeley), and his many colleagues, for developing logics for dealing with fuzzy statements, including Fuzzy probabilities (Zadeh, 1983; Negoita and Ralescu, 1975). In his methods for relating verbal assessments of uncertainty with numerical equivalents, Zadeh employed what he termed a *possibility function*, μ, to indicate ranges of numerical probabilities a person might associate with a verbal expression of uncertainty. Zadeh reasoned that a person might not be able to identify a single precise number he or she would always associate with a verbal statement or Fuzzy probability. Here is an example of a possibility function for the Fuzzy probability "very probable."

Asked to grade what numerical probabilities might be associated with an analyst's Fuzzy probability of "very probable," the analyst might respond as follows:

> For me, "very probable" means a numerical probability of at least 0.75 and at most 0.95. If it were any value above 0.95, I might use a stronger term, such as "very, very probable." I would further say that I would not use the term "very probable" if I thought the probability was less than 0.75. In such cases, I would weaken my verbal assessment. Finally, I think it is most possible ($\mu = 1.0$) that my use of the verbal assessment "very probable" means something that has about 0.85 of occurring. If the analyst decides that "very probable" declines linearly on either side of $\mu = 1.0$, we would have the possibility function shown in Figure 1.8.

1.3.5.2 Fuzzy Probability of Boolean Expressions

As an example of using fuzzy probabilities, suppose we have three events, or propositions A, B, and C. We consider the following Fuzzy probabilities (F) for these events, and we say the following:

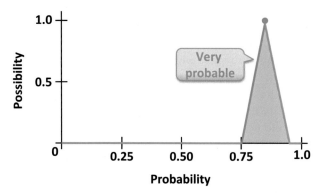

Figure 1.8. Possibilities and Fuzzy probabilities.

- Event A is very likely.
- Event B is likely.
- Event C is very unlikely.

We express this by saying that F(A) > F(B) > F(C).

Fuzzy Conjunction: The Fuzzy conjunction of several events is the *minimum* Fuzzy probability of these events. For example, F(A and B and C) = F(C), which is the minimum Fuzzy probability of these three events.

Fuzzy Disjunction: The Fuzzy disjunction of several events is the *maximum* Fuzzy probability of these events. For example, F(A or B or C) = F(A), which is the maximum Fuzzy probability of these three events.

Notice that both in the Baconian system and in the Fuzzy system we have MIN/MAX rules for combining probabilities for complex events.

Fuzzy Negation: Fuzzy negation is complementary: F(A) = 1 – F(¬A).

More details about the Fuzzy probabilities are provided in Schum (1994 [2001a], pp. 261–269).

1.3.5.3 On Verbal Assessments of Probabilities

Let us also consider the critics who sneer at *verbal assessments of probabilities*, saying that only *numerical assessments*, conforming to the Kolmogorov axioms, are acceptable. As a top-ranking analyst, you are asked by an equally high-ranking customer for the probability of a crucial hypothesis H_K. All the evidence in this case is for a one-of-a-kind event, so your assessment is necessarily subjective. You tell the customer, "Sir, the probability of H_K, on our analysis is 78 percent." The customer asks, "This is a very precise number. How did you arrive at it, given the subjective nature of your assessment?" You reply, "Yes, sir, what I really should have said was that my probability is between 73 percent and 83 percent, and 78 percent seemed like a good figure to quote." The customer then says, "But the limits to the probability interval you quoted are also precise. How did you arrive at them?" You might say, "Well, my lower limit is really between 70 percent and 76 percent and my upper limit is between 80 percent and 86 percent." Your customer says, "But these are also precise numbers." There is, as you see, an infinite regress of similar questions regarding the basis for subjective numerical assessments.

There are many places to begin a defense of verbal or *Fuzzy probability statements*. The most obvious one is law. All of the forensic standards of proof are given verbally: "beyond reasonable doubt," "clear and convincing evidence," "balance of probabilities," "sufficient evidence," and "probable cause." Over the centuries, attempts have been made to supply numerical probability values and ranges for each of these standards, but none of them has been successful. The reason, of course, is that every case is unique and rests upon many subjective and imprecise judgments. Wigmore (1913, 1937) understood completely that the catenated inferences in his Wigmorean networks were probabilistic in nature. Each of the arrows in a chain of reasoning describes the force of one hypothesis on the next one, such as E → F. Wigmore graded the force of such linkages verbally, using such terms as "strong force," "weak force," "provisional force," and so on. Toulmin (1963) also used fuzzy qualifiers in the probability statements of his system, which grounds the Rationale analytical tool (van Gelder, 2007). There are many other examples of situations in which it is difficult or impossible for people to find numerical equivalents for verbal probabilities they assess. Intelligence analysis so often supplies very good examples in spite of what Sherman Kent (1994) said some years ago. Indeed, using words is quite often necessary in analyses based on masses of evidence that are so complex that they resist even the most devoted attention to the construction of inference networks. Couple this with the fact that different analysts might disagree substantially about what specific probability should be assigned to a conclusion. In addition an analyst might assign a different probability to the same conclusion, based on the same evidence, on different occasions. What this says is that there will be inter-analyst and intra-analyst variation in the assessment of probabilities. Words are less precise than numbers, so there will often be less disagreement about a verbal or a Fuzzy probability.

We conclude this discussion by recalling what the well-known probabilist Professor Glenn Shafer said years ago (Shafer, 1988):

> Probability is more about structuring arguments than it is about numbers. All probabilities rest upon arguments. If the arguments are faulty, the probabilities, however determined, will make no sense.

1.3.6   A Summary of Uncertainty Methods and What They Best Capture

Evidence-based reasoning is necessarily probabilistic in nature because our evidence is always *incomplete* (we can look for more, if we have time), usually *inconclusive* (it is consistent with the truth of more than one hypothesis or possible explanation), frequently *ambiguous* (we cannot always determine exactly what the evidence is telling us), commonly *dissonant* (some of it favors one hypothesis or possible explanation, but other evidence favors other hypotheses), and with various degrees of *believability* shy of perfection.

As illustrated in Table 1.1 and discussed in this section, each of the alternative views of probability previously discussed captures best some of these characteristics of evidence, but no single view captures best all of them. We include in this table just the four views concerning nonenumerative situations. One can easily find many works on statistics, frequentistic or Bayesian, in enumerative situations in which they can estimate probabilities from observed relative frequencies.

The first entry in Table 1.1 lists a major strength that is exclusive to the Baconian system: its concern about how much favorable evidence was taken into account in an

Table 1.1. A Summary of Nonenumerative Uncertainty Methods and What They Best Capture

Major Strength	Subjective Bayes	Belief Functions	Baconian	Fuzzy
Accounting for **incompleteness** of coverage of evidence			☑	
Coping with **inconclusiveness** in evidence	☑	☑	☑	☑
Coping with **ambiguities** or **imprecision** in evidence and judgmental indecision		☑		☑
Coping with **dissonance** in evidence	☑	☑	☑	☑
Coping with **source believability** issues	☑		☑	

analysis, and how completely this evidence covered matters judged relevant to conclusions that could be reached. A major question this form of analysis allows us to address is the extent to which questions that have not been answered by existing evidence could have altered the conclusion being reached. It would be quite inappropriate to assume that answers to the remaining unanswered questions would, if they were obtained, all favor the conclusion that was being considered. This, of course, requires us to consider carefully matters relevant to any conclusion that are not addressed by available evidence.

The second entry in Table 1.1 notes that all four of the probabilistic methods have very good ways for dealing with the inconclusive nature of most evidence, but they do so in different ways. The Subjective Bayesian does so by assessing nonzero likelihoods for the evidence under every hypothesis being considered. Their relative sizes indicate the force that the evidence is judged to have on each hypothesis. But the Belief Functions advocate assigns numbers indicating the *support* evidence provides for hypotheses or subsets of them. We should be quick to notice that Bayesian likelihoods do not grade evidential support, since in Belief Functions one can say that an item of evidence provides no support at all to some hypothesis. But a Bayesian likelihood of zero under a particular hypothesis would mean that this hypothesis is impossible and should be eliminated. Offering no support in Belief Functions does not entail that this hypothesis is impossible, since some support for this hypothesis may be provided by further evidence. The Baconian acknowledges the inconclusive nature of evidence by assessing how completely, as well as how strongly, the evidence favors one hypothesis over others. In Fuzzy probabilities, it would be quite appropriate to use words in judging how an item or body of evidence bears on several hypotheses. For example, one might say, "This evidence is indeed consistent with H_1 and H_2, but I believe it *strongly favors* H_1 over H_2."

The third entry in the table first acknowledges the Belief Functions and Fuzzy concerns about ambiguities and imprecision in evidence. In the Belief Functions approach, one is entitled to *withhold belief* for some hypotheses in the face of ambiguous evidence. In such cases, one may not be able to decide upon the extent to which the evidence may support any hypothesis being considered, or even whether the evidence supports any of them. Judgmental indecision is not allowed in the Bayesian system since it assumes one can say precisely how strongly evidence judged relevant favors every hypothesis being considered. Ambiguities in evidence may be commonly encountered. The Fuzzy advocate will argue that ambiguities or imprecision in evidence hardly justifies precise numerical judgments. In the face of fuzzy evidence, we can make only fuzzy judgments of uncertainty.

The fourth entry in Table 1.1 shows that all four probability systems have very good mechanisms for coping with dissonant evidence in which there are patterns of contradictory and divergent evidence. Dissonant evidence is directionally inconsistent; some of it will favor certain hypotheses and some of it will favor others. In resolving such inconsistencies, both the Bayesian and Belief Functions approaches will side with the evidence having the strongest believability. The Bayesian approach to resolving contradictions is especially interesting since it shows how "counting heads" is not the appropriate method for resolving contradictions. In times past, "majority rule" was the governing principle. Bayes' rule shows that what matters is the aggregate believability on either side of a contradiction. The Baconian approach also rests on the strength and aggregate believability in matters of dissonance, but it also rests on how much evidence is available on either side and upon the questions that remain unanswered. In Fuzzy terms, evidential dissonance, and how it might be resolved, can be indicated in verbal assessments of uncertainty. In such instances, one might say, "We have dissonant evidence favoring both H_1 and H_2, but I believe the evidence favoring H_1 predominates because of its very strong believability."

Row five in Table 1.1 concerns the vital matter of assessing the believability of evidence. From considerable experience, we find that the Bayesian and Baconian systems are especially important when they are combined. In many cases, these two radically different schemes for assessing uncertainty are not at all antagonistic but are entirely complementary. Let us consider a body of evidence about a human intelligence (HUMINT) asset or informant. Ideas from the Baconian system allow us to ask, "How much evidence do we have about this asset, and how many questions about this asset remain unanswered?" Ideas from the Bayesian system allow us to ask, "How strong is the evidence we do have about this asset?" (Schum, 1991; Schum and Morris, 2007)

1.4 EVIDENCE-BASED REASONING

1.4.1 Deduction, Induction, and Abduction

These three types of inference involved in evidence-based reasoning may be intuitively summarized as shown in the following.

Deduction shows that something is *necessarily* true:

A ➔ *necessarily* B
Socrates is a man ➔ *necessarily* Socrates is mortal

Induction shows that something is *probably* true:

A ➔ *probably* B
Julia was born in Switzerland ➔ *probably* Julia speaks German

Abduction shows that something is *possibly* or *plausibly* true:

A → *possibly* B
There is smoke in the East building → *possibly* there is fire
in the East building

These types of inference are described more formally in the following.

Deductive Inference:

$\forall x, U(x) \rightarrow V(x)$	Whenever $U(x)$ is true, $V(x)$ is also true
$U(a_1)$	$U(a_1)$ is true
Necessarily $V(a_1)$	Therefore $V(a_1)$ is *necessarily* true

Inductive Inference:

$U(a_1)$ and $V(a_1)$	When $U(a_1)$ was true, it was observed that $V(a_1)$ was also true
$U(a_2)$ and $V(a_2)$	When $U(a_2)$ was true, it was observed that $V(a_2)$ was also true
. . .	. . .
$U(a_n)$ and $V(a_n)$	When $U(a_n)$ was true, it was observed that $V(a_n)$ was also true
$\forall x, U(x) \rightarrow$ Probably $V(x)$	Therefore, whenever $U(x)$ is true, $V(x)$ is also *probably* true

Abductive Inference:

$U(a_1) \rightarrow V(a_1)$	If $U(a_1)$ were true then $V(a_1)$ would follow as a matter of course
$V(a_1)$	$V(a_1)$ is true
Possibly $U(a_1)$	Therefore $U(a_1)$ is *possibly* true

1.4.2   The Search for Knowledge

We can extend Oldroyd's *Arch of Knowledge* from Figure 1.2, as indicated in Figure 1.9, to show how abduction, deduction, and induction are used in the search for knowledge. They are at the basis of collaborative processes of evidence in search of hypotheses, hypotheses in search of evidence, and evidentiary testing of hypotheses in a complex dynamic world.

Through *abductive reasoning* (which shows that something is *possibly* true), we search for hypotheses that explain our observations; through *deductive reasoning* (which shows that something is *necessarily* true), we use our hypotheses to generate new lines of inquiry and discover new evidence; and through *inductive reasoning* (which shows that something is *probably* true), we test our hypotheses by evaluating our evidence. Now the discovery of new evidence may lead to new hypotheses or the refinement of the existing ones. Also, when there is more than one most likely hypothesis, we need to search for additional evidence to determine which of them is actually the most likely. Therefore, the processes of evidence in search of hypotheses, hypotheses in search of evidence, and evidentiary

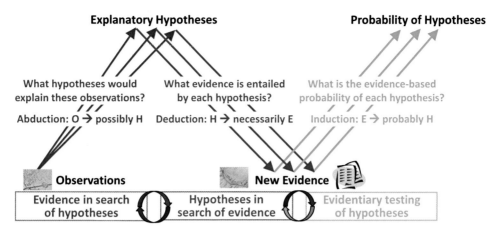

Figure 1.9. The search for knowledge.

testing of hypotheses also take place in response to one another, as indicated by the feedback loops from the bottom of Figure 1.9.

1.4.3 Evidence-based Reasoning Everywhere

As illustrated in Figure 1.10, evidence-based reasoning is at the core of many problem-solving and decision-making tasks in a wide variety of domains, including physics, chemistry, history, archaeology, medicine, law, forensics, intelligence analysis, cyber-curity, and many others. This is not surprising, because, as Jeremy Betham stated over two centuries ago, "The field of evidence is no other than the field of knowledge" (Betham, 1810, p. 5).

Scientists from various domains, such as physics, chemistry, or biology, may recognize this as a formulation of the scientific method.

In medicine, a doctor makes observations with respect to a patient's complaints and attempts to generate possible diagnoses (hypotheses) that would explain them. He or she then performs various medical tests that provide further evidence for or against the various hypothesized illnesses. After that, the doctor uses the obtained evidence to determine the most likely illness.

In law, an attorney makes observations in a criminal case and seeks to generate hypotheses in the form of charges that seem possible in explaining these observations. Then, assuming that a charge is justified, attempts are made to deduce further evidence bearing on it. Finally, the obtained evidence is used to prove the charge.

In forensics, observations made at the site of an explosion in a power plant lead to the formulation of several possible causes. Analysis of each possible cause leads to the discovery of new evidence that eliminates or refines some of the causes, and may even suggest new ones. This cycle continues until enough evidence is found to determine the most likely cause.

In intelligence analysis, an analyst formulates alternative hypotheses that would explain the evidence about an event. Then the analyst puts each of the hypotheses at work to guide him or her in the collection of additional evidence, which is used to assess the probability of each hypothesis.

In cybersecurity, a suspicious connection to our computer from an external one triggers the automatic generation of alternative threat and nonthreat hypotheses. Each generated

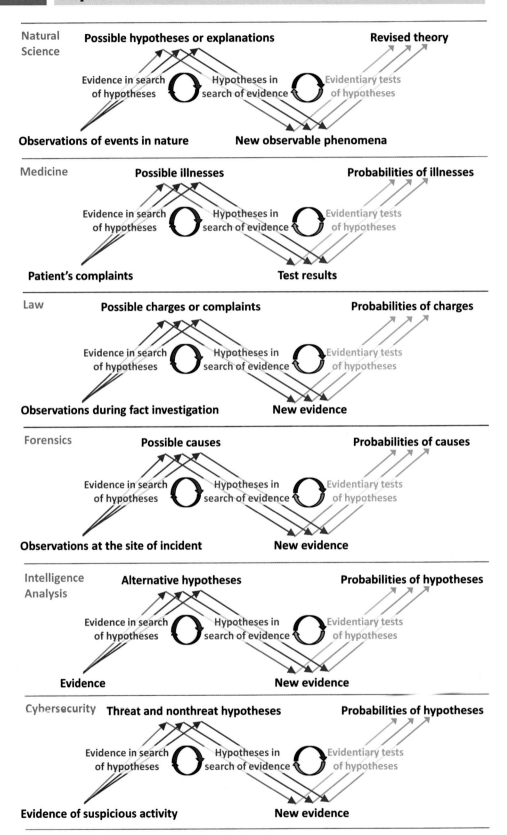

Figure 1.10. Evidence-based reasoning everywhere.

hypothesis guides the collection of additional evidence, which is used to assess the probability of each hypothesis (Meckl et al., 2015).

The following, for instance, are different hypotheses one may be interested in assessing based on evidence:

- University U would be a good university for student S.
- Professor P would be a good PhD Advisor for student S.
- House H would be a good house to be bought by person P.
- Country C will be a world leader in nonconventional energy sources within the next decade.
- Country C has nuclear weapons.
- Person P was murdered by suspect S.
- Patient P has illness I.
- Building B has collapsed because of the use of low-quality materials.
- Connection C is part of APT1 intrusion using malware M.

Evidence-based reasoning, however, is often highly complex, and the conclusions are necessarily probabilistic in nature because our evidence is always *incomplete*, usually *inconclusive*, frequently *ambiguous*, commonly *dissonant*, and has imperfect *believability* (Schum, 1994 [2001a]; Tecuci et al., 2010b). Arguments requiring both imaginative and critical reasoning, and involving all known types of inference (deduction, induction, and abduction), are necessary in order to estimate the probability of the considered hypotheses. Therefore, evidence-based reasoning can be best approached through the mixed-initiative integration of human imagination and computer knowledge-based reasoning (Tecuci et al., 2007a, 2007b), that is, by using knowledge-based intelligent agents for evidence-based reasoning. Therefore, in the next section, we briefly review the field of artificial intelligence.

1.5 ARTIFICIAL INTELLIGENCE

Artificial intelligence (AI) is the science and engineering domain concerned with the theory and practice of developing systems that exhibit the characteristics we associate with intelligence in human behavior, such as perception, natural language processing, problem solving and planning, learning and adaptation, and acting on the environment. Its main scientific goal is understanding the principles that enable intelligent behavior in humans, animals, and artificial agents. This scientific goal directly supports several engineering goals, such as developing intelligent agents, formalizing knowledge and mechanizing reasoning in all areas of human endeavor, making working with computers as easy as working with people, and developing human-machine systems that exploit the complementariness of human and automated reasoning.

Artificial intelligence is a very broad interdisciplinary field that has roots in and intersects with many domains, not only all the computing disciplines, but also mathematics, linguistics, psychology, neuroscience, mechanical engineering, statistics, economics, control theory and cybernetics, philosophy, and many others. The field has adopted many concepts and methods from these domains, but it has also contributed back.

While some of the developed systems, such as an expert system or a planning system, can be characterized as pure applications of AI, most of the AI systems are developed as components of complex applications to which they add intelligence in various ways, for instance, by enabling them to reason with knowledge, to process natural language, or to learn and adapt.

Artificial intelligence researchers investigate powerful techniques in their quest for realizing intelligent behavior. But these techniques are pervasive and are no longer considered AI when they reach mainstream use. Examples include time-sharing, symbolic programming languages (e.g., Lisp, Prolog, and Scheme), symbolic mathematics systems (e.g., Mathematica), graphical user interfaces, computer games, object-oriented programming, the personal computer, email, hypertext, and even the software agents. While this tends to diminish the merits of AI, the field is continuously producing new results and, due to its current level of maturity and the increased availability of cheap computational power, it is a key technology in many of today's novel applications.

1.5.1   Intelligent Agents

It has become common to describe an AI system using the agent metaphor (Russell and Norvig, 2010, pp. 34–63). *An agent is a system that perceives its environment (which may be the physical world, a user via a graphical user interface, a collection of other agents, the Internet, or other complex environment); reasons to interpret perceptions, draw inferences, solve problems, and determine actions; and acts upon that environment to realize a set of goals or tasks for which it has been designed.* An intelligent knowledge-based agent will continuously improve its knowledge and performance through learning from input data, from a user, from other agents, and/or from its own problem-solving experience. While interacting with a human or some other agents, it may not blindly obey commands, but may have the ability to modify requests, ask clarification questions, or even refuse to satisfy certain requests. It can accept high-level requests indicating what the user wants and can decide how to satisfy each request with some degree of independence or autonomy, exhibiting goal-directed behavior and dynamically choosing which actions to take and in what sequence. It can collaborate with users to improve the accomplishment of their tasks or can carry out such tasks on their behalf, based on knowledge of their goals or desires. It can monitor events or procedures for the users, can advise them on performing various tasks, can train or teach them, or can help them collaborate (Tecuci, 1998, pp. 1–12).

Figure 1.11 shows the main components of a knowledge-based agent:

- The *knowledge base* is a type of long-term memory that contains data structures representing the objects from the application domain, general laws governing them, and actions that can be performed with them.
- The *perceptual processing module* implements methods to process natural language, speech, and visual inputs.
- The *problem-solving engine* implements general problem-solving methods that use the knowledge from the knowledge base to interpret the input and provide an appropriate output.
- The *learning engine* implements learning methods for acquiring, extending, and refining the knowledge in the knowledge base.
- The *action processing module* implements the agent's actions upon that environment aimed at realizing the goals or tasks for which it was designed (e.g., generation of

answers to questions, solutions of input problems, manipulation of objects, or navigation to a new position).

- The *reasoning area* is a type of short-term memory where the actual reasoning takes place.

An intelligent agent has an internal representation of its external environment that allows it to reason about the environment by manipulating the elements of the representation. For each relevant aspect of the environment, such as an object, a relation between objects, a class of objects, a law, or an action, there is an expression in the agent's knowledge base that represents that aspect. For example, the left side of Figure 1.12 shows one way to represent the simple world from the right side of Figure 1.12. The upper part is a hierarchical representation of the objects and their relationships (an ontology). Under it is a rule to be used for reasoning about these objects. This mapping between real entities and their representations allows the agent to reason about the environment by manipulating its internal representations and creating new ones. For example, by employing natural deduction and its *modus ponens* rule, the agent may infer that cup1 is on table1. The actual algorithm that implements natural deduction is part of the problem-solving engine, while the actual reasoning is performed in the reasoning area (see Figure 1.11). Since such an agent integrates many of the intelligent behaviors that we observe in humans, it is also called a *cognitive agent or system* (Langley, 2012).

Most of the current AI agents, however, will not have all the components from Figure 1.11, or some of the components will have very limited functionality. For example, a user may speak with an automated agent (representing her Internet service provider) that will guide her in troubleshooting the Internet connection. This agent may have

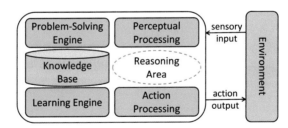

Figure 1.11. Notional architecture of an intelligent agent.

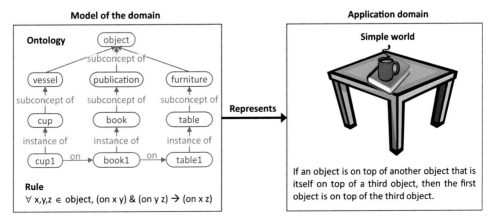

Figure 1.12. An ontology fragment and a reasoning rule representing a simple agent world.

advanced speech, natural language, and reasoning capabilities, but no visual or learning capabilities. A natural language interface to a database may have only natural language processing capabilities, while a face recognition system may have only learning and visual perception capabilities.

1.5.2   Mixed-Initiative Reasoning

Table 1.2 lists some of the complementary abilities of humans and computer agents. Humans are slow, sloppy, forgetful, implicit, and subjective, but have common sense and intuition, and may find creative solutions in new situations. In contrast, computer agents are fast, rigorous, precise, explicit, and objective, but they lack common sense and the ability to deal with new situations (Turoff, 2007). Moreover, in contrast to an agent, a human has a very limited attention span and can analyze only a small number of alternatives at a time (Pomerol and Adam, 2006). That is why we have claimed that the evidence-based reasoning tasks are best performed in a problem-solving and decision-making environment that synergistically integrates the complementary capabilities of humans and computer agents, taking advantage of their relative strengths to compensate for each other's weaknesses. Such an integration becomes even more important in face of the globalization and the rapid evolution toward the knowledge economies (Filip, 2001; Rooney et al., 2005). Indeed, these developments present additional challenges to decision makers who need to cope with dynamic and increasingly complex situations and make good decisions in face of an overwhelming amount of incomplete, uncertain, and mostly irrelevant information.

Mixed-initiative reasoning is a type of collaboration between humans and computer agents that mirrors the flexible collaboration between people. It is based on an efficient, natural interleaving of contributions by people and agents that is determined by their relative knowledge and skills and the problem-solving context, rather than by fixed roles, enabling each participant to contribute what it does best, at the appropriate moment (Horvitz, 1999; Tecuci et al., 2007a, 2007b).

Table 1.2. Complementary Computational Abilities of Humans and Computer Agents

Humans are	Computer agents are
slow	fast
sloppy	rigorous
forgetful	precise
implicit	explicit
subjective	objective
but	**but**
have common sense	lack common sense
have intuition	lack intuition
may find creative solutions in new situations	have poor ability to deal with new situations

Mixed-initiative systems can either accomplish goals unachievable by the component agents, assuming they work independently, or they can achieve the same goals more effectively.

An example of a good problem-solving and decision-making environment is one where the human acts as the orchestrator of the reasoning process, guiding the high-level exploration, while the agent implements this guidance by taking into account the human's preferred problem-solving strategies, assumptions, and biases (Tecuci et al., 2007c). In such an environment, the agent is an extension of the reasoning capabilities of the human, much like a calculator is an extension of the computational capabilities of an accountant. The emphasis is on enhancing human's creativity (Filip, 1989), relying on the human to take the most critical decisions and only to critique and correct the more routine ones that are proposed by the agent (Tecuci et al., 2007c).

Developing such an environment requires an automatic approach to problem solving that is very natural and easy to understand. Moreover, the human and the agent should collaborate in a natural way, similarly to how humans collaborate, as opposed to the usual human–computer interaction that is inflexible and mostly unidirectional. Also, because most of the complex decisions are based on incomplete and imperfect information, the decision-making environment should allow the investigation of what-if scenarios, where the decision maker can make various assumptions about a situation.

In the following section, we discuss the development of knowledge-based agents that could be used for mixed-initiative reasoning.

1.6   KNOWLEDGE ENGINEERING

Knowledge engineering is the area of artificial intelligence that is concerned with the design, development, and maintenance of agents that use knowledge and reasoning to perform problem solving and decision making tasks.

Knowledge engineering is a central discipline in the *Knowledge Society, the society where knowledge is the primary production resource instead of capital and labor* (Druker, 1993). Currently, human societies are rapidly evolving toward knowledge societies and an *Integrated Global Knowledge Society* because of the development of the information technologies, the Internet, the World Wide Web, and the Semantic Web that no longer restrict knowledge societies to geographic proximity and that facilitate the sharing, archiving, retrieving, and processing of knowledge (Schreiber et al., 2000; David and Foray, 2003; UNESCO, 2005). Moreover, the *Semantic Web, an extension of the World Wide Web in which Web content is expressed both in a natural form for humans, and in a format that can be understood by software agents,* is becoming the main infrastructure for the Knowledge Society, allowing knowledge-based agents to automatically find, integrate, process, and share information (Allemang and Hendler, 2011; W3C, 2015).

1.6.1   From Expert Systems to Knowledge-based Agents and Cognitive Assistants

Expert systems are among the most successful applications of artificial intelligence. According to Edward Feigenbaum (1982, p. 1), their founding father, *"An 'expert system' is an intelligent computer program that uses knowledge and inference procedures to solve problems that are difficult enough to require significant human expertise for their solution.*

The knowledge necessary to perform at such a level, plus the inference procedures used, can be thought of as a model of the expertise of the best practitioners in that field."

Two early and very influential expert systems were DENDRAL (Buchanan and Feigenbaum, 1978) and MYCIN (Buchanan and Shortliffe, 1984). DENDRAL, an expert system for organic chemistry, analyzed mass spectral data and inferred a complete structural hypothesis of a molecule. MYCIN, a medical expert system, produced diagnoses of infectious diseases and advised the physician on antibiotic therapies for treating them.

Expert systems and *knowledge-based systems* are often used as synonyms since all expert systems are knowledge-based systems. However, not all the knowledge-based systems are expert systems, such as the Watson natural language question-answering system (Ferrucci et al., 2010), and the Siri personal assistant (2011).

Continuous advances in artificial intelligence, particularly with respect to knowledge representation and reasoning, learning, and natural language processing, are reflected in more and more powerful and useful knowledge-based systems that, as discussed Section 1.5.1, are now more commonly called *knowledge-based agents,* or simply *intelligent agents.*

In this book, we are primarily concerned with a very important and newer class of intelligent agents, namely *cognitive assistants,* which have the following capabilities:

- *Learn complex problem-solving expertise directly from human experts*
- *Assist nonexpert users in solving problems requiring subject matter expertise*
- *Assist human experts in complex problem solving and decision making*
- *Teach problem solving and decision making to students*

Expert systems, knowledge-based agents, and cognitive assistants are used in business, science, engineering, manufacturing, military, intelligence, and many other areas (Durkin, 1994; Giarratano and Riley, 1994; Tecuci, 1998; Tecuci et al., 2001; 2008b). They are everywhere.

The following are examples of such successful systems.

Digital Equipment Corporation's R1 (McDermott, 1982), which helped configure orders for new computers, is considered the first successful commercial system. By 1986, it was saving the company an estimated $40 million a year.

Intuit's TurboTax, an American tax preparation software package initially developed by Michael A. Chipman of Chipsoft in the mid-1980s (Forbes, 2013), helps you fill in your taxes with the maximal deductions, according to the law.

The Defense Advanced Research Projects Agency's (DARPA) DARP logistics planning system was used during the Persian Gulf crisis of 1991 (Cross and Walker, 1994). It planned with up to fifty thousand vehicles, cargo, and people, and reportedly more than paid back DARPA's thirty-year investment in artificial intelligence.

IBM's Deep Blue chess playing system defeated Gary Kasparov, the chess world champion, in 1997 (Goodman and Keene, 1997).

Disciple-COG agent for center of gravity analysis helped senior military officers from the U.S. Army War College to learn how to identify the centers of gravity of the opposing forces in complex war scenarios (Tecuci et al., 2002a; 2002b; 2008b).

NASA's planning and scheduling systems helped plan and control the operations of NASA's spacecraft. For example, MAPGEN, a mixed-initiative planner, was deployed as a mission-critical component of the ground operations system for the Mars Exploration Rover mission (Bresina and Morris, 2007).

IBM's Watson natural language question-answering system defeated the best human players at the quiz show *Jeopardy* in 2011 (Ferrucci et al., 2010).

Apple's Siri, running on a cell phone, answers questions, makes recommendations on nearby places of interest, and provides directions (2011).

TIACRITIS (Tecuci et al., 2011a, 2011b) and Disciple-CD (Tecuci et al., 2014) are intelligent agents for evidence-based hypothesis analysis that help analysts in analyzing complex hypotheses and teach new analysts.

In the following section, we present an overview of the types of tasks that can be performed by expert systems, knowledge-based agents, and cognitive assistants.

1.6.2 An Ontology of Problem-Solving Tasks

Immanuel Kant, in his *Critique of Pure Reason* (Kant, 1781), considered that the two main reasoning operations are analysis and synthesis. *Analysis* comes from the Greek word *analyein*, which means "to break up." *It is a reasoning operation by which we break down a system or problem into parts or components to better understand or solve it. Synthesis* also comes from a Greek word, *syntithenai*, which means "to put together." *It is the complementary reasoning operation by which we combine system or solution components to form a coherent system or solution.*

Analysis and synthesis can be used as organizing principles for an ontology of problem-solving tasks for knowledge-based agents, as was done by Clancey (1985), Breuker and Wielinga (1989), and Schreiber et al. (2000, pp. 123–166). A fragment of such an ontology is presented in Figure 1.13.

An analytic task is one that takes as input some data about a system or object and produces a characterization of it as output. For example, in diagnosis, one analyzes the symptoms of a malfunctioning system in order to determine their cause.

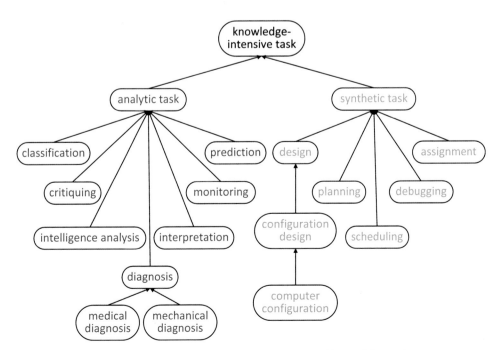

Figure 1.13. Ontology of knowledge-intensive problem-solving tasks.

A synthetic task is one which takes as input the requirements of an object or system and produces the corresponding object or system, as, for instance, in designing a car based on given specifications.

Under each type of analytic or synthetic task, one may consider more specialized versions of that task. For example, special cases of diagnosis are medical diagnosis and mechanical diagnosis. Special cases of mechanical diagnosis are car diagnosis, airplane diagnosis, and so on.

The importance of identifying such types of tasks is that one may create general models for solving them (e.g., a general model of diagnosis) that could guide the development of specialized systems (e.g., a system to diagnose Toyota cars).

Schreiber et al. (2000, pp. 123–166) present abstract problem-solving models for many of the task types in Figure 1.13. These abstract models can provide initial guidance when developing knowledge-based agents to perform such tasks.

1.6.2.1 Analytic Tasks

The following is a brief characterization with examples of the analytic tasks from Figure 1.13.

Classification means determining the class to which an object belongs as, for instance, determining that a plant is a rose based on its characteristics. Credit card companies, for instance, use classification software learned from examples that classify applicants into various categories corresponding to the type of card to be approved for them (if any).

Critiquing means expressing judgments about something according to certain standards. For example, one may identify strengths and weaknesses in a military course of action by considering the principles of war and the tenets of Army operations and determining how well each principle or tenet is illustrated by that course of action, as done by the Disciple-COA agent (Tecuci et al., 2001), which will be presented in Section 12.3.

Interpretation means inferring situation description from sensory data as, for example, interpreting gauge readings in a chemical process plant to infer the status of the process.

Monitoring means comparing observations of a dynamic system or process with the expected outcomes, to identify changes in its state and take appropriate actions. Examples include monitoring instrument readings in a nuclear reactor to detect accident conditions, or monitoring a patient in an intensive care unit based on the data from the monitoring equipment.

Prediction means inferring likely consequences of given situations, such as predicting the damage to crops from some type of insect, estimating global oil demand from the current geopolitical world situation, or forecasting the weather.

Diagnosis means inferring system malfunctions from observables, such as determining the disease of a patient from the observed symptoms, locating faults in electrical circuits, finding defective components in the cooling system of nuclear reactors, or diagnosing the faults in an electrical network.

Intelligence analysis means analyzing information to estimate the probability of various hypotheses, such as estimating the probability that Al Qaeda has nuclear weapons. Examples of systems for intelligence analysis are Disciple-LTA (Tecuci et al., 2005a; 2008a), TIACRITIS (Tecuci et al., 2011a, 2011b), and Disciple-CD (Tecuci et al., 2014).

1.6.2.2 Synthetic Tasks

The following is a brief characterization with examples of the synthetic tasks from Figure 1.13.

Design means configuring objects under constraints, such as designing an elevator with a certain capacity and speed, as done by the SALT system (Marcus, 1988), or designing a computer system with certain memory, speed, and graphical processing characteristics, based on a set of predefined components.

Planning means finding a set of actions that achieve a certain goal, such as determining the actions that need to be performed in order to repair a bridge, as done by the Disciple-WA agent (Tecuci et al., 2000), which will be discussed in Section 12.2. A more complex example is collaborative emergency response planning, illustrated by Disciple-VPT (Tecuci et al., 2008c), which is presented in Section 12.5.

Scheduling means allocating sequences of activities or jobs to resources or machines on which they can be executed, such as scheduling the lectures in the classrooms of a university, or scheduling the sequence of operations needed to produce an object on the available machines in a factory.

Debugging means prescribing remedies for malfunctions, such as determining how to tune a computer system to reduce a particular type of performance problem.

Assignment means creating a partial mapping between two sets of objects, such as allocating offices to employees in a company or allocating airplanes to gates in an airport.

1.6.3   Building Knowledge-based Agents

1.6.3.1 How Knowledge-based Agents Are Built and Why It Is Hard

As shown in the right-hand side of Figure 1.14, the basic components of a knowledge-based agent are the problem-solving engine and the knowledge base.

The problem-solving engine implements a general method of solving the input problems based on the knowledge from the knowledge base. An example of such a general method is problem reduction and solution synthesis, which will be discussed in detail in Chapter 4. As illustrated in the right side of Figure 1.15, this method consists in solving a problem, such as P_1, by successively reducing it, from the top down, to simpler and simpler problems; finding the solutions of the simplest problems; and successively combining these solutions, from the bottom up, into the solution of the initial problem (i.e., S_1).

Knowledge of the actual problems to solve and how they can be solved depends on the expertise domain. This knowledge is represented into the knowledge base of the system by using different representation formalisms. The left and middle parts of Figure 1.15 illustrate the representation of this knowledge by using an ontology of concepts and a set of rules expressed with these concepts. The ontology describes the types of objects in the application domain, as well as the relationships between them. Some of the rules are

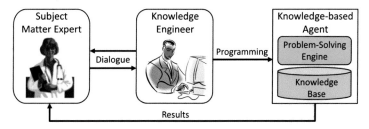

Figure 1.14. Conventional approach to building a knowledge-based agent.

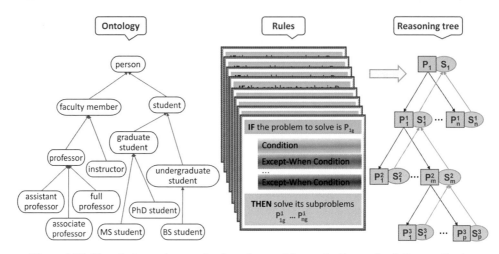

Figure 1.15. Knowledge and reasoning based on problem reduction and solution synthesis.

if-then structures that indicate the conditions under which a general complex problem (such as P_{1g}) can be reduced to simpler problems. Other rules indicate how the solutions of simpler problems can be combined into the solution of the more complex problem. These rules are applied to generate the reasoning tree from the right part of Figure 1.15.

Figure 1.14 illustrates the conventional approach to building a knowledge-based agent. A knowledge engineer interviews the subject matter expert to understand how the expert reasons and solves problems, identifies the knowledge used by the expert, and then represents it into the agent's knowledge base. For instance, the knowledge engineer may represent the knowledge acquired from the expert as an ontology of concepts and a set of reasoning rules expressed with these concepts, like those from Figure 1.15. Then the agent is used to solve typical problems, and the subject matter expert analyzes the generated solutions (e.g., the reasoning tree from the right side of Figure 1.15), and often the knowledge base itself, to identify errors. Referring to the identified errors, the knowledge engineer corrects the knowledge base.

After more than two decades of work on expert systems, Edward Feigenbaum (1993) characterized the knowledge-based technology as a tiger in a cage:

> The systems offer remarkable cost savings; some dramatically "hot selling" products; great return-on-investment; speedup of professional work by factors of ten to several hundred; improved quality of human decision making (often reducing errors to zero); and the preservation and "publishing" of knowledge assets of a firm. ... These stories of successful applications, repeated a thousand fold around the world, show that knowledge-based technology is a tiger. Rarely does a technology arise that offers such a wide range of important benefits of this magnitude. Yet as the technology moved through the phase of early adoption to general industry adoption, the response has been cautious, slow, and "linear" (rather than exponential).

The main reason for this less than exponential growth of expert systems lies in the difficulty of capturing and representing the knowledge of the subject matter expert in the system's knowledge base. This long, difficult, and error-prone process is known as the "knowledge acquisition bottleneck" of the system development process. But why is knowledge acquisition so difficult? First, much of an expert's problem-solving knowledge is in the form of tacit knowledge, which is difficult to make explicit (Nonaka and Krogh, 2009). Second, when describing their knowledge, experts use natural language, visual representations, and common sense, often omitting essential details that are implicit in human communication. This is very different from the way in which knowledge has to be represented into the knowledge base, which is formal, precise, and sufficiently complete. Finally, the knowledge engineer needs domain training in order to understand properly the expert's problem-solving knowledge, and this takes time and effort.

1.6.3.2 Teaching as an Alternative to Programming: Disciple Agents

In an interesting way, the difficulty of building knowledge-based systems confirms Turing's intuition that building an intelligent machine by programming is too difficult and that a simpler way might be to teach a learning agent: *"Instead of trying to produce a program to simulate the adult mind, why not rather try to produce one which simulates the child's? If this were then subjected to an appropriate course of education one would obtain the adult brain"* (Turing, 1950).

The Disciple learning and reasoning agents, which will be presented in detail in this book, represent one realization of Turing's intuition. A subject matter expert can teach a Disciple agent how to solve problems in ways that are similar to how the expert would teach a student or a collaborator (Tecuci, 1988; Tecuci, 1998; Boicu et al., 2000). For example, the expert will show the agent examples of how to solve specific problems, helping it to understand the solutions, and will supervise and correct the problem-solving behavior of the agent. The agent will learn from the expert by generalizing the examples and building its knowledge base. In essence, this creates a synergism between the expert who has the knowledge to be formalized and the agent that knows how to formalize it. This approach is based on methods for mixed-initiative problem solving, integrated teaching and learning, and multistrategy learning. In mixed-initiative problem solving (Tecuci et al., 2007a, 2007b), the expert solves the more creative parts of the problem and the agent solves the more routine ones. In integrated teaching and learning (Tecuci and Kodratoff, 1995; Tecuci, 1998), for example, the agent helps the expert to teach it by asking relevant questions, and the expert helps the agent to learn by providing examples, hints, and explanations. In multistrategy learning (Tecuci, 1993; Michalski and Tecuci, 1994), the agent integrates multiple learning strategies, such as learning from examples, learning from explanations, and learning by analogy, to learn from the expert how to solve problems.

Disciple agents have been developed in many domains, including intelligence analysis (Tecuci et al., 2011a, 2011b; 2014; 2015), modeling of the behavior of violent extremists, military center of gravity determination (Tecuci et al., 2002b; 2008b), course of action critiquing (Tecuci et al, 2001), planning (Tecuci et al, 2000; 2008c), financial services, and education (Tecuci and Keeling, 1999).

As illustrated in Figure 1.16, learning agents such as the Disciple agents contribute to a new age in the software systems development process. In the age of mainframe computers, the software systems were both built and used by computer science experts. In the current age of personal computers, such systems are still being built by computer science experts, but many of them (such as text processors, email programs, and Internet browsers) are regularly used by persons who have no formal computer science education. We think that this trend will continue, with the next age being that of cognitive assistants on the

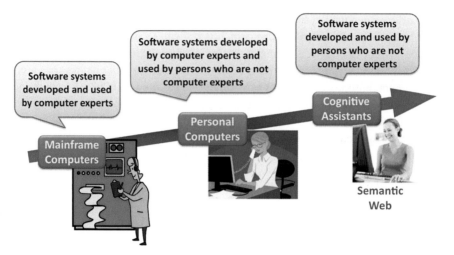

Figure 1.16. Evolution of software development and use.

Semantic Web, where typical computer users will be able to both develop and use special types of software agents.

The learning agent technology illustrated by the Disciple approach attempts to change the way the knowledge-based agents are built, from "being programmed" by a knowledge engineer to "being taught" by a user who does not have prior knowledge engineering or computer science experience. This approach will allow typical computer users, who are not trained knowledge engineers, to build by themselves cognitive assistants. Thus, non–computer scientists will no longer be only users of generic programs developed by others (such as word processors or Internet browsers), as they are today, but also agent developers themselves. They will be able to train their cognitive assistants to help them with their increasingly complex tasks in the Knowledge Society, which should have a significant beneficial impact on their work and life. This goal is consistent with the Semantic Web vision of enabling typical users to author Web content that can be understood by automated agents (Allemang and Hendler, 2011; W3C, 2015). Bill Gates has also stressed the great potential and importance of software assistants (Simonite, 2013).

Because the subject matter expert teaches a Disciple agent similarly to how the expert would teach a student, through explicit examples and explanations, a trained Disciple agent can be used as an assistant by a student, learning from the agent's explicit reasoning. Alternatively, Disciple may behave as a tutoring system, guiding the student through a series of lessons and exercises. Educational Disciple agents have been developed for intelligence analysis (Tecuci et al., 2011a, 2011b) and for center of gravity determination (Tecuci et al., 2008b). Thus the Disciple agents also contribute to advancing "Personalized Learning," which is one of the fourteen Grand Challenges for the Twenty-first Century identified by the U.S. National Academy of Engineering (NAE, 2008).

1.6.3.3 Disciple-EBR, Disciple-CD, and TIACRITIS

The Disciple learning agents theory and technology has been continuously developed over many years, with significant stages presented in a series of PhD theses (Tecuci, 1988; Dybala, 1996; Hieb, 1996; Keeling, 1998; Boicu M., 2002; Bowman, 2002; Boicu C., 2006;

Le 2008; Marcu 2009), and several books (e.g., Tecuci, 1998; Tecuci et al., 2008b). Some of the most representative implementations of this evolving theory and technology are discussed in Chapter 12. The rest of this book, however, focuses on the most recent advances of this theory and technology that enables the development of Disciple agents for evidence-based reasoning (EBR) tasks such as those introduced in Section 1.4.3. The corresponding agent development environment is called Disciple-EBR, which can be used by a subject matter expert, with support from a knowledge engineer, to develop a knowledge-based agent incorporating his or her expertise.

Disciple-EBR (the Disciple learning agent shell for evidence-based reasoning) will be used throughout this book to explain knowledge engineering concepts, principles, and methods using a hands-on approach. It will also be the software environment used in the agent design and development project.

There is also a reduced version of Disciple-EBR, called Disciple-CD (the Disciple cognitive assistant for "Connecting the Dots"). This version was created for the end-user who has no knowledge engineering experience and receives no support from a knowledge engineer (Tecuci et al., 2014). Therefore, when using Disciple-CD, the user does not have access to any Disciple-EBR module that may require any kind of knowledge engineering support, such as Ontology Development, Rule Learning, or Rule Refinement.

We have written a book for intelligence analysis courses, titled *Intelligence Analysis as Discovery of Evidence, Hypotheses, and Arguments: Connecting the Dots* (Tecuci et al., 2016), which uses Disciple-CD. This is because Disciple-CD incorporates a significant amount of knowledge about evidence and its properties, uses, and discovery to help the students acquire the knowledge, skills, and abilities involved in discovering and processing of evidence and in drawing defensible and persuasive conclusions from it, by employing an effective learning-by-doing approach. The students can practice and learn how to link evidence to hypotheses through abductive, deductive, and inductive reasoning that establish the basic credentials of evidence: its relevance, believability or credibility, and inferential force or weight. They can experiment with "what-if" scenarios and can study the influence of various assumptions on the final result of analysis. So, their learning experience will be a joint venture involving the intelligence analysis book together with their interaction with Disciple-CD.

Disciple-CD is a significant improvement over an earlier system that we have developed for intelligence analysis, called TIACRITIS (Teaching Intelligence Analysts Critical Thinking Skills), and it subsumes all the reasoning and learning capabilities of TIACRITIS that have been described in several papers (Tecuci et al., 2010b; 2011a; 2011b).

1.7 OBTAINING DISCIPLE-EBR

Disciple-EBR (Disciple, for short) is a learning agent shell for evidence-based reasoning. It is a research prototype implemented in Java and tested on PC. Disciple-EBR is a stand-alone system that needs to be installed on the user's computer.

For installation requirements and to download the system, visit http://lac.gmu.edu/KEBook/Disciple-EBR/. At this address, you will also find instructions on how to install and uninstall Disciple-EBR, a section with frequently asked questions (FAQs), and a section that allows users to submit error reports to the developers of the system.

REVIEW QUESTIONS

1.1. Consider the following illustrations of the concepts data, information, and knowledge:

Data: the color red.
Information: red tomato.
Knowledge: If the tomato is red, then it is ripe.

Data: the sequence of dots and lines "...–..."
Information: the "S O S" emergency alert.
Knowledge: If there is an emergency alert, then start rescue operations.

Provide two other illustrations of these concepts.

1.2. What is evidence?

1.3. Provide an example of an item of evidence.

1.4. Why does evidence differ from data or items of information?

1.5. Give an example of a fact F and of evidence about F. In general, what is the difference between a fact and evidence about that fact?

1.6. Formulate a hypothesis. Indicate an item of evidence that favors this hypothesis, an item of evidence that disfavors this hypothesis, and an item of information that is not evidence for this hypothesis.

1.7. What is deduction? Provide an example of deductive reasoning.

1.8. What is abduction? Give an example of abductive reasoning. Provide other explanations or hypotheses that are less plausible. Specify a context where one of these alternative explanatory hypotheses would actually be more plausible.

1.9. A doctor knows that the disease hepatitis causes the patient to have yellow eyes 90 percent of the time. The doctor also knows that the probability that a patient has hepatitis is one in one hundred thousand, and the probability that any patient has yellow eyes is one in ten thousand. What is the probability that a patient with yellow eyes has hepatitis?

1.10. Suppose that in answering a multiple-choice test question with five choices, a student either knows the answer, with probability p, or she guesses it with probability 1 – p. Assume that the probability of answering a question correctly is 1 for a student who knows the answer. If the student guesses the answer, she chooses one of the options with equal probability. What is the probability that a student knew the answer, given that she answered it correctly? What is this probability in the case of a true-false test question?

1.11. Consider a hypothesis H and its negation $\neg H$. Suppose you believe, before you have any evidence, that the prior probability of H is $P(H) = 0.30$. Now you receive an item of evidence E^* and ask yourself how likely is this evidence E^* if H were true, and how likely is this evidence E^*, if H were not true. Suppose you say that $P(E^*|H) = 0.70$ and $P(E^*|\neg H) = 0.10$. What are your prior odds $Odds(H : \neg H)$, and how have these odds changed as a result of the evidence E^*? What is the posterior probability $P(H|E^*)$?

1.12. Suppose in Question 1.11 you said that the prior probability of H is $P(H) = 0.20$ and the posterior probability $P(H|E^*) = 0.95$. What would be the force of evidence E^* (i.e., the likelihood ratio L_{E^*}) that is implied by these assessments you have made?

1.13. Think back to the very first time you were ever tutored about probability, what it means, and how it is determined. What were you told about these matters? Then describe your present views about these probability matters.

1.14. As we noted, the subjective Bayesian view of probability lets us assess probabilities for singular, unique, or one-of-a-kind events, provided that our assessed probabilities obey the three Kolmogorov axioms we discussed regarding enumerative probabilities. First, is there any way of showing that these axioms for enumerative probabilities also form the basis for ideal or optimal probability assessments in the nonenumerative case? Second, can this really be the rational basis for all probability assessments based on evidence?

1.15. Show how Bayes' rule supplies no method for incorporating "pure evidence" as does the Belief Function system.

1.16. Provide an example showing how an analyst's numerical assessment of a probability applied to a conclusion can invite criticism.

1.17. What is induction? Provide an example of inductive reasoning.

1.18. Consider the following statements:

(a) All the beans from this bag are white.
(b) These beans are from this bag.
(c) These beans are white.

We will arrange these statements in three different ways and you will have to identify what type of inference it represents (Walton, 2004).

(1) **Premise One:** (a) All the beans from this bag are white.
     Premise Two: (b) These beans are from this bag.
     Conclusion: (c) These beans are white.

(2) **Premise One:** (b) These beans are from this bag.
     Premise Two: (c) These beans are white.
     Conclusion: (a) All the beans from this bag are white.

(3) **Premise One:** (a) All the beans from this bag are white.
     Premise Two: (c) These beans are white.
     Conclusion: (b) These beans are from this bag.

1.19. Consider the following statements:

(a) These persons are French nationals.
(b) All the French nationals speak French.
(c) These persons speak French.

Arrange these statements in three different ways so that the reasoning is the indicated one (using a word in the conclusion that is characteristic to that type of reasoning):

Deductive Inference

Premise One:
Premise Two:
Conclusion:

Inductive Inference

Premise One:
Premise Two:
Conclusion:

Abductive Inference

Premise One:
Premise Two:
Conclusion:

1.20. Provide examples of evidence-based reasoning in law, medicine, geography, cyber-security, and intelligence analysis.

1.21. Give an example of an observation and of several hypotheses that would explain it.

1.22. Define artificial intelligence.

1.23. What is an intelligent agent?

1.24. Describe the generic architecture of an intelligent agent and the role of each main component.

1.25. Which are two main types of knowledge often found in the knowledge base of an agent?

1.26. What are some of the complementary abilities of humans and computer agents?

1.27. What would be a good mixed-initiative environment for problem solving and decision making? What are some key requirements for such an environment?

1.28. How do assumptions enable mixed-initiative problem solving? How do they enable problem solving in the context of incomplete information?

1.29. What is a knowledge-based system?

1.30. Which are some other examples of the analytic tasks introduced in Section 1.6.2.1?

1.31. Which are some other examples of the synthetic tasks introduced in Section 1.6.2.2?

1.32. Why is building a knowledge-based system difficult?

2 Evidence-based Reasoning: Connecting the Dots

In Section 1.4.3, we have briefly introduced evidence-based reasoning in various domains (see Figure 1.10, p. 28). In this section, we start with discussing the complexity of evidence-based reasoning by using the "connecting the dots" metaphor. Then we discuss in more detail evidence-based reasoning in a representative EBR domain, intelligence analysis. We conclude this section with other examples of evidence-based reasoning. Then the following chapters will address the development of such systems and of knowledge-based agents in general.

2.1 HOW EASY IS IT TO CONNECT THE DOTS?

The "connecting the dots" metaphor seems appropriate for characterizing evidence-based reasoning. This metaphor may have gained its current popularity following the terrorist attacks in New York City and Washington, D.C., on September 11, 2001. It was frequently said that the intelligence services did not connect the dots appropriately in order to have possibly prevented the catastrophes that occurred. Since then, we have seen and heard this metaphor applied in the news media to inferences in a very wide array of contexts, in addition to the intelligence, including legal, military, and business contexts. For example, we have seen it applied to allegedly faulty medical diagnoses; to allegedly faulty conclusions in historical studies; to allegedly faulty or unpopular governmental decisions; and in discussions involving the conclusions reached by competing politicians. What is also true is that the commentators on television and radio, or the sources of written accounts of inferential failures, never tell us what they mean by the phrase "connecting the dots." A natural explanation is that they have never even considered what this phrase means and what it might involve.

But we have made a detailed study of what "connecting the dots" entails. We have found this metaphor very useful, and quite intuitive, in illustrating the extraordinary complexity of the evidential and inferential reasoning required in the contexts we have mentioned. Listening or seeing some media accounts of this process may lead one to believe that it resembles the simple tasks we performed as children when, if we connected some collection of *numbered* dots correctly, a figure of Santa Claus, or some other familiar figure, would emerge. Our belief is that critics employing this metaphor in criticizing intelligence analysts and others have very little awareness of how astonishingly difficult the process of connecting *unnumbered* dots can be in so many contexts (Schum, 1987).

A natural place to begin our examination is by trying to define what is meant by the metaphor "connecting the dots" when it is applied to evidence-based reasoning tasks:

"Connecting the Dots" refers to the task of marshaling thoughts and evidence in the generation or discovery of productive hypotheses and new evidence, and in the construction of defensible and persuasive arguments on hypotheses we believe to be most favored by the evidence we have gathered and evaluated.

The following represents an account of seven complexities in the process of "connecting the dots."

2.1.1   How Many Kinds of Dots Are There?

It is so easy to assume that the only kind of dot to be connected concerns details in the observable information or data we collect that may eventually be considered as evidence in some analysis. We might refer to these dots as being *evidential dots*. Sherlock Holmes had another term for the details in observations he made, calling them *trifles*. As he told Dr. Watson: "You know my method, it is based on the observance of trifles." A related problem here is that most items of evidence may contain many details, dots, or trifles, some of which are interesting and others not. What this means is the information must be carefully parsed in order to observe its significant evidential dots. *Not all data or items of information we have will ever become evidence in an analysis task.*

Consider the bombing during the Boston Marathon that took place on April 15, 2013. Many images were taken during this event. One is a widely televised videotape of two young men, one walking closely behind the other, both carrying black backpacks. This is the evidential dot shown in the bottom-left of Figure 2.1. Why should we be interested in this evidence dot? Because it suggests ideas or hypotheses of what might have actually happened. Consider our ideas or thoughts concerning the relevance of the backpack dot just described. We have other evidence that the two bombs that were set off were small enough to be carried in backpacks. This allows the inference that the backpacks carried by the two young men might have contained explosive devices and that they should be considered as suspects in the bombing. A further inference is that these two men were the ones who actually detonated the two bombs.

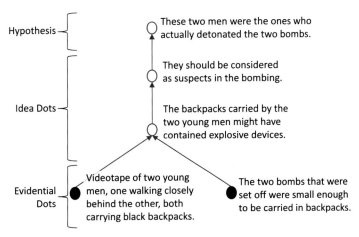

Figure 2.1. Types of dots to be connected: evidence, ideas, and hypotheses.

Thus, the second type of dot concerns ideas we have about how some evidential dots are connected to matters we are trying to prove or disprove. We commonly refer to the matters to be proved or disproved as *hypotheses*. Hypotheses commonly refer to possible alternative conclusions we could entertain about matters of interest in an analysis. The other dots, which we call *idea dots*, come in the form of links in chains of reasoning or arguments we construct to link evidential dots to hypotheses. Of course, hypotheses are also ideas. Each of these idea dots refers to sources of uncertainty or doubt we believe to be interposed between our evidence and our hypotheses. This is precisely where imaginative reasoning is involved. The essential task for the analyst is to *imagine* what evidential dots mean as far as hypotheses or possible conclusions are concerned. Careful *critical reasoning* is then required to check on the logical coherence of sequences of idea dots in our arguments or chains of reasoning. In other words, does the meaning we have attached to sequences of idea dots make logical sense?

2.1.2 Which Evidential Dots Can Be Believed?

The next problem we discuss is one of the most important, challenging, and interesting problems raised in any area of analysis. From some source, a sensor of some sort, or from a person, we obtain an evidential dot saying that a certain event has occurred. Just because this source says that this event occurred does not entail that it did occur. So, as discussed in Section 1.1.3, *what is vitally necessary is to distinguish between evidence of an event and the event itself.* We adopt the following notational device to make this distinction:

- E represents the actual occurrence of event E
- E^*_i represents the reported occurrence of event E from source I.

So, a basic inference we encounter is whether or not E did occur based on our evidence E^*_i. Clearly, this inference rests upon what we know about the *believability* of source I. There are some real challenges here in discussing the believability of source I. Section 4.7 of this book is devoted to the task of assessing the believability of the sources of our evidence. As we will see, Disciple-EBR (as well as Disciple-CD and TIACRITIS, introduced in Section 1.6.3.3) already knows much about this crucial task.

But there are even distinctions to be made in what we have called *evidential dots*. Some of these dots arise from objects we obtain or from sensors that supply us with records or images of various sorts. So one major kind of evidential dot involves what we can call *tangible evidence* that we can observe for ourselves to see what events it may reveal. In many other cases, we have no such tangible evidence but must rely upon the reports of human sources who allegedly have made observations of events of interest to us. Their reports to us come in the form of *testimonial evidence* or assertions about what they have observed. Therefore, an evidential dot E^*_i can be one of the following types:

- *Tangible evidence,* such as objects of various kinds, or sensor records such as those obtained by signals intelligence (SIGINT), imagery intelligence (IMINT), measurement and signature intelligence (MASINT), and other possible sources
- *Testimonial evidence* obtained from human sources (HUMINT)

The origin of one of the greatest challenges in assessing the *believability* of evidence is that we must ask different questions about the sources of tangible evidence than those we ask about the sources of testimonial evidence. Stated another way, the believability attributes of tangible evidence are different from the believability attributes of testimonial evidence. Consider again the evidential dot concerning the two men carrying backpacks. This is an example of *tangible evidence*. We can all examine this videotape to our heart's content to see what events it might reveal. The most important attribute of tangible evidence is its *authenticity:* Is this evidential dot what it is claimed to be? The FBI claims that this videotape was recorded on April 15, 2013, on Boyleston Street in Boston, Massachusetts, where the bombings occurred, and recorded before the bombings occurred. Our imaginations are excited by this claim and lead to questions such as those that would certainly arise in the minds of defense attorneys during trial. Was this videotape actually recorded on April 15, 2013? Maybe it was recorded on a different date. If it was recorded on April 15, 2013, was it recorded before the bombings occurred? Perhaps it was recorded after the bombings occurred. And, was this videotape actually recorded on Boyleston Street in Boston, Massachusetts? It may have been recorded on a different street in Boston, or perhaps on a street in a different city.

But there is another difficulty that is not always recognized that can cause endless trouble. While, in the case of tangible evidence, believability and credibility may be considered as equivalent terms, human sources of evidence have another characteristic apart from credibility; this characteristic involves their *competence*. As we discuss in Section 4.7.2, the credibility and competence characteristics of human sources must not be confused; to do so invites *inferential catastrophes*, as we will illustrate. The questions required to assess human source competence are different from those required to assess human source credibility. Competence requires answers to questions concerning the source's actual *access* to, and *understanding* of, the evidence he or she reports. Credibility assessment for a testimonial source requires answers to questions concerning the *veracity, objectivity*, and *observational sensitivity or accuracy* of the source. Disciple-EBR knows the credibility-related questions to ask of tangible evidence and the competence- and credibility-related questions to ask of HUMINT sources.

There is no better way of illustrating the importance of evidence believability assessments than to show how such assessments form the very foundation for all arguments we make from evidence to possible conclusions. In many situations, people will mistakenly base inferences on the assumption that an event E has occurred just because we have evidence E^*_i from source I. This amounts to the suppression of any uncertainty we have about the believability of source I (whatever this source might be). In Figure 2.2 is a

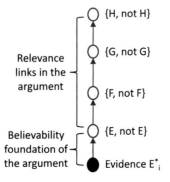

Figure 2.2. The believability foundation for an argument.

simple example illustrating this believability foundation; it will also allow us to introduce the next problem in connecting the dots.

What this figure shows is an argument from evidence E^*_i as to whether or not hypothesis H is true. As shown, the very first stage in this argument concerns an inference about whether or not event E actually occurred. This is precisely where we consider whatever evidence we may have about the believability of source I. We may have considerable uncertainty about whether or not event E occurred. All subsequent links in this argument concern the *relevance* of event E on hypothesis H. As we noted in Figure 2.1, these relevance links connect the *idea dots* we discussed. As Figure 2.2 shows, each idea dot is a source of uncertainty associated with the logical connection between whether or not event E did occur and whether or not H is true. Consideration of these relevance links is our next problem in connecting the dots.

2.1.3   Which Evidential Dots Should Be Considered?

In all of the contexts we have considered, there is usually no shortage of potential evidential dots. In fact, in many of these contexts, persons drawing conclusions about matters of importance are swamped with information or data. This situation is currently being called the "big data problem." Here we begin to consider vital matters concerning the discovery-related or investigative tasks and the imaginative or creative reasoning these tasks involve. Unfortunately, in many situations people or organizations try to collect *everything* in the hope of finding *something* useful in an inference task. This wasteful practice is one reason why the big data problem exists, since only a minute fraction of the information collected will be relevant in any inference of concern. In our work, we have paid great attention to the process of discovery that necessarily takes place in a world that keeps changing all the while we are trying to understand parts of it of interest to us in our inference tasks. As will be discussed in Section 2.2, this is an ongoing, seamless activity in which we have evidence in search of hypotheses, hypotheses in search of evidence, and the testing of hypotheses *all going on at the same time*. Hypotheses you entertain, questions you ask, particular evidence items, and your accumulated experience all allow you to examine which evidential dots to consider. Part of our objectives here is to make the process of discovery more efficient. As was discussed in Section 1.4.2, these discovery tasks involve mixtures of three different forms of reasoning: *deduction, induction* (probabilistic), and *abduction* (imaginative, creative, or insightful) reasoning. These forms of reasoning provide the bases for our idea dots.

2.1.4   Which Evidential Dots Should We Try to Connect?

Here comes a matter of great complexity. It usually happens that hypotheses we entertain are generated from observations we have made involving potential evidential dots. On limited occasions, we can generate a hypothesis from a single evidential dot. For example, in a criminal investigation finding a fingerprint will suggest a possible suspect in the case. But in most cases, it takes consideration of *combinations of evidential dots* in order to generate plausible and useful hypotheses, as illustrated in the following example based on accounts given in *Time Magazine* and the *Washington Post*. From European sources came word that terrorists of Middle Eastern origin would make new attempts to destroy the World Trade Center, this time *using airliners*. Many threats are received every day, most of which come to nothing. However, from several civilian flying schools in the United States came word (to the FBI) that persons from the Middle East were taking flying lessons, paying for them in cash, and wanting only to learn how to steer and navigate heavy aircraft but not how to make takeoffs and landings in these aircraft. By itself, this information, though admittedly strange, may not have seemed very important. But, *taken together*, these two items of information might have caused even Inspector Lestrade (the rather incompetent police investigator in Sherlock Holmes stories) to generate the hypothesis that there would be attacks on the World Trade Center using hijacked airliners. The hijackers would not need to learn how to make takeoffs; the aircrafts' regular pilots would do this. There would be no need for the hijackers to know how to land aircraft, since no landings were intended, only crashes into the World Trade Center and the Pentagon. Why were these two crucial items of information *not considered together*? The answer seems to be that they were not *shared* among relevant agencies. Information not shared cannot be considered jointly, with the result that their joint inferential impact could never have been assessed. For all time, this may become the best (or worst) example of failure to consider evidence items together. Even Sherlock Holmes would perhaps not have inferred what happened on September 11, 2001, if he had not been given these two items of information together.

The problem, however, is that here we encounter a combinatorial explosion, since the number of possible combinations of two or more evidential dots is *exponentially* related to the number of evidential dots we are considering. Suppose we consider having some number N of evidential dots. We ask the question: How many combinations C of two or more evidential dots are there when we have N evidential dots? The answer is given by the following expression: $C = 2^N - (N + 1)$. This expression by itself does not reveal how quickly this combinatorial explosion takes place. Here are a few examples showing how quickly C mounts up with increases in N:

- For $N = 10$, $C = 1013$
- For $N = 25$, $C = 33,554,406$
- For $N = 50$, $C = 1.13 \times 10^{15}$
- For $N = 100$, $C = 1.27 \times 10^{30}$

There are several important messages in this combinatorial analysis for evidence-based reasoning. The first concerns the size of N, the number of potential evidential dots that might be connected. Given the array of sensing devices and human observers available, the number N of potential evidential dots is as large as you wish to make it. In most analyses, N would certainly be greater than one hundred and would increase as time passes. Remember that we live in a nonstationary world in which things change and we find out about new things all the time. So, in most cases, even if we had access to the world's fastest computer, we could not possibly examine all possible evidential dot combinations, even when N is quite small.

Second, trying to examine all possible evidential dot combinations would be the act of looking through *everything* with the hope of finding *something*. This would be a silly thing to do, even if it were possible. The reason, of course, is that most of the dot combinations would tell us nothing at all. What we are looking for are combinations of evidential dots that interact or are dependent in ways that suggest new hypotheses or possible conclusions. If we would examine these dots separately or independently, we would not perceive these new possibilities. A tragic real-life example is what happened on September 11, 2001.

Figure 2.3 is an abstract example involving four numbered evidential dots. The numbers might indicate the order in which we obtained them. In part (a) of the figure, we show an instance where these four dots have been examined separately or independently, in which case they tell us nothing interesting. Then someone notices that, taken together, these four dots combine to suggest a new hypothesis H_K that no one has thought about before, as shown in part (b) of the figure. What we have here is a case of *evidential synergism* in which two or more evidence items mean something quite different when they are examined jointly than they would mean if examined separately or independently. Here we come to one of the most interesting and crucial evidence subtleties or complexities that have, quite frankly, led to intelligence failures in the past: *failure to identify and exploit evidential synergisms*. We will address this matter in other problems we mention concerning connecting the dots.

It might be said that the act of looking through everything in the hope of finding something is the equivalent of giving yourself a prefrontal lobotomy, meaning that you are ignoring any imaginative capability you naturally have concerning which evidential dot combinations to look for in your analytic problem area. What is absolutely crucial in selecting dot combinations to examine is an analyst's experience and imaginative reasoning capabilities. What we should like to have is a conceptual "magnet" that we could direct at a base of evidential dots that would "attract" interesting and important dot combinations.

2.1.5   How to Connect Evidential Dots to Hypotheses?

As will be discussed in Section 4.4, all evidence has three major credentials or properties: *relevance, believability or credibility*, and *inferential force or weight*. No evidence ever comes to us with these three credentials already attached; they must be established by defensible and persuasive arguments linking the evidence to the hypotheses we are considering. As we will see, *relevance* answers the question: So what? How is this datum or information item linked to something we are trying to prove or disprove? If such relevance linkage cannot be established, this datum is irrelevant or useless. As discussed previously, *believability* answers the question: Can we believe what this evidence is telling us? The *force or weight* credential asks: How strong is this evidence in favoring or disfavoring the hypothesis? This is where probability enters our picture, since, for very good reasons, the force or weight of evidence is always graded in probabilistic terms.

A relevance argument is precisely where the *idea dots* become so important. Considering an item of information, an analyst must imagine how this item could be linked to some hypothesis being considered before it could become an item of evidence. These idea dots

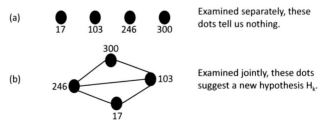

Figure 2.3. Evidential synergism.

forming this linkage come in the form of propositions or statements indicating possible sources of doubt or uncertainty in the imagined linkage between the item of information and hypotheses being considered. For a simple example, look again at Figure 2.2 (p. 49), where we show a connection between evidence E^*_i and hypothesis H. An analyst has an item of information from source I concerning the occurrence of event E that sounds very interesting. This analyst attempts to show how event E, if it did occur, would be relevant in an inference about whether hypothesis H is true or not. So the analyst forms the following chain of reasoning involving idea dots. The analyst says, "If event E were true, this would allow us to infer that event F might be true, and if F were true, this would allow us to infer that event G might be true. Finally, if event G were true, this would make hypothesis H more probable." If this chain of reasoning is defensible, the analyst has established the *relevance* of evidence E^*_i on hypothesis H.

In forming this argument, the analyst wisely begins with the believability foundation for this whole argument: Did event E really occur just because source I says it did? Also notice in Figure 2.2 that we have indicated the uncertainty associated with each idea dot in this argument. For example, the analyst only infers from E that F might have occurred and so we note that we must consider F and 'not F' as possibilities. The same is true for the other idea dot G and for the hypothesis dot H.

There are several important things to note about relevance arguments; the first concerns their defense. Suppose the argument in Figure 2.2 was constructed by analyst $\mathcal{A}$. $\mathcal{A}$ shows this argument to analyst $\mathcal{B}$, who can have an assortment of quibbles about this argument. Suppose $\mathcal{B}$ says, "You cannot infer F directly from E; you need another step here involving event K. From E you can infer that K occurred, and then if K occurred, then you can infer F." Now comes analyst $\mathcal{C}$, who also listens to $\mathcal{A}$'s argument. $\mathcal{C}$ says, "I think your whole argument is wrong. I see a different reasoning route from E to hypothesis H. From E we can infer event R, and from R we can infer event S, and from S we can infer T, which will show that hypothesis H is less probable." Whether or not there is any final agreement about the relevance of evidence E^*_i, analyst $\mathcal{A}$ has performed a real service by making the argument openly and available for discourse and criticism by colleagues. There are several important messages here.

First, there is no such thing as a uniquely correct argument from evidence to hypotheses. What we all try to avoid are disconnects or non sequiturs in the arguments we construct. But even when we have an argument that has no disconnects, someone may be able to come up with a better argument. Second, we have considered only the simplest possible situation in which we used just a single item of potential evidence. But intelligence analysis and other evidence-based reasoning tasks are based on masses of evidence of many different kinds and from an array of different sources. In this case, we are obliged to consider multiple lines of argument that can be connected in different ways. It is customary to call these complex arguments *inference networks*.

From years of experience teaching law students to construct defensible and persuasive arguments from evidence, we have found that most of them often experience difficulty in constructing arguments from single items of evidence; they quickly become overwhelmed when they are confronted with argument construction involving masses of evidence. But they gain much assistance in such tasks by learning about argument construction methods devised nearly a hundred years ago by a world-class evidence scholar named John H. Wigmore (1863–1943). Wigmore (1913, 1937) was the very first person to study carefully what today we call inference networks. We will encounter Wigmore's work in several places in our discussions, and you will see that Disciple-EBR employs elements of Wigmore's methods of argument construction.

There is also a message here for critics, such as newswriters and the talking heads on television. These critics always have an advantage never available to practicing intelligence analysts. Namely, they know how things turned out or what actually happened in some previously investigated matter. In the absence of clairvoyance, analysts studying a problem will never know for sure, or be able to predict with absolute certainty, what will happen in the future. A natural question to ask these critics is, "What arguments would you have constructed if all you knew was what the analysts had when they made their assessments?" This would be a very difficult question for them to answer fairly, even if they were given access to the classified evidence the analysts may have known at the time.

2.1.6   What Do Our Dot Connections Mean?

The previous topic concerns efforts designed to establish the *defensibility* of complex arguments. But what do these arguments mean to persons for whom these arguments are being constructed? This question raises matters concerning how *persuasive* are our arguments when they are taken all together. Our view is that the persuasiveness of an argument structure depends, in large part, upon the nature of the probabilities we assess and combine in making our arguments and in stating our major conclusions.

Here we consider the *direction* and *force* of our arguments based on the combined evidence we have considered. *Direction* refers to the hypothesis we believe our evidence favors most. *Force* means how strongly we believe the evidence favors this hypothesis over alternative hypotheses we have considered. There are two uncontroversial statements we can make about the force or weight of evidence. The first is that the force or weight of evidence has *vector-like* properties. What this means is that evidence points us in the direction of certain hypotheses or possible conclusions with varying degrees of strength. The second is that the force or weight of evidence is always graded in *probabilistic terms,* indicating our uncertainties or doubts about what the evidence means in terms of its inferential direction and force. But beyond these two statements, controversies begin to arise.

Before we consider assorted controversies, it is advisable to consider where our uncertainties or doubts come from in the conclusions we reach from evidence. Have a look once again at Figure 2.2, involving a simple example based on a single item of evidence. Our evidence here was E^*_i, from source I, saying that event E occurred. We ask the question: How strongly does this evidence E^*_i favor hypothesis H over not H? As we discussed, this argument was indicated by what we termed *idea dots*, each one indicating what the analyst constructing this argument believed to be sources of doubt or uncertainty associated with the argument from the evidence to the hypothesis. As you see, there are two major origins of uncertainty: those associated with the *believability* of source I, and those associated with links in the analyst's *relevance* argument. So, the force of evidence E^*_i on hypotheses H and not H depends on how much uncertainty exists in this entire argument involving each one of its believability and relevance links. The interesting message here is that the evidence force or weight credential depends on its other two credentials: believability and relevance.

In the simple example just discussed, there are four major origins of uncertainty, one associated with believability and three associated with relevance. But this is the easiest possible situation since it involves only one item of evidence. Think of how many sources of uncertainty there might be when we have a mass of evidence together with multiple complex and possibly interrelated arguments. The mind boggles at the enormity of the task of assessing the force or weight of a mass of evidence commonly encountered in intelligence analysis when we have some untold numbers of sources of believability and relevance uncertainties to assess and combine (Schum, 1987). We are certain that critics of intelligence analysts have never considered how many evidential and idea dots there would be to connect.

So, the question remains: How do we assess and combine the assorted uncertainties in complex arguments in intelligence analysis and in any other context in which we have the task of trying to make sense out of masses of evidence? Here is where controversies arise. The problem is that there are several quite different views among probabilists about what the force or weight of evidence means and how it should be assessed and combined across evidence in either simple or complex arguments: Bayesian, Belief Functions, Baconian, and Fuzzy (Schum, 1994[2001a]). Each of these views has something interesting to say, but no one view says it all, as discussed in Section 1.3.6.

Later in this book, we will discuss how Disciple-EBR allows you to assess and combine probabilistic judgments in situations in which many such judgments are required. There is further difficulty as far as judgments of the weight or force of evidence are concerned. Analysts, or teams of analysts, may agree about the construction of an argument but disagree, often vigorously, about the extent and direction of the force or weight this argument reveals. There may be strong disagreements about the believability of sources of evidence or about the strength of relevance linkages. These disagreements can be resolved only when arguments are made carefully and are openly revealed so that they can be tested by colleagues. A major mission of Disciple-EBR is to allow you to construct arguments carefully and critically and encourage you to share them with colleagues so that they can be critically examined.

There is one final matter of interest in making sense out of masses of evidence and complex arguments. Careful and detailed argument construction might seem a very laborious task, no matter how necessary it is. Now consider the task of revealing the conclusions resulting from an analysis to some policy-making "customer" who has decisions to make that rest in no small part on the results of an intelligence analysis. What this customer will probably not wish to see is a detailed inference network analysis that displays all of the dots that have been connected and the uncertainties that have been assessed and combined in the process. A fair guess is that this customer will wish to have a narrative account or a story about what the analysis predicts or explains. In some cases, customers will require only short and not extensive narratives. This person may say, "Just tell me the conclusions you have reached and briefly why you have reached them." So the question may be asked: Why go to all the trouble to construct defensible and persuasive arguments when our customers may not wish to see their details?

There is a very good answer to the question just raised. Your narrative account of an analysis *must be appropriately anchored on the evidence you have*. What you wish to be able to tell is a story that you believe contains some truth; that is, it is not just a good story. The virtue of careful and critical argument construction is that it will allow you to anchor your narrative not only on your imagination, but also on the care you have taken to subject your analysis to critical examination. There is no telling what questions you might be asked about your analysis. Rigor in constructing your arguments from your evidence is the best protection you have in dealing with customers and other critics who might have entirely different views regarding the conclusions you have reached. Disciple-EBR is designed to allow you and others to evaluate critically the arguments you have constructed.

2.2   SAMPLE EVIDENCE-BASED REASONING TASK: INTELLIGENCE ANALYSIS

The purpose of intelligence analysis is to answer questions arising in the decision-making process by analyzing evidence about the world, such as, "Does Al Qaeda have nuclear weapons?" or, "Will the United States be the world leader in nonconventional energy sources within the next decade?" This is done by determining the probabilities of alternative (hypothesized) answers, based on evidence, and by selecting the most likely answer.

As discussed in Section 1.4.2, intelligence analysis, like other evidence-based reasoning tasks, can be viewed as ceaseless discovery of evidence, hypotheses, and arguments in a nonstationary world, involving collaborative processes of evidence in search of hypotheses, hypotheses in search of evidence, and evidentiary testing of hypotheses (see Figure 1.9, p. 27). Since these processes are generally very complex and involve both imaginative and critical reasoning, they can be best approached through the synergistic integration of the analyst's imaginative reasoning and the computer's knowledge-based critical reasoning, as was discussed in Section 1.5.2, and will be illustrated with the use of the Disciple-EBR cognitive assistant.

The following sections illustrate this systematic approach to intelligence analysis by using a specific example of anticipatory analysis. At the same time, this example introduces the main concepts related to evidence and inference.

2.2.1   Evidence in Search of Hypotheses

Consider that you are an intelligence analyst and you read in today's *Washington Post* an article that concerns how safely radioactive materials are stored in this general area. Willard, the investigative reporter and author of this piece, begins by noting how the storage of nuclear and radioactive materials is so frequently haphazard in other countries and wonders how carefully these materials are guarded here in the United States, particularly in this general area. In the process of his investigations, the reporter notes his discovery that a canister containing cesium-137 has gone missing from the XYZ Company in Maryland, just three days ago. The XYZ Company manufactures devices for sterilizing medical equipment and uses cesium-137 in these devices along with other radioactive materials. This piece arouses your curiosity because of your concern about terrorists planting dirty bombs in our cities. The question is: *What hypotheses would explain this observation?* You experience a flash of insight that a dirty bomb may be set off in the Washington, D.C., area (see Figure 2.4).

However, no matter how imaginative or important this hypothesis is, no one will take it seriously unless you are able to justify it. So you develop the chain of abductive inferences shown in Table 2.1 and in Figure 2.5.

The chain of inferences from Table 2.1 and Figure 2.5 shows clearly the possibility that a dirty bomb will be set off in the Washington, D.C., area. Can you then conclude that this will actually happen? No, because there are many other hypotheses that may explain this evidence, as shown in Figure 2.6 and discussed in the following paragraphs.

Just because there is evidence that the cesium-137 canister is missing does not mean that it is indeed missing. At issue here is the believability of Willard, the source of this information. What if this Willard is mistaken or deceptive? Thus an alternative hypothesis is that the cesium-137 canister is not missing.

Table 2.1 Abductive Reasoning Steps Justifying a Hypothesis

There is evidence that the cesium-137 canister is missing (E^*).

Therefore, it is possible that the cesium-137 canister is indeed missing (H_1).

Therefore, it is possible that the cesium-137 canister was stolen (H_2).

Therefore, it is possible that the cesium-137 canister was stolen by someone associated with a terrorist organization (H_3).

Therefore, it is possible that the terrorist organization will use the cesium-137 canister to construct a dirty bomb (H_4).

Therefore, it is possible that the dirty bomb will be set off in the Washington, D.C., area (H_5).

H: A dirty bomb will be set off in the Washington, D.C., area

Insight

E*: Article on cesium-137 canister missing

What hypotheses would explain this observation?

Figure 2.4. Hypothesis generation through imaginative reasoning.

But let us assume that the cesium-137 canister is indeed missing. Then it is possible that it was stolen. But it is also possible that it was misplaced, or maybe it was used in a project at the XYZ Company without being checked out from the warehouse?

However, let us assume that the cesium-137 canister was indeed stolen. It is then possible that it might have been stolen by a terrorist organization, but it is also possible that it might have been stolen by a competitor or by an employee, and so on.

This is the process of *evidence in search of hypotheses*, shown in the left side of Figure 1.9 (p. 27). You cannot conclude that a dirty bomb will be set off in the Washington, D.C., area (i.e., hypothesis H_5) until you consider all the alternative hypotheses and show that those on the chain from E^* to H_5 are actually more likely than their alternatives. But to analyze all these alternative hypotheses and make such an assessment, you need additional evidence. How can you get it? As represented in the middle of Figure 1.9, you put each hypothesis to work to guide you in the collection of additional evidence. This process is discussed in the next section.

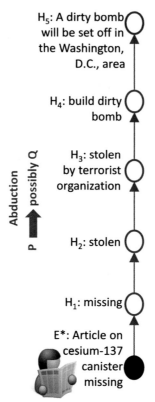

What hypotheses would explain this observation?

Evidence in search of hypotheses

Figure 2.5. Justification of the generated hypothesis.

2.2.2 Hypotheses in Search of Evidence

Let us first consider the hypothesis "H_1: missing" from the bottom of Figure 2.6, shown as "H_1: cesium-137 canister is missing from warehouse," in the top-left of Figure 2.7. The question is: *Assuming that this hypothesis is true, what other things should be observable?* Which are the necessary and sufficient conditions for an object to be missing from a warehouse? It was in the warehouse, it is no longer there, and no one has checked it out.

This suggests the decomposition of the hypothesis H_1 into three simpler hypotheses, as shown in the left part of Figure 2.7. This clearly indicates that you should look for evidence that indeed the cesium-137 canister was in the warehouse, that it is no longer there, and that no one has checked it out. That is, by putting hypothesis H_1 to work, you were guided to perform the collection tasks from Table 2.2, represented in Figure 2.7 by the gray circles.

Guided by the evidence collection tasks in Table 2.2, you contact Ralph, the supervisor of the XYZ warehouse, who provides the information shown in Table 2.3 and in Figure 2.7.

When you are given testimonial information, or descriptions of tangible items, the information might contain very many details, dots, or trifles. Some of the details might be interesting and relevant evidence, and others not. What you always have to do is to parse the information to extract the information that you believe is relevant in the inference task

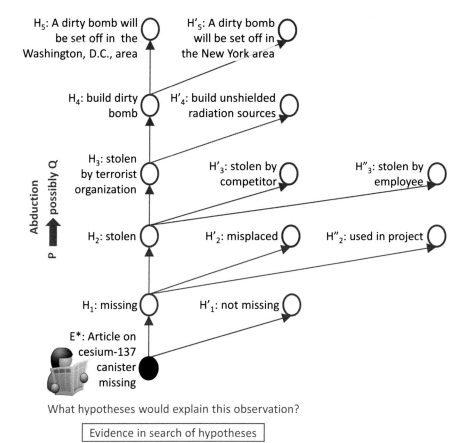

What hypotheses would explain this observation?

Evidence in search of hypotheses

Figure 2.6. Competing hypotheses explaining an item of evidence.

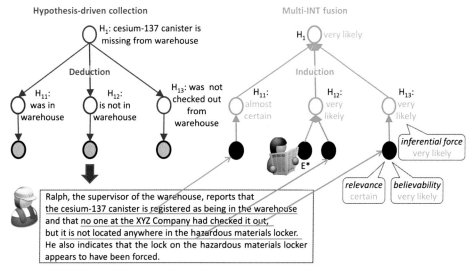

Figure 2.7. Hypothesis-driven evidence collection and hypothesis testing.

Table 2.2 Evidence Collection Tasks Obtained from the Analysis in Figure 2.7

Collection Task1: Look for evidence that the cesium-137 canister was in the XYZ warehouse before being reported as missing.

Collection Task2: Look for evidence that the cesium-137 canister is no longer in the XYZ warehouse.

Collection Task3: Look for evidence that the cesium-137 canister was not checked out from the XYZ warehouse.

Table 2.3 Information Obtained through the Collection Tasks in Table 2.2

INFO-002-Ralph: Ralph, the supervisor of the warehouse, reports that the cesium-137 canister is registered as being in the warehouse and that no one at the XYZ Company had checked it out, but it is not located anywhere in the hazardous materials locker. He also indicates that the lock on the hazardous materials locker appears to have been forced.

Table 2.4 Dots or Items of Evidence Obtained from Willard and Ralph

E001-Willard: Willard's report in the *Washington Post* that a canister containing cesium-137 was missing from the XYZ warehouse in Baltimore, MD.

E002-Ralph: Ralph's testimony that the cesium-137 canister is registered as being in the XYZ warehouse.

E003-Ralph: Ralph's testimony that no one at the XYZ Company had checked out the cesium-137 canister.

E004-Ralph: Ralph's testimony that the canister is not located anywhere in the hazardous materials locker.

E005-Ralph: Ralph's testimony that the lock on the hazardous materials locker appears to have been forced.

---

at hand. Consider, for example, the information provided by Willard in his *Washington Post* article. You parse it to extract the relevant information represented as E001-Willard in Table 2.4. Similarly, Ralph's testimony from Table 2.3 provides you with several dots or items of evidence that are relevant to assessing the hypotheses from Figure 2.7. These items of evidence are represented in Table 2.4.

This is the process of *hypotheses in search of evidence* that guides you in collecting new evidence. The next step now is to assess the probability of hypothesis H₁ based on the collected evidence, as represented in the right-hand side of Figure 1.9 (p. 27), and discussed in the next section.

2.2.3   Evidentiary Testing of Hypotheses

Having identified evidence relevant to the leaf hypotheses in Figure 2.7, the next step is to use it in order to assess these hypotheses. The assessments of the hypotheses will be done by using probabilities that are expressed in words rather than in numbers. In particular, we will use the ordered symbolic probability scale from Table 2.5. This is based on a combination of ideas from the Baconian and Fuzzy probability systems (Schum, 1994 [2001a], pp. 243–269). As in the Baconian system, "no support" for a hypothesis means that we have no basis to consider that the hypothesis might be true. However, we may later find evidence that may make us believe that the hypothesis is "very likely," for instance.

To assess the hypotheses, you first need to attach each item of evidence to the hypothesis to which it is relevant, as shown in the right side of Figure 2.7. Then you need to establish the *relevance* and the *believability* of each item of evidence, which will result in the *inferential force* of that item of evidence on the corresponding hypothesis, as illustrated in the right side of Figure 2.7 and explained in the following.

So let us consider the hypothesis "H_{13}: cesium-137 canister was not checked out from the warehouse" and the item of evidence "E003-Ralph: Ralph's testimony that no one at the XYZ Company had checked out the cesium-137 canister."

Relevance answers the question: So what? How does E003-Ralph bear on the hypothesis H_{13} that you are trying to prove or disprove? If you believe what E003-Ralph is telling us, then H_{13} is "certain."

Believability answers the question: To what extent can you believe what E003-Ralph is telling you? Let us assume this to be "very likely."

Inferential force or weight answers the question: How strong is E003-Ralph in favoring H_{13}? Obviously, an item of evidence that is not relevant to the considered hypothesis will have no inferential force on it and will not convince you that the hypothesis is true. An item of evidence that is not believable will have no inferential force either. Only an item of evidence that is both very relevant and very believable will make you believe that the hypothesis is true. In general, the inferential force of an item of evidence (such as E003-Ralph) on a hypothesis (such as H_{13}) is the minimum of its relevance and its believability. You can therefore conclude that, based on E003-Ralph, the probability of the hypothesis H_{13} is "very likely" (i.e., the minimum of "certain" and "very likely"), as shown in Figure 2.7.

Notice in Figure 2.7 that there are two items of evidence that are relevant to the hypothesis H_{12}. In this case, the probability of H_{12} is the result of the combined (maximum) inferential force of these two items of evidence.

Once you have the assessments of the hypotheses H_{11}, H_{12}, and H_{13}, the assessment of the hypothesis H_1 is obtained as their minimum, because these three subhypotheses are necessary and sufficient conditions for H_1. Therefore, all need to be true in order for H_1 to be true, and H_1 is as weak as its weakest component.

Thus, as shown at the top-right side of Figure 2.7, you conclude that it is "very likely" that the cesium-137 canister is missing from the warehouse.

Notice that this is a process of *multi-intelligence fusion* since, in general, the assessment of a hypothesis involves fusing different types of evidence.

Figure 2.8 summarizes the preceding analysis, which is an illustration of the general framework from Figure 1.9 (p. 27).

Table 2.5 Ordered Symbolic Probability Scale

no support < likely < very likely < almost certain < certain

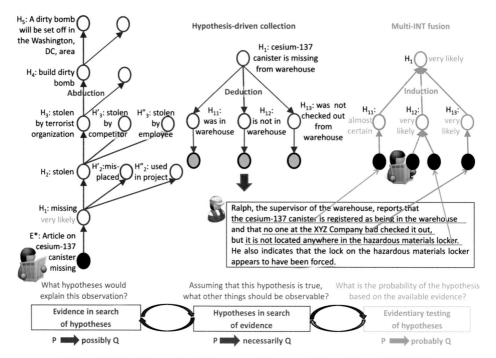

Figure 2.8. An illustration of the general framework from Figure 1.9 (p. 27).

Now that you have concluded "H_1: missing," you repeat this process for the upper hypotheses (i.e., H_2: stolen, H'_2: misplaced, and H''_2: used in project), as will be discussed in the next section.

2.2.4 Completing the Analysis

Let us first consider the hypothesis "H_2: stolen." You need to put this hypothesis to work to guide you in collecting relevant evidence for its analysis. During your investigation of the security camera of the warehouse, you discover a video segment showing a person loading a container into a U-Haul panel truck (E007-SecurityCamera). This new item of evidence, together with Ralph's testimony that the lock on the hazardous materials locker appears to have been forced (E005-Ralph in Table 2.4), suggests the following scenario of how the cesium-137 canister might have been stolen (see Figure 2.9): *The truck entered the company, the canister was stolen from the locker, the canister was loaded into the truck, and the truck left with the canister.*

Such scenarios have enormous heuristic value in advancing the investigation because they consist of mixtures of what is taken to be factual and what is conjectural. Conjecture is necessary in order to fill in natural gaps left by the absence of existing evidence. Each such conjecture opens up new avenues of investigation, and the discovery of additional evidence, if the scenario turns out to be true. For instance, the first hypothesized action from the scenario ("Truck entered company") leads you to check the record of the security guard, which shows that a panel truck bearing Maryland license plate number MDC-578 was in the XYZ parking area the day before the discovery that the cesium-137 canister was missing (E008-GuardReport).

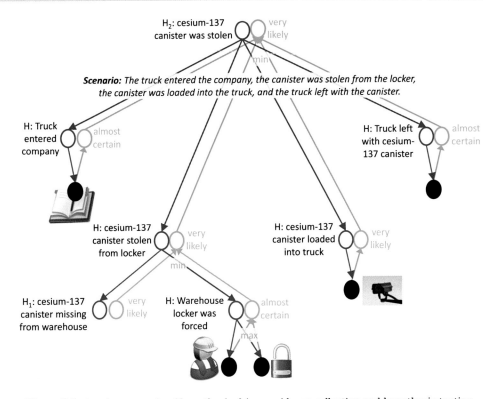

Figure 2.9. Another example of hypothesis-driven evidence collection and hypothesis testing.

The second hypothesized action in the scenario (i.e., "cesium-137 canister stolen from locker") is further decomposed into two hypotheses. The first one was already analyzed: "It is very likely that the cesium-137 canister is missing from the warehouse." The second subhypothesis ("Warehouse locker was forced") is supported both by Ralph's testimony (i.e., E005-Ralph in Table 2.4) and by the professional locksmith Clyde who was asked to examine it (E006-Clyde: Professional locksmith Clyde testimony that the lock has been forced, but it was a clumsy job).

After continuing the process for the remaining hypothesized actions in the scenario and fusing all the discovered evidence, you and Disciple-EBR conclude that it is "very likely" that the cesium-137 canister was stolen.

You repeat the same process for the other two competing hypotheses, "H'$_2$: misplaced," and "H"$_2$: used in project." However, you find no evidence that the cesium-137 canister might have been misplaced. Moreover, you find disfavoring evidence for the second competing hypothesis: Grace, the Vice President for Operations at XYZ, tells us that no one at the XYZ Company had checked out the canister for work on any project (E014-Grace).

Thus you conclude that the canister-137 was stolen and you continue the analysis with investigating the next level up of competing hypotheses: "H$_3$: stolen by terrorist organization"; "H'$_3$: stolen by competitor"; and "H"$_3$: stolen by employee." Of course, at any point, the discovery of new evidence may lead you to refine your hypotheses, define new hypotheses, or eliminate existing hypotheses.

This example is not as simple as it may be inferred from this presentation. It is the methodology that guides you and makes it look simple. Many things can and will indeed go wrong. But the computational theory of evidence-based reasoning and Disciple-EBR provide you the means to deal with them. Based on evidence, you come up with some hypotheses, but then you cannot find evidence to support any of them. So you need to come up with other hypotheses, and you should always consider alternative hypotheses. The deduction-based decomposition approach guides you on how to look for evidence, but your knowledge and imagination also play a crucial role. As illustrated here, you imagined a scenario where the cesium-137 canister was stolen with a truck. But let us now assume that you did not find supporting evidence for this scenario. Should you conclude that the cesium-137 canister was not stolen? No, because this was just one scenario. If you can prove it, you have an assessment of your hypothesis. However, if you cannot prove it, there still may be another scenario on how the cesium-137 canister might have been stolen. Maybe the cesium-137 canister was stolen by someone working at the XYZ Company. Maybe it was stolen by Ralph, the administrator of the warehouse. The important thing is that each such scenario opens a new line of investigation and a new way to prove the hypothesis.

Having established that the cesium-137 canister was stolen, you would further like to determine by whom and for what purpose. If it is for building and setting off a dirty bomb, you would like to know who will do this; where exactly in the Washington, D.C., area will the bomb be set off; precisely when this action will happen; what form of dirty bomb will be used; and how powerful it will be. These are very hard questions that the computational theory of evidence-based reasoning (as well as its current implementation in Disciple-EBR) will help you answer.

One major challenge in performing such an analysis is the development of argumentation structures. An advantage of using an advanced tool, such as Disciple-EBR, is that it can learn reasoning rules from the user to greatly facilitate and improve the analysis of similar hypotheses, as will be shown in the next chapters of this book.

In conclusion, the computational theory of evidence-based reasoning presented in this volume, as well as its current implementation in Disciple-EBR, provides a framework for integrating the art and science of evidence-based reasoning, to cope with its astonishing complexity.

More details about intelligence analysis are presented in our book *Intelligence Analysis as Discovery of Evidence, Hypotheses, and Arguments: Connecting the Dots* (Tecuci et al., 2016). Other examples of applications of evidence-based reasoning are presented in the next section.

2.3   OTHER EVIDENCE-BASED REASONING TASKS

2.3.1   Cyber Insider Threat Discovery and Analysis

Cyber insider threats are persons who operate inside an organization and use legitimate access and normal tactics to accomplish abnormal and malicious cyber-missions, such as to perform data reconnaissance, collection, and exfiltration, or to create vulnerabilities for cyber-attacks by outsiders. These persons represent a major national security concern, a critical concern for businesses that need to protect their intellectual property, as well as a huge privacy concern.

In the following, we will present a hypothetical agent for cyber-insider threat discovery and analysis. This example was developed with the assistance of Professor Angelos Stavrou from George Mason University. We will assume that we have a set of monitoring agents that perform persistent surveillance of a computer network and host systems. They include login monitors, file system monitors, internal network monitors, port monitors, outside network monitors, and others. These monitoring agents are constantly looking for indicators and warnings of insider missions.

Let us further assume that the evidence collection agents have detected a record inside network logs involving an instance of denied access from the device with the Internet Protocol address IP_1 to the device with the address IP_2, at time T. This is *evidence* E^* at the bottom of Figure 2.10. While this *denied service access* might be a normal event of an accidental access to a shared resource generated by legitimate browsing on a local host, it can also be an indication of an improper attempt to access a shared network resource. Therefore, the question is: *What insider missions might explain this observation?*

By means of *abductive reasoning*, which shows that something is *possibly* true, the analysis agent may formulate the chain of explanatory hypotheses from the left side of Figure 2.10:

It is possible that the observed denied access from IP_1 to IP_2 is part of a sequence of attempted network service accesses from IP_1 to other IPs (hypothesis H_{11}). It is further possible that this is part of a network scan for files (hypothesis H_{21}). It is possible that this network scan is in fact a malicious attempt to discover network shared files (hypothesis H_{31}), part of malicious covert reconnaissance (hypothesis H_{41}), which may itself be part of a covert reconnaissance, collection, and exfiltration mission (hypothesis H_{51}).

As one can notice, these hypotheses are very vague at this point. Moreover, for each of these hypotheses there are alternative hypotheses, as shown in the right-hand side of Figure 2.10. For example, the denied access may be part of a single isolated attempt (hypothesis H_{12}). However, even in the case where we have established that the denied service access is part of a sequence of accesses (hypothesis H_{11}), it is still possible that this

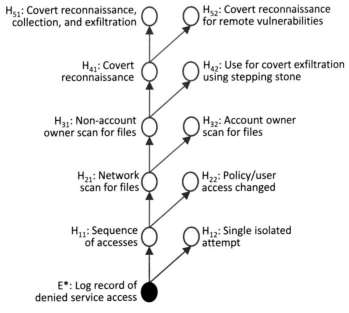

Figure 2.10. Evidence in search of insider missions (abductive reasoning).

sequence of accesses is due to recent policy changes that affected the user's access to specific services or objects (hypothesis H_{22}).

What the agent needs to do is to test each of these alternative hypotheses, *starting from bottom up,* to make sure that, if an insider mission is actually being performed, it is promptly detected. Each of the bottom-level alternative hypotheses (i.e., H_{11} and H_{12}) is put to work to guide the collection of relevant evidence (see Figure 2.11). The discovered evidence may lead to the refinement of the hypotheses, including the possible formulation of new hypotheses, and these refined hypotheses may lead to new evidence. Next, the discovered evidence is used to assess the probabilities of the bottom-level alternative hypotheses.

Assuming that the most likely hypothesis was determined to be H_{11}, this process continues with the next level up of alternative hypotheses (i.e., H_{21} and H_{22}), using them to collect evidence, and assessing which of them is most likely, as illustrated in Figure 2.12.

Now, since H_{21} was assessed as being "very likely," it is possible that H_{31} is true. But it is also possible that H_{32} is true. The right-hand side of Figure 2.13 illustrates the process of using the hypothesis H_{31} in order to guide the collection of evidence to test it:

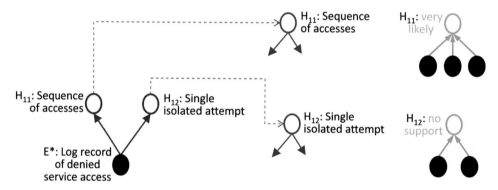

Figure 2.11. Evidence collection and assessment of the bottom-level hypotheses in Figure 2.10.

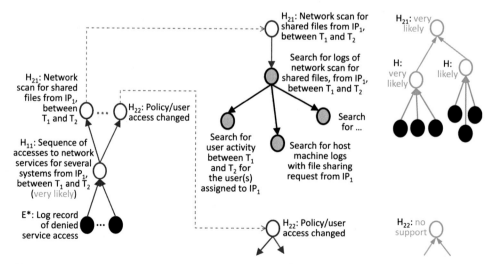

Figure 2.12. Evidence collection and assessment for the next level up of alternative hypotheses.

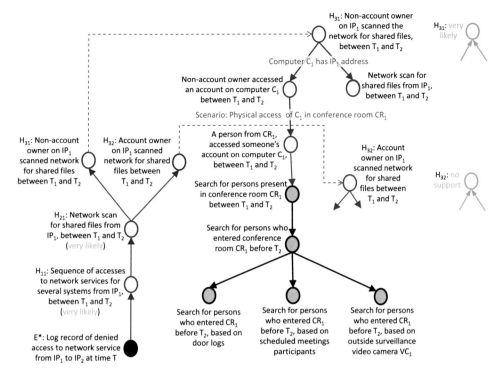

Figure 2.13. Evidence collection and assessment of higher-level alternative hypotheses.

If "H_{31}: Non-account owner on IP_1 scanned the network for shared files, between T_1 and T_2" were true

Then the following subhypotheses would also be true:
"Non-account owner accessed an account on computer C_1 between T_1 and T_2"
"Network scan for shared files from IP_1, between T_1 and T_2"

To collect evidence for the first subhypothesis, we need to consider possible scenarios for a non-account owner to access computer C_1. The scenario illustrated in Figure 2.13 is a physical access to C_1 in the conference room CR_1 where C_1 is located. Another possible scenario is a virtual access to C_1.

As discussed in Section 2.2.4, such scenarios have *enormous heuristic value* in advancing the investigation. In this case, for example, we are guided toward searching for persons who were present in CR_1 between T_1 and T_2. As indicated at the bottom of Figure 2.13, there are several possible strategies to look for such persons:

Search for persons who entered CR_1 before T_2, based on door logs.
Search for persons who entered CR_1 before T_2, based on scheduled meetings participants.
Search for persons who entered CR_1 before T_2, based on outside surveillance video camera VC_1.

Notice that these are precise queries that can be answered very fast. Notice also that, in this particular case, they involve all-source (non-computer) evidence. *It is very important to be able to use both computer and non-computer evidence* to discover cyber insider threats.

This process will continue until the top-level hypothesis is assessed, as illustrated in Figure 2.14.

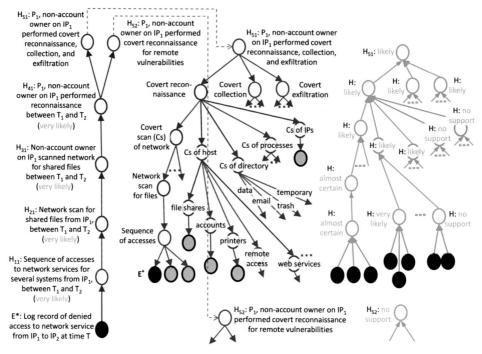

Figure 2.14. Evidence collection and assessment of top-level alternative hypotheses.

2.3.2   Analysis of Wide-Area Motion Imagery

Capabilities exist today to persistently monitor fixed geographic locations (such as conflict areas) as wide as 100 km^2, for long periods of time, using electro-optic sensors (see Figure 2.15). This leads to the collection of huge amounts of data to be used either in *real-time analysis* or in *forensic analysis*. During real-time analysis, analysts attempt to discover impeding threat events (e.g., ambush, kidnapping, rocket launch, false check-point, suicide bomber, and improvised explosive devices [IEDs]) in time to react. During forensic analysis, the analysts backtrack from such an event (e.g., an ambush) in order to discover the participants, possible related locations and events, and the specific movement patterns (Desai, 2009). The problem, however, is that the manual analysis of these huge amounts of data would require thousands of analysts. Thus the use of a cognitive assistant, such as Disciple-EBR, is very helpful.

Let us consider an analyst who performs *real-time analysis* of the wide area motion imagery of a region characterized by insurgency operations. Road work at a highway intersection suggests the hypothesis that there is an ambush threat to the U.S. forces. Table 2.6 shows a chain of abductive inferences leading to this hypothesis. The corresponding intermediary hypotheses and their alternatives are also shown in the left-hand side of Figure 2.16. All these hypotheses would need to be analyzed.

The analyst uses Disciple-EBR to analyze these hypotheses. Because Disciple-EBR was previously taught how to analyze such hypotheses, it automatically decomposes them into increasingly simpler hypotheses that guide the collection of relevant evidence. This is illustrated in the middle of Figure 2.16 with the top hypothesis "H$_k$: Ambush threat to U.S. forces at Al Batha highway junction." Thus, as indicated in the middle of Figure 2.16, an ambush threat at a certain location requires that location to be good for ambush

---

Table 2.6 Evidence in Search of Hypotheses through Abductive Reasoning

E^*_i: *There is evidence of road work at 1:17 am at the Al Batha highway junction.*

→ E_i: *It is possible that there is indeed road work at the Al Batha highway junction.*

→ H_a: *It is possible that the road work is for blocking the road.*

→ H_c: *It is possible that there is ambush preparation at the Al Batha highway junction.*

→ H_k: *It is possible that there is an ambush threat at the Al Batha highway junction.*

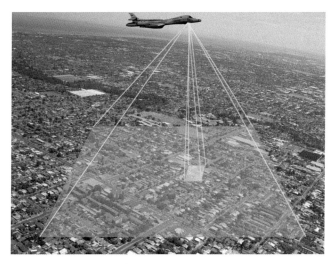

Figure 2.15. Wide-area motion imagery (background image reprinted from www.turbophoto.com/
Free-Stock-Images/Images/Aerial%20City%20View.jpg).

(H_b: Ambush location), and there should also be some observable ambush preparation activities (H_c: Ambush preparation). Further on, to be a good location for ambush requires the corresponding route to be used by the U.S. forces (H_d: Blue route), and there should also be cover at that location (H_e: Cover). This directly guides the analyst to check whether the U.S. forces are using that route. It also guides the analyst to analyze images of that location for the existence of cover. Having obtained the corresponding evidence, the analyst assesses its support of the corresponding subhypotheses, and Disciple-EBR automatically aggregates these assessments, concluding that it is almost certain that the location is good for ambush.

The rest of the analysis is developed in a similar way. The "H_c: Ambush preparation" activity is automatically decomposed into three simpler activities: "H_f: Deployment," "H_a: Road blocking," and "H_p: Move to cover." Further on, "H_f: Deployment" is decomposed into "H_g: Vehicle deployment" and "H_m: Insurgent vehicle," the last one being further decomposed into two subhypotheses. All these simpler subhypotheses guide the collection of corresponding relevant evidence which, in this example, is found and evaluated, leading Disciple-EBR to infer that the top-level hypothesis is very likely.

Let us now consider that the analyst does not perform real-time analysis, but *forensic analysis*. The ambush has already taken place (hence a third subhypothesis, "H_q: Ambush execution," of the top-level hypothesis), and the goal is to trace back the wide-area motion

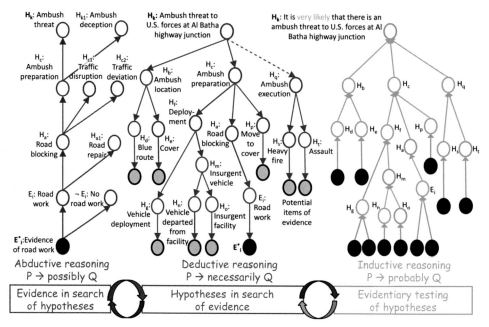

Figure 2.16. Another illustration of the general reasoning framework from Figure 1.9 (p. 27).

imagery in order to identify the participants together with the related locations and events. The analyst and Disciple-EBR develop a similar analysis tree, as discussed previously, which leads to the following hypotheses from the bottom of Figure 2.16: "H_n: Vehicle departed from facility" and "H_o: Insurgent facility." Thus, forensic analysis leads to the discovery of the facility from which the insurgents have departed, identifying it as an insurgent facility.

The same approach can also be used as a basis for the development of *collaborative autonomous agents* engaged in persistent surveillance and interpretation of unconstrained dynamic environments, continuously generating and testing hypotheses about the state of the world. Consider, for example, the use of such agents in counterinsurgency operations with the mission to automatically discover threat activities, such as IEDs, suicide bombers, rocket launches, kidnappings, or ambushes. Discovery by sensor agents of road work at a location that is often used by the U.S. forces leads to the hypothesis that there is an ambush threat at that location. This hypothesis is then automatically decomposed into simpler and simpler hypotheses, as discussed previously, guiding the agents to discover additional evidence. Then the ambush threat hypothesis is automatically assessed and an alert is issued if its probability is above a certain threshold.

2.3.3   Inquiry-based Teaching and Learning in a Science Classroom

2.3.3.1 Need for Inquiry-based Teaching and Learning

Significant progress has been made in K–12 science education with the development of the National Science Education Standards (NRC, 1996). These standards call for inquiry-based teaching and learning that, according to the standards, "refers to the diverse ways in which scientists study the natural world and propose explanations based on the evidence derived from their work. Inquiry also refers to the activities of students in which they develop knowledge and understanding of scientific ideas, as well as an understanding of how scientists study the natural world" (NRC, 1996, p. 23). "The research base on learning and on effective learning environments makes a strong case for inquiry-based approaches" (NRC, 2000, p. 128). The standards indicate that "teaching through inquiry is effective" (NRC, 2000, p. 126) and that the appropriate use of inquiry by the teachers "can have a powerful influence on their students' science learning" (NRC, 2000, p. 128).

However, "for students to understand inquiry and use it to learn science, their teachers need to be well-versed in inquiry and inquiry-based methods. Yet most teachers have not had opportunities to learn science through inquiry or to conduct scientific inquiries themselves. Nor do many teachers have the understanding and skills they need to use inquiry thoughtfully and appropriately in their classrooms" (NRC 2000, p. 87). "Currently, K–12 science education in the United States ... does not provide students with engaging opportunities to experience how science is actually done" (NRC, 2011, p. 1). "Instruction throughout K–12 education is likely to develop science proficiency if it provides students with opportunities for a range of scientific activities and scientific thinking, including, but not limited to: inquiry and investigation, collection and analysis of evidence, logical reasoning, and communication and application of information" (NRC, 2010, p. 137).

In this section, we will illustrate the use of a hypothetical Disciple-EBR agent in the science classroom. We will call this hypothetical agent *Inquirer*, to emphasize its purpose.

2.3.3.2 Illustration of Inquiry-based Teaching and Learning

The illustration presented in this section follows closely the introductory example of inquiry in a science classroom from *Inquiry and the National Science Education Standards* (NRC, 2000, pp. 5–11), modified only to show a hypothetical use of Inquirer.

Several of the students in Mrs. Graham's science class were excited when they returned to their room after recess one fall day. They pulled their teacher over to a window, pointed outside, and said, 'We noticed something about the trees on the playground. The left tree had lost all its leaves while the right tree had lush, green leaves. Why are those trees different? They used to look the same, didn't they?' Mrs. Graham didn't know the answer.

Mrs. Graham knew that her class was scheduled to study plants later in the year, and this was an opportunity for them to investigate questions about plant growth that they had originated and thus were especially motivated to answer. Although she was uncertain about where her students' questions would lead, Mrs. Graham chose to take the risk of letting her students pursue investigations with Inquirer's assistance and her guidance. "Let's make a list of hypotheses that might explain what's happening to the left tree." They came up with a list of competing explanatory hypotheses, including the following ones (shown also in the top-left of Figure 2.17):

H_1:   The left tree has lost its leaves because there is too much water at its root.
H_2:   The left tree has lost its leaves because it is older than the right tree.
H_3:   The left tree has lost its leaves because it is ill.

She then invited each student to pick one explanatory hypothesis, which led to several groups: a "water" group, an "age" group, an "illness" group, and so on. She asked each group to use the Inquirer assistant in order to plan and conduct a simple investigation to test their preferred hypothesis.

For the next three weeks, science periods were set aside for each group to carry out its investigation. Each group used the Inquirer assistant to conduct its investigation,

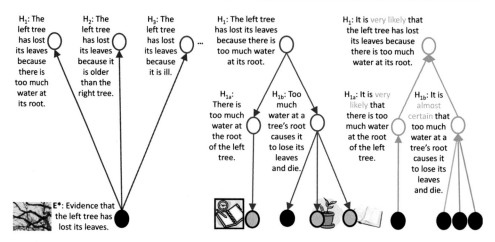

Figure 2.17. Systematic inquiry with a cognitive assistant (based on NRC, 2000, pp. 5–11).

discovering a variety of sources with information about characteristics of trees, their life cycles, and their environments. For example, the water group entered the following hypothesis into Inquirer:

H₁: The left tree has lost its leaves because there is too much water at its root.

The group's members reasoned that, if this hypothesis were true, then two simpler subhypotheses need to be true:

H₁ₐ: There is too much water at the root of the left tree.
H₁ᵦ: Too much water at a tree's root causes it to lose its leaves and die.

Therefore, they decomposed H₁ into H₁ₐ and H₁ᵦ by entering them into Inquirer (see the middle part of Figure 2.17) and decided to assess them based on evidence. As a result, Inquirer guided the students to look for both favoring and disfavoring evidence for each of these two subhypotheses.

To collect relevant evidence for H₁ₐ, the students decided to look at the ground around the two trees every hour that they could. They took turns on making individual observations, and since some of them lived near the school, their observations continued after school hours and on weekends. Even though they missed some hourly observations, they had sufficient data that they introduced into Inquirer as evidence E*₁ favoring H₁ₐ, because their observations confirmed the presence of excessive water at the root of the tree. As a result, Inquirer extended the analysis of H₁ₐ from the middle of Figure 2.17 with the blue tree shown in Figure 2.18, asking the students to assess the relevance of E₁ (the event indicated by the evidence E*₁) with respect to H₁ₐ, as well as the believability of the evidence E*₁.

Inquirer reminded the students that *relevance* answers the question: So what? May E₁ change my belief in the truthfulness of H₁ₐ? The students' answer was: Assuming that E*₁ is believable, it is very likely that there is too much water at the root of the left tree. They did this by selecting one value from the following list of probabilistic assessments displayed by Inquirer: {no support, likely, very likely, almost certain, certain}. They also justified their choice with the fact that during their observations, the tree was standing in water, which means that it is very likely that there is too much water there.

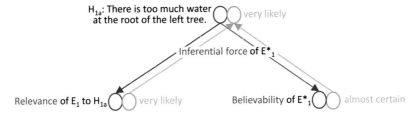

Figure 2.18. Evidence-based assessment of an elementary hypothesis.

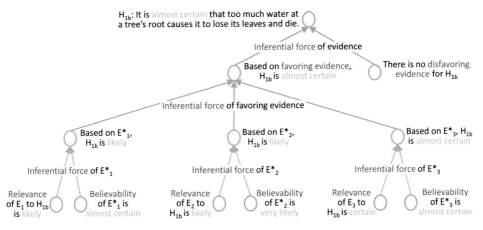

Figure 2.19. Inferential force of evidence on an elementary hypothesis.

Inquirer also reminded them that *believability* answers the question: Can we believe what E^*_1 is telling us? Here the students' answer was: Believability of E^*_1 is almost certain, since a few data points were missing and, on rare occasions, the left tree was not standing in water.

Based on the students' assessments, Inquirer determined the inferential force of E^*_1 on H_{1a}, as shown by the green reasoning tree in Figure 2.18: Based on E^*_1, it is very likely that there is too much water at the root of the left tree. Inquirer explained the students that *inferential force* answers the question: How strong is E^*_1 in favoring H_{1a}? An item of evidence, such as E^*_1, will make us believe that the hypothesis H_{1a} is true if and only if E_1^* is both highly relevant and highly believable. Therefore, the inferential force of E^*_1 on H_{1a} was computed as the minimum of the relevance of E_1 (very likely) and the believability of E^*_1 (almost certain), the minimum of which is very likely.

The students agreed that E_1^* also supports the hypothesis "H_{1b}: Too much water at a tree's root causes it to lose its leaves and die." They assessed the relevance of E_1 as likely (because E_1 is only one instance of this phenomenon), and the believability of E_1^* as almost certain, leading Inquirer to assess the inferential force of E_1^* on H_{1b} as likely, which is the minimum of the two (see the left part of Figure 2.19).

One of the students recalled that several months ago the leaves on one of his mother's geraniums had begun to turn yellow. She told him that the geranium was getting too much water. This item of information was represented in Inquirer as item of evidence E^*_2 favoring the hypothesis H_{1b}. The students agreed to assess E_2's relevance as likely (because geranium is a different type of plant) and E^*_2's believability as very likely (because although the mother has experience with plants, she is not a professional), leading Inquirer to compute E^*_2's inferential force on H_{1b} as likely (see the bottom-middle part of Figure 2.19). Additionally, Mrs. Graham gave the group a pamphlet from a local nursery entitled *Growing Healthy Plants*. The water group read the pamphlet and found that when plant roots are surrounded by water, they cannot take in air from the space around the roots and they essentially "drown." This item of information was represented in Inquirer as item of evidence E^*_3 favoring the hypothesis H_{1b}. The students agreed to assess E_3's relevance as certain (since it, in fact, asserted the hypothesis) and the believability of E^*_3 as almost certain (because this information is from a highly credible expert), leading Inquirer to compute E^*_3's inferential force on H_{1b} as almost certain (see the bottom-right part of Figure 2.19). Additionally, Inquirer computed the inferential force of all favoring evidence (i.e., E^*_1, E^*_2, and E^*_3) on H_{1b} as almost certain, by taking the maximum of them. This is also the probability of H_{1b}, because no disfavoring evidence was found. However, if any disfavoring evidence would have been found, then the Inquirer would have needed to determine whether, on balance, the totality of evidence favors or disfavors H_{1b}, and to what degree.

Having assessed the probability of H_{1a} as very likely and that of H_{1b} as almost certain, the students and Inquirer inferred that the probability of their top-level hypothesis H_1 is the minimum of the two because both are required to infer H_1 (see the top-right part of Figure 2.17). Finally, Inquirer automatically generated a report describing the analysis logic, citing sources of data used and the manner in which the analysis was performed. The report was further edited by the water group before being presented to the class, together with the reports of the other teams.

As different groups presented and compared their analyses, the class learned that some evidence – such as that from the group investigating whether the trees were different – did not explain the observations. The results of other investigations, such as the idea that the trees could have a disease, partly supported the observations. But the explanation that seemed most reasonable to the students, that fit all the observations and conformed with what they had learned from other sources, was "too much water." After their three weeks of work, the class was satisfied that together the students had found a reasonable answer to their question.

2.3.3.3 Other Examples of Inquiry-based Teaching and Learning

The preceding scenario illustrates one form of classroom inquiry where the investigations are free-ranging explorations of unexplained phenomena. However, depending on the educational goals for students, other forms of inquiry can be much more structured, allowing Inquirer to provide even more guidance and assistance, as discussed in the following.

According to the National Science Education Standards, "Inquiry is a multifaceted activity that involves making observations; posing questions; examining books and other sources of information to see what is already known; planning investigations; reviewing what is already known in light of experimental evidence; using tools to gather, analyze, and interpret data; proposing answers, explanations, and predictions; and communicating the results. Inquiry requires identification of assumptions, use of critical and logical thinking, and consideration of alternative explanations" (NRC, 1996, p. 23). "Developing the ability to understand and engage in this kind of activity requires direct experience and continued practice with the processes of inquiry. Students do not come to understand inquiry simply by learning words such as 'hypothesis' and 'inference' or by memorizing procedures such as 'the steps of the scientific method.' They must experience inquiry directly to gain a deep understanding of its characteristics" (NRC 2000, p. 14).

The Inquirer cognitive assistant illustrates a computational view of the inquiry process as ceaseless discovery of evidence, hypotheses, and arguments, through evidence in search of hypotheses, hypotheses in search of evidence, and evidentiary testing of hypotheses. This allows students hands-on experiences with this process, as illustrated in the previous section and described in a more general way in Section 1.4.2. The hypothetical Inquirer cognitive assistant incorporates this general model of inquiry, together with a significant amount of knowledge about the properties, uses, discovery, and marshaling of evidence. This allows it to be used as a general tool supporting the learning of those inquiry-based practices that all sciences share, as advocated by the National Research Council (NRC) framework for K–12 science education (NRC, 2011). This can be done through a sequence of hands-on exercises in biology, chemistry, or physics, allowing the students to experience the same inquiry-based scientific practices in multiple domains. For example, in one exercise, Inquirer will teach the students how a complex hypothesis is decomposed into simpler hypotheses, and how the assessments of the simpler hypotheses are combined into the assessment of the top-level hypothesis, as was illustrated in Figure 2.17.

In another exercise, Inquirer will teach the students how to assess the relevance and the believability of evidence. This case study will provide both a decomposition tree (like the one in the middle of Figure 2.17, with the elementary hypotheses H_{1a} and H_{1b}) and a set of items of information, some relevant to the considered hypotheses and some irrelevant. The students will be asked to determine which item of information is relevant to which elementary hypothesis, and whether it is favoring or disfavoring evidence. They will also be asked to assess and justify the relevance and the believability of each item of evidence. After completing their analysis, the teacher and Inquirer will provide additional information, asking the students to update their analysis in the light of the new evidence. Finally, the students will present, compare, and debate their analyses in class.

In yet another exercise, Inquirer will provide an analysis tree like the one from the middle of Figure 2.17 but no items of information, asking the students to look for relevant evidence (e.g., by searching the Internet or by performing various experiments) and to complete the analysis.

In a more complex exercise, Inquirer will present a scenario with some unusual characteristics, like the two trees previously discussed. The students will be asked to formulate competing hypotheses that may explain the surprising observations, use the formulated hypotheses to collect evidence, and use the evidence to assess each hypothesis. Then they will compare their analyses of the competing hypotheses in terms of the evidence used and assessments made, and will select the most likely hypothesis. Inquirer will assist the students in this process by guiding them in decomposing hypotheses, searching for evidence, assessing the elementary hypotheses, combining the assessments of the simpler hypotheses, comparing the analyses of the competing hypotheses, and producing an analysis report.

Inquirer can also provide many opportunities for collaborative work, in addition to those that we have illustrated. For example, a complex hypothesis will be decomposed into simpler hypotheses, each assessed by a different student. Then the results obtained by different students will be combined to produce the assessment of the complex hypothesis. Or different students will analyze the same hypothesis. Then they will compare and debate their analysis and evidence and work together toward producing a consensus analysis.

Consistent with the writers of the National Science Education Standards, who "treated inquiry as both a learning goal and as a teaching method" (NRC 2000, p. 18), Inquirer is envisioned as both a teaching tool for teachers and as a learning assistant for students. For example, the teacher will demonstrate some of these exercises in class. Other exercises will be performed by the students, under the guidance of the teacher and with the assistance of Inquirer.

2.4   HANDS ON: BROWSING AN ARGUMENTATION

The use of the various modules of Disciple-EBR will be introduced with the help of case studies with associated instructions that will provide detailed guidance. We will illustrate this process by running the case study stored in the knowledge base called "01-Browse-Argumentation." This case study concerns the hypothesis "The cesium-137 canister is missing from the XYZ warehouse," which is part of the analysis example discussed in Section 2.2.1. This case study has three objectives:

- Learning how to run a case study
- Learning how to browse a reasoning tree or argumentation
- Understanding the process of hypothesis analysis through problem reduction and solution synthesis

Figure 2.20 shows an example of an argumentation or reasoning tree in the interface of the Reasoner. The left panel shows an abstract view of the entire reasoning tree. It consists of brief names for the main hypotheses and their assessments, if determined. You can expand (or show the decomposition of) a hypothesis by clicking on it or on the plus sign (+) on its left. To collapse a decomposition, click on the minus sign (–). You can expand or collapse the entire tree under a hypothesis by right-clicking on it and selecting **Expand** or **Collapse**.

When you click on a hypothesis in the left panel, the right panel shows the detailed description of the reasoning step abstracted in the left panel (see Figure 2.20). If you click on [HIDE SOLUTIONS] at the top of the window, the agent will no longer display the solutions/assessments of the hypotheses in the right panel. You may show the solutions again by clicking on [SHOW SOLUTIONS].

The detailed argumentation from the right panel may be a single decomposition or a deeper tree. In both cases, the leaves of the tree in the right panel are the detailed descriptions of the subhypotheses of the hypothesis selected in the left panel (see the arrows in Figure 2.20 that indicate these correspondences).

A detailed description shows the entire name of a hypothesis. It also shows the question/answer pair that justifies the decomposition of the hypothesis into subhypotheses. The detailed descriptions with solutions also show the synthesis functions that were used to obtain those solutions from children solutions in the tree. These functions will be discussed in Section 4.3.

Notice that, in the actual interface of Disciple-EBR, some of the words appear in bright blue while others appear in dark blue (this distinction is not clearly shown in this book). The bright blue words are names of specific entities or instances, such as "cesium-137 canister." The dark blue words correspond to more general notions or concepts, such as "evidence." If you click on such a (blue) word in the right panel, the agent automatically

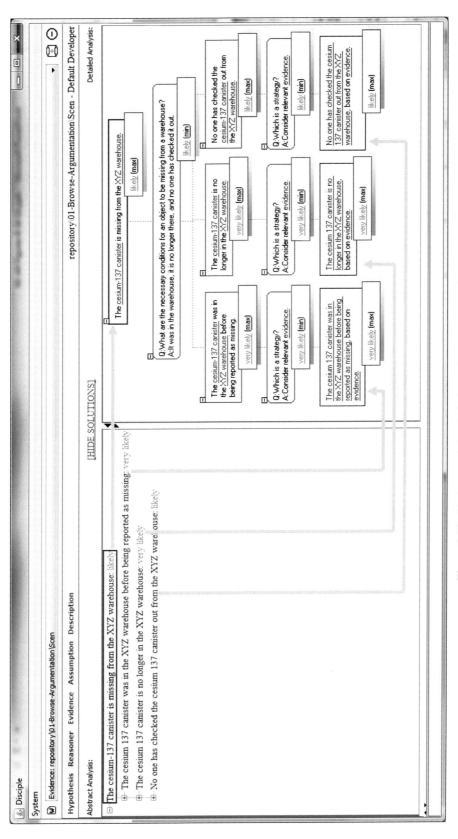

Figure 2.20. Abstract and detailed views of an argumentation.

switches to the Description module and displays its description. To view the reasoning tree again, just click on Reasoner on the top of the window.

Figure 2.21 shows another part of the reasoning tree from Figure 2.20 to be browsed in this case study. Notice that some of the solutions in the left panel have a yellow background. This indicates that they are assessments or assumptions made by the user, as will be discussed in Sections 4.4 and 4.9.

In this case study, you will practice the aforementioned operations. You will first select the hypothesis "The cesium-137 canister is missing from the XYZ warehouse." Then you will browse its analysis tree to see how it is decomposed into simpler hypotheses and how the assessments of these simpler hypotheses are composed. You will visualize both detailed descriptions of these decomposition and synthesis operations, as well as abstract ones, including an abstract view of the entire tree. Then you will visualize the descriptions of the concepts and instances to which the analysis tree refers. Start by following the instructions described in Operation 2.1 and illustrated in Figure 2.22.

Operation 2.1. Run a case study

- Start Disciple-EBR.
- In the **System Workspace Manager**, click on the knowledge base icon containing the plus sign (+).
- The **Knowledge Manager** window opens, showing all the knowledge bases from the repository.
- Click on the plus sign (+) of the case study domain knowledge base to be run. This will display one or several scenario knowledge bases.
- Click on the scenario knowledge base corresponding to the case study to be run.
- Click on the **Select** button. This will both load the case study knowledge bases in memory (i.e., the domain KB and the scenario KB) and select them as the current ones to work with. Because they are loaded in memory, their names will be shown in bold in the **Knowledge Manager** window.
- Follow the instructions at the bottom of the displayed window and run the case study. After running the case study, you have to close the corresponding knowledge base, as instructed in the following steps.
- Close all the workspaces open on the current knowledge base (case study) by selecting one of them and clicking on the minus sign (−) to the right of the knowledge base icon containing the plus sign (+).
- Click on the knowledge base icon containing the plus sign (+) situated at the right of the workspace selector (see Figure 3.23).
- The **Knowledge Manager** window will be opened, showing all the knowledge bases.
- Click on the **Scen** node corresponding to the case study knowledge base that was run.
- Click on the **Close** button in the right side of the window.
- Click on the **X** button to close the **Knowledge Manager** window.

This case study has also illustrated the following basic operations:

Operation 2.2. Browse the analysis of a hypothesis

- In the Hypothesis module, select a hypothesis.
- The Reasoner module will be automatically selected, showing the corresponding reasoning tree.

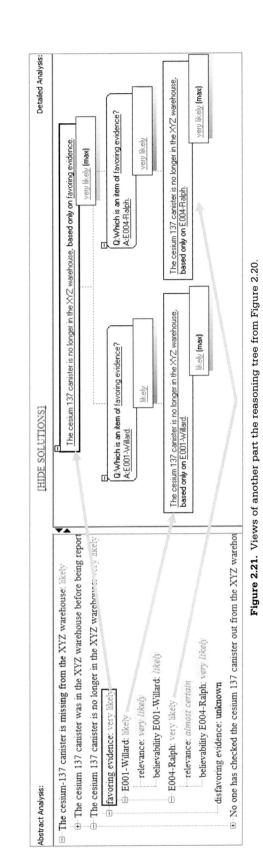

Figure 2.21. Views of another part the reasoning tree from Figure 2.20.

Figure 2.22. Running a case study.

- To browse the entire reasoning tree, step by step, click on the hypotheses in the left panel, or one of the + and – signs preceding them.
- To expand or collapse the entire subtree of a hypothesis, right-click on it and select the corresponding action.
- To view the detailed description of an abstract decomposition of a hypothesis in the left panel, click on the hypothesis, and the detailed decomposition will be displayed in the right panel.
- To browse a detailed reasoning tree in the right panel click on the + and – signs.

Operation 2.3. End a case study

- Select the Scenario workspace (repository\KB-name\Scen)
- From the **System** menu, select **Save All** to save the knowledge bases.

- Close all the workspaces open on the current knowledge bases (case studies) by clicking on the minus sign (–) to the right of the knowledge base icon containing the plus sign (+).
- Close the opened knowledge bases corresponding to the case study by following the instructions from Operation 3.3.

2.5 PROJECT ASSIGNMENT 1

This is the first of a sequence of assignments in which you will develop a knowledge-based agent for analyzing hypotheses in a domain of interest to you. Since you will develop the knowledge base of the agent, you will have to consider a familiar domain. Select a domain and illustrate the process of evidence-based reasoning with a diagram such as those in Figures 2.8, 2.14, 2.26, or 2.27. That is, specify an item of evidence, an abductive reasoning chain from that evidence to a hypothesis of interest, alternative hypotheses to those from the reasoning chain, and the analysis of one of these hypotheses.

2.6 REVIEW QUESTIONS

2.1. Consider the intelligence analysis problem from Section 2.2.1. What might constitute an item of evidence for the hypothesis that the cesium-137 canister was misplaced?

2.2. What might by an alternative hypothesis for "H_5: A dirty bomb will be set off in the Washington, D.C., area"?

2.3. A terrorist incident occurred two weeks ago in an American city involving considerable destruction and some loss of life. After an investigation, two foreign terrorist groups have been identified as possible initiators of this terrorist action: Group A and Group B. Which are some hypotheses we could entertain about this event?

2.4. Consider the hypothesis that Group A from Country W was involved in a recent terrorist incident in an American city. What evidence we might find concerning this hypothesis?

2.5. Sometimes we have evidence in search of hypotheses or possible explanations. For example, consider the dog-tag containing the name of one of our soldiers who has been missing since the end of our conflict with Country X. This tag was allegedly given to a recent visitor in Country X, who then gave it to us. One possibility is that this soldier is still being held as a prisoner in Country X. What are some other possibilities?

2.6. Sometimes we have hypotheses in search of evidence. Suppose our hypothesis is that Person X was involved in a recent terrorist incident in an American city. So far, all we have is evidence that he was at the scene of the incident an hour before it happened. If this hypothesis were true, what other kinds of evidence about X might we want to look for?

2.7. Consider the hypothesis that the leadership of Country A is planning an armed conflict against Country B. You have just obtained a report that says that there has just been an attempt on the life of the president of Country B by an unknown assailant. Why is this report, if believable, relevant evidence on the hypothesis that the leadership of Country A is planning an armed conflict against Country B?

2.8.   Defendant Dave is accused of shooting a victim Vic. When Dave was arrested sometime after the shooting he was carrying a 32 caliber Colt automatic pistol. Let H be the hypothesis that it was Dave who shot Vic. A witness named Frank appears and says he saw Dave fire a pistol at the scene of the crime when it occurred; that's all Frank can tell us. Construct a simple chain of reasoning that connects Frank's report to the hypothesis that it was Dave who shot Vic.

2.9.   Consider the situation from Question 2.8. The chain of reasoning that connects Frank's report to the hypothesis that it was Dave who shot Vic shows only the possibility of this hypothesis being true. What are some alternative hypotheses?

2.10.   Consider again the situation from Questions 2.8 and 2.9. In order to prove the hypothesis that it was Dave who shot Vic, we need additional evidence. As discussed in Section 2.2.2, we need to put this hypothesis to work to guide us in collecting new evidence. Decompose this hypothesis into simpler hypotheses, as was illustrated by the blue trees in Figures 2.8 and 2.9, in order to discover new evidence.

2.11.   Our investigation described in Questions 2.8, 2.9, and 2.10 has led to the discovery of additional evidence. By itself, each evidence item is hardly conclusive that Dave was the one who shot Vic. Someone else might have been using Dave's Colt automatic. But Frank's testimony, along with the fact that Dave was carrying his weapon and with the ballistics evidence, puts additional heat on Dave. Analyze the hypothesis that it was Dave who shot Vic, based on all these items of evidence, as was illustrated by the green trees in Figures 2.8 and 2.9. In Chapter 4, we will discuss more rigorous methods for making such probabilistic assessments. In this exercise, just use your common sense.

2.12.   A car bomb was set off in front of a power substation in Washington, D.C., on November 25. The building was damaged but, fortunately, no one was injured. From the car's identification plate, which survived, it was learned that the car belonged to Budget Car Rental Agency. From information provided by Budget, it was learned that the car was last rented on November 24 by a man named M. Construct an argument from this evidence to the hypothesis that Person M was involved in this car-bombing incident.

2.13.   Consider again the situation from Question 2.12, and suppose that we have determined that the evidence that M rented a car on November 24 is believable. We want now to assess whether M drove the car on November 25. For this, we need additional evidence. As discussed in Section 2.2.2, we need to put this hypothesis to work to guide us in collecting new evidence. Decompose this hypothesis into simpler hypotheses, as was illustrated by the blue trees in Figures 2.8 and 2.9, in order to discover new evidence.

3 Methodologies and Tools for Agent Design and Development

3.1 A CONVENTIONAL DESIGN AND DEVELOPMENT SCENARIO

3.1.1 Conventional Design and Development Phases

Table 3.1 shows the main development phases for a knowledge-based agent. As in the case of developing a typical software system, there are feedback loops between all these phases. We will illustrate these phases with a conventional scenario of developing a knowledge-based agent. This scenario is an adaptation of the one described in Buchanan et al. (1983).

3.1.2 Requirements Specification and Domain Understanding

The development process starts with identifying a problem that may be solved by developing a knowledge-based agent. Table 3.2 shows an example of such a problem.

A *knowledge engineer*, who is a person specialized in developing knowledge-based agents, is assigned the job of building an agent that incorporates the expertise of *subject matter experts,* who are people familiar with the detection, monitoring, and containment of the spills of hazardous materials. The goal of the system is to assist its users in performing such tasks. The knowledge engineer has to identify a subject matter expert from whom to capture the domain expertise and represent it into the agent's knowledge base, as was briefly discussed in Section 1.6.3.1.

Table 3.1 Main Phases in the Development of a Knowledge-based Agent

1. Requirements specification (specifying the types of problems to be solved or hypotheses to be analyzed, and the agent to be built).
2. Domain understanding.
3. Ontology design and development.
4. Development of problem-solving rules or methods.
5. Refinement of the knowledge base (ontology and rules/methods).
6. Verification, validation, and certification of the agent.

Table 3.2 Problem to Be Solved with a Knowledge-based Agent (from Buchanan et al., p. 132).

The director of the Oak Ridge National Lab (ORNL) faces a problem. Environmental Protection Agency (EPA) regulations forbid the discharge of quantities of oil or hazardous chemicals into or upon waters of the United States when this discharge violates specified quality standards. ORNL has approximately two thousand buildings on a two-hundred-square-mile government reservation, with ninety-three discharge sites entering White Oak Creek. Oil and hazardous chemicals are stored and used extensively at ORNL. The problem is to detect, monitor, and contain spills of these materials, and this problem may be solved with a knowledge-based agent.

Table 3.3 Specification of the Actual Problem to Be Solved (from Buchanan et al., p.133).

When an accidental inland spill of an oil or chemical occurs, an emergency situation may exist, depending on the properties and the quantity of the substance released, the location of the substance, and whether or not the substance enters a body of water.

The observer of a spill should:

1. Characterize the spill and the probable hazards.
2. Contain the spill material.
3. Locate the source of the spill and stop any further release.
4. Notify the Department of Environmental Management.

What issues may concern the subject matter expert? First of all, the expert may be concerned that once his or her expertise is represented into the agent, the organization may no longer need him or her because the job can be performed by the agent. Replacing human experts was a bad and generally inaccurate way of promoting expert systems. Usually, the knowledge-based agents and even the expert systems are used by experts in order to better and more efficiently solve problems from their areas of expertise. They are also used by people who need the expertise but do not have access to a human expert, or the expert would be too expensive.

What are some examples of knowledge-based agents? Think, for instance, of any tax-preparation software. Is it a knowledge-based agent? What about the software systems that help us with various legal problems, such as creating a will? They all are based on large amounts of subject matter expertise that are represented in their knowledge bases.

Once the subject matter expert is identified and agrees to work on this project, the knowledge engineer and the expert have a series of meetings to better define the actual problem to be solved, which is shown in Table 3.3.

The knowledge engineer has many meetings with the subject matter expert to elicit his or her knowledge on how to solve the specified problem. There are several knowledge elicitation methods that can be employed, as discussed later in Section 6.3. Table 3.4 illustrates the unstructured interview, where the questions of the knowledge engineer and the responses of the expert are open-ended.

Table 3.4 Unstructured Interview to Elicit Subject Matter Expertise (from Buchanan et al., p. 134)

KE: Suppose you were told that a spill had been detected in White Oak Creek one mile before it enters White Oak Lake. What would you do to contain the spill?

SME: That depends on a number of factors. I would need to find the source in order to prevent the possibility of further contamination, probably by checking drains and manholes for signs of the spill material. And it helps to know what the spilled material is.

KE: How can you tell what it is?

SME: Sometimes you can tell what the substance is by its smell. Sometimes you can tell by its color, but that's not always reliable since dyes are used a lot nowadays. Oil, however, floats on the surface and forms a silvery film, while acids dissolve completely in the water. Once you discover the type of material spilled, you can eliminate any building that either doesn't store the material at all or doesn't store enough of it to account for the spill.

Table 3.5 Identification of the Basic Concepts and Features Employed by the Subject Matter Expert

KE: Suppose you were told that a spill had been detected in White Oak Creek one mile before it enters White Oak Lake. What would you do to contain the spill?

SME: That depends on a number of factors. I would need to find the source in order to prevent the possibility of further contamination, probably by checking drains and manholes for signs of the spill material. And it helps to know what the spilled material is.

KE: How can you tell what it is?

SME: Sometimes you can tell what the substance is by its smell. Sometimes you can tell by its color, but that's not always reliable since dyes are used a lot nowadays. Oil, however, floats on the surface and forms a silvery film, while acids dissolve completely in the water. Once you discover the type of material spilled, you can eliminate any building that either doesn't store the material at all or doesn't store enough of it to account for the spill.

3.1.3 Ontology Design and Development

The main goal of the initial interview sessions is to identify the basic concepts and features from the application domain. Some of these domain concepts and features are underlined in Table 3.5.

The identified concepts, instances, and features are used to design and develop the ontology of the system to be built. A fragment of the developed concept and instance hierarchy is shown in Figure 3.1.

The nodes in light blue (such as "*building 3023*") represent specific objects or instances. The nodes in dark blue (such as "building") represent sets of instances and are called concepts. The instances and concepts may have features that are represented in green, as for instance, "*spill-1* has as type acid" and "*spill-1* has as odor vinegar odor."

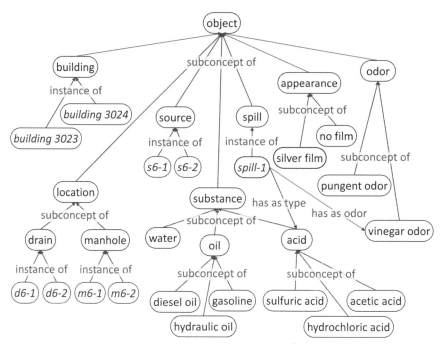

Figure 3.1. Hierarchy of domain concepts and instances.

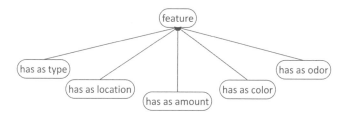

Figure 3.2. Features used to describe the instances and concepts.

The features are also represented hierarchically, as shown in Figure 3.2. Ontologies are discussed in detail in Chapter 5.

3.1.4   Development of the Problem-Solving Rules or Methods

Once an initial ontology is developed, the knowledge engineer and the subject matter expert use the component concepts and features to represent the expert's methods of determining the spill material as a set of rules. Consider, for example, the reasoning of the subject matter expert (SME) from the top of Table 3.6. What IF-THEN rules may represent this reasoning?

In an iterative process, the knowledge engineer represents the expert's reasoning as rules, asks the expert to critique them, and correspondingly updates the rules, as illustrated in Table 3.7. As would be expected, this is quite a long and difficult process, for the reasons discussed in Section 1.6.3.1.

Table 3.6 Representing the Expert's Reasoning as If-Then Rules

SME: Sometimes you can tell what the <u>substance</u> is by its <u>smell</u>. Sometimes you can tell by its <u>color</u>, but that's not always reliable since dyes are used a lot nowadays. *Oil*, however, <u>floats</u> on the surface and <u>forms a silvery film</u>, while <u>acid dissolves completely</u> in the <u>water</u>.

IF   the spill ...
THEN   the substance of the spill is oil

IF   the spill ...
THEN   the substance of the spill is acid

Table 3.7 Iterative Process of Rules Development and Refinement (Based on Buchanan et al., p.138)

KE: Here are some rules I think capture your explanation about determining the substance of the spill. What do you think?

IF   the spill does not dissolve in water
        and the spill forms a silvery film
THEN   the substance of the spill is oil

IF   the spill dissolves in water
        and the spill does not form a film
THEN   the substance of the spill is acid

SME: Uh-huh (long pause). Yes, that begins to capture it. Of course, if the substance is silver nitrate, it will dissolve only partially in water.

KE: I see. Rather than talking about a substance dissolving or not dissolving in water, we should talk about its solubility, which we may consider as being high, moderate, or low. Let's add that information to the knowledge base and see what it looks like.

IF   the solubility of the spill is low
        and the spill forms a silvery film
THEN   the substance of the spill is oil

IF   the solubility of the spill is moderate
THEN   the substance of the spill is silver-nitrate

SME: If the solubility of the spill is moderate, I would be about 60 percent sure that the substance of the spill is silver-nitrate.

KE: Okay, we will represent this information in the rule.

IF   the solubility of the spill is moderate
THEN   the substance of the spill is silver-nitrate with certainty 0.6

3.1.5 Verification, Validation, and Certification

Once the ontology and the rules are defined and represented into the knowledge base of the agent, the knowledge engineer and the subject matter expert can run the prototype agent and analyze its solutions, which are generated by the chaining of the rules.

Testing of the agent involves three types of activity: verification, validation, and certification (O'Keefe et al., 1987; Awad, 1996).

In essence, *verification* attempts to answer the question: *Are we building the agent right?* Its goal is to test the consistency and the completeness of the agent with respect to its initial specification. For example, in the case of a rule-based agent, one would check the rules to identify various types of errors, such as the existence of rules that are redundant, conflicting, subsumed, circular, dead-end, missing, unreachable, or with unnecessary IF conditions.

Validation, on the other hand, attempts to answer the question: *Are we building the right agent?* In essence, this activity checks whether the agent meets the user's needs and requirements.

Finally, *certification* is a written guarantee that the agent complies with its specified requirements and is acceptable for operational use.

3.2   DEVELOPMENT TOOLS AND REUSABLE ONTOLOGIES

Various types of tools can be used to develop a knowledge-based agent. We will briefly discuss three different types: expert system shells, learning agent shells, and learning agent shells for evidence-based reasoning. We will also discuss the reuse of knowledge in the development of a knowledge-based agent.

3.2.1   Expert System Shells

These tools exploit the architectural separation in a knowledge-based system between the knowledge base and the inference engine (see the right-hand side of Figure 1.14, p. 37). Given this separation, two knowledge-based agents, one for diagnosing ships and the other for diagnosing airplanes, may potentially use the same inference engine for diagnosis. The difference between the two agents will be in the content of their knowledge bases (e.g., ship parts versus airplane parts).

An expert system shell is a tool that consists of an inference engine for a certain class of tasks (e.g., planning, design, diagnosis, monitoring, prediction, interpretation, etc.); a representation formalism in which the knowledge base can be encoded; and mechanisms for acquiring, verifying, and revising knowledge expressed in that formalism.

If the inference engine of an expert system shell is adequate for a certain expertise task (e.g., planning), then the process of building an expert system or agent for that type of tasks is, in principle, reduced to the building of the knowledge base.

Different expert system shells trade generality (i.e., their domain of applicability) against power (i.e., the assistance given to the expert and the knowledge engineer in the development process), covering a large spectrum.

At the generality end of the spectrum are very general shells that can be used to build almost any type of expert system, but they do not provide too much assistance in building a specific system. Examples of such shell are:

- OPS (Cooper and Wogrin, 1988), which has a general rule engine
- CLIPS (Giarratano and Riley, 1994), which also has a general rule engine
- CYC (Lenat, 1995; CYC, 2008; 2016), a very large knowledge base with ontologies covering many domains, and with several rule engines
- EXPECT (Gil and Paris, 1995; EXPECT 2015), a shell that enables the acquisition of problem-solving knowledge both from knowledge engineers and from end-users

- JESS (Friedman-Hill, 2003; JESS, 2016), which is a version of CLIPS with a Java-based rule engine
- CommonKADS (Schreiber et al., 2000), which is a general methodology with supporting tools for the development of knowledge-based systems
- Jena, which is a toolkit for developing applications for the Semantic Web (Jena, 2012)
- Pellet, an ontology (OWL2) reasoner that can be used to develop knowledge-based applications for the Semantic Web (Pellet, 2012)
- Protégé (Musen, 1989; Protégé, 2015), an ontology editor and knowledge base framework, also used to develop knowledge-based applications for the Semantic Web
- TopBraid Composer (Allemang and Hendler, 2011; TopBraid Composer, 2012) Ontology Development Tool for Semantic Web applications

At the power end of the spectrum are shells that employ much more specific problem-solving methods, such the *propose-and-revise* design method used in SALT (Marcus, 1988) to design elevators. The knowledge for such a system can be elicited by simply filling in forms, which are then automatically converted into rules. Thus the shell provides significant assistance in building the system, but the type of systems for which it can be used is much more limited.

In between these two types of shells are the shells applicable to a certain type of problems (such as planning, or diagnosis, or design). A representative example is EMYCIN (van Melle et al., 1981), a general rule-based shell for medical diagnosis.

3.2.2 Foundational and Utility Ontologies and Their Reuse

The use of an expert system shell facilitates the development of an expert system because it reduces the process of developing the system to that of developing the knowledge base for the provided inference engine. However, it is this development of the knowledge base that is the most challenging part of developing the system.

Despite the fact that building the knowledge base is such a difficult problem, historically knowledge bases were very rarely reused, primarily for two reasons. First, the knowledge in the knowledge base is usually very specific to a particular domain and type of problems and cannot be applied directly to a different application area. Second, even if the knowledge base of a system is directly relevant to the new area, its reuse by a system with a different knowledge representation is likely to be very difficult because of the differences between the knowledge models of the two systems.

Progress in knowledge engineering has changed this situation. A new architectural separation has emerged at the level of the knowledge base, which is structured into two main components: an ontology that defines the concepts of the application domain, and a set of problem-solving rules or methods expressed with these concepts, as was illustrated in Section 1.6.3.1. The ontology is the more general part, being characteristic to an entire application domain, such as military or medicine. In the military domain, for example, the ontology includes descriptions of military units and of military equipment. These descriptions are most likely needed in almost any specific military application and can therefore be reused. The rules are the more specific part of the knowledge base, corresponding to a certain type of application. For example, there may be rules for an agent, such as Disciple-COA, that assists a commander in critiquing courses of action, or rules for an agent, such as Disciple-WA, that assists in planning the repair of damaged bridges or roads. These rules offer much fewer opportunities for reuse, if any.

As a result of terminological standardization to facilitate automatic processing of information, particularly in the context of the Semantic Web, many domain and general-purpose ontologies have been developed. The general-purpose (domain-independent) ontologies are also called *upper, foundational,* or *universal ontologies* because they provide high-level, domain-independent concepts and relationships that can be included in the top part of a domain ontology (Obrst et al., 2012). Examples of such ontologies are Cyc/OpenCyc (2016; Lenat, 1995), Suggested Upper Merged Ontology (SUMO) (Pease, 2011), WordNet (2012; Fellbaum 1988), Descriptive Ontology for Linguistic and Cognitive Engineering (DOLCE, 2012), Basic Formal Ontology (BFO, 2012), Object-centered High-level Reference (OCHRE) (Schneider, 2003), General Formal Ontology (GFO, 2012), Unified Medical Language System (UMLS) (Humphreys and Lindberg, 1993), and Unified Foundational Ontology (UFO) (Guizzardi and Wagner, 2005a, 2005b).

There are also *utility ontologies* (Obrst et al., 2012) that include representations of commonly used concepts, such as persons, social roles, and organizations (Masolo et al., 2004; FOAF, 2012), temporal concepts (Hobbs and Pan, 2004; Pan and Hobbs, 2004; 2012), and geospatial concepts (Ressler et al., 2010; Geonames, 2012).

The Open Knowledge Base Connectivity (OKBC) protocol (OKBC, 2008) has been defined to facilitate knowledge sharing and reuse (Chaudhri et al., 1998). OKBC is a standard for accessing knowledge bases stored in different frame-representation systems. It provides a set of operations for a generic interface to such systems. As a result, OKBC servers for various frame-based systems, such as Ontolingua (Ontolingua 1997; 2008; Farquhar et al., 1997) and Loom (Loom, 1999; MacGregor, 1991), have been developed. These servers are repositories of reusable ontologies and domain theories and can be accessed using the OKBC protocol.

Additionally, there are many tools that can query existing ontologies on the Semantic Web or simply import them into the knowledge base to be built, including Jena (2012), OWLIM (2012), Pellet (2012), Protégé (2015), and TopBraid Composer (2012).

3.2.3   Learning Agent Shells

While part of the ontology of the agent to be developed can be imported from previously developed ontologies, the reasoning rules of the agent are application-specific and cannot be reused. An alternative approach to rules development is to employ a learning agent that is able to learn the rules. In addition to containing the knowledge base and the inference engine, the architecture of a learning agent includes a learning engine consisting of the programs that create and update the data structures in the knowledge base. The learning agent may learn from a variety of information sources in the environment. It may learn from its user or from other agents, either by being directly instructed by them or just by observing and imitating their behavior. It may learn from a repository of information (such as a database), or it may learn from its own experience. Building a practical autonomous learning agent that can acquire and update its knowledge by itself is not yet practical, except for very simple problems, such as classification. Therefore, a more practical approach is to develop an interactive learning agent that can interact with an expert. Such an agent can perform many of the functions of the knowledge engineer. It allows the human expert to communicate expertise in a way familiar to him or her and is responsible for building, updating, and reorganizing the knowledge base. We call such a tool a learning agent shell.

A learning agent shell is an advanced tool for building knowledge-based agents. It contains a general problem-solving engine, a learning engine, and a general knowledge base structured into an ontology and a set of rules (see Figure 3.3). Building a knowledge-based agent for a specific application consists of customizing the shell for that application and developing the knowledge base. The learning engine facilitates the building of the knowledge base by subject matter experts and knowledge engineers.

Examples of learning agent shells are Disciple-LAS (Tecuci et al., 1999), Disciple-COA (Tecuci et al., 2001), and Disciple-COG/RKF (Tecuci et al., 2005b), the last two being presented in Section 12.4.

3.2.4 Learning Agent Shell for Evidence-based Reasoning

As discussed in Section 1.4.3, tasks in many domains, such as law, intelligence analysis, cybersecurity, forensics, medicine, physics, chemistry, history, or archaeology, involve evidence-based reasoning. All these tasks use general evidence-based reasoning concepts and rules. Examples of general concepts are different types of evidence, such as tangible evidence and testimonial evidence. An example of a general rule is to assess the credibility of a human source of information by assessing his or her veracity, objectivity, and observational sensitivity. Since all this knowledge is domain-independent, it makes sense to develop a general knowledge base for evidence-based reasoning that can be reused each time we are developing an agent that also needs to perform this kind of reasoning. To facilitate this process, the knowledge base of the agent is structured into a hierarchy of knowledge bases, with the knowledge base for evidence-based reasoning at top of the hierarchy.

A learning agent shell for evidence-based reasoning is a learning agent shell that contains a hierarchy of knowledge bases the top of which is a knowledge base for evidence-based reasoning (see Figure 3.4). As will be illustrated in the following sections, building an agent for a specific evidence-based reasoning application consists in extending the knowledge base with domain-specific knowledge through learning from a subject matter expert.

An example of a learning agent shell for evidence-based reasoning is Disciple-EBR, the architecture of which is shown in the center of Figure 3.5. It includes multiple modules for problem solving, learning, tutoring, evidence-based reasoning, mixed-initiative inter-action, as well as a hierarchically organized knowledge base with domain-independent knowledge for evidence-based reasoning at the top of the knowledge hierarchy. The Disciple-EBR shell can learn complex problem-solving expertise directly from human experts, and in doing so it evolves into a cognitive assistant that can support experts and nonexperts in problem solving and can teach expert problem-solving to students.

The outside hexagon in Figure 3.5 summarizes a possible life cycle of a Disciple cognitive assistant for evidence-based reasoning. The first stage is *shell customization,*

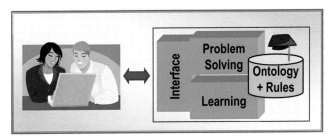

Figure 3.3. The overall architecture of a learning agent shell.

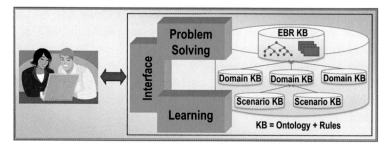

Figure 3.4. The overall architecture of a learning agent shell for evidence-based reasoning.

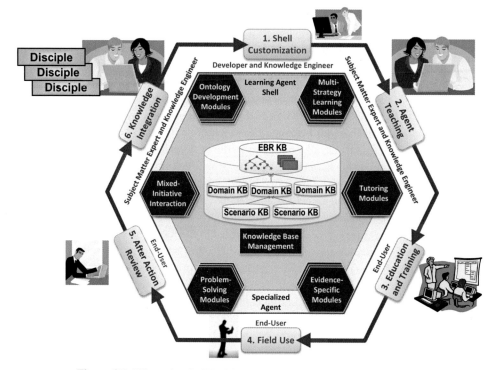

Figure 3.5. Life cycle of a Disciple agent for evidence-based reasoning.

where, based on the specification of the type of problems to be solved and the agent to be built, the developer and the knowledge engineer may decide that some extensions of the Disciple shell may be necessary or useful. It is through such successive extensions during the development of Disciple agents for various applications that the current version of the Disciple shell for evidence-based reasoning problems (which includes the EBR knowledge base) has emerged.

The next stage is *agent teaching* by the subject matter expert and the knowledge engineer, supported by the agent itself, which simplifies and speeds up the knowledge base development process (Tecuci et al., 2001; 2002b; 2005b). Once an operational agent is developed, it is used for the *education and training* of the end-users, possibly in a classroom environment.

The fourth stage is *field use*, where copies of the developed agent support users in their operational environments. During this stage, an agent assists its user both in solving problems and in collaborating with other users and their cognitive assistants. At the same time, it continuously learns from this problem-solving experience by employing a form of nondisruptive learning. In essence, it learns new rules from examples. However, because there is no learning assistance from the user, the learned rules will not include a formal applicability condition. It is during the next stage of *after action review*, when the user and the agent analyze past problem-solving episodes, that the formal applicability conditions are learned based on the accumulated examples.

In time, each cognitive assistant extends its knowledge with expertise acquired from its user. This results in different agents and creates the opportunity to develop a more competent agent by integrating the knowledge of all these agents. This can be accomplished by a knowledge engineer, with assistance from a subject matter expert, during the next stage of *knowledge integration*. The result is an improved agent that may be used in a new iteration of a spiral process of development and use.

3.3   AGENT DESIGN AND DEVELOPMENT USING LEARNING TECHNOLOGY

In Section 3.1, we briefly illustrated a conventional scenario for building knowledge-based agents. Now that we have reviewed several learning-based agent building tools, we can illustrate the development of a knowledge-based agent using learning technology. While the main design and development phases are, in essence, still those from Table 3.1, the way they are performed is different. The tasks of the knowledge engineer are reduced because part of them will be performed by the subject matter expert (e.g., explaining to the agent shell the sequence of reasoning steps to solve a problem), and part by the agent shell (e.g., learning rules from example reasoning steps rather than having them defined by the knowledge engineer).

3.3.1   Requirements Specification and Domain Understanding

Let us consider the development of an agent that will assist a PhD student in assessing a potential PhD advisor, a case study that will be used throughout this book.

The agent should receive a hypothesis, such as "John Doe would be a good PhD advisor for Bob Sharp," and should return the probability that this hypothesis is true, such as "very likely," together with an easy-to-understand reasoning that has led this assessment.

To build such an agent, one needs first to understand the expertise domain. In this case, a simple search on the Internet will lead to the discovery of many papers written on this subject (see Figure 3.6), which may supplement the expertise of a specific subject matter expert.

Reading some of these papers, you will discover that assessing a PhD advisor is a very complex task. Many questions need to be addressed whose answers need to be aggregated to evaluate a potential PhD advisor. A few of these questions, identified by the knowledge engineer and the subject matter expert (in such a case, an experienced professor), are shown in Table 3.8.

3.3.2   Rapid Prototyping

The next agent development phase is to develop rapidly a prototype that can be validated by the end-users.

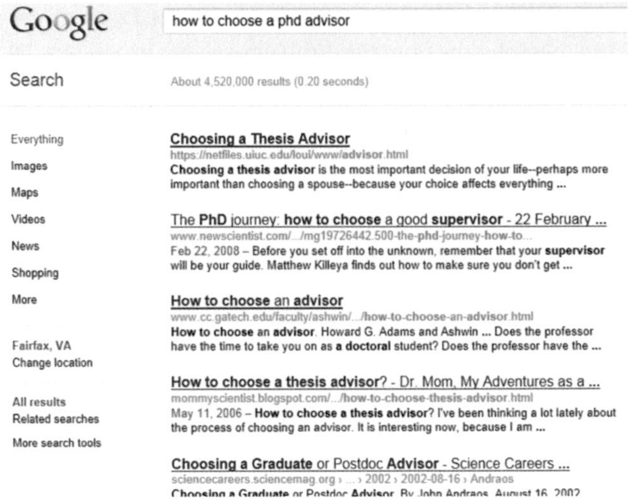

Figure 3.6. Understanding the expertise domain.

Table 3.8 Some Relevant Questions to Consider When Assessing a Potential PhD Advisor

(1) What is the reputation of the PhD advisor within the professional community at large?
(2) Does the advisor have many publications?
(3) Is his or her work cited?
(4) What is the opinion of the peers of this PhD advisor?
(5) What do the students think about this PhD advisor?
(6) Is the PhD advisor likely to remain on the faculty for the duration of your degree program?
(7) What is the placement record of the students of this PhD advisor? Where do they get jobs?
(8) Is the PhD advisor expert in your areas of interest?
(9) Does the PhD advisor publish with students?
(10) Does the PhD advisor have a research group or merely a string of individual students?
(11) Is the PhD advisor's research work funded?

An analysis of the questions in Table 3.8 shows that some of them point to necessary conditions that need to be satisfied by the PhD advisor, while others refer to various desirable qualities. Which questions from Table 3.8 point to necessary conditions? The answers to questions (6) and (8) need to be "yes" in order to further consider a potential PhD advisor.

Now let us consider the desirable qualities of a PhD advisor revealed by the other questions in Table 3.8. Some of these qualities seem to be more closely related than others. It would be useful to organize them in classes of quality criteria. Could you identify a class of related criteria? Questions (2), (3), (4), and (11) all characterize aspects of the professional reputation of the advisor.

What might be other classes of related criteria suggested by the questions in Table 3.8? Questions (7) and (9) characterize the results of the students of the PhD advisor, while questions (5) and (10) characterize their learning experience.

Based on these observations, we can develop the ontology of criteria from Figure 3.7.

Each of the criteria from the right side corresponds to one of the questions in Table 3.8. They are components of the higher-order criteria shown in the middle of the figure, which are all components of a top-level criterion that characterizes the quality of the PhD advisor. This is what is called a *part-of hierarchy*. All these individual criteria are all instances of the "criterion" concept.

The preceding analysis suggests that, in order to assess a PhD advisor, one needs to check that the advisor satisfies the necessary conditions and to assess his or her advisor qualities.

The knowledge engineer and the subject matter expert need to develop a formal, yet intuitive way of representing the assessment logic. This has to be natural enough, such that subject matter experts who do not have knowledge engineering experience are able to express how to solve different problems by themselves, with no or limited support from knowledge engineers. But the assessment logic also needs to be formal enough so that an agent can learn general rules from such problem-solving examples.

A general problem-solving paradigm, called *problem reduction and solution synthesis*, which has been illustrated in Section 2.2 and will be discussed in detail in Chapter 4, satisfies both these requirements. It will be again illustrated in this case.

To clarify the reduction logic, the knowledge engineer and the subject matter expert consider a particular hypothesis:

John Doe would be a good PhD advisor for Bob Sharp.

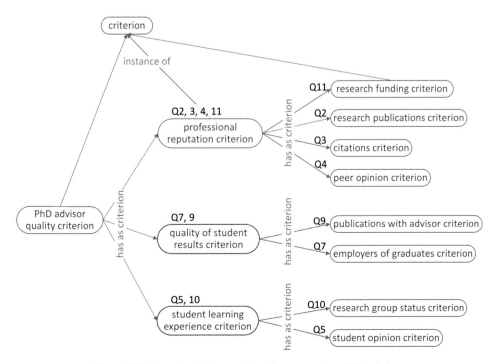

Figure 3.7. Sample criteria ontology for assessing a PhD advisor.

They express the hypothesis in natural language and select the phrases that may be different for other similar hypotheses, such as the names of the advisor and student. The selected phrases will appear in blue, guiding the agent to learn a general hypothesis pattern:

?O1 would be a good PhD advisor for ?O2.

This top-level hypothesis will be successively reduced to simpler and simpler hypotheses, guided by questions and answers, as shown in Figure 3.8 and discussed in this section.

John Doe would be a good PhD advisor for Bob Sharp.
Which are the necessary conditions?
Bob Sharp should be interested in an area of expertise of John Doe who should stay on the faculty of George Mason University for the duration of the PhD dissertation of Bob Sharp, and should have the qualities of a good PhD advisor.

Therefore, the initial hypothesis can be reduced to three simpler hypotheses:

Bob Sharp is interested in an area of expertise of John Doe.
John Doe will stay on the faculty of George Mason University for the duration of the PhD dissertation of Bob Sharp.
John Doe would be a good PhD advisor with respect to the PhD advisor quality criterion.

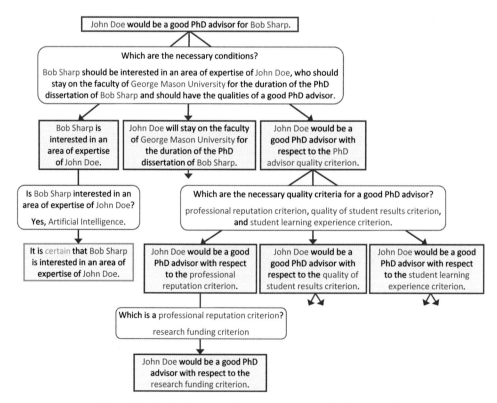

Figure 3.8. Reduction logic for assessing a specific hypothesis.

The reductions of the subhypotheses continues in the same way, until solutions are obtained for them:

Bob Sharp is interested in an area of expertise of John Doe.
Is Bob Sharp interested in an area of expertise of John Doe?
Yes, Artificial Intelligence.

Therefore, one may conclude:

It is certain that Bob Sharp is interested in an area of expertise of John Doe.

Consider now the third subhypothesis of the initial hypothesis:

John Doe would be a good PhD advisor with respect to the PhD advisor quality criterion.

Its reduction is also guided by a question/answer pair:

Which are the necessary quality criteria for a good PhD advisor?
professional reputation criterion, quality of student results criterion, and student learning experience criterion.

Therefore, the preceding hypothesis can be reduced to three simpler hypotheses:

John Doe would be a good PhD advisor with respect to the professional reputation criterion.
John Doe would be a good PhD advisor with respect to the quality of student results criterion.
John Doe would be a good PhD advisor with respect to the student learning experience criterion.

Each of these subhypotheses can now be reduced to simpler hypotheses, each corresponding to one of the elementary criteria from the right side of Figure 3.7 (e.g., research funding criterion). Since each of these reductions reduces a criterion to a subcriterion, the agent could be asked to learn a general reduction pattern, as shown in Figure 3.9.

Why is pattern learning useful? One reason is that the pattern can be applied to reduce a criterion to its subcriteria, as shown in Figure 3.10. Additionally, as will be illustrated later, the pattern will evolve into a rule that will automatically generate all the reductions of criteria to their sub-criteria. If, instead of learning a pattern and

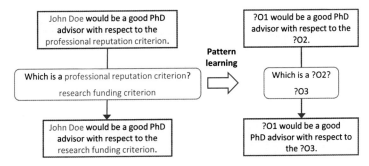

Figure 3.9. Pattern learning.

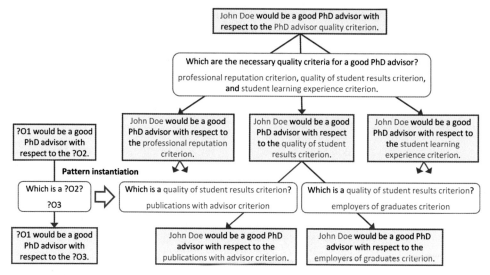

Figure 3.10. Uniform modeling through the instantiation of a learned pattern.

applying it, the user would manually define these reductions, then any syntactic differences between these reductions would lead to the learning of different rules. These rules would only be superficially different, leading to an inefficient and difficult to maintain agent.

After the top-level criterion (i.e., PhD advisor quality criterion) is reduced to a set of elementary criteria, specific knowledge and evidence about the advisor need to be used to evaluate John Doe with respect to each such elementary criterion. For example, the following hypothesis will be evaluated based on favoring and disfavoring evidence from John Doe's peers:

John Doe would be a good PhD advisor with respect to the peer opinion criterion.

A learning agent shell for evidence-based reasoning already knows how to assess such hypotheses based on evidence.

Through this process, the initial hypothesis is reduced to elementary hypotheses for which assessments are made. Then these assessments are successively combined, from bottom-up, until the assessment of the initial hypothesis is obtained, as illustrated in Figure 3.11.

Notice at the bottom-right side of Figure 3.11 the assessments corresponding to the subcriteria of the quality of student results criterion:

It is likely that John Doe would be a good PhD advisor with respect to the publications with advisor criterion.

It is very likely that John Doe would be a good PhD advisor with respect to the employers of graduates criterion.

These assessments are combined by taking their maximum, leading to an evaluation of "very likely" for the quality of student results criterion:

It is very likely that John Doe would be a good PhD advisor with respect to the quality of student results criterion.

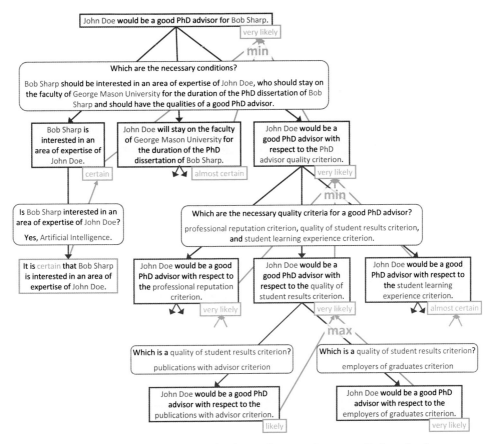

Figure 3.11. Reduction and synthesis tree for assessing a specific hypothesis.

Then this assessment is combined with the assessments corresponding to the other major criteria (very likely for the professional reputation criterion, and almost certain for the student learning experience criterion), through a minimum function (because they are necessary conditions), to obtain the assessment very likely for the PhD advisor quality criterion.

Finally, consider the assessments of the three subhypotheses of the top-level hypothesis:

It is certain that Bob Sharp is interested in an area of expertise of John Doe.

It is almost certain that John Doe will stay on the faculty of George Mason University for the duration of the PhD dissertation of Bob Sharp.

It is very likely that John Doe would be a good PhD advisor with respect to the PhD advisor quality criterion.

These assessments are combined by taking their minimum, leading to the following assessment of the initial hypothesis:

It is very likely that John Doe would be a good PhD advisor for Bob Sharp.

Could you justify the preceding solution synthesis function? We used minimum because each of the three subhypotheses of the initial hypothesis corresponds to a necessary condition. If any of them has a low probability, we would like this to be reflected in the overall evaluation.

Notice that, at this point, the knowledge engineer and the subject matter expert have completely modeled the assessment of the specific hypothesis considered. This is the most creative and the most challenging part of developing the agent. Once such a model for assessing hypotheses (or solving problems, in general) is clarified, the agent can be rapidly prototyped by modeling a set of typical hypotheses. The rest of the agent development process consists of developing its knowledge base so that the agent can automatically assess other hypotheses. The knowledge base will consist of an ontology of domain concepts and relationships and of problem/hypothesis reduction and solution synthesis rules, as was discussed in Section 1.6.3.1 and illustrated in Figure 1.15 (p. 38). As will be discussed in the following, the way the preceding assessments were modeled will greatly facilitate this process.

3.3.3   Ontology Design and Development

We want the developed agent to generate by itself reasoning trees like that shown in Figure 3.11. What knowledge does it need in its ontology to perform this kind of reasoning?

Consider, for example, the reasoning step from the bottom-left of Figure 3.8, shown again in the left-hand side of Figure 3.12. What knowledge does the agent need in order to answer the question from this reasoning step? It needs the knowledge from the right-hand side of Figure 3.12.

But this is just an example. We want the agent to be able to answer similar questions, corresponding to similar hypotheses. Therefore, the ontological knowledge from the right-hand side of Figure 3.12 is just a *specification* for the ontological knowledge needed by the agent.

What other concepts and instances should we add to the ontology, based on the specification in Figure 3.12? We would obviously need to consider other areas of expertise, since we want to develop a general advisor assistant, capable of assessing advisors from different disciplines. Thus the ontology can be expanded as shown in Figure 3.13.

The knowledge engineer and the subject matter expert will consider all the reasoning steps from the developed reasoning trees and will correspondingly develop the ontology of the agent.

What resources could be used to develop the ontology? Obvious resources are the many foundational and utility ontologies for the Semantic Web that were discussed in Section 3.2.2.

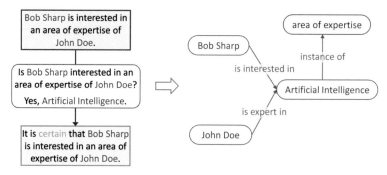

Figure 3.12. Modeling-based ontology specification.

The goal of this phase is to develop an ontology that is as complete as possible. This will enable the agent to learn reasoning rules based on the concepts and the features from the ontology, as will be briefly illustrated in the following.

3.3.4 Rule Learning and Ontology Refinement

During this phase, the subject matter expert will interact with the learning agent shell to explain to it a specific reasoning tree. From each reasoning step, the agent will learn a general reasoning rule, as shown in Figure 3.14.

Figure 3.15 illustrates the learning of a general hypothesis reduction rule from a specific hypothesis reduction step. Notice that the specific instances from the example (e.g., Bob Sharp or John Doe) are generalized to variables (i.e., ?O1, ?O2). In essence, the rule

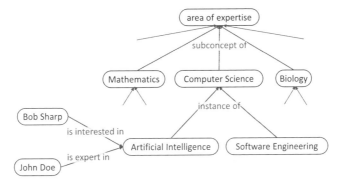

Figure 3.13. Expanded ontology based on the specification from Figure 3.12.

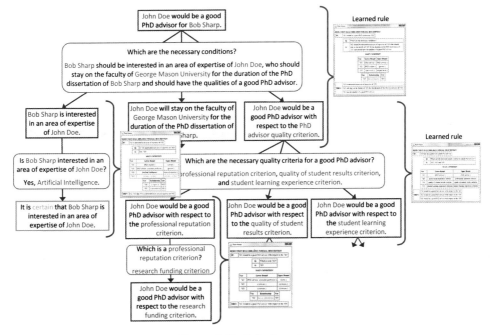

Figure 3.14. Rules learning.

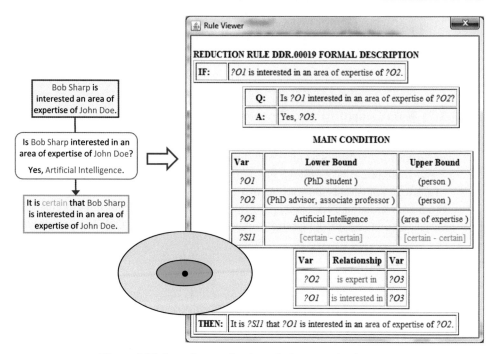

Figure 3.15. Learning a reduction rule from a reduction step.

indicates the conditions that need to be satisfied by these variables so that the IF hypothesis can be assessed as indicated in the example. For example, ?O1 should be a PhD student or possibly a person (the agent does not yet know precisely what concept to apply because the rule is only partially learned), ?O1 should be interested in ?O3, and ?O3 should be Artificial Intelligence or possibly any area of expertise.

The way the question and its answer from the reduction step are formulated is very important for learning. What could the agent learn if the answer were simply "yes"? The agent would only be able to learn the fact that "Bob Sharp is interested in an area of expertise of John Doe." By providing an explanation of why this fact is true ("Yes, Artificial Intelligence" meaning: "Yes, because Bob Sharp is interested in Artificial Intelligence which is an area of expertise of John Doe"), we help the agent to learn a general rule where it will check that the student ?O1 is interested in some area ?O3, which is an area of expertise of the advisor ?O2. This is precisely the condition of the rule that can be easily verified because this type of knowledge was represented in the ontology, as discussed previously and shown in Figure 3.12.

What is the difference between the pattern learning illustrated in Figure 3.9 and the rule learning illustrated in Figure 3.15? The difference is in the formal applicability condition of the rule, which restricts the possible values of the rule variables and allows the automatic application of the rule in situations where the condition is satisfied. A learned pattern, such as that from Figure 3.9, cannot be automatically applied because the agent does not know how to instantiate its variables correctly. Therefore, its application, during the modeling phase, is controlled by the user, who selects the instances of the variables.

A remarkable capability of the agent is that it learns a general rule, like the one in Figure 3.15, from a single example rather than requiring the rule to be manually developed by the knowledge engineer and the subject matter expert. Rule learning will be discussed in detail in Chapter 9.

As indicated in the preceding, the rule in Figure 3.15 is only partially learned, because instead of an exact applicability condition, it contains an upper and a lower bound for this condition. The upper bound condition (represented as the larger ellipse from Figure 3.15) corresponds to the most general generalization of the example (represented as the point from the center of the two ellipses) in the context of the agent's ontology, which is used as a generalization hierarchy for learning. The lower bound condition (represented as the smaller ellipse) corresponds to the least general generalization of the example.

The next phase is to refine the learned rules and, at the same time, test the agent with new hypotheses. Therefore, the subject matter expert will formulate new hypotheses, for example:

Dan Smith would be a good PhD advisor for Bob Sharp.

Using the learned rules, the agent will automatically generate the reasoning tree from Figure 3.16. Notice that, in this case, the area of common interest/expertise of Dan Smith and Bob Sharp is Information Security. The expert will have to check each reasoning step. Those that are correct represent new positive examples that are used to generalize the lower bound conditions of the corresponding rules. Those that are incorrect are used as negative examples. The expert will interact with the agent to explain to it why a reasoning step is incorrect, and the agent will correspondingly specialize the upper bound condition of the rule, or both conditions. During the rule refinement process, the rule's conditions will converge toward one another and toward the exact applicability condition. During this process, the ontology may also be extended, for instance to include the new concepts used to explain the agent's error. Rule refinement will be discussed in detail in Chapter 10.

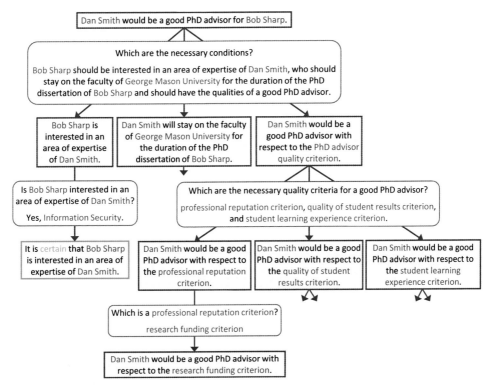

Figure 3.16. Reasoning tree automatically generated by the agent.

3.3.5   Hierarchical Organization of the Knowledge Repository

Figure 3.17 illustrates the organization of a knowledge repository developed with the Disciple-EBR learning agent shell, which was trained to assess different types of hypotheses in different domains.

The top of the knowledge repository is the Shared KB, which contains general knowledge for evidence-based reasoning applicable in all the domains.

Under the Shared KB are Domain KBs, each corresponding to a different application domain. One of these domain KBs will correspond to PhD advisor assessment. This PhD advisor domain KB will contain general knowledge for assessing a PhD advisor, such as the criteria for assessing a PhD advisor shown in Figure 3.7, and the learned reasoning rules. This knowledge is, in principle, applicable for assessing any PhD advisor from any university.

Let us assume that we are using this agent to assess PhD advisors at three different universities: George Mason University, Old Dominion University, and the University of Virginia. How many scenario knowledge bases do we need and what knowledge will be stored in each of them?

For each university there is at least one Scenario KB containing knowledge specific to that university, such as individual professors and their characteristics.

When we need to assess PhD advisors at a specific university, the agent will use only the corresponding Scenario KB, the Domain KB for PhD advisor assessment, and the Shared KB for evidence-based reasoning.

The left-hand side of Figure 3.17 shows a reasoning step in the assessment of John Doe. In which knowledge base will the following elements be represented: John Doe, Bob Sharp, Artificial Intelligence, and certain?

John Doe and Bob Sharp are individuals at a specific university and are therefore represented as *specific instances* in the Scenario KB corresponding to that university.

Artificial Intelligence is an instance to be used in reasoning in the context of any university and is therefore represented as a *generic instance* in the Domain KB corresponding to the assessment of PhD advisors.

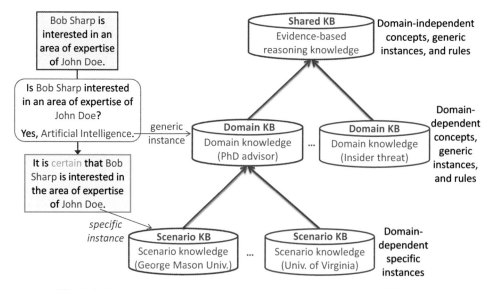

Figure 3.17. Organization of the knowledge repository of a Disciple-EBR agent.

Finally, certain is a constant to be used in evidence-based reasoning in any application domain and is therefore represented in the Shared KB.

3.3.6   Learning-based Design and Development Phases

Figure 3.18 summarizes the main phases of agent development when using learning technology. The first phase is *agent specification,* during which a knowledge engineer and a subject matter expert define the types of hypotheses to assess (or problems to be solved) by the agent. For example, the hypotheses might be to assess potential PhD advisors.

The second phase is *rapid prototyping,* where the knowledge engineer supports the subject matter expert to develop reasoning trees for specific but representative hypotheses (or problems). An example of a reasoning tree is the one from Figure 3.8. In this reasoning tree, a complex hypothesis is assessed as illustrated in Figure 3.11 by:

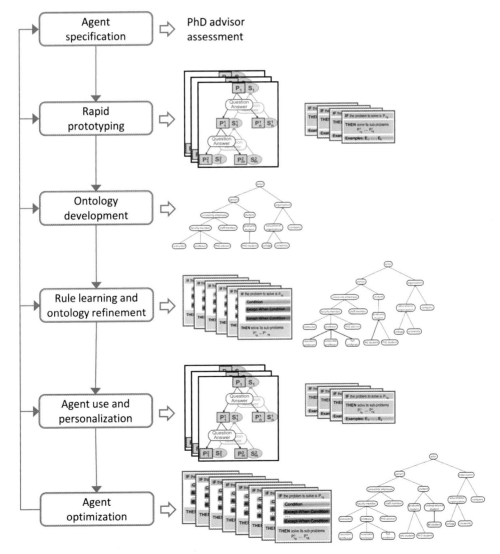

Figure 3.18. Main phases of agent development when using learning technology.

- Successively reducing it, from the top down, to simpler and simpler hypotheses
- Assessing the simplest hypotheses
- Successively combining, from the bottom up, the assessments of the subhypotheses, until the assessment of the top-level hypothesis is obtained

During this phase, the agent also learns reduction patterns.

The next phase is that of *ontology development*. The guiding question is: What are the domain concepts, relationships, and instances that would enable the agent to automatically generate the reasoning trees developed during rapid prototyping, as well as similar ones? From each reasoning step, the knowledge engineer and the subject matter expert identify the ontology elements mentioned in it, as illustrated in Figure 3.12. Such semantic network fragments represent a specification of the needed ontology. In particular, this fragment suggests the need for the ontology fragment shown in Figure 3.13. Based on such specifications, and using the ontology development tools of the Disciple-EBR shell, the knowledge engineer develops an ontology that is sufficiently complete. As part of ontology development, a knowledge engineer may reuse concepts and relationships from previously developed ontologies, including those on the Semantic Web.

The next phase in agent development is that of *rule learning and ontology refinement*. From each hypothesis reduction step of a reasoning tree developed during rapid prototyping, the agent will learn a general hypothesis reduction rule by using the ontology as a generalization hierarchy. This was illustrated in Figures 3.14 and 3.15. During this phase, the expert teaches the agent to assess other similar hypotheses. The expert instantiates a learned hypothesis pattern, such as "Dan Smith would be a good PhD advisor for Bob Sharp," and the agent automatically generates a reasoning tree, by applying the learned rules, as was illustrated in Figure 3.16. The expert then critiques the agent's reasoning, guiding it in refining the rules.

Now the assistant is ready for the typical end-user, as part of the next phase, *agent use and personalization*. Typically, the user will specify the hypothesis to assess by simply instantiating a corresponding pattern. Then the agent will automatically generate a reduction tree like the one in Figure 3.16 by automatically applying the learned reduction rules. This tree reduces the top-level hypothesis to elementary hypotheses to be directly assessed based on knowledge and evidence. The assessments of these elementary hypotheses are then automatically combined, from the bottom up, until the probability of the initial hypothesis is obtained.

The end-user may also assess an entirely new hypothesis, but in this case he or she also needs to indicate its decomposition, either to elementary hypotheses or to known hypotheses.

So when does the additional learning take place? It may be the case that the agent does not know how to decompose a specific hypothesis. In such a case, the user can indicate the desired decomposition, which will be used in the current analysis. As a result, the agent will automatically learn a decomposition pattern, such as the one from the right-hand side of Figure 3.9.

As mentioned previously, an important difference between a learned rule and a learned pattern concerns its use in problem solving. A learned rule is always automatically applied, while a pattern will be proposed to the user who may decide to select it and instantiate it appropriately. If this is done, the corresponding instances will be added to the pattern. Thus this type of learning is much simpler for the end-user, who only needs to specify, in natural language, the decomposition of a hypothesis into simpler hypotheses.

Periodically, the agent can undergo an *optimization* phase, which is the last phase in Figure 3.18. During this phase, the knowledge engineer and the subject matter expert will review the patterns learned from the end-user, will learn corresponding rules from them, and will correspondingly refine the ontology. The current version of the Disciple-EBR shell reapplies its rule and ontology learning methods to do this. However, improved methods can be used when the pattern has more than one set of instances, because each represents a different example of the rule to be learned. This is part of future research.

Figure 3.19 compares the conventional knowledge engineering process of developing a knowledge-based agent (which was discussed in Section 3.1) with the process discussed in this section, which is based on the learning agent technology.

The top part of Figure 3.19 shows the complex knowledge engineering activities that are required to build the knowledge base. The knowledge engineer and the subject matter expert have to develop a model of the application domain that will make explicit the way the subject matter expert assesses hypotheses. Then the knowledge engineer has to develop the ontology. He or she also needs to define general hypotheses decomposition rules and to debug them, with the help of the subject matter expert.

As shown at the bottom of Figure 3.19, each such activity is replaced with an equivalent activity that is performed by the subject matter expert and the agent, with limited assistance from the knowledge engineer. The knowledge engineer still needs to help the subject matter expert to define a formal model of how to assess hypotheses and to develop the ontology. After that, the subject matter expert will teach the agent how to assess hypotheses, through examples and explanations, and the agent will learn and refine the rules by itself.

The next chapters discuss each phase of this process in much more detail.

3.4 HANDS ON: LOADING, SAVING, AND CLOSING KNOWLEDGE BASES

The knowledge bases developed with Disciple-EBR are located in the repository folder, which is inside the installation folder. As shown in Figure 3.17, the knowledge bases are

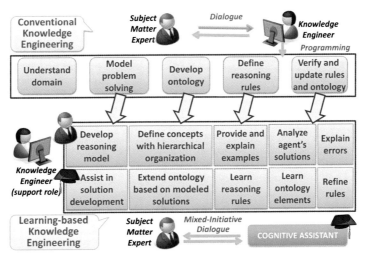

Figure 3.19. Conventional knowledge engineering versus learning-based knowledge engineering.

organized hierarchically, with the knowledge base for evidence-based reasoning at the top of the hierarchy. The user cannot change this knowledge base, whose knowledge elements are inherited in the domain and scenario knowledge bases. From the user's point of view, each knowledge base consists of a top-level domain part (which contains knowledge common to several applications or scenarios in a domain) and one scenario part (containing knowledge specific to a particular application or scenario). As illustrated in Figure 3.17, there can be more than one scenario under a domain. In such a case, the domain and each of the scenarios correspond to a different knowledge base. Loading, saving, or closing a scenario will automatically load, save, or close both the scenario part and the corresponding domain part of the knowledge base.

Loading and selecting a knowledge base are described in Operation 3.1 and illustrated in Figure 3.20.

Operation 3.1. Load and select a knowledge base

- In the **System Workspace Manager**, click on the knowledge base icon containing the plus sign (+).
- The **Knowledge Manager** window opens, showing all the knowledge bases from the repository.
- Click on the plus sign (+) of the domain knowledge base to be loaded, to display all its scenario knowledge bases.
- Click on the scenario knowledge base to be loaded.
- Click on the **Select** button. This both loads the scenario and domain KBs and selects them as the current ones to work with. Their names will be shown in bold in the **Knowledge Manager** window.

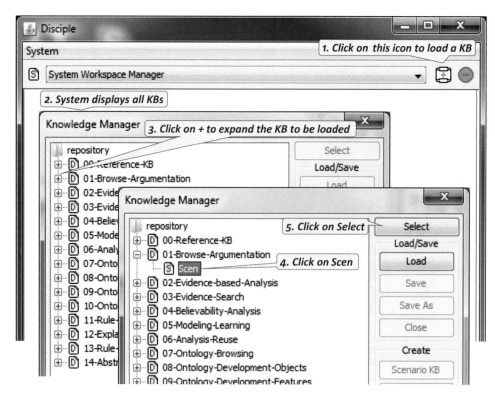

Figure 3.20. Loading and selecting a knowledge base.

Once a knowledge base is selected, you can invoke different modules of Disciple-EBR to use it. Each module is accessible in a specific workspace. As illustrated in Figure 3.21, there are three workspaces:

Evidence workspace: "Evidence: repository\KB-name\Scen"
Scenario workspace: "repository\KB-name\Scen"
Domain workspace: "repository\KB-name"

The user can switch between the workspaces to use the corresponding modules. For example, you must switch to the Evidence workspace to work with evidence items. Then, to save the knowledge base, you must switch to the Scenario workspace.

The user should work with only one set of the three workspaces at a time (corresponding to the same KB). Therefore, you should close the workspaces corresponding to a knowledge base (by clicking on the icon with the minus sign [–]) before opening the workspaces corresponding to another knowledge base.

The steps to save all the knowledge bases loaded in memory are described in Operation 3.2 and illustrated in Figure 3.22.

Operation 3.2. Save all the knowledge bases

- Select the Scenario workspace ("repository\KB-name\Scen").
- Select the **System** menu.
- Select **Save All**.

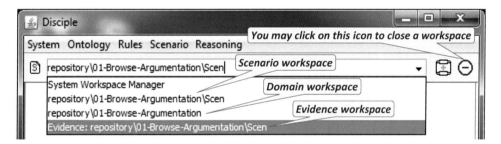

Figure 3.21. Workspaces in Disciple-EBR.

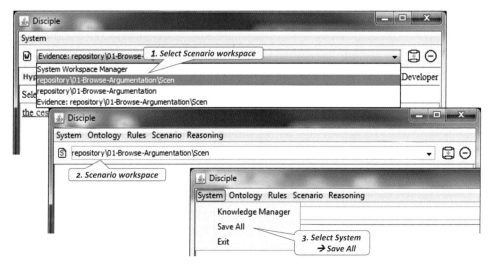

Figure 3.22. Saving all the knowledge bases.

It is highly recommended to have only one knowledge base loaded in memory. Therefore, before loading a new knowledge base, you should close all the opened ones by following the instructions described in Operation 3.3 and illustrated in Figure 3.23.

Operation 3.3. Close a knowledge base

- Click on the knowledge base icon containing the plus sign (+) situated at the right of the workspace selector.
- The **Knowledge Manager** window opens, showing all the knowledge bases.
- Click on the scenario knowledge base to be closed.
- Click on the **Close** button in the right side of the window.
- Click on the **X** button to close the **Knowledge Manager** window.

The predefined knowledge base "00-Reference-KB" contains general knowledge for evidence-based reasoning, an empty domain, and an empty scenario. Users can create their knowledge bases as renamed copies of "00-Reference-KB," as indicated in Operation 3.4. They should never work with "00-Reference-KB," which should be kept as a reference knowledge base.

Operation 3.4. Create a user knowledge base

- Open the "repository" folder from the "installation" directory in **Windows Explorer**.
- Make a copy of the entire "00-Reference-KB" folder and give it a new name.
- Use the Disciple-EBR modules to develop the newly created knowledge base.

Figure 3.23. Closing a knowledge base.

3.5   KNOWLEDGE BASE GUIDELINES

The following are knowledge engineering guidelines for knowledge base development.

Guideline 3.1. Work with only one knowledge base loaded in memory

To maintain the performance of the Disciple-EBR modules, work with only one knowledge base loaded in memory. Therefore, close all the knowledge bases before loading a new one.

If several knowledge bases are loaded, work only with the set of three workspaces corresponding to the knowledge base you are currently using. Close all the other workspaces.

Guideline 3.2. Create a knowledge base and save successive versions

A user can introduce errors into the knowledge base while developing it. When Disciple-EBR attempts to load a knowledge base, it makes a rigorous check of its correctness and will not load the knowledge base if it contains errors. It is therefore important to save successive versions of the knowledge base being developed in order to fall back to a previous version in case the latest one contains errors.

Create your knowledge base by making a copy of "00-Reference-KB" and giving it a new name, for instance "WA." From now on, you will work only with "WA," but as you develop it, you will have to save successive copies of it with different names, as explained in the following.

Suppose that you have developed "WA" to contain part of the modeling for a hypothesis. Save "WA" in Disciple-EBR, then using Windows Explorer make a copy of it, and rename the copy as "WA-1m." Continue working with "WA" and expand the modeling of the hypothesis. Save and make a copy of "WA." Then rename the copy as "WA-2m," and so on.

Through such a process, you will save a sequence of knowledge bases: "WA-1m," "WA-2m," "WA-3o," "WA-4o," and so on, each corresponding to a given stage in your development of "WA." In this way, if your "WA" knowledge base is damaged for any reason, you can always resume from the most recently saved version, as illustrated in the following scenario:

- "WA" has errors, and the most recently saved version is "WA-4o."
- Delete "WA" in Windows Explorer, copy "WA-4o," and rename this copy as "WA."
- Continue with the development of "WA."

3.6   PROJECT ASSIGNMENT 2

Finalize the project team, specify the type of hypotheses to be analyzed by the agent to be developed, and study the application domain. Prepare a short presentation of the following:

- The application domain of your agent and why your agent is important.
- A bibliography containing the expertise domain and your current familiarity with the domain, keeping in mind that you should choose a domain where you already are or could become an expert without investing a significant amount of time.
- Three examples of hypotheses and a probability for each.

3.7   REVIEW QUESTIONS

3.1.   Which are the main phases in the development of a knowledge-based agent?

3.2.   Which are the required qualifications of a knowledge engineer?

3.3.   Which are the required qualifications of a subject matter expert?

3.4.   Briefly define "verification," "validation," and "certification."

3.5.   Consider the fact that a knowledge-based agent may need to have hundreds or thousands of rules. What can be said about the difficulty of defining and refining these rules through the conventional process discussed in Section 3.1.4?

3.6.   Use the scenario from Section 3.1 to illustrate the different difficulties of building a knowledge-based agent discussed in Section 1.6.3.1.

3.7.   What is an expert system shell?

3.8.   Which are different types of expert system shells?

3.9.   What is a learning agent shell?

3.10.   What is a learning agent shell for evidence-based reasoning?

3.11.   What is the organization of the knowledge repository of a learning agent shell for evidence-based reasoning?

3.12.   What is the difference between a specific instance and a generic instance? Provide an example of each.

3.13.   Are there any mistakes in the reasoning step from Figure 3.24 with respect to the goal of teaching the agent? If the answer is yes, explain and indicate corrections.

3.14.   Which are the main stages of developing a knowledge-based agent using learning agent technology?

3.15.   Compare the manual knowledge engineering process of developing a knowledge-based agent, as described in Section 3.1, with the process using learning agent technology, described in Section 3.3.

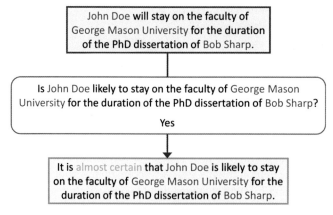

Figure 3.24. Reduction step.

4 Modeling the Problem-Solving Process

4.1 PROBLEM SOLVING THROUGH ANALYSIS AND SYNTHESIS

Analysis and synthesis, introduced in Section 1.6.2, form the basis of a general divide-and-conquer problem-solving strategy that can be applied to a wide variety of problems. The general idea, illustrated in Figure 4.1, is to decompose or reduce a complex problem P_1 to n simpler problems P_{11}, P_{12}, ..., P_{1n}, which represent its components. If we can then find the solutions S_{11}, S_{12}, ..., S_{1n} of these subproblems, then these solutions can be combined into the solution S_1 of the problem P_1.

If any of the subproblems is still too complex, it can be approached in a similar way, by successively decomposing or reducing it to simpler problems, until one obtains problems whose solutions are known, as illustrated in Figure 4.2.

Figures 4.3 and 4.4 illustrate the application of this divide-and-conquer approach to solve a symbolic integration problem. Notice that each reduction and synthesis operation is justified by a specific symbolic integration operator.

4.2 INQUIRY-DRIVEN ANALYSIS AND SYNTHESIS

Cognitive assistants require the use of problem-solving paradigms that are both natural enough for their human users and formal enough to be automatically executed by the agents. Inquiry-driven analysis and synthesis comprise such a problem-solving paradigm where the reduction and synthesis operations are guided by corresponding questions and answers. The typical questions are those from Rudyard Kipling's well-known poem "I Keep Six Honest . . ."

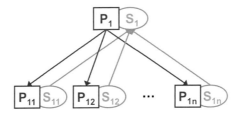

Figure 4.1. Problem reduction (decomposition) and solutions synthesis (composition).

I keep six honest serving-men
(They taught me all I knew);
Their names are What and Why and When
And How and Where and Who.

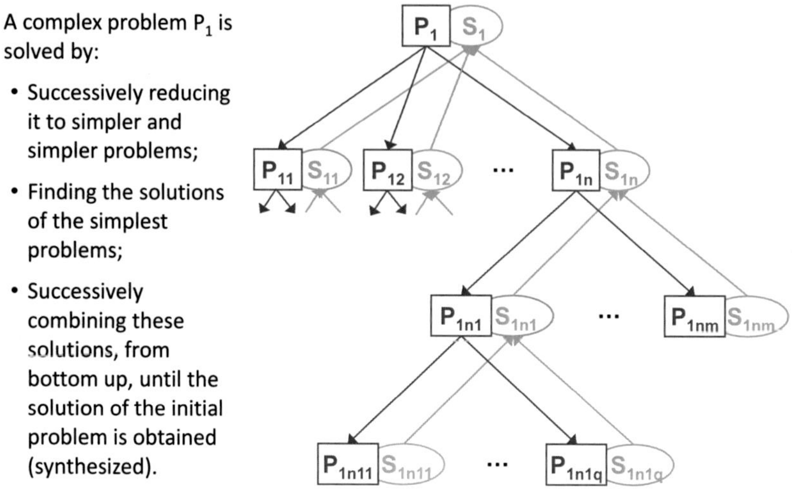

A complex problem P_1 is solved by:

- Successively reducing it to simpler and simpler problems;

- Finding the solutions of the simplest problems;

- Successively combining these solutions, from bottom up, until the solution of the initial problem is obtained (synthesized).

Figure 4.2. Problem solving through analysis and synthesis.

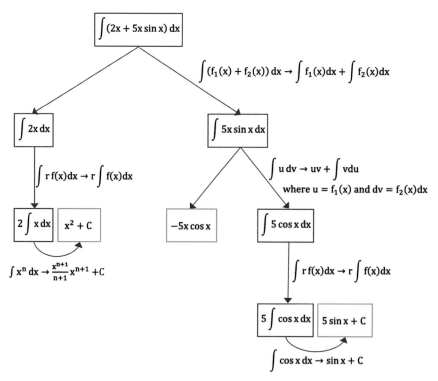

Figure 4.3. Reduction of a symbolic integration problem.

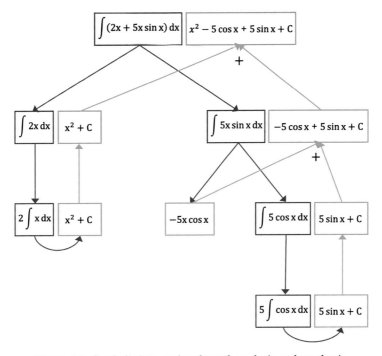

Figure 4.4. Symbolic integration through analysis and synthesis.

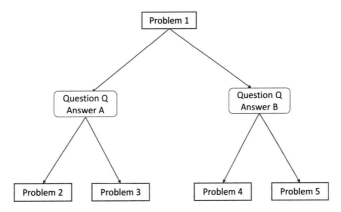

Figure 4.5. Inquiry-driven problem reduction.

We have already illustrated this paradigm in Sections 2.2 and 3.3.2. To better understand it, let us consider the simple abstract example from Figure 4.5. To solve Problem 1, one asks Question Q related to some aspect of Problem 1. Let us assume that there are two answers to Q: Answer A and Answer B. For example, the question, "Which is a sub-criterion of the quality of student results criterion?" has two answers, "publications with advisor criterion" and "employers of graduates criterion."

Let us further assume that Answer A leads to the reduction of Problem 1 to two simpler problems, Problem 2 and Problem 3. Similarly, Answer B leads to the reduction of Problem 1 to the other simpler problems, Problem 4 and Problem 5.

Let us now assume that we have obtained the solutions of these four subproblems. How do we combine them to obtain the solution of Problem 1? As shown in Figure 4.6, first the solutions to Problem 2 and Problem 3 are combined to obtain a solution to Problem 1 corresponding to Answer A (called Solution A). Also the solutions to Problem 4 and Problem 5 are combined to obtain a solution to Problem 1 corresponding to Answer B (called Solution B). Each of these two synthesis (or composition) operations is called a *reduction-level synthesis* because it corresponds to a *specific* reduction of the top-level problem. Second, we need to combine Solution A with Solution B into the final solution of Problem 1. This synthesis operation is called *problem-level synthesis* because it corresponds to *all* reductions of Problem 1.

Figures 4.7 and 4.8 illustrate inquiry-driven analysis and synthesis in the context of the military center of gravity (COG) determination problem (Tecuci et al., 2005b; 2008b), which will be discussed in Section 12.4. Figure 4.7 shows the reduction of a problem to three simpler problems, guided by a question/answer pair.

Figure 4.8 illustrates the composition of the solutions of the three subproblems into the solution of the problem. One aspect to notice is that the reduction-level synthesis operation is guided by a question/answer pair, while the problem-level synthesis operation is not. Thus the use of questions and answers is actually optional.

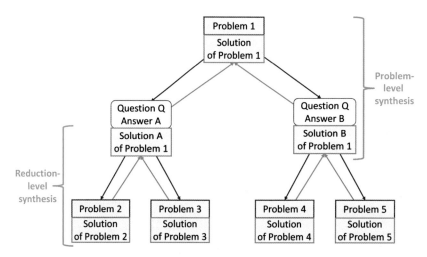

Figure 4.6. A more detailed view of the analysis and synthesis process.

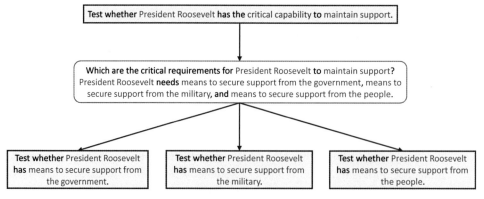

Figure 4.7. Illustration of a reduction operation in the COG domain.

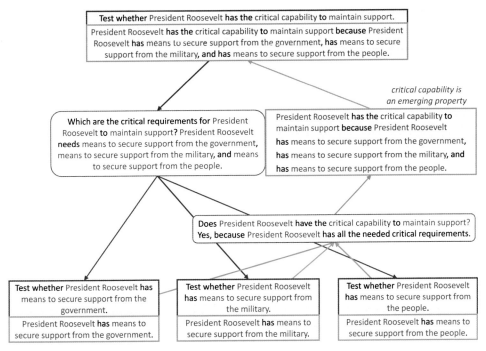

Figure 4.8. Illustration of reduction and synthesis operations in the COG domain.

Moreover, it is assumed that the questions guiding the synthesis operations may have only one answer, which typically indicates how to combine the solutions. Allowing more questions and more answers in the synthesis tree would lead to a combinatorial explosion of solutions.

Another interesting aspect is that the three leaf solutions in Figure 4.8 are about the means of President Roosevelt, while their composition is about a capability. Thus this illustrates how synthesis operations may lead to emerging properties.

A third aspect to notice is how the reduction-level composition is actually performed. In the example from Figure 4.8, the solutions to combine are:

President Roosevelt has means to secure support from the government.
President Roosevelt has means to secure support from the military.
President Roosevelt has means to secure support from the people.

The synthesized solution is obtained by concatenating substrings from these solutions because, as indicated in corresponding question/answer pair, President Roosevelt has all the needed critical requirements:

President Roosevelt has the critical capability to maintain support because President Roosevelt has means to secure support from the government, has means to secure support from the military, and has means to secure support from the people.

The preceding synthesis operation in the interface of Disciple-COG is shown in Figure 12.28 (p. 373) from Section 12.4.2.

Figure 4.9 shows another example of reduction and synthesis in the COG domain. In this case, the solutions to combine are:

PM Mussolini has means to secure support from the government.
PM Mussolini has means to secure support from the military.
PM Mussolini does not have means to secure support from the people.

In this case, the synthesized solution is no longer obtained by concatenating substrings from these solutions because, as indicated in corresponding question/answer pair, PM Mussolini does not have all the needed critical requirements:

PM Mussolini does not have the critical capability to maintain support because PM Mussolini does not have means to secure support from the people.

Additional examples of solution synthesis from the COG domain are presented in Figures 12.27 (p. 372), 12.28 (p. 373), 12.29 (p. 373), and 12.30 (p. 374) from Section 12.4.2.

As suggested by the preceding examples, there are many ways in which solutions may be combined.

One last important aspect related to problem solving through analysis and synthesis is that the solutions of the elementary problems may be obtained by applying any other type of reasoning strategy. This enables the solving of problems through a multistrategy approach.

Chapter 12 presents Disciple cognitive assistants for different types of tasks, illustrating the use of the inquiry-driven analysis and synthesis in different domains. Section 12.2 discusses this problem-solving paradigm in the context of military engineering planning. Section 12.3 discusses it in the context of course of action critiquing. Section 12.4 discusses it in the context of center of gravity analysis, and Section 12.5 discusses it in the context of collaborative emergency response planning.

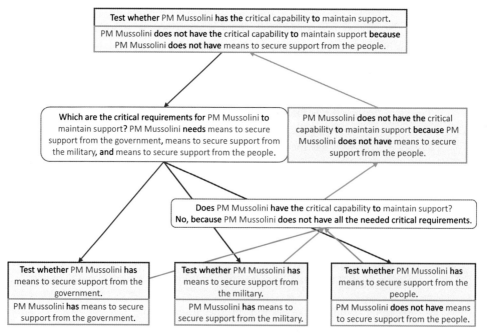

Figure 4.9. Another illustration of reduction and synthesis operations in the COG domain.

INQUIRY-DRIVEN ANALYSIS AND SYNTHESIS FOR
        EVIDENCE-BASED REASONING

4.3.1   Hypothesis Reduction and Assessment Synthesis

In this section, we discuss the specialization of the inquiry-driven analysis and synthesis paradigm for evidence-based reasoning where one assesses the probability of hypotheses based on evidence, as was illustrated in Section 2.2. In this case, a complex hypothesis is assessed by:

- Successively reducing it, from the top down, to simpler and simpler hypotheses (guided by introspective questions and answers).
- Assessing the simplest hypotheses based on evidence.
- Successively combining, from the bottom up, the assessments of the simpler hypotheses, until the assessment of the top-level hypothesis is obtained.

Figure 4.10 shows a possible analysis of the hypothesis that Country X has nuclear weapons.

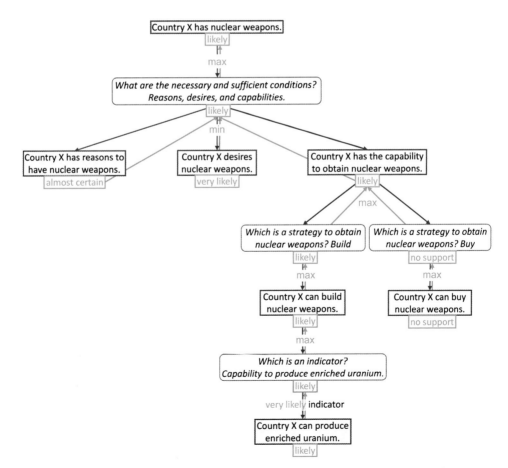

Figure 4.10. An example of different types of reductions and corresponding synthesis functions.

As pointed out by Alvin Toffler (1984, p. xi):

> One of the most highly developed skills in contemporary Western civilization is dissection; the split-up of problems into their smallest possible components. We are good at it. So good, we often forget to put the pieces back together again.

Evidence-based reasoning offers an opportunity to simplify the more complex synthesis process. Indeed, in this case, the solution of a hypothesis may no longer need to be a complex phrase or expression, but just its probability of being true, given the available evidence. The actual solution synthesis function depends on the type of reduction strategy used.

In the following section, we will review different types of reduction strategies and the corresponding synthesis functions.

4.3.2   Necessary and Sufficient Conditions

Ideally, a hypothesis would be reduced to several subhypotheses that would represent necessary and sufficient conditions. That is, the hypothesis is true *if and only if* all the subhypotheses are true. An example is the top-level reduction from Figure 4.10, where the top-level hypothesis is reduced to three subhypotheses. Let us assume that we have obtained the following assessments of these subhypotheses: almost certain, very likely, and likely, respectively. Then the assessment of the top hypothesis, corresponding to this necessary and sufficient condition, is the minimum of the three assessments (i.e., likely), because each of the three subhypotheses would need to be true to ensure that the top-level hypothesis is true. This value and the minimum (min) function that produced it are associated with the question/answer pair.

In general, as will be illustrated later in this chapter, there may be more than one strategy to reduce a hypothesis to simpler hypotheses, each resulting in a possibly different assessment. In such a case, the assessment of the hypothesis should be taken as the maximum of all these possible assessments. In this particular example, since we have only one strategy, the assessment of the top-level hypothesis is max(likely) = likely.

4.3.3   Sufficient Conditions and Scenarios

Many times it is not easy or even possible to identify necessary and sufficient conditions to reduce a hypothesis. In such a case, a second-best reduction would be a sufficient condition. This means that if the subhypotheses are true, then the hypothesis is true. But, as we have discussed previously, there may be more than one sufficient condition for a hypothesis. For example, the middle part of Figure 4.10 shows two possible strategies for Country X to obtain nuclear weapons: It can build them, or it can buy them. Each strategy has to be assessed and the maximum assessment represents the assessment of the hypothesis that Country X has the capability to obtain nuclear weapons.

A special type of a sufficient condition for a hypothesis is a scenario in which the hypothesis would be true, such as the one illustrated in Figure 2.9 (p. 63) from Section 2.2.4. But, as we have discussed in Section 2.2.4, there may be multiple alternative scenarios. Figure 4.11 shows an abstract example where there are two alternative scenarios for Hypothesis 1 to be true. Scenario 1 consists of action 2 and action 3. For this scenario to have happened, both these actions should have happened. Therefore, we combine their

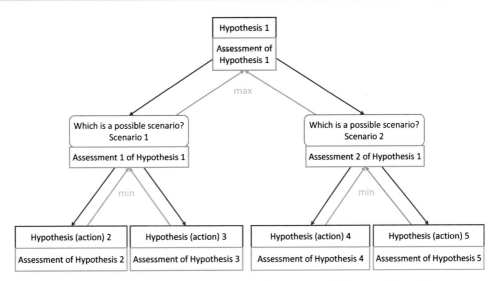

Figure 4.11. Reductions and syntheses corresponding to two sufficient conditions (scenarios).

corresponding assessments with a minimum function, as shown at the bottom-left of Figure 4.11. Hypothesis 1, however, would be true if either of the two scenarios would happen. Therefore, we combine the assessments corresponding to the two scenarios through a maximum function.

4.3.4 Indicators

Many times when we are assessing a hypothesis, we have only indicators. For example, as shown at the bottom part of Figure 4.10, having the capability to produce enriched uranium is an indicator that a country can build nuclear weapons. An indicator is, however, weaker than a sufficient condition. If we determine that a sufficient condition is satisfied (e.g., a scenario has actually happened), we may conclude that the hypothesis is true. But we cannot draw such a conclusion just because we have discovered an indicator. However, we may be more or less inclined to conclude that the hypothesis is true, based on the relevance (strength) of the indicator. Therefore, given the symbolic probabilities from Table 2.5, we distinguish between three types of indicators of different relevance (strength): "likely indicator," "very likely indicator," and "almost certain indicator."

A "likely indicator" is one that, if discovered to be true, would lead to the conclusion that the considered hypothesis is likely. Similarly, a "very likely indicator" would lead to the conclusion that the hypothesis is very likely, and an "almost certain indicator" would lead to the conclusion that the hypothesis is almost certain.

In the example from the bottom part of Figure 4.10 it is likely that Country X can produce enriched uranium, and this is a very likely indicator that Country X can build nuclear weapons. Therefore, we can conclude that the probability of the hypothesis that Country X can build nuclear weapons is likely, the minimum between likely (the probability of the indicator) and very likely (the strength of the indicator).

In general, *the probability of a hypothesis H based on an indicator I is the minimum between the probability of the indicator and the relevance (strength) of the indicator* (which could be likely, very likely, or almost certain).

It makes no sense to consider the type "certain indicator," because this would be a sufficient condition. Similarly, it makes no sense to consider the type "no support indicator," because this would not be an indicator.

As an abstract example, Figure 4.12 shows a hypothesis that has two likely indicators, A and B, if only one of them is observed. However, if both of them are observed, they synergize to become an almost certain indicator.

As a concrete example, consider Person Υ, who has been under surveillance in connection with terrorist activities. We suspect that Υ will attempt to leave the country in a short while. Three days ago, we received information that Υ sold his car. Today, we received information that he closed his account at his bank. Each of these is only a likely indicator of the hypothesis that Υ plans to leave the country. He could be planning to buy a new car, or he could be dissatisfied with his bank. But, taken together, these two indicators suggest that it is almost certain that Υ is planning to leave the country.

Coming back to the abstract example in Figure 4.12, let us assume that indicator A is almost certain and indicator B is very likely. In such a case, the assessment of Hypothesis 1, based only on indicator A, is minimum(almost certain, likely) = likely. Similarly, the assessment of Hypothesis 1, based only on indicator B, is minimum(very likely, likely) = likely. But the assessment of Hypothesis 1, based on both indicators A and B, is minimum(minimum(almost certain, very likely), almost certain) = very likely. Also, the assessment of Hypothesis 1 based on all the indicators is the maximum of all the individual assessments (i.e., very likely), because these are three alternative solutions for Hypothesis 1.

4.4   EVIDENCE-BASED ASSESSMENT

Now we discuss the assessment of the leaf hypotheses of the argumentation structure, based on the identified relevant evidence. Let us consider an abstract example where the leaf hypothesis to be directly assessed based on evidence is **Q** (see Figure 4.13).

We begin by discussing how to assess the probability of hypothesis **Q** based only on one item of favoring evidence E_k^* (see the bottom of Figure 4.13). First notice that we call this *likeliness* of **Q**, and not *likelihood*, because in classic probability theory, likelihood is

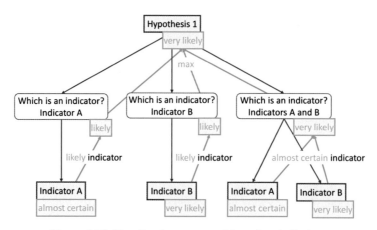

Figure 4.12. Hypothesis assessment based on indicators.

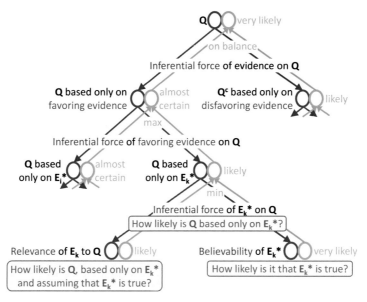

Figure 4.13. The relevance, believability, and inferential force of evidence.

P(E$_k$*|Q), while here we are interested in P(Q|E$_k$*), the posterior probability of **Q** given **E$_k$***. To assess **Q** *based only on* **E$_k$***, there are three judgments to be made by answering three questions:

The *relevance* question is: *How likely is **Q**, based only on **E$_k$*** and assuming that **E$_k$*** is true?* If **E$_k$*** tends to favor **Q**, then our answer should be one of the values from likely to certain. If **E$_k$*** is not relevant to **Q**, then our answer should be no support, because **E$_k$*** provides no support for the truthfulness of **Q**. Finally, if **E$_k$*** tends to disfavor **Q**, then it tends to favor the complement of **Q**, that is, **Q^c**. Therefore, it should be used as favoring evidence for **Q^c**, as discussed later in this section.

The *believability* question is: *How likely is it that **E$_k$*** is true?* Here the answer should be one of the values from no support to certain. The maximal value, certain, means that we are sure that the event **E$_k$** reported in **E$_k$*** did indeed happen. The minimal value, no support, means that **E$_k$*** provides us no reason to believe that the event **E$_k$** reported in **E$_k$*** did happen. For example, we believe that the source of **E$_k$*** has lied to us.

The *inferential force or weight* question is: *How likely is **Q** based only on **E$_k$***?* The agent automatically computes this answer as the minimum of the relevance and believability answers. What is the justification for this? Because to believe that **Q** is true *based only on* **E$_k$***, **E$_k$*** should be both relevant to **Q** and believable.

When we assess a hypothesis **Q**, we may have several items of evidence, some favoring **Q** and some disfavoring **Q**. The agent uses the favoring evidence to assess the probability of **Q** and the disfavoring evidence to assess the probability of **Q^c**. As mentioned previously, because the disfavoring evidence for **Q** is favoring evidence for **Q^c**, the assessment process for **Q^c** is similar to the assessment for **Q**.

When we have several items of favoring evidence, we evaluate **Q** based on each of them (as was explained previously), and then we compose the obtained results. This is illustrated in Figure 4.13, where the assessment of **Q** *based only on* **E$_i$*** (almost certain) is composed with the assessment of **Q** *based only on* E_k* (likely), through the maximum function, to obtain the assessment of **Q** *based only on favoring evidence* (almost certain). In this case, the use of the maximum function is justified because it is enough to have one item of evidence that is both very relevant and very believable to persuade us that the hypothesis **Q** is true.

Let us assume that **Q^c** *based only on disfavoring evidence* is likely. How should we combine this with the assessment of **Q** *based only on favoring evidence*? As illustrated at the top of Figure 4.13, the agent uses an *on-balance* judgment: Because **Q** is almost certain and **Q^c** is likely, it concludes that, *based on all available evidence*, **Q** is very likely.

In general, as indicated in the right and upper side of Table 4.1, if the assessment of **Q^c** (based on disfavoring evidence for **Q**) is higher than or equal to the assessment of **Q** (based on favoring evidence), then we conclude that, based on all the available evidence, there is no support for **Q**. If, on the other hand, the assessment of **Q** is strictly greater than the assessment of **Q^c**, then the assessment of **Q** is decreased, depending on the actual assessment of **Q^c** (see the left and lower side of Table 4.1).

One important aspect to notice is that the direct assessment of hypotheses based on favoring and disfavoring evidence is done automatically by the agent, once the user assesses the relevance and the believability of evidence.

Another important aspect to notice is that the evaluation of upper-level hypotheses (such as those from Figure 4.10) requires the user to indicate what function to use when composing the assessments of their direct subhypotheses. This was discussed in Section 4.3.

4.5   HANDS ON: WAS THE CESIUM STOLEN?

To illustrate further the divide-and-conquer approach to hypothesis analysis, let us continue with the cesium example introduced in Section 2.2, where we have already

Table 4.1 An "On-Balance" Synthesis Function

Q based on all evidence	Q^c based only on disfavoring evidence				
	no support	likely	very likely	almost certain	certain
no support	no support	no support	no support	no support	no support
likely	likely	no support	no support	no support	no support
very likely	very likely	likely	no support	no support	no support
almost certain	almost certain	very likely	likely	no support	no support
certain	certain	almost certain	very likely	likely	no support

Q based only on favoring evidence

established that the cesium-137 canister is missing (see Figure 2.8 on p. 62). The next step is to consider the competing hypotheses:

H_2: The cesium-137 canister was stolen.

H_2': The cesium-137 canister was misplaced.

H_2'': The cesium-137 canister is used in a project without being checked out from the XYZ warehouse.

We have to put each of these hypotheses to work, to guide the collection of relevant evidence. In Section 2.2.4, we have already discussed, at a conceptual level, the collection of evidence for hypothesis H_2. Table 4.2 shows the result of our information collection efforts.

The collected information from Table 4.2 suggests that the cesium-137 canister was stolen with the panel truck having Maryland license MDC-578. This has led to the development of the analysis tree in Figure 2.9 (p. 63). In this case study, you are going to actually perform this analysis. You have to identify the "dots" in the information from

---

Table 4.2 Additional Information on the Missing Cesium-137 Canister

INFO-003-Clyde: We talked to a professional locksmith named Clyde, who said that the lock had been forced, but it was a clumsy job.

INFO-004-SecurityCamera: The security camera of the XYZ warehouse contains a video segment showing a person loading a container into a U-Haul panel truck.

INFO-005-Guard: There is a security perimeter around the XYZ warehouse and employee parking area having just one gate that is controlled by a guard. On the day before the missing canister was observed, the security guard, Sam, recorded that a panel truck having Maryland license plate MDC-578 was granted entry at 4:45 pm just before the XYZ closing hour at 5:00 pm. The driver of this vehicle showed the guard a manifest containing items being delivered to the XYZ warehouse. This manifest contained a list of packing materials allegedly ordered by the XYZ Company. The vehicle was allowed to enter the parking area. At 8:30 pm, this same vehicle was allowed to exit the parking area. A different guard was on duty in the evenings and noticed that his records showed that this vehicle had been permitted entry, and so he allowed the vehicle to exit the parking area.

INFO-006-TRUXINC: Maryland DOT's record indicates that the panel truck carrying the license plate number MDC-578 is registered in the name of a truck-rental company called TRUXINC, located in Silver Spring, MD. The manager of this agency showed records indicating that this truck was rented to a person who gave his name as Omer Riley, having as his listed address 6176 Williams Ave. in Silver Spring. The truck was rented on the day before Willard's discovery about the missing cesium-137, and it was returned the day after he made the discovery.

INFO-007-SilverSpring: Silver Spring city record according to which there is no residence at 6176 Williams Ave. in Silver Spring, MD.

INFO-008-InvestigativeRecord: An examination of the panel truck rented by Omer Riley, using a Geiger counter, revealed minute traces of cesium-137.

INFO-009-Grace: Grace, the Vice President for Operations at XYZ, tells us that no one at the XYZ Company had checked out the canister for work on any project the XYZ Company was working on at the time. She says that the XYZ Company had other projects involving hazardous materials, but none that involved the use of cesium-137.

Table 4.2, which are fragments representing relevant items of evidence for the leaf hypotheses in Figure 2.9. These dots are presented in Table 4.3.

This case study has several objectives:

- Learning to associate with a hypothesis in an argument the evidence that is relevant to it
- Learning to evaluate the relevance and the believability of evidence
- Learning to select synthesis functions
- Better understanding the process of evaluating the probability or likeliness of a hypothesis based on the available evidence

When you associate an item of evidence with a hypothesis, the agent automatically generates a decomposition tree like the one in Figure 4.14. The bottom part of Figure 4.14 shows the abstraction of the tree that is automatically generated by the agent when you indicate that the item of evidence E005-Ralph favors the leaf hypothesis "The XYZ hazardous material locker was forced."

The agent also automatically generates the reduction from the top of Figure 4.14, where the leaf hypothesis, "The XYZ hazardous material locker was forced," is reduced to the elementary hypothesis with the name, "The XYZ hazardous material locker was forced," to be directly assessed based on evidence. Although these two hypotheses are composed of the same words, internally they are different, the latter being an instance introduced in the agent's ontology. This elementary hypothesis corresponds to the hypothesis **Q** in Figure 4.13. The agent decomposes this hypothesis as shown in the bottom part of Figure 4.14, which corresponds to the tree in Figure 4.13 except that there is only one

---

Table 4.3 Dots from Table 4.2

E006-Clyde: Locksmith Clyde's report that the lock was forced.

E007-SecurityCamera: Video segment of the security camera of the XYZ warehouse, showing a person loading a container into a U-Haul panel truck.

E008-GuardReport: The record, made by Sam, security guard at the XYZ Company, that a panel truck bearing Maryland license plate number MDC-578 was in the XYZ parking area on the day before Willard's discovery about the missing cesium-137 canister.

E009-MDDOTRecord: Maryland DOT's record that the truck bearing license plate number MDC-578 is registered in the name of the TRUXINC Company in Silver Spring, MD.

E010-TRUXINCRecord1: TRUXINC's record that the truck bearing MD license plate number MDC-578 was rented to a man who gave his name as Omer Riley on the day before Willard's discovery of the missing cesium-137 canister.

E011-TRUXINCRecord2: TRUXINC's record that Omer Riley gave his address as 6176 Williams Ave.

E012-SilverSpringRecord: Silver Spring city record according to which there is no residence at 6176 Williams Ave. in Silver Spring, MD.

E013-InvestigativeRecord: Investigative record that traces of cesium-137 were found in the truck bearing license plate number MDC-578.

E014-Grace: Grace, the Vice President for Operations at XYZ, tells us that no one at the XYZ Company had checked out the canister for work on any project.

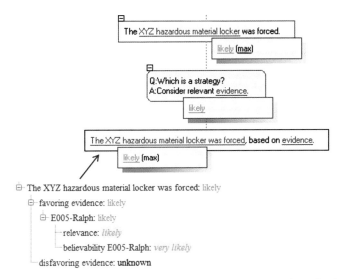

Figure 4.14. Evidence-based assessment of an elementary hypothesis.

item of favoring evidence, namely E005-Ralph. After that, you have to assess the relevance of this item of evidence to the considered hypothesis (e.g., likely), as well as its believability (e.g., very likely), and the agent automatically composes them, from the bottom up, to obtain the assessment of the leaf hypothesis. When you add additional items of evidence as either favoring or disfavoring evidence, the agent extends the reasoning tree from Figure 4.14 as indicated in Figure 4.13.

Figure 4.15 illustrates the selection of a synthesis function indicating how to evaluate the probability of a node based on the probability of its children. You have to right-click on the node (but not on any word in blue), select **New Solution with**. . ., and then select the function from the displayed list.

Now you can perform the case study. Start Disciple-EBR, select the case study knowledge base "02-Evidence-based-Analysis/Scen," and proceed as indicated in the instructions from the bottom of the opened window.

This case study illustrates several basic hypothesis analysis operations described in the following.

Operation 4.1. Associate evidence to hypotheses

- In the Evidence workspace, click on the Evidence menu at the top of the window.
- Notice the four modes of operations from the top part of the left panel. Because the selected one is [AVAILABLE EVIDENCE], the left panel shows the current evidence from the knowledge base.
- In the left panel, click on the item of evidence you would like to associate with a leaf hypothesis from the current argumentation. As a result, the upper part of the right panel shows the main characteristics of this item of evidence, followed by all the leaf hypotheses in the analysis tree (see Figure 4.16). You will have to decide whether the selected item of evidence favors or disfavors any of the hypotheses under the **Irrelevant to** label, and indicate this by clicking on [FAVORS] or [DISFAVORS] following that hypothesis.
- Clicking on [FAVORS] or [DISFAVORS] automatically creates an elementary hypothesis to be assessed based on evidence, and moves it under the **Favors** (or **Disfavors**)

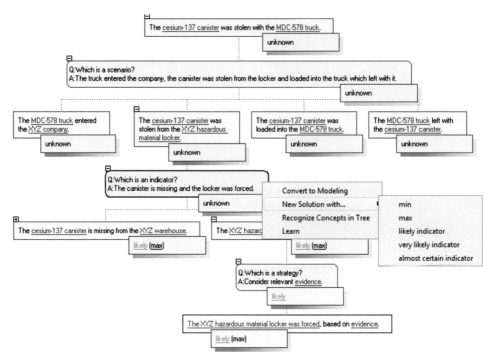

Figure 4.15. Selecting the synthesis function for a node.

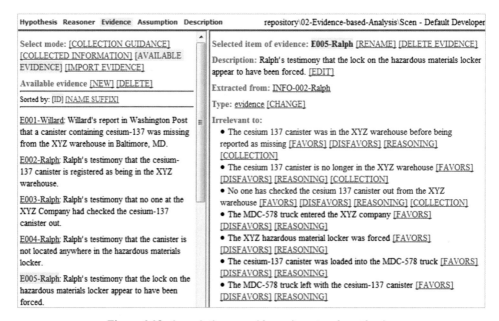

Figure 4.16. Associating an evidence item to a hypothesis.

label. Clicking on [REMOVE] will restore the leaf hypothesis under the **Irrelevant to** label.

- To associate another evidence item to a hypothesis, click on it in the left panel and repeat the preceding operations.
- To return to the **Reasoner** module, click on [REASONING] following the hypothesis.

Operation 4.2. Update the name of an elementary hypothesis

- In the right panel of the Reasoner module, right-click on a hypothesis that was reduced to an elementary hypothesis to be assessed based on evidence, and select **Improve Phrasing**.
- In the opened editor, update the phrasing of the hypothesis and then click outside the box.
- Notice that both this hypothesis and the corresponding elementary hypothesis have been updated accordingly.

Operation 4.3. Assess evidence

- In the Reasoner module, in the left panel, click on the name of the item of evidence to assess. You may need to right-click on the top hypothesis and select **Expand**, to make the evidence item visible. As a result, the right panel shows the decomposition of evidence assessment into a relevance assessment (the left leaf) and a believability assessment (the right leaf), as illustrated in Figure 4.17.
- If the right panel does not show the solutions of the hypotheses, then click on [SHOW SOLUTIONS] at the top of the panel.
- In the right panel, right-click on the left (relevance) leaf and select **New Assumption**. As a result, the agent proposes the default solution (e.g., certain).
- If necessary, click on the default solution (the underlined text) and, from the displayed list, select (double-click) the appropriate value.
- In the right panel, right-click on the right (believability) leaf and select **New Assumption** (as illustrated in Figure 4.17). As a result, the agent proposes the default solution.
- If necessary, click on the default solution and, from the displayed list, select the appropriate value.
- The agent automatically determines the inferential force of the item of evidence.

Operation 4.4. Select the synthesis function

- In the Reasoner module, in the right panel, right-click on the node for which you have to select the synthesis function, select **New Solution with**..., and then select the function from the displayed list (see Figure 4.18).
- To select a function for a node, all its children must have solutions.

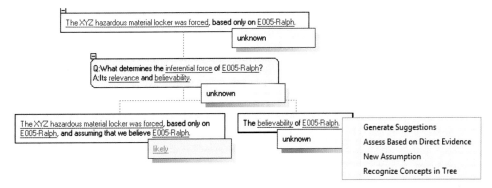

Figure 4.17. Assessing an item of evidence.

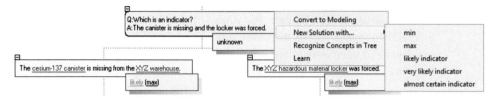

Figure 4.18. Selecting a synthesis function.

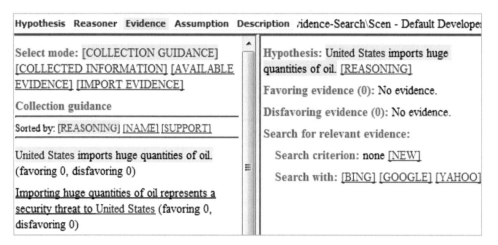

Figure 4.19. Evidence collection guidance for a selected hypothesis.

4.6   HANDS ON: HYPOTHESIS ANALYSIS AND EVIDENCE SEARCH AND REPRESENTATION

The objective of this case study is to learn how to use Disciple-EBR to analyze hypotheses based on evidence retrieved from the Internet, by associating search criteria with elementary hypotheses, invoking various search engines (such as Google, Yahoo!, or Bing), identifying relevant information, extracting evidence from it, and using the evidence to evaluate the hypotheses.

This case study concerns the hypothesis that the United States will be a global leader in wind power within the next decade.

To search for evidence that is relevant to a leaf hypothesis, the agent guides you to associate search criteria with it and to invoke various search engines on the Internet. Figure 4.19 shows the corresponding interface of the Evidence module. Because the [COLLECTION GUIDANCE] mode is selected in the left panel, it shows all the leaf hypotheses and their current evidential support. If you click on one of these hypotheses, such as "United States imports huge quantities of oil," it displays this hypothesis in the right panel, enabling you to define search criteria for it. You just need to click on the [NEW] button following the Search criterion label, and the agent will open an editor in which you can enter the search criterion.

Figure 4.20 shows two defined search criteria: "oil import by United States" and "top oil importing countries." You can now invoke Bing, Google, or Yahoo! with any one of these criteria to search for relevant evidence on the Internet. This will open a new window with the results of the search, as shown in Figure 4.21.

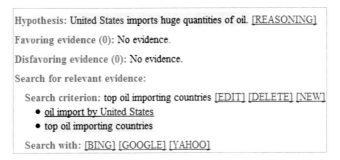

Hypothesis: United States imports huge quantities of oil. [REASONING]

Favoring evidence (0): No evidence.

Disfavoring evidence (0): No evidence.

Search for relevant evidence:

Search criterion: top oil importing countries [EDIT] [DELETE] [NEW]
- oil import by United States
- top oil importing countries

Search with: [BING] [GOOGLE] [YAHOO]

Figure 4.20. Defined search criteria for a selected hypothesis.

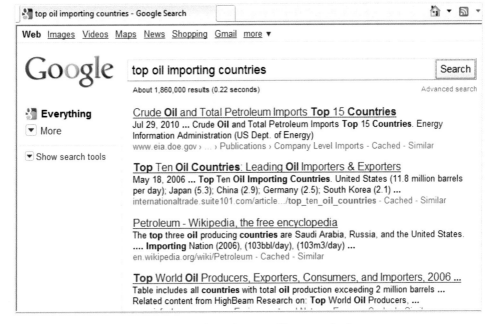

Figure 4.21. Searching relevant evidence on the Internet.

You have to browse the retrieved documents shown in Figure 4.21 and determine whether any of them contains information that is relevant to the hypothesis that the United States imports huge quantities of oil. Such a document is the second one, whose content is shown in Figure 4.22.

You can now define one or several items of evidence with information copied from the retrieved document, as illustrated in Figure 4.23. In the left panel of the Evidence module, you switch the selection mode to [AVAILABLE EVIDENCE] and then click on [NEW]. As a result, the right panel displays a partial name for the evidence E001- to be completed by you. You then have to click on the [EDIT] button, which opens an editor where you can copy the description of this item of evidence from the retrieved document. The result is shown in the right panel of Figure 4.23.

You can define additional characteristics of this item of evidence, such as its type (as will be discussed in Section 4.7), and you should indicate whether this item of evidence favors or disfavors the hypothesis that the United States imports huge quantities of oil, as explained previously.

Figure 4.22. Selected document providing relevant information.

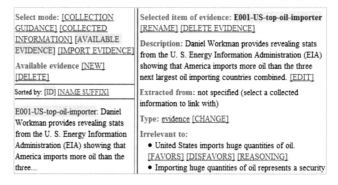

Figure 4.23. Defining an item of evidence.

In this case study, you will first select the hypothesis, "United States will be a global leader in wind power within the next decade," and then you will browse its analysis tree to see how it is reduced to simpler hypotheses that you have to assess by searching evidence on the Internet. You will associate specific search criteria with the leaf hypotheses, invoke specific search engines with those criteria, identify relevant Web information, define evidence from this information, associate evidence with the corresponding hypotheses, and evaluate its relevance and believability, with the goal of assessing the probability of the top-level hypothesis.

Start Disciple-EBR, select the case study knowledge base "03-Evidence-Search/Scen," and proceed as indicated in the instructions from the bottom of the opened window.

This case study illustrates the following hypothesis analysis operation:

Operation 4.5. Associate search criteria with hypotheses

- In the Evidence workspace, click on the Evidence menu and then click on [COLLECTION GUIDANCE]. The left panel shows the leaf hypotheses and their evidential support.

- In the left panel, select a hypothesis.
- In the right panel, after **Search criterion**, click on [NEW] to define a new criterion.
- Type the search criterion and click on [SAVE].
- You may define additional criteria by repeating the preceding two steps.
- Select one of the search criteria by clicking on it.
- After **Search with**, click on one of the available search engines (i.e., [BING], [GOOGLE], [YAHOO]) to search the Internet with the selected criterion.
- Browse the documents returned by the search engine, select the relevant ones, and define items of evidence based on them, as indicated in Operation 4.6, later in this chapter.

4.7   BELIEVABILITY ASSESSMENT

In the previous sections, we have discussed and illustrated how you may directly assess the believability of an item of evidence. However, the Disciple-EBR agent has a significant amount of knowledge about the various types of evidence and its believability credentials, enabling you to perform a much deeper believability analysis, as will be discussed in this section. You may wish to perform such a detailed believability analysis for those items of evidence that are critical to the final result of the analysis. We will start with presenting a classification or ontology of evidence.

Attempts to categorize evidence in terms of its substance or content would be a fruitless task, the essential reason being that the substance or content of evidence is virtually unlimited. What we have termed a *substance-blind* classification of evidence refers to a classification of recurrent forms and combinations of evidence, based not on substance or content, but on the inferential properties of evidence (Schum, 1994 [2001a], pp. 114–130; Schum, 2011). In what follows, we identify specific attributes of the believability of various recurrent types of evidence without regard to their substance or content.

Here is an important question you are asked to answer regarding the individual kinds of evidence you have: *How do you stand in relation to this item of evidence?* Can you examine it for yourself to see what events it might reveal? If you can, we say that the evidence is *tangible* in nature. But suppose instead you must rely upon other persons to tell you about events of interest. Their reports to you about these events are examples of *testimonial evidence*. Figure 4.24 shows a substance-blind classification of evidence based on its believability credentials. This classification is discussed in the following sections.

4.7.1   Tangible Evidence

There is an assortment of tangible items you might encounter. Both imagery intelligence (IMINT) and signals intelligence (SIGINT) provide various kinds of sensor records and images that can be examined. Measurement and signature intelligence (MASINT) and technical intelligence (TECHINT) provide various objects, such as soil samples and weapons, that can be examined. Communications intelligence (COMINT) can provide audio recordings of communications that can be overheard and translated if the communication has occurred in a foreign language. Documents, tabled measurements, charts, maps, and diagrams or plans of various kinds are also tangible evidence.

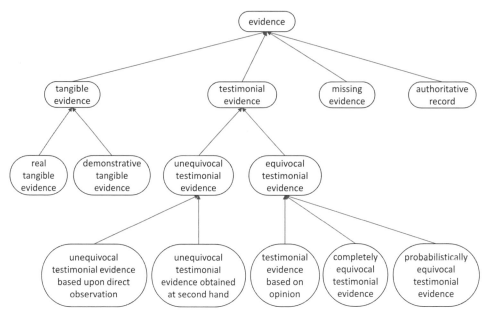

Figure 4.24. Substance-blind classification of evidence.

There are two different kinds of tangible evidence: *real tangible evidence* and *demonstrative tangible evidence* (Lempert et al., 2000, pp. 1146–1148). Real tangible evidence is an actual thing and has only one major believability attribute: *authenticity. Is this object what it is represented as being or is claimed to be?* There are as many ways of generating deceptive and inauthentic evidence as there are persons wishing to generate it. Documents or written communications may be faked, captured weapons may have been tampered with, and photographs may have been altered in various ways. One problem is that it usually requires considerable expertise to detect inauthentic evidence.

Demonstrative tangible evidence does not concern things themselves but only representations or illustrations of these things. Examples include diagrams, maps, scale models, statistical or other tabled measurements, and sensor images or records of various sorts such as IMINT, SIGINT, and COMINT. Demonstrative tangible evidence has three believability attributes. The first concerns its *authenticity*. For example, suppose we obtain a hand-drawn map from a captured insurgent showing the locations of various groups in his insurgency organization. Has this map been deliberately contrived to mislead our military forces, or is it a genuine representation of the location of these insurgency groups?

The second believability attribute is *accuracy* of the representation provided by the demonstrative tangible item. The *accuracy question* concerns the extent to which the device that produced the representation of the real tangible item had a degree of sensitivity (resolving power or accuracy) that allows us to tell what events were observed. We would be as concerned about the accuracy of the hand-drawn map allegedly showing insurgent groups locations as we would about the accuracy of a sensor in detecting traces of some physical occurrence. Different sensors have different resolving power that also depends on various settings of their physical parameters (e.g., the settings of a camera).

The third major attribute, *reliability*, is especially relevant to various forms of sensors that provide us with many forms of demonstrative tangible evidence. *A system, sensor, or test of any kind is reliable to the extent that the results it provides are repeatable or consistent.* You say that a sensing device is reliable if it provides the same image or report on successive occasions on which this device is used.

The left side of Figure 4.25 shows how the agent assesses the believability of an item of demonstrative tangible evidence E_i^* as the minimum of its authenticity, accuracy, and reliability.

Here are additional examples involving evidence that is tangible and that you can examine personally to see what events it reveals.

Have a look at evidence item E009-MDDOTRecord in Table 4.3 (p. 126). The Maryland DOT record, in the form of a tangible document, could be given to the analyst to verify that the vehicle carrying MD license plate number MDC-578 is registered in the name of the TRUXINC Company in Silver Spring, Maryland.

Now consider evidence item E008-GuardReport in Table 4.3. Here we have a document in the form of a log showing that the truck bearing license plate number MDC-578 exited the XYZ parking lot at 8:30 PM on the day in question. This tangible item could also be made available to analysts investigating this matter.

4.7.2   Testimonial Evidence

For *testimonial evidence,* we have two basic sources of uncertainty: *competence* and *credibility.* This is one reason why it is more appropriate to talk about the *believability* of testimonial evidence, which is a broader concept that includes both competence and credibility considerations. The first question to ask related to competence is whether this source actually made the observation the source claims to have made or had *access* to the information the source reports. The second competence question concerns whether this source *understood* what was being observed well enough to provide us with an intelligible account of what was observed. Thus competence involves *access* and *understandability.*

Assessments of human source credibility require consideration of entirely different attributes: *veracity* (or *truthfulness*), *objectivity,* and *observational sensitivity under the conditions of observation* (Schum, 1989). Here is an account of why these are the major attributes of testimonial credibility. First, is this source telling us about an event this source believes to have occurred? This source would be untruthful if he or she did not believe the reported event actually occurred. So, this question involves the source's *veracity.* The second question involves the source's *objectivity.* The question is: Did this source base a belief on sensory evidence received during an observation, or did this source believe the reported event occurred because this source either expected or wished it to occur?

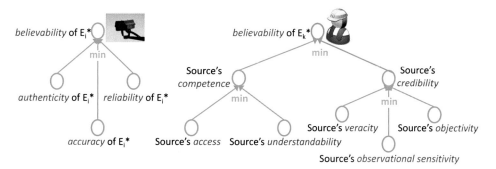

Figure 4.25. Assessing the believability of evidence with Disciple-EBR.

An objective observer is one who bases a belief on the sensory evidence instead of desires or expectations. Finally, if the source did base a belief on sensory evidence, how good was this evidence? This involves information about the source's relevant *sensory capabilities and the conditions under which a relevant observation was made.*

As indicated in Figure 4.24, there are several types of testimonial evidence. If the source does not hedge or equivocate about what the source observed (i.e., the source reports that he or she is certain that the event did occur), then we have *unequivocal testimonial evidence.* If, however, the source hedges or equivocate in any way (e.g., "I'm fairly sure that E occurred"), then we have *equivocal testimonial evidence.* The first question we would ask a source of *unequivocal testimonial evidence* is: How did you obtain information about what you have just reported? It seems that this source has three possible answers to this question. The first answer is, "I made a *direct observation* myself." In this case, we have *unequivocal testimonial evidence based upon direct observation.* The second possible answer is, "I did not observe this event myself but heard about its occurrence (or nonoccurrence) from another person." Here we have a case of second hand or hearsay evidence, called *unequivocal testimonial evidence obtained at second hand.* A third answer is possible: "I did not observe event E myself nor did I hear about it from another source. But I did observe events C and D and inferred from them that event E definitely occurred." This is called *testimonial evidence based on opinion,* and it requires some very difficult questions. The first concerns the source's credibility as far as his or her observation of events C and D; the second involves our examination of whether we ourselves would infer E based on events C and D. This matter involves our assessment of the source's *reasoning ability.* It might well be the case that we do not question this source's credibility in observing events C and D, but we question the conclusion that the source has drawn from his or her observations that event E occurred. We would also question the certainty with which the source has reported the opinion that E occurred. Despite the source's conclusion that "event E definitely occurred," and because of many sources of uncertainty, we should consider that *testimonial evidence based on opinion* is a type of *equivocal testimonial evidence.*

There are two other types of equivocal testimonial evidence. The first we call *completely equivocal testimonial evidence.* Asked whether event E occurred or did not, our source says, "I don't know," or, "I can't remember."

But there is another way a source of HUMINT can equivocate: The source can provide *probabilistically equivocal testimonial evidence* in various ways: "I'm 60 percent sure that event E happened"; or "I'm fairly sure that E occurred"; or, "It is very likely that E occurred." We could look upon this particular probabilistic equivocation as an assessment by the source of the source's own observational sensitivity.

The right side of Figure 4.25 shows how a Disciple-EBR agent assesses the believability of an item of testimonial evidence based upon direct observation E_k^* by a source, as the minimum of the source's competence and credibility. The source's competence is assessed as the minimum of the source's access and understandability, while the source's credibility is assessed as the minimum of the source's veracity, objectivity, and observational sensitivity.

Here are some examples involving testimonial evidence from human sources that is not hedged or qualified in any away.

Evidence item E014-Grace in Table 4.3 (p. 126) is Grace's testimony that no one at the XYZ Company had checked out the canister for work on any project. Grace states this unequivocally. You should also note that she has given *negative evidence* saying the cesium-137 was *not* being used by the XYZ Company. This negative evidence is very important, because it strengthens our inference that the cesium-137 canister was stolen.

E006-Clyde in Table 4.3 is unequivocal testimonial evidence. It represents positive evidence.

Here are some examples involving testimonial evidence given by human sources who equivocate or hedge in what they tell us.

Consider the evidence item E005-Ralph in Table 2.4 (p. 60). Here Ralph hedges a bit by saying that the lock on the hazardous materials storage area *appears to* have been forced. He cannot say for sure that the lock had been forced, so he hedges in what he tells us.

In new evidence regarding the dirty bomb example, suppose we have a source code-named "Yasmin." She tells us that she knew a man in Saudi Arabia named Omar al-Massari. Yasmin says she is "quite sure" that Omar spent two years "somewhere" in Afghanistan "sometime" in the years 1998 to 2000.

4.7.3 Missing Evidence

To say that evidence is missing entails that we must have had some basis for expecting we could obtain it. There are some important sources of uncertainty as far as missing evidence is concerned. In certain situations, missing evidence can itself be evidence. Consider some form of tangible evidence, such as a document, that we have been unable to obtain. There are several reasons for our inability to find it, some of which are more important than others. First, it is possible that this tangible item never existed in the first place; our expectation that it existed was wrong. Second, the tangible item exists, but we have simply been looking in the wrong places for it. Third, the tangible item existed at one time but has been destroyed or misplaced. Fourth, the tangible item exists, but someone is keeping it from us. This fourth consideration has some very important inferential implications, including denial and possibly deception. An adverse inference can be drawn from someone's failure to produce evidence.

We should not confuse negative evidence with missing evidence. To adopt a common phrase, "evidence of absence (negative evidence) is not the same as absence of evidence (missing evidence)." Entirely different conclusions can be drawn from evidence that an event did not occur than can be drawn from our failure to find evidence. We are obliged to ask different questions in these two situations.

Consider our discussion on the cesium-137 canister. Upon further investigation, we identify the person who rented the truck as Omar al-Massari, alias Omer Riley. We tell him that we wish to see his laptop computer. We are, of course, interested in what it might reveal about the terrorists with whom he may be associating. He refuses to tell us where it is. This we referred to as the nonproduction of evidence.

4.7.4 Authoritative Record

This final category of evidence would never oblige an analyst to assess its believability. Tabled information of various sorts such as tide tables, celestial tables, tables of physical or mathematical results such as probabilities associated with statistical calculations, and many other tables of information we would accept as being believable provided that we used these tables correctly. For example, we would not be obliged to prove that temperatures in Iraq can be around 120 degrees Fahrenheit during summer months or that the population of Baghdad is greater than that of Basra.

4.7.5   Mixed Evidence and Chains of Custody

We have just described a categorization of individual items of evidence. But there are situations in which individual items can reveal various mixtures of the types of evidence shown in Figure 4.24. One example is testimonial evidence about tangible evidence where a source describes a weapon observed at a scene of a crime. Another example is a tangible document containing a testimonial assertion based on other alleged tangible evidence. Figure 4.26, for example, shows how one would need to assess the believability of tangible evidence about testimonial evidence.

Here is an example of a mixture of two or more items of tangible evidence; it is called a *passport*. A passport is a tangible document alleging the existence of other tangible documents recording the place of birth and country of origin of the holder of the passport. In other words, a passport sets up a *paper trail* certifying the identity of the holder of the passport. In addition to needing to check the authenticity of the passport itself, we are also interested in the authenticity of all the other tangible documents on which this passport is based.

Here is another mixture of forms of evidence, this time recording a mixture of tangible and testimonial evidence. We return to our asset "Yasmin," who has given us further evidence about Omar al-Massari in our cesium-137 example. Suppose we have a tangible document recording Yasmin's account of her past experience with Omar al-Massari. This document records Yasmin's testimony about having seen a document, detailing plans for constructing weapons of various sorts, that was in Omar al-Massari's possession. As far as believability issues are concerned, we first have the authenticity of the transcription of her testimony to consider. Yasmin speaks only in Arabic, so we wonder how adequate the translation of her testimony has been. Also, we have concerns about Yasmin's competence and credibility to consider in her recorded testimony. Finally, we have further interest in the authenticity of the document she allegedly saw in Omar al-Massari's possession.

But the believability analysis of an item of evidence can be even more complicated. For example, very rarely, if ever, has an analyst access to the original evidence. Most often, what is being analyzed is an item of evidence that has undergone a series of transformations through a *chain of custody* (Schum et al., 2009). Here we have borrowed an

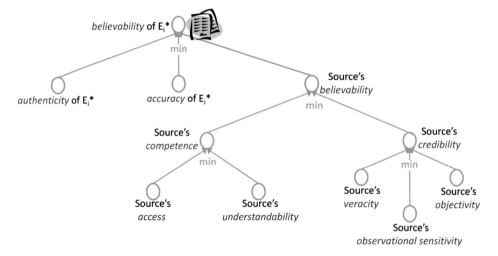

Figure 4.26. Believability analysis of tangible evidence about testimonial evidence.

important concept from the field of law, where a chain of custody refers to the persons or devices having access to the original evidence, the time at which they had such access, and what they did to the original evidence when they had access to it. These chains of custody add three major sources of uncertainty for intelligence analysts to consider, all of which are associated with the persons in the chains of custody, whose competence and credibility need to be considered. The first and most important question involves *authenticity*: Is the evidence received by the analyst exactly what the initial evidence said, and is it complete? The other questions involve assessing the *reliability* and *accuracy* of the processes used to produce the evidence if it is tangible in nature or also used to take various actions on the evidence in a chain of custody, whether the evidence is tangible or testimonial. As an illustration, consider the situation from Figure 4.27. We have an item of testimonial HUMINT coming from a foreign national whose code name is "Wallflower," who does not speak English. Wallflower gives his report to the *case officer* Bob. This report is *recorded* by Bob and then *translated* by Husam. Then Wallflower's translated report is *transmitted* to the *report's officer* Marsha, who *edits* it and *transmits* it to the analyst Clyde, who evaluates it.

Figure 4.28 shows how a Disciple-EBR agent may determine the believability of the evidence received by the analyst. A more detailed discussion is provided in Schum et al. (2009).

The case officer might have intentionally overlooked details in his recording of Wallflower's report. Thus, as shown at the bottom of Figure 4.28, the believability of the recorded testimony of Wallflower is the minimum between the believability of Wallflower and the believability of the recording. Then Husam, the translator, may have intentionally altered or deleted parts of this report. Thus, the believability of the translated recording is the minimum between the believability of the recorded testimony and the believability of the translation by Husam. Then Marsha, the report's officer, might have altered or deleted parts of the translated report of Wallflower's testimony in her editing of it, and so on.

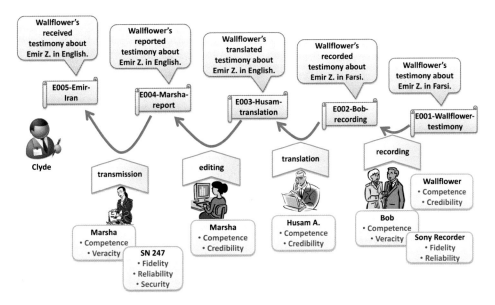

Figure 4.27. The chain of custody of the Wallflower's testimony.

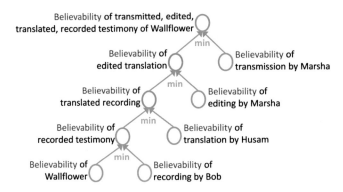

Figure 4.28. Assessing the believability of Wallflower's testimony.

The result of these actions is that the analyst receiving this evidence almost certainly did not receive an authentic and complete account of it, nor did he receive a good account of its reliability and accuracy. What Clyde received was the transmitted, edited, translated, and recorded testimony of Wallflower. Although the information to make such an analysis may not be available, the analyst should adjust the confidence in his conclusion in recognition of these uncertainties.

4.8   HANDS ON: BELIEVABILITY ANALYSIS

This case study, which continues the analysis from Section 4.5 with the analysis of the hypothesis, "The cesium-137 canister is used in a project without being checked-out from the XYZ warehouse," has two main objectives:

- Learning to define a more detail representation of an item of evidence
- Better understanding the process of believability analysis

In Section 4.6, we have presented how you can define an item of evidence, and Figure 4.23 (p. 132) shows the definition of E001-US-top-oil-importer with type evidence. You can specify the type by clicking on the [CHANGE] button. Figure 4.29, for instance, shows the definition of E014-Grace. After you click on the [CHANGE] button, the agent displays the various evidence types from the right panel. You just need to click on the [SELECT] button following the correct type, which in this case is unequivocal testimonial evidence based upon direct observation.

Once you have selected the type of E014-Grace, the agent displays it after the label **Type** and asks for its source, which is Grace (see Figure 4.30).

As shown in Figure 4.30, we have also indicated that this item of evidence disfavors the hypothesis "The missing cesium-137 canister is used in a project at the XYZ company." As a result, the agent introduced it into the analysis tree and generated a more detailed analysis of its believability, which is shown in Figure 4.31.

You can now perform a more detailed believability analysis, as illustrated in Figure 4.32, where we have assessed the competence, veracity, objectivity, and observational sensitivity of Grace, and the agent has automatically determined her believability.

In this case study, you will practice the preceding operations. You will first select the hypothesis, "The cesium-137 canister is used in a project without being checked out from

E009-MDDOTRecord: Maryland DOT's record that the truck bearing license plate # MDC-578 is registered in the name of the TRUXINC Company in Silver Spring, MD.

E010-TRUXINCRecord1: TRUXINC's record that the truck bearing MD license plate number MDC-597 was rented to a man who gave his name as Omer Riley on the day before...

E011-TRUXINCRecord2: TRUXINC's record that Omer Riley gave his address as 6176 Williams Ave.

E012-SilverSpringRecord: Silver Spring city record according to which there is no residence at 6176 Williams Ave in Silver Spring.

E013-InvestigativeRecord: Investigative record that traces of cesium-137 were found by a Geiger counter in the truck bearing license plate # MDC-578.

E014-Grace: Grace, the Vice President for Operations at XYZ, tells us that no one at the XYZ Company had checked out the canister for work on any project.

Selected item of evidence: **E014-Grace**

Description: Grace, the Vice President for Operations at XYZ, tells us that no one at the XYZ Company had checked out the canister for work on any project.

Extracted from: not specified

Select the type: [CANCEL]
- evidence [SELECT]
  - testimonial evidence
    - unequivocal testimonial evidence
      - unequivocal testimonial evidence based upon direct observation [SELECT]
      - unequivocal testimonial evidence obtained at second hand [SELECT]
    - equivocal testimonial evidence
      - testimonial evidence based on opinion [SELECT]
      - probabilistically equivocal testimonial evidence [SELECT]
      - completely equivocal testimonial evidence [SELECT]
  - tangible evidence
    - real tangible evidence [SELECT]
    - demonstrative tangible evidence [SELECT]
  - authoritative record
  - processed evidence
    - testimonial evidence about tangible evidence [SELECT]
    - tangible evidence about testimonial evidence [SELECT]
    - evidence from chain of custody [SELECT]

Figure 4.29. Selecting the type of evidence.

Hypothesis Reasoner Evidence Assumption Description   repository\04-Believability-Analysis\Scen - Default Developer

that the truck bearing license plate # MDC-578 is registered in the name of the TRUXINC Company in Silver Spring, MD.

E010-TRUXINCRecord1: TRUXINC's record that the truck bearing MD license plate number MDC-597 was rented to a man who gave his name as Omer Riley on the day before...

E011-TRUXINCRecord2: TRUXINC's record that Omer Riley gave his address as 6176 Williams Ave.

E012-SilverSpringRecord: Silver Spring city record according to which there is no residence at 6176 Williams Ave in Silver Spring.

E013-InvestigativeRecord: Investigative record that traces of cesium-137 were found by a Geiger counter in the truck bearing license plate # MDC-578.

E014-Grace: Grace, the Vice President for Operations at XYZ, tells us that no one at the XYZ Company had checked out the canister for work on any project.

Selected item of evidence: **E014-Grace** [RENAME] [DELETE EVIDENCE]

Description: Grace, the Vice President for Operations at XYZ, tells us that no one at the XYZ Company had checked out the canister for work on any project. [EDIT]

Extracted from: not specified (select a collected information to link with)

Type: unequivocal testimonial evidence based upon direct observation [CHANGE]

By the source: Grace [RENAME] [CHANGE]

Disfavors:
- The missing cesium 137 canister is used in a project at the XYZ company [REMOVE] [REASONING] [COLLECTION]

Irrelevant to:
- The cesium 137 canister was in the XYZ warehouse before being reported as missing [FAVORS] [DISFAVORS] [REASONING] [COLLECTION]
- The cesium 137 canister is no longer in the XYZ warehouse [FAVORS] [DISFAVORS] [REASONING] [COLLECTION]
- No one has checked the cesium 137 canister out from the XYZ warehouse [FAVORS] [DISFAVORS] [REASONING] [COLLECTION]

Figure 4.30. Definition of an item of evidence.

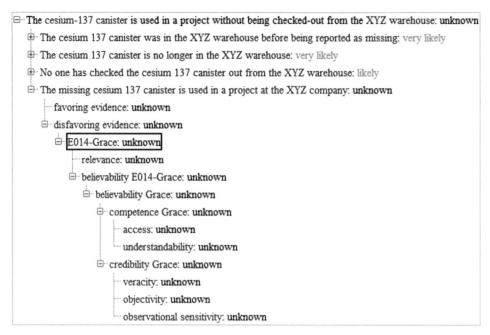

Figure 4.31. Decomposition of the believability assessment for an item of testimonial evidence.

Figure 4.32. More detailed believability analysis.

the XYZ warehouse." Then you will browse its analysis to see how it is reduced to simpler hypotheses that need to be assessed based on the evidence. After that, you will represent a new item of evidence, will associate it with the hypothesis to which it is relevant, assess its relevance, evaluate its believability by assessing its credentials, and browse the resulting analysis tree.

Start Disciple-EBR, select the case study knowledge base "04-Believability-Analysis/ Scen," and proceed as indicated in the instructions from the bottom of the opened window.

This case study illustrates the general operation of defining an item of evidence, summarized as follows.

Operation 4.6. Define an item of evidence

- In the Evidence workspace, click on the Evidence menu at the top of the window.
- Notice the four modes of operations from the top part of the left panel. Because the selected one is [AVAILABLE EVIDENCE], the left panel shows the current evidence (if any) from the knowledge base.
- In the left panel, click on [NEW]. The right panel now shows a partially defined item of evidence, such as E002-. You will complete the definition of this item of evidence.
- Complete the name E...- at the top of the right panel and click on [SAVE].
- Click on [EDIT] for **Description**, click inside the pane and type the description of the item of evidence.
- Click on [SAVE].
- You may now provide additional information about the item of evidence (as indicated in the following steps) or define additional items of evidence (by repeating the preceding steps).
- After "**Type:** evidence," click on [CHANGE] to specify the type of this item of evidence.
- Inspect the different evidence types and click on [SELECT] following the type corresponding to the current item of evidence.
- Provide the additional, type-related information, requested by the system (e.g., the source in the case of a testimonial item of evidence).

4.9 DRILL-DOWN ANALYSIS, ASSUMPTION-BASED REASONING, AND WHAT-IF SCENARIOS

An important feature of the Disciple-EBR agent is that it allows you to perform analyses at different levels of detail. What this means is that a hypothesis may be reduced to many levels of subhypotheses or just a few levels that are then assessed based on relevant evidence. The same applies to assessing the believability of evidence. You may directly assess it, as was illustrated in Figure 4.14 (p. 127), where the believability of E005-Ralph was assessed as very likely. But if an item of evidence has an important influence on the analysis, then you may wish to perform a deeper believability analysis, as was illustrated in Figure 4.32, where the user assessed lower-level believability credentials. The user could have drilled even deeper to assess the source's access and understandability instead of his or her competence.

It may also happen that you do not have the time or the evidence to assess a subhypothesis, in which case you may make various assumptions with respect to its probability. Consider, for example, the analysis from the case study in Section 4.5, partially shown in Figure 4.15 (p. 128) and the four subhypotheses of the top-level hypothesis. The first three of these subhypotheses have been analyzed as discussed in the previous sections. However, for the last subhypothesis, you have made the following assumption:

It is certain that the MDC-578 truck left with the cesium-137 canister.

Assumptions are distinguished from system-computed assessments by the fact that the assumed probabilities have a yellow background.

You may provide justifications for the assumptions made. You may also experiment with various what-if scenarios, where you make different assumptions to determine their influence on the final result of the analysis.

Thus the agent gives you the flexibility of performing the analysis that makes the best use of your time constraints and available evidence.

The Disciple-EBR shell includes a customized modeling assistant to model the hypothesis analysis process. The following two case studies demonstrate its use.

4.10   HANDS ON: MODELING, FORMALIZATION, AND PATTERN LEARNING

The objective of this case study is to learn how to use Disciple-EBR to model the analysis of a hypothesis. More specifically, you will learn how to:

- Specify a new hypothesis
- Specify a question/answer pair that suggests how the hypothesis can be reduced to simpler hypotheses
- Specify the subhypotheses suggested by the question/answer pair
- Select ontology names to be used in hypotheses, questions, and answers
- Convert a hypothesis to an elementary solution (assessment)
- Formalize a reasoning tree or a part of it to learn reduction patterns
- Convert formalized nodes back to modeling to further update them

This case study will guide you through the process of defining and analyzing a hypothesis by using, as an example, the following hypothesis: "CS580 is a potential course for Mike Rice." You will first define the reduction tree shown in Figure 4.33. Then you will formalize it and specify the synthesis functions.

Start Disciple-EBR, select the case study knowledge base "05-Modeling-Learning/Scen," and proceed as indicated in the instructions from the bottom of the opened window.

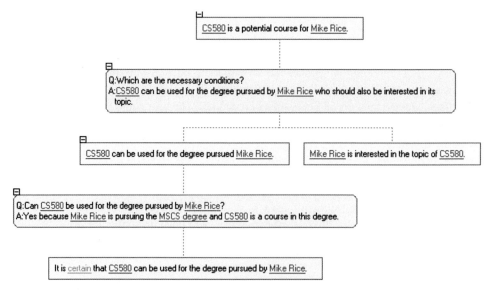

Figure 4.33. Hypotheses reduction tree.

This case study illustrates several important operations, which are described in the following.

Operation 4.7. Specify a new hypothesis

- In the Evidence workspace, click on the Hypothesis menu at the top of the window.
- Click on [NEW].
- At the top of the window, click on [NEW EXAMPLE]. The Reasoner module is automatically selected.
- Double-click on the red-border box and define the hypothesis: "CS580 is a potential course for Mike Rice."
- Define instances and concepts as indicated in Operation 4.8.
- Click outside the editing box when finished.

Operation 4.8. Define instances and constants

- In the Evidence workspace, in the Reasoner module, while editing a node in the reasoning tree, select the text representing the instance or constant, right-click on it, and select the corresponding type, as illustrated in Figure 4.34.

Operation 4.9. Specify question/answer nodes, subhypotheses, and solutions

- In the Evidence workspace, in the right panel of the Reasoner module, right-click on the node under which the new node will be defined and select **Generate Suggestions**.
- If only a generic suggestion is made, double-click on that node and write the desired text.
- If several suggestions are made, right-click on one of them and select **Accept Suggestion**.

Operation 4.10. Insert an intermediary hypothesis

- In the Evidence workspace, in the right panel of the Reasoner module, right-click on the hypothesis node above which an intermediary hypothesis is to be inserted and select **New Hypothesis Above**.

Operation 4.11. Move a hypothesis to the left or right

- In the Evidence workspace, in the right panel of the Reasoner module, right-click on a subhypothesis that has siblings, and select **Move Left** or **Move Right** to move it to the left of its left sibling or to the right of its right sibling.

Operation 4.12. Delete question/answer nodes, subhypotheses, and solutions

- When a node is deleted, the entire subtree under it is also deleted.
- In the Evidence workspace, in the right panel of the Reasoner module, right-click on the node to be deleted and select **Remove Node**.

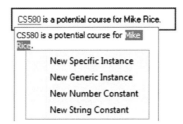

Figure 4.34. Defining Mike Rice as a specific instance.

Operation 4.13. Convert between modeled and formalized hypotheses and solutions/assessments

- In the Evidence workspace, in the right panel of the Reasoner module, right-click on the node to be converted and select the desired and applicable conversion option, for example, **Convert to Modeling** (to convert a formalized node), **Learn Hypothesis Pattern** (to formalize a modeled hypothesis and learn a hypothesis pattern), **Learn Tree Patterns** (to formalize the entire tree under a hypothesis and learn reduction patterns), **Change to Assessment** (to convert a hypothesis into an assessment), or **Change to Hypothesis** (to convert an assessment into a hypothesis to be assessed).

Operation 4.14. Define an assumption

- In the Evidence workspace, in the right panel of the Reasoner module, right-click on a formalized or learned hypothesis node and select **New Assumption**.
- If several assumption patterns are proposed, select the desired one from the displayed list.
- If necessary, change the automatically selected probability value by clicking on it and selecting another one from the displayed list.

Operation 4.15. Define an assumption with justification

- Define an assumption following the steps from Operation 4.14.
- Click on the Assumption menu at the top of the window.
- Click on [MODIFY].
- Click on the underlined space following **Justification** and write your justification in the opened editor. Then click outside the box.
- Click on [SAVE] and then on the Reasoner menu.

Operation 4.16. Delete an assumption

- In the Evidence workspace, in the right panel of the Reasoner module, right-click on the hypothesis node with the assumption to be deleted and select **Delete Assumption**.

4.11   HANDS ON: ANALYSIS BASED ON LEARNED PATTERNS

The objective of this case study is to learn how to use Disciple-EBR to model the analysis of a hypothesis by reusing learned patterns. More specifically, you will learn how to:

- Specify a new hypothesis by instantiating a learned pattern
- Specify the reduction of a hypothesis by reusing a learned reduction pattern
- Instantiate variables in a reduction
- Understand how the solution composition functions from the employed patterns are automatically applied

You will first define the hypothesis by selecting an existing pattern and instantiating it to: "CS681 is a potential course for Dan Bolt." Then you will successively reduce it to simpler hypotheses by reusing learned patterns. This will include the instantiation of variables from the learned patterns.

Start Disciple-EBR, select the case study knowledge base "06-Analysis-Reuse/Scen" and proceed as indicated in the instructions from the bottom of the opened window.

This case study illustrates several important operations described in the following.

Operation 4.17. Specify a new hypothesis by instantiating a pattern

- In the Evidence workspace, click on the Hypothesis menu at the top of the window.
- Click on [NEW].
- Click on the pattern to instantiate and notice that each pattern variable is replaced with "..."
- Click on each "..." and, in the text field that appears under it, write the desired value and press the **Enter** key.
- Select an answer from those proposed by the system.
- After all the values have been defined, click on [CREATE].

**Operation 4.18. Specify the reduction of a hypothesis by reusing
a learned pattern**

- In the Evidence workspace, in the right panel of the Reasoner module, right-click on a formalized hypothesis node and select **Generate Suggestions**.
- If the knowledge base has applicable learned patterns, it will propose them together with a generic suggestion.
- If a generated pattern to be selected contains variables, click on each of them and select the desired values.
- When the pattern to be selected is completely instantiated, right-click on its Q/A node and select **Accept Suggestion**.

4.12   MODELING GUIDELINES

The following are several knowledge engineering guidelines for modeling the reasoning process. In general, we will refer to hypotheses in these guidelines, although the guidelines are applicable to problems as well. To make this clearer, Guideline 4.1 uses the form "problem/hypothesis," and we will illustrate it with planning problems. However, the rest of the guidelines refer only to "hypothesis," although "hypothesis" may be replaced with "problem."

Guideline 4.1. Structure the modeling process based on the agent's specification

A main result of the agent specification phase (see Table 3.1, p. 83) is the identification of the types of problems to be solved by the envisioned agent or the types of hypotheses to be analyzed. The entire modeling process can be structured based on the types or classes of these problems or hypotheses, as indicated Table 4.4.

Table 4.4 General Structure of the Modeling Process

- Partition the domain into classes of problems/hypotheses.
- Select representative problems/hypotheses for each class.
- Model one class at a time.
- Model one example solution at a time.
- Organize the top-level part of the reasoning tree to identify the class of the problem/hypothesis.

As an illustration, consider developing a workaround military planning agent that needs to determine the actions to be performed in order to work around damage to transportation infrastructures, such a tunnels, bridges, or roads (Tecuci et al., 2000). This agent, called Disciple-WA, will be presented in Section 12.2. Figure 4.35 shows a possible organization of the top-level part of the reasoning tree of this agent, which identifies the class of the current problem to be solved.

Guideline 4.2. Define reduction trees in natural language using simple questions

Table 4.5 shows a recommended sequence of steps to be followed when developing the reduction tree for a specific hypothesis.

Guideline 4.3. Identify the specific instances, the generic instances, and the constants

After defining each hypothesis and question/answer pair, identify the specific instances, the generic instances, and the constants, such as "certain" or "5." The agent will automatically add all the instances under a temporary concept called "user instance," as shown in Figure 4.36. The concepts will be identified later as part of ontology development.

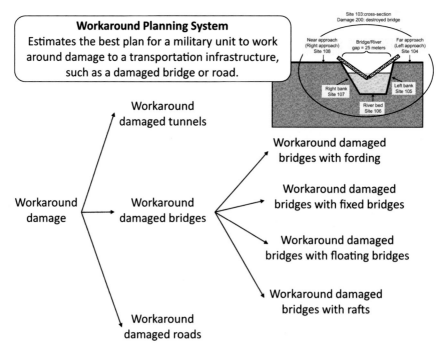

Figure 4.35. Sample top-level structuring of the reasoning tree.

Table 4.5 The Reduction Tree Modeling Process

1. Identify the hypothesis to be assessed and express it with a clear natural language sentence.

2. Select the instances and constants in the hypothesis.

3. Follow each hypothesis or subhypothesis with a single, concise, question relevant to decomposing it. Ask small, incremental questions that are likely to have a single category of answer (but not necessarily a single answer). This usually means asking who, what, where, what kind of, whether it is this or that, and so on, not complex questions such as "Who and what?" or, "What and where?"

4. Follow each question with one or more answers to that question. Express answers as complete sentences, restating key elements of the question in the answer. Even well-formed, simple questions are likely to generate multiple answers. Select the answer that corresponds to the example solution being modeled and continue down that branch.

5. Select instances and constants in the question/answer pair.

6. Evaluate the complexity of each question and its answers. When a question leads to apparently overly complex answers, especially answers that contain an "and" condition, rephrase the question in a simpler, more incremental manner leading to simpler answers.

7. For each answer, form a new subhypothesis, several subhypotheses, or an assessment corresponding to that answer by writing a clear, natural language sentence describing the new subhypotheses or assessment. To the extent that it is practical, incorporate key relevant phrases and elements of preceding hypothesis names in subhypotheses' names to portray the expert's chain-of-reasoning thought and the accumulation of relevant knowledge. If the answer has led to several subhypotheses, then model their solutions in a depth-first order.

8. Select instances and constants in each subhypothesis.

9. Utilize the formalization and reuse capabilities of Disciple to minimize the amount of new modeling required, both for the current hypothesis and for other hypotheses.

Guideline 4.4. Guide the reduction by the possible need of future changes

Use the reduction pattern in Figure 4.37 when you know all the n factors (i.e., A, B, C) that lead to the reduction of the top-level hypothesis to n simpler hypotheses. Adding, changing, or deleting factors after a rule was learned from that reduction is a more difficult operation that also requires deleting the old rule and learning a new one, so you want to avoid making such changes.

If, however, you anticipate adding new factors in the future, then you can use the reduction pattern illustrated in Figure 4.38. You can easily add, change, or delete factors after the rule is learned by adding, changing, or deleting them in the ontology.

Guideline 4.5. Learn and reuse reduction patterns

Disciple-EBR will learn different rules from reduction steps that have different patterns, even though their meaning is the same and the only difference is in their wording, such as "with respect to" as opposed to "wrt" or "from the point of view of." To avoid the learning

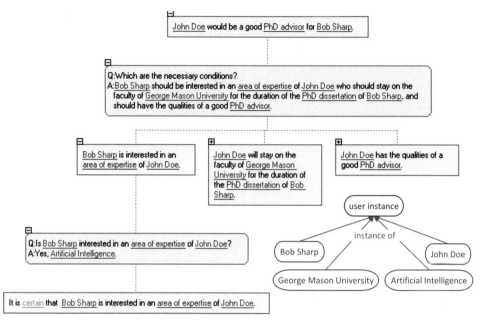

Figure 4.36. Identification of instances and constants in the reasoning tree.

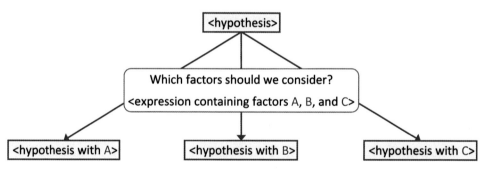

Figure 4.37. Reduction used when all the relevant factors are known.

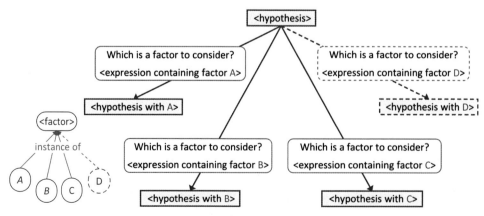

Figure 4.38. Reduction used when new relevant factors may be added in the future.

of semantically redundant rules, you should learn and reuse reduction patterns, as illustrated in Figure 4.39.

4.13 PROJECT ASSIGNMENT 3

Prototype a preliminary version of the agent that you will develop as part of your project by working as a team to:

- Define a domain knowledge base as a copy of 00-Reference-KB.
- Think of three hypotheses to analyze.
- Model the reduction of one hypothesis down to the level of hypotheses that will be addressed by individual team members.

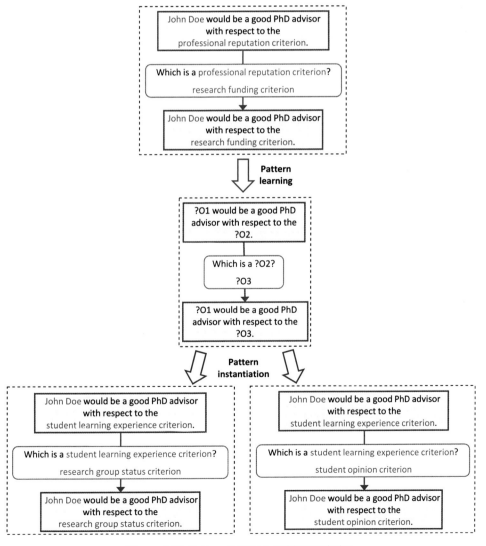

Figure 4.39. Pattern learning and instantiation.

- Formalize the reduction tree and define the composition functions.
- Analyze the other two hypotheses by reusing the learned patterns, if applicable.
- Present the prototype agent in class.

4.14   REVIEW QUESTIONS

4.1. Review again Figures 4.3 and 4.4. Then illustrate the application of problem reduction and solution synthesis with another symbolic integration problem.

4.2. Consider the reductions of Problem1 from Figure 4.40. Indicate the corresponding solution syntheses.

4.3. Illustrate the reasoning in Figure 4.5 with the problem "Travel from Boston to New York." Hint: Consider the question, "Which is a transportation means I can use?"

4.4. How could you use the problem-level synthesis from Question 4.3 to obtain an optimal solution? What might be some possible optimization criteria?

4.5. Illustrate the reasoning in Figure 4.6 with an example of your own.

4.6. You are considering whether a statement S is true. You search the Internet and find two items of favoring evidence, E_1* and E_2*. You estimate that the relevance and the believability of E_1* are "almost certain" and "very likely," respectively. You also estimate that the relevance and the believability of E_2* are "certain" and "likely," respectively. Based on this evidence, what is the probability that S is true? Draw a reasoning tree that justifies your answer.

4.7. Define the concepts of relevance, believability, and inferential force of evidence. Then indicate the appropriate synthesis functions and the corresponding solutions in the reasoning tree from Figure 4.41.

4.8. What are the different types of tangible evidence? Provide an example of each type.

4.9. What items of tangible evidence do you see in Table 4.3?

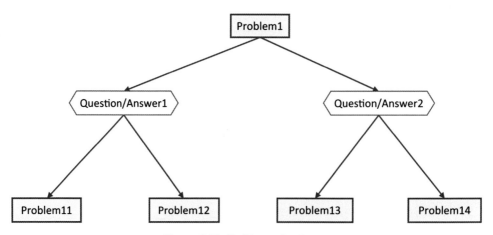

Figure 4.40. Problem reductions.

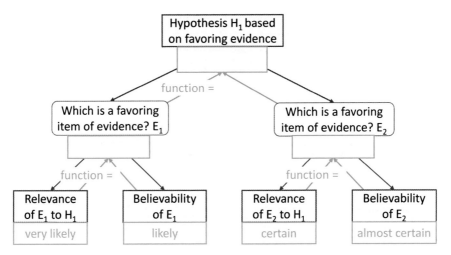

Figure 4.41. Sample reasoning tree for assessing the inferential force of evidence.

4.10. Provide some examples of tangible evidence for the hypothesis that John Doe would be a good PhD advisor for Bob Sharp.

4.11. Define the believability credentials of demonstrative tangible evidence.

4.12. What is testimonial evidence? Give an example.

4.13. What are the different types of testimonial evidence? Provide an example of each type.

4.14. Give some examples from your own experience when you have heard people providing information about which they hedge or equivocate.

4.15. Provide some examples of testimonial evidence for the hypothesis that John Doe would be a good PhD advisor for Bob Sharp.

4.16. Define missing evidence. Provide an example of missing evidence.

4.17. Consider our discussion on the cesium-137 canister. Upon further investigation, we identify the person who rented the truck as Omar al-Massari, alias Omer Riley. We tell him that we wish to see his laptop computer. We are, of course, interested in what it might reveal about the terrorists with whom he may be associating. He refuses to tell us where his laptop is. What inferences might we draw from Omar al-Massari's refusal to provide us with his laptop computer?

4.18. What other items of evidence are missing so far in our discussion of the cesium-137 case?

4.19. Provide some examples of missing evidence for the hypothesis that John Doe would be a good PhD advisor for Bob Sharp.

4.20. Define the term *authoritative record*. Provide an example of an authoritative record.

4.21. Define the believability credentials of a source of testimonial evidence.

4.22. What are some types of mixed evidence? Provide an example. Do you see any example of mixed evidence in Table 4.3?

4.23. Provide some examples of mixed evidence for the hypothesis that John Doe would be a good PhD advisor for Bob Sharp.

4.24. Can you provide other examples of mixed evidence from your own experience?

4.25. Which is the general reduction and synthesis logic for assessing a PhD advisor? Indicate another type of problem that can be modeled in a similar way.

4.26. Use the knowledge engineering guidelines to develop a problem reduction tree for assessing the following hypothesis based on knowledge from the ontology (not evidence): "John Doe would be a good PhD advisor with respect to the employers of graduates criterion." You do not need to develop the ontology, but the questions and answers from your reasoning tree should make clear what knowledge would need to be represented in the ontology. The logic should be clear, all the statements should be carefully defined, and the question/answer pairs should facilitate learning. Mark all the instances in the reasoning tree.

4.27. Rapidly prototype an agent that can assess the following hypothesis and others with a similar pattern: "John Doe would be a good PhD advisor with respect to the research publication criterion." Hint: You may consider that a certain number of publications corresponds to a certain probability for the research publications criterion. For example, if someone has between 41 and 60 publications, you may consider that it is very likely that he or she would be a good PhD advisor with respect to that criterion.

4.28. Rapidly prototype an agent that can assess the following hypothesis and others with a similar pattern: "John Doe would be a good PhD advisor with respect to the research funding criterion." Hint: You may consider that a certain average amount of annual funding corresponds to a certain probability for the research funding criterion. For example, if someone has between $100,000 dollars and $200,000, you may consider that it is very likely that he or she would be a good PhD advisor with respect to that criterion.

4.29. Rapidly prototype an agent that can assess the following hypothesis and others with a similar pattern: "John Doe would be a good PhD advisor with respect to the publications with advisor criterion." Hint: You may consider that a certain number of publications of PhD students with the advisor corresponds to a certain probability for the publications with advisor criterion.

4.30. Rapidly prototype an agent that can assess the following hypothesis and others with a similar pattern: "John Doe would be a good PhD advisor with respect to the research group status criterion."

5 Ontologies

5.1 WHAT IS AN ONTOLOGY?

An *ontology* is an explicit formal specification of the terms that are used to represent an agent's world (Gruber, 1993).

In an ontology, definitions associate names of entities in the agent's world (e.g., classes of objects, individual objects, relations, hypotheses, problems) with human-readable text and formal axioms. The text describes what a name means. The axioms constrain the interpretation and use of a term. Examples of terms from the ontology of the PhD advisor assessment agent include student, PhD student, professor, course, and publication. The PhD advisor assessment agent is a Disciple agent that helps a PhD student in selecting a PhD advisor based on a detailed analysis of several factors, including professional reputation, learning experience of an advisor's students, responsiveness to students, support offered to students, and quality of the results of previous students (see Section 3.3). This agent will be used to illustrate the various ontology issues discussed in this chapter.

The ontology is a hierarchical representation of the objects from the application domain. It includes both descriptions of the different types of objects (called concepts or classes, such as professor or course) and descriptions of individual objects (called instances or individuals, such as CS580), together with the properties of each object and the relationships between objects.

The underlying idea of the ontological representation is to represent knowledge in the form of a graph (similar to a concept map) in which the nodes represent objects, situations, or events, and the arcs represent the relationships between them, as illustrated in Figure 5.1.

The ontology plays a crucial role in cognitive assistants, being at the basis of knowledge representation, user–agent communication, problem solving, knowledge acquisition, and learning.

First, the ontology provides the basic representational constituents for all the elements of the knowledge base, such as the hypotheses, the hypothesis reduction rules, and the solution synthesis rules. It also allows the representation of partially learned knowledge, based on the plausible version space concept (Tecuci, 1998), as discussed in Section 7.6.

Second, the agent's ontology enables the agent to communicate with the user and with other agents by declaring the terms that the agent understands. Consequently, the ontology enables knowledge sharing and reuse among agents that share a common vocabulary that they understand. An agreement among several agents to use a shared vocabulary in a coherent and consistent manner is called *ontological commitment*.

Third, the problem-solving methods or rules of the agent are applied by matching them against the current state of the agent's world, which is represented in the ontology. The use of partially learned knowledge (with plausible version spaces) in reasoning allows assessing hypotheses (or solving problems) with different degrees of confidence.

Fourth, a main focus of knowledge acquisition is the elicitation of the domain concepts and of their hierarchical organization, as will be discussed in Section 6.3.

And fifth, the ontology represents the generalization hierarchy for learning, in which specific problem-solving episodes are generalized into rules by replacing instances with concepts from the ontology.

5.2   CONCEPTS AND INSTANCES

A *concept* (or *class*) is a general representation of what is common to a set of *instances* (or *individuals*). Therefore, a concept may be regarded as a representation of that set of instances. For example, professor in Figure 5.2 represents the set of all professors, which includes Amanda Rice and Dan Smith.

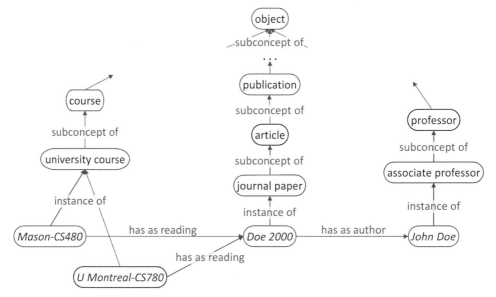

Figure 5.1. Fragment of an ontology.

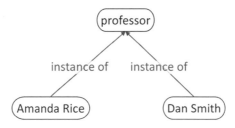

Figure 5.2. A concept and two of its instances.

An *instance (individual)* is a representation of a particular entity in the application domain, such as Amanda Rice. We indicate that an instance belongs to a concept by using the relation instance of:

Amanda Rice instance of professor

5.3   GENERALIZATION HIERARCHIES

Generalization is a fundamental relation between concepts. *A concept P is said to be more general than* (or *a generalization of) another concept Q if and only if the set of instances represented by P includes the set of instances represented by Q.*

Figure 5.3 shows several concepts with different degrees of generality. For example, person is more general than student because any student must be a person or, in other words, the set of all persons includes the set of all students.

Let us notice that the preceding definition of generalization is extensional, based upon the instance sets of concepts. In order to show that P is more general than Q, this definition would require the computation of the (possibly infinite) sets of the instances of P and Q. Therefore, it is useful in practice only for showing that P is not more general than Q. Indeed, according to this definition, it is enough to find an instance of Q that is not an instance of P because this shows that the set represented by Q is not a subset of the set represented by P. Section 8.3 discusses generalization rules that allow the agent to compare the generality of the concepts by working with their descriptions rather than their sets of instances.

One may express the generality relation between two concepts by using the relation subconcept of:

student subconcept of person

Other names used for expressing this type of relation are subclass of, type, and isa.

A concept Q is a direct subconcept of *a concept P if an only if Q is a subconcept of P and there is no other concept R such that Q is a subconcept of R and R is a subconcept of P.*

One may represent the generality relations between the concepts in the form of a partially ordered graph that is usually called a *generalization hierarchy* (see Figure 5.4). The leaves of the hierarchy in Figure 5.4 are instances of the concepts that are represented by the upper-level nodes. Notice that (the instance) John Doe is both an associate professor and a PhD advisor. Similarly, a concept may be a direct subconcept of several concepts.

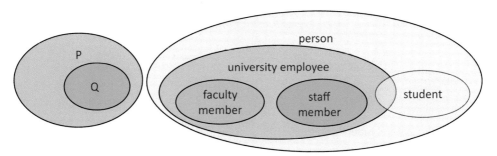

Figure 5.3. Concepts of different generality.

5.4   OBJECT FEATURES

The objects in an application domain may be described in terms of their properties and their relationships with each other. For example, Figure 5.5 represents Mark White as an associate professor employed by George Mason University. In general, the value of a feature may be a number, a string, an instance, a symbolic probability, an interval, or a concept (see Section 5.9).

5.5   DEFINING FEATURES

A feature is itself characterized by several features that have to be specified when defining a new feature. They include its domain, range, superfeatures, subfeatures, and documentation.

The *domain* of a feature is the concept that represents the set of objects that could have that feature. The *range* is the set of possible values of the feature.

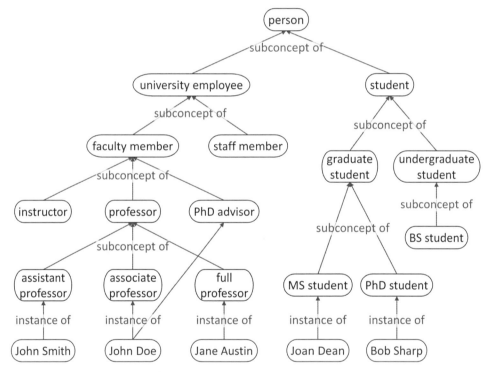

Figure 5.4. A generalization hierarchy.

Figure 5.5. Sample object description.

For example, Figure 5.6 shows the representation of the has as employer feature. Its domain is person, which means that only entities who are persons may have an employer. Its range is organization, meaning that any value of such a feature should be an organization.

There are several types of ranges that could be defined with Disciple-EBR: Concept, Number, Symbolic interval, Text, and Any element.

We have already illustrated a range of type "Concept" (see Figure 5.6). A range of type "Number" could be either a set or an interval of numbers, and the numbers could be either integer or real. A range of type "Symbolic interval" is an ordered set of symbolic intervals. A range of type "Text" could be any string, a set of strings, or a natural language text. Finally, a range of type "Any element" could be any of the aforementioned entities.

As will be discussed in more detail in Chapter 7, the knowledge elements from the agent's knowledge base, including features, may be partially learned. Figure 5.7 shows an example of the partially learned feature has as employer. The exact domain is not yet known, but its upper and lower bounds have been learned as person and professor, respectively. This means that the domain is a concept that is less general than or as general as person. Similarly, the domain is more general than or as general as professor.

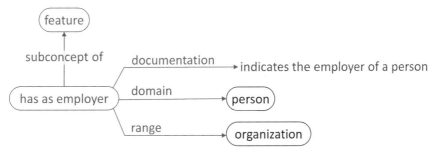

Figure 5.6. The representation of a feature.

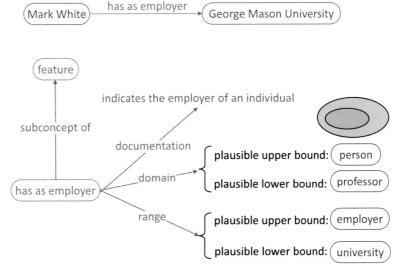

Figure 5.7. Partially learned feature.

Through further learning, the agent will learn that the actual domain is person, as indicated in Figure 5.6.

Features are also organized in a generalization hierarchy, as illustrated in Figure 5.8.

5.6   REPRESENTATION OF N-ARY FEATURES

Let us suppose that we want to represent the following information in the ontology: "John Doe has written *Windows of Opportunities*." This can be easily represented by using a binary feature:

John Doe has as writing Windows of Opportunities.

But let us now suppose that we want to represent "John Doe has written *Windows of Opportunities* from 2005 until 2007." This information can no longer be represented with a binary feature, such as has as writing, that can link only two entities in the ontology. We need to represent this information as an instance (e.g., Writing 1) of a concept (e.g., writing), because an instance may have any number of features, as illustrated in Figure 5.9.

Disciple-EBR can, in fact, represent n-ary features, and it generates them during learning, but the ontology tools can display only binary features, and the user can define only binary features.

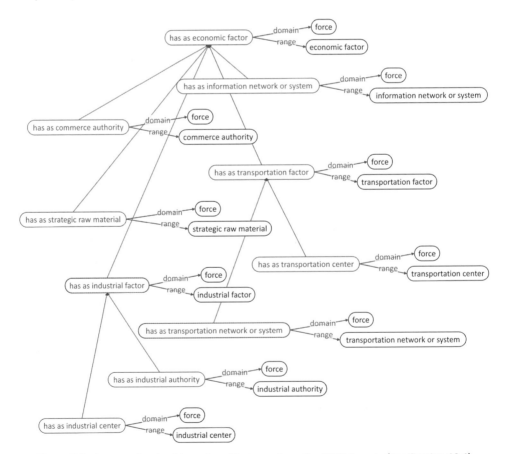

Figure 5.8. A generalization hierarchy of features from the COG domain (see Section 12.4).

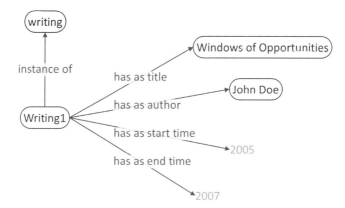

Figure 5.9. Representation of an n-ary relation as binary features.

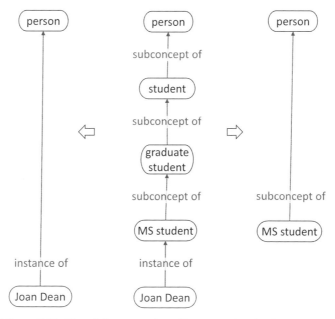

Figure 5.10. Use of the properties of instance of and subconcept of.

5.7   TRANSITIVITY

The instance of and subconcept of relations have the following properties:

∀x,∀y,∀z, (x subconcept of y) ∧ (y subconcept of z) → (x subconcept of z)
∀x,∀y,∀z, (x instance of y) ∧ (y subconcept of z) → (x instance of z)

As one can see, subconcept of is a transitive relation and, in combination with instance of, allows inferring new instance of relations. Let us consider, for example, the hierarchy fragment from the middle of Figure 5.10. By applying the aforementioned properties of instance of and subconcept of, one may infer that:

Joan Dean instance of person
MS student subconcept of person

5.8   INHERITANCE

A theorem that is implicitly represented in an ontology is the inheritance of features from a more general concept to a less general concept or an instance.

An instance inherits the features of the concepts to which it belongs:

$$\forall x, \forall y, \forall z, (x \text{ instance of } y) \wedge (y \text{ feature } z) \rightarrow (x \text{ feature } z)$$

Similarly, a concept inherits the properties of its superconcepts:

$$\forall x, \forall y, \forall z, (x \text{ subconcept of } y) \wedge (y \text{ feature } z) \rightarrow (x \text{ feature } z)$$

For example, in the case of the ontology in Figure 5.11, one can infer:

    professor retirement age 66
    assistant professor retirement age 66
    John Smith retirement age 66

by inheriting the retirement age property from

    faculty member retirement age 66

The inheritance of properties is one of the most important strengths of an ontology, allowing a compact and economical representation of knowledge. Indeed, if all the instances of a concept C have the property P with the same value V, then it is enough to associate the property P with the concept C because it will be inherited by each of the concept's instances. There are, however, two special cases of inheritance to which one should pay special attention: default inheritance and multiple inheritance. They are discussed in the following subsections.

5.8.1   Default Inheritance

In many domains, exceptions to general rules exist. For example, it is generally useful to assume that all birds can fly. Certain birds, however, such as the ostrich and the kiwi, cannot fly. In such a case, it is reasonable to use a representation scheme in which properties associated with concepts in a hierarchy are assumed to be true for all sub-concepts and instances, unless specifically overridden by a denial or modification associated with the subconcepts or the instances.

Let us consider again the hypothetical example in Figure 5.11. The fact that the retirement age of assistant professor is 66 is inherited from faculty member. On the other hand, full professor does not inherit this property from faculty member because it is explicitly represented that the retirement age of full professor is 70. This overrides the default inherited from faculty member. Therefore, to find a feature of some object, the agent will first check whether the feature is explicitly associated with the object and take the corresponding value. Only if the feature is not explicitly associated with the object will the agent try to inherit it from the superconcepts of the object, by climbing the generalization hierarchy.

5.8.2   Multiple Inheritance

It is possible for a concept or an instance to have more than one direct superconcept. For example, in the ontology from Figure 5.11, John Doe is both an associate professor and

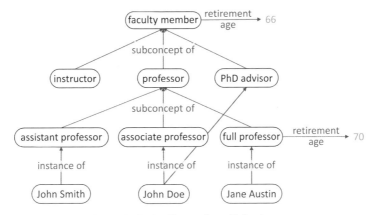

Figure 5.11. An illustration of inheritance.

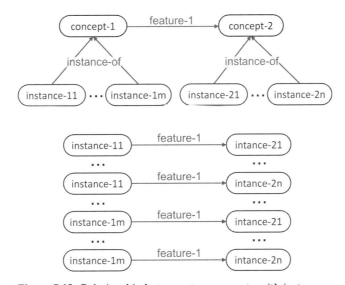

Figure 5.12. Relationship between two concepts with instances.

a PhD advisor. Therefore, John Doe will inherit features from both of them and there is a potential for inheriting conflicting values. In such a case, the agent should use some strategy in selecting one of the values. A better solution, however, is to detect such conflicts when the ontology is built or updated, and to associate the correct feature value directly with each element that would otherwise inherit conflicting values.

5.9   CONCEPTS AS FEATURE VALUES

The previous section has discussed how the features of the concepts are inherited. However, in all the examples given, the value of the feature was a number. The same procedure will work if the value is an instance or a string. But what happens if the value is a concept, which has itself a set of instances, as shown in the top part of Figure 5.12?

In this case, each instance of concept-1 inherits feature-1, the value of which is concept-2, which is the set of all the instances of concept-2, as shown in the bottom part of Figure 5.12.

One has to exercise care when defining features between concepts. For example, the correct way to express the fact that a parent has a child is to define the following feature:

has as child

domain parent

range child

On the contrary, the expression, "parent has as child child" means that each parent is the parent of each child.

5.10   ONTOLOGY MATCHING

Ontology matching allows one to ask questions about the objects in the ontology, such as: "Is there a course that has as reading a publication by John Doe?"

We first need to express the question as a network fragment with variables, as illustrated in the top part of Figure 5.13. The variables represent the entities we are looking for. We then need to match the network fragment with the ontology to find the values of the variables, which represent the answer to our question.

For example, *John Doe* in the pattern is matched with *John Doe* in the ontology, as shown in the right-hand side of Figure 5.13. Then, following the has as author feature (in reverse), ?O2 is successfully matched with *Doe 2000* because each of them is a publication. Finally, following the has as reading feature (also in reverse), ?O1 is successfully matched with *Mason-CS480* and with *U Montreal-CS780*, because each of them is an instance of a course. Therefore, one obtains two answers of the asked question:

Yes, *Mason-CS480* has as reading *Doe 2000*, and *Doe 2000* has as author *John Doe*.

Yes, *U Montreal-CS780* has as reading *Doe 2000*, and *Doe 2000* has as author *John Doe*.

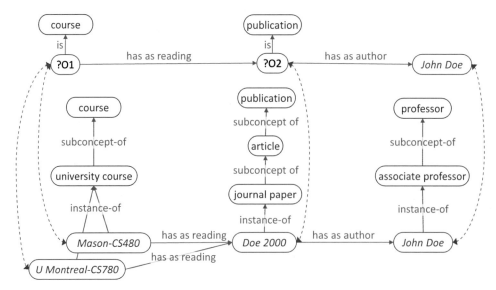

Figure 5.13. Ontology matching.

One important aspect to notice is that the structure of the ontology is also a guide in searching it. This significantly speeds up the matching process as compared, for example, to a representation of the same information as a set of predicates.

5.11   HANDS ON: BROWSING AN ONTOLOGY

The objective of this case study is to learn how to use the various ontology browsers of Disciple-EBR: the Hierarchical Browser, the Feature Browser and the Feature Viewer, the Association Browser, the Object Browser, and the Object Viewer. These tools are very similar to the ontology browsers from many other knowledge engineering tools, such as Protégé (2015) and TopBraid Composer (2012).

Figure 5.14 shows the interface and the main functions of the Hierarchical Browser of Disciple-EBR, an ontology tool that may be used to browse a hierarchy of concepts and instances. The hierarchy in Figure 5.14 is rotated, with the most general concept (object) on the left-hand side and its subconcepts on its right-hand side. The hierarchy can be rotated by clicking on the **Rotate View** button. Clicking on the **Expand View** button leads to showing additional levels of the hierarchy, while clicking on the **Reduce View** button leads to showing fewer levels.

Figure 5.15 shows the interface and the main functions of the Association Browser of Disciple-EBR, which may be used to browse the objects and their features. This browser is centered on a given object (e.g., John Doe), showing its features (e.g., John Doe has as employer George Mason University), the features for which it is a value (e.g., Adam Pearce has as PhD advisor John Doe), its direct concepts (e.g., PhD advisor and associate professor) and, in the case of a concept, its direct subconcepts or its direct instances. Double-clicking on any entity in the interface will center the Association Browser on that entity.

One may also browse the objects and their features by using the Object Browser and the Object Viewer, as illustrated in Figure 5.16 and described in Operation 5.1.

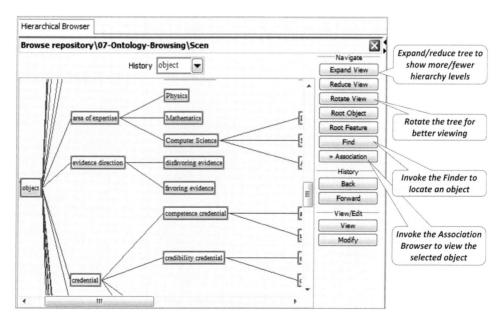

Figure 5.14. The interface and the main functions of the Hierarchical Browser.

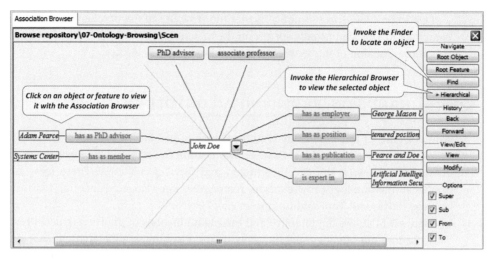

Figure 5.15. The Association Browser and its functions.

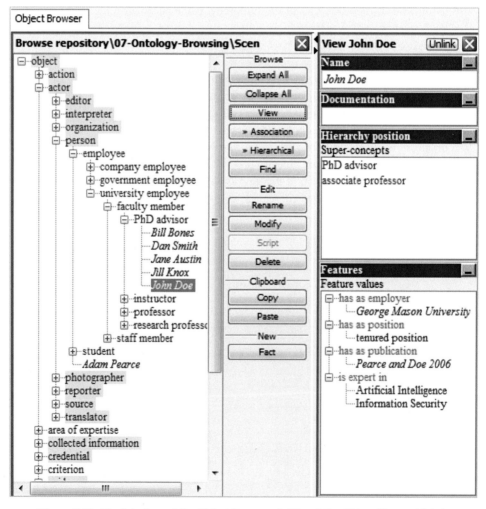

Figure 5.16. The interface of the Object Browser (left) and the Object Viewer (right).

Operation 5.1. View an object

- Select the Scenario workspace.
- Click on the **Ontology** menu and select **Object Browser**.
- Click on the object in the Object Browser (e.g., John Doe on the left-hand side of Figure 5.16).
- Click on the **View** button to view the object's features with the Object Viewer (see the right-hand side of Figure 5.16).
- Click on the **Association** button to view the object's features with the Association Browser.

You can browse the feature generalization hierarchy by using the Feature Browser, which is illustrated in the left-hand side of Figure 5.17. To view the definition of a specific feature, you may follow the steps in Operation 5.2.

Operation 5.2. View a feature definition

- Select the Scenario workspace.
- Click on the **Ontology** menu and select **Feature Browser**.
- Click on the feature in the Feature Browser (e.g., is expert in on the left-hand side of Figure 5.17).
- Click on the **View** button to view the feature with the Feature Viewer (see the right-hand side of Figure 5.17).
- Click on the **Association** button to view the feature with the Association Browser.

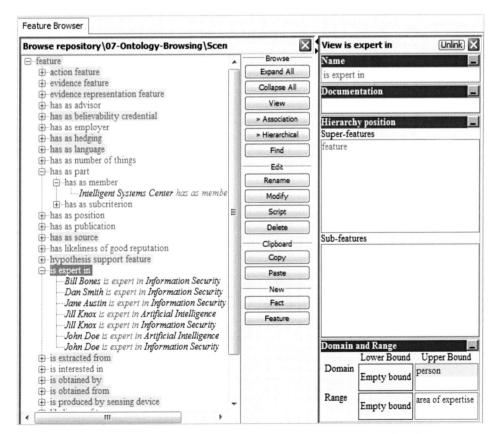

Figure 5.17. The Feature Browser (left) and the Feature Viewer (right).

Start Disciple-EBR, select the case study knowledge base "07-Ontology-Browsing/Scen," and proceed as indicated in the instructions from the bottom of the opened window.

5.12   PROJECT ASSIGNMENT 4

Extend the preliminary version of the agent that you will develop as part of your project by analyzing one leaf hypothesis based on several items of evidence, as discussed in Section 4.4 and practiced in the case study from Section 4.5.

5.13   REVIEW QUESTIONS

5.1. What is an ontology?

5.2. Why are ontologies important?

5.3. What is a concept?

5.4. What is an instance?

5.5. What does it mean for a concept P to be more general than a concept Q?

5.6. What are the possible relationships between two concepts A and B, from a generalization point of view? Provide examples of concepts A and B in each of the possible relationships.

5.7. How could one prove that a concept A is more general than a concept B? Is the proposed procedure likely to be practical?

5.8. How can one prove that a concept A is *not* more general than a concept B? Is the proposed procedure likely to be practical?

5.9. Consider the feature hierarchy from Figure 5.18. Indicate the necessary relationship between: (a) Domain B and Domain 1; (b) Range B and Range 1; (c) Domain A2 and Domain 1; (d) Domain A and Domain B; (e) Domain 1 and Range 1.

5.10. Consider the knowledge represented in Figure 5.11 (p. 163). What is the retirement age of John Smith? What is the retirement age of Jane Austin?

5.11. Insert the additional knowledge that platypus lays eggs into the object ontology from Figure 5.19. Explain the result.

5.12. Explain in English what information is represented in Figure 5.20.

5.13. Explain in English what information is represented in Figure 5.21. How could one encode the additional information that Clyde owned nest1 from spring 2013 to fall 2013? Hint: You need to restructure the ontology and represent an n-ary relationship.

5.14. Represent the following information as an ontology fragment: "Bob Sharp enrolled at George Mason University in fall 2014."

5.15. Consider the generalization hierarchy from Figure 5.4 (p. 158). Consider the following information: In general, the retirement age of a faculty member is 66,

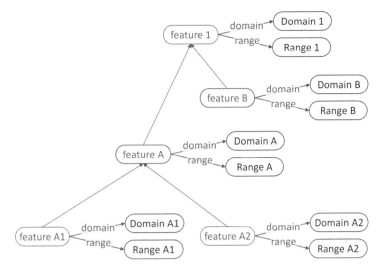

Figure 5.18. Sample feature hierarchy.

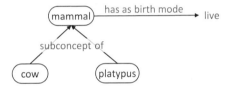

Figure 5.19. Ontology fragment.

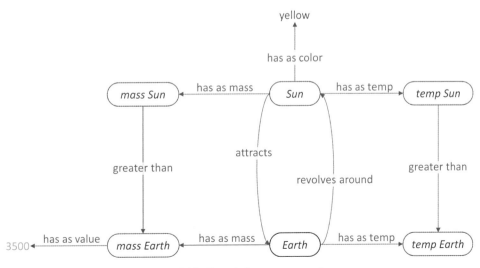

Figure 5.20. Knowledge representation.

but a full professor may retire at 70, although Jane Austin opted to retire at 66. How could you represent this information?

5.16. How can we deal with the inheritance of contradictory properties? Provide an example.

5.17. Define the main features of a feature and illustrate each of them with an example.

5.18. Provide an example of a partially learned feature.

5.19. Why it is very important to carefully define the features of a feature?

5.20. What is the meaning of the ontology fragment from Figure 5.22?

5.21. How could one represent the fact that a bird has a nest?

5.22. Explain how the following questions are answered based on the ontology fragment from Figure 5.23, specifying the types of inference used in each case, and providing the corresponding answers:

What is the color of membrane?
What does contact adhesive1 glue?
Which are the loudspeaker components made of metal?

5.23. Consider the background knowledge consisting of the object hierarchy from Figure 5.23.
(a) Which are all the answers to the following question: "Is there a part of a loudspeaker that is made of metal?"
(b) Which are the reasoning operations that need to be performed in order to answer this question?
(c) Consider one of the answers that require all these operations and show how the answer is found.

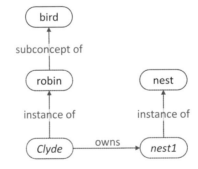

Figure 5.21. Representation with binary predicates.

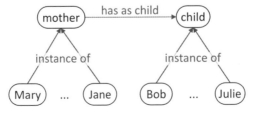

Figure 5.22. Example of a wrong concept feature.

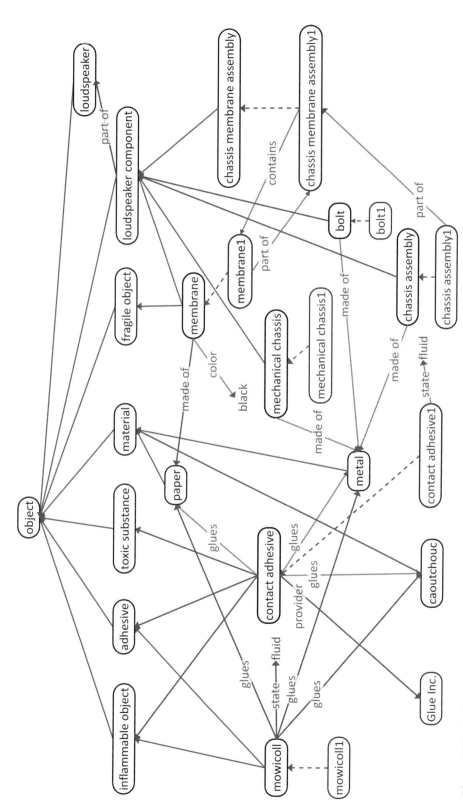

Figure 5.23. Ontology fragment from the loudspeaker domain (Tecuci, 1998). Dotted links indicate instance of relationships while continuous unnamed links indicate subconcept of relationships.

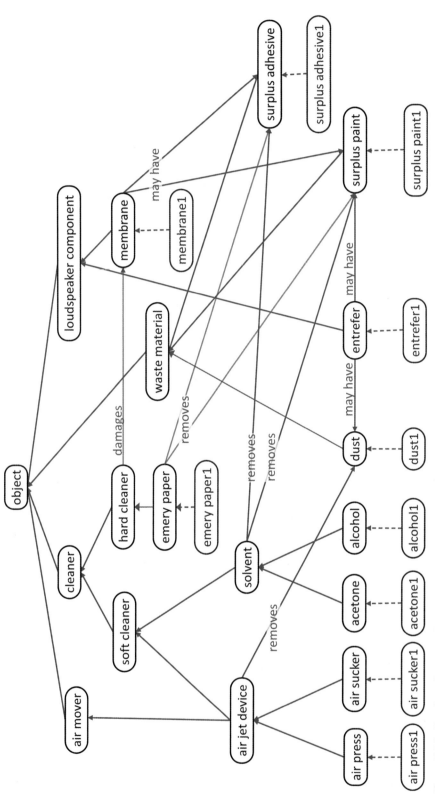

Figure 5.24. Ontology fragment from the loudspeaker domain (Tecuci, 1998). Dotted links indicate instance of relationships while unnamed continuous links indicate subconcept of relationships.

5.24. Consider the ontology fragment from Figure 5.24. Notice that each of the most specific concepts, such as dust or air press, has an instance, such as dust1 and air press1, respectively.

(a) Represent the question "Is there a cleaner X that removes dust?" as a network fragment.

(b) Find all the possible answers to this question based on the information in the ontology fragment.

(c) In order to answer this question, the agent would need to use several reasoning operations. Which are these operations?

5.25. Consider the following description in the context of the ontology fragment from Figure 5.24:

```
?z    is          cleaner
      removes  surplus-paint1
```

Determine all the possible values of ?z.

5.26. Consider the following action description in the context of the ontology fragment from Figure 5.24:

```
clean   object   ?x
        of       ?y
        with     ?z
condition
    ?x   is   entrefer
         may have  ?y
    ?y   is   object
    ?z   is   cleaner
         removes   ?y
```

Find all the possible values for the variables ?x, ?y, and ?z. Indicate some of the corresponding actions.

6 Ontology Design and Development

6.1 DESIGN AND DEVELOPMENT METHODOLOGY

Ontology design is a creative process whose first step is determining the scope of the ontology by specifying its main concepts, features, and instances. One approach is to elicit them from a subject matter expert or some other sources, as will be discussed in Section 6.3.

Another approach is to extract a specification of the ontology from the reasoning trees developed as part of the rapid prototyping of the agent. During this phase, the subject matter expert and the knowledge engineer define a set of typical hypotheses (or problems) that the envisioned agent should be able to assess (or solve). Then they actually assess these hypotheses the way they would like Disciple-EBR to assess them. This process identifies very clearly what concepts and features should be present in the ontology to enable the agent to assess those types of hypotheses. This modeling-based ontology specification strategy will be discussed in Section 6.4. Once a specification of the ontology has been developed, one has to complete its design.

Because ontology design and development is a complex process, it makes sense to import relevant concepts and features from previously developed ontologies (including those from the Semantic Web) rather than defining them from scratch. In particular, one may wish to look for general-purpose ontologies, such as an ontology of time, space, or units of measures, if they are necessary to the agent under development. Significant foundational and utility ontologies have been developed and can be reused (Obrst et al., 2012), as discussed in Section 3.2.2.

The actual development of the ontology is performed by using ontology tools such as Protégé (Noy and McGuinness, 2001) or those that will be presented in this section. As will be discussed next, ontology development is an iterative process during which additional concepts, features, and instances are added while teaching the agent to assess hypotheses (or solve problems).

An important aspect to emphasize is that the ontology will always be incomplete. Moreover, one should not attempt to represent all of the agent's knowledge in the ontology. On the contrary, the ontology is intended to represent only the terms of the representation language that are used in the definitions of hypotheses and rules. The more complex knowledge will be represented as rules.

6.2 STEPS IN ONTOLOGY DEVELOPMENT

Table 6.1 presents the ontology development steps, which are also illustrated in Figure 6.1.

Table 6.1 Ontology Development Steps

1. Define basic concepts (types of objects) and their organization into a hierarchical structure (the generalization hierarchy).
2. Define object features by using the previously defined concepts to specify their domains and ranges.
3. Define instances (specific objects) by using the previously defined concepts and features.
4. Extend the ontology with new concepts, features, and instances.
5. Repeat the preceding steps until the ontology is judged to be complete enough.

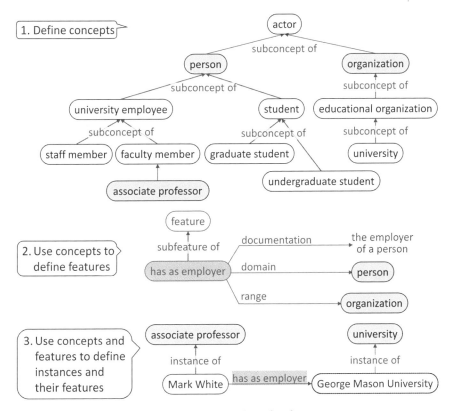

Figure 6.1. Steps in ontology development.

First one needs to define basic concepts and to organize them into a hierarchical structure. This may be performed by using the Object Browser of Disciple-EBR, as will be discussed in Section 6.5.

Once a set of basic concepts have been defined, one can define features that use these concepts as their domains and ranges. For example, one may define the feature has as employer with the domain person and range organization, which are previously defined concepts. The features are defined and organized in a hierarchy by using the Feature Browser and the Feature Editor, as discussed in Section 6.7.

With some of the concepts and features defined, one can define instances of these concepts and associate features with them, as discussed in Section 6.8. For example, one can define Mark White as an instance of associate professor and specify its feature has as employer with the value George Mason University.

Ontology development is an iterative process, as indicated by the last step in Table 6.1.

In the case of Disciple-EBR, one does not develop an ontology from scratch. Rather, one extends the shared ontology for evidence-based reasoning. Moreover, as part of the rapid prototyping phase, the user has defined the specific instances and the generic instances used in the sample reasoning trees. All these entities are represented as instances of the "user instance" concept. Thus, as part of ontology development, one needs to move all these instances under their proper concepts, as illustrated in Figure 6.2.

6.3   DOMAIN UNDERSTANDING AND CONCEPT ELICITATION

Concept elicitation consists of determining which concepts apply in the domain, what do they mean, what is their relative place in the domain, what are the differentiating criteria distinguishing similar concepts, and what is the organizational structure giving these concepts a coherence for the expert (Gammack, 1987).

What are some natural ways of eliciting the basic concepts of a domain? Table 6.2 lists the most common concept elicitation methods. The methods are briefly described in the following subsections.

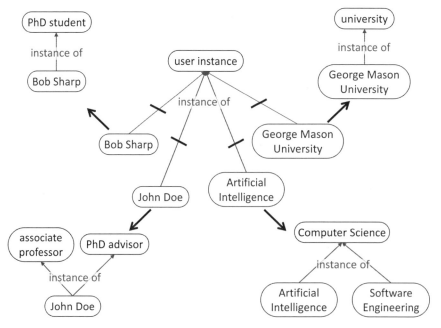

Figure 6.2. Moving the instances of "user instance" under their corresponding concepts.

> **Table 6.2 Basic Concept Elicitation Methods**
>
> - Preliminary methods
>   - Tutorial session delivered by expert
>   - Ad-hoc list created by expert
>   - Book index
> - Interviews with expert
>   - Unstructured interview
>   - Structured interview
>   - Multiple-choice questions
>   - Dichotomous questions
>   - Ranking scale questions
> - Protocol analysis
> - Concept hierarchy elicitation

6.3.1 Tutorial Session Delivered by the Expert

The knowledge engineer asks the subject matter expert to prepare an introductory talk outlining the whole domain and to deliver it as a tutorial session. Then the knowledge engineer extracts concepts from the transcript of the talk.

6.3.2 Ad-hoc List Created by the Expert

The knowledge engineer asks the subject matter expert to generate a list of typical concepts and then systematically probe for more relevant information (e.g., using free association).

6.3.3 Book Index

The knowledge engineer identifies a representative book on the expertise domain and extracts concepts from the index of the book.

6.3.4 Unstructured Interviews with the Expert

These are goal-oriented methods used when the knowledge engineer wants to explore an issue, where the questions and the responses are open-ended. Examples of unstructured interview fragments have been presented in Tables 3.4 (p. 85), 3.6 (p. 87), and 3.7 (p. 87) in Section 3.1.

6.3.5 Structured Interviews with the Expert

These are interviews where the questions are fixed in advance. The types of structured questions include multiple-choice questions (see Table 6.3); dichotomous (yes/no) questions (see Table 6.4); and ranking scale questions, where the expert is asked to arrange some items in a list in the order of their importance or preference (see Table 6.5).

Table 6.3 Multiple-Choice Question for the Diabetic Foot Advisor (Awad, 1996)

If a diabetic patient complains of foot problems, who should he or she see first *(check one)*:

☐ Podiatrist

☐ General practitioner

☐ Orthopedic surgeon

☐ Physical therapist

Table 6.4 Dichotomous Question for the Diabetic Foot Advisor (Awad, 1996)

Do patients with neuropathy come for regular checkups?

☐ Yes

☐ No

Table 6.5 Example of a Ranking Scale Question

Please rank the following professional reputation criteria for a PhD advisor in the order of their importance from your point of view. Give a rank of 1 to the most important criterion, a rank of 2 to the second most important one, and so on:

___ research funding criterion

___ publications criterion

___ citations criterion

___ peer opinion criterion

What are the main characteristics of the structured interview method? It offers specific choices, enables faster tabulation, and has less bias due to the way the questions are formulated. However, this method is restricted by the requirement to specify choices.

6.3.6   Protocol Analysis (Think-Aloud Technique)

This is the systematic collection and analysis of the thought processes or problem-solving methods of an expert where the expert is asked to solve problems and to verbalize what goes through his or her mind, stating directly what the expert thinks. The solving process is carried out in an automatic fashion while the expert talks. The knowledge engineer does not interrupt or ask questions. The structuring of the information elicited occurs later when the knowledge engineer analyzes the protocol. Table 6.6 shows an example of a protocol where a doctor verbalizes the diagnosis of a diabetic foot patient.

Which are the main strengths and weaknesses of all of the preceding concept elicitation methods? These methods give the knowledge engineer an orientation to the domain,

---

Table 6.6. Sample Protocol (Adapted from Awad, 1996)

1. This woman is in her mid- to late forties.
2. The patient being quite overweight and a diabetic, blisters are common occurrences.
3. Pain is symptomatic of the blister.
4. Patient is experiencing this blister for the first time. She's probably more worried than being in pain.
5. Being diabetic, blisters take a long time to heal. It is not likely to get worse.

. . .

40. I don't see broken skin or pus accumulating, which is a good sign.
41. I'm going to recommend NSD and soaking the foot in warm water before going to bed and after getting up.
42. Her husband will have to help.
43. I'm going to recommend that patient wear wide-toed shoes.

. . .

64. So, for the moment, I am going to tell the patient to see me in two weeks.
65. Right now, I wouldn't recommend any medical treatment. Surgery is the last thing on my mind.
66. I'll relay this diagnosis and decision to the patient.

---

generate much knowledge cheaply and naturally, and do not require a significant effort on the part of the expert. However, they have an incomplete and arbitrary coverage, and the knowledge engineer needs appropriate training and/or social skills.

6.3.7 The Card-Sort Method

This is a simple method to develop a hierarchy of concepts. Its main steps are shown in Table 6.7.

An example of a concept hierarchy elicited through the card-sort method for the development of a domestic gas-fired hot water and central heating system is shown in Figure 6.3.

Which are the main strengths and weaknesses of the card-sort method? This method produces clusters of concepts and hierarchical organization, splits large domains into manageable subareas, is easy to use, and is widely applicable. However, it is incomplete and unguided, produces strict hierarchies that are usually too restrictive, and does not comply with the knowledge engineering guidelines for ontology structuring.

How could we modify the card-sort method to build a tangled hierarchy? We simply need to write the same concept on more cards, so that it can be included into different groups.

6.4 MODELING-BASED ONTOLOGY SPECIFICATION

Modeling-based ontology specification has already been introduced in Section 3.3. The knowledge engineer and the subject matter expert analyze each step of the reasoning trees

Table 6.7 The Card-Sort Method (Gammack, 1987)

1. Type the concepts on small individual index cards.

2. Ask the expert to group together the related concepts into as many small groups as possible.

3. Ask the expert to label each of the groups.

4. Ask the expert to combine the groups into slightly larger groups and to label them.

5. Ask the expert to repeat step 4 until a single group is obtained.

The result will be a hierarchical organization of the concepts.

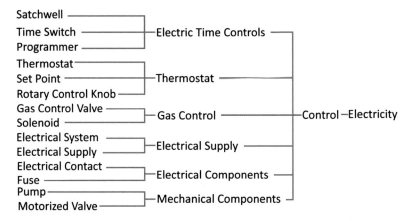

Figure 6.3. Concept hierarchy elicited through the card-sort method (Gammack, 1987).

developed as part of the rapid prototyping phase of agent development, in order to identify the concepts and the features that should be in the ontology to enable the agent to perform that reasoning.

Let us consider the reasoning step from the left-hand side of Figure 6.4. To enable the agent to answer the question from this step, we may define the ontology fragment from the right-hand side of Figure 6.4.

However, this reasoning step is just an example. We want the agent to be able to answer similar questions, corresponding to similar hypotheses. Therefore, the ontology fragment from the right-hand side of Figure 6.4 should be interpreted only as a *specification* of the ontological knowledge needed by the agent. This specification suggests that we should define various university positions, as well as various employers in the ontology, as shown in Figure 6.5. It also suggests defining two features, has as position and has as employer, as illustrated in Figure 6.6.

6.5   HANDS ON: DEVELOPING A HIERARCHY OF CONCEPTS AND INSTANCES

The hierarchy of concepts and instances can be developed by using the Object Browser, which was introduced in Section 5.11. Its interface and main functions are shown in Figure 6.7. This tool shows the hierarchy in a tree structure, which the user can expand or collapse by selecting a node (e.g., educational organization) and then clicking on **Expand**

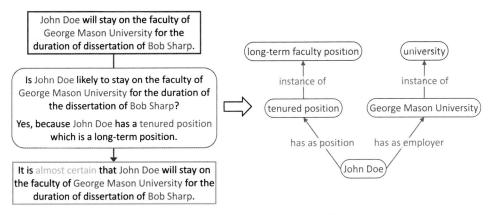

Figure 6.4. Modeling-based ontology specification.

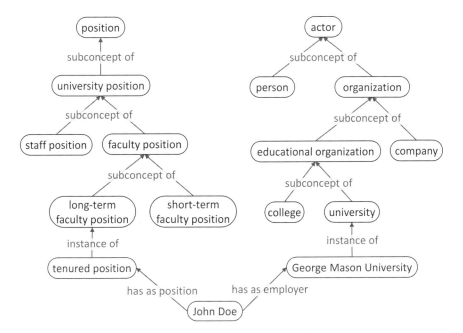

Figure 6.5. Concept hierarchy design.

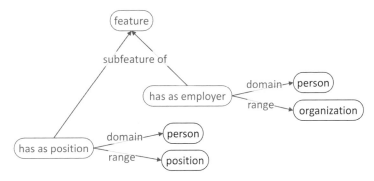

Figure 6.6. Feature hierarchy design.

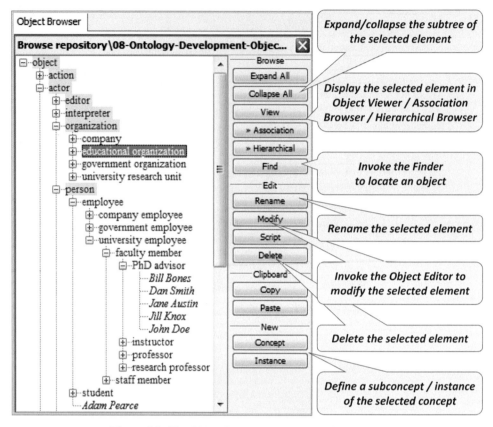

Figure 6.7. The Object Browser and its main functions.

All and **Collapse All**, respectively. Similar effects may be obtained by clicking on the – and + nodes. Selecting a node and then clicking on the **Hierarchical** button will open the Hierarchical Browser with that node as the top of the displayed hierarchy.

The Object Browser can be used to develop a generalization hierarchy by defining concepts and instances, as described in Operation 6.1 and illustrated in Figure 6.8.

Operation 6.1. Define a subconcept or an instance of a concept
- Open the Object Browser.
- Click on the concept name to select the concept.
- Click on the **Concept** button (to define a subconcept) or on the **Instance** button (to define an instance).
- Write the name of the subconcept/instance.
- Press the **Enter** key.

If an instance is to be used only in the current scenario, then it should be defined in the *Scenario* part of the knowledge base, as described in Operation 6.2. The system will create it as a *specific instance*.

Operation 6.2. Define a specific instance of a concept
- Select the Scenario workspace.
- Open the Object Browser and notice that it displays both generic instances and specific instances.

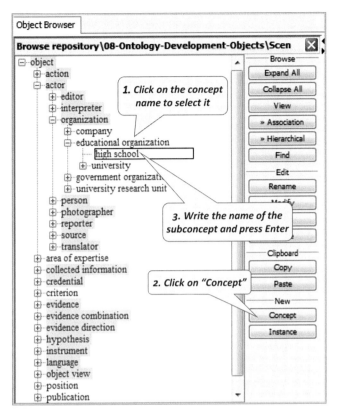

Figure 6.8. Defining a subconcept of a concept.

- Define the instance (see Operation 6.1).
- Notice that the instance is displayed in italics, indicating that it is a specific instance.

If an instance needs to be used in more than one scenario, then you have to define it as a *generic instance* in the *Domain* part of the knowledge base, as described in Operation 6.3 and illustrated in Figure 6.9. Such an instance is visible both in the Domain KB and in all its Scenario KBs and is displayed in regular font, as shown in Figure 6.10.

Operation 6.3. Define a generic instance of a concept

- Select the Domain workspace.
- Open the Object Browser and notice that it displays only generic instances.
- Define the instance (see Operation 6.1).
- Notice that the instance is displayed in regular font, indicating that it is a generic instance.

In the case of the PhD advisor assessment agent, the following instances have been defined in the *Domain* part of the knowledge base, and are therefore generic instances:

- The criteria to assess a PhD advisor (e.g., professional reputation criterion)
- Faculty positions (e.g., tenured position)
- PhD research areas (e.g., Artificial Intelligence)

The *Scenario* part still contains specific instances, such as *John Doe*, *Bob Sharp*, and *George Mason University*. A *specific instance* is visible only in the corresponding Scenario KB and is displayed in italics, as shown in Figure 6.10.

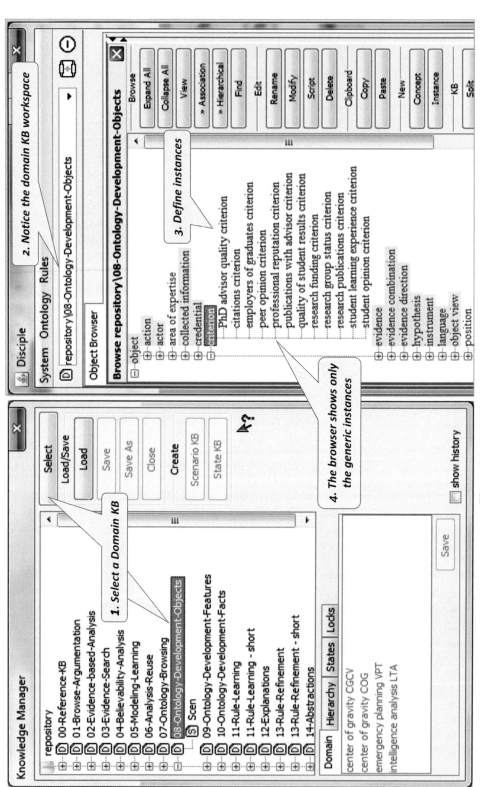

Figure 6.9. Defining a generic instance.

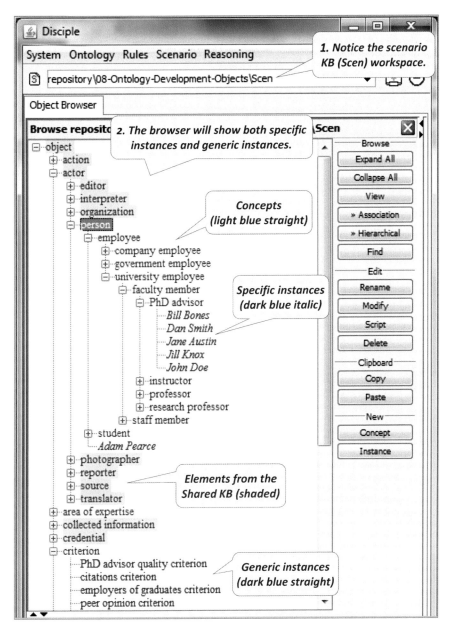

Figure 6.10. Specific instances and generic instances.

Notice that the specific instances are displayed with italic font only in the ontology interfaces. In all the other interfaces, they are displayed in the regular font.

In addition to defining concepts and instances, one should also be able to rename or delete them. These operations are performed as explained in Operations 6.4 and 6.5, respectively. Deletion is a particularly complex operation. Disciple-EBR prevents the deletion of an entity if this would lead to an inconsistent knowledge base where some of the knowledge base elements refer to the element to be deleted.

Operation 6.4. Rename a concept or an instance

- Open the Object Browser.
- Click on the concept or instance to select it.
- Click on the **Rename** button.
- Write the new name.
- Press the **Enter** key.

Operation 6.5. Delete a concept or an instance

- Open the Object Browser.
- Click on the concept or instance to select it.
- Click on the **Delete** button.

Start Disciple-EBR, select the knowledge base "08-Ontology-Development-Objects/Scen," and use the Object Browser to extend the ontology with the following information:

- course subconcept of object
- operating systems course subconcept of course
- artificial intelligence course subconcept of course
- CS571 instance of operating systems course
- CS580 instance of artificial intelligence course

6.6   GUIDELINES FOR DEVELOPING GENERALIZATION HIERARCHIES

6.6.1   Well-structured Hierarchies

Siblings in a generalization hierarchy are the concepts (or instances) that are direct subconcepts (instances) of the same concept. For example, assistant professor, associate professor, and full professor in Figure 5.4 (p. 158) are siblings because they are all direct subconcepts of professor.

Guideline 6.1. Define similar siblings

In a well-structured generalization hierarchy, all the siblings should have a comparable level of generality. In particular, they should be either all concepts or all instances. If some of them are instances, insert one or several concepts that include them, as illustrated in Figure 6.11.

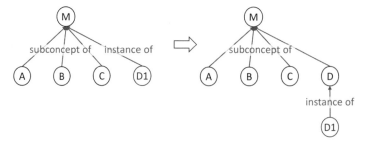

Figure 6.11. Define similar siblings.

Guideline 6.2. **Group similar siblings under natural concepts**

The siblings should reflect concepts from the real world. However, if there are too many siblings, consider whether some of them may be grouped under another (natural) concept, as illustrated in Figure 6.12.

Guideline 6.3. **Recognize that a single subconcept may indicate ontology incompleteness or error**

A case of a single subconcept, such as ABC in Figure 6.13, may be an indication of either an incomplete ontology (where the siblings of ABC are missing) or a modeling error (where ABC should not defined and A, B, and C are linked directly to M).

6.6.2 Instance or Concept?

In general, a set of individuals is represented as a concept, while a single individual is represented as an instance. But sometimes a set can be regarded as an individual and represented as an instance. Consider the hierarchy from Figure 6.14. In that hierarchy,

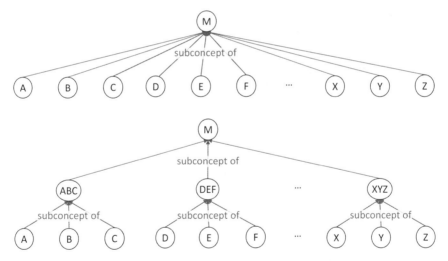

Figure 6.12. Grouping of similar siblings under natural concepts.

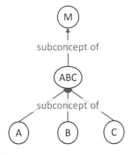

Figure 6.13. Single subconcept of a concept.

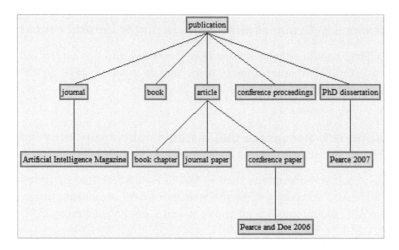

Figure 6.14. Representation of entities as concepts or as instances.

Artificial Intelligence Magazine is represented as an instance of a journal. But one could have also represented it as a concept, the instances of which would have been specific issues of the Artificial Intelligence Magazine. Whether something is represented as an instance or as a concept influences how Disciple-EBR learns. In particular, when learning a reduction rule from a reduction example, instances are generalized while the concepts are preserved as such. Therefore, *in many cases, learning considerations determine whether an entity is represented as an instance or as a concept.*

6.6.3   Specific Instance or Generic Instance?

If an instance needs to be used in more than one scenario (such as Artificial Intelligence, which is needed to evaluate advisors at various universities), then you have to create it in the Domain knowledge base, and it will be automatically defined as a *generic instance*.

Similarly, if it would make sense to have general rules that explicitly mention that instance, then again it should be defined as a generic instance. For example, we may envision a general rule related to Artificial Intelligence, but not a general rule related to *John Doe*. Thus Artificial Intelligence may be defined as a *generic instance*, but *John Doe* should be defined as a *specific instance*.

The instances created in the Scenario KB will automatically be defined as *specific instances*.

Notice that, in the ontology interfaces, the names of the generic instances are displayed in dark blue straight characters (such as Artificial Intelligence), while the names of the specific instances are displayed in dark blue italics characters (such as *John Doe*).

6.6.4   Naming Conventions

The following guidelines suggest conventions for naming concepts.

Guideline 6.4. **Adopt and follow a naming convention**

It is recommended to adopt a naming convention and to strictly adhere to it. This will both facilitate the understanding of the ontology and will help avoid modeling mistakes.

In Disciple-EBR, it is recommended to use lowercase letters for concept names. It is also recommended to use either singular or plural consistently, but not both, in naming the concepts.

Guideline 6.5. **Name subconcepts based on superconcepts**

Often the names of the subconcepts of a concept include the name of the concept, as shown in several places in Figure 5.4 (p. 158) and illustrated in Figure 6.15.

6.6.5 Automatic Support

Disciple-EBR will not accept ontology operations that will make the ontology inconsistent or introduce a circularity, where a concept is both a superconcept and a subconcept of another concept. Disciple-EBR will not accept definitions of concepts or instances that have the same names as previously defined ones.

6.7 HANDS ON: DEVELOPING A HIERARCHY OF FEATURES

The hierarchy of features can be developed by using the Feature Browser. Its interface and main functions are shown in Figure 6.16. Like the Object Browser, this tool shows the feature hierarchy in a tree structure that the user can expand or collapse by selecting a node (e.g., has as part) and then by clicking on **Expand All** and **Collapse All**, respectively. Similar effects may be obtained by clicking on the – and + nodes. Selecting a node and then clicking on the **Hierarchical** button opens the Hierarchical Browser with that node at the top of the displayed hierarchy.

The features are defined and organized in a hierarchy by using the Feature Browser, similarly to how the Object Browser is used to develop a concept hierarchy. The steps needed to define a new feature (e.g., works for) are those described in Operation 6.6.

Operation 6.6. Define a feature

- Open the Feature Browser.
- Select the superfeature (e.g., feature) of the feature to be defined (e.g., works for).
- Click on the **Feature** button.
- Specify the name of the feature to be defined (i.e., works for).
- Press the **Enter** key.

When a user defines a subfeature of a given feature, the domain and the range of the subfeature are set to be the ones of the superfeature. The user can change them by clicking on the **Modify** button of the Feature Browser. This invokes the Feature Editor, which is

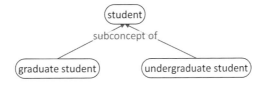

Figure 6.15. Naming concepts.

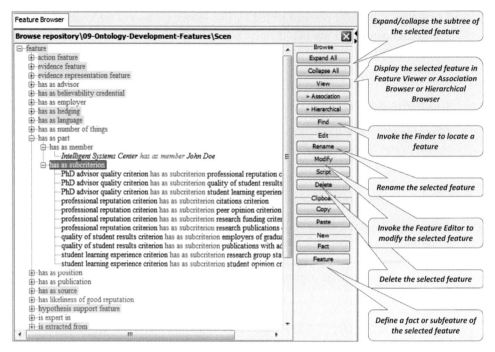

Figure 6.16. The Feature Browser and its main functions.

illustrated in Figure 6.17. Using the Feature Editor, the user can add or delete super-features or subfeatures of the selected feature, in addition to modifying its domain and range.

Figure 6.18 illustrates the process of changing the domain of the works for feature from object to actor. This process consists of the steps described in Operation 6.7.

Operation 6.7. Change the domain of a feature

- Open the Feature Browser.
- Select the feature with the domain to be changed (e.g., works for).
- Click on the **Modify** button to invoke the Feature Editor.
- Select the **<P1>[domain]** tab in the Feature Editor.
- Click on the **Add** button to open an Object Browser pane.
- Browse and select a concept for the new domain (e.g., actor).
- Click on the **Add to domain** button in the Object Browser pane.
- Click on the **Apply Domain** button in the **<P1>[domain]** tab to commit the addition in the ontology.

A range of type "Concept" is modified in the same way as a domain (see Operation 6.8).

Operation 6.8. Change the range of a feature

- Open the Feature Browser.
- Select the feature with the range to be changed (e.g., works for).
- Click on the **Modify** button to invoke the Feature Editor.
- Select the **<P2>[range]** tab in the Feature Editor.
- Click on the **Add** button to open an Object Browser pane.

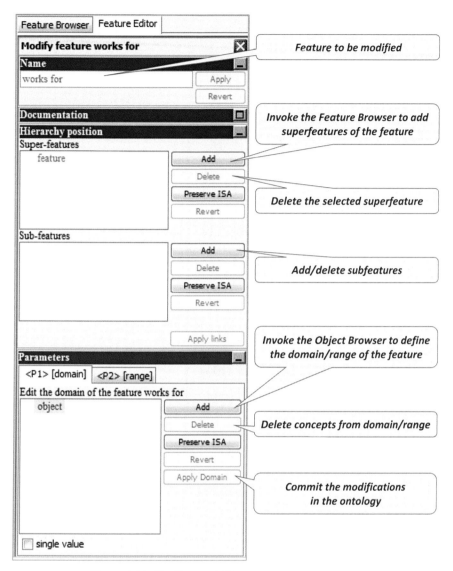

Figure 6.17. The Feature Editor and its main functions.

- Browse and select a concept for the new range (e.g., actor).
- Click on the **Add to range** button in the Object Browser pane.
- Click on the **Apply** button in the **<P2>[range]** tab to commit the addition in the ontology.

For range types other than "Concept," a type-specific editor is invoked after clicking on the **Add** button. For example, Figure 6.19 illustrates the definition of a range, which is the integer interval [0, 10].

Start Disciple-EBR, select the knowledge base "09-Ontology-Development-Features/Scen," and use the Feature Browser and the Feature Editor to represent the following related features in a hierarchy:

- works for, a subfeature of feature, with domain actor and range actor
- is employed by, a subfeature of works for, with domain employee and range organization

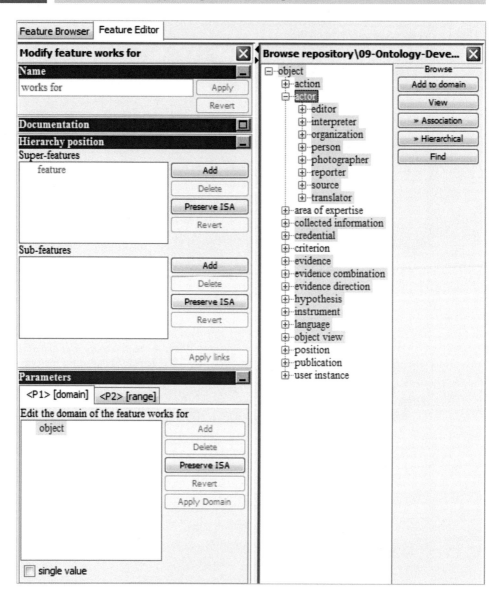

Figure 6.18. Changing the domain of a feature.

Optionally, you may also add the following feature:

- contracts to, a subfeature of works for, with domain actor (inherited from works for) and range organization

6.8   HANDS ON: DEFINING INSTANCES AND THEIR FEATURES

With some concepts and features defined, one may use the Object Editor to define instances of these concepts (as discussed in Section 6.5) and associate features with them. Figure 6.20 illustrates the process of defining the is interested in feature of *John Doe*. The steps of this process are those described in Operation 6.9.

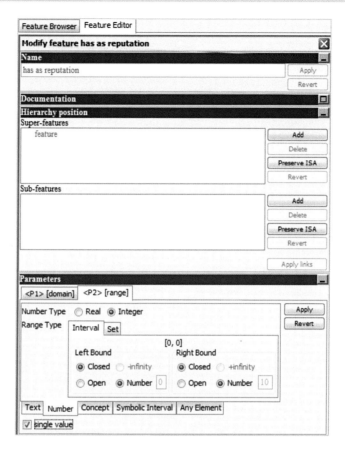

Figure 6.19. Defining a feature range as an integer interval.

Operation 6.9. Define a feature of an object

- Open the Object Browser and select the object (e.g., *John Doe*).
- Click on the **Modify** button to open the Object Editor.
- Click on the **Add feature** button in the Object Editor to open a Feature Browser pane.
- Browse and select the feature to be added to the object (e.g., is interested in).
- Click on the **Define for object** button in the Feature Browser pane.
- The Finder is automatically opened to locate its value in the ontology (see Figure 6.21).
- Write a part of the name of the value in the Finder text field.
- Click on the **Find** button.
- Click on the correct value from the list returned by the Finder.
- Click on the **Select** button.
- If the range of the feature is a symbolic interval or a set of values, a selection pane is opened in which you can choose the right value of the feature. For a number, simply type it.

The Object Editor can also be used to update the list of the direct superconcepts of an object (instance or concept) and the list of the direct subconcepts or instances of a concept. The actual steps to perform are presented in Operations 6.10 and 6.11. As with all the ontology operations, Disciple-EBR will not perform them if they would lead to an inconsistent ontology or a cycle along the subconcept of relation.

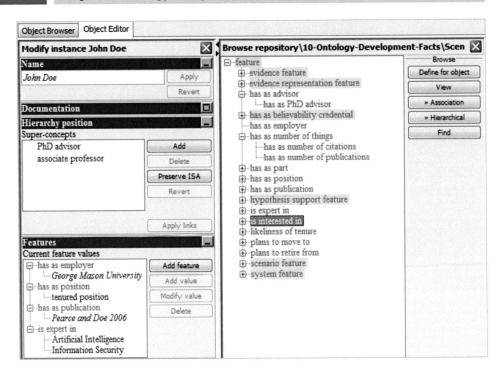

Figure 6.20. Defining a feature of an instance.

Operation 6.10. Add a direct superconcept to an object

- Locate the object (e.g., *John Doe*) with the Object Browser and the Finder and click on the **Modify** button to open the Object Editor (see Figure 6.20).
- Click on the **Add** button in the "Super-concepts" pane to open an Object Browser pane.
- Browse and select the superconcept.
- Click on the **Add as parent** button in the Object Browser pane.
- Click on the **Apply links** button in the Object Editor to commit the addition in the ontology.

Operation 6.11. Add a direct subconcept or an instance to a concept

- Locate the concept with the Object Browser and the Finder and click on the **Modify** button to open the Object Editor.
- Click on the **Add** button in the "Sub-concepts and instances" pane to open an Object Browser pane.
- Browse and select the subconcept or the instance to be added.
- Click on the **Add as child** button in the Object Browser pane.
- Click on the **Apply links** button in the Object Editor to commit the addition in the ontology.

Start Disciple-EBR, select the knowledge base "10-Ontology-Development-Facts/Scen," and use the Ontology tools to extend the representation of *John Doe* with the following fact:

John Doe is interested in Software Engineering

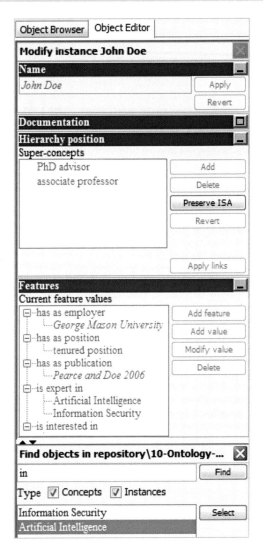

Figure 6.21. Using the Finder to define the value of a feature.

GUIDELINES FOR DEFINING FEATURES AND VALUES

6.9.1 Concept or Feature?

***Guideline 6.6.* Represent well-established categories from the real world as concepts**

Almost any distinction from the real world may be represented either as a concept, or as a feature. While there are no absolute rules for this difficult modeling decision, several guidelines are useful to follow. For example, two alternative ways of representing the fact that Bob Evens is a PhD student are:

Bob Evens instance of PhD student
Bob Evens has as student level PhD

The first one is preferable because PhD student is a well-established category.

Guideline 6.7. Define concepts and instances to represent knowledge corresponding to n-ary relations

A feature in an ontology can naturally represent a binary relation. However, if the relation is not binary, you need to define a concept or an instance with which you can associate any number of features. Let us consider the fact that John Doe has written "Windows of Opportunities." This can be represented as:

John Doe has as writing *Windows of Opportunities*

But what if we want to represent the additional knowledge that he has written it from 2005 until 2007? We can no longer associate this information with the has as writing feature. A solution is to define the concept writing and its instance *Writing1*, instead of the feature has as writing, as was illustrated in Figure 5.9 (p. 161).

6.9.2   Concept, Instance, or Constant?

Another modeling issue is to decide whether to represent the value of a feature as a concept, as an instance, or as a constant (i.e., a string).

If one needs to associate additional properties with a value, then it cannot be represented as a constant.

Let us consider again the representation from Figure 5.9 (p. 161). If we want to represent any additional features of *Windows of Opportunities* (e.g., that it is 258 pages long), then we have to represent it as an instance (which will have number of pages as a property with value 258).

If one anticipates learning concepts that will be characterized by various subsets of values, then one may elect to define the colors as strings, such as white, yellow, and orange. A learned concept might then be {white, orange}. However, if concepts such as warm color or cold color are important in the application domain, then one should define a hierarchy of colors where white, yellow, and orange are defined as generic instances or concepts.

The same considerations apply to numbers. While generally they are represented as values, one may wish to define an ordered set of intervals (see Section 8.3.6). In this case, each interval will have a specific name (such as toddler, youth, or mature), which can be used as value.

6.9.3   Naming of Features

Guideline 6.8. Define feature names that distinguish them from concept names

It is useful to define names that allow for easy distinction between a concept and a feature. For example, "author" would not be a good name for a feature because it would not be clear that "author" denotes a feature. Indeed, you may have a concept named "author."

Two common practices are to add the "has as" prefix or the "of" suffix to the feature name, resulting in has as author or author of, respectively.

6.9.4   Automatic Support

The ontology tools of Disciple-EBR have several features that facilitate their use. For example, when modifying the domain or the range of a feature (see the right-hand side of Figure 6.18 on p. 192), Disciple-EBR will display only the concepts that are acceptable values.

When defining a new feature for a given concept or an instance (see the right-hand side of Figure 6.20, p. 194), Disciple-EBR will only display the features the domain of which include the given concept or instance.

When defining the value of a given feature (see Figure 6.21 on p. 195), the Finder will display only those values that are in the range of the feature.

6.10   ONTOLOGY MAINTENANCE

Maintaining the consistency of the ontology is a very complex knowledge engineering activity because the definitions of the objects and features interact in complex ways. For example, deleting a concept requires the updating of all the knowledge base elements that refer to it, such as any feature that contains it in its range or domain, or any concept that inherits its features.

Consider the ontology fragment from the left part of Figure 6.22. Let us assume that in the initial state of this ontology, the domain of the feature f is the concept A. Let us further assume that the instance C has the feature f with value 7. If we now delete the relation "B subconcept of A" (i.e., B is no longer a subconcept of A), the modified ontology is inconsistent. Indeed, in the initial state C can have the feature f because the domain of f is A, and C is included in A (C is an instance of B, which is a subconcept of A). In the modified ontology however, C can no longer have the feature f because it is no longer included in A. The important thing to remember from this example is that a modification done to B generated an error in another part of the knowledge base (at C).

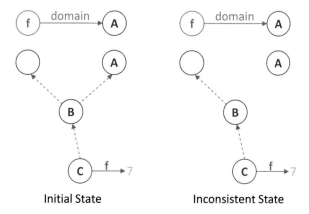

Initial State   Inconsistent State

Figure 6.22. Complexity of ontology maintenance.

6.11   PROJECT ASSIGNMENT 5

Use the reasoning trees developed as part of the rapid prototyping of your agent and employ the modeling-based ontology specification method to extend the ontology of your agent.

6.12   REVIEW QUESTIONS

6.1.   What are the basic concept elicitation methods? What are their main strengths? What are their main weaknesses?

6.2.   Briefly describe the card-sort method. What are its main strengths? What are its main weaknesses? How could one modify this method to build a tangled hierarchy?

6.3.   Describe and illustrate the "Well-structured Hierarchies" knowledge engineering guidelines presented in Section 6.6.1.

6.4.   Describe and illustrate the decision of representing an entity as instance or concept.

6.5.   Describe and illustrate the "Concept or Feature?" knowledge engineering guidelines presented in Section 6.9.1.

6.6.   Describe and illustrate the decision of representing an entity as concept, instance, or constant.

6.7.   Describe and illustrate the "Naming Conventions" guidelines, presented in Section 6.6.4 for concepts, and in Section 6.9.3 for features.

6.8.   Consider the question/answer pair from Figure 6.23. Specify the ontology fragments that are suggested by this question/answer pair, including instances, concepts, and features definitions (with appropriate domains and ranges that will facilitate learning). Do not limit yourself to the concepts that are explicitly referred to, but define additional ones as well, to enable the agent to assess similar hypotheses in a similar way.

Hint 1: Notice that the answer represents an n-ary relation while in an ontology you may only represent binary relations.
Hint 2: You need to define a hierarchy of concepts that will include those used in the domains and ranges of the defined features.
Hint 3: Your solution should reflect the use of knowledge engineering guidelines.

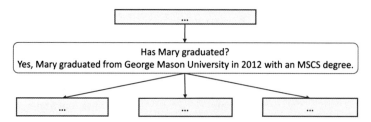

Figure 6.23. Question/answer pair corresponding to a reduction step.

6.9.   Consider the reduction step from Figure 6.24. Specify the ontology fragments that are suggested by this reasoning step. Do not limit yourself to the concepts and features that are explicitly mentioned, but define additional ones as well, to enable the agent to assess similar hypotheses in a similar way.

6.10.   What instances, concepts, and relationships should be defined in the agent's ontology, based on the analysis of the reduction step from Figure 6.25?

6.11.   What instances, concepts, and relationships should be defined in the agent's ontology, based on the analysis of the reduction step from Figure 6.26?

6.12.   What instances, concepts, and relationships should be defined in the agent's ontology, based on the analysis of the reduction step from Figure 6.27?

6.13.   Consider the design of an agent for assessing whether some actor (e.g., Aum Shinrikyo) is developing weapons of mass destruction (e.g., chemical weapons). We would like our agent to be able to perform the sample reasoning step from Figure 6.28, where the entities in blue are represented as specific instances.

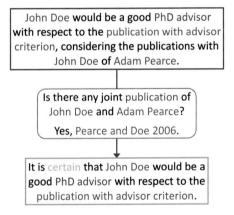

Figure 6.24. Reduction step for modeling-based ontology specification.

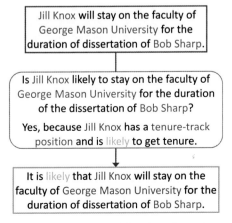

Figure 6.25. Reduction step for modeling-based ontology specification.

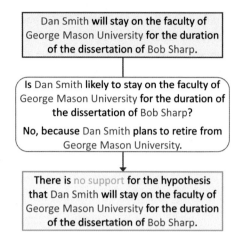

Figure 6.26. Reduction step for modeling-based ontology specification.

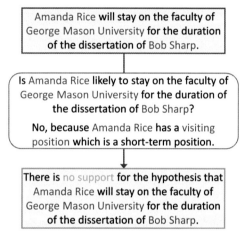

Figure 6.27. Reduction step for modeling-based ontology specification.

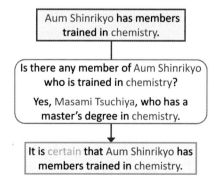

Figure 6.28. Reduction step for modeling-based ontology specification.

(a) What relationships should you define in the agent's ontology in order to represent the meaning of the question/answer pair?

(b) Represent this meaning as a network fragment showing the relationships and the related instances.

(c) Network fragments such as the one at (b) represent a specification of the needed ontology, guiding you in defining a hierarchy of concepts to which the identified instances belong, as well as the siblings of these concepts. Indicate eight such concepts. Also indicate which might be the domain and the range of each of the identified feature.

6.14. Develop an ontology that represents the following information:

Apple1 is an apple.
The color of Apple1 is red.
Apple2 is an apple.
The color of Apple2 is green.
Apples are fruits.
Hint: You should define concepts, features, and instances.

6.15. Develop an ontology that represents the following information:

Puss is a calico.
Herb is a tuna.
Charlie is a tuna.
All tunas are fishes.
All calicos are cats.
All cats like to eat all kinds of fish.
Cats and fishes are animals.
Hint: You should define concepts, features, and instances.

6.16. Develop an ontology that represents the following information:

Basketball players are tall.
Muresan is a basketball player.
Muresan is tall.
Hint: Define concepts, features, and instances.

6.17. Develop an ontology that represents the following information:

Birds are animals.
Birds have feathers, fly, and lay eggs.
Albatross is a bird.
Donald is a bird.
Tracy is an albatross.
Hint: Define concepts, features, and instances.

6.18. Explain why maintaining the consistency of the ontology is a complex knowledge engineering activity.

6.19. One of the principles in the development of a knowledge base with a tool such as Disciple-EBR is to maintain its consistency because correcting an inconsistent knowledge base is a very complex problem. Therefore, the tool will not allow the deletion of a knowledge base element (e.g., an instance, a fact, a concept, or a feature definition) if that operation will make the knowledge base inconsistent. List and explain five possible ways in which the deletion of a concept may render the knowledge base inconsistent.

7 Reasoning with Ontologies and Rules

7.1   PRODUCTION SYSTEM ARCHITECTURE

In Chapter 4, we presented the problem reduction and solution synthesis paradigm. In this chapter, we will present how a knowledge-based agent can employ this paradigm to solve problems and assess hypotheses.

Figure 7.1 shows the architecture of the agent, which is similar to that of a production system (Waterman and Hayes-Roth, 1978). The knowledge base is the long-term memory, which contains an ontology of concepts and a set of rules expressed with these concepts. When the user formulates an input problem, the problem reduction and solution synthesis inference engine applies the learned rules from the knowledge base to develop a problem reduction and solution synthesis tree, as was discussed in Section 4. This tree is developed in the reasoning area, which plays the role of the short-term memory.

The ontology from the knowledge base describes the types of objects (or concepts) in the application domain, as well as the relationships between them. Also included are the instances of these concepts, together with their properties and relationships.

The rules are IF-THEN structures that indicate the conditions under which a general problem (or hypothesis) can be reduced to simpler problems (hypotheses), or the solutions of the simpler problems (hypotheses) can be combined into the solution of the more complex problem (hypothesis).

The applicability conditions of these rules are complex concepts that are expressed by using the basic concepts and relationships from the ontology, as will be discussed in Section 7.2. The reduction and synthesis rules will be presented in Section 7.3. This section

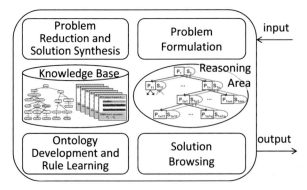

Figure 7.1. Production system architecture of the knowledge-based agent.

will also present the overall reduction and synthesis algorithm. Section 7.4 will present the simplified reduction and synthesis rules used for evidence-based hypotheses analysis, and Section 7.5 will present the rule and ontology matching process. Finally, Section 7.6 will present the representation of partially learned knowledge, and Section 7.7 will present the reasoning with this type of knowledge.

7.2   COMPLEX ONTOLOGY-BASED CONCEPTS

Using the concepts and the features from the ontology, one can define more complex concepts as logical expressions involving these basic concepts and features. For example, the concept "PhD student interested in an area of expertise" may be expressed as shown in [7.1].

?O1	instance of	PhD student	[7.1]
	is interested in	?O2	
?O2	instance of	area of expertise	

Because a concept represents a set of instances, the user can interpret the preceding concept as representing the set of instances of the tuple (?O1, ?O2), which satisfy the expression [7.1], that is, the set of tuples where the first element is a student and the second one is the research area in which the student is interested. For example, Bob Sharp, a PhD student interested in artificial intelligence, is an instance of the concept [7.1]. Indeed, the following expression is true:

Bob Sharp	instance of	PhD student
	is interested in	Artificial Intelligence
Artificial Intelligence	instance of	area of expertise

In general, the basic representation unit (BRU) for a more complex concept has the form of a tuple (?O1, ?O2, ... , ?On), where each ?Oi has the structure indicated by [7.2], called a *clause*.

?Oi	instance of	$concept_i$	[7.2]
	$feature_{i_1}$	$?Oi_1$	
	...		
	$feature_{i_q}$	$?Oi_m$	

$Concept_i$ is either an object concept from the object ontology (such as PhD student), a numeric interval (such as [50 , 60]), a set of numbers (such as {1, 3, 5}), a set of strings (such as {white, red, blue}), or an ordered set of intervals (such as (youth, mature)). $?Oi_1$ ... $?Oi_m$ are distinct variables from the sequence (?O1, ?O2, ... , ?On).

A concept may be a conjunctive expression of form [7.3], meaning that any instance of the concept satisfies BRU and does not satisfy BRU1 and ... and does not satisfy BRUp.

BRU ∧ not BRU1 ∧ ... ∧ not BRUp   [7.3]

However, instead of "not," we write "Except-When," as shown in [7.4].

BRU ∧ Except-When BRU1 ∧ ... ∧ Except-When BRUp   [7.4]

For example, expression [7.5] represents the concept "PhD student interested in an area of expertise that does not require programming."

?O1	instance of	PhD student	[7.5]
	is interested in	?O2	
?O2	instance of	area of expertise	
Except-When			
?O2	instance of	area of expertise	
	requires	programming	

7.3   REDUCTION AND SYNTHESIS RULES AND THE INFERENCE ENGINE

An agent can solve problems through reduction and synthesis by using problem reduction rules and solution synthesis rules. The rules are IF-THEN structures that indicate the conditions under which a general problem can be reduced to simpler problems, or the solutions of the simpler problems can be combined into the solution of the more complex problem.

The general structure of a *problem reduction rule* R^i is shown in Figure 7.2. This rule indicates that solving the problem P can be reduced to solving the simpler problems $P^i_1, \ldots, P^i_{ni}$, if certain conditions are satisfied. These conditions are expressed in two equivalent forms: one as a question/answer pair in natural language that is easily understood by the user of the agent, and the other as a formal applicability condition expressed as a complex concept having the form [7.4], as discussed in the previous section.

Consequently, there are two interpretations of the rule in Figure 7.2:

(1) If the problem to solve is P, and the answer to the question QR^i is AR^i, then one can solve P by solving the subproblems $P^i_1, \ldots, P^i_{ni}$.

(2) If the problem to solve is P, and the condition CR^i is satisfied, and the conditions $ER^i_1, \ldots, ER^i_{ki}$ are not satisfied, then one can solve P by solving the subproblems $P^i_1, \ldots, P^i_{ni}$.

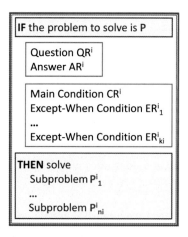

Figure 7.2. Structure of a problem reduction rule R^i.

An example of a problem reduction rule is shown in Figure 7.3. It reduces the IF problem to two simpler problems. This rule has a main condition and no Except-When conditions. Notice also that the main condition is expressed as the concept (?O1, ?O2, ?O3, ?O4).

As discussed in Section 4.2 and illustrated in Figure 4.6 (p. 116), there are two synthesis operations associated with a reduction operation: a reduction-level synthesis and a problem-level synthesis. These operations are performed by employing two solution synthesis rules that are tightly coupled with the problem reduction rule, as illustrated in Figure 7.4 and explained in the following paragraphs.

For each problem reduction rule R^i that reduces a problem P to the subproblems $P^i_1, \ldots, P^i_{ni}$ (see the left-hand side of Figure 7.4), there is a *reduction-level solution synthesis rule* (see the upper-right-hand side of Figure 7.4). This reduction-level solution synthesis rule is an IF-THEN structure that expresses the condition under which the solutions $S^i_1, \ldots, S^i_{ni}$ of the subproblems $P^i_1, \ldots, P^i_{ni}$ of the problem P can be combined into the solution S^i of P corresponding to the rule R^i.

Let us now consider all the reduction rules $R^i, \ldots, R^m$ that reduce problem P to simpler problems, and the corresponding synthesis rules $SR^i, \ldots, SR^m$. In a given situation, some of these rules will produce solutions of P, such as the following ones: Based on R^i, the

IF the problem to solve is

Analyze a strategic COG candidate corresponding to the ?O1 which is an industrial economy.

Q: Who or what is a strategically critical element with respect to the ?O1 ?

A: ?O2 because it is an essential generator of war material for ?O3 from the strategic perspective.

Main Condition

?O1   is   industrial economy

?O2   is   industrial capacity
generates essential war material from the strategic perspective of   ?O3

?O3   is   multistate force
has as member   ?O4

?O4   is   force
has as economy   ?O1
has as industrial factor   ?O2

THEN solve the subproblems

Identify ?O2 as a strategic COG candidate with respect to the ?O1.

Test ?O2 which is a strategic COG candidate with respect to the ?O1.

Figure 7.3. An example of a problem reduction rule.

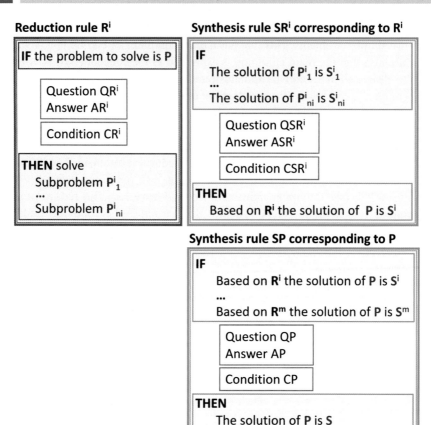

Figure 7.4. A reduction rule and the corresponding synthesis rules.

solution of P is S^i, ... , and based on R^m, the solution of P is S^m. The synthesis rule SP corresponding to the problem P combines all these rule-specific solutions of the problem P (named S^i, ... , S^m) into the solution S of P (see the bottom-right side of Figure 7.4).

The problem-solving algorithm that builds the reduction and synthesis tree is presented in Table 7.1.

7.4 REDUCTION AND SYNTHESIS RULES FOR EVIDENCE-BASED HYPOTHESES ANALYSIS

In Section 4.3, we discussed the specialization of inquiry-driven analysis and synthesis for evidence-based reasoning, where one assesses the probability of hypotheses based on evidence, such as the following one:

John Doe would be a good PhD advisor for Bob Sharp.

Moreover, the assessment of any such hypothesis has the form, "It is <probability> that H," which can be abstracted to the actual probability, as in the following example, which can be abstracted to "very likely:"

It is very likely that John Doe would be a good PhD advisor for Bob Sharp.

Table 7.1 The Basic Operation of the Inference Engine

Procedure SOLVE(PN(n_0, P, x_0))
Input
  P – a problem class;
  x_0 – parameters instantiation
  P(x_0) – a specific problem
  n_0 – the index of the problem node in the reasoning tree
  PN(n_0, P, x_0) – a problem node for problem P(x_0) with index n_0
SOL={ }
FOR ALL R^i ∈ GET-APPLICABLE-RULES-OF(P)
  FOR ALL y_j ∈ GENERATE-RULE-INSTANTIATIONS (R^i, x_0)
    RN(n_{ij}, R^i, y_j) = GENERATE-REDUCTION-NODE (PN(n_0,P,x_0), R^i (y_j))
    FOR ALL TN_{nk}(n^k, T_k, z_k) ∈ GET-THEN-STATEMENT-NODE (RN(n_{ij}, R^i, y_j))
    IF TN_{nk} IS PROBLEM-NODE THEN
      SN_{nk} ← SOLVE(TN_{nk})
    IF ALL TN_{nk} HAVE SOLUTIONS THEN
      SN(n_{ij}, S, u_k)← COMPUTE-FIRST-REDUCTION-LEVEL-SOLUTION-NODE
                                                    (RN(n_{ij}, R^i, y_j), $(SN_{nk})_k$)

    IF SN(n_{ij}, S, u_k) THEN
SOL ← SOL ∪ {S(u_k)}
IF SOL ≠ ∅ THEN
  SN(n_0, S, u) ← COMPUTE-FIRST-PROBLEM-LEVEL-SOLUTION-NODE (PN(n_0, P, x_0), SOL)
RETURN SN_{n0}

As a result, the solution synthesis rules have a simplified form, as shown in Figure 7.5. In particular, notice that the condition of a synthesis rule is reduced to computing the probability of the THEN solution based on the probabilities for the IF solutions.

In the current implementation of Disciple-EBR, the function for a reduction-level synthesis rule SR could be one of the following (as discussed in Section 4.3): **min, max, likely indicator, very likely indicator, almost certain indicator,** or **on balance**. The function for a problem-level synthesis can be only **min** or **max**.

Figure 7.6 shows an example of a reduction rule and the corresponding synthesis rules. The next section will discuss how such rules are actually applied in problem solving.

7.5   RULE AND ONTOLOGY MATCHING

Let us consider the following hypothesis to assess:

Bob Sharp is interested in an area of expertise of John Doe.

The agent (i.e., its inference engine) will look for all the reduction rules from the knowledge base with an IF hypothesis that matches the preceding hypothesis. Such a rule is the one from the right-hand side of Figure 7.7. As one can see, the IF hypothesis becomes identical with the hypothesis to be solved if ?O1 is replaced with Bob Sharp and ?O2 is replaced with John Doe. The rule is applicable if the condition of the rule is satisfied for these values of ?O1 and ?O2.

Reduction rule R^i   **Synthesis rule SR^i corresponding to R^i**

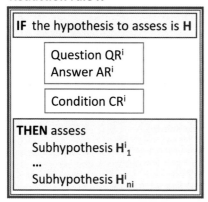

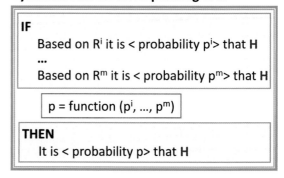

Synthesis rule SH corresponding to H

IF
  Based on R^i it is < probability p^i> that H
  ...
  Based on R^m it is < probability p^m> that H

  p = function (p^i, ..., p^m)

THEN
  It is < probability p> that H

Figure 7.5. Reduction and synthesis rules for evidence-based hypotheses analysis.

The partially instantiated rule is shown in the right-hand side of Figure 7.8. The agent has to check that the partially instantiated condition of the rule can be satisfied. This condition is satisfied if there is any instance of ?O3 in the object ontology that satisfies all the relationships specified in the rule's condition, which is shown also in the left-hand side of Figure 7.8. ?Sl1 is an output variable that is given the value certain, without being constrained by the other variables.

The partially instantiated condition of the rule, shown in the left-hand side of Figures 7.8 and 7.9, is matched successfully with the ontology fragment shown in the right-hand side of Figure 7.9. The questions are: How is this matching performed, and is it efficient?

John Doe from the rule's condition (see the left-hand side of Figure 7.9) is matched with John Doe from the ontology (see the right-hand side of Figure 7.9).

Following the feature is expert in, ?O3 has to match Artificial Intelligence:

    John Doe   is expert in   ?O3

    John Doe   is expert in   Artificial Intelligence

This matching is successful because both ?O3 and Artificial Intelligence are areas of expertise, and both are the values of the feature is interested in of Bob Sharp. Indeed, Artificial Intelligence is an instance of Computer Science, which is a subconcept of area of expertise.

Reduction Rule R^i

IF the hypothesis to assess is

?O1 would be a good PhD advisor for ?O2.

> Q: Which are the necessary conditions?
>
> A: ?O2 should be interested in the area of expertise of ?O1 who should stay on the faculty of ?O3 for the duration of the dissertation of ?O2, and should have the qualities of a good PhD advisor.

Main Condition

?O1	is	PhD advisor
	has as employer	?O3
?O2	is	PhD student
?O3	is	university
?O4	is	PhD advisor quality criterion

THEN assess the subhypotheses

?O2 is interested in an area of expertise of ?O1.

?O1 will stay on the faculty of ?O3 for the duration of dissertation of ?O2.

?O1 would be a good PhD advisor with respect to the ?O4.

Synthesis Rule SR^i corresponding to R^i

IF

It is <probability p^i_1> that ?O2 is interested in an area of expertise of ?O1.

It is <probability p^i_2> that ?O1 will stay on the faculty of ?O3 for the duration of dissertation of ?O2.

It is <probability p^i_3> that ?O1 would be a good PhD advisor with respect to the ?O4.

$$p^i = \min(p^i_1, p^i_2, p^i_3)$$

THEN

Based on R^i it is <probability p^i> that ?O1 would be a good PhD advisor for ?O2.

Synthesis Rule SH

IF

Based on R$_i$ it is <probability p^i> that ?O1 would be a good PhD advisor for ?O2.

...

Based on R$_m$ it is <probability p^m> that ?O1 would be a good PhD advisor for ?O2.

$$I = \max(p^i,..., p^m)$$

THEN

It is <probability I> that ?O1 would be a good PhD advisor for ?O2.

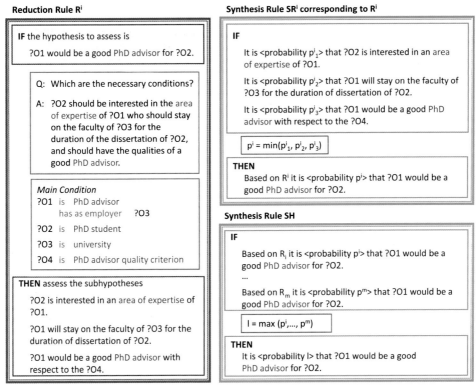

Figure 7.6. Examples of reduction and synthesis rules for evidence-based hypotheses analysis.

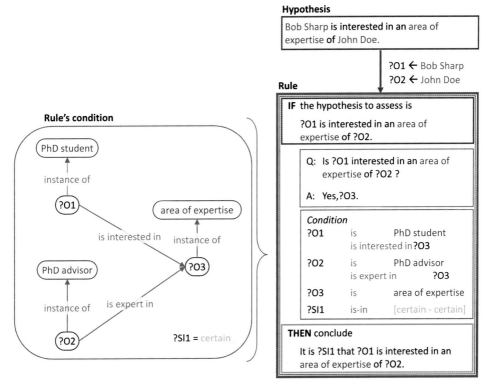

Hypothesis

Bob Sharp is interested in an area of expertise of John Doe.

?O1 ← Bob Sharp
?O2 ← John Doe

Rule

IF the hypothesis to assess is

?O1 is interested in an area of expertise of ?O2.

> Q: Is ?O1 interested in an area of expertise of ?O2 ?
>
> A: Yes, ?O3.

Condition

?O1	is	PhD student
	is interested in	?O3
?O2	is	PhD advisor
	is expert in	?O3
?O3	is	area of expertise
?SI1	is-in	[certain - certain]

THEN conclude

It is ?SI1 that ?O1 is interested in an area of expertise of ?O2.

Rule's condition

PhD student

instance of

?O1

is interested in

area of expertise

instance of

PhD advisor

?O3

instance of   is expert in

?O2

?SI1 = certain

Figure 7.7. Rule selection based on hypotheses matching.

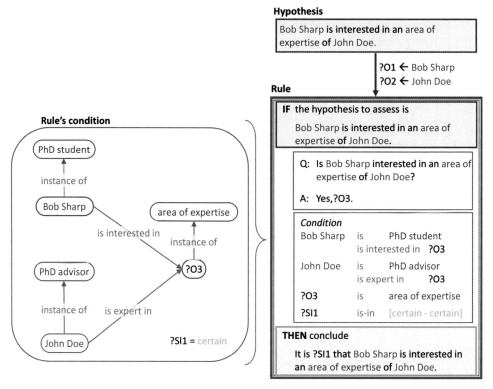

Figure 7.8. Partial instantiation of the rule based on hypotheses matching.

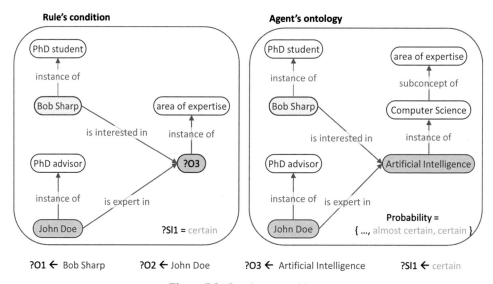

Figure 7.9. Ontology matching.

As the result of this matching, the rule's ?O3 variable is instantiated to Artificial Intelligence:

?O3 ⟵ Artificial Intelligence

Also, ?Sl1 will take the value certain, which is one of the values of probability, as constrained by the rule's condition.

The matching is very efficient because the structure used to represent knowledge (i.e., the ontology) is also a guide for the matching process, as was illustrated previously and discussed in Section 5.10.

Thus the rule's condition is satisfied for the following instantiations of the variables:

?O1 ← Bob Sharp

?O2 ← John Doe

?O3 ← Artificial Intelligence

?SI1 ← certain

Therefore, the rule can be applied to reduce the IF hypothesis to an assessment. This entire process is summarized in Figure 7.10, as follows:

(1) The hypothesis to assess is matched with the IF hypothesis of the rule, leading to the instantiations of ?O1 and ?O2.

(2) The corresponding instantiation of the rule's condition is matched with the ontology, leading to instances for all the variables of the rule.

(3) The question/answer pair and the THEN part of the rule are instantiated, generating the following reasoning step shown also in the left-hand side of Figure 7.10:

Hypothesis to assess:

Bob Sharp is interested in an area of expertise of John Doe.

Q: Is Bob Sharp interested in an area of expertise of John Doe?
A: Yes, Artificial Intelligence.

Assessment:

It is certain that Bob Sharp is interested in an area of expertise of John Doe.

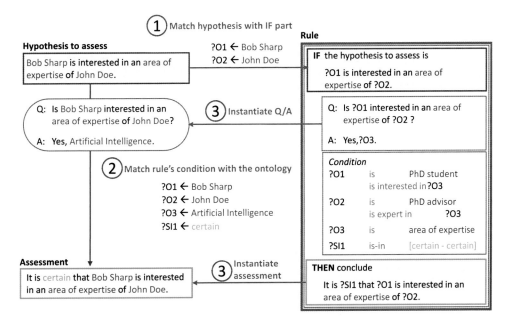

Figure 7.10. Application of a rule in problem solving.

In the preceding example, the agent has found one instance for each rule variable, which has led to a solution. What happens if it cannot find instances for all the rule's variables? In such a case, the rule is not applicable.

But what happens if it finds more than one set of instances? In that case, the agent will generate an assessment for each distinct set of instances.

What happens if there is more than one applicable reduction rule? In such a case, the agent will apply each of them to find all the possible reductions.

All the obtained assessments will be combined into the final assessment of the hypothesis, as was discussed in the previous section.

Figure 7.11 shows the successive applications of two reduction rules to assess an initial hypothesis. Rule 1 reduces it to three subhypotheses. Then Rule 2 finds the assessment of the first subhypothesis.

7.6   PARTIALLY LEARNED KNOWLEDGE

7.6.1   Partially Learned Concepts

An incremental learning system will maintain representations of the partially learned concepts. Disciple-EBR is such an incremental learner that learns general concepts from examples and explanations (Tecuci, 1998; Tecuci et al., 2005b), as will be discussed in the following chapters. During the learning process, the agent maintains a set of possible versions of the concept to be learned, called a *version space* (Mitchell, 1978, 1997; Tecuci, 1988). The concepts in this space are partially ordered, based on the generalization relationship. For that reason, the version space can be represented by an upper bound and a lower bound. The *upper bound* of the version space contains the most

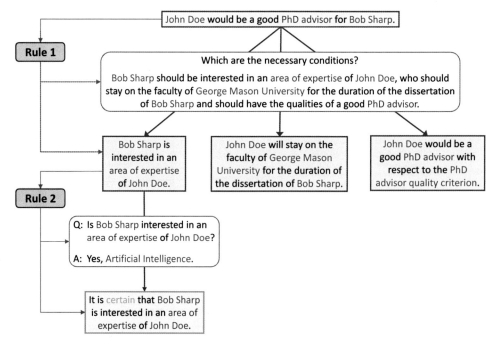

Figure 7.11. Successive rules applications.

general concepts from the version space, and the *lower bound* contains the least general concepts from the version space. Any concept that is more general than (or as general as) a concept from the lower bound and less general than (or as general as) a concept from the upper bound is part of the version space and may be the actual concept to be learned. Therefore, a version space may be regarded as a *partially learned concept.*

The version spaces built by Disciple-EBR during the learning process are called *plausible version spaces* because their upper and lower bounds are generalizations based on an incomplete ontology. Therefore, a plausible version space is only a plausible approximation of the concept to be learned, as illustrated in Figure 7.12.

The plausible upper bound of the version space from the right-hand side of Figure 7.12 contains two concepts: "a faculty member interested in an area of expertise" (see expression [7.6]) and "a student interested in an area of expertise" (see expression [7.7]).

Concept 1:	?O1	instance of	faculty member	[7.6]
	is interested in	?O2		
	?O2	instance of	area of expertise	
Concept 2:	?O1	instance of	student	[7.7]
	is interested in	?O2		
	?O2	instance of	area of expertise	

The plausible lower bound of this version space also contains two concepts, "an associate professor interested in Computer Science," and "a graduate student interested in Computer Science."

The concept to be learned (see the left side of Figure 7.12) is, *as an approximation,* less general than one of the concepts from the plausible upper bound, and more general than one the concepts from the plausible lower bound.

The notion of plausible version space is fundamental to the knowledge representation, problem-solving, and learning methods of Disciple-EBR because all the partially learned concepts are represented using this construct, as discussed in the following.

7.6.2 Partially Learned Features

As discussed in Section 5.5, a feature is characterized by a domain and a range. Most often, the domains and the ranges of the features are basic concepts from the object ontology. However,

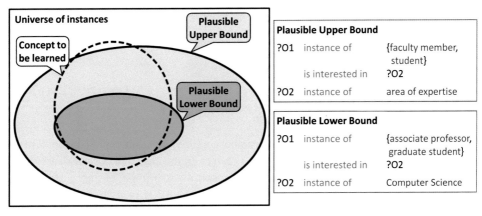

Figure 7.12. The plausible version space of a concept to be learned.

they could also be complex concepts of the form shown in Section 7.2. Moreover, in the case of partially learned features, they are plausible version spaces, as illustrated in Figure 5.7 (p. 159).

7.6.3   Partially Learned Hypotheses

A specific hypothesis consists of a natural language sentence that includes at least one instance and, optionally, additional instances, concepts, numbers, and strings. An example of a specific hypothesis is the following one:

> John Doe is a potential PhD advisor for Bob Sharp.   [7.8]

As will be discussed in Section 9.10, the agent learns general hypotheses with applicability conditions from specific hypotheses. An example of a general hypothesis learned from [7.8] in shown in [7.9].

> Name   [7.9]
>   ?O1 is a potential PhD advisor for ?O2.
> Condition
>   ?O1   instance of   faculty member
>   ?O2   instance of   person

The condition is a concept that, in general, may have the form [7.4] (p. 203). The purpose of the condition is to ensure that the hypothesis makes sense for each hypothesis instantiation that satisfies it. For example, the hypothesis from [7.8] satisfies the condition in [7.9] because John Doe is a faculty member and Bob Sharp is a person. However, the hypothesis instance in [7.10] does not satisfy the condition in [7.9] because 45 is not a faculty member. The condition in [7.9] will prevent the agent from generating the instance in [7.10].

> 45 is a potential PhD advisor for Bob Sharp.   [7.10]

A partially learned hypothesis will have a plausible version space condition, as illustrated in [7.11].

> Name   [7.11]
>   ?O1 is a potential PhD advisor for ?O2.
> Plausible Upper Bound Condition
>   ?O1   instance of   person
>   ?O2   instance of   person
> Plausible Lower Bound Condition
>   ?O1   instance of   {associate professor, PhD advisor}
>   ?O2   instance of   PhD student

7.6.4   Partially Learned Rules

As discussed in Section 7.3, the applicability condition of a rule is the concept representing the set of instances for which the rule is correct. In the case of a partially learned rule, the applicability condition is a plausible version space. An example of such a rule is presented in Figure 7.13. Its lower bound condition requires that ?O1 be a PhD student interested in artificial intelligence, while the upper bound allows ?O1 to be any person interested in any area of expertise. Similarly, the lower bound condition requires ?O2 to be either a PhD

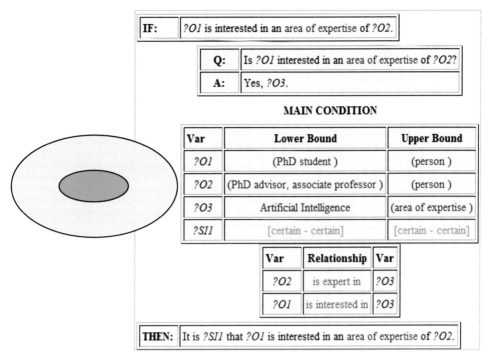

Figure 7.13. Partially learned hypothesis reduction rule.

advisor or an associate professor who is an expert in artificial intelligence, while the upper bound allows ?O2 to be any person who is an expert in any area of expertise ?O3 in which ?O1 is interested.

7.7 REASONING WITH PARTIALLY LEARNED KNOWLEDGE

A learning agent should be able to reason with partially learned knowledge. Figure 7.14 shows an abstract rule with a partially learned applicability condition. It includes a *Main plausible version space condition* (in light and dark green) and an *Except-When plausible version space condition* (in light and dark red). The reductions generated by a partially learned rule will have different degrees of plausibility, as indicated in Figure 7.14. For example, a reduction r1 corresponding to a situation where the plausible lower bound condition is satisfied and none of the Except-When conditions is satisfied is most likely to be correct. Similarly, r2 (which is covered by the plausible upper bound, and is not covered by any bound of the Except-When condition) is plausible but less likely than r1.

The way a partially learned rule is used depends on the current goal of the agent. If the current goal is to support its user in problem solving, then the agent will generate the solutions that are more likely to be correct. For example, a reduction covered by the plausible lower bound of the Main condition and not covered by any of the Except-When conditions (such as the reduction r1 in Figure 7.14) will be preferable to a reduction covered by the plausible upper bound of the Main condition and not covered by any of the Except-When conditions (such as the reduction r2), because it is more likely to be correct.

However, if the current goal of the agent is to improve its reasoning rules, then it is more useful to generate the reduction r2 than the reduction r1. Indeed, no matter how the user characterizes r2 (either as correct or as incorrect), the agent will be able to use it to

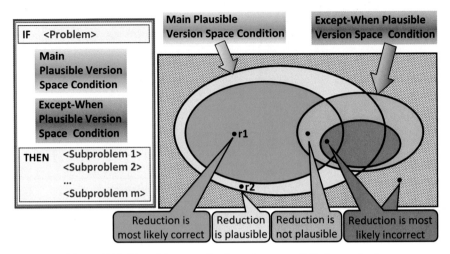

Figure 7.14. Plausible reasoning based on a partially learned rule.

refine the rule, either by generalizing the plausible lower bound of the Main condition to cover r2 (if r2 is a correct reduction), or by specializing the plausible upper bound of the Main to uncover r2 (if r2 is an incorrect reduction), or by learning an additional Except-When condition based on r2 (again, if r2 is an incorrect reduction).

7.8   REVIEW QUESTIONS

7.1. What does the following concept represent? What would be an instance of it?

?O1	instance of	course
	has as reading	?O2
?O2	instance of	publication
	has as author	?O3
?O3	instance of	professor

7.2. Illustrate the problem-solving process with the hypothesis, the rule, and the ontology from Figure 7.15.

7.3. Consider the reduction rule and the ontology fragment from Figure 7.16. Indicate whether this agent can assess the hypothesis, "Bill Bones is expert in an area of interest of Dan Moore," and if the answer is yes, indicate the result.

7.4. Consider the following problem:

Analyze a strategic COG candidate corresponding to the economy of US 1943, which is an industrial economy.

Explain how this problem is reduced by applying the reduction rule from Figure 7.17, in the context of the ontology from Figure 7.18. Show the generated reduction step.

7.5. Illustrate the problem-solving process with the hypothesis, rule, and ontology fragment from Figure 7.19.

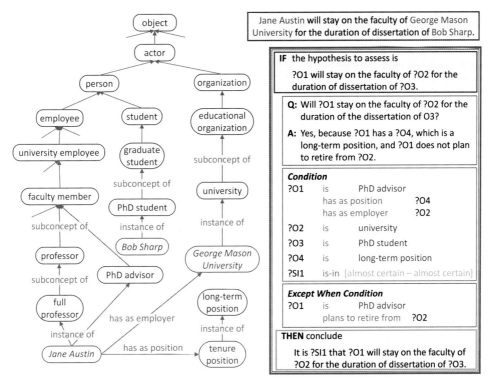

Figure 7.15. Ontology fragment, hypothesis, and reduction rule.

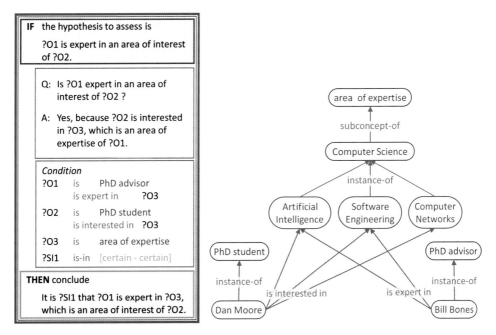

Figure 7.16. Reduction rule and ontology fragment.

7.6.   Consider the partially learned concept and the nine instances from Figure 7.20. Order the instances by the plausibility of being instances of this concept and justify the ordering.

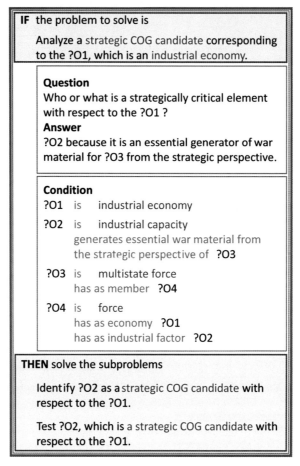

Figure 7.17. Reduction rule from the center of gravity analysis domain.

7.7.   Consider the ontology fragment from the loudspeaker manufacturing domain shown in Figure 5.24 (p. 172). Notice that each most specific concept, such as dust or air press, has an instance, such as dust1 or air press1.

Consider also the following rule:

IF the task to perform is
    Clean ?x   of   ?y
Condition
      ?x   is   object
         may have ?y
     ?y   is   object
     ?z   is   cleaner
        removes ?y
THEN perform the task
    Clean ?x of   ?y   with ?z

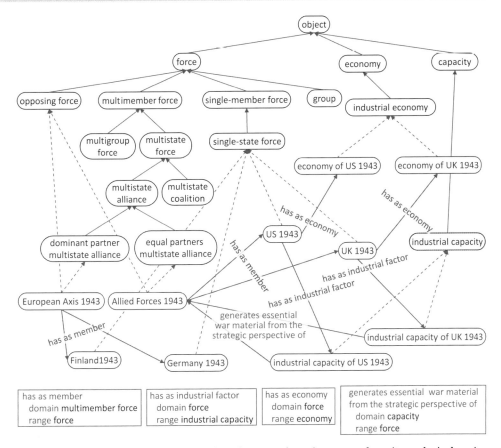

Figure 7.18. Feature definitions and ontology fragment from the center of gravity analysis domain. Dotted links indicate "instance of" relationships while unnamed continuous links indicate "sub-concept of" relationships.

Describe how this rule is applied to solve the problem:

Clean   entrefer1 of   dust1

What will be the result?
Describe how this rule is applied to solve the problem:

Clean   membrane1 of   surplus-adhesive1

What will be the result?

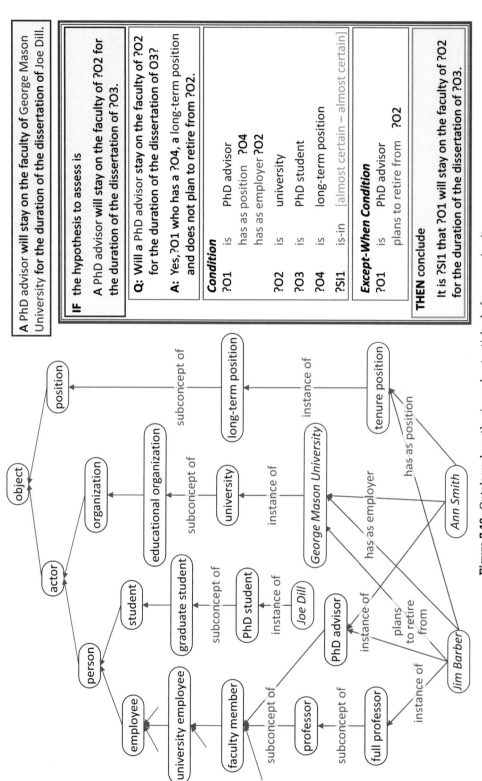

Figure 7.19. Ontology, hypothesis, and potential rule for assessing it.

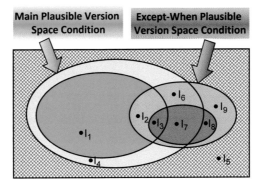

Figure 7.20. A partially learned concept and several instances.

8 Learning for Knowledge-based Agents

The previous chapters introduced the main knowledge elements from the knowledge base of an agent, which are all based on the notion of concept. This chapter presents the basic operations involved in learning, including comparing the generality of concepts, generalizing concepts, and specializing concepts. We start with a brief overview of several machine learning strategies that are particularly useful for knowledge-based agents.

8.1 INTRODUCTION TO MACHINE LEARNING

8.1.1 What Is Learning?

The following are definitions of learning given by some of the most prominent researchers in this field:

- "Learning denotes changes in the system that are adaptive in the sense that they enable the system to do the same task or tasks drawn from the same population more efficiently and more effectively the next time" (Simon, 1983, p. 28).
- "'Learning' is making useful changes in the workings of our minds" (Minsky, 1986, p. 120).
- "Learning is constructing or modifying representations of what is being experienced" (Michalski, 1986, p. 10).
- "A computer program is said to **learn** from experience E with respect to some class of tasks T and performance measure P, if its performance at tasks in T, as measured by P, improves with experience E." (Mitchell, 1997, p. 2).

Given the preceding definitions, we may characterize *learning as denoting the way in which people and computers*:

- *Acquire, discover, and organize knowledge by building, modifying, and organizing internal representations of some external reality.*
- *Acquire skills by gradually improving their motor or cognitive abilities through repeated practice, sometimes involving little or no conscious thought.*

There are two complementary dimensions of learning: competence and efficiency. A system is improving its *competence* if it learns to solve a broader class of problems and to make fewer mistakes in problem solving. The system is improving its *efficiency* if it learns to solve the problems from its area of competence faster or by using fewer resources.

Machine learning is the domain of artificial intelligence that is concerned with building adaptive computer systems that are able to improve their performance (competence and/or efficiency) through learning from input data, from a user, or from their own problem-solving experience.

Research in machine learning has led to the development of many basic learning strategies, each characterized by the employment of a certain type of:

- *Inference* (e.g., deduction, induction, abduction, analogy)
- *Computational or representational mechanism* (e.g., rules, trees, neural networks)
- *Learning goal* (e.g., to learn a concept, discover a formula, acquire new facts, acquire new knowledge about an entity, refine an entity)

The following are some of the most representative learning strategies:

- Rote learning
- Version space learning
- Decision trees induction
- Clustering
- Rule induction (e.g., Learning rule sets, Inductive logic programming)
- Instance-based strategies (e.g., K-nearest neighbors, Locally weighted regression, Collaborative filtering, Case-based reasoning and learning, Learning by analogy)
- Bayesian learning (e.g., Naïve Bayes learning, Bayesian network learning)
- Neural networks and Deep learning
- Model ensembles (e.g., Bagging, Boosting, ECOC, Staking)
- Support vector machines
- Explanation-based learning
- Abductive learning
- Reinforcement learning
- Genetic algorithms and evolutionary computation
- Apprenticeship learning
- Multistrategy learning

In the next sections, we will briefly introduce four learning strategies that are particularly useful for agent teaching and learning.

8.1.2   Inductive Learning from Examples

The goal of inductive learning from examples is to learn a general description of a concept, for instance, the concept of "cup," by analyzing *positive examples* of cups (i.e., objects that are cups) and *negative examples* of cups (i.e., objects that are not cups).

The learning agent will attempt to find out what is common to the cups and what distinguishes them from non-cups. For instance, in the illustration from Figure 8.1, the agent may learn that a cup should have a handle because all the positive examples of cups have handles, and the negative examples of cups do not have handles. However, the color does not seem to be important for a cup because a particular color is encountered for both cups and non-cups.

Learning a good concept description through this learning strategy requires a very large number of positive and negative examples. On the other hand, this is the only information

Figure 8.1. Illustration of inductive concept learning from examples.

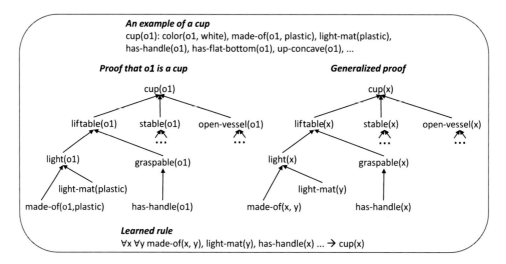

Figure 8.2. Illustration of explanation-based learning.

the agent needs. For instance, the agent does not require any prior knowledge to perform this type of learning.

The result of this learning strategy is the increase of the problem-solving competence of the agent. Indeed, the agent will learn to perform tasks it was not able to perform before, such as recognizing the cups from a set of objects.

8.1.3   Explanation-based Learning

The goal of explanation-based learning is to improve the agent's efficiency in problem solving. The agent is able to perform some task, for example, to recognize cups, but in an inefficient manner. Through explanation-based learning, the agent learns to perform its tasks faster, as illustrated in the following.

Let us assume that the agent receives the description of the cup o1 from the top part of Figure 8.2. Using its prior knowledge, it will recognize that this object is a cup by performing a complex reasoning process demonstrating that o1 is indeed a cup. This process is illustrated by the proof tree from the left-hand side of Figure 8.2.

The agent's reasoning process proceeds as follows:

- o1 is made of plastic, which is a light material. Therefore, o1 is light.
- o1 has a handle, and it is therefore graspable.

- Being light and graspable, o1 is liftable.

- . . .

- Being liftable, stable, and an open vessel, o1 is a cup.

Notice that the agent used the fact that o1 has a handle in order to prove that o1 is a cup. This means that having a handle is an important feature. On the other hand, the agent did not use the color of o1 to prove that o1 is a cup. This means that color is not important. Notice how the agent reaches the same conclusions as in inductive learning from examples, but through a different line of reasoning, and based on a different type of information (i.e., prior knowledge instead of multiple examples).

The next step in the learning process is to generalize the proof tree from the left-hand side of Figure 8.2 into the general tree from the right-hand side. This is done by using the agent's prior knowledge of how to generalize the individual inferences from the specific tree.

While the tree from the left-hand side proves that the specific object o1 is a cup, the tree from the right-hand side proves that any object x that satisfies the leaves of the general tree is a cup. Thus the agent has learned the general cup recognition rule from the bottom of Figure 8.2.

To recognize that another object, o2, is a cup, the agent needs only to check that it satisfies the rule, that is, to check for the presence of these features discovered as important (i.e., light-mat, has-handle, etc.). The agent no longer needs to build a complex proof tree. Therefore, cup recognition is done much faster.

Finally, notice that the agent needs only one example from which to learn. However, it needs a lot of prior knowledge to prove that this example is a cup. Providing such prior knowledge to the agent is a very complex task.

8.1.4   Learning by Analogy

Learning by analogy is the process of learning new knowledge about some entity by transferring it from a known similar entity. The central intuition supporting the learning by analogy paradigm is that if two entities are similar in some respects, then they could be similar in other respects as well.

An important result of the learning by analogy research (Winston, 1980; Carbonell, 1983, 1986; Gentner, 1983; Davies and Russell, 1990; Forbus et al., 1994; Veloso, 1994) is that the analogy involves mapping some underlying causal network of relations between analogous situations. A causal network of relations generally means a set of relations related by higher-order causal-like relations, such as "physical-cause(ri, rj)," "logically-implies(ri, rj)," "enables (ri, rj)," "explains(ri, rj)," "justifies(ri, rj)," "determines(ri, rj)," and so on. The idea is that such similar "causes" are expected to have similar effects. This idea is illustrated in Figure 8.3.

Because A' is similar to A, which causes B, A' is expected to cause something (B') that is similar to B. Thus analogy involves mapping some underlying "causal network of relations" between a (better-known) source entity A and a (less-known) target entity B, with the goal of transferring knowledge from A to B.

For instance, we can teach students about the structure of the hydrogen atom by using the analogy with the solar system (see Figure 8.4): The hydrogen atom is like our Solar System.

We are telling the students that the hydrogen atom has a similar structure with that of the Solar System, where the electrons revolve around the nucleus as the planets revolve around the sun.

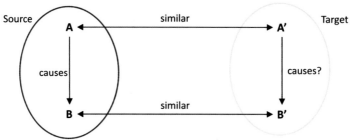

A causes B and A is similar to A'.
Therefore, it is possible that A' causes something (B'), which is similar to B.

Figure 8.3. Analogical reasoning.

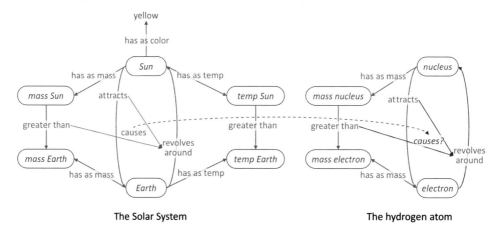

The Solar System   The hydrogen atom

Figure 8.4. Illustration of analogical learning.

The students may then infer that other features of the Solar System are also features of the hydrogen atom. For instance, in the Solar System, the greater mass of the sun and its attraction of the planets cause the planets to revolve around it. Therefore, the students may hypothesize that this causal relationship is also true in the case of the hydrogen atom: The greater mass of the nucleus and its attraction of the electrons cause the electrons to revolve around the nucleus. This is indeed true and represents a very interesting discovery.

The main problem with analogical reasoning is that not all the features of the Solar System are true for the hydrogen atom. For instance, the sun is yellow, but the nucleus is not. Therefore, the information derived by analogy has to be verified.

8.1.5   Multistrategy Learning

As illustrated in Table 8.1, the individual learning strategies have complementary strengths and weaknesses. For instance, inductive learning from example requires a lot of examples while explanation-based learning requires only one example. On the other hand, inductive learning from examples does not require any prior knowledge while explanation-based learning requires complete prior knowledge.

Multistrategy learning attempts to integrate synergistically such complementary learning strategies in order to take advantage of their relative strengths to compensate for

---

Table 8.1 Illustration of the Complementariness of the Learning Strategies

	Inductive learning from examples	Explanation-based learning	Multistrategy learning
Examples needed	many	one	several
Prior knowledge	very little	complete	incomplete
Type of inference	induction	deduction	induction, deduction, . . .
Effect on agent's behavior	improves competence	improves efficiency	improves competence and/or efficiently

---

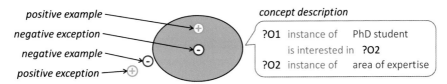

Figure 8.5. Examples and exceptions of a concept.

---

their relative weaknesses. *Multistrategy learning is concerned with developing learning agents that synergistically integrate two or more learning strategies in order to solve learning problems that are beyond the capabilities of the individual learning strategies that are integrated* (Tecuci and Michalski, 1991; Tecuci 1993; Michalski and Tecuci, 1994).

An example of multistrategy learning system is Disciple which integrates learning from examples, learning from explanations, and learning by analogy and experimentation, as will be discussed in Chapters 9 and 10.

8.2   CONCEPTS

8.2.1   Concepts, Examples, and Exceptions

As discussed in Section 5.2, *a concept represents a set of instances.*

With respect to the description of a concept, an instance can be a positive example of the concept, a negative example, a positive exception, or a negative exception, as illustrated in Figure 8.5.

A positive example is an instance of the concept that is covered by the description of the concept.

A negative example is an instance that does not belong to the concept and is not covered by the description of the concept.

A positive exception is a positive example that is not covered by the description of the concept, and any generalization of the description that would cover it would also cover some negative examples.

A negative exception is a negative example that is covered by the description of the concept, and any specialization of the description that would uncover it would also uncover some positive examples.

The generalization and the specialization of concepts will be discussed in the following sections.

8.2.2   Examples and Exceptions of a Partially Learned Concept

Figure 8.6 shows the representation of a partially learned concept consisting of the *Plausible Version Space of the Main Condition* (with the plausible upper bound in light green and the plausible lower bound in dark green) and *the Plausible Version Space of an Except-When Condition* (with the plausible upper bound in light red and the plausible lower bound in dark red). In general, a partially learned concept has a plausible version space of a Main condition, and none, one, or several plausible version spaces of Except-When conditions.

A partially learned concept may have known positive and negative examples. For the other instances of the representation space, one may estimate their nature based on their actual position with respect to the plausible bounds of the concept, as illustrated in Figure 8.6 and defined in the following.

An instance covered by the plausible lower bound of the Main condition of the concept and not covered by the plausible version space of any Except-When condition is *most likely* a positive example of the concept.

An instance covered by the plausible upper bound of the Main condition of the concept, but not covered by the plausible lower bound of the Main condition and not covered by the plausible version space of any Except-When condition, is *likely* to be a positive example of the concept.

An instance covered by the plausible lower bound of one of the Except-When plausible version space conditions of the concept is *most likely* a negative example of the concept.

Finally, an instance covered by the plausible upper bound of an Except-When plausible version space condition of the concept is *likely* to be a negative example of the concept.

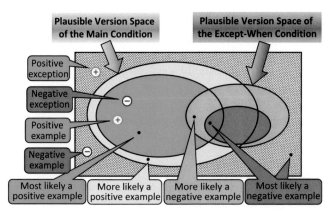

Figure 8.6. Examples and exceptions of a partially learned concept.

In the next sections, we will describe in detail the basic learning operations dealing with concepts: the *generalization of concepts*, the *specialization concepts,* and the *comparison of the generality of the concepts.*

8.3 GENERALIZATION AND SPECIALIZATION RULES

A concept was defined as representing a set of instances. In order to show that a concept P is more general than a concept Q, this definition would require the computation and comparison of the (possibly infinite) sets of the instances of P and Q. In this section, we will introduce generalization and specialization rules that will allow one to prove that a concept P is *more general than* another concept Q by manipulating the descriptions of P and Q, without computing the sets of instances that they represent.

A generalization rule is a rule that transforms (the description of) a concept into (the description of) a more general concept. The generalization rules are usually inductive transformations. The inductive transformations are not truth preserving but falsity preserving. That is, if P is true and is inductively generalized to Q, then the truth of Q is not guaranteed. However, if P is false, then Q is also false.

A specialization rule is a rule that transforms a concept into a less general concept. The reverse of any generalization rule is a specialization rule. Specialization rules are deductive, truth-preserving transformations.

A reformulation rule transforms a concept into another, logically equivalent concept. Reformulation rules are also deductive, truth-preserving transformations.

If one can transform concept P into concept Q by applying a sequence of generalization rules, then Q is more general than P.

Consider the phrase, "Students who have majored in computer science at George Mason University between 2007 and 2008." The following are some of the phrases that are obvious generalizations of this phrase:

- "Students who have majored in computer science between 2007 and 2008"
- "Students who have majored in computer science between 2000 and 2012"
- "Students who have majored in computer science at George Mason University"
- "Students who have majored in computer science"

Some of the phrases that are specializations of the preceding phrase follow:

- "Graduate students who have majored in computer science at George Mason University between 2007 and 2008"
- "Students who have majored in computer science at George Mason University in 2007"
- "Undergraduate students who have majored in both computer science and mathematics at George Mason University in 2008"

It will be easy to demonstrate the generalization relationships between the preceding phrases by using some of the following generalization rules, which will be described in the following sections:

- Turning constants into variables
- Turning occurrences of a variable into different variables
- Climbing the generalization hierarchies

- Dropping conditions
- Extending intervals
- Extending ordered sets of intervals
- Extending discrete sets
- Using feature definitions
- Using inference rules

8.3.1   Turning Constants into Variables

The turning constants into variables generalization rule consists in generalizing an expression by replacing a constant with a variable. For example, expression [8.1] represents the following concept: "The set of professors with 55 publications."

E1 = ?O1	instance of	professor	[8.1]
	number of publications	55	

By replacing 55 with the variable ?N1, which can take any value, we generalize this concept to the one shown in [8.2]: "The set of professors with any number of publications." In particular, ?N1 could be 55. Therefore the second concept includes the first one.

E2 = ?O1	instance of	professor	[8.2]
	number of publications	?N1	

Conversely, by replacing ?N1 with 55, we specialize the concept [8.2] to the concept [8.1]. The important thing to notice here is that by a simple syntactic operation (turning a number into a variable), we can generalize a concept. This is one way in which an agent generalizes concepts.

8.3.2   Turning Occurrences of a Variable into Different Variables

According to this rule, the expression [8.3] may be generalized to the expression [8.4] by turning the two occurrences of the variable ?O3 in E1 into two variables, ?O31 and ?O32:

E1 = ?O1	instance of	paper	[8.3]
	is authored by	?O3	
?O2	instance of	paper	
	is authored by	?O3	
?O3	instance of	professor	
E2 = ?O1	instance of	paper	[8.4]
	is authored by	?O31	
?O2	instance of	paper	
	is authored by	?O32	
?O31	instance of	professor	
?O32	instance of	professor	

E1 may be interpreted as representing the concept: "the papers ?O1 and ?O2 authored by the professor ?O3." E2 may be interpreted as representing the concept: "the papers ?O1 and ?O2 authored by the professors ?O31 and ?O32, respectively." In particular, ?O31 and ?O32 may represent the same professor. Therefore, the second set includes the first one, and the second expression is more general than the first one.

8.3.3 Climbing the Generalization Hierarchies

One can generalize an expression by replacing a concept from its description with a more general concept, according to some generalization hierarchy. For instance, the expression [8.5] may be generalized to [8.6] by replacing the concept assistant professor with the more general concept professor (see the generalization hierarchy in Figure 5.4, p. 158). The reverse operation of replacing a concept with a less general one leads to the specialization of an expression.

E1 = ?O1	instance of	assistant professor	[8.5]
	has as employer	?O2	
?O2	instance of	state university	
E2 = ?O1	instance of	professor	[8.6]
	has as employer	?O2	
?O2	instance of	state university	

8.3.4 Dropping Conditions

The agent can generalize a concept by dropping a condition, that is, by dropping a constraint that its instances must satisfy. For example, the expression [8.7] may be generalized to [8.8] by removing the constraint on the professor to be employed by a state university.

E1 = ?O1	instance of	assistant professor	[8.7]
	has as employer	?O2	
?O2	instance of	state university	
E2 = ?O1	instance of	assistant professor	[8.8]

8.3.5 Extending Intervals

A number may be generalized to an interval containing it. For example, the expression [8.9] (the set of professors with 55 publications) may be generalized to [8.10] (the set of professors with 50 to 60 publications), which in turn may be generalized to [8.11] (the set of professors with 25 to 75 publications).

E1 = ?O1	instance of	professor	[8.9]
	number of publications	55	
E2 = ?O1	instance of	professor	[8.10]
	number of publications	?N1	
?N1	is in	[50, 60]	
E3 = ?O1	instance of	professor	[8.11]
	number of publications	?N1	
?N1	is in	[25, 75]	

8.3.6   Extending Ordered Sets of Intervals

An ordered set of intervals is an ordered set of symbols where each symbol corresponds to an interval. For example, "infant" corresponds to the interval "(0.0, 1.0)," and "toddler" corresponds to the interval "[1.0, 4.5)." Obviously infant < toddler. Such an ordered set of intervals may be regarded as an ordered generalization hierarchy, where the nodes are ordered from left to right, as illustrated in Figure 8.7.

Using such an ordered set of intervals, one may generalize the expression [8.12] (persons from youth to teen) to the expression [8.13] (persons from youth to mature) by replacing the symbolic interval "[youth – teen]" with the larger interval "[youth – mature]."

E1 = ?O1	instance of	person	[8.12]
	has as age	[youth – teen]	
E1 = ?O1	instance of	person	[8.13]
	has as age	[youth – mature]	

8.3.7   Extending Symbolic Probabilities

A symbolic probability may be generalized by replacing it with a symbolic probability interval containing it. For example, "very likely" may be generalized to the interval "[likely – very likely]" (which includes the values "likely" and "very likely"). This interval can be further generalized by replacing it with a larger interval, such as "[likely – certain]."

8.3.8   Extending Discrete Sets

An expression may be generalized by replacing a discrete set with a larger discrete set that includes the first set. For example, the expression [8.14] (the set of flags with white color, or red color, or both) may be generalized to the expression [8.15] (the set of flags with white color, or red color, or blue color, or any combination of these colors).

E1 = ?O1	instance of	flag	[8.14]
	includes colors from	{white, red}	
E2 = ?O1	instance of	flag	[8.15]
	includes colors from	{white, red, blue}	

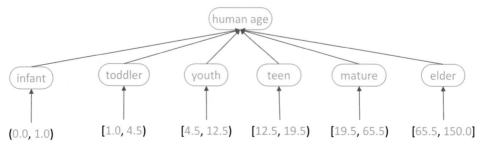

Figure 8.7. Ordered set of intervals as an ordered generalization hierarchy.

8.3.9   Using Feature Definitions

This rule generalizes an expression containing a feature, such as, "A feature B," by replacing A and B with the domain and the range of feature, respectively.

This rule is illustrated by the generalization of the expression [8.16] (professors who are experts in computer science) to the expression [8.17] (persons who are experts in some area of expertise).

E1 = ?O1	instance of	professor	[8.16]
	is expert in	?O2	
?O2	instance of	Computer Science	
E2 = ?O1	instance of	person	[8.17]
	is expert in	?O2	
?O2	instance of	area of expertise	

In the preceding example, professor was generalized to person (the domain of is expert in), and Computer Science was generalized to area of expertise (the range of is expert in).

In general, a generalization rule indicates how one can generalize a concept through a simple syntactic transformation without suggesting the actual generalization to perform, but only a set of possible generalizations. The *using feature definition rule* actually suggests a generalization to perform, which will be useful during learning. In fact, it indicates the most general generalization that can be performed. Indeed, ?O1 in [8.16] has the feature is expert in. Therefore, it has to be in the domain of this feature, which is person. Similarly, ?O2 is the value of the feature is expert in. Therefore, it has to be in the range of this feature, which is area of expertise.

8.3.10   Using Inference Rules

Given an inference rule of the form "A ➔ B," one may generalize an expression by replacing A with B. For example, using the theorem [8.18] one may generalize the expression [8.19] (students and their PhD advisors) to the expression [8.20] (students and the professors they know).

∀X, ∀Y ((X has as PhD advisor Y) ➔ (X knows Y))			[8.18]

E1 = ?O1	instance of	student	[8.19]
	has as PhD advisor	?O2	
?O2	instance of	professor	
E2 = ?O1	instance of	student	[8.20]
	knows	?O2	
?O2	instance of	professor	

Indeed, by applying the preceding inference rule, one may transform E1 into the equivalent expression E'1 shown in [8.21]. Then, by dropping the relation has as PhD advisor, one generalizes E'1 into E2.

E'1 = ?O1	instance of	student	[8.21]
	has as PhD advisor	?O2	
	knows	?O2	
?O2	instance of	professor	

8.4   TYPES OF GENERALIZATIONS AND SPECIALIZATIONS

Up to this point we have only defined when a concept is more general than another concept. Learning agents, however, would need to generalize sets of examples and concepts. In the following we define some of these generalizations.

8.4.1   Definition of Generalization

As defined in Section 5.3, a concept P is said to be more general than another concept Q if and only if the set of instances represented by P includes the set of instances represented by Q.

If a concept Q can be transformed into another concept P by applying a sequence of generalization rules, then P is more general than Q. Indeed, the application of each successive generalization rule generalizes the concept Q, as shown in the previous sections. As an illustration, consider the concept C1 in [8.22] and the concept C2 in [8.23].

C1 = ?O1	instance of	assistant professor	[8.22]
	number of publications	10	
	is employed by	George Mason University	
C2 = ?O1	instance of	professor	[8.23]
	number of publications	?N1	
?N1	is in	[10, 35]	

To show that [8.23] is more general than [8.22] it is enough to show that [8.22] can be transformed into [8.23] by applying a sequence of generalization rules. The sequence is the following one:

- Generalize assistant professor to professor (climbing the generalization hierarchy).
- Generalize 10 to [10, 35] (extending a number to an interval).
- Drop "?O1 is employed by George Mason University" (dropping condition).

8.4.2   Minimal Generalization

The concept P is a minimal generalization of a different concept Q if and only if P is a generalization of Q, and P is not more general than any other generalization of Q.

Consider the generalization hierarchy from Figure 8.8 and the concepts from Figure 8.9. G3 is a minimal generalization of G2 because there is no concept in Figure 8.8 which is more general than student and less general than person.

However, G3 is not a minimal generalization of G1. Indeed, the concept G4 in [8.24] is more general than G1 and less general than G3.

G4 = ?O1	instance of	employee	[8.24]
	is interested in	?O2	
?O2	instance of	area of expertise	

If the minimal generalization of a concept is unique, it is called the *least general generalization*.

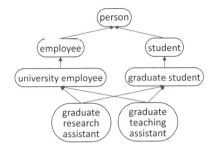

Figure 8.8. Fragment of a generalization hierarchy.

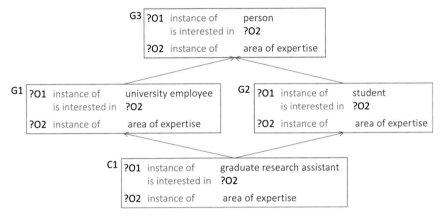

Figure 8.9. Illustration of a minimal generalization.

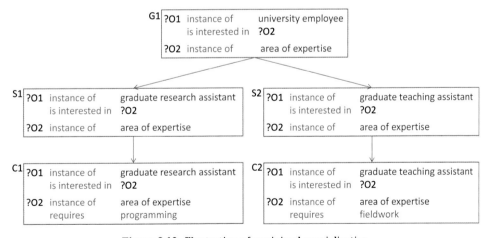

Figure 8.10. Illustration of a minimal specialization.

8.4.3   Minimal Specialization

The concept Q is a minimal specialization of a different concept P if and only if Q is a specialization of P, and no other specialization of P is more general than Q. For example, consider the generalization hierarchy from Figure 8.8 and the concepts from Figure 8.10. Clearly C1 and C2 are not minimal specializations of G1. However, both S1 and S2 are minimal specializations of G1.

8.4.4   Generalization of Two Concepts

The concept Cg is a generalization of the concepts C1 and C2 if and only if Cg is more general than C1 and Cg is more general than C2. One may show that if both the concept C1 and the concept C2 can be transformed into the concept Cg by applying generalization rules, then Cg is a generalization of C1 and C2.

As an illustration, consider the concept C1 described by the expression [8.25], and the concept C2 described by the expression [8.26]. One may easily show that the concept C described by the expression [8.27] is a generalization of C1 and C2. Indeed, by generalizing assistant professor to professor (through climbing the generalization hierarchy), by generalizing 10 to [10, 35] (through replacing a number with an interval containing it), and by dropping the condition "?O1 is employed by George Mason University," one generalizes C1 to C. Similarly, by generalizing associate professor to professor, and 35 to [10, 35], one generalizes C2 into C. Therefore, C is a generalization of C1 and C2.

C1 = ?O1	instance of	assistant professor	[8.25]
	number of publications	10	
	is employed by	George Mason University	
C2 = ?O1	instance of	associate professor	[8.26]
	number of publications	35	
C = ?O1	instance of	professor	[8.27]
	number of publications	?N1	
?N1	is in	[10, 35]	

In general, to determine a generalization of two concepts, each represented as a clause, such as [8.25] and [8.26], one first matches the features of the two concepts. Then one applies the dropping condition rule to remove the unmatched features (and possibly even matched features). Finally, one applies other generalization rules to determine the generalizations of the matched feature values. Notice that usually there are several generalizations of two concepts.

In a similar way, one can determine a generalization G of two more complex expressions E1 and E2, each consisting of a conjunction of clauses. G will consist of the conjunction of the generalizations of some of the corresponding clauses in the two expressions E1 and E2.

8.4.5   Minimal Generalization of Two Concepts

The concept G is a minimal generalization of the concepts C1 and C2 if and only if G is a generalization of C1 and C2, and G is not more general than any other generalization of C1 and C2.

To determine a minimal generalization of two clauses, one has to keep *all* the common features of the clauses and determine a minimal generalization of each of the matched feature values. In a similar way, one determines the minimal generalization of two conjunctions of clauses by matching the clauses and determining the minimal generalizations of the matched clauses. These procedures are correct if we assume that there are no other common features due to theorems. Otherwise, all the common features will have to first be made explicit by applying the theorems.

Notice, however, that there may be more than one minimal generalization of two expressions. For instance, according to the generalization hierarchy from the middle of Figure 8.8, there are two minimal generalizations of graduate research assistant and graduate teaching assistant. They are university employee and graduate student. Consequently, there are two minimal generalizations of S1 and S2 in Figure 8.11: mG1 and mG2. The generalization mG1 was obtained by generalizing graduate research assistant and graduate teaching assistant to university employee. mG2 was obtained in a similar fashion, except that graduate research assistant and graduate teaching assistant were generalized to graduate student. Neither mG1 nor mG2 is more general than the other. However, G3 is more general than each of them.

Disciple agents employ minimal generalizations, also called maximally specific generalizations (Plotkin, 1970; Kodratoff and Ganascia, 1986). They also employ maximal generalizations, also called maximally general generalizations (Tecuci and Kodratoff, 1990; Tecuci, 1992; Tecuci 1998).

8.4.6 Specialization of Two Concepts

The concept Cs is a specialization of the concepts C1 and C2 if and only if Cs is less general than C1 and Cs is less general than C2. For example, research professor is a specialization of researcher and professor.

One can easily show that if both the concept C1 and the concept C2 can be transformed into the concept Cs by applying specialization rules (or Cs can be transformed into C1, and it can also be transformed into C2 by applying generalization rules), then Cs is a specialization of C1 and C2.

8.4.7 Minimal Specialization of Two Concepts

The concept C is a minimal specialization of two concepts C1 and C2 if and only if C is a specialization of C1 and C2 and no other specialization of C1 and C2 is more general than C.

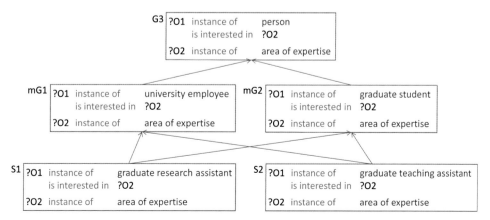

Figure 8.11. Several generalizations of the concepts S1 and S2.

The minimal specialization of two clauses consists of the minimal specialization of the matched feature-value pairs, and of all the unmatched feature-value pairs. This procedure assumes that no new clause feature can be made explicit by applying theorems. Otherwise, one has first to make all the features explicit.

The minimal specialization of two conjunctions of clauses C1 and C2 consists of the conjunction of the minimal specializations of each of the matched clauses of C1 and C2, and of all the unmatched clauses from C1 and C2.

Figure 8.12 shows several specializations of the concepts G1 and G2. mS1 and mS2 are two minimal specializations of G1 and G2 because graduate research assistant and graduate teaching assistant are two minimal specializations of university employee and graduate student.

Notice that in all the preceding definitions and illustrations, we have assumed that the clauses to be generalized correspond to the same variables. If this assumption is not satisfied, then one would need first to match the variables and then compute the generalizations. In general, this process is computationally expensive because one will need to try different matchings.

INDUCTIVE CONCEPT LEARNING FROM EXAMPLES

Inductive concept learning from examples has already been introduced in Section 8.1.2. In this section, we will discuss various aspects of this learning strategy that are relevant to agent teaching and learning. The problem of inductive concept learning from examples can be more precisely defined as indicated in Table 8.2.

The *bias* of the learning agent is any basis for choosing one generalization over another, other than strict consistency with the observed training examples (Mitchell, 1997). In the following, we will consider two agents that employ two different preference biases: a cautious learner that always prefers minimal generalizations, and an aggressive learner that always prefers maximal generalizations.

Let us consider the positive examples [8.28] and [8.29], and the negative example [8.30] of a concept to be learned by these two agents in the context of the generalization hierarchies from Figure 8.13.

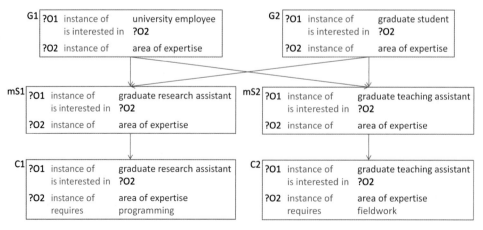

Figure 8.12. Several specializations of the concepts G1 and G2.

Table 8.2 The Problem of Inductive Concept Learning from Examples

Given

- A language of instances.
- A language of generalizations.
- A set of positive examples ($E_1, \ldots, E_n$) of a concept.
- A set of negative (or counter) examples ($C_1, \ldots, C_m$) of the same concept.
- A learning bias.
- Other background knowledge.

Determine
A concept description that is a generalization of the positive
examples and that does not cover any of the negative examples.

Purpose of concept learning
Predict if an instance is a positive example of the learned concept.

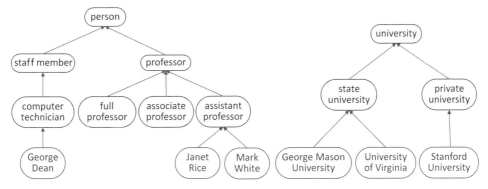

Figure 8.13. Two generalization hierarchies.

Positive examples:

Mark White	instance of	assistant professor	[8.28]
	is employed by	George Mason University	
Janet Rice	instance of	assistant professor	[8.29]
	is employed by	University of Virginia	

Negative example:

| George Dean | instance of | computer technician | [8.30] |
| | is employed by | Stanford University | |

What concept might be learned by the cautious learner from the positive examples [8.28] and [8.29], and the negative example [8.30]? The cautious learner would learn a minimal generalization of the positive examples, which does not cover the negative example. Such a minimal generalization might be the expression [8.31], "an assistant professor employed by a state university," obtained by minimally generalizing George Mason University and University of Virginia to state university.

?O1	instance of	assistant professor	[8.31]
	is employed by	?O2	
?O2	instance of	state university	

The concept learned by the cautious learner is represented in Figure 8.14 as the minimal ellipse that covers the positive examples without covering the negative example. Assuming a complete ontology, the learned concept is included into the actual concept.

How will the cautious learner classify each of the instances represented in Figure 8.14 as black dots? It will classify the dot covered by the learned concept as positive example, and the two dots that are not covered by the learned concept as negative examples.

How confident are you in the classification, when the learner predicts that an instance is a positive example? When a cautious learner classifies an instance as a positive example of a concept, this classification is correct because an instance covered by the learned concept is also covered by the actual concept.

But how confident are you in the classification, when the learner predicts that an instance is a negative example? The learner may make mistakes when classifying an instance as a negative example, such as the black dot that is covered by the actual concept but not by the learned concept. This type of error is called "error of omission" because some positive examples are omitted – that is, they are classified as negative examples.

Let us now consider the concept that might be learned by the aggressive learner from the positive examples [8.28] and [8.29], and the negative example [8.30]. The aggressive learner will learn a maximal generalization of the positive examples that does not cover the negative example. Such a maximal generalization might be the expression [8.32], "a professor employed by a university." This is obtained by generalizing assistant professor to professor (the most general generalization that does not cover computer technician from the negative example) and by maximally generalizing George Mason University and University of Virginia to university. Although university covers Stanford University, this is fine because the obtained concept [8.32] still does not cover the negative example [8.30].

?O1	instance of	professor	[8.32]
	is employed by	?O2	
?O2	instance of	university	

An alternative maximally general generalization of the positive examples [8.28] and [8.29], which does not cover the negative example [8.30], is [8.33].

?O1	instance of	person	[8.33]
	is employed by	?O2	
?O2	instance of	state university	

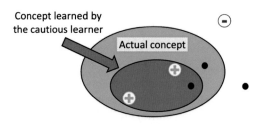

Figure 8.14. Learning and classifications by a cautious learner.

The concept learned by the aggressive learner is represented in Figure 8.15 as the maximal ellipse that covers the positive examples without covering the negative example. Assuming a complete ontology, the learned concept includes the actual concept.

How will the aggressive learner classify each of the instances represented in Figure 8.15 as black dots? It will classify the dot that is outside the learned concept as a negative example, and the other dots as positive examples.

How confident are you in the classification when the learner predicts that an instance is negative example? When the learner predicts that an instance is a negative example, this classification is correct because that instance is not covered by the actual concept, which is itself covered by the learned concept.

But, how confident are you in the classification when the learner predicts that an instance is a positive example? The learner may make mistakes when predicting that an instance is a positive example, as is the case with the dot covered by the learned concept, but not by the actual concept. This type of error is called "error of commission" because some negative examples are committed – that is, they are classified as positive examples.

Notice the interesting fact that the aggressive learner is correct when it classifies instances as negative examples (they are indeed outside the actual concept because they are outside the concept learned by the aggressive learner) while the cautious learner is correct when it classifies instances as positive examples (they are inside the actual concept because they are inside the concept learned by the cautious learner). How could one synergistically integrate these two learning strategies to take advantage of their complementariness? An obvious solution is to use both strategies, learning both a minimal and a maximal generalization from the examples, as illustrated in Figure 8.16.

What class will be predicted by a dual-strategy learner for the instances represented as black dots in Figure 8.16? The dot covered by the concept learned by the cautious learner

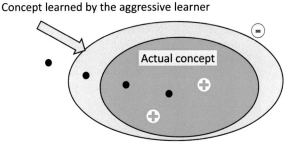

Figure 8.15. Learning and classifications by an aggressive learner.

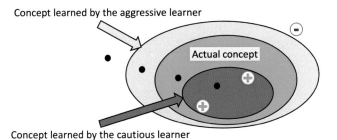

Figure 8.16. Learning and classifications by a dual-strategy learner.

will be classified, with high confidence, as a positive example. The dot that is not covered by the concept learned by the aggressive learner will be classified, again with high confidence, as a negative example. The dual-strategy learner will indicate that it cannot classify the other two dots.

8.6   LEARNING WITH AN INCOMPLETE REPRESENTATION LANGUAGE

Let us consider the ontology from Figure 8.17. What is the maximal generalization of the positive examples John Doe and Jane Austin that does not cover the given negative example Bob Sharp, in the case where graduate research assistant is included into the ontology? The maximal generalization is faculty member.

But what is the maximal generalization in the case where graduate research assistant is missing from the ontology? In this case, the maximal generalization is employee, which is, in fact, an *overgeneralization*.

What is the minimal specialization of person that does not cover Bob Sharp in the case where graduate research assistant is included into the ontology? It is faculty member.

But what is the minimal specialization in the case where graduate research assistant is missing from the ontology? In this case, the minimal specialization is employee, which is an *underspecialization*.

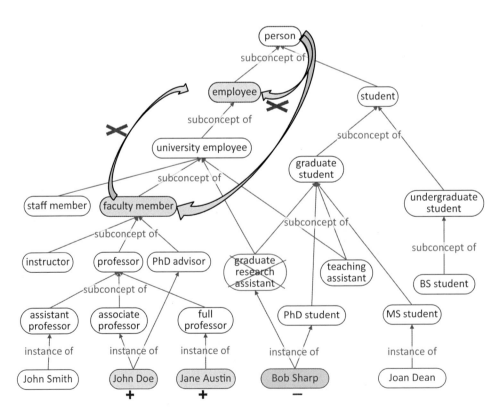

Figure 8.17. Plausible generalizations and specializations due to ontology incompleteness.

Notice that the incompleteness of the ontology causes the learner both to overgeneralize and underspecialize. In view of the preceding observations, what can be said about the relationships between the concepts learned using minimal and maximal generalizations and the actual concept when the ontology and the representation language are incomplete? The minimal and maximal generalizations are only approximations of the actual concept, as shown in Figure 8.18.

Why is the concept learned with an aggressive strategy more general than the one learned with a cautious strategy? Because they are based on the same ontology and generalization rules.

8.7   FORMAL DEFINITION OF GENERALIZATION

8.7.1   Formal Representation Language for Concepts

A knowledge representation language defines the syntax and the semantics for expressing knowledge in a form that an agent can use. We define a formal representation language for concepts as follows:

- Let $\mathcal{V}$ be a set of *variables.* For convenience in identifying variables, their names start with "?," as in, for instance, ?O1. Variables are used to denote unspecified instances of concepts.
- Let $\mathcal{C}$ be a set of *constants.* Examples of constants are the numbers (such as "5"), strings (such as "programming"), symbolic probability values (such as "very likely"), and instances (such as "John Doe"). We define a *term* to be either a variable or a constant.
- Let $\mathcal{F}$ be a set of *features.* The set $\mathcal{F}$ includes the domain independent features "instance of," "subconcept of," and "direct subconcept of," as well as other domain-specific features, such as "is interested in."
- Let O be an object ontology consisting of a set of concepts and instances defined using the clause representation [7.2] presented in Section 7.2, where the feature values $(v_{i1} \ldots v_{im})$ are constants, concepts, instances, or intervals (numeric or symbolic). That is, there are no variables in the definition of a concept or an instance from O, such as the following one:

instance-k   instance of   concept-i

                    feature-i_1 vi_1

                    . . .

                    feature-i_n vi_m

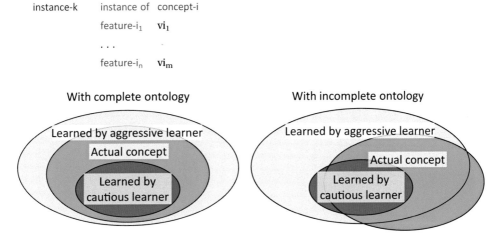

Figure 8.18. The influence of the ontology on concept learning.

- The concepts and the instances from O are related by the generalization relations "instance of" and "subconcept of." O includes the concept object, which represents all the instances from the application domain and is therefore more general than any other object concept.
- Let $\mathcal{H}$ be the set of the theorems and the properties of the features, variables, and constants.
- Two properties of any feature are its domain and its range. Other features may have special properties. For instance, the relation subconcept of is transitive (see Section 5.7). Also, a concept or an instance inherits the features of the concepts that are more general than it (see Section 5.8).
- Let $\mathcal{N}$ be a set of connectors. $\mathcal{N}$ includes the logical connectors AND ($\wedge$), OR ($\vee$), and NOT (Except–When), the connectors "{" and "}" for defining alternative values of a feature, the connectors "[" and "]" as well as "(" and ")" for defining a numeric or a symbolic interval, the delimiter "," (a comma), and the symbols "Plausible Upper Bound" and "Plausible Lower Bound."

We call the tuple $\mathcal{L} = (\mathcal{V}, \mathcal{C}, \mathcal{F}, O, \mathcal{H}, \mathcal{N})$ a *representation language* for concepts.

The basic representation unit (BRU) for a concept in $\mathcal{L}$ has the form of a tuple (?O1, ?O2,..., ?On), where each ?Oi is a *clause*:

?O1	instance of	concept-i
	feature-1_1	?Oj
	. . .	
	feature-1_i	?Ol
	. . .	
?On	instance of	concept-n
	feature-n_1	?Op
	. . .	
	feature-n_k	?Ot

In the preceding expression, each of concept-i . . . concept-n is either an object concept from the object ontology (such as PhD student), a numeric interval (such as [50, 60]), a set of numbers (such as {1, 3, 5}), a set of strings (such as {white, red, blue}), a symbolic probability interval (such as [likely - very likely]), or an ordered set of intervals (such as [youth - mature]). ?Oj, . . . , ?Ol,. . ., ?Op, . . . , ?Ot are distinct variables from the sequence (?O1, ?O2, . . . , ?On). When concept-n is a set or interval such as "[50, 60]," we use "is in" instead of "instance of."

A more complex concept is defined as a conjunctive expression "BRU $\wedge$ not BRU$_1$ $\wedge$ ... $\wedge$ not BRU$_p$," where "BRU" and each "BRU$_k$ (k = 1, . . . , p)" is a conjunction of clauses. This is illustrated by the following example, which represents the set of instances of the tuple (?O1, ?O2, ?O3), where ?O1 is a professor employed by a university ?O2 in a long-term position ?O3, such that it is not true that ?O1 plans to retire from ?O2 or to move to some other organization:

?O1	instance of	professor
	has as employer	?O2
	has as position	?O3
?O2	instance of	university
?O3	instance of	long-term faculty position

Not

?O1	instance of	professor
	plans to retire from	?O2
?O2	instance of	university

Not

?O1	instance of	professor
	plans to move to	?O4
?O4	instance of	organization

We generally use "Except-When" instead of "Not."

In the following sections, we will provide a formal definition of generalization in the representation language $\mathcal{L}$, based on substitutions.

A substitution is a function $\sigma = (x_1 \leftarrow t_1, \ldots, x_n \leftarrow t_n)$, where each x_i ($i = 1, \ldots, n$) is a variable and each t_i ($i = 1, \ldots, n$) is a term.

If l_i is an expression in the representation language $\mathcal{L}$, then σl_i is the expression obtained by substituting each variable x_i from l_i with the term t_i.

8.7.2 Term Generalization

In the representation language $\mathcal{L}$, a term is a constant (e.g., number, string, symbolic interval, or instance) or a variable. An unrestricted variable ?X is more general than any constant and is as general as any other unrestricted variable (such as ?Y).

8.7.3 Clause Generalization

Let us consider two concepts described by the following two clauses, C1 and C2, respectively, where $v_1, v_2, v_{11}, \ldots, v_{2n}$ are variables, b_1 and b_2 are concepts, and $f_{11}, \ldots, f_{2n}$ are features from the ontology.

C1 =	v_1	instance of	b_1
		f_{11}	v_{11}
		$\ldots$	
		f_{1m}	v_{1m}
C2 =	v_2	instance of	b_2
		f_{21}	v_{21}
		$\ldots$	
		f_{2n}	v_{2n}

We say that the clause C1 is *more general than* the clause C2 if there exists a substitution σ such that:

$$\sigma v_1 = v_2$$
$$b_1 = b_2$$
$$\forall i \in \{1, \ldots, m\}, \exists j \in \{1, \ldots, n\} \text{ such that } f_{1i} = f_{2j} \text{ and } \sigma v_{1i} = v_{2j}.$$

For example, the concept

C1 =	?X	instance of	student
		enrolled at	George Mason University

is more general than the concept

C2 =	?Y	instance of	student
	enrolled at	George Mason University
	has as sex	female

Indeed, let $\sigma = (?X \leftarrow ?Y)$. As one can see, $\sigma C1$ is a part of C2, that is, each feature of $\sigma C1$ is also a feature of C2. The first concept represents the set of all students enrolled at George Mason University, while the second one represents the set of all female students enrolled at George Mason University. Obviously the first set includes the second one, and therefore the first concept is more general than the second one.

Let us notice, however, that this definition of generalization does not take into account the theorems and properties of the representation language $\mathcal{L}$. In general, one needs to use these theorems and properties to transform the clauses C1 and C2 into equivalent clauses C'1 and C'2, respectively, by making explicit all the properties of these clauses. Then one shows that C'1 is *more general than* C'2. Therefore, the definition of the *more general than* relation in $\mathcal{L}$ is the following one:

A clause C1 is *more general than* another clause C2 if and only if there exist C'1, C'2, and a substitution σ, such that:

$$C'1 =_{\mathcal{L}} C1$$

$$C'2 =_{\mathcal{L}} C2$$

$$\sigma v_1 =_{\mathcal{L}} v_2$$

$$b_1 \text{ is more general than } b_2 \text{ in } \mathcal{L}$$

$$\forall\, i \in \{1, \ldots, m\}, \exists\, j \in \{1, \ldots, n\} \text{ such that } f'_{1i} =_{\mathcal{L}} f'_{2j} \text{ and } \sigma v'_{1i} =_{\mathcal{L}} v'_{2j}.$$

In the following sections, we will always assume that the equality is in $\mathcal{L}$ and we will no longer indicate this.

8.7.4 BRU Generalization

As discussed in Section 8.7.1, a basic representation unit (BRU) is a conjunction of clauses. An example of BRU is the following one where, for notational convenience, we have dropped the AND connector between the clauses:

?O1	instance of	course
	has as reading	?O2
?O2	instance of	publication
	has as author	?O3
?O3	instance of	professor

Therefore, anytime there is a sequence of clauses, they are to be considered as being connected by AND ($\wedge$).

Let us consider two concepts, A and B, defined by the following expressions

$$A = A_1 \wedge A_2 \wedge \ldots \wedge A_n$$

$$B = B_1 \wedge B_2 \wedge \ldots \wedge B_m$$

where each A_i ($i = 1, \ldots, n$) and each B_j ($j = 1, \ldots, m$) is a clause.

A is *more general than* B if and only if there exist A', B', and σ such that:

$$A' = A, A' = A'_1 \wedge A'_2 \wedge \ldots \wedge A'_p$$

$$B' = B, B' = B'_1 \wedge B'_2 \wedge \ldots \wedge B'_q$$

$$\forall \, i \in \{1, \ldots, p\}, \exists \, j \in \{1, \ldots, q\} \text{ such that } \sigma A'_i = B'_j.$$

Otherwise stated, one transforms the concepts A and B, using the theorems and the properties of the representation language, so as to make each clause from A' more general than a corresponding clause from B'. Notice that some clauses from B' may be "left over," that is, they are not matched by any clause of A'.

8.7.5 Generalization of Concepts with Negations

By concept with negations, we mean an expression of the following form:

$$\text{BRU} \wedge \text{not BRU}_1 \wedge \ldots \wedge \text{not BRU}_p$$

where each BRU is a conjunction of clauses.

Let us consider two concepts with negations, A and B, defined by the following expressions:

$$A = \text{BRU}_a \wedge \text{not BRU}_{a1} \wedge \ldots \wedge \text{not BRU}_{ap}$$

$$B = \text{BRU}_b \wedge \text{not BRU}_{b1} \wedge \ldots \wedge \text{not BRU}_{bq}$$

A is *more general than* B if and only if there exist A', B', and σ, such that:

$$A' = A, A' = \text{BRU}'_a \wedge \text{not BRU}'_{a1} \wedge \ldots \wedge \text{not BRU}'_{ap}$$

$$B' = B, B' = \text{BRU}'_b \wedge \text{not BRU}'_{b1} \wedge \ldots \wedge \text{not BRU}'_{bq}$$

$$\sigma\text{BRU}'_a \text{ is more general than } \text{BRU}'_b$$

$$\forall \, i \in \{1, \ldots, p\}, \exists \, j \in \{1, \ldots, q\} \text{ such that } \text{BRU}'_{bj} \text{ is more general than } \sigma\text{BRU}'_{ai}.$$

8.7.6 Substitutions and the Generalization Rules

One can use the definition of generalization based on substitution to prove that the generalization rules transform concepts into more general concepts.

As an illustration, let us consider the turning constants into variables generalization rule (see Section 8.3.1) that transformed the expression E1 from [8.1] on p. 230, into the expression E2 from [8.2] on p. 230. E2 is indeed a generalization of E1 because E1 = σE2, where σ = (?N1←55).

8.8 REVIEW QUESTIONS

8.1. What is a positive example of a concept? What is a negative example of a concept?

8.2. What is a generalization rule? What is a specialization rule? What is a reformulation rule?

8.3.   Name all the generalization rules you know.

8.4.   Define and illustrate the following generalization rule: climbing generalization hierarchies.

8.5.   Briefly describe and illustrate the "turning constants into variables" generalization rule.

8.6.   Define and illustrate the "dropping conditions" generalization rule.

8.7.   Define the minimal generalization G of two concepts A and B. Then define their least general generalization. Do these generalizations always exist?

8.8.   What is a negative exception? What is a positive exception?

8.9.   Indicate three different generalizations of the phrase "History books in the Fenwick Library," and demonstrate that each of them is more general than the given phrase.

8.10.   Give an example of a natural language phrase C that has a concept interpretation.

    (a) Formulate a phrase G that is a generalization of C, and use the generalization rules to demonstrate that G is a generalization of C.
    (b) Formulate a phrase S that is a specialization of C, and use the generalization rules to demonstrate that S is a specialization of C.
    (c) Formulate a phrase D that is neither a generalization of C nor a specialization of C.

8.11. P_3 in Figure 8.19 is a natural language sentence that represents a concept. Fill in each of the other boxes with sentences such that the arrows from the figure represent *all* the "subconcept of" relationships between these concepts. This means, for instance, that P_3 is less general than P_5, P_3 is more general than P_1, and P_3 is more general than P_2. However, P_3 is not more general than P_4, and P_4 is not more general than P_3. Justify each shown "subconcept of" relationship by labeling it with the name of the generalization rule(s) that transform the less general concept into the more general concept. You should use at least three different generalization rules while solving this problem.

8.12.   Draw a picture representing a plausible version space, as well as a positive example, a negative example, a positive exception, and a negative exception. Then briefly define each of these notions.

8.13.   Consider the cells consisting of two bodies, each body having two attributes, number of nuclei (1 or 2), and color (yellow or green). The relative position of

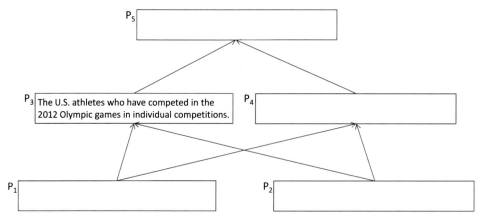

Figure 8.19. Determining concepts that satisfy given "subconcept of" relationships.

the bodies is not relevant because they can move inside the cell. For example, ((1 green) (2 yellow)) is the same with ((2 yellow) (1 green)) and represents a cell where one body has one nucleus and is green, while the other body has two nuclei and is yellow. You should also assume that any generalization of a cell is also described as a pair of pairs ((s t) (u v)).

(a) Indicate *all* the possible generalizations of the cell from Figure 8.20 and the generalization relations between them.

(b) Determine the number of the distinct sets of instances and the number of the concept descriptions from this problem.

(c) Consider the cell descriptions from Figure 8.21 and determine the following minimal generalizations: g(E1, E2), g(E2, E3), g(E3, E1), g(E1, E2, E3).

8.14. Consider the ontology fragment from the loudspeaker manufacturing domain, shown in Figure 5.23 (p. 171), and the following expressions:

E1: ?X	instance of membrane		E2: ?X	instance of mechanical chassis
	made of ?M			made of ?M
?M	instance of paper		?M	instance of metal
?Z	instance of contact adhesive		?Z	instance of mowicoll
	glues ?M			glues ?M
	state fluid			

(a) Find the minimal generalizations of E1 and E2.

(b) Find two generalizations of E1 and E2 that are not minimal generalizations.

(c) Consider one of the generalizations found at (b) and demonstrate that it is a generalization of E1 and E2 but it is not a minimal generalization.

(d) What would be the least general generalization of E1 and E2? Does it exist?

(e) Indicate a specialization of E1.

8.15. Consider the ontology fragment from the loudspeaker manufacturing domain, shown in Figure 5.24 (p. 172). Notice that each most specific concept, such as dust or air press, has an instance, such as dust1 or air press1.

Consider also the following two expressions:

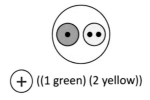

+ ((1 green) (2 yellow))

Figure 8.20. An example of a cell.

E1: ((1 green) (1 green))   E2: ((1 yellow) (2 green))   E3: ((1 green) (2 green))

Figure 8.21. The descriptions of three cells.

E1:	?X	instance of	soft cleaner
		removes	?Z
	?Y	instance of	membrane
	?Z	instance of	waste material
E2:	?X	instance of	air sucker
		removes	?Z
	?Y	instance of	membrane
	?Z	instance of	dust

Use the generalization rules to show that E1 is more general than E2.

8.16. Determine a generalization of the following two expressions in the context of the ontology fragment from Figure 5.24 (p. 172):

E1:	?X	instance of	entrefer
		may have	?Y
	?Y	instance of	dust
	?Z	instance of	air sucker
		removes	?Y
E2:	?X	instance of	membrane
		may have	?Y
	?Y	instance of	surplus adhesive
	?Z	instance of	alcohol
		removes	?Y

8.17. Consider the background knowledge represented by the generalization hierarchies shown in Figure 8.22.
Consider also the following concept:

E:	?O	instance of	object
		color	yellow
		shape	circle
		radius	5

Indicate five different generalization rules. For each such rule, determine an expression Eg that is more general than E according to that rule.

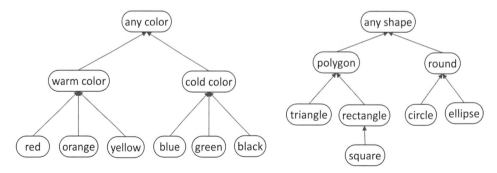

Figure 8.22. Generalization hierarchies for color and shape.

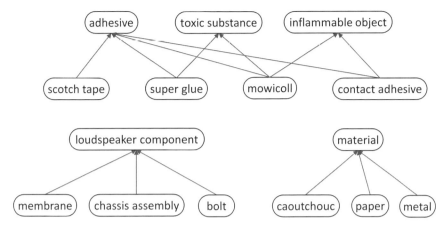

Figure 8.23. Ontology fragments.

8.18. Consider the following two concepts:

C1: ?X	instance of screw	C2: ?X	instance of	nut
	head ?M		cost	6
	cost 5			

Indicate two different generalizations of them.

8.19. Consider the following two concepts G1 and G2, and the ontology fragments in Figure 8.23. Indicate four specializations of G1 and G2 (including a minimal specialization).

G1:?X	instance of	loudspeaker component	G2: ?X	instance of	loudspeaker component
	made of	?M		made of	?M
?M	instance of	material	?M	instance of	material
?Z	instance of	adhesive	?Z	instance of	inflammable object
	glues	?M		glues	?M

8.20. Illustrate the clause generalization defined in Section 8.7.3 with an example from the PhD Advisor Assessment domain.

8.21. Illustrate the BRU generalization defined in Section 8.7.4 with an example from the PhD Advisor Assessment domain.

8.22. Illustrate the generalization of concepts with negations defined in Section 8.7.5 by using an example from the PhD Advisor Assessment domain.

8.23. Use the definition of generalization based on substitution to prove that each of the generalization rules discussed in Section 8.3 transforms a concept into a more general concept.

9 Rule Learning

In this and the next chapter on rule refinement, we will refer to both problems and hypotheses, interchangeably, to emphasize the fact that the learning methods presented are equally applicable in the context of hypotheses analysis and problem solving.

9.1 MODELING, LEARNING, AND PROBLEM SOLVING

Figure 9.1 summarizes the interactions between the subject matter expert and the learning agent that involve modeling, learning, and problem solving.

The expert formulates the problem to be solved (or the hypothesis to be analyzed), and the agent uses its knowledge to generate a (problem-solving or argumentation) tree to be verified by the expert.

Several cases are possible. If the problem is not completely solved, the expert will extend the tree with additional reductions and provide solutions for the leaf problems/hypotheses.

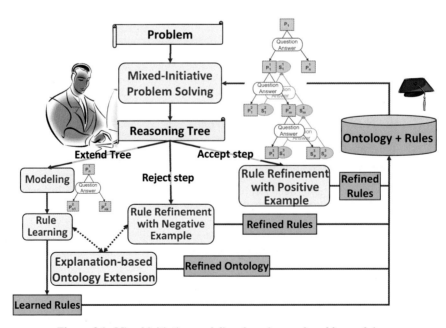

Figure 9.1. Mixed-initiative modeling, learning, and problem solving.

From each new reduction provided by the expert, the agent will learn a new rule, as will be presented in the following sections.

If the expert rejects any of the reasoning steps generated by the agent, then an explanation of why that reduction is wrong needs to be determined, and the rule that generated it will be refined to no longer generate the wrong reasoning step.

If the expert accepts a reasoning step as correct, then the rule that generated it may be generalized. The following section illustrates these interactions.

9.2   AN ILLUSTRATION OF RULE LEARNING AND REFINEMENT

As will be discussed in the following, the subject matter expert helps the agent to learn by providing examples and explanations, and the agent helps the expert to teach it by presenting attempted solutions.

First, as illustrated in Figure 9.2, the expert formulates the problem to solve or the hypothesis to analyze which, in this illustration, is the following hypothesis:

John Doe would be a good PhD advisor for Bob Sharp.

In this case, we will assume that the agent does not know how to assess this hypothesis. Therefore, the expert has to teach the agent how to assess it. The expert will start by developing a reduction tree, as discussed in Chapter 4 and illustrated in the middle of Figure 9.2. The initial hypothesis is first reduced to three simpler hypotheses, guided by a question/answer pair. Then each of the subhypotheses is further reduced, either to a solution/assessment or to an elementary hypothesis to be assessed based on evidence. For example, the bottom part of Figure 9.2 shows the reduction of the first subhypothesis to an assessment.

After the reasoning tree has been developed, the subject matter expert interacts with the agent, helping it "understand" why each reduction step is correct, as will be discussed in Section 9.5. As a result, from each reduction step the agent learns a plausible version

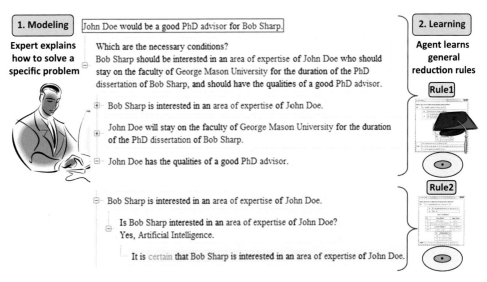

Figure 9.2. Modeling and rule learning.

space rule, as a justified generalization of it. This is illustrated in the right-hand side of Figure 9.2 and discussed in Section 9.7. These rules are not shown to the expert, but they may be viewed with the Rule Browser.

The agent can now use the learned rules to assess by itself similar hypotheses formulated by the expert, as illustrated in Figure 9.3, where the expert formulated the following hypothesis:

Dan Smith would be a good PhD advisor for Bob Sharp.

The reduction tree shown in Figure 9.3 was generated by the agent. Notice how the agent concluded that Bob Sharp is interested in an area of expertise of Dan Smith, which is Information Security, by applying the rule learned from John Doe and Bob Sharp, who share a common interest in Artificial Intelligence.

The expert has to inspect each reduction generated by the agent and indicate whether it is correct or not. Because the reductions from Figure 9.3 are correct, the agent generalizes the lower bound conditions of the applied rules, if the reductions were generated based on the upper bound conditions of these rules.

The bottom part of Figure 9.4 shows a reduction generated by the agent that is rejected by the expert. While Dan Smith has indeed a tenured position, which is a long-term faculty position, he plans to retire. It is therefore wrong to conclude that it is almost certain that he will stay on the faculty of George Mason University for the duration of the dissertation of Bob Sharp.

Such failure explanations are either proposed by the agent and accepted by the expert, or are provided by the expert, as discussed in Section 9.5.2.

Based on this failure explanation, the agent specializes the rule that generated this reduction by adding an Except-When plausible version space condition, as illustrated in the right-hand side of Figure 9.4. From now on, the agent will check not only that the faculty member has a long-term position (the main condition of the rule), but also that he or she does not plan to retire (the Except-When condition). The refined rule is not shown to the expert, but it may be viewed with the Rule Browser.

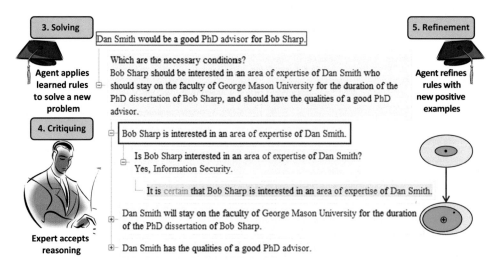

Figure 9.3. Problem solving, critiquing, and rule refinement.

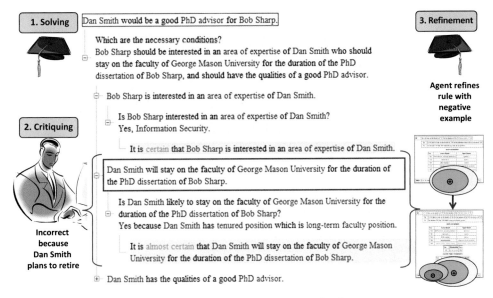

Figure 9.4. Problem solving, critiquing, and refinement.

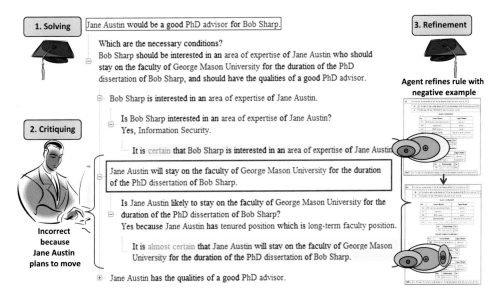

Figure 9.5. Problem solving, critiquing, and refinement.

Figure 9.5 shows another reasoning tree generated by the agent for an expert-formulated hypothesis. Again the expert rejects one of the reasoning steps: Although Jane Austin has a tenured position and does not plan to retire, she plans to move from George Mason University and will not stay on the faculty for the duration of the dissertation of Bob Sharp.

Based on this failure explanation, the agent specializes the rule that generated the reduction by adding an additional Except-When plausible version space condition, as shown in the right-hand side of Figure 9.5. From now on, the agent will check not only that the faculty member has a long-term position, but also that he or she does not plan to retire or move from the university.

The refined rule is shown in Figure 9.6. Notice that this is a quite complex rule that was learned based only on one positive example, two negative examples, and their explanations. The rule may be further refined based on additional examples.

The following sections describe in more detail the rule-learning and refinement processes. Before that, however, let us notice a significant difference between the development of a knowledge-based learning agent and the development of a (nonlearning) knowledge-based agent. As discussed in Sections 1.6.3.1 and 3.1, after the knowledge base of the (nonlearning) agent is developed by the knowledge engineer, the agent is tested with various problems. The expert has to analyze the solutions generated by the agent, and the knowledge engineer has to modify the rules manually to eliminate any identified problems, testing the modified rules again.

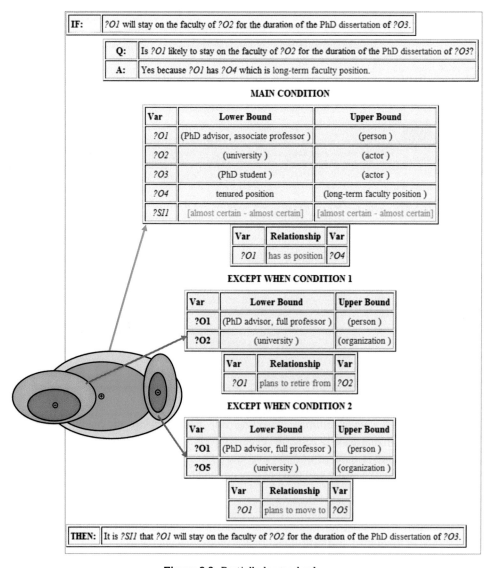

Figure 9.6. Partially learned rule.

In the case of a learning agent, both rule learning and rule refinement take place as part of agent teaching. Testing of the agent is included into this process. This process will also continue as part of knowledge base maintenance. If we would like to extend the agent to solve new problems, we simply need to teach it more. Thus, in the case of a learning agent, such as Disciple-EBR, there is no longer a distinction between knowledge base development and knowledge base maintenance. This is very important because it is well known that knowledge base maintenance (and system maintenance, in general) is much more challenging and time consuming than knowledge base (system) development. Thus knowledge base development and maintenance are less complex and much faster in the case of a learning agent.

9.3 THE RULE-LEARNING PROBLEM

The rule-learning problem is defined in Table 9.1 and is illustrated in Figures 9.7 and 9.8. The agent receives an example of a problem or hypothesis reduction and learns a plausible version space rule that is an analogy-based generalization of the example. There is no restriction with respect to what the example actually represents. However, it has to be described as a problem or hypothesis that is reduced to one or several subproblems, elementary hypotheses, or solutions. Therefore, this example may also be referred to as a problem-solving episode. For instance, the example shown in the top part of Figure 9.8 reduces a specific hypothesis to its assessment or solution, guided by a question and its answer.

The expert who is training the agent will interact with it to help it understand why the example is a correct reduction. The understanding is done in the context of the agent's ontology, a fragment of which is shown in Figure 9.7.

The result of the rule-learning process is a general plausible version space rule that will allow the agent to solve problems by analogy with the example from which the rule was learned. The plausible version space rule learned from the example at the top of Figure 9.8 is shown at the bottom part of the figure. It is an IF-THEN structure that specifies the conditions under which the problem from the IF part has the solution from the THEN part. The rule is only partially learned because, instead of a single applicability condition, it has two conditions:

Table 9.1 The Rule-Learning Problem

GIVEN
- A knowledge base that includes an ontology and a set of (previously learned) rules
- An example of a problem reduction expressed with the concepts and instances from the agent's knowledge base
- An expert who will interact with the agent to help it understand why the example is correct

DETERMINE
- A plausible version space rule, where the upper bound is a maximal generalization of the example, and the lower bound is a minimal generalization that does not contain any specific instance
- An extended ontology, if any extension is needed for the understanding of the example

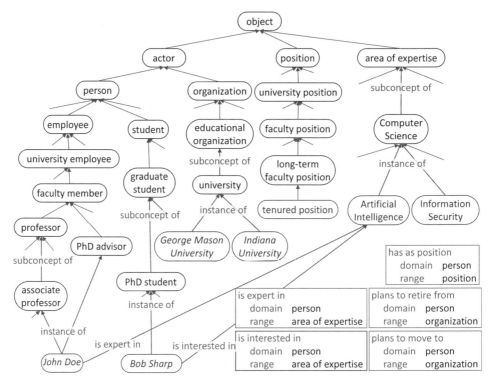

Figure 9.7. Fragment of the agent's ontology.

- A plausible upper bound condition that is a maximal generalization of the instances and constants from the example (e.g., Bob Sharp, certain), in the context of the agent's ontology
- A plausible lower bound condition that is a minimal generalization that does not contain any specific instance

The relationships among the variables ?O1, ?O2, and ?O3 are the same for both conditions and are therefore shown only once in Figure 9.8, under the conditions.

Completely learning the rule means learning an exact condition, where the plausible upper bound is identical with the plausible lower bound.

During rule learning, the agent might also extend the ontology with new features or concepts, if they are needed for the understanding the example.

9.4   **OVERVIEW OF THE RULE-LEARNING METHOD**

An overview of the rule-learning method is presented in Figure 9.9 and in Table 9.2. As in explanation-based learning (DeJong and Mooney, 1986; Mitchell et al., 1986), it consists of two phases: an explanation phase and a generalization phase. However, in the explanation phase the agent does not automatically build a deductive proof tree but an explanation structure through mixed-initiative understanding. Also, the generalization is not a deductive one, but an analogy-based one.

In the following, we will describe this learning method in more detail and illustrate it. First we will present the mixed-initiative process of explanation generation and example

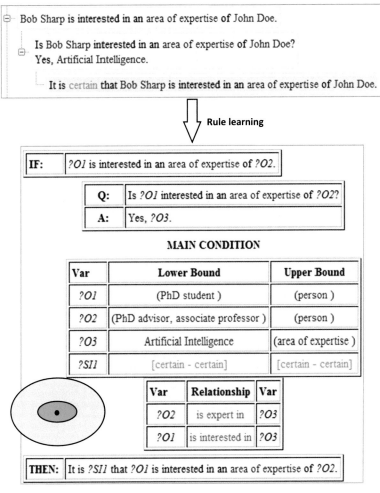

Figure 9.8. Rule learned from an example.

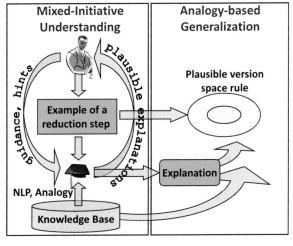

Figure 9.9. The rule-learning method.

Table 9.2 Basic Steps of the Rule-Learning Method

(1) Mixed-Initiative Understanding (Explanation Generation)
Through a mixed-initiative interaction with the subject matter expert, determine the set of relationships EX from the agent's ontology that collectively explain why the example is correct. EX represents the explanation of the example E. In general, these relationships express the meaning of the question/answer pair from the example E, as well as other conditions that need to be satisfied by the instances and constants from the example E. During this process, new objects and features may be elicited from the expert and added to the ontology, if the ontology is incomplete.

(2) Example Reformulation
Generate a variable for each instance and each constant (i.e., number, string, or symbolic probability) that appears in the example E and its explanation EX. Then use these variables to create an instance I of the concept C representing the applicability condition of the rule R to be learned. C is the concept to be learned as part of rule learning and refinement. Finally, reformulate the example as a very specific IF-THEN rule with I as its applicability condition. The IF problem, the question, the answer, and the THEN subproblems (or solutions) are obtained by replacing each instance or constant from the example E with the corresponding variable.

(3) Analogy-based Generalizations
Generate the plausible upper bound condition of the rule R as the maximal generalization of I in the context of the agent's ontology. Generate the plausible lower bound condition of the rule R as the minimal generalization of I, which does not contain any specific instance.

(4) Rule Analysis
If there is any variable from the THEN part of a rule that is not linked to some variable from the other parts of the rule, or if the rule has too many instances in the knowledge base, then interact with the expert to extend the explanation of the example and update the rule if new explanation pieces are found.

(5) Determining the Generalized Example
Generate a minimal generalization of the example E and its explanation EX that does not contain any specific instance, and associate it with the learned rule.

---

understanding, which is part of the first phase. Then we will present and justify the generalization method, which is based on analogical reasoning.

9.5   MIXED-INITIATIVE EXAMPLE UNDERSTANDING

9.5.1   What Is an Explanation of an Example?

The mixed-initiative example understanding process is illustrated in Figure 9.10. The expert has defined the example during the modeling process. Now the expert and the agent have to collaborate to learn a general rule from this specific example.

The first step consists in finding the set of relationships from the agent's ontology that collectively explain why the example is correct. In general, these relationships express the meaning of the question/answer pair from the example, as well as other conditions that need to be satisfied by the instances and constants from the example.

Consider the following question/answer pair:

Is Bob Sharp interested in an area of expertise of John Doe?
Yes, Artificial Intelligence.

The following is an approximate representation of the meaning of the question/answer pair using the terms from the agent's ontology:

Bob Sharp is interested in Artificial Intelligence
John Doe is expert in Artificial Intelligence

Adding "Probability of solution is always certain" to the preceding relationships results in the explanation of the example, which is shown on the left-hand side of Figure 9.10. This is a formal explanation of the example and consists of a set of relationships (or explanation pieces) involving the instances and the constants from the example.

One can distinguish between different types of explanation pieces, as shown in Table 9.3. Formally, the explanation of the example consists of several explanation pieces. Each explanation piece corresponds to a path in the ontology between an object in the example and another object or constant, as illustrated in Figure 9.10. In principle, the path could have any length. In practice, however, one has to limit the maximum length of the path for a certain type of explanation, in order to reduce the combinatorial explosion in the generation of plausible explanations by the agent.

Table 9.3 Types of Explanation Pieces

- *Association* – a relation between two objects from the example
- *Correlation* – a common feature of two objects from the example
- *Property* – a property of an object from the example
- *Relation* – a relation between an object from the example and one from the knowledge base
- *Generalization* – a generalization of an object from the example
- *Specific value* – a specific value for an entity from the example (constant or generic instance)

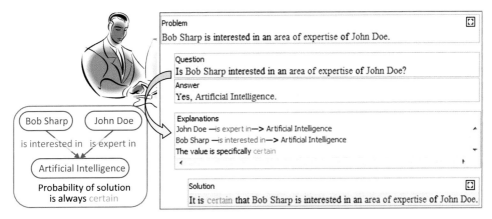

Figure 9.10. Example understanding.

Because the agent's ontology is incomplete, sometimes the explanation includes only an approximate representation of the meaning of the question/answer (natural language) sentences.

The next section presents the explanation generation method.

9.5.2 Explanation Generation

Fully automatic explanation generation by the agent, while highly desirable, is problematic because it would require human-like natural language understanding capabilities from an agent that has only an incomplete ontology.

Manual explanation definition by an expert who is not a knowledge engineer is also problematic. For one thing, he or she would need to use the formal language of the agent. But this would not be enough. The expert would also need to know the names of the potentially many thousands of concepts and features from the agent's ontology (such as "is interested in").

While defining the formal explanation of a reduction step is beyond the individual capabilities of both the expert and the agent, it is not beyond their joint complementary capabilities. Therefore, finding such explanation pieces is modeled as a *mixed-initiative process* (Tecuci et al., 2007a), based on the following observations:

- It is easier for an expert to understand sentences in the formal language of the agent than it is to produce such formal sentences
- It is easier for the agent to generate formal sentences than it is to understand sentences in the natural language of the expert

In essence, the agent will use basic natural language processing, various heuristics, analogical reasoning, and help from the expert in order to identify and propose a set of plausible explanation pieces, ordered by their plausibility of being correct explanations. Then the expert will select the correct ones from the generated list.

The left-hand side of Figure 9.11 shows an example to be understood, and the upper-right part of Figure 9.11 shows all the instances and constants from the example. The agent will look for plausible explanation pieces of the types from Table 9.3, involving those instances and constants. The most plausible explanation pieces identified, in plausibility

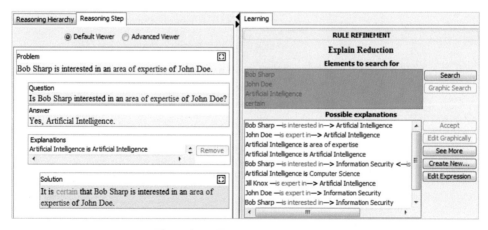

Figure 9.11. Explanation generation.

order, are shown in the bottom-right of Figure 9.11. Notice that the two most plausible explanation pieces from Figure 9.11 are the correct explanation pieces shown in Figure 9.10. The expert will have to select each of them and click on the **Accept** button. As a result, the agent will move them in the Explanations pane from the left side of Figure 9.11.

Notice in the upper-right of Figure 9.11 that all the objects and constants from the example are selected. Consequently, the agent generates the most plausible explanations pieces related to all these objects and displays those with the highest plausibility. The expert may click on the **See More** button, asking the agent to display the next set of plausible explanations.

The expert may also deselect some of the objects and constants, asking the agent to generate only plausible explanations involving the selected elements. For example, Figure 9.12 illustrates a situation where only the constant "certain" is selected. As a result, the agent generated only the explanation "The value is specifically certain," which means that this value should be kept as such (i.e., not generalized) in the learned rule.

The expert may also provide a new explanation, even using new instances, concepts, or features. In such a case, the expert should first define the new elements in the ontology. After that, the expert may guide the agent to generate the desired explanations.

If the example contains any generic instance, such as "Artificial Intelligence," the agent will automatically select the explanation piece "Artificial Intelligence is Artificial Intelligence" (see Explanation pane on the left side of Figure 9.11), meaning that this instance will appear as such in the learned rule. If the expert wants Artificial Intelligence to be generalized, he or she should simply remove that explanation by clicking on it and on the **Remove** button at its right.

The expert may also define explanations involving functions and comparisons, as will be discussed in Sections 9.12.3 and 9.12.4.

Notice, however, that the explanation of the example may still be incomplete for at least three reasons:

- The ontology of the agent may be incomplete, and therefore the agent may not be able to propose all the explanation pieces of the example simply because they are not present in the ontology

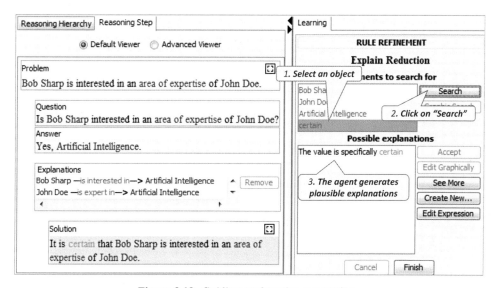

Figure 9.12. Guiding explanation generation.

- The agent shows the plausible explanation pieces incrementally, as guided by the expert, and if one of the actual explanation pieces is not among the first ones shown, it may not be seen and selected by the expert
- It is often the case that the human expert forgets to provide explanations that correspond to common-sense knowledge that also is not represented in the question/answer pair

The incompleteness of the explanation is not, however, a significant problem because the explanation may be further extended during the rule refinement process, as discussed in Chapter 10.

To conclude, Table 9.4 summarizes the mixed-initiative explanation generation method. Once the expert is satisfied with the identified explanation pieces, the agent will generate the rule, as discussed in the following sections.

9.6 EXAMPLE REFORMULATION

As indicated in Table 9.2 (p. 260), once the explanation of the example is found, the agent generates a very specific IF-THEN rule with an applicability condition that covers only that example. The top part of Figure 9.13 shows an example, and the bottom part shows the generated specific rule that covers only that example. Notice that each instance (e.g., Bob Sharp) and each constant (e.g., certain) is replaced with a variable (i.e., ?O1, ?Sl1). However, the applicability condition restricts the possible values of these variables to those from the example (e.g., "?O1 is Bob Sharp"). The applicability condition also includes the properties and the relationships from the explanation. Therefore, the rule from the bottom of Figure 9.13 will cover only the example from the top of Figure 9.13. This rule will be further generalized to the rule from Figure 9.8, which has a plausible upper bound condition and a plausible lower bound condition, as discussed in the next section. In particular, the plausible upper bound condition will be obtained as the maximal generalization of the specific condition in the context of the agent's ontology. Similarly, the plausible lower bound condition will be obtained as the minimal generalization of the specific condition that does not contain any specific instance.

Table 9.4 Mixed-Initiative Explanation Generation

Let E be an example.

Repeat

- The expert focuses the agent's attention by selecting some of the instances and constants from the example.
- The agent proposes what it determines to be the most plausible explanation pieces related to the selected entities, ordered by their plausibility.
- The expert chooses the relevant explanation pieces.
- The expert may ask for the generation of additional explanation pieces related to the selected instances and constants, may select different ones, or may directly specify explanation pieces.

until the expert is satisfied with the explanation of the example.

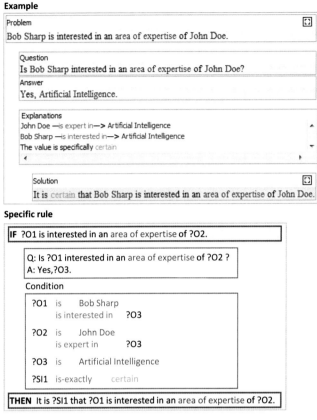

Figure 9.13. Specific rule covering only the example.

9.7 ANALOGY-BASED GENERALIZATION

9.7.1 Analogical Problem Solving Based on Explanation Similarity

The goal of the learning agent is to learn a general rule that will enable it to solve new problems by analogy with the example provided by the expert. As discussed in Section 8.1.4, analogy involves mapping some underlying "causal network of relations" between a source and a target, with the goal of transferring knowledge from the source to the target. This applies to analogical problem solving as illustrated in Figure 9.14.

The explanation in the upper-left part of Figure 9.14 explains why the input example in the lower-left part is correct. The expression from the upper-right part of Figure 9.14 is similar with this explanation because both have the same structure. Therefore, one may infer, by analogy, that this expression explains an example that is similar to the initial example. This example is shown in the bottom-right part of Figure 9.14.

The more general question is: *When should we consider that two expressions or explanations are similar?* In general, one considers that two expressions, explanations, or situations are similar if they match within a certain predefined threshold (Winston, 1980). As shown in Kodratoff and Ganascia (1986), generalization may be reduced to structural matching. Therefore, we may consider that two expressions (explanations) are similar if

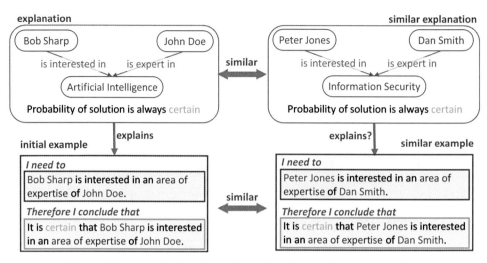

Figure 9.14. Analogical problem solving based on explanation similarity.

they are both less general then a given expression that represents the analogy criterion. Consequently, the preceding question may be rephrased as:

Given the explanation EX of an example E, which generalization of EX should be considered an analogy criterion, enabling the agent to generate reductions that are analogous to E?

There are two interesting answers of this question, one given by a cautious learner, and the other given by an aggressive learner, as discussed in the next sections.

9.7.2   Upper Bound Condition as a Maximally General Analogy Criterion

An aggressive learner always prefers maximal generalizations, as discussed in Section 8.5. Consequently, it will determine the analogy criterion as a maximal generalization of the explanation, as illustrated in Figure 9.15 and explained in the following.

The explanation of the initial example corresponds to the applicability condition of the specific rule representing the example (see Figure 9.13). Thus the aggressive learner will learn a rule by maximally generalizing the specific applicability condition, as illustrated in the upper right side of Figure 9.16.

The specific instance Bob Sharp is generalized to the most general concept from the ontology that covers it and satisfies all the constraints imposed by the domains and the ranges of the features related to it in the specific condition (explanation). As shown in the left-hand side of Figure 9.16, the most general generalization of Bob Sharp in the ontology is object. On the other hand, in the specific condition (explanation), Bob Sharp has the feature "is interested in," the domain of which is person. Thus the maximal generalization of Bob Sharp is: object ∩ domain(is interested in) = object ∩ person = person.

In general, if an instance in the explanation has the features $f_{11}, \ldots, f_{1m}$, and appears as value of the features $f_{21}, \ldots, f_{2n}$, then its maximal general generalization is:

$$\text{object} \cap \text{domain}(f_{11}) \cap \ldots \cap \text{domain}(f_{1m}) \cap \text{range}(f_{21}) \cap \ldots \cap \text{range}(f_{2n})$$

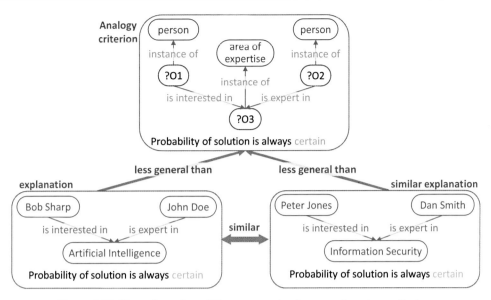

Figure 9.15. Upper bound condition as a maximally general analogy criterion.

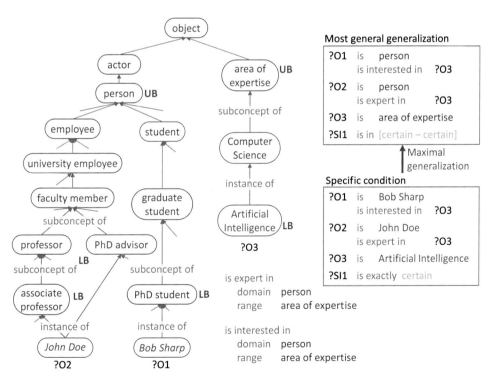

Figure 9.16. Maximal generalization of the specific applicability condition.

Now consider John Doe. Its most general generalization is object ∩ domain(is expert in) = object ∩ person = person.

Consider now Artificial Intelligence. It appears as a value of the features "is interested in" and "is expert in." Therefore, its maximal generalization is: object ∩ range(is interested in) ∩ range(is expert in) = object ∩ area of expertise ∩ area of expertise = area of expertise.

On the other hand, the maximal generalization of "certain" is the interval with a single value "[certain – certain]" because ?Sl1 is restricted to this value by the feature "is exactly."

Let us consider again the example from the top part of Figure 9.13, but now let us assume that "The value is specifically certain" was not identified as an explanation piece. That is, the explanation of the example consists only of the following pieces:

Bob Sharp is interested in Artificial Intelligence
John Doe is expert in Artificial Intelligence

In this case, the generated specific condition is the one from the bottom of Figure 9.17, and its maximal generalization is the one from the top of Figure 9.17. Notice that the maximal generalization of "certain" is the entire interval [no support – certain] because there is no restriction on the possible values of ?Sl1.

9.7.3   Lower Bound Condition as a Minimally General Analogy Criterion

A cautious learner prefers minimal generalizations, as discussed in Section 8.5. Consequently, it will determine the analogy criterion as a minimal generalization of the explanation, as illustrated in Figure 9.18.

The explanation of the initial example corresponds to the applicability condition of the specific rule representing the example (see Figure 9.13). Thus the cautious learner will learn a rule by minimally generalizing the specific applicability condition, as illustrated in Figure 9.19.

The specific instance Bob Sharp is minimally generalized to the most specific concept from the ontology that covers it, that is, to PhD student. This generalization is allowed because the domain of the feature "is interested in" is person, which includes PhD student.

Most general generalization

?O1	is	person	
		is interested in	?O3
?O2	is	person	
		is expert in	?O3
?O3	is	area of expertise	
?SI1	is in	[no support – certain]	

↑ Maximal generalization

Specific condition

?O1	is	Bob Sharp	
		is interested in	?O3
?O2	is	John Doe	
		is expert in	?O3
?O3	is	Artificial Intelligence	
?SI1	is	certain	

Figure 9.17. Maximal generalization of a symbolic probability value when no explanation is identified.

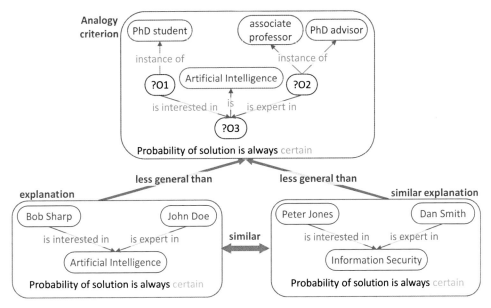

Figure 9.18. Lower bound condition as a minimally general analogy criterion.

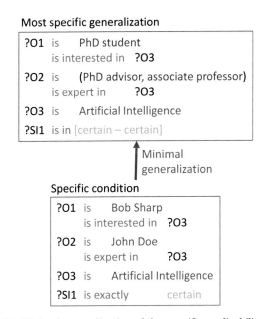

Figure 9.19. Minimal generalization of the specific applicability condition.

Similarly, the specific instance John Doe is minimally generalized to PhD advisor or associate professor, because these are the minimal generalizations of John Doe and neither is more specific than the other. Additionally, both these concepts are subconcepts of person, the domain of is expert in.

Because Artificial Intelligence is a generic instance, it can appear in the learned rule (as opposed to the specific instances Bob Sharp and John Doe). Therefore, its minimal generalization is Artificial Intelligence itself. Similarly, the constants (such as certain) can also appear in the learned rule, and they are kept as such in the minimal generalization.

Notice that if you want an instance to appear in the condition of a learned rule, it needs to be defined as a generic instance. Specific instances are always generalized to concepts and will never appear in the condition.

9.8   RULE GENERATION AND ANALYSIS

The partially learned rule is shown in the bottom part of Figure 9.8 (p. 259). Notice that the features are listed only once under the bounds because they are the same for both bounds.

The generated rule is analyzed to determine whether there are any variables in the THEN part that are not linked to some variable from the IF part. If such an unlinked variable exists, then it can be instantiated to any value, leading to solutions that make no sense. Therefore, the agent will interact with the expert to find an additional explanation that will create the missing link and update the rule accordingly.

The generated rule is also analyzed to determine whether it has too many instances in the knowledge base, which is also an indication that its explanation is incomplete and needs to be extended.

9.9   GENERALIZED EXAMPLES

The rule learned from an example and its explanation depends on the ontology of the agent at the time the rule was generated. If the ontology changes, the rule may need to be updated, as will be discussed in Chapter 10. For example, the minimal generalization of a specific instance will change if a new concept is inserted between that instance and the concept above it. To enable the agent to update its rules automatically when relevant changes occur in the ontology, minimal generalizations of the examples and their explanations are associated with the learned rules.

Why is the agent maintaining minimal generalizations of examples instead of the examples themselves? Because the examples exist only in Scenario KBs, where the specific instances are defined, while the rules are maintained in the Domain KB. If a scenario is no longer available, the corresponding examples are no longer defined. However, generalized examples (which do not contain specific instances) will always be defined in the Domain KB. Thus the generalized examples represent a way to maintain a history of how a rule was learned, independent of the scenarios. They are also a compact way of preserving this history because one generalized example may correspond to many actual examples.

Figure 9.20 shows the minimal generalization of the example and its explanation from which the rule in Figure 9.8 (p. 259) was learned.

One should notice that the minimal generalization of the example shown at the top part of Figure 9.20 is not the same with the plausible lower bound condition of the learned rule from Figure 9.8. Consider the specific instance John Doe from the example.

In the ontology, John Doe is both a direct instance of PhD advisor and of associate professor (see Figure 9.16). In the lower bound condition of the rule, John Doe is generalized to PhD advisor *or* associate professor, indicated as (PhD advisor, associate professor), because each of these two concepts is a minimal generalization of John Doe in the ontology. Thus the agent maintains the two concepts as part of the lower bound of the rule's version space: one corresponding to PhD advisor, and the other corresponding to

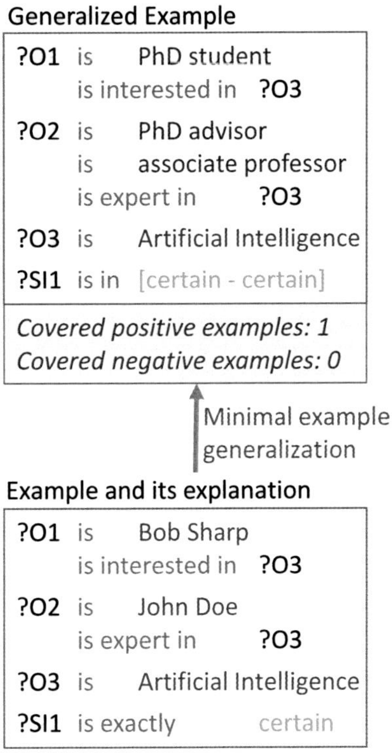

Generalized Example

?O1	is	PhD student
	is interested in	?O3
?O2	is	PhD advisor
	is	associate professor
	is expert in	?O3
?O3	is	Artificial Intelligence
?SI1	is in	[certain - certain]

Covered positive examples: 1
Covered negative examples: 0

Minimal example
generalization

Example and its explanation

?O1	is	Bob Sharp
	is interested in	?O3
?O2	is	John Doe
	is expert in	?O3
?O3	is	Artificial Intelligence
?SI1	is exactly	certain

Figure 9.20. Determining the generalized example.

associate professor. During further learning, the agent will choose one of these generalizations or a more general generalization that covers both of them.

In the minimal generalization of the example, John Doe is generalized to PhD advisor **and** associate professor because this is the best representation of the minimal generalization of the example that can be used to regenerate the rule, when changes are made to the ontology. This minimal generalization is expressed as follows:

?O2	is	PhD advisor
	is	associate professor

Initially, the generalized example shown at the top of Figure 9.20 covers only one specific example. However, when a new (positive or negative) example is used to refine the rule, the agent checks whether it is already covered by an existing generalized example and records this information. Because a generalized example may cover any number of specific positive and negative examples, its description also includes the number of specific examples covered, as shown in the top part of Figure 9.20.

Cases of using generalized examples to regenerate previously learned rules are presented in Section 10.2.

9.10   HYPOTHESIS LEARNING

In addition to learning a general reduction rule from a specific reduction example, Disciple-EBR also learns general hypotheses (or problems). The left-hand side of Figure 9.21 shows

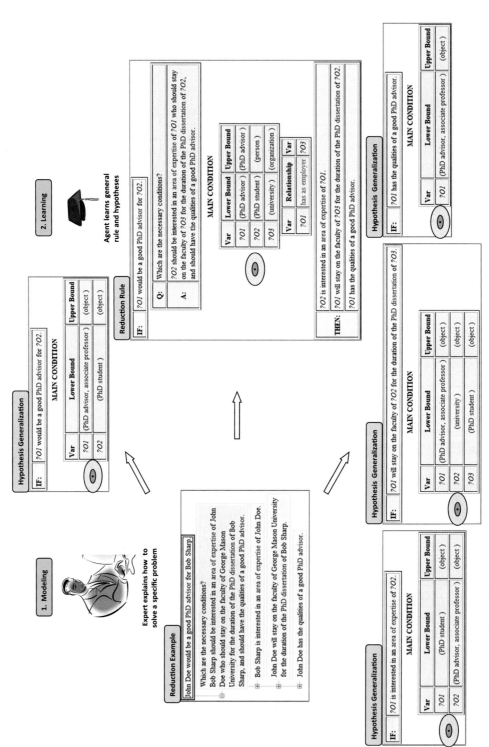

Figure 9.21. A reduction rule and four hypotheses learned from a specific hypothesis reduction.

an example of a reduction where a hypothesis is reduced to three subhypotheses. From this example, Disciple-EBR learns five general knowledge pieces that share the same variables:

- A general hypothesis reduction rule that is a generalization of the reduction example where each instance was replaced with a variable
- A generalization of the top hypothesis with a plausible version space condition
- Generalizations of the three subhypotheses, each with its own plausible version space condition

The hypothesis learning method, shown in Table 9.5, is very similar with the rule-learning method.

Figure 9.22 illustrates the automatic learning of a general hypothesis from the specific hypothesis, "John Doe would be a good PhD advisor for Bob Sharp," when no explanation is provided.

The specific instances, John Doe and Bob Sharp, are replaced with the variables ?O1 and ?O2, respectively, as in the reduction rule.

The lower bounds of these variables are obtained as the minimal generalizations of John Doe and Bob Sharp, according to the agent's ontology from the left-hand side of Figure 9.22, because both of them are specific instances. Notice that there are two minimal generalizations of John Doe: PhD advisor and associate professor. The minimal generalization of Bob Sharp is PhD student.

The upper bounds are obtained as the maximum generalizations of John Doe and Bob Sharp, according to the agent's ontology from the left-hand side of Figure 9.22. They are both object.

During the explanation generation process, the user may wish to restrict the generalization of the hypothesis by providing the following explanations:

Table 9.5 Basic Steps of the Hypothesis Learning Method

(1) Mixed-Initiative Understanding (Explanation Generation)
Through a mixed-initiative interaction with the subject matter expert, determine the set of constraints EX that need to be satisfied by the instances and constants from the example hypothesis EH in order for the hypothesis statement to make sense. These include the types of the instances from the hypothesis.

(2) Hypothesis Reformulation
Use the constraints EX and the variables generated during the learning of the corresponding reduction rule to create an instance I of the concept C representing the applicability condition of the hypothesis H to be learned. Then reformulate the specific hypothesis as a hypothesis pattern with I as its applicability condition.

(3) Analogy-based Generalizations
Generate the plausible upper bound condition of the general hypothesis H as the maximal generalization of I in the context of the agent's ontology. Generate the plausible lower bound condition of the hypothesis H as the minimal generalization of I that does not contain any specific instance.

(4) Determining the Generalized Example
Generate a minimal generalization of the example hypothesis EH and its explanation EX that does not contain any specific instance and associate it with the learned hypothesis.

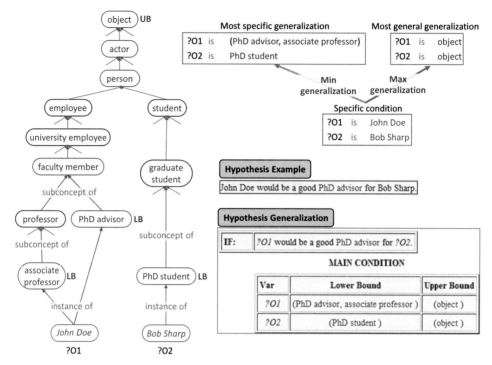

Figure 9.22. Generation of the applicability conditions of a hypothesis.

John Doe is faculty member
Bob Sharp is student

In this case, the lower bound condition of the learned hypothesis remains the same, but the upper bound condition becomes:

?O1 is faculty member
?O2 is student

In general, hypothesis learning is done automatically, as a byproduct of rule learning, but the explanations found for learning the reduction rule will not be used for learning the hypothesis. Indeed, these explanations indicate only why this particular reduction is correct. There may be other reductions of the same hypothesis, which will have different explanations. If desired, the user may provide specific explanations for the hypothesis that limit the possible instantiations of the learned hypothesis to those that make sense, as illustrated previously.

Notice that for each specific hypothesis, the agent may learn a single general hypothesis but several reduction rules. Then, when trying to reduce a hypothesis to simpler hypotheses, the agent checks that both the applicability condition of the corresponding general hypothesis and that of the considered rule are satisfied. It is therefore important that the applicability condition of the general hypothesis is general enough to enable the use of all the learned reduction rules associated with that general hypothesis.

A general hypothesis may be learned in several circumstances. As illustrated in Figure 9.21, a hypothesis may be learned as a byproduct of rule learning. It may also be learned during the modeling and formalization of a reasoning tree by using the **Learn**

Hypothesis Pattern or the **Learn Tree Patterns** commands that were introduced in Section 4.10. Finally, it may be learned by specifically invoking hypothesis (problem) learning when working with the Mixed-Initiative Reasoner. But it is only this last situation that also allows the definitions of explanations, as will be discussed later in this section. In all the other situations, a hypothesis is automatically learned, with no explanations, as was illustrated in Figure 9.22.

The overall user–agent interactions during the hypothesis explanation process are illustrated in Figure 9.23 and described in Operation 9.1. Here it is assumed that the reasoning tree was already formalized and thus a hypothesis pattern was already learned. If it was not learned, the pattern will be automatically learned before the explanations are identified.

Operation 9.1. Define explanations for a hypothesis

- Select the Scenario workspace.
- Click on the **Reasoning** menu and select **Mixed-Initiative Reasoner**.
- Select the hypothesis to analyze, and click on the **Select** button on the right side of the window.
- In the Reasoning Hierarchy viewer of the **Mixed-Initiative Reasoner**, select a hypothesis by clicking on it.
- In the right panel, click on the **Modify Explanations** button.
- Explanation generation is automatically invoked, the left pane showing the hypothesis in the Reasoning Step viewer, and the right pane showing the selected entities and a corresponding ordered list of plausible explanations (see the upper-right part of Figure 9.23).
- Inspect the explanation pieces proposed by the agent in the right panel, click on a correct explanation piece (if any), and then click on the **Accept** button.
- Repeat explanation selection and acceptance to select all the needed explanation pieces.
- If necessary, click on the **See More** button, asking the agent to generate additional possible explanation pieces related to the selected entities.
- If necessary, select a subset of instances and constants and click on the **Search** button, asking the agent to generate explanations related to the selected entities.
- All the accepted explanations are added to the hypothesis (see the bottom-left part of Figure 9.23). You may delete any of them by clicking on it and then clicking on the **Remove** button.
- Click on the **Finish** button to end the learning of the current hypothesis.

9.11 HANDS ON: RULE AND HYPOTHESES LEARNING

This case study will guide you to use Disciple-EBR to learn rules and hypotheses from examples. More specifically, you will learn how to:

- Invoke the rule learning module
- Interact with the agent to find the explanation of the example
- Learn the rule (and the associated hypotheses)

The overall user–agent interactions during the rule- (and hypotheses-) learning process are illustrated in Figure 9.24 and described in Operation 9.2. It is assumed that the

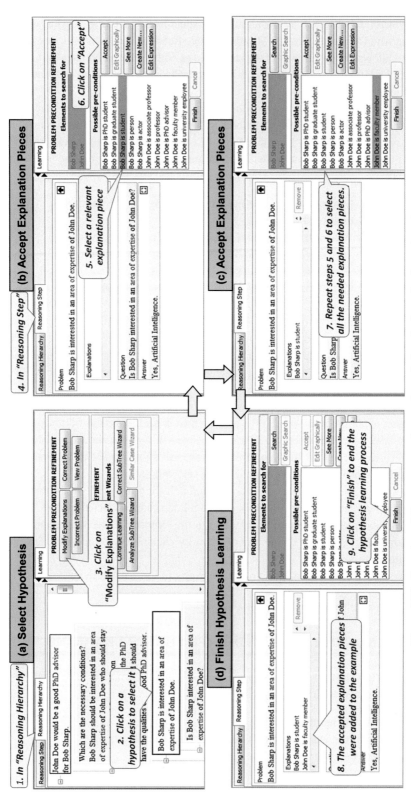

Figure 9.23. Overview of the user-agent interactions during the hypothesis explanation process.

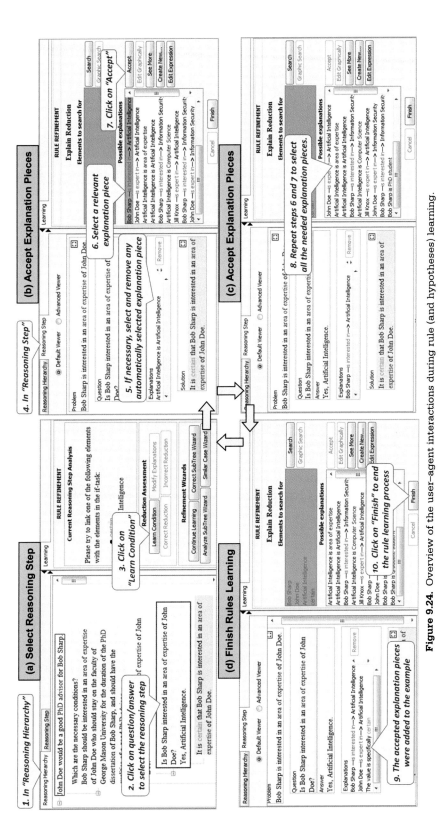

Figure 9.24. Overview of the user-agent interactions during rule (and hypotheses) learning.

reasoning tree is formalized. If not, one can easily formalize it in the Evidence workspace before invoking rule learning by simply right-clicking on the top node and selecting **Learn Tree**.

Operation 9.2. Learn rule

- Select the Scenario workspace.
- Click on the **Reasoning** menu and select **Mixed-Initiative Reasoner**.
- Select the hypothesis to analyze, and click on the **Select** button on the right side of the window.
- In the Reasoning Hierarchy viewer, select a reasoning step by clicking on the corresponding Q/A node (see the upper-left part of Figure 9.24).
- In the right panel, click on the **Learn Condition** button.
- Explanation generation is automatically invoked, the left pane showing the reduction in the Reasoning Step viewer, and the right pane showing the selected entities and a corresponding ordered list of plausible explanations (see the upper-right part of Figure 9.24).
- If the example contains generic instances, check whether you want to remove any of the corresponding explanations that were automatically accepted by the agent. To remove such an explanation piece, click on it in the left panel and then click on the **Remove** button.
- Inspect the explanation pieces proposed by the agent in the right panel, click on a correct explanation piece (if any), and then click on the **Accept** button.
- Repeat explanation selection and acceptance to select all the needed explanation pieces.
- If necessary, click on the **See More** button, asking the agent to generate additional possible explanation pieces related to the selected entities.
- If necessary, select a subset of instances and constants and click on the **Search** button, asking the agent to generate explanations related to the selected entities.
- All the accepted explanations are added to the reduction (see the bottom-left part of Figure 9.24). You may delete any of them by clicking on them and then clicking on the **Remove** button.
- Click on the **Finish** button to end the learning of the current rule.
- Continue with selecting another reasoning step and learning the corresponding rule.

You are now ready to perform a rule-learning case study. There are two of them, a shorter one and a longer one. In the shorter case study, you will guide the agent to learn the rule from Figure 9.8, as discussed in the previous sections. In the longer case study, you will guide the agent to learn several rules, including the rule from Figure 9.8.

Start Disciple-EBR, select one of the case study knowledge bases (either "11-Rule-Learning-short/Scen" or "11-Rule-Learning/Scen"), and proceed as indicated in the instructions at the bottom of the opened window.

A learned rule can be displayed as indicated in the following operation.

Operation 9.3. Display a learned rule with the Rule Viewer

- In the Scenario workspace, in the Reasoning Hierarchy viewer select a reasoning step for which a rule has already been learned by clicking on the corresponding Q/A node.
- At the bottom of the right panel, click on the **Reduction Rule** button to see the rule that generated the reduction step.

- At the top of the **Rule Viewer**, notice the name of the rule (e.g., DDR.00018). You may also display or delete this rule with the **Rule Browser**, as described in Operations 10.4 and 10.5.
- Click on the **X** button of the **Rule Viewer** to close it.

Operation 9.4. Display a learned hypothesis with the Problem Viewer

- In the Scenario workspace, in the Reasoning Hierarchy viewer click on a hypothesis to select one for which a general hypothesis has already been learned.
- In the right panel, click on the **View Problem** button to see the learned hypothesis.
- Click on the **X** button of the **Problem Viewer** to close it.

9.12   EXPLANATION GENERATION OPERATIONS

An important part of rule learning is finding an explanation of the example that is as complete as possible. The following sections discuss various operations that support this process.

9.12.1   Guiding Explanation Generation

You can guide the agent in explanation generation by selecting the instances and constants from the example for which explanation pieces will be proposed. As a result, the agent generates a list of potential explanations, ordered by their plausibility, from which you can select the correct ones. The corresponding user–agent interaction is described in Operation 9.5 and illustrated in Figure 9.25.

Operation 9.5. Guide the generation of explanations

- In the Scenario workspace, during rule learning, in the Reasoning Hierarchy viewer, select a reasoning step by clicking on the corresponding Q/A node.
- In the right panel, click on the **Learn Condition** button.

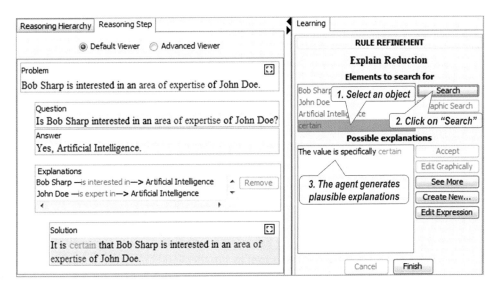

Figure 9.25. Guiding explanation generation.

- Select one or several entities from the "Elements to search for" pane, such as certain in Figure 9.25. You may also need to deselect some entities by clicking on them.
- Click on the **Search** button, asking the agent to generate explanation pieces related to the selected entities.
- Select an explanation piece and click on the **Accept** button.
- Click on the **See More** button to see more of the generated explanation pieces.
- Repeat the preceding steps until all the desired explanations are generated and selected.

9.12.2 Fixing Values

You may block the generalizations of numbers (e.g., "5"), symbolic probability values (e.g., "certain"), or generic instances (e.g., "Artificial Intelligence") by selecting explanations of the following forms, as described in Operation 9.6:

> The value is specifically 5
> The value is specifically certain
> Artificial Intelligence is Artificial Intelligence

Operation 9.6. Generate explanations with fixed values

- In the Scenario workspace, during rule learning, in the Reasoning Hierarchy viewer, select a reasoning step by clicking on the corresponding Q/A node.
- In the right panel, click on the **Learn Condition** button.
- Select one or several generic instances or constants (e.g., certain in Figure 9.25) in the "Elements to search for" pane. No specific instances should be selected.
- If a selected element is a constant, then the agent will generate a possible explanation piece of the form "The value is specifically <selected constant>."
- If a selected element is a generic instance, then the agent will generate a possible explanation piece of the form "<selected instance> is <selected instance>," as well as other explanations containing the selected instance.
- Accept the explanation "The value is specifically <selected constant>" (or "<selected instance> is <selected instance>") to fix that value in the learned rule.

Notice that these types of explanation pieces are generated when only constants or generic instances are selected in the "Elements to search for" pane. For example, only "certain" was selected in the "Elements to search for" pane in the upper-right part of Figure 9.25, and therefore the potential explanation piece "The value is specifically certain" was generated.

Notice also that explanations such as "Artificial Intelligence is Artificial Intelligence" can be generated only for generic instances. They cannot be generated for specific instances because these instances are always generalized in the learned rules.

9.12.3 Explanations with Functions

We will illustrate these explanations based on the reasoning tree in Figure 9.26. Notice that all the numbers are correctly recognized as numbers and appear in green.

The Q/A pair from the first reduction explains how the price of the Apple iPad 16GB is computed. The corresponding explanation pieces express the meaning of the Q/A pair by

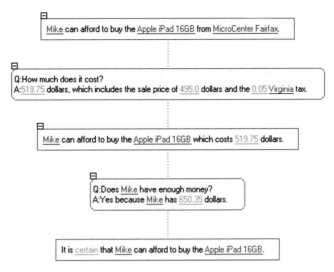

Figure 9.26. Reasoning tree involving numbers.

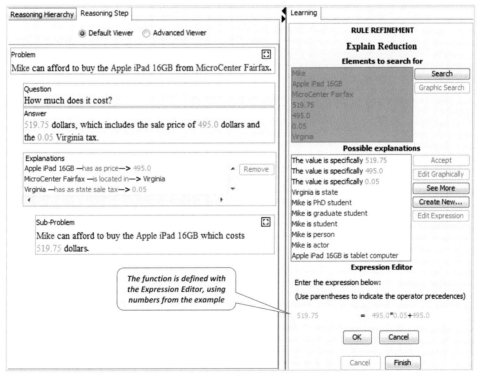

Figure 9.27. Explanations with functions.

using relationships from the agent's ontology. They are the following ones, and are shown also in the left-hand side of Figure 9.27:

Apple iPad 16GB has as price 495.0
MicroCenter Fairfax is located in Virginia
Virginia has as state sale tax 0.05

Additionally, you have to teach the agent how the price is actually computed. You invoke the Expression Editor by clicking on the **Edit Expression** button, which displays a pane to define the expression (see the bottom right of Figure 9.27). Then you fill in the left side of the equality with the price, and the right side with the expression that leads to this price, by using the numbers from the example:

$$519.75 = 495.0 * 0.05 + 495.0$$

Each of these numbers is generalized to a variable, and a general relationship between these variables is learned (i.e., "?N1 = ?N2 * ?N3 + ?N2"). The learned rule, containing this expression in its applicability condition, is shown in Figure 9.28.

In general, to define an explanation containing a function, you have to follow the steps from Operation 9.7.

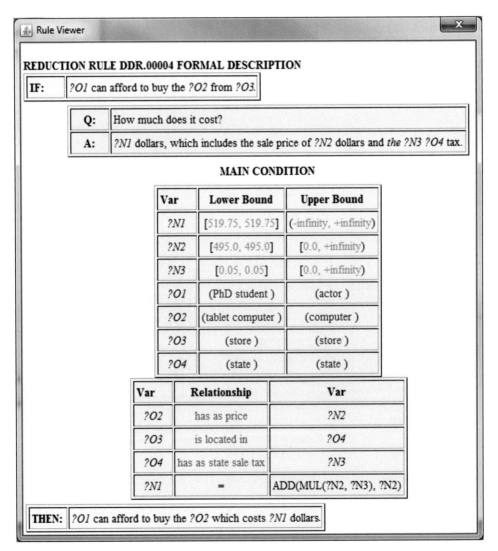

Figure 9.28. Learned rule with a learned function in the applicability condition.

Operation 9.7. Define explanations containing functions

- In the Scenario workspace, during rule learning, in the Reasoning Hierarchy viewer, select a reasoning step by clicking on the corresponding Q/A node.
- In the right panel, click on the **Learn Condition** button.
- In the "Possible explanations" pane, click on the **Edit Expression** button.
- The agent displays the Expression Editor.
- In the left part of the Expression Editor, start typing the result of the expression (e.g., the actual price of "519.75" shown in Figure 9.27) and select it from the completion pop-up.
- In the right part of the Expression Editor, type the expression used to compute the result (i.e., "495.0 * 0.05 + 495.0"), making sure you select the values from the completion pop-up.
- Click on the **OK** button under the Expression Editor to define the expression.

9.12.4 Explanations with Comparisons

We will illustrate these explanations based on the reasoning tree from Figure 9.26. Notice that the Q/A pair corresponding to the bottom reduction explains why Mike has enough money to buy the Apple iPad 16GB. The following is the corresponding explanation piece:

> Mike has as available funds 650.35

Additionally, you have to indicate that 650.35 is greater than 519.75. You click on the **Create New…** button, which opens a window allowing you to define a new explanation as an object-feature-value triplet (see the bottom of Figure 9.29). In the left editor, you start typing the amount of money Mike has (i.e., 650.35) and select it from the completion

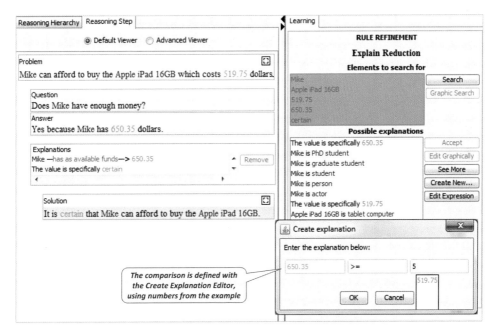

Figure 9.29. Defining explanations with comparisons.

pop-up. In the center editor, you type >=. Then, in the right editor, you start typing the actual cost (519.75) and select it from the completion pop-up. Finally, you click on the **OK** button in the **Create explanation** window to select this explanation:

$$650.35 >= 519.75$$

Each of these numbers is generalized to a variable, and a general relationship between these variables is learned (i.e., "?N2 >= ?N1"). The learned rule, containing this relationship in its applicability condition, is shown in Figure 9.30.

In general, to define an explanation containing a comparison you have to follow the steps from Operation 9.8.

Operation 9.8. Define explanations containing comparisons

- In the Scenario workspace, during rule learning, in the Reasoning Hierarchy viewer, select a reasoning step by clicking on the corresponding Q/A node.
- In the right panel, click on the **Learn Condition** button.
- In the "Possible explanations" pane, click on the **Create New...** button.
- The agent opens a window for defining an explanation as an object-feature-value triplet (see the bottom of Figure 9.29).
- In the left editor, type the number corresponding to the left side of the comparison (e.g., "650.35" in Figure 9.29) and select it from the completion pop-up.

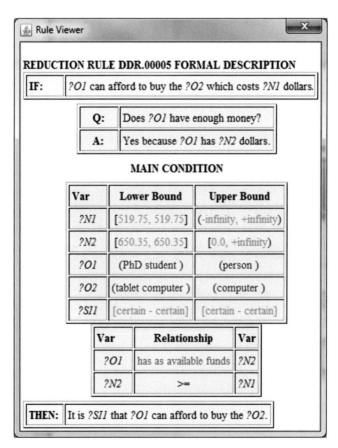

Figure 9.30. Learned rule with a condition containing a comparison.

- In the center editor, type the comparison operator ($<$, $<=$, $=$, $!=$, $>=$, or $>$).
- In the right editor, type the number corresponding to the right side of the comparison.
- Click on the **OK** button in the **Create explanation** window to accept the explanation.

9.12.5 Hands On: Explanations with Functions and Comparisons

The objective of this case study is to learn how to define explanations involving functions (as discussed in Section 9.12.3) and comparisons (as discussed in Section 9.12.4).

Start Disciple-EBR, select the case study knowledge base "12-Explanations/Scen," and proceed as indicated in the instructions at the bottom of the opened window.

9.13 GUIDELINES FOR RULE AND HYPOTHESIS LEARNING

Guideline 9.1. Properly identify all the entities in the example before starting rule learning

Before starting rule learning, make sure that all the elements are properly recognized as instances, numbers, symbolic intervals, or strings. This is important because only the entities with one of these types will be replaced with variables as part of rule learning, as shown in the top part of Figure 9.31. Recognizing concepts is also recommended, but it is optional, since concepts are not generalized. However, recognizing them helps the agent in explanation generation.

Notice the case from the middle part of Figure 9.31. Because "the United States" appears as text (in black) and not as instance (in blue), it will not be replaced with a variable in the learned rule. A similar case is shown at the bottom of Figure 9.31. Because 600.0 is not recognized as number (in green), it will appear as such in the learned rule, instead of being generalized to a variable.

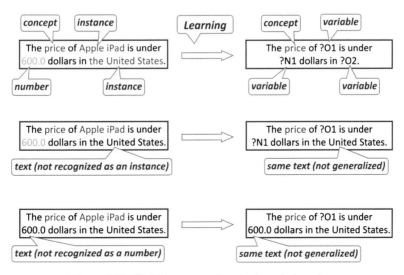

Figure 9.31. Variables generation during rule learning.

Guideline 9.2. Avoid learning from examples that are too specific

It is important to teach the agent with good examples from which it can learn general rules. A poor example is illustrated in the upper-left part of Figure 9.32. In this case, the amount of money that Mike has is the same as the price of the Apple iPad 16GB. As a result, both occurrences of 519.75 are generalized to the same variable ?N1, and the agent will learn a rule that will apply only to cases where the amount of money of the buyer is exactly the same as the price of the product (see the upper-right part of Figure 9.32).

You need instead to teach the agent with an example where the numbers are different, such as the one from the bottom-left part of Figure 9.32. In this case, the agent will generalize the two numbers to two different variables. Notice that the learned rule will also apply to cases where ?N1 = ?N2.

Guideline 9.3. Use modeling-based ontology extension before starting rule learning

Let us consider the reduction step from the left-hand side of Figure 9.33.

If you have used modeling-based ontology specification, then the ontology contains the basic explanation piece of this reduction step:

John Doe has as number of publications 53

Therefore, before starting rule learning, review the modeling and check that you have defined the features suggested by the Q/A pair in the ontology.

What are the other explanation pieces for this reduction step? You will need to define two additional explanation pieces involving comparisons, as well as explanation pieces fixing the values 41, 53, and very likely, as shown in the left-hand side of Figure 9.34. The learned rule is shown in the right-hand side of Figure 9.34.

Guideline 9.4. Carefully define the domains and the ranges of the features

Thoughtfully defined features significantly simplify and speed up the rule-learning process because their domains and ranges are used in determining the minimal and maximal generalizations of the examples, as discussed in Sections 9.7.2 and 9.7.3.

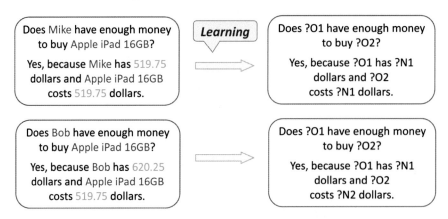

Figure 9.32. Variable generation for identical entities.

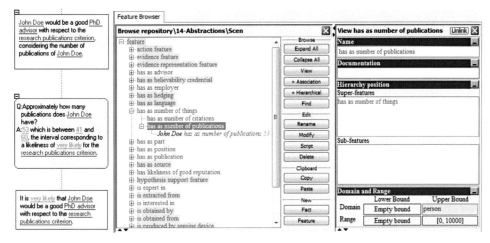

Figure 9.33. Specification of the ontology knowledge for learning.

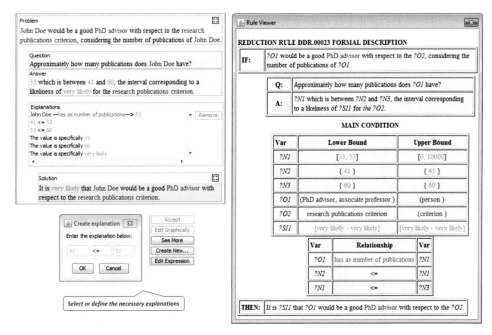

Figure 9.34. Another example of rule learning.

When you define a new feature, make sure you define both the domain and the range. Do not leave the ones generated automatically. The automatically generated range (Any Element) is too general, and features with that range are not even used in explanations. Therefore, make sure that you select a more specific domain and range, such as a concept, a number interval, or a symbolic interval.

If you have already defined facts involving that feature, you need to remove them first before you can change the domain and the range of the feature.

Guideline 9.5. **Provide hints to guide explanation generation**

You may guide explanation generation by selecting one or several entities from the example, asking the agent to propose only plausible explanation pieces involving those entities, as was discussed in Section 9.12.1. This is a very effective way of reducing the combinatorial explosion of explanation generation.

Guideline 9.6. **Avoid learning rules without explanations**

When you invoke **Learn Condition** and then **Finish** without selecting any explanation, the agent automatically generates a plausible version space rule with a very general upper bound condition. The rule is then automatically applied to reduce problems. There is a danger that the rule will generate too many reductions, which may even block the system. To alleviate this situation, the current implementation of Disciple-EBR uses the following heuristic:

> *Generalization heuristic: When no explanation is provided for a reduction step, the upper bound of the learned rule is obtained by generalizing each instance not to "object," but to a direct child of it.*

Even with this heuristic, the plausible upper bound condition is still very general. To alleviate this situation further, consider selecting explanations of the form "<specific instance> is <concept>," such as "John Doe is PhD advisor." You can always provide such explanations that limit the possible values in similar reductions to those that make sense.

An additional explanation type to consider is "<generic instance> is <generic instance>," such as "Artificial Intelligence is Artificial Intelligence." However, make sure that such an explanation makes sense. Do you want "Artificial Intelligence" in all the similar reductions? If yes, then this explanation is necessary. Otherwise, use "Artificial Intelligence is <some concept>."

Yet another explanation type to consider is, "The value is specifically <some value>," such as, "The value is specifically 5.0," or, "The value is specifically certain." However, make sure that these explanations make sense. Do you want 5.0 in all the similar reductions? Do you want "certain" in all the similar reductions?

Guideline 9.7. **Recognize concepts in the reasoning tree**

When editing a node in the reasoning tree, Disciple-EBR proposes completions of the current word based on the names of the instances, concepts, and symbolic probabilities from the ontology. Selecting one of the proposed completions introduces it into the edited statement with a color characteristic to its type (e.g., dark blue for concepts).

Even if the concepts were not recognized at the time of the development of the reasoning tree, they can later be recognized automatically by right-clicking on the top hypothesis and selecting **Recognize Concepts in Tree**. However, only the concepts that appear exactly as in the ontology will be recognized, and only in the nodes that have not yet been formalized.

Having the concepts recognized in the reasoning tree helps the agent in identifying the relevant explanation pieces during the explanation generation process.

Operation 9.9. Recognize concepts in the reasoning tree
- In the Evidence workspace, click on the **Reasoner** menu at the top of the window.
- In the right panel, right-click on the top hypothesis and select **Recognize Concepts in Tree**.

9.14 PROJECT ASSIGNMENT 6

Learn rules from the reasoning trees developed in the previous project assignments.

9.15 REVIEW QUESTIONS

9.1. Define the rule-learning problem.

9.2. What are the basic steps of rule learning?

9.3. Consider the following expression, where both *Jane Austin* and *Bob Sharp* are specific instances:

?O1	is	*Jane Austin*	
?O2	is	*Bob Sharp*	
	has as advisor	?O1	

Find its minimal generalization that does not contain any instance, in the context of the ontological knowledge from Figure 9.35. Find also its maximal generalization.

9.4. Consider the following explanation of a reduction:

Dan Smith plans to retire from *George Mason University*.

(a) Reformulate this explanation as a concept with variables.
(b) Determine the minimal generalization of the concept, in the context of the ontology from Figure 9.36, where all the instances are specific instances.
(c) Determine the maximal generalization of the concept.

9.5. Consider the following explanation of a reduction:

Jane Austin plans to move to *Indiana University*.

(a) Reformulate this explanation as a concept with variables.
(b) Determine the minimal generalization of the concept, in the context of the ontology from Figure 9.36, where all the instances are specific instances.
(c) Determine the maximal generalization of the concept.

9.6. Consider the ontological knowledge from Figure 9.37, where *Dana Jones*, *Rutgers University*, and *Indiana University* are specific instances.
(a) What are the minimal generalization and the maximal generalization of the following expression?

?O1	is	*Dana Jones*	
	plans to move to	?O2	
?O2	is	*Indiana University*	

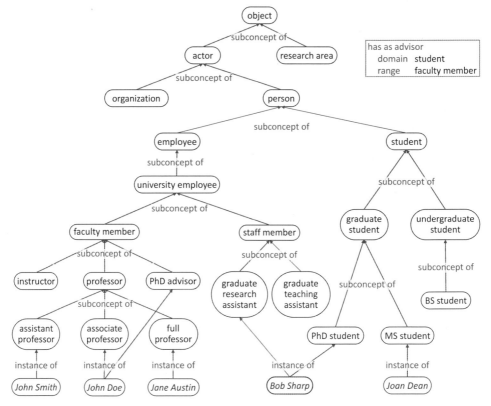

Figure 9.35. Ontology fragment.

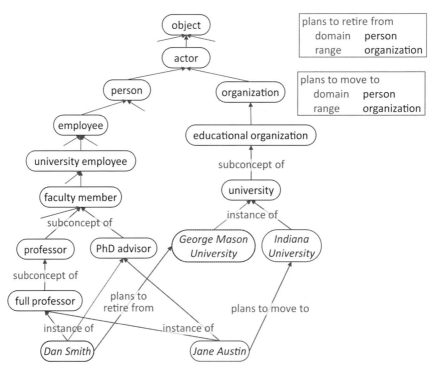

Figure 9.36. Ontology fragment.

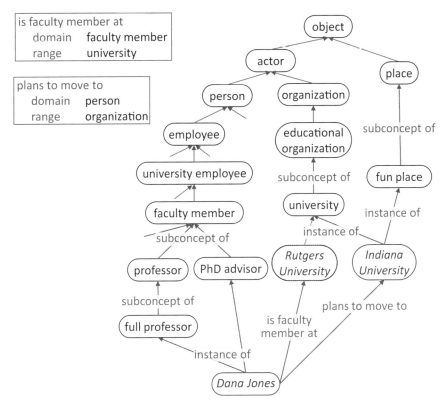

Figure 9.37. Ontology fragment.

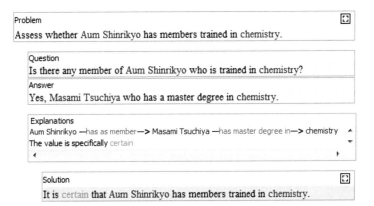

Figure 9.38. A reduction example and its explanation.

(b)   What are the minimal generalization and the maximal generalization of the following expression?

?O1   is   *Dana Jones*

?O2   is   *Indiana University*

9.7.   Consider the example problem reduction and its explanation from Figure 9.38. Which is the specific rule condition covering only this example? What rule will be learned from this example and its explanation, assuming the ontology fragment from Figure 9.39? What general problem will be learned from the specific IF problem of this reduction?

Notice that some of the instances are specific (e.g., *Aum Shinrikyo* and *Masami Tsuchiya*), while others are generic (e.g., chemistry).

9.8.   Consider the problem reduction example and its explanation from Figure 9.40. Which is the specific rule covering only this example? What rule will be learned from this example and its explanation, assuming the ontology fragment from Figure 9.41? What general problems will be learned from this example? Assume that all the instances are specific instances.

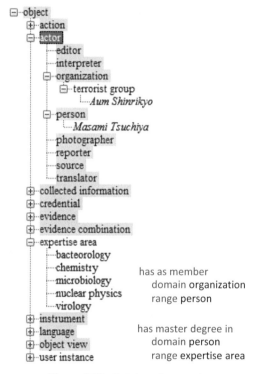

Figure 9.39. Ontology fragment.

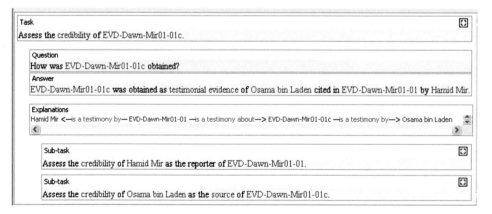

Figure 9.40. A problem reduction example and its explanation.

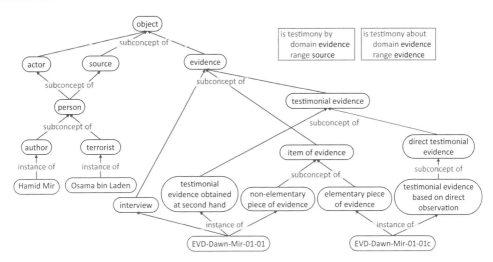

Figure 9.41. Ontology fragment.

9.9. Compare the rule-learning process with the traditional knowledge acquisition approach, where a knowledge engineer defines such a rule by interacting with a subject matter expert. Identify as many similarities and differences as possible, and justify the relative strengths and weaknesses of the two approaches, but be as concise as possible.

10 Rule Refinement

10.1 INCREMENTAL RULE REFINEMENT

10.1.1 The Rule Refinement Problem

The triggering event for rule refinement is the discovery of a new positive or negative example of the rule. There are several possible origins for such an example:

- It is generated by the agent during its regular problem solving
- It is generated by the agent through active experimentation for rule testing
- It is provided by the expert
- It is obtained from an external source (e.g., a repository of examples)

Regardless of the origin of the example, the goal of the agent is to refine the rule to be consistent with the example. A possible effect of rule refinement is the extension of the ontology.

The rule refinement problem is defined in Table 10.1 and an overview of the rule refinement method is presented in the next section.

Table 10.1 The Rule Refinement Problem

GIVEN
- A plausible version space reduction rule
- A positive or a negative example of the rule (i.e., a correct or an incorrect reduction)
- A knowledge base that includes an ontology and a set of (previously learned) reduction rules
- An expert who will interact with the agent, helping it understand why the example is positive (correct) or negative (incorrect)

DETERMINE
- An improved rule that covers the example if it is positive, and does not cover the example if it is negative
- An extended ontology, if this is needed for rule refinement

---

10.1.2 Overview of the Rule Refinement Method

Figure 10.1 shows an overview of rule refinement during problem solving. The agent applies existing partially learned rules to solve the current problem or assess the current hypothesis. As discussed in Section 9.7, the reductions generated by a rule R are analogous with the reduction from which the rule was initially learned. Thus this process can be understood as learning by analogy and experimentation, as indicated in the top part of Figure 10.1.

The subject matter expert has to verify the generated reduction and accept it if it is correct, or reject it otherwise. In both cases, the rule will be improved to become consistent with this new example. We therefore refer to this learning phase as learning from examples, as indicated in the bottom part of Figure 10.1.

If the generated reduction is correct, then it is a new positive example of the rule, which may need to be generalized to cover it, by minimally generalizing its applicability condition. There are various ways to generalize the applicability condition, depending on the position of the positive example with respect to it. For instance, if the example is covered by the plausible upper bound of the main condition (the light green ellipse), but it is not covered by the plausible lower bound (the dark green ellipse), then the plausible lower bound is generalized as little as possible to cover this new positive example, while still remaining less general than (or included into) the plausible upper bound.

If the generated example is incorrect, then the expert has to interact with the agent to help it understand why the reduction is wrong. This interaction is similar to that taking place during the explanation generation phase of rule learning (see Section 9.5). The identified failure explanation will be used to refine the rule. We therefore refer to this phase as learning from explanations, as indicated in the left part of Figure 10.1.

There are various strategies to refine the rule based on a negative example and its failure explanation (if identified), as illustrated in the top part of Figure 10.1. For instance, if the negative example is covered only by the upper bound of the main condition, then this bound is minimally specialized to no longer cover the negative example, while still remaining more general than the plausible lower bound. Or, a new Except-When plausible

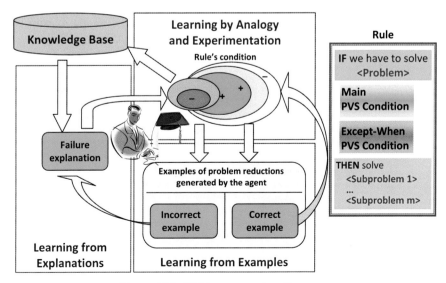

Figure 10.1. Multistrategy rule refinement.

version space condition may be learned, starting from that negative example and its failure explanation. This plausible version space Except-When condition is represented by the red ellipses at the top of Figure 10.1.

The refined rule is shown in the right-hand side of Figure 10.1. The applicability condition of a partially learned rule consists of a main applicability condition and zero, one, or more Except-When conditions. The way the rule is refined based on a new example depends on the type of the example (i.e., positive or negative), on its position with respect to the current conditions of the rule, and on the type of the explanation of the example (if identified). The refinement strategies will be discussed in more detail in the next sections by considering a rule with a main condition and an Except-When condition, as shown in Figure 10.2. We will consider all the possible nine positions of the example with respect to the bounds of these conditions. Notice that the presented methods will similarly apply when there is no Except-When condition or more than one Except-When condition.

We will first illustrate rule refinement with a positive example and then we will present the general method.

10.1.3 Rule Refinement with Positive Examples

10.1.3.1 Illustration of Rule Refinement with a Positive Example

The upper-left part of Figure 10.3 shows an example generated by the agent based on the partially learned rule shown in the right-hand side of the figure. This example is generated because it satisfies the plausible upper bound condition of the rule. Indeed, the condition corresponding to this example, shown in the bottom-left part of Figure 10.3, is covered the plausible upper bound condition: Bob Sharp is a person, Dan Smith is a person, Information Security is an area of expertise, and certain is in the interval [certain – certain]. Additionally, the entities from the example are in the relationships from the rule's condition, that is, "Bob Sharp is interested in Information Security," and "Dan Smith is expert in Information Security."

Notice also that the example is not covered by the plausible lower bound condition of the rule because Dan Smith (corresponding to ?O2) is a full professor, and Information

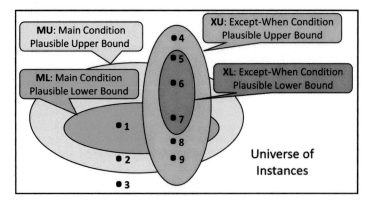

Figure 10.2. Partially learned condition and various positions of a new example.

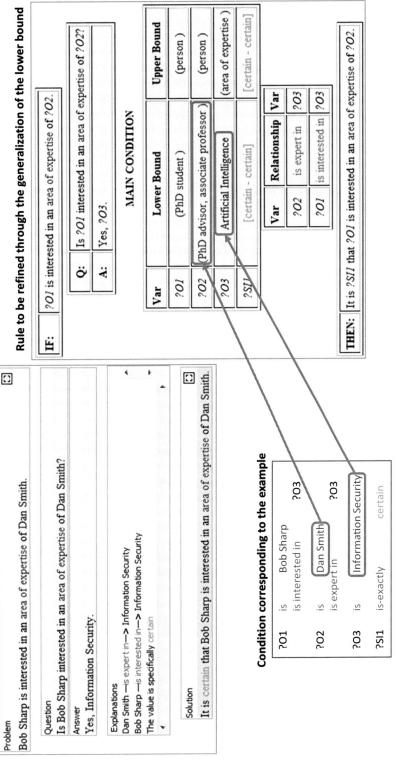

Figure 10.3. Positive example generated by the agent.

Security (corresponding to ?O3) is different from Artificial Intelligence. Therefore, this example corresponds to Case 2 in Figure 10.2.

Because the example is accepted as correct by the expert, the agent will minimally generalize the plausible lower bound condition of the rule to cover it, while still keeping this condition less general than the plausible upper bound condition, as shown in Figure 10.4.

Notice that, with respect to the variable ?O3, Artificial Intelligence and Information Security are generalized to Computer Science, which is the least general concept covering both of them, and is less general than area of expertise, the corresponding concept from the plausible upper bound. With respect to the variable ?O2, PhD advisor does not need to be generalized because it already covers Dan Smith. However, associate professor is minimally generalized to professor to cover Dan Smith, which is a full professor. This is possible because professor is less general than person, the concept from the plausible upper bound. The refined rule is shown in Figure 10.5.

10.1.3.2 The Method of Rule Refinement with a Positive Example

The general rule refinement method illustrated by the preceding example (i.e., Case 2 in Figure 10.2) is presented in Table 10.2. It is similar with the part of the Candidate Elimination Algorithm (Mitchell, 1997) corresponding to the treatment of a positive example.

The method described in Table 10.2 corresponds to the more complex case where the entity E_X from the example is an instance, such as Bob Sharp or Information Security, and the "climbing the generalization hierarchies" rule is used (see Section 8.3.3). Similar methods apply when the entity E_X corresponds to a number, string, or symbolic probability, except that other generalization rules are used, as discussed in Section 8.3.

One of the most difficult problems in computing a good generalization of some expressions is to establish the objects to be matched (Kodratoff and Ganascia, 1986). This

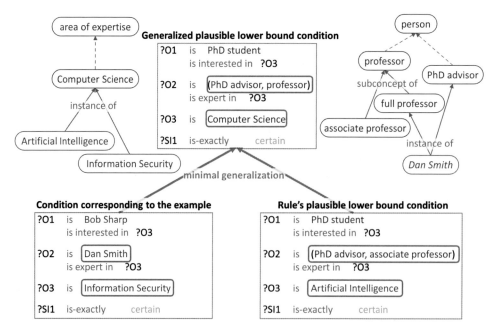

Figure 10.4. Minimal generalization of the rule's plausible lower bound condition.

Table 10.2 The Example-based Incremental Inductive Generalization Method

Let R be a plausible version space rule, U its main plausible upper bound condition, L its main plausible lower bound condition, and P a positive example of R covered by U and not covered by L.

Repeat for each variable **?X** from U
- Let the concept corresponding to **?X** from U be $U_X = \{u_1 \ldots u_m\}$.
- Let the concept corresponding to **?X** from L be $L_X = \{l_1 \ldots l_n\}$.
  Each concept u_i from U_X is a maximal generalization of all the known positive examples of **?X** that does not cover any of the known negative examples of **?X** and is more general than (or as general as) at least one concept l_k from L_X. Also, u_i is not covered by any other element u_k of U_X.
  Each concept l_i is a minimal generalization of the known positive examples of **?X** that does not cover any of the known negative examples of **?X** and is less general than (or as general as) at least one concept u_k from U_X. Also l_i does not cover any other element l_k of L_X.
- Let E_X be the new positive example of **?X** from the rule's example P. E_X is covered by at least one element u_i of U_X.
- Remove from U_X any element that does not cover E_X.

Repeat for each l_i from L_X that does not cover E_X
- Remove l_i from L_X.
- Add to L_X all minimal generalizations of l_i and E_X that are less general or at most as general as an element of U_X.
- Remove from L_X all the elements that are more general than or as general as other elements from L_X.

end

end

Determine P_g, the minimal generalization of the example P (see Section 9.9).

Return the generalized rule R with the updated conditions U and L, and P_g in the list of generalized examples of R.

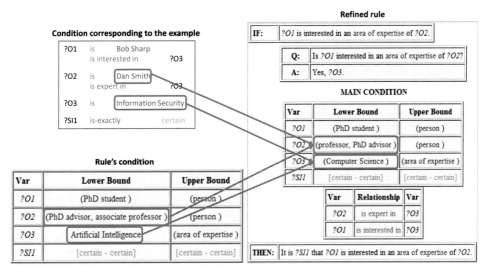

Figure 10.5. Rule generalization based on a positive example.

problem, however, is trivial in Disciple-EBR because both the plausible lower bound condition and the condition corresponding to the example have exactly the same structure, and the corresponding variables have the same names, as shown in Figure 10.5. This is a direct consequence of the fact that the example is generated from the plausible upper bound condition of the rule.

10.1.3.3 Summary of Rule Refinement with a Positive Example

The general method for rule refinement with a positive example, covering all the nine cases from Figure 10.2, is presented in Table 10.3. Notice that a positive example covered by an Except-When condition leads to the specialization of that condition to no longer cover it. This is similar with a negative example covered by the main applicability condition, which is discussed in the next section.

Next we will illustrate rule refinement with negative examples, and then we will present the general refinement method.

10.1.4 Rule Refinement with Negative Examples

10.1.4.1 Illustration of Rule Refinement with Except-When Conditions

The left side of Figure 10.6 shows an example generated by the agent based on the partially learned rule shown in the right-hand side of Figure 10.6. This example is generated because it satisfies the plausible upper bound condition of the rule. However, the example is rejected as incorrect by the expert, with the following explanation:

Dan Smith plans to retire from George Mason University

Based on this failure explanation, the agent generates an Except-When plausible version space condition by applying the method described in Sections 9.6 and 9.7. First it reformulates the explanation as a specific condition by using the corresponding variables from the rule, or by generating new variables (see also the bottom-left part of Figure 10.7):

?O1	is	Dan Smith
	plans to retire from	?O2
?O2	is	George Mason University

Then the agent generates a plausible version space by determining maximal and minimal generalizations of the preceding condition. Finally, the agent adds it to the rule as an Except-When plausible version space condition, as shown in the bottom-right part of Figure 10.7. The Except-When condition should not be satisfied to apply the rule. Thus, in order to conclude that a professor will stay on the faculty for the duration of the dissertation of a student, the professor should have a long-term position (the main condition) and it should not be the case that the professor plans to retire from the university (the Except-When condition).

Figure 10.8 shows the further refinement of the rule with an additional negative example. This example satisfies the rule in Figure 10.7. Indeed, Jane Austin has a long-term position and she does not plan to retire from George Mason University. Nevertheless, the expert rejects the reasoning represented by this example because Jane Austin plans to move to Indiana University. Therefore, she will not stay on the faculty of George Mason University for the duration of the dissertation of Bob Sharp.

Table 10.3 Rule Refinement with a Positive Example

1. If the positive example E is covered by ML and is not covered by XU (case 1), then the rule does not need to be refined because the example is correctly classified as positive by the current rule.

2. If E is covered by MU, is not covered by ML, and is not covered by XU (case 2), then minimally generalize ML to cover E and remain less general than MU. Remove from MU the elements that do not cover E.

3. If E is not covered by MU (cases 3 and 5), or if E is covered by XL (cases 5, 6, and 7), then keep E as a positive exception of the rule. Alternatively, learn a new rule starting from this example.

4. If E is not covered by MU but is covered by XU (case 4), then E is kept as a positive exception (or a new rule is learned). Additionally, interact with the expert to find an explanation of the form, "The problem reduction step is correct because I_i is C_i," where I_i is an instance from the example E and C_i is a concept from the ontology. If such an explanation is found, then XU is minimally specialized to no longer cover E.

5. If E is covered by ML and XU, but it is not covered by XL (case 8), then interact with the expert to find an explanation of the form, "The problem reduction step is correct because I_i is C_i," where I_i is an instance from the example E and C_i is a concept from the ontology. If such an explanation is found, then XU is minimally specialized to no longer cover E. Otherwise, E is kept as a positive exception.

6. If E is covered by MU and XU, it is not covered by ML, and it is not covered by XL (case 9), then minimally generalize ML to cover E and remain less general than MU. Also remove from MU the elements that do not cover E. Then interact with the expert to find an explanation of the form, "The problem reduction step is correct because I_i is C_i," where I_i is an instance from the example E and C_i is a concept from the ontology. If such an explanation is found, then XU is minimally specialized to no longer cover E. Otherwise, E is kept as a positive exception.

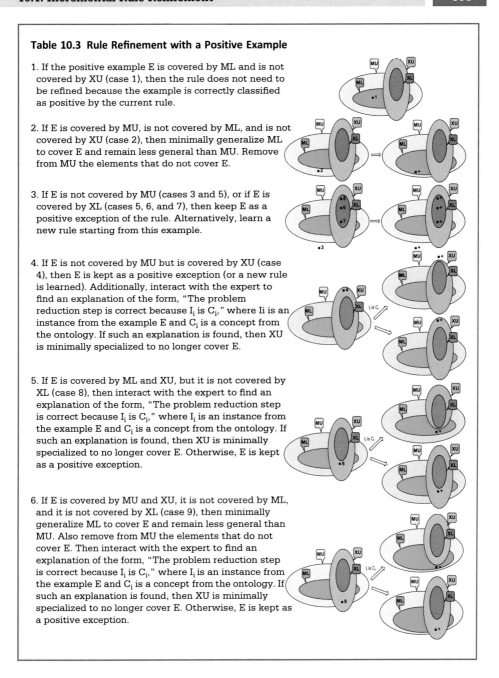

As in the case of the previous negative example, the failure explanation

Jane Austin plans to move to Indiana University

is rewritten as a specific condition

?O1	is	Jane Austin
	plans to move to	?O5
?O5	is	Indiana University

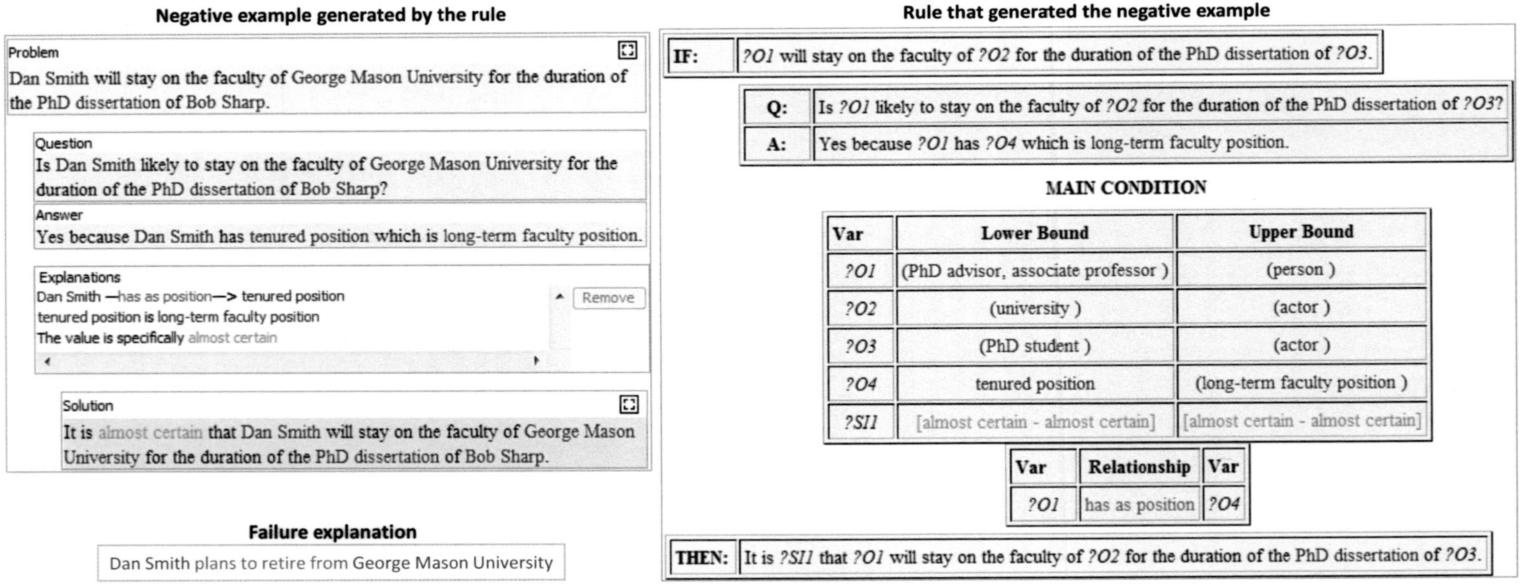

Negative example generated by the rule

Problem

Dan Smith will stay on the faculty of George Mason University for the duration of the PhD dissertation of Bob Sharp.

Question

Is Dan Smith likely to stay on the faculty of George Mason University for the duration of the PhD dissertation of Bob Sharp?

Answer

Yes because Dan Smith has tenured position which is long-term faculty position.

Explanations

Dan Smith —has as position—> tenured position
tenured position is long-term faculty position
The value is specifically almost certain

Remove

Solution

It is almost certain that Dan Smith will stay on the faculty of George Mason University for the duration of the PhD dissertation of Bob Sharp.

Failure explanation

Dan Smith plans to retire from George Mason University

Rule that generated the negative example

IF: ?O1 will stay on the faculty of ?O2 for the duration of the PhD dissertation of ?O3.

Q: Is ?O1 likely to stay on the faculty of ?O2 for the duration of the PhD dissertation of ?O3?

A: Yes because ?O1 has ?O4 which is long-term faculty position.

MAIN CONDITION

Var	Lower Bound	Upper Bound
?O1	(PhD advisor, associate professor)	(person)
?O2	(university)	(actor)
?O3	(PhD student)	(actor)
?O4	tenured position	(long-term faculty position)
?SI1	[almost certain - almost certain]	[almost certain - almost certain]

Var	Relationship	Var
?O1	has as position	?O4

THEN: It is ?SI1 that ?O1 will stay on the faculty of ?O2 for the duration of the PhD dissertation of ?O3.

Figure 10.6. Negative example generated by the agent.

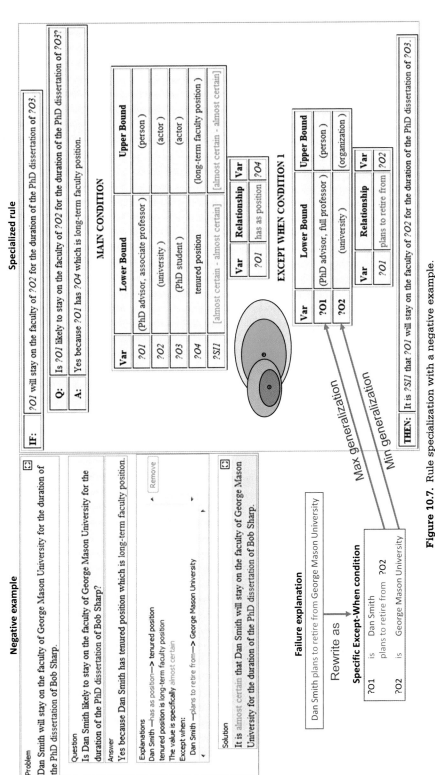

Figure 10.7. Rule specialization with a negative example.

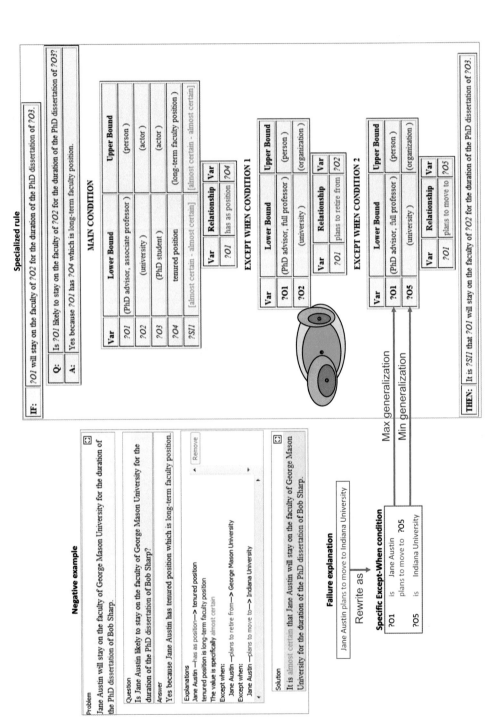

Figure 10.8. Rule refinement with an additional negative example.

Notice that the agent has introduced a new variable ?O5 because Indiana University does not correspond to any entity from the previous form of the rule (as opposed to Jane Austin who corresponds to ?O1).

Then the agent generates a plausible version space by determining maximal and minimal generalizations of the preceding condition. Finally, the agent adds it to the rule as an additional Except-When plausible version space condition, as shown at the bottom-right part of Figure 10.8.

10.1.4.2 The Method of Rule Refinement with Except-When Conditions

The basic steps for learning an Except-When condition based on the explanation of a negative example are summarized in Table 10.4.

10.1.4.3 Illustration of Rule Refinement through Condition Specialization

The preceding two sections presented the refinement of a rule through the addition of Except-When plausible version space conditions. This section will illustrate rule refinement through the specialization of the upper bound of the main applicability condition of the rule.

Figure 10.9 illustrates the mixed-initiative development of a reasoning tree. The expert formulated the hypothesis:

Jill Knox would be a good PhD advisor for Peter Jones.

Then the agent developed a partial reasoning tree, but it was unable to assess one of the subhypotheses:

Jill Knox will stay on the faculty of George Mason University for the duration of the dissertation of Peter Jones.

Table 10.4 Basic Steps for Learning an Except-When Condition

Let R be a plausible version space rule, N an instance of R rejected by the expert as an incorrect reasoning step (a negative example of R), and EX an explanation of why N is incorrect (a failure explanation).

(1) Reformulation of the Failure Explanation

Generate a new variable for each instance and each constant (i.e., number, string, or symbolic probability) that appears in the failure explanation EX but does not appears in the negative example N. Use the new variables and the rule's variables to reformulate the failure explanation EX as an instance I of the concept EC representing an Except-When condition of the rule R.

(2) Analogy-based Generalizations of the Failure Explanation

Generate the plausible upper bound XU of the concept EC as the maximal generalization of I in the context of the agent's ontology.

Generate the plausible lower bound LU of the concept EC as the minimal generalization of I that does not contain any specific instance.

(3) Rule Refinement with an Except-When Plausible Version Space Condition

Add an Except-When plausible version space condition (XU, LU) to the existing conditions of the rule R. This condition should not be satisfied for the rule to be applicable in a given situation.

Therefore, the expert defined the reduction of this hypothesis, which includes its assessment, as shown at the bottom of Figure 10.9.

Based on this example, the agent learned a general rule, as illustrated in the right-hand side of Figure 10.9 and as discussed in Chapter 9. The rule is shown in Figure 10.10.

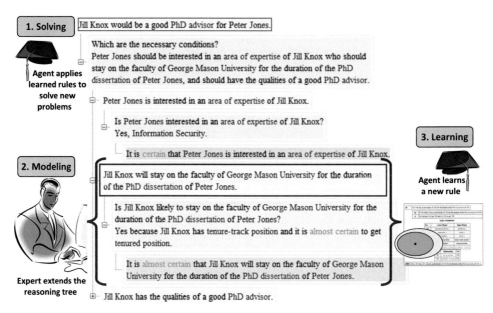

Figure 10.9. Problem solving, modeling, and learning.

IF:	?O1 will stay on the faculty of ?O2 for the duration of the PhD dissertation of ?O3.

Q:	Is ?O1 likely to stay on the faculty of ?O2 for the duration of the PhD dissertation of ?O3?
A:	Yes because ?O1 has ?O4 and it is ?SI1 to get ?O5.

MAIN CONDITION

Var	Lower Bound	Upper Bound
?O1	(assistant professor)	(professor)
?O2	(university)	(actor)
?O3	(PhD student)	(actor)
?O4	tenure-track position	tenure-track position
?O5	tenured position	tenured position
?SI1	[almost certain - almost certain]	[no support - certain]

Var	Relationship	Var
?O1	has as position	?O4
?O1	probability of tenure	?SI1

THEN:	It is ?SI1 that ?O1 will stay on the faculty of ?O2 for the duration of the PhD dissertation of ?O3.

Figure 10.10. Partially learned rule.

This and the other learned rules enabled the agent to develop the reasoning tree from Figure 10.11 for assessing the following hypothesis:

Bill Bones would be a good PhD advisor for June Allison.

However, the expert rejected the bottom reasoning step as incorrect. Indeed, the correct answer to the question, "Is Bill Bones likely stay on the faculty of George Mason University for the duration of the PhD dissertation of June Allison?" is, "No," not, "Yes," because there is no support for Bill Bones getting tenure.

The user–agent interaction during example understanding is illustrated in Figure 10.12. The agent identified an entity in the example (the symbolic probability "no support") that would enable it to specialize the upper bound of the main condition of the rule to no longer cover the negative example. Therefore, it proposed the failure explanation shown at the right-hand side of Figure 10.12:

The example is incorrect because of the value no support.

The expert accepted this explanation by clicking on OK, and the rule was automatically specialized as indicated in Figure 10.13. More precisely, the upper bound of the main condition for the variable ?Sl1 was minimally specialized from the interval [no support – certain] to the interval [likely – certain], in order to no longer cover the value no support, while continuing to cover the interval representing the lower bound, which is [almost certain – almost certain].

10.1.4.4 The Method of Rule Refinement through Condition Specialization

The previous example illustrated the specialization of an upper bound of a condition with a negative example. The corresponding general method is presented in Table 10.5.

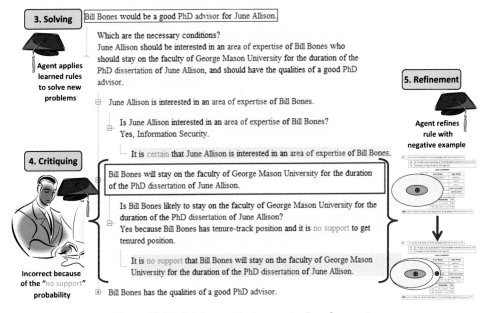

Figure 10.11. Solving, critiquing, and rule refinement.

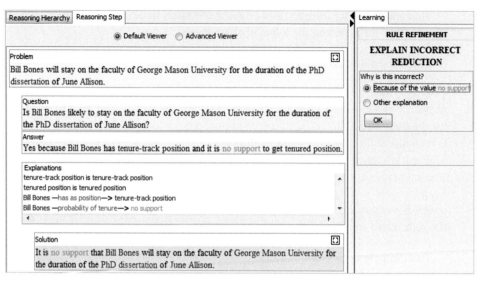

Figure 10.12. Explaining why the problem reduction is incorrect.

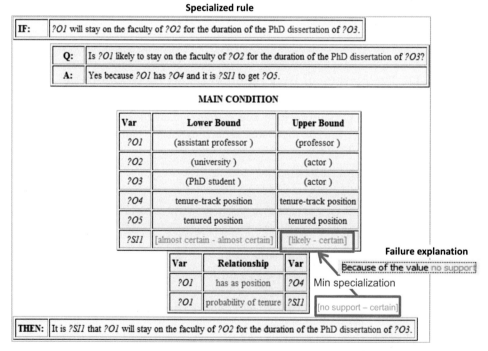

Figure 10.13. Specialization of the upper bound of a plausible version space condition.

10.1.4.5 Summary of Rule Refinement with a Negative Example

We have illustrated only some of the nine cases of negative examples from Figure 10.2 (p. 296). The general method for rule refinement with a negative example, covering all the cases, is presented in Table 10.6.

Table 10.5 The Example-based Incremental Inductive Specialization Method

Let R be a plausible version space rule, U the plausible upper bound of the main condition, L the plausible lower bound of the main condition, N a negative example covered by U and not covered by L, and C an entity from N that is blamed for the failure.

1. Let ?X be the variable from the rule's conditions that corresponds to the blamed entity C.

   Let U_X and L_X be the classes of ?X in the two bounds.

       If each concept from L_X covers C

           then   Continue with step 2.

           else   Continue with step 3.

2. The rule cannot be specialized to uncover the current negative example.
   The negative example N is associated with the rule as a negative exception.
   Return the rule R.

3. There are concepts in L_X that do not cover C. The rule can be specialized to uncover N by specializing U_X, which is known to be more general than C.

   3.1. Remove from L_X any element that covers C.

   3.2. **Repeat** for each element u_i of U_X that covers C

       • Remove u_i from U_X.

       • Add to U_X all minimal specializations of u_i that do not cover C and are more general than or at least as general as a concept from L_X.

       • Remove from U_X all the concepts that are less general than or as general as other concepts from U_X.

       end

4. Return the specialized rule R.

LEARNING WITH AN EVOLVING ONTOLOGY

10.2.1   The Rule Regeneration Problem

The applicability conditions of the learned rules depend of the agent's ontology, which is used as a generalization hierarchy. When the ontology changes in significant ways, the rules need to be updated accordingly. Let us consider that the ontology fragment shown in Figure 9.7 (p. 258) has evolved into the one from Figure 10.14. The changed elements are underlined. In particular, PhD advisor was moved from under professor to above professor. A new concept, expert, was introduced between PhD advisor and person. Additionally, the domains of the features is expert in, has as position, and plans to retire from have been changed from person to expert, employee, and employee, respectively. These are all changes that affect the minimal and the maximal generalizations of the examples from which the rules have been learned. Therefore, the rules need to be updated.

In Disciple-EBR, the adaptation of the rules to a changed ontology is done by simply automatically regenerating the rules based on the minimal generalizations of the examples

Table 10.6 Rule Refinement with a Negative Example

1. If the negative example N is covered by ML and it is not covered by XU (case 1), then interact with the subject matter expert to find an explanation of why N is an incorrect problem reduction step. If an explanation EX is found, then generate a new Except-When plausible version space condition and add it to the rule. Otherwise, keep N as a negative exception.

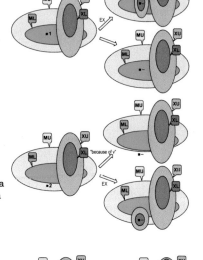

2. If N is covered by MU but it is not covered by ML and by XU (case 2), then interact with the expert to find an explanation of why N is an incorrect problem reduction step. If an explanation EX is found and it has the form "because of v," then minimally specialize MU to no longer cover N while still remaining more general than ML. Otherwise, if another type of explanation EX is found, then learn a new Except-When plausible version space condition based on it, and add it to the rule.

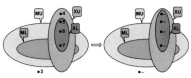

3. If N is not covered by MU (cases 3, 5), or it is covered by XL (cases 5, 6, 7), then the rule does not need to be refined because the example is correctly classified as negative by the current rule. If N is not covered by MU, is not covered by XL, and is covered by XU (case 4), then minimally generalize XL to cover N and remain less general than XU.

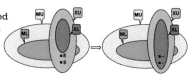

4. If N is covered by ML and by XU, but it is not covered by XL (case 8), or N is covered by MU and by XU, but it is not covered by ML and XL (case 9), then minimally generalize XL to cover N while still remaining less general than XU.

and their explanations in the context of the updated ontology. This is, in fact, the reason why the generalized examples are maintained with each rule, as discussed in Section 9.9.

The rule regeneration problem is presented in Table 10.7. Notice that not all the changes of an ontology lead to changes in the previously learned rules. For example, adding a new concept that has no instance, or adding a new instance, will not affect the previously learned rules. Also, renaming a concept or a feature in the ontology automatically renames it in the learned rules, and no additional adaptation is necessary.

10.2.2 On-Demand Rule Regeneration

Rules adaptation in response to changes in the ontology is an expensive operation if it means regenerating all the rules after each significant change of the ontology. Therefore, the question is: When should the rules be regenerated? The solution adopted in Disciple-EBR is on-demand regeneration. That is, a rule is regenerated only when the agent needs to apply it in problem solving, and only if the current version of the ontology is different from the one when the rule was last refined or regenerated. Thus, the agent associates with the ontology a version, and each time a rule is learned or refined, it associates the version of the ontology with the rule. The version of the ontology is incremented each time a significant change – that is, a change that may affect the conditions of the previously learned rules – is made. Then, before using a rule in problem solving, the agent checks the rule's ontology version with the current version of the ontology. If the versions are the same, the rule is up to date and can be used. Otherwise, the agent regenerates the rule based on the current ontology and also updates the rule's ontology version to the current version of the ontology. The on-demand rule regeneration method is presented in Table 10.8.

Table 10.7 The Rule Regeneration Problem

GIVEN
- A plausible version space reduction rule R corresponding to a version v of the ontology
- Minimal generalizations of the examples and explanations from which the rule R was learned, in the context of the version v of the ontology
- An updated ontology with a new version v'

DETERMINE
- An updated rule that corresponds to the same generalized examples, but in the context of the new version v' of the ontology
- Updated minimal generalizations of the specific examples from the current scenario, if any

---

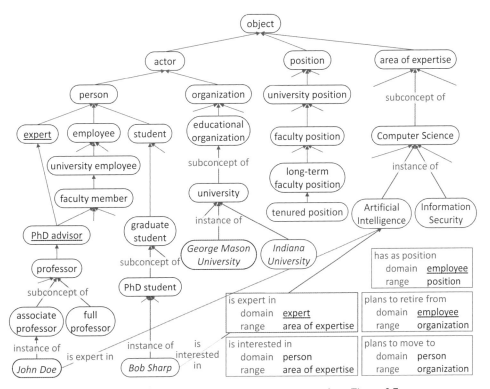

Figure 10.14. Evolution of the ontology fragment from Figure 9.7.

We will first illustrate the regeneration of the rules presented in the previous sections and then provide the general regeneration method.

10.2.3   Illustration of the Rule Regeneration Method

Let us first consider the rule from the right-hand side of Figure 10.5 (p. 299). This rule was learned from two positive examples and their explanations, based on the ontology from Figure 9.7 (p. 258), as discussed in Section 10.1.3.1. This rule can be automatically relearned from its generalized examples, in the context of the updated ontology, as illustrated in Figure 10.15. The bottom part of Figure 10.15 shows the generalized examples of the rule, which were determined in the context of the ontology from Figure 9.7 (p. 258), as discussed

---

Table 10.8 On-Demand Rule Regeneration

Let R be a plausible version space rule, and O the current ontology with version v.

If R's ontology version is v, the same as the version of the current ontology O

    then   Return R (no regeneration is needed).

    else   Regenerate rule R (see Table 10.9).

            Set R's ontology version to v.

            Return R

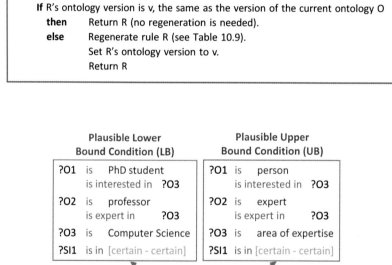

Figure 10.15. The updated conditions of the rule from Figure 10.5 in the context of the ontology from Figure 10.14.

in Section 9.9. The top part of Figure 10.15 shows the updated bounds of the rule, in the context of the updated ontology from Figure 10.14. The new plausible lower bound condition is the minimal generalization of the generalized examples, in the context of the updated ontology. Similarly, the new plausible upper bound condition is the maximal generalization of the generalized examples in the context of the updated ontology.

Notice that in the updated plausible lower bound condition (shown in the upper-left part of Figure 10.15), ?O2 is now a professor, instead of a professor *or* PhD advisor. Indeed, note the following expression from the first generalized example shown in the lower-left part of Figure 10.15:

?O2	is	PhD advisor	[10.1]
	is	associate professor	
	is expert in	?O3	

Based on the updated ontology, where associate professor is a subconcept of PhD advisor, this expression is now equivalent to the following:

| ?O2 | is | associate professor | [10.2] |
| | is expert in | ?O3 | |

Similarly, note the following expression from the second generalized example shown in the lower-right part of Figure 10.15:

?O2	is	PhD advisor	[10.3]
	is	full professor	
	is expert in	?O3	

Because full professor is now a subconcept of PhD advisor, this expression is now equivalent to the following:

| ?O2 | is | full professor | [10.4] |
| | is expert in | ?O3 | |

Then the minimal generalization of the expressions [10.2] and [10.4] is the following expression because professor is the minimal generalization of associate professor and full professor:

| ?O2 | is | professor | [10.5] |
| | is expert in | ?O3 | |

Also, in the updated plausible upper bound condition (shown in the upper-right part of Figure 10.15), ?O2 is an expert instead of a person, because this is the maximal generalization of associate professor and full professor, which is included into the domain of the is expert in feature of ?O2, which is expert.

Let us now consider the rule from the right-hand part of Figure 10.8 (p. 304). The minimal generalizations of the examples from which this rule was learned are shown under the updated conditions in Figure 10.16. They were determined based on the ontology from Figure 9.7. You remember that this rule was learned from one positive example and two negative examples. However, each of the negative examples was used as a positive example of an Except-When plausible version space condition. That is why each of the generalized examples in Figure 10.16 has a positive example.

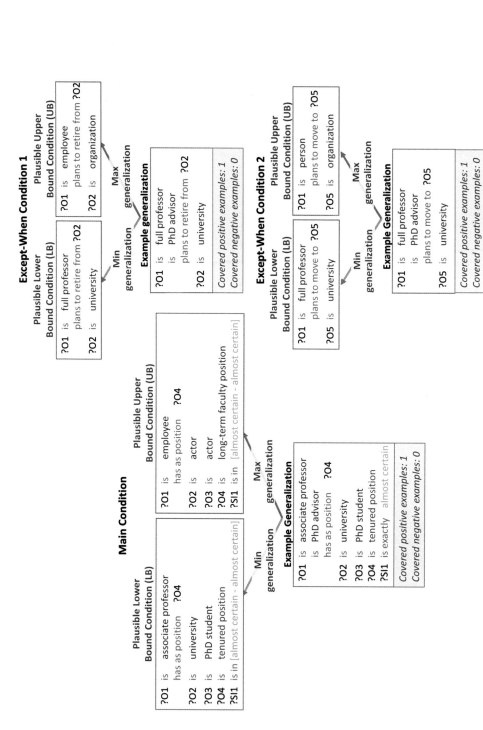

Figure 10.16. The updated conditions of the rule from Figure 10.8, in the context of the ontology from Figure 10.14.

The lower and upper bounds of the rule in Figure 10.8 (p. 304) were updated by computing the minimal and maximal generalizations of these generalized examples in the context of the updated ontology from Figure 10.14. Let us first consider the updated version space of the main condition. Notice that in the lower bound, ?O1 is now associate professor, instead of PhD advisor *or* associate professor (see Figure 10.8). Also, in the upper bound, ?O1 is employee instead of person. The version spaces of the Except-When conditions have also been updated. In the first Except-When condition, ?O1 is now full professor in the lower bound and employee in the upper bound, instead of PhD advisor *or* full professor and person, respectively. Similarly, in the second Except-When condition, ?O1 is now full professor in the lower bound, instead of PhD advisor *or* full professor.

Finally, let us consider the rule from Figure 10.13 (p. 308), which was learned based on the ontology from Figure 9.7, as discussed in Section 10.1.4. The minimal generalizations of the positive and negative examples from which this rule was learned are shown at the bottom of Figure 10.17. They were determined based on the ontology from Figure 9.7. Notice that these generalized examples include all the explanations from which the rule was learned. In particular, the explanation that fixed the value of "tenure-track position" is represented as "?O4 is exactly tenure-track position" and that which excluded the value "no support" is represented as "?SI1 is-not no support *in main condition.*"

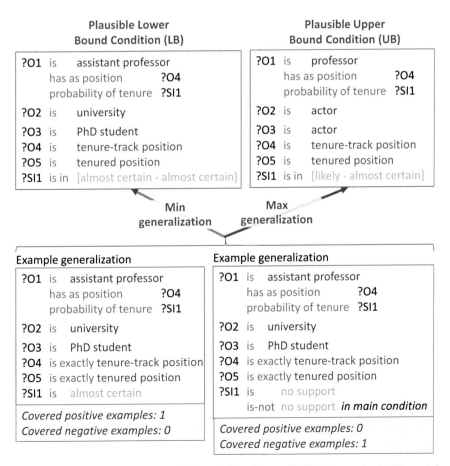

Plausible Lower Bound Condition (LB)

?O1	is	assistant professor
	has as position	?O4
	probability of tenure	?SI1
?O2	is	university
?O3	is	PhD student
?O4	is	tenure-track position
?O5	is	tenured position
?SI1	is in	[almost certain - almost certain]

Plausible Upper Bound Condition (UB)

?O1	is	professor
	has as position	?O4
	probability of tenure	?SI1
?O2	is	actor
?O3	is	actor
?O4	is	tenure-track position
?O5	is	tenured position
?SI1	is in	[likely - almost certain]

Min generalization   Max generalization

Example generalization

?O1	is	assistant professor
	has as position	?O4
	probability of tenure	?SI1
?O2	is	university
?O3	is	PhD student
?O4	is exactly	tenure-track position
?O5	is exactly	tenured position
?SI1	is	almost certain

Covered positive examples: 1
Covered negative examples: 0

Example generalization

?O1	is	assistant professor
	has as position	?O4
	probability of tenure	?SI1
?O2	is	university
?O3	is	PhD student
?O4	is exactly	tenure-track position
?O5	is exactly	tenured position
?SI1	is	no support
	is-not	no support *in main condition*

Covered positive examples: 0
Covered negative examples: 1

Figure 10.17. The updated conditions of the rule from Figure 10.13 in the context of the ontology from Figure 10.14.

The new lower and upper bounds of the rule in the context of the updated ontology from Figure 10.14 are shown at the top of Figure 10.17. Notice that in this case, the regenerated rule is actually the same with the previous rule. The changes made to the ontology did not affect this rule. However, the agent did recompute it because it cannot know, a priori, whether the rule will be changed or not. The only change made to the rule is to register that it was determined based on the new version of the ontology.

10.2.4 The Rule Regeneration Method

The previous section has illustrated the automatic rule regeneration method. Table 10.9 and the ones following it describe the actual method in a more formal way.

10.3 HYPOTHESIS REFINEMENT

Hypothesis refinement is performed using methods that are very similar to the preceding methods for rule refinement, as briefly summarized in this section.

Remember that general hypotheses are automatically learned as a byproduct of reduction rule learning, if they have not been previously learned. When a reduction rule is refined with a positive example, each included hypothesis is also automatically refined with its corresponding positive example. Indeed, when you say that a reduction is correct, you are also implicitly saying that each of the included hypotheses is correct.

However, when a reduction rule is refined with a negative example, the hypotheses are not affected. Indeed, a negative reduction example means that the corresponding reduction is not correct, not that the any of the involved hypotheses is incorrect. For this reason, an explanation of why a specific reduction is incorrect does not automatically apply to the hypotheses from that reduction. If you want to say that a specific hypothesis is incorrect, you have to select it and click on the **Incorrect problem** button. Then the

---

Table 10.9 Rule Regeneration Method

Let O be the current ontology with version v, and R a plausible version space rule with a different version.
1. Recompute the formal parameters P for rule R (see Table 10.10).
2. Refresh examples for rule R (see Table 10.11).
3. **If** R is no longer valid (i.e., the rule has no longer any generalized positive example)
    then   Return null
4. Recompute plausible version space for rule R (see Table 10.12).
5. **Repeat** for each specific example EX of R
    If the upper bound of the main plausible version space condition (PVS) of R does not cover EX and EX is a positive example
        then make EX a positive exception.
    If the upper bound of PVS of R does cover EX and EX is a negative example
        then make EX a negative exception.
    end
6. Return R

Table 10.10 Method for Recomputing the Formal Parameters of a Rule

Let R be a plausible version space rule having the list of parameters P.
Recompute the parameters P of R as follows:
  1. P = IF task parameters ∪ question parameters ∪ answer parameters
  2. **Repeat** for each THEN statement of R
      P = P ∪ THEN statement parameters
  end
  3. **Repeat** for each explanation of R
      P = P ∪ explanation parameters
  end
  4. Return P

Table 10.11 Method for Refreshing the Examples of a Rule

Let R be a plausible version space rule.
  1. **Repeat** for each specific example EX of the rule R
      Keep only the values corresponding to the current list of parameters in the rule R.
  end
  2. **Repeat** for each generalized example GE of the rule R
      Keep only the values corresponding to the current list of parameters in the rule R.
  end
  3. **Repeat** for each specific example EX of the rule R
      If the stored generalized example is no longer a minimal generalization **then**
         Unregister the example from the generalized example.
         If the generalized example has no examples any more
           then delete the generalized example.
         Register the example with its new minimal generalization.
  end
  4. **If** the rule R has no generalized or specific positive examples any more
      then Remove the rule R.

---

selected hypothesis will be refined basically using the same methods as those for rule refinement.

Just as a refined rule, a refined hypothesis may include, in addition to the plausible version space of the main condition, one or several plausible version spaces of Except-When conditions, and generalized positive and negative examples. When the ontology is changed, the hypotheses can be automatically regenerated based on the associated generalized examples. They are actually regenerated when the corresponding rules are regenerated.

10.4   CHARACTERIZATION OF RULE LEARNING AND REFINEMENT

The presented rule learning and refinement methods have the following characteristics:

- They use multistrategy learning that synergistically integrates mixed-initiative learning from examples, from explanations, and by analogy, to take advantage of the

---

Table 10.12 Method for Recomputing the Plausible Version Space of a Rule

Let R be a plausible version space rule having the main condition M and the list of the Except-When conditions LX.

1. Let MP be the list of the parameters from the main condition M.
   Let IP be the list of parameters from the natural language part of the rule R, referred to as informal parameters.
   MP = IP
2. **Repeat** for each explanation of a positive example EP in the rule R
   MP = MP ∪ the new parameters from EP
   end
3. Let LGS be the list of the generalized examples that have at least one specific positive example.
   Let LEP be the list of the explanations EP of the positive examples in the rule R.
   Create the multivariable condition MC based on MP, LGS, LEP, IP (see Table 10.13).
4. Let LX be the list of Except-When conditions.
   LX = [ ]
5. **Repeat** for each group EEp of Except-When explanations in R.
   Let EP be the list of parameters used in EEp.
   Let EX be the list of the generalized negative examples associated with EEp that have at least one specific negative example.
   Create the multivariable condition XC based on MP = EP, LGS = EX, LEP = EEp, and IP = ∅ (see Table 10.13).
   LX = LX ∪ XC
   end
6. Return R

---

complementary strengths of these individual learning strategies and compensate for their relative weaknesses.

- The methods efficiently capture the expert's tacit knowledge, significantly reducing the complexity of developing cognitive assistants.
- They use the explanation of the first positive example and analogical reasoning to generate a much smaller initial version space than Mitchell's classical version space method (Mitchell, 1997).
- The methods efficiently search the version space, guided by explanations obtained through mixed-initiative interaction with the user (both the upper bounds and the lower bounds being both generalized and specialized to converge toward one another).
- They learn from only a few examples, in the context of an incomplete and evolving ontology.
- These methods enable agents to learn even in the presence of exceptions.
- They keep minimally generalized examples and explanations to regenerate the rules automatically when the ontology changes.
- The methods have been successfully applied to develop cognitive assistants for many complex real-world domains (e.g., intelligence analysis, military strategy and planning, education, collaborative emergency response planning), because they enable agents to learn within a complex representation language.

Table 10.13 Method for Creating the Multivariable Condition Structure

Let R be a plausible version space rule, MP be the list of the parameters from the main condition, LGS be the list of generalized examples that have at least one specific positive example, LEP be the list of the explanations EP of the positive examples in the rule R, and IP be the list of informal parameters of R.

1. Let A be the list of the generalized explanations fragments (such as "$?O_i$ is interested in $?O_j$") from the generalized examples of R.
   Compute A based on MP and LEP.
2. Let D be the domains of the variables from MP, each domain consisting of a lower bound and an upper bound.
   D = [ ]
3. **Repeat** for each parameter $?O_i$ in MP
   Determine the list GE = {ge_1, ..., ge_g} of the concepts from LGS corresponding to $?O_i$ (e.g., "assistant professor" from "$?O_i$ is assistant professor").
   Determine the list PC = {PC_1, ..., PC_p} of the concepts to which $?O_i$ must belong, corresponding to positively constraining explanations
   (e.g., "$?O_i$ is exactly tenured position").
   Determine the list NC = {NC_1, ..., NC_n} of the concepts to which $?O_i$ must not belong, corresponding to negatively constraining explanations (e.g., "SI1 is-not no support").
   Create the domains D_o from the examples GE and the constraints PC and NC (see Table 10.14).
   $D = D \cup D_o$
   end
4. Create the multivariable condition structure from MP, D, and A.
   Return MVC

HANDS ON: RULE REFINEMENT

There are two rule refinement case studies, a shorter one and a longer one. In the shorter case study, you will guide the agent to refine the rule from Figure 9.8 (p. 259), as discussed in the previous sections. In the longer case study, you will guide the agent to refine several rules, including the rule from Figure 9.8. You may perform the short case study, or the long one, or both of them.

Start Disciple-EBR, select the case study knowledge base (either "13-Rule-Refinement-short/Scen" or "13-Rule-Refinement/Scen"), and proceed as indicated in the instructions at the bottom of the opened window.

The following are the basic operations for rule refinement, as well as additional operations that are useful for knowledge base refinement, such as changing a generated reasoning step into a modeling step, visualizing a rule with the Rule Editor, and deleting a rule.

Operation 10.1. Refine rule with positive example

- In the Scenario workspace, during rule refinement, in the Reasoning Hierarchy viewer, select a reasoning step for which a rule has already been learned by clicking on the corresponding Q/A node.
- In the right panel, click on the **Correct Reduction** button.

Table 10.14 Method for Creating Domains from Examples and Constraints

Let $?O_i$ be a parameter for which we compute a plausible version space.
  $GE = \{ge_1, \ldots, ge_g\}$ be the set of generalized examples corresponding to variable $?O_i$.
  $PC = \{PC_1, \ldots, PC_p\}$ be the set of concepts to which $?O_i$ must belong, representing positive constraints.
  $NC = \{NC_1, \ldots, NC_n\}$ be the set of concepts to which $?O_i$ must not belong, representing negative constraints.
  1. Compute UB, the maximal generalization of the generalized examples in GE.
  2. Compute LB, the minimal generalization of the generalized examples in GE.
  3. Compute UB, the minimal specialization of UB based on all the positive constraints PC.
  4. Compute LB by selecting from LB the elements covered by UB.
  5. **Repeat** for each NC_i in NC
       Compute LB, the minimal specialization of LB that is disjoint with the negative constraint NC_i.
       Compute UB, the minimal specialization of UB covering LB that is disjoint with the negative constraint NC_i.
     end
  6. Create the list (UB, LB) as the domain D_o for $?O_i$.
  7. Return D_o

Operation 10.2. Refine rule with negative example

- In the Scenario workspace, during rule refinement, in the Reasoning Hierarchy viewer, select a reasoning step by clicking on the corresponding Q/A node.
- In the right panel, click on the **Incorrect Reduction** button.
- Follow the agent's instructions to select or provide a failure explanation.

Operation 10.3. Replace a generated reasoning step with a modeling step

- In the Scenario workspace, in the Reasoning Hierarchy viewer, right-click on the Q/A node of the reasoning step that was generated through the application of a learned rule and select **Replace with modeling**.
- As a result, the reasoning step is replaced with a modeled one that can be changed. Additionally, the initial reasoning step becomes a negative exception of the rule.

Operation 10.4. View a rule with the Rule Browser

- Select the Scenario workspace.
- Click on the **Rules** menu and select **Rule Browser**.
- The left pane displays the names of the rules.
- Click on one of these rules (e.g., DDR.00018) and the right pane displays its description in a given format (e.g., "Formal Description") when you select it in the corresponding tab.
- Generally, you would first find the name of a rule of interest from a reasoning tree (e.g., DDR.00018), as described in Operation 9.3, and then you can view or delete it with the Rule Browser.
- Click on the **X** button of the Rule Browser, to close it.

Operation 10.5. Delete a rule with the Rule Browser

- Generally, you would first find the name of the rule to be deleted (e.g., DDR.00018) by inspecting the reasoning tree, as described in Operation 9.3.
- In the Scenario workspace, click on the **Rules** menu and select **Rule Browser**.
- The left pane displays the names of the rules.
- Click on the name of the rule to be deleted (e.g., DDR.00018), and the right pane displays its description in a given format (e.g., "Formal Description") when you select it in the corresponding tab.
- At the bottom of the right pane, click on the **Edit Rule** button. As a result, new options are displayed.
- At the bottom of the right pane, click on the **Delete Rule** button.
- Click on the **X** button of the Rule Browser to close it.

10.6   GUIDELINES FOR RULE REFINEMENT

Guideline 10.1. Assess similar hypotheses to refine the rules

Formulate hypotheses (or problems) that are similar to those from which the rules were learned. Refine the rules with positive examples by selecting (clicking on) the corresponding Q/A pair, and then clicking on **Correct Reduction** (see the right-hand side of Figure 10.18). You can also click on **Modify Explanations** to interact with the agent and update the explanations (e.g., by adding new ones and/or deleting some of the existing ones).

Refine the rules with negative examples by selecting (clicking on) the corresponding Q/A pair and then clicking on **Incorrect Reduction** (see the right-hand side of Figure 10.18). Then interact with the agent to identify an explanation of why the reduction is incorrect.

Guideline 10.2. Extend the ontology to define failure explanations

If necessary, extend the ontology to provide explanations for negative examples. However, do not limit yourself to a minimal extension of the ontology (that consists of only the failure explanation) if you anticipate that related concepts and features may be needed in the future for related hypotheses or problems.

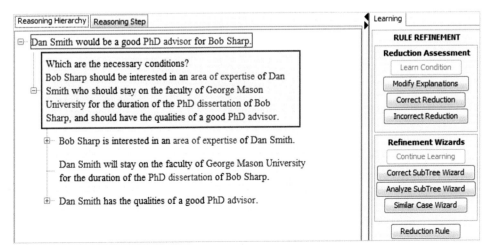

Figure 10.18. Rule refinement with a selected example.

10.7 PROJECT ASSIGNMENT 7

Refine the learned reduction rules by assessing hypotheses that are similar to the ones considered in the previous assignments.

10.8 REVIEW QUESTIONS

10.1. Define the rule refinement problem.

10.2. What are the basic steps of rule refinement?

10.3. Consider the version space from Figure 10.19. In light of the refinement strategies studied in this chapter, how will the plausible version space be changed as a result of a new negative example labeled 1? Draw the new version space(s).

10.4. Consider the version space from Figure 10.20. In light of the refinement strategies studied in this chapter, what are three alternative ways in which this version space may be changed as a result of the negative example 2?

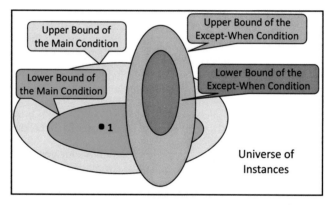

Figure 10.19. Version space and a negative example covered by the lower bound of the main condition.

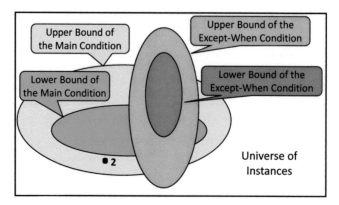

Figure 10.20. Version space and a negative example covered by the upper bound of the main condition.

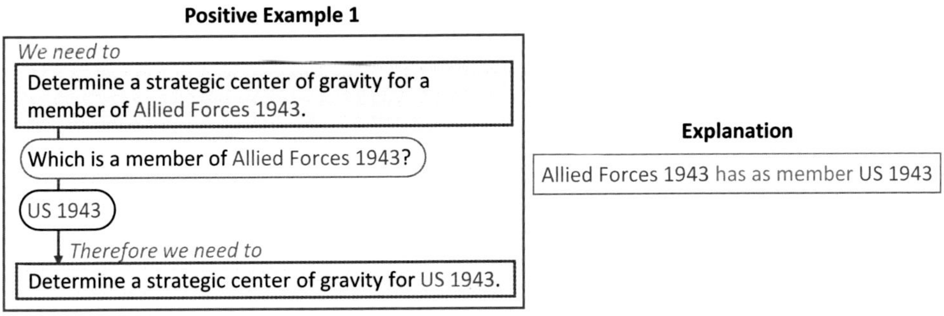

Positive Example 1
We need to
Determine a strategic center of gravity for a member of Allied Forces 1943.
Which is a member of Allied Forces 1943?
US 1943
Therefore we need to
Determine a strategic center of gravity for US 1943.
Explanation
Allied Forces 1943 has as member US 1943

Figure 10.21. A reduction example and its explanation.

object
...
force
force goal
opposing force
multimember force
single-member force
group
multigroup force
multistate force
single-state force
single-group force
illegal group
legal group
multistate alliance
multistate coalition
dominant partner multistate alliance
equal partners multistate alliance
US 1943
UK 1943
Allied Forces 1943
has as member
has as member
European Axis 1943
has as member
Germany 1943
has as member
Finland 1943
has as member
domain multimember force
range force

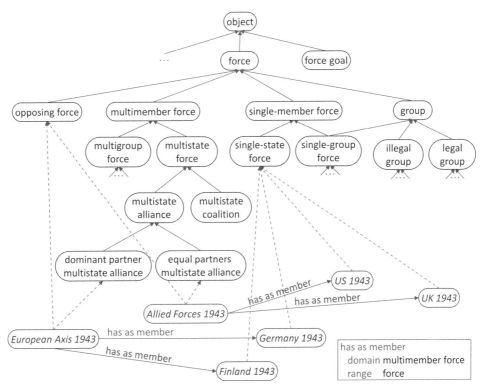

Figure 10.22. Ontology fragment from the center of gravity analysis domain. Dotted links indicate instance of relationships while continuous unnamed links indicate subconcept of relationships.

10.5. (a) Consider the example and its explanation from Figure 10.21. What rule will be learned from them, assuming the ontology from Figure 10.22, where all the instances are considered specific instances?

(b) Consider the additional positive example from Figure 10.23. Indicate the refined rule.

(c) Consider the negative example, its failure explanation, and the additional ontological knowledge from Figure 10.24. Indicate the refined rule.

Positive Example 2

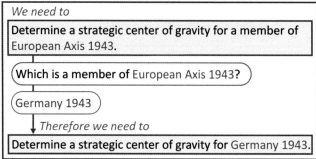

Figure 10.23. An additional positive example.

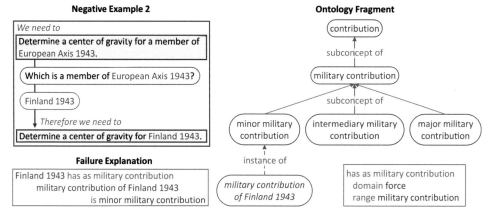

Figure 10.24. Negative example, failure explanation, and additional ontology fragment.

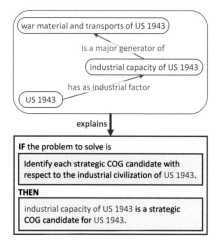

Figure 10.25. An example and its explanation.

10.6. Consider the example and its explanation shown in Figure 10.25. Find the plausible version space rule that will be learned based on the ontology fragments from Figures 10.26, 10.27, and 10.28, where all the instances are defined as generic instances.

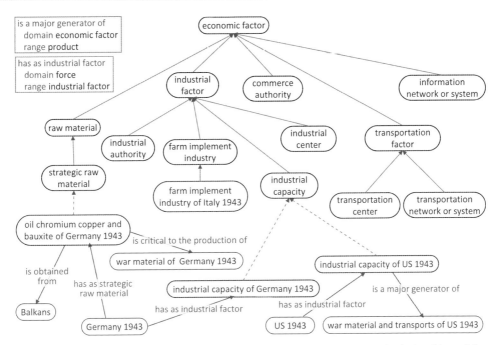

Figure 10.26. Ontology of economic factors. Dotted links indicate instance of relationships while continuous unnamed links indicate subconcept of relationships.

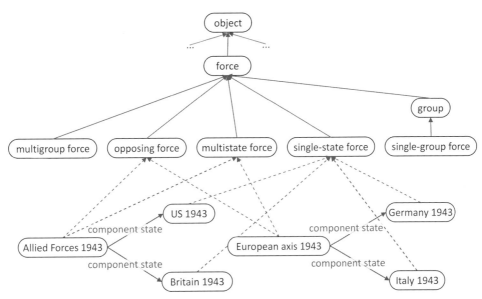

Figure 10.27. An ontology of forces. Dotted links indicate instance of relationships while continuous unnamed links indicate subconcept of relationships.

10.7. Minimally generalize the rule from the left side of Figure 10.29 in order to cover the positive example from the right side of Figure 10.29, considering the background knowledge from Figures 10.26, 10.27, and 10.28.

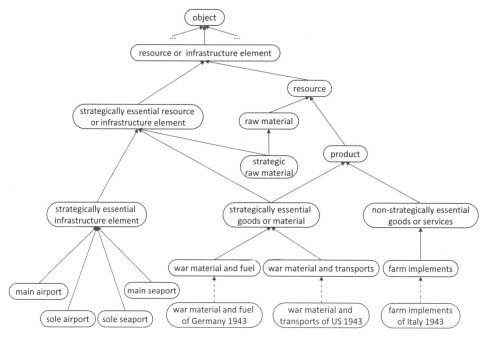

Figure 10.28. An ontology of resources. Dotted links indicate instance of relationships while continuous unnamed links indicate subconcept of relationships.

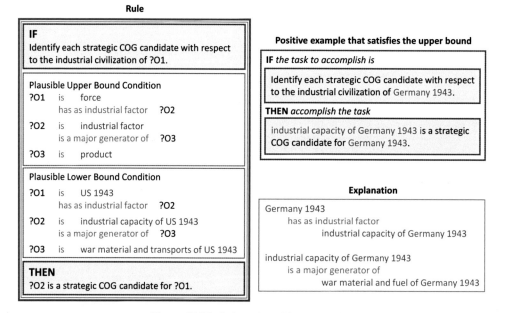

Figure 10.29. Rule and positive example.

10.8.   Minimally specialize the rule from the left side of Figure 10.30, in order to cover the positive example from the right side of Figure 10.30, considering the background knowledge from Figures 10.26, 10.27, and 10.28.

Table 10.15 Rule Refinement with Learning Agent versus Rule Refinement by Knowledge Engineer

	Rule Refinement with Learning Agent	Rule Refinement by Knowledge Engineer
Description (highlighting differences and similarities)		
Strengths		
Weaknesses		

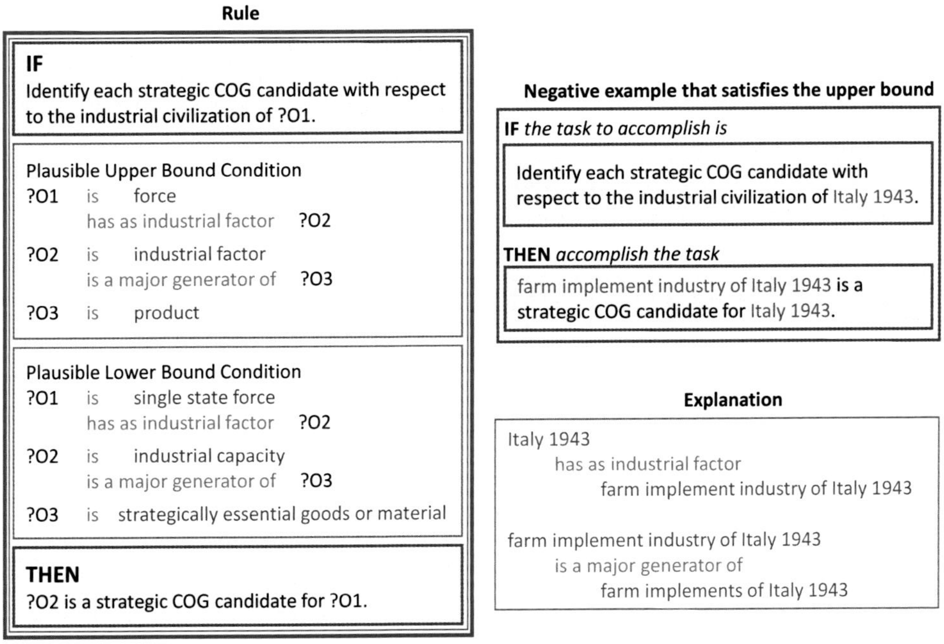

Rule

IF
Identify each strategic COG candidate with respect to the industrial civilization of ?O1.

Plausible Upper Bound Condition
?O1   is   force
         has as industrial factor   ?O2

?O2   is   industrial factor
         is a major generator of   ?O3

?O3   is   product

Plausible Lower Bound Condition
?O1   is   single state force
         has as industrial factor   ?O2

?O2   is   industrial capacity
         is a major generator of   ?O3

?O3   is   strategically essential goods or material

THEN
?O2 is a strategic COG candidate for ?O1.

Negative example that satisfies the upper bound

IF *the task to accomplish is*

Identify each strategic COG candidate with respect to the industrial civilization of Italy 1943.

THEN *accomplish the task*

farm implement industry of Italy 1943 **is a strategic COG candidate for** Italy 1943.

Explanation

Italy 1943
    has as industrial factor
        farm implement industry of Italy 1943

farm implement industry of Italy 1943
    is a major generator of
        farm implements of Italy 1943

Figure 10.30. Rule and negative example.

10.9.   Consider the problem reduction step and its explanation from Figure 10.25, as well as the ontology of economic factors from Figure 10.26. Show the corresponding analogy criterion generated by a cautious learner, and an analogous reduction made by that cautious learner.

10.10.   Indicate five qualitatively different possible uses of an ontology in an instructable agent such as Disciple-EBR.

10.11.   Compare the learning-based rule refinement process discussed in this chapter with the traditional knowledge acquisition approach discussed in Section 3.1.4 by filling in Table 10.15. Identify similarities and differences and justify the relative strengths and weaknesses of the two approaches.

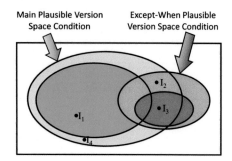

Figure 10.31. A partially learned concept and several instances.

10.12. Consider the partially learned concept and the four instances from Figure 10.31. Order the instances by the plausibility of being positive examples of this concept and justify the ordering.

11 Abstraction of Reasoning

Up until this point, the methodology for developing intelligent agents has encouraged the expert to be very explicit and detailed, to provide clear descriptions of the hypotheses (or problems), and to formulate detailed questions and answers that guide the reduction of hypotheses (or problems) to subhypotheses (or subproblems). This is important because it facilitates a clear and correct logic and the learning of the reasoning rules.

The developed agents can solve complex problems through the generation of reasoning trees that can be very large, with hundreds or even thousands of nodes. In such cases, browsing and understanding these reasoning trees become a challenge.

In this section, we will discuss an approach to abstract a large reasoning tree that involves abstracting both hypotheses/problems and subtrees. The goal is to obtain a simpler representation where the abstract tree has fewer nodes and each node has a simpler description. At the same time, however, we want to maintain the correspondence between the abstract tree and the original tree, in order to have access to the full descriptions of the nodes.

11.1 STATEMENT ABSTRACTION

By abstraction of a statement (hypothesis or problem), we simply mean a shorter statement summarizing its meaning. Consider, for example, the following hypothesis:

John Doe will stay on the faculty of George Mason University for the duration of the PhD dissertation of Bob Sharp.

Any of the following shorter statements is an abstraction of the preceding hypothesis:

John Doe will stay on the faculty of George Mason University.

John Doe will stay on the faculty.

John Doe will not leave.

The expert needs to define abstractions that are short enough to simplify the display of the reasoning tree while still conveying the meaning of the original hypotheses. One abstraction technique is to eliminate some of the words, as illustrated by the first two of the preceding examples. Additionally, one may abstract phrases by using new words, as illustrated by the last example.

The specific hypothesis, "John Doe will stay on the faculty of George Mason University for the duration of the PhD dissertation of Bob Sharp," is shown also in the upper-left part of

Figure 11.1. As discussed in Section 9.10, from each specific hypothesis Disciple-EBR automatically learns a general hypothesis with applicability conditions, which can be further refined. The bottom-left part of Figure 11.1 shows the learned hypothesis whose upper bound condition was further refined. Let us assume that the expert abstracts the specific hypothesis to "John Doe will stay on the faculty" (see the upper-right part of Figure 11.1). As a result, the agent automatically learns the abstraction pattern "?O1 will stay on the faculty," which corresponds to the abstraction of the learned hypothesis (see the lower-right part of Figure 11.1).

The data structures and their relationships illustrated in Figure 11.1 have several consequences. First, all the instances of the learned hypothesis will have the same abstraction pattern. For example, the instance, "Dan Barker will stay on the faculty of University of Virginia for the duration of the PhD dissertation of Sandra Lee," will automatically be abstracted to "Dan Barker will stay on the faculty."

Conversely, if you change the abstraction of a specific hypothesis, the pattern of the learned abstraction will change accordingly. For example, if you now change the abstraction of "Dan Barker will stay on the faculty of University of Virginia for the duration of the PhD dissertation of Sandra Lee," to "Dan Barker will stay with University of Virginia," then the abstraction of the learned hypothesis in Figure 11.1 is automatically changed to "?O1 will stay with ?O2." Therefore, the abstraction of the specific hypothesis from Figure 11.1 is automatically changed to "John Doe will stay with George Mason University."

Thus, although at the beginning of this section we have provided several examples of abstracting a hypothesis, each hypothesis may have only one abstraction at a time. Notice, however, that the same abstract pattern may be an abstraction of different learned hypotheses. Consequently, different specific hypotheses may also have the same abstraction.

Finally, notice that the agent automatically abstracts the probabilistic solution of a hypothesis to the actual probability. Thus, the solution, "It is almost certain that John Doe will stay on the faculty of George Mason University for the duration of the PhD dissertation of Bob Sharp," is automatically abstracted to "almost certain."

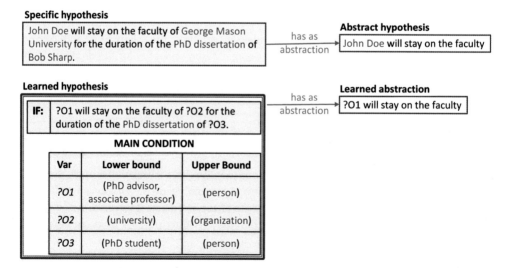

Figure 11.1. Hypotheses and their abstractions.

11.2   REASONING TREE ABSTRACTION

One simple way of abstracting a reasoning step is to abstract all the hypotheses and to eliminate the question/answer pair, as illustrated in Figure 11.2. The right-hand side of Figure 11.2 shows the complete description of a reasoning step. The left-hand side shows only the abstraction of the top hypothesis and the abstractions of its subhypotheses.

Notice that the meaning of an abstract subhypothesis is to be understood in the context of its parent abstract hypothesis, and therefore it can be shorter. For example, "reasons" is understood as "United States has reasons to be a global leader in wind power." Notice also that the abstraction of a hypothesis also includes the abstraction of its assessment, or "unknown" (if an assessment has not yet been made). The assessments (or solutions) may also be made visible in the detailed reasoning tree by clicking on [SHOW SOLUTIONS] at the top of the window.

One may also abstract an entire subtree, not just a reduction step. The right-hand side of Figure 11.3 shows the reasoning tree that is abstracted in the left-hand side of the figure. In particular, the abstract tree consists of the abstraction of the top hypothesis and the abstractions of the leaf hypotheses from the detailed tree.

11.3   REASONING TREE BROWSING

Once a reasoning tree has been abstracted, it can be browsed as illustrated in Figure 11.4. The left-hand side of Figure 11.4 shows the entire abstract tree. Each node in this tree is an abstraction of a hypothesis and of its assessment (or "unknown" if an assessment has not yet been made). The user can browse this tree by expanding or collapsing its nodes through clicking on the + or – nodes. Once you click on a node in the abstract tree, such as "desire: unknown," the detailed description of that node is shown in the right-hand side.

11.4   HANDS ON: ABSTRACTION OF REASONING

The objective of this case study is to learn how to use Disciple-EBR to abstract a reasoning tree. More specifically, you will learn how to:

- Introduce a hypothesis/problem into the abstract tree (see Operation 11.1)
- Define the abstraction of a hypothesis/problem (see Operation 11.2)
- Remove a hypothesis/problem from the abstract tree (see Operation 11.3)
- Browse the abstract tree

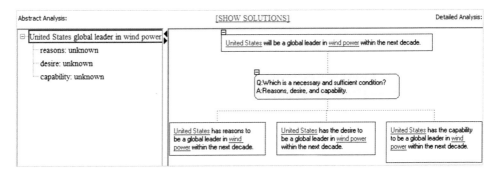

Figure 11.2. Abstraction of a reasoning step.

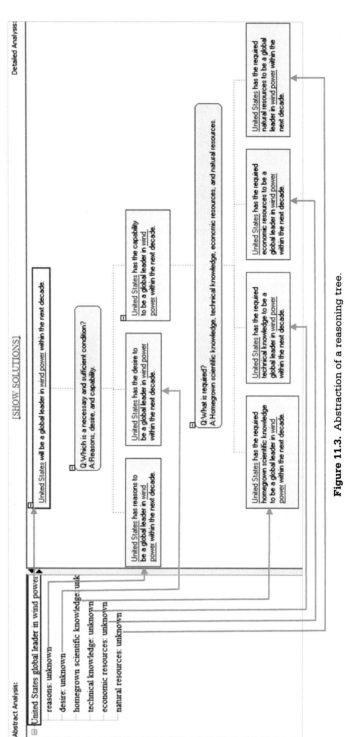

Figure 11.3. Abstraction of a reasoning tree.

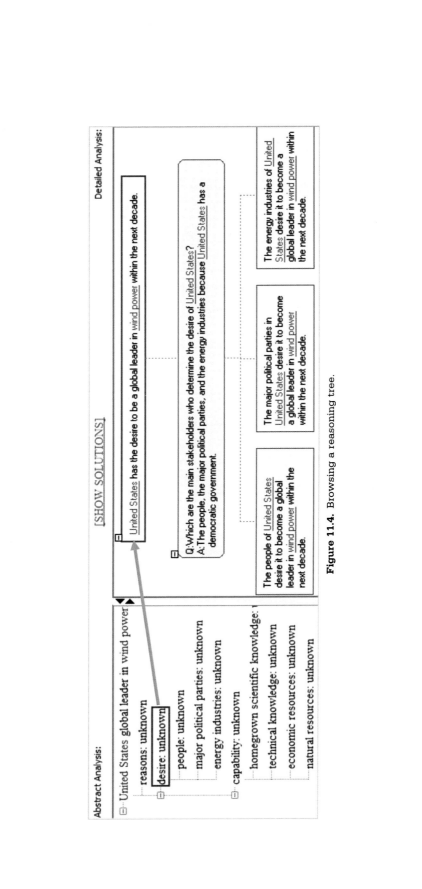

Figure 11.4. Browsing a reasoning tree.

This case study will guide you through the process of abstracting the analysis of the hypothesis, "John Doe would be a good PhD advisor for Bob Sharp," with which you have practiced in the previous case studies.

Start Disciple-EBR, select the case study knowledge base "14-Abstractions/Scen" and proceed as indicated in the instructions at the bottom of the opened window.

This case study illustrates the following operations for the abstraction of reasoning:

Operation 11.1. Introduce a hypothesis into the abstract reasoning tree

- In the Evidence workspace, in the right panel of the Reasoner module, right-click on the hypothesis to be abstracted and select **Add to TOC**.
- Notice that the hypothesis is now displayed in the left panel, while the right panel no longer displays its reasoning subtree.
- If you click on the hypothesis in the left panel, you will see its subtree in the right panel.

Operation 11.2. Modify the abstraction of a hypothesis

- In the Evidence workspace, in the left panel of the Reasoner module, right-click on the hypothesis to be abstracted and select **Modify**.
- In the opened editor, edit the hypothesis to abstract it, making sure that all the remaining instances and constants are recognized (i.e., appear in blue or green). Then click outside the editor.

Operation 11.3. Remove a hypothesis from the abstract reasoning tree

- In the Evidence workspace, in the left panel of the Reasoner module, right-click on the hypothesis to be deleted and select **Remove from TOC**.
- Notice that the hypothesis is no longer displayed in the left panel, while the right panel now displays its reasoning subtree.

11.5   ABSTRACTION GUIDELINE

Guideline 11.1. Define short context-dependent hypothesis names for the abstract tree

Because you always have access to the complete description of an abstracted hypothesis, define the shortest possible abstraction, taking into account that its meaning is to be understood in the context of its upper-level hypotheses. Consider, for example, the abstract hypothesis "US Democratic Party," selected in the left-hand side of Figure 11.5. Its upper-level hypotheses indicate that this refers to one of the "major political parties,"

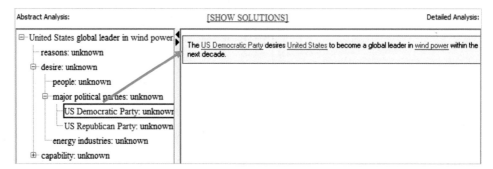

Figure 11.5. Understanding the meaning of an abstracted hypothesis in the context of its upper hypotheses.

which contributes to the "desire" component for the hypothesis "United States global leader in wind power."

11.6   PROJECT ASSIGNMENT 8

Abstract the reasoning trees developed in the previous project assignments.

11.7   REVIEW QUESTIONS

11.1. How is the abstraction of a hypothesis defined? Provide an example.

11.2. How is the abstraction of a reasoning tree defined? Provide an example.

11.3. Consider that the top hypothesis is "John Doe would be a good PhD advisor for Bob Sharp," and that "John Doe would be a good PhD advisor with respect to the professional reputation criterion" is one of its subhypotheses. Indicate several possible abstractions of this subhypothesis, where each such abstraction is to be understood in the context of the top hypothesis.

11.4. Consider the hypothesis, "John Doe would be a good PhD advisor with respect to the professional reputation criterion," and its subhypothesis, "John Doe would be a good PhD advisor with respect to the peer opinion criterion." Indicate abstractions of these two hypotheses, where these abstractions are to be understood in the context of the top hypothesis "John Doe would be a good PhD advisor for Bob Sharp."

11.5. Consider the detailed reasoning tree from Figure 11.6. Provide a corresponding abstract tree, thinking carefully about how to best abstract each of the hypotheses.

11.6. Consider the detailed reasoning tree from Figure 11.7. Provide a corresponding abstract tree, thinking carefully about how to best abstract each of the hypotheses.

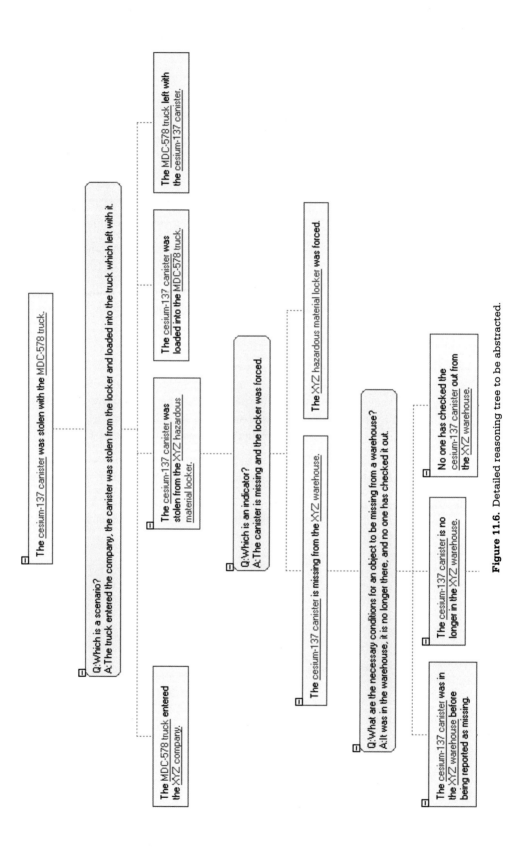

Figure 11.6. Detailed reasoning tree to be abstracted.

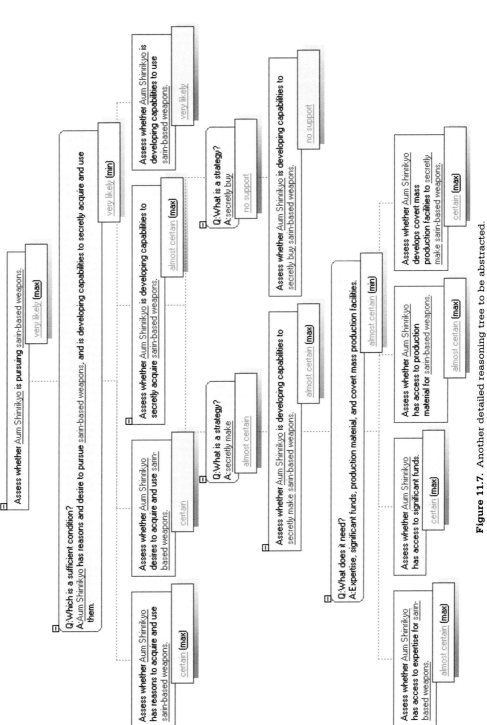

Figure 11.7. Another detailed reasoning tree to be abstracted.

12 Disciple Agents

12.1 INTRODUCTION

The agent building theory, methodology and tool presented in this book evolved over many years, with developments presented in numerous papers and a series of PhD theses (Tecuci, 1988; Dybala, 1996; Hieb, 1996; Keeling, 1998; Boicu 2002; Bowman, 2002; Boicu, 2006; Le, 2008; Marcu, 2009). Although this book has emphasized the development of Disciple agents for evidence-based reasoning applications, the learning agent theory and technology are applicable and have been applied to a wide range of knowledge-intensive tasks, such as those discussed in Section 1.6.2.

A previous book (Tecuci, 1998) presented the status of this work at that time and included descriptions of Disciple agents for designing plans for loudspeaker manufacturing, for assessing students' higher-order thinking skills in history or in statistics, for configuring computer systems, and for representing a virtual armored company commander in distributed interactive simulations.

More recent Disciple agents and their applications include Disciple-WA, an agent for the development of military engineering plans; Disciple-COA, for the critiquing of military courses of action; Disciple-COG, for military center of gravity determination; Disciple agents representing virtual experts for collaborative emergency response planning; Disciple-LTA, for intelligence analysis; Disciple-FS, for regulatory compliance in financial services industries; Disciple-WB, for assessing the believability of websites; and Disciple agents for modeling the behavior of violent extremists.

The following sections present four of these agents and their applications. While all illustrate the general agent development approach discussed in this book, they differ in some of their capabilities and appearance, each reflecting a different stage or trajectory in the development of the Disciple approach.

12.2 DISCIPLE-WA: MILITARY ENGINEERING PLANNING

12.2.1 The Workaround Planning Problem

The workaround planning problem consists of assessing how rapidly and by what method a military unit can reconstitute or bypass damage to a transportation infrastructure, such as a damaged and/or mined bridge, a blocked tunnel, or a cratered road (Cohen et al. 1998; Jones, 1998).

The input to the agent includes three elements:

- A description of the military unit that needs to work around some damage (e.g., an armored tank brigade or a supply company)
- A description of the damage (e.g., a span of the bridge is dropped and the area is mined) and of the terrain (e.g., the soil type; the slopes of the riverbanks; the river's speed, depth, and width)
- A detailed description of the resources in the area that could be used to repair the damage. This includes a description of the engineering assets of the military unit that has to work around the damage, as well as the descriptions of other military units in the area that could provide additional resources

The output of the agent consists of the most likely repair strategies, each described in terms of three elements:

- A reconstitution schedule, giving the transportation capacity of the repaired link (bridge, road, or tunnel), as a function of time, including both a minimum time and an expected time
- A time line of engineering actions to perform the repair, the minimum as well as the expected time that these actions require, and the temporal constraints among them
- A set of required assets for the entire strategy and for each action

Workaround plan generation requires detailed knowledge about the capabilities of the engineering equipment and its use. For example, repairing damage to a bridge typically involves different types of mobile bridging equipment and earth-moving equipment. Each kind of mobile bridge takes a characteristic amount of time to deploy, requires different kinds of bank preparation, and is owned by different echelons in the military hierarchy. This information was available from military experts and U.S. Army field manuals.

Figure 12.1 illustrates a sample input problem for Disciple-WA, a destroyed bridge over a 25-meter-wide river that needs to be crossed by UNIT 91010.

Disciple-WA automatically generates all the possible plans and selects the one that has the minimum duration. The best plan for the problem illustrated in Figure 12.1 is shown in

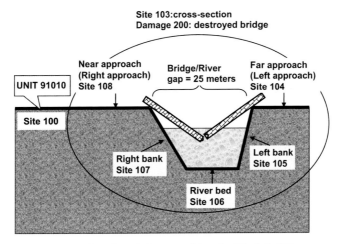

Figure 12.1. Sample input problem for Disciple-WA.

Figure 12.2. Notice that, in Disciple-WA, we used a structured representation of the actions, each consisting of a name and a sequence of feature-value pairs.

The top part of Figure 12.2 shows a summary of the plan. It consists of installing an armored vehicle launched bridge (AVLB) over the river gap. It is estimated that this will take a minimum of 11h:4m:58s, but it is expected to take 14h:25m:56s. UNIT91010 will need the help of UNIT202, which has the AVLB equipment, and of UNIT201, which has a bulldozer. After the bridge is installed, it will allow a traffic rate of 135.13 vehicles per hour.

Initial task:
WORKAROUND-DAMAGE
    FOR-DAMAGE   DAMAGE200
    BY-INTERDICTED-UNIT   UNIT91010

Engineering action: INSTALL AVLB
    MIN-DURATION   11H:4M:58S
    EXPECTED-DURATION   14H:25M:56S
    RESOURCES-REQUIRED AVLB-UNIT202
                      BULLDOZER-UNIT201
    LINK CAPACITY-AFTER-RECONSTRUCTION
                      135.13 VEHICLES/HR

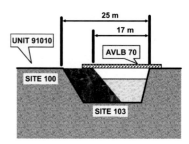

Detailed plan:

S1 OBTAIN-OPERATIONAL-CONTROL-FROM-CORPS
    OF-UNIT   UNIT202
    BY-UNIT   UNIT91010
    MIN-DURATION   4H:0M:0S
    EXPECTED-DURATION   6H:0M:0S
    TIME-CONSTRAINTS   NONE

S2 MOVE-UNIT
    FOR-UNIT   UNIT202
    FROM-LOCATION   SITE0
    TO-LOCATION   SITE100
    MIN-DURATION   1H:8M:14S
    EXPECTED-DURATION   1H:8M:14S
    TIME-CONSTRAINTS   AFTER S1

S3 REPORT-OBTAINED-EQUIPMENT
    FOR-EQ-SET   AVLB-UNIT202
    MIN-DURATION   0S
    EXPECTED-DURATION   0S
    TIME-CONSTRAINTS   AFTER S2

S4 OBTAIN-OPERATIONAL-CONTROL-FROM-CORPS
    OF-UNIT   UNIT201
    BY-UNIT   UNIT91010
    MIN-DURATION   4H:0M:0S
    EXPECTED-DURATION   6H:0M:0S
    TIME-CONSTRAINTS   NONE

S5 MOVE UNIT
    FOR-UNIT   UNIT201
    FROM-LOCATION   SITE0
    TO-LOCATION   SITE100
    MIN-DURATION   1H:8M:14S
    EXPECTED-DURATION   1H:8M:14S
    TIME-CONSTRAINTS   AFTER S4

S6 REPORT-OBTAINED-EQUIPMENT
    FOR-EQ-SET   BULLDOZER-UNIT201
    MIN-DURATION   0S
    EXPECTED-DURATION   0S
    TIME-CONSTRAINTS   AFTER S5

S7 NARROW-GAP-BY-FILLING-WITH-BANK
    FOR-GAP   SITE103
    FOR-BR-DESIGN   AVLB70
    MIN-DURATION   5H:19M:44S
    EXPECTED-DURATION   6H:7M:42S
    RESOURCES-REQUIRED BULLDOZER-UNIT201
    TIME-CONSTRAINTS   AFTER S6

S8 EMPLACE-AVLB
    FOR-BR-DESIGN   AVLB70
    MIN-DURATION   5M:0S
    EXPECTED-DURATION   10M:0S
    RESOURCES-REQUIRED AVLB-UNIT202
    TIME-CONSTRAINTS   AFTER S3, S7

S9 REPORT-EMPLACED-FIXED-BRIDGE
    FOR-MIL-BRIDGE   AVLB-UNIT202
    MIN-DURATION   0S
    EXPECTED-DURATION   0S
    TIME-CONSTRAINTS   AFTER S8

S10 MOVE-EQUIPMENT-OVER-UNSTABILIZED-MIL-BRIDGE
    FOR-EQ-SET   BULLDOZER-UNIT201
    FOR-BR-DESIGN   AVLB70
    MIN-DURATION   2M:0S
    EXPECTED-DURATION   10M:0S
    RESOURCES-REQUIRED AVLB-UNIT202
    TIME-CONSTRAINTS   AFTER S9

S11 MINOR-BANK-PREPARATION
    OF-BANK   SITE105
    MIN-DURATION   30M:0S
    EXPECTED-DURATION   50M:0S
    RESOURCES-REQUIRED BULLDOZER-UNIT201
    TIME-CONSTRAINTS   AFTER S10

S12 RESTORE-TRAFFIC-LINK
    FOR-UNIT   UNIT91010
    FOR-LINK   AVLB70
    LINK-CAPACITY   135.13 VEHICLES/H
    MIN-DURATION   0S
    EXPECTED-DURATION   0S

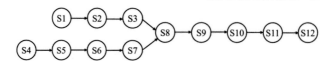

Figure 12.2. The best workaround plan.

The detailed plan is shown under its summary and consists of twelve elementary actions. UNIT91010 has to obtain operational control of UNIT202, which has the AVLB. Then UNIT202 has to come to the site of the destroyed bridge. Also, UNIT91010 has to obtain operational control of UNIT201, which has a bulldozer. Then UNIT201 will have to move to the site of the destroyed bridge and to narrow the river gap from 25 meters to 17 meters. These actions can take place in parallel with the actions of bringing UNIT202 to the bridge site, as shown at the bottom of Figure 12.2. Then the AVLB bridge is emplaced, and the bulldozer moves over the bridge to clear the other side of the river in order to restore the flow of traffic. This plan was generated by successively reducing the WORKAROUND-DAMAGE task to simpler subtasks, until this task was reduced to the twelve tasks shown in Figure 12.2.

The process of developing this agent has followed the general Disciple methodology, as briefly discussed in the next sections.

12.2.2 Modeling the Workaround Planning Process

As discussed in Section 4.2, the subject matter expert has to model the planning process of the agent as problem/task reduction and solution synthesis. The top-level organization of the reasoning tree was already introduced in Figure 4.35 (p. 148), as part of Guideline 4.1. Figure 12.3 shows the reduction tree corresponding to the workaround problem from Figure 12.1.

The top-level task is to work around whatever obstacle is encountered by UNIT91010. This general task is successively reduced to simpler and simpler tasks, guided by questions whose answers either are obtained from the description of the problem or indicate ways to perform an action. In this case, for instance, the obstacle is a damaged bridge but without having any mines, at SITE100. Possible solutions to work around this obstacle are to ford the river, to use a fixed bridge over the river, or to use a floating bridge. All these alternatives are considered, but the tree in Figure 12.3 shows only the fixed bridge solution. There are also alternatives ways to use a fixed bridge. In the case of the considered problem, the river is too wide to install a fixed bridge directly, but it is narrow enough to be further narrowed in order to install the bridge. Therefore, the solution is first to reduce the gap by moving dirt into it with a bulldozer, and then to install an AVLB. However, because UNIT91010 has neither the bulldozer nor the fixed bridge, it has to obtain them from other units. As a result, the task, USE-FIXED-BRIDGE-WITH-GAP-REDUCTION-OVER-GAP, is reduced to three subtasks:

OBTAIN-AVLB
OBTAIN-BULLDOZER-AND-NARROW-GAP
INSTALL-AVLB-OVER-NARROWED-GAP

Each of these subtasks is further reduced to elementary tasks that will constitute the generated plan shown in Figure 12.2. For example, OBTAIN-AVLB is reduced to the following elementary tasks:

S1 OBTAIN-OPERATIONAL-CONTROL-FROM-CORPS
S2 MOVE-UNIT
S3 REPORT-OBTAINED-EQUIPMENT

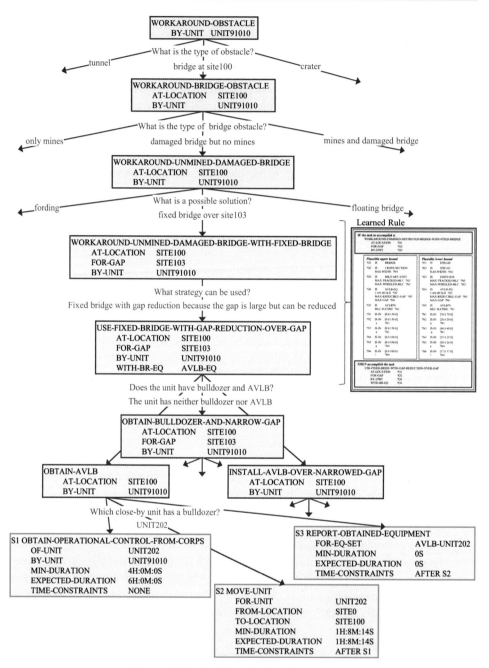

Figure 12.3. Modeling the planning process.

Since these are elementary tasks that can be directly performed by the actual units, they have known minimum and expected durations that are specified in military manuals. Notice that these durations are specified in the descriptions of these tasks, as shown at the bottom of Figure 12.3.

Similarly, OBTAIN-BULLDOZER-AND-NARROW-GAP from Figure 12.3 is reduced to the tasks S4, S5, S6, and S7, as shown in Figure 12.2. Also, INSTALL-AVLB-OVER-NARROWED-GAP is reduced to the tasks S8, S9, S10, S11, and S12.

Notice that the generated plan is a partially ordered one, where some of the actions are actually performed in parallel. Disciple-WA uses a very simple strategy to generate such plans that does not require maintaining complex state descriptions and operators with preconditions and effects, as other planning systems do. Instead, it generates REPORT actions with duration 0 that mark the achievement of conditions used in ordering elementary actions generated in different parts of the planning tree. For example, the action S8 EMPLACE-AVLB from Figure 12.2 can be performed only after S3 (a REPORT action) and S7:

S3 REPORT-OBTAINED-EQUIPMENT
S7 NARROW-GAP-BY-FILLING-WITH-BANK

12.2.3   Ontology Design and Development

As discussed in Section 6.4, modeling trees like the one in Figure 12.3 provide a specification of the concepts and features to be represented in the ontology of the agent. We have defined these entities by using information from several military engineering manuals. We have also imported elements of the military unit ontology, as well as various characteristics of military equipment (such as their tracked and wheeled vehicle military load classes) from the Loom server (MacGregor, 1991). Figure 12.4, for instance, presents a fragment of the hierarchy of concepts from the ontology of the workaround agent. Included are several types of military bridges that can be used to cross a river. Notice that, in Disciple-WA, we used "CLASS" to refer to a concept, and "SUBCLASS-OF" to denote a "subconcept of" relation.

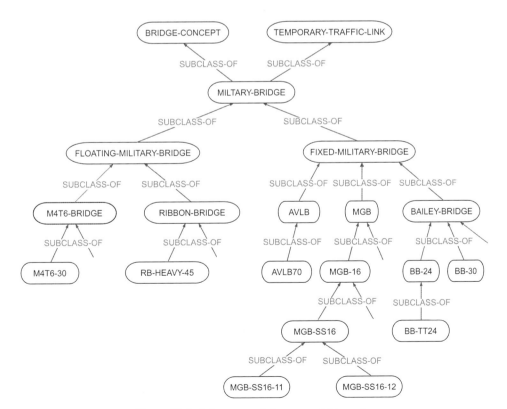

Figure 12.4. A fragment of the concept hierarchy.

Figure 12.5 contains the descriptions of two concepts from the hierarchy in Figure 12.4, AVLB and AVLB70. An AVLB is a subclass of fixed military bridge that has additional features. AVLB70 is a subclass of AVLB bridge. Each such concept inherits all of the features of its superconcepts. Therefore, all the features of AVLB are also features of AVLB70.

The features are defined in the same way as the concepts, in terms of more general features. Figure 12.6, for instance, presents a fragment of the feature hierarchy. Two important characteristics of any feature are its domain (the set of objects that could have this feature) and its range (the set of possible values of the feature). The features may also specify functions for computing their values.

AVLB	SUBCLASS-OF	FIXED-MILITARY-BRIDGE
	MIN-CROSSING-TIME-FOR-UNSTABILIZED-END	2 MIN
	EXPECTED-CROSSING-TIME-FOR-UNSTABILIZED-END	10 MIN
	MIN-EMPLACEMENT-TIME	5 MIN
	EXPECTED-EMPLACEMENT-TIME	10 MIN
	MAX-DOWNHILL-SLOPE-FOR-EQ	19 %
	MAX-TRANSVERSE-SLOPE	11 %
	MAX-UPHILL-SLOPE-FOR-EQ	28 %
AVLB70	SUBCLASS-OF	AVLB
	HAS-WIDTH	19.2 METERS
	MAX-GAP	17 METERS
	MAX-REDUCIBLE-GAP	26 METERS
	MLC-RATING	70 TONS
	WEIGHT	15 TONS

Figure 12.5. Descriptions of two concepts from the hierarchy in Figure 12.4.

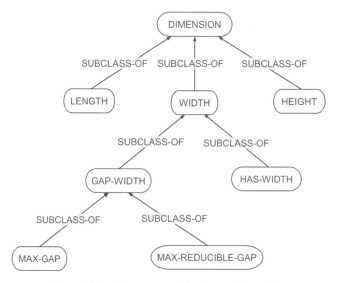

Figure 12.6. A fragment of the feature hierarchy.

12.2.4   Rule Learning

As presented in Chapters 9 and 10, a Disciple agent learns rules from individual reasoning steps and their explanations, as illustrated in the middle of Figure 12.3. That task reduction step is shown again in the top part of Figure 12.7. It states that in order to work around the damaged bridge at SITE100, one can use a bridge equipment of type AVLB-EQ and to reduce the size of the gap.

The bottom part of Figure 12.7 shows the explanation of this task reduction step, obtained through an interaction with the expert. The first two explanation pieces justify why one can use gap reduction.

The width of the SITE103 gap is 25 meters, and the AVLB-EQ allows building a bridge of type AVLB70 that can span gaps only as long as 17 meters. Therefore, the gap is too wide to install an AVLB70 directly. However, any gap that is smaller than 26 meters can be reduced to a 17 meter gap on which one can install an AVLB70 bridge.

The next two explanation pieces show that an AVLB70 bridge is strong enough to sustain the vehicles of UNIT91010.

The maximum load class of the wheeled vehicles of UNIT91010 is 20 tons, and AVLB70 can sustain vehicles with a load of up to 70 tons. Similarly, the AVLB70 bridge can sustain the tracked vehicles of UNIT91010.

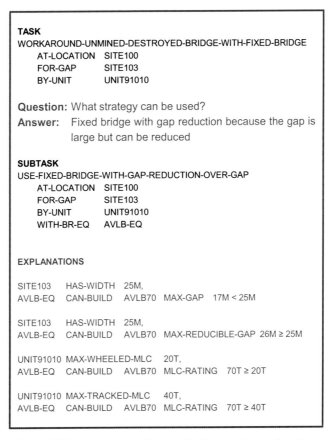

Figure 12.7. An example of task reduction and its explanation.

Figure 12.8 shows the plausible version space rule learned from the task reduction example and its explanation in Figure 12.7.

12.2.5 Experimental Results

Disciple-WA (Tecuci et al., 1999; 2000) was tested together with three other systems in a two-week intensive study, in June 1998, as part of the Defense Advance Research Projects Agency's (DARPA) annual High Performance Knowledge Bases (HPKB) program evaluation (Cohen et al. 1998). The evaluation, performed by Alphatech, consisted of two phases, each comprising a test and a retest. In the first phase, the systems were tested on twenty problems that were similar to those used for systems development. Then the solutions were provided, and the developers had one week to improve their systems, which were tested again on the same problems. In the second phase, the systems were tested on five new problems, partially or completely out of the scope of the systems. For instance, they specified a new type of damage (cratered roads) or required the use of new types of engineering equipment (TMM bridges, ribbon rafts, and M4T6 rafts). Then again the correct solutions were provided, and the developers had one week to improve and develop their systems, which were tested again on the same five problems and five new ones. Solutions were scored along five equally weighted dimensions: (1) generation of the best workaround solutions for all the viable options; (2) correctness of the overall

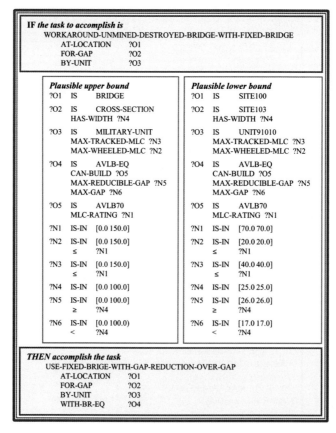

Figure 12.8. Rule learned by Disciple-WA from the example and the explanation in Figure 12.7.

time estimate for each workaround solution; (3) correctness of each solution step; (4) correctness of temporal constraints among these steps; and (5) appropriateness of engineering resources used. Scores were assigned by comparing the systems' answers with those of Alphatech's human expert. Bonus points were awarded when systems gave better answers than the expert, and these answers were used as standard for the next phase of the evaluation.

The participating teams were not uniform in terms of prior system development and human resources. Consequently, only one of them succeeded to enter the evaluation with a system that had a fully developed knowledge base. The other three teams (including the Disciple team) entered the evaluation with systems that had incompletely developed knowledge bases. Figure 12.9 shows a plot of the overall coverage of each system against the overall correctness of that system for each of the two phases of the evaluation.

The Disciple team entered the evaluation with a workaround agent the knowledge base of which was covering only about 40 percent of the workaround domain (equivalent to 11,841 binary predicates). The coverage of our agent was declared prior to each release of the testing problems, and all the problems falling within its scope were attempted and scored. During the evaluation period, we continued to extend the knowledge base to cover more of the initially specified domain, in addition to the developments required by the modification phase. At the end of the two weeks of evaluation, the knowledge base of our agent grew to cover about 80 percent of the domain (equivalent to 20,324 binary predicates). This corresponds to a rate of knowledge acquisition of approximately 787 binary predicates per day, as indicated in Figure 12.10. This result supports the claim that the Disciple approach enables rapid acquisition of relevant problem-solving knowledge from subject matter experts.

With respect to the quality of the generated solutions, within its scope, the Disciple-WA agent performed at the level of the human expert. There were several cases during the evaluation period where the Disciple-WA agent generated more correct or more complete

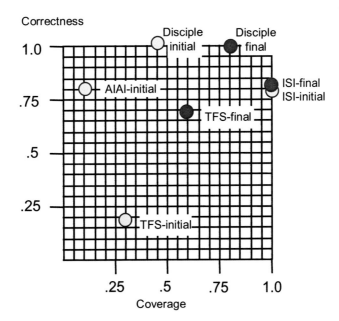

Figure 12.9. Evaluation results for the coverage of the problem space and the correctness of the solutions (reprinted with permission from Eric Jones).

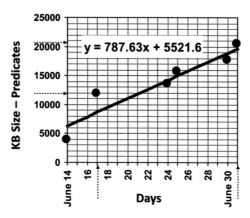

Figure 12.10. Knowledge base development time.

solutions than those of the human expert. There were also cases where the agent generated new solutions that the human expert did not initially consider. For instance, it generated solutions to work around a cratered road by emplacing a fixed bridge over the crater in a way similar to emplacing a fixed bridge over a river gap. Or, in the case of several craters, it generated solutions where some of the craters were filled while for others fixed bridges were emplaced. These solutions were adopted by the expert and used as standard for improving all the systems. For this reason, although the agent also made some mistakes, the overall correctness of its solutions was practically as high as that of the expert's solutions. This result supports the second claim that the acquired problem-solving knowledge is of good enough quality to ensure a high degree of correctness of the solutions generated by the agent.

Finally, our workaround generator had also a very good performance, being able to generate a solution in about 0.3 seconds, on a medium-power PC. This supports the third claim, that the acquired problem-solving knowledge ensures high performance of the problem solver.

Based on the evaluation results, the Disciple-WA agent was selected by DARPA and Alphatech to be further extended and was integrated by Alphatech into a larger system that supports air campaign planning by the Joint Force Air Component Commander (JFACC) and his or her staff. The integrated system was one of the systems selected to be demonstrated at EFX'98, the Air Force's annual showcase of promising new technologies.

12.3   DISCIPLE-COA: COURSE OF ACTION CRITIQUING

12.3.1   The Course of Action Critiquing Problem

A military course of action (COA) is a preliminary outline of a plan for how a military unit might attempt to accomplish a mission. A COA is not a complete plan in that it leaves out many details of the operation, such as exact initial locations of friendly and enemy forces. After receiving orders to plan for a mission, a Commander and staff complete a detailed and practiced process of analyzing the mission. They conceive and evaluate potential COAs, select a COA, and prepare detailed plans to accomplish the mission based on the selected COA. The general practice is for the staff to generate several COAs for a mission and then to compare those COAs based on many factors, including the situation, the commander's guidance, the principles of war, and the tenets of Army operations. Then the Commander makes the final decision on which COA will be used to generate his or her plan based on the recommendations of the staff and his or her own experience with the same factors considered by the staff (Jones, 1998).

The COA critiquing problem consisted of developing a knowledge-based agent that can automatically critique COAs for ground force operations, can systematically assess selected aspects of a COA, and can suggest repairs to it. The role of this agent is to act as an assistant to the military Commander, helping the Commander in choosing between several COAs under consideration for a certain mission. The agent could also help military students learn how to develop courses of action.

The input to the COA critiquing agent consists of the description of a COA that includes the following aspects:

1. The COA sketch, such as the one in the top part of Figure 12.11, which is a graphical depiction of the preliminary plan being considered. It includes enough of the high-level structure and maneuver aspects of the plan to show how the actions of each unit fit together to accomplish the overall purpose, while omitting much of the execution detail that will be included in the eventual operational plan. The three primary elements included in a COA sketch are (a) control measures that limit and control interactions between units; (b) unit graphics that depict known, initial locations and makeup of friendly and enemy units; and (c) mission graphics that depict actions and tasks assigned to friendly units. The COA sketch is drawn using a palette-based sketching utility.

2. The COA statement, such as the partial one shown in the bottom part of Figure 12.11, which clearly explains what the units in a course of action will do to accomplish the assigned mission. This text includes a description of the mission and the desired end state, as well as standard elements that describe purposes, operations, tasks, forms of maneuver, units, and resources to be used in the COA. The COA statement is expressed in a restricted but expressive subset of English.

3. Selected products of mission analysis, such as the areas of operations of the units, avenues of approach, key terrain, unit combat power, and enemy COAs.

Based on this input, the critiquing agent has to assess various aspects of the COA, such as its viability (i.e., its suitability, feasibility, acceptability, and completeness), its correctness (which considers the array of forces, the scheme of maneuver, and the command and control), and its strengths and weaknesses with respect to the principles of war and the tenets of Army operations. The critiquing agent should also be able to clearly justify the assessments made and to propose improvements to the COA.

Disciple-COA was developed in the DARPA's HPKB program to solve part of the COA critiquing problem (Cohen et al., 1998). In particular, Disciple-COA identifies the strengths and the weaknesses of a course of action with respect to the principles of war and the tenets of Army operations (FM 100–5, 1993). There are nine principles of war: objective, offensive, mass, economy of force, maneuver, unity of command, security, surprise, and simplicity. They provide general guidance for the conduct of war at the strategic, operational, and tactical levels. For example, Table 12.1 provides the definition of the principle of mass.

The tenets of Army operations describe the characteristics of successful operations. They are initiative, agility, depth, synchronization, and versatility.

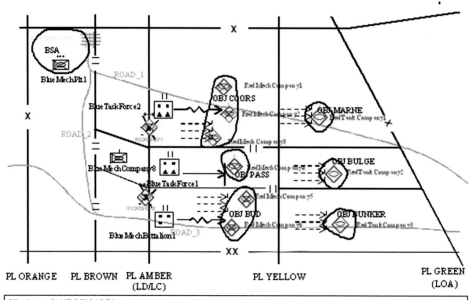

PL ORANGE	PL BROWN	PL AMBER		PL YELLOW	PL GREEN
		(LD/LC)			(LOA)

Mission:	BLUE-BRIGADE2 attacks to penetrate RED-MECH-REGIMENT2 at 130600 Aug in order to enable the completion of seize OBJ-SLAM by BLUE-ARMOR-BRIGADE1.
Close:	BLUE-TASK-FORCE1, a balanced task force (MAIN-EFFORT) attacks to penetrate RED-MECH-COMPANY4, then clears RED-TANK-COMPANY2 in order to enable the completion of seize OBJ-SLAM by BLUE-ARMOR-BRIGADE1.
	BLUE-TASK-FORCE2, a balanced task force (SUPPORTING-EFFORT1) attacks to fix RED-MECH-COMPANY1 and RED-MECH-COMPANY2 and RED-MECH-COMPANY3 in order to prevent RED-MECH-COMPANY1 and RED-MECH-COMPANY2 and RED-MECH-COMPANY3 from interfering with conducts of the MAIN-EFFORT1, then clears RED-MECH-COMPANY1 and RED-MECH-COMPANY2 and RED-MECH-COMPANY3 and RED-TANK-COMPANY1.
	BLUE-MECH-BATTALION1, a mechanized infantry battalion (SUPPORTING-EFFORT2) attacks to fix RED-MECH-COMPANY5 and RED-MECH-COMPANY6 in order to prevent RED-MECH-COMPANY5 and RED-MECH-COMPANY6 from interfering with conducts of the MAIN-EFFORT1, then clears RED-MECH-COMPANY5 and RED-MECH-COMPANY6 and RED-TANK-COMPANY3
Reserve:	The reserve, BLUE-MECH-COMPANY8, a mechanized infantry company, follows MAIN-EFFORT, and is prepared to reinforce MAIN-EFFORT.
Security:	SUPPORTING-EFFORT1 destroys RED-CSOP1 prior to begin moving across PL-AMBER by MAIN-EFFORT in order to prevent RED-MECH-REGIMENT2 from observing MAIN-EFFORT.
	SUPPORTING-EFFORT2 destroys RED-CSOP2 prior to begin moving across PL-AMBER by MAIN-EFFORT in order to prevent RED-MECH-REGIMENT2 from observing MAIN-EFFORT.
Deep:	Deep operations will destroy RED-TANK-COMPANY1 and RED-TANK-COMPANY2 and RED-TANK-COMPANY3.
Rear:	BLUE-MECH-PLT1, a mechanized infantry platoon secures the brigade support area.
Fire:	Fires will suppress RED-MECH-COMPANY1 and RED-MECH-COMPANY2 and RED-MECH-COMPANY3 and RED-MECH-COMPANY4 and RED-MECH-COMPANY5 and RED-MECH-COMPANY6.
End State:	At the conclusion of this operation, BLUE-BRIGADE2 will enable accomplishing conducts forward passage of lines through BLUE-BRIGADE2 by BLUE-ARMOR-BRIGADE1.
	MAIN-EFFORT will complete to clear RED-MECH-COMPANY4 and RED-TANK-COMPANY2.
	SUPPORTING-EFFORT1 will complete to clear RED-MECH-COMPANY1 and RED-MECH-COMPANY2 and RED-MECH-COMPANY3 and RED-TANK-COMPANY1.
	SUPPORTING-EFFORT2 will complete to clear RED-MECH-COMPANY5 and RED-MECH-COMPANY6 and RED-TANK-COMPANY3.

Figure 12.11. COA sketch and a fragment of a COA statement (reprinted with permission from Eric Jones).

Table 12.2, for instance, shows some of the strengths of the COA from Figure 12.11 with respect to the principle of mass, identified by Disciple-COA.

In addition to generating answers in natural language, Disciple-COA also provides the reference material based on which the answers are generated, as shown in the bottom part of Table 12.2. Also, the Disciple-COA agent can provide justifications for the generated

---

Table 12.1 The Principle of Mass (from FM 100–5)

Mass the effects of overwhelming combat power at the decisive place and time.
Synchronizing all the elements of combat power where they will have decisive effect on an enemy force in a short period of time is to achieve mass. To mass is to hit the enemy with a closed fist, not poke at him with fingers of an open hand. Mass must also be sustained so the effects have staying power. Thus, mass seeks to smash the enemy, not sting him. This results from the proper combination of combat power with the proper application of other principles of war. Massing effects, rather than concentrating forces, can enable numerically inferior forces to achieve decisive results, while limiting exposure to enemy fire.

Table 12.2 Strengths of the COA from Figure 12.11 with Respect to the Principle of Mass, Identified by Disciple-COA

Major Strength: There is a major strength in COA411 with respect to mass because BLUE-TASK-FORCE1 is the MAIN-EFFORT1 and it acts on the decisive point of the COA (RED-MECH-COMPANY4) with a force ratio of 10.6, which exceeds a recommended force ratio of 3.0. Additionally, the main effort is assisted by supporting action SUPPRESS-MILITARY-TASK1, which also acts on the decisive point. This is good evidence of the allocation of significantly more than minimum combat power required at the decisive point and is indicative of the proper application of the principle of mass.

Strength: There is a strength in COA411 with respect to mass because BLUE-TASK-FORCE1 is the main effort of the COA and it has been allocated 33% of available combat power, but this is considered just a medium-level weighting of the main effort.

Strength: There is a strength in COA411 with respect to mass because BLUE-MECH-COMPANY8 is a COMPANY-UNIT-DESIGNATION level maneuver unit assigned to be the reserve. This is considered a strong reserve for a BRIGADE-UNIT-DESIGNATION–level COA and would be available to continue the operation or exploit success.

Reference: FM 100–5 pg 2–4, KF 113.1, KF 113.2, KF 113.3, KF 113.4, KF 113.5 – To mass is to synchronize the effects of all elements of combat power at the proper point and time to achieve decisive results. Observance of the principle of mass may be evidenced by allocation to the main effort of significantly greater combat power than the minimum required throughout its mission, accounting for expected losses. Mass is evidenced by the allocation of significantly more than the minimum combat power required at the decisive point.

---

answers at three levels of detail, from a very abstract one that shows the general line of reasoning followed, to a very detailed one that indicates each of the knowledge pieces used in generating the answer.

12.3.2 Modeling the COA Critiquing Process

To critique a course of action with respect to a specific principle or tenet, one needs a certain amount of information about that course of action, information related to that principle or tenet. This information is obtained by asking a series of questions. The answer to each question allows one to reduce the current critiquing task to a more specific and simpler one. This process continues until one has enough information to recognize a weakness or a strength. Consider, for example, the principle of surprise, whose definition is provided in Table 12.3. As you can see, this is a very general description. How to apply this general principle in actual situations is knowledge that is learned by military officers during their lifetime. Therefore, developing an agent able to identify to what extent a specific COA conforms to the principle of surprise involves capturing and representing the knowledge of a military expert into the agent's knowledge base.

Guided by this general definition and the COA from Figure 12.11, our subject matter expert (Colonel Michael Bowman) has developed the reduction tree from Figure 12.12. Notice how each successive question identifies a surprise-related feature of the COA until a strength is recognized.

Through this kind of modeling of the COA critiquing process, each leaf may lead to the identification of a strength or weakness. Then, the bottom-up solution synthesis process consists only in accumulating all the identified strengths and weaknesses, just as in the case of Disciple-WA, where the solution synthesis process accumulates the elementary actions.

Notice also that, as in the case of Disciple-WA, the tasks are structured, consisting of a name and a sequence of feature-value pairs.

12.3.3   Ontology Design and Development

For Disciple-COA, an initial ontology was defined by importing the input ontology built by Teknowledge and Cycorp for the COA challenge problem (Boicu et al., 1999). The imported ontology was further developed by using the ontology building tools of Disciple-COA. Figure 12.13, for instance, presents a fragment of the COA ontology.

The top part represents the upper level of the ontology that identifies the types of concepts represented in the ontology (called classes in Disciple-COA). They include GEOGRAPHICAL-REGION, ORGANIZATION, EQUIPMENT, and ACTION. Each of these concepts is the top of a specialized hierarchy, such as the hierarchy of organizations, a fragment of which is shown in the left part of Figure 12.13. The leaves of this hierarchy are specific military units (e.g., BLUE-TASK-FORCE1), corresponding to a specific COA to be critiqued by Disciple-COA. Each concept and instance of the object hierarchy is described

---

Table 12.3 The Principle of Surprise (from FM 100–5)

Strike the enemy at a time or place or in a manner for which he is unprepared.
Surprise can decisively shift the balance of combat power. By seeking surprise, forces can achieve success well out of proportion to the effort expended. Rapid advances in surveillance technology and mass communication make it increasingly difficult to mask or cloak large-scale marshaling or movement of personnel and equipment. The enemy need not be taken completely by surprise, but only become aware too late to react effectively. Factors contributing to surprise include speed, effective intelligence, deception, application of unexpected combat power, operations security (OPSEC), and variations in tactics and methods of operation. Surprise can be in tempo, size of force, direction or location of main effort, and timing. Deception can aid the probability of achieving surprise.

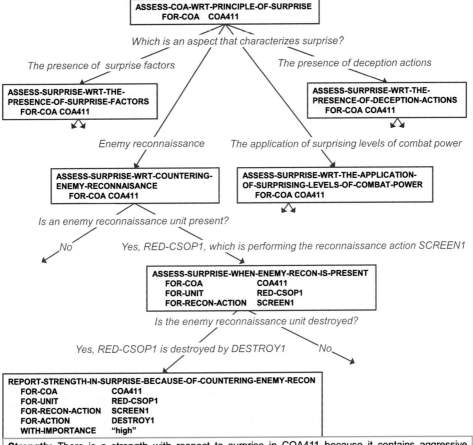

Figure 12.12. Sample modeling of the COA critiquing process.

by specific features and values. For instance, the bottom part of Figure 12.13 shows the description of the specific military unit called BLUE-TASK-FORCE1. BLUE-TASK-FORCE1 is described as being both an ARMORED-UNIT-MILITARY-SPECIALTY and a MECHANIZED-INFANTRY-UNIT-MILITARY-SPECIALTY. The other features describe BLUE-TASK-FORCE1 as being at the battalion level; belonging to the blue side; being designated as the main effort of the blue side; performing two tasks, PENETRATE1 and CLEAR1; having a regular strength; and having four other units under its operational control. The values of the features of BLUE-TASK-FORCE1 are themselves described in the same way. For instance, one of the tasks performed by BLUE-TASK-FORCE1 is PENETRATE1.

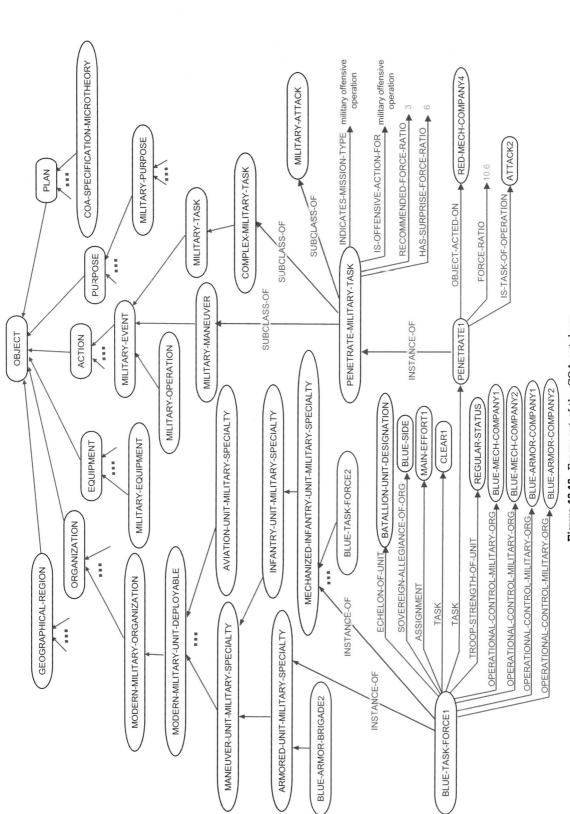

Figure 12.13. Fragment of the COA ontology.

PENETRATE1 is defined as being a penetration task, and therefore inherits all the features of the penetration tasks, in addition to the features that are directly associated with it.

The hierarchy of objects is used as a generalization hierarchy for learning by the Disciple-COA agent. For instance, one way to generalize an expression is to replace an object with a more general one from such a hierarchy. In particular, PENETRATE1 from the bottom-right side of Figure 12.13 can be generalized to PENETRATE-MILITARY-TASK, COMPLEX-MILITARY-TASK, MILITARY-MANEUVER, etc. The goal of the learning process is to select the right generalization.

The features used to describe the objects are themselves represented in the feature hierarchy.

12.3.4 Training the Disciple-COA Agent

The next step in the development of the Disciple-COA critiquer was to teach it to critique COAs with respect to the principles of war and the tenets of Army operations, based on the developed models. The expert loads the description of a specific COA, such as COA411 represented in Figure 12.11, and then invokes the Problem Solver with a task of critiquing the COA with respect to a certain principle or tenet. Disciple-COA uses its task reduction rules to reduce the current task to simpler tasks, showing the expert the reductions found. The expert may accept a reduction proposed by the agent, reject it, or decide to define a new reduction. From each such interaction, Disciple-COA either refines a previously learned rule or learns a new task reduction rule. After a new rule is learned or an existing rule is refined, the Problem Solver resumes the task reduction process until a solution to the initial problem is found.

Initially Disciple-COA does not contain any rules. Therefore, all the problem-solving steps (i.e., task reductions) must be provided by the expert, as illustrated in Figure 12.14 and explained in the following.

To assess COA411 with respect to the principle of surprise, the expert and Disciple-COA need a certain amount of information, which is obtained by asking a series of questions, as already illustrated in Section 12.3.2. The answer to each question allows the expert and the agent to reduce the current assessment task to a more detailed one. This process continues until the expert and Disciple-COA have enough information about COA411 to make the assessment. As shown in Figure 12.14, the initial task is reduced to that of assessing the surprise of COA411 with respect to the countering of enemy reconnaissance. Then one asks whether there is any enemy reconnaissance unit present in COA411. The answer identifies RED-CSOP1 as being such a unit because it is performing the task SCREEN1. Therefore, the task of assessing surprise for COA411 with respect to countering enemy reconnaissance is now reduced to the better defined task of assessing surprise when enemy reconnaissance is present. The next question to ask is whether the enemy reconnaissance unit is destroyed or not. In the case of COA411, RED-CSOP1 is destroyed by the task DESTROY1. Therefore, one can conclude that there is a strength in COA411 with respect to the principle of surprise because the enemy reconnaissance unit is countered.

Figure 12.15 illustrates the process of teaching Disciple-COA. The left-hand side represents the reasoning process of the expert, the question and the answer being in free natural language format. While this line of reasoning is very natural to a human expert, a learning agent cannot understand it. The explanation that would be understood by the agent is represented in the upper-right part of Figure 12.15 and consists of various

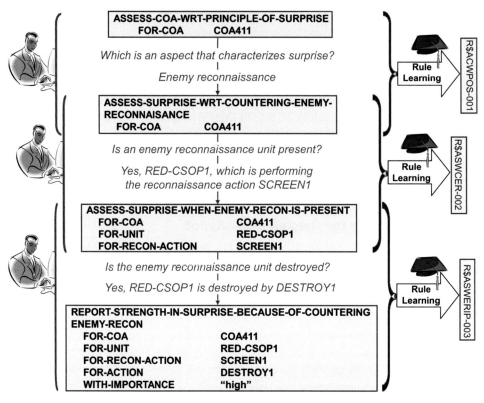

Figure 12.14. Task reductions indicated by the expert.

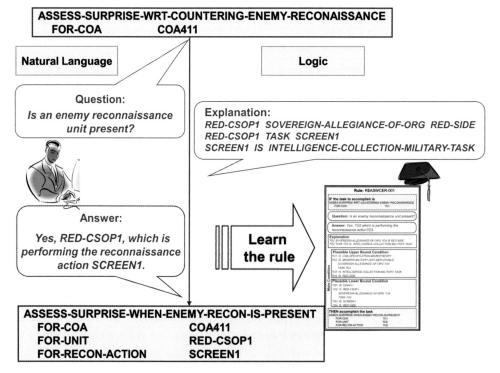

Figure 12.15. Teaching Disciple-COA to reduce a task.

relations between certain elements from its ontology. The first explanation piece states, in the formal language of Disciple-COA, that RED-CSOP1 is an enemy unit. The second explanation piece expresses the fact that RED-CSOP1 is performing the action SCREEN1. Finally, the last explanation piece expresses the fact that SCREEN1 is a reconnaissance action. While an expert can understand the meaning of these formal expressions, he cannot easily define them because he or she is not a knowledge engineer. For one thing, the expert would need to use the formal language of the agent. But this would not be enough. The expert would also need to know the names of the potentially many thousands of concepts and features from the agent's ontology.

While defining the formal explanations of this task reduction step is beyond the individual capabilities of the expert or the agent, it is not beyond their joint capabilities. Finding these explanation pieces is a mixed-initiative process of searching the agent's ontology, an explanation piece being a path of objects and relations in this ontology, as discussed in Section 9.5. In essence, the agent uses analogical reasoning and help from the expert to identify and propose a set of plausible explanation pieces from which the expert has to select the correct ones. One explanation generation strategy is based on an ordered set of heuristics for analogical reasoning. These heuristics exploit the hierarchies of objects, features, and tasks to identify the rules that are similar to the current reduction and to use their explanations as a guide to search for similar explanations of the current example.

From the example reduction and its explanation in Figure 12.15, Disciple-COA automatically generated the plausible version space rule in Figure 12.16. This is an IF-THEN rule, the components of which are generalizations of the elements of the example in Figure 12.15.

The rule in Figure 12.16 also contains two conditions for its applicability: a plausible lower bound condition and a plausible upper bound condition. These conditions approximate an exact applicability condition that Disciple-COA attempts to learn. Initially, the plausible lower bound condition covers only the example in Figure 12.15, restricting the variables from the rule to take only the values from this example. It also includes the relations between these variables that have been identified as relevant in the explanation of the example. The plausible upper bound condition is the most general generalization of the plausible lower bound condition. It is obtained by taking into account the domains and the ranges of the features from the plausible lower bound condition and the tasks, in order to determine the possible values of the variables. The domain of a feature is the set of objects that may have that feature. The range is the set of possible values of that feature. For instance, ?O2 is the value of the task feature FOR-UNIT, and has as features SOVEREIGN-ALLEGENCE-OF-ORG and TASK. Therefore, any value of ?O2 has to be in the intersection of the range of FOR-UNIT, the domain of SOVEREIGN-ALLEGENCE-OF-ORG, and the domain of TASK. This intersection is MODERN-MILITARY-UNIT-DEPLOYABLE.

The learned rules, such as the one in Figure 12.16, are used in problem solving to generate task reductions with different degrees of plausibility, depending on which of their conditions are satisfied. If the plausible lower bound condition is satisfied, then the reduction is very likely to be correct. If the plausible lower bound condition is not satisfied, but the plausible upper bound condition is satisfied, then the solution is considered only plausible. Any application of such a partially learned rule, however, either successful or not, provides an additional (positive or negative) example, and possibly an additional explanation, that are used by the agent to improve the rule further through the generalization and/or specialization of its conditions.

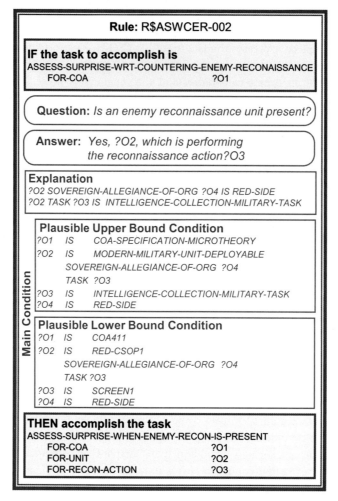

Rule: R$ASWCER-002

IF the task to accomplish is
ASSESS-SURPRISE-WRT-COUNTERING-ENEMY-RECONAISSANCE
    FOR-COA   ?O1

Question: *Is an enemy reconnaissance unit present?*

Answer: *Yes, ?O2, which is performing*
                the reconnaissance action?O3

Explanation
?O2 SOVEREIGN-ALLEGIANCE-OF-ORG ?O4 IS RED-SIDE
?O2 TASK ?O3 IS INTELLIGENCE-COLLECTION-MILITARY-TASK

Main Condition

Plausible Upper Bound Condition
?O1	IS	COA-SPECIFICATION-MICROTHEORY
?O2	IS	MODERN-MILITARY-UNIT-DEPLOYABLE
		SOVEREIGN-ALLEGIANCE-OF-ORG ?O4
		TASK ?O3
?O3	IS	INTELLIGENCE-COLLECTION-MILITARY-TASK
?O4	IS	RED-SIDE

Plausible Lower Bound Condition
?O1	IS	COA411
?O2	IS	RED-CSOP1
		SOVEREIGN-ALLEGIANCE-OF-ORG ?O4
		TASK ?O3
?O3	IS	SCREEN1
?O4	IS	RED-SIDE

THEN accomplish the task
ASSESS-SURPRISE-WHEN-ENEMY-RECON-IS-PRESENT
    FOR-COA   ?O1
    FOR-UNIT   ?O2
    FOR-RECON-ACTION   ?O3

Figure 12.16. Plausible version space rule learned from the example and the explanation in Figure 12.15.

Let us consider again the specific task reductions from Figure 12.14. At least for the elementary tasks, such as the one at the bottom of the figure, the expert needs also to express them in natural language: "There is a strength with respect to surprise in COA411 because it contains aggressive security/counter-reconnaissance plans, destroying enemy intelligence collection units and activities. Intelligence collection by RED-CSOP1 will be disrupted by its destruction by DESTROY1."

Similarly, the expert would need to indicate the reference (source) material for the concluded assessment. The learned rules contain generalizations of these phrases that are used to generate answers in natural language, as illustrated in the bottom part of Figure 12.12. Similarly, the generalizations of the questions and the answers from the rules applied to generate a solution are used to produce an abstract justification of the reasoning process.

As Disciple-COA learns plausible version space rules, it can use them to propose routine or innovative solutions to the current problems. The *routine solutions* are those that satisfy the plausible lower bound conditions of the rules and are very likely to be correct. Those that are not correct are kept as exceptions to the rule. The *innovative solutions* are those that do not satisfy the plausible lower bound conditions but satisfy the plausible upper bound conditions. These solutions may or may not be correct, but in each case they lead to the refinement of the rules that generated them. Let us consider the situation illustrated in Figure 12.17. After it has been shown how to critique COA411 with respect to the principle of security, Disciple-COA is asked to critique COA421. COA421 is similar to COA411, except that in this case the enemy recon unit is not destroyed. Because of this similarity, Disciple-COA is able to propose the two top reductions in Figure 12.17. Both of them are innovative reductions that are accepted by the expert. Therefore, Disciple-COA generalizes the plausible lower bound conditions of the corresponding rules, as little as possible, to cover these reductions and to remain less general or at most as general as the corresponding plausible upper bound conditions.

The last reduction step in Figure 12.17 has to be provided by the expert because no rule of Disciple-COA is applicable. We call the expert-provided reduction a *creative* problem-solving step. From each such reduction, Disciple-COA learns a new task reduction rule, as was illustrated in the preceding example.

Through refinement, the task reduction rules may become significantly more complex than the rule in Figure 12.16. For instance, when a reduction proposed by Disciple-COA is rejected by the expert, the agent attempts to find an explanation of why the reduction is wrong. Then the rule may be refined with an Except-When plausible version space condition. The bounds of this version space are generalizations of the explanations that should not hold in order for the reduction rule to be applicable.

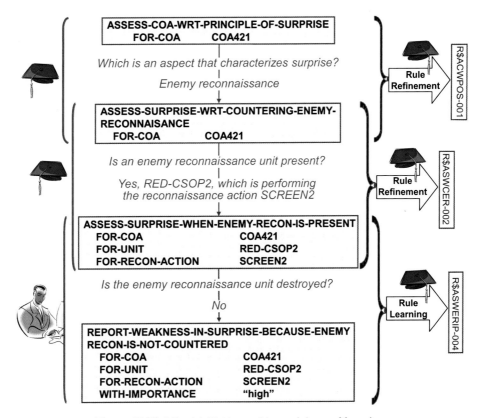

Figure 12.17. Mixed-initiative problem solving and learning.

In any case, comparing the left-hand side of Figure 12.15 (which is defined by the domain expert) with the rule from Figure 12.16 (which is learned by Disciple-COA) suggests the usefulness of a Disciple agent for knowledge acquisition. In the conventional knowledge engineering approach, a knowledge engineer would need to manually define and debug a rule such as the one in Figure 12.16. With Disciple, the domain expert needs only to define an example reduction, because Disciple learns and refines the corresponding rule.

12.3.5   Experimental Results

Like Disciple-WA, Disciple-COA has also been developed and evaluated as part of the DARPA's High Performance Knowledge Bases Program, as discussed in the following (Tecuci et al., 2001).

In addition to George Mason University (GMU), three other research groups have developed COA critiquers as part of the HPKB program. Teknowledge and Cycorp have developed a critiquer based on the Cyc system (Lenat, 1995). The other two critiquers have been developed at the Information Sciences Institute (ISI) at the University of Southern California (USC), one based on the Expect system (Kim and Gil, 1999), and the other based on the Loom system (Loom, 1999). All the critiquers were evaluated as part of the HPKB's annual evaluation that took place during the period from July 6 to July 16, 1999, and included five evaluation items of increasing difficulty. Each item consisted of descriptions of various COAs and a set of questions to be answered about each of them. Item1 consisted of COAs and questions that were previously provided by DARPA to guide the development of the COA critiquing agents. Item2 included new test questions about the same COAs. Items 3, 4, and 5 consisted of new COAs that were increasingly more complex and required further development of the COA agents in order to answer the asked questions properly. Each of the Items 3, 4, and 5 consisted of two phases. In the first phase, each team had to provide initial system responses. Then the evaluator issued the model answers, and each team had a limited amount of time to repair its system, to perform further knowledge acquisition, and to generate revised system responses.

The responses of each system were scored by a team of domain experts along the following dimensions and associated weights: (1) Correctness, 50 percent (matches model answer or is otherwise judged to be correct); (2) Justification, 30 percent (scored on presence, soundness, and level of detail); (3) Lay Intelligibility, 10 percent (degree to which a lay observer can understand the answer and the justification); (4) Sources, 10 percent (degree to which appropriate references or sources are noted); and (5) Pro-activity, 10 percent extra credit (appropriate corrective actions or other information suggested to address the critique). Based on these scores, several classes of metrics have been computed, including Recall and Precision. Recall is obtained by dividing the score for all answers provided by a critiquer to the total number of model answers for the asked questions. This was over 100 percent in the case of the Disciple-COA critiquer, primarily because of the extra credit received for generating additional critiques that were not among the model answers provided by the evaluator. The Precision score is obtained by dividing the same score by the total number of answers provided by that system (both the model answers provided by the evaluator and the new answers provided by the critiquer). The results obtained by the four evaluated critiquers are presented in Figure 12.18. These graphs show also the averages of these results, which represent the recall and the precision of the integrated system consisting of the four critiquers.

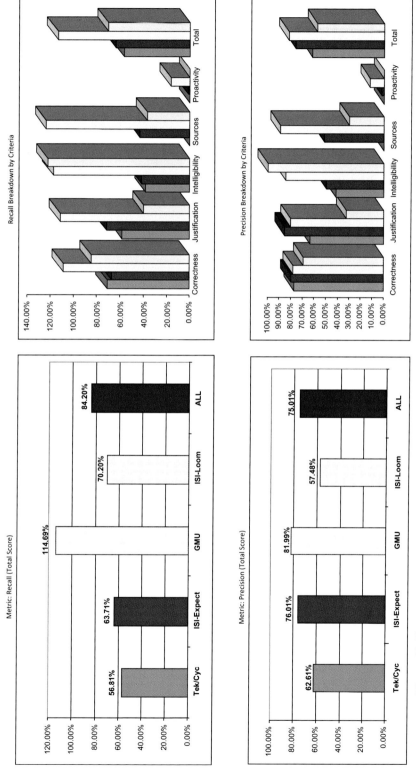

Figure 12.18. The performance of the COA critiquers and of the integrated system (reprinted with permission from Eric Jones).

Figure 12.19 compares the recall and the coverage of the developed critiquers for the last three most complex items of the evaluation. For each item, the beginning of each arrow shows the coverage and recall for the initial testing phase, and the end of the arrow shows the same data for the modification phase. In this graph, the results that are above and to the right are superior to the other results. This graph also shows that all the systems increased their coverage during the evaluation. In particular, the knowledge base of Disciple-COA increased by 46 percent (from the equivalent of 6,229 simple axioms to 9,092 simple axioms), which represents a very high rate of knowledge acquisition of 286 simple axioms per day.

During August 1999, we conducted a one-week knowledge acquisition experiment with Disciple-COA, at the U.S. Army Battle Command Battle Lab, in Fort Leavenworth, Kansas, to test the claim that domain experts who do not have prior knowledge engineering experience can teach Disciple-COA (Tecuci et al., 2001). The experiment involved four such military experts and had three phases: (1) a joint training phase during the first three days, (2) an individual teaching experiment on day four, and (3) a joint discussion of the experiment on day five. The entire experiment was videotaped. The training for the experiment included a detailed presentation of Disciple's knowledge representation, problem-solving, and learning methods and tools. For the teaching experiment, each expert received a copy of Disciple-COA with a partial knowledge base. This knowledge base was obtained by removing the tasks and the rules from the complete knowledge base of Disciple-COA. That is, the knowledge base contained the complete ontology of objects,

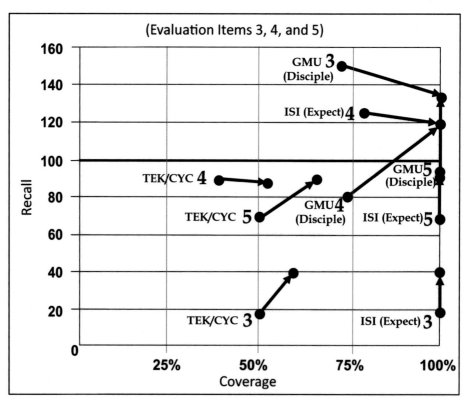

Figure 12.19. Coverage versus recall, pre-repair and post-repair (reprinted with permission from Eric Jones).

object features, and task features. We also provided the experts with the descriptions of three COAs (COA411, COA421, and COA51), to be used for training Disciple-COA. These were the COAs used in the final phases of the DARPA's evaluation of all the critiquers. Finally, we provided and discussed with the experts the modeling of critiquing these COAs with respect to the principles of offensive and security. That is, we provided the experts with specific task reductions, similar to the one from Figure 12.17, to guide them in teaching Disciple-COA. After that, each expert taught Disciple-COA independently while being supervised by a knowledge engineer, whose role was to help the expert if he or she reached an impasse while using Disciple-COA.

Figure 12.20 shows the evolution of the knowledge base during the teaching process for one of the experts, being representative for all the four experts. In the morning, the expert taught Disciple-COA to critique COAs with respect to the principle of offensive, and in the afternoon he taught it to critique COAs with respect to the principle of security. In both cases, the expert used first COA411, then COA422, and then COA51. As one can see from Figure 12.20, Disciple-COA initially learned more rules, and then the emphasis shifted on rule refinement. Therefore, the increase in the size of the knowledge base is greater toward the beginning of the training process for each principle. The teaching for the principle of offensive took 101 minutes. During this time, Disciple-COA learned fourteen tasks and fourteen rules (147 simple axioms' equivalent). The teaching for security took place in the afternoon and consisted of 72 minutes of interactions between the expert and Disciple-COA. During this time, Disciple-COA learned fourteen tasks and twelve rules (136 simple axioms' equivalent). There was no or very limited assistance from the knowledge engineer with respect to teaching. The knowledge acquisition rate obtained during the experiment was very high (approximately nine tasks and eight rules per hour, or ninety-eight simple axioms' equivalent per hour). At the end of this training process, Disciple-COA was able to correctly identify seventeen strengths and weaknesses of the three COAs with respect to the principles of offensive and security.

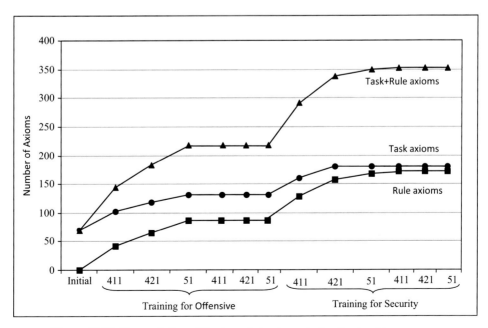

Figure 12.20. The evolution of the knowledge base during the teaching process.

After the experiment, each expert was asked to fill in a detailed questionnaire designed to collect subjective data for usability evaluation. All the answers took into account that Disciple-COA was a research prototype and not a commercial product and were rated based on a scale of agreement with the question from 1 to 5, with 1 denoting "not at all" and 5 denoting "very". For illustration, Table 12.4 shows three questions and the answers provided by the four experts.

In conclusion, Disciple-COA demonstrated the generality of its learning methods that used an object ontology created by another group, namely Teknowledge and Cycorp (Boicu et al., 1999). It also demonstrated high rule learning rates, as compared with manual definition of rules, and better performance than the evaluating experts, with many unanticipated solutions.

12.4 DISCIPLE-COG: CENTER OF GRAVITY ANALYSIS

12.4.1 The Center of Gravity Analysis Problem

Military literature distinguishes among three levels of war – strategic, operational, and tactical – that help clarify the links between national strategic objectives and tactical actions. There are no finite limits or boundaries between the levels of war (Joint Chiefs of Staff, 2008, II–1).

One of the most difficult problems that senior military leaders face at the strategic level is the determination and analysis of the centers of gravity for friendly and opposing forces. The concept of the center of gravity of an entity (state, alliance, coalition, or group) was

Table 12.4 Sample Questions Answered by the Four Experts

Questions	Answers
Do you think that Disciple is a useful tool for knowledge acquisition?	• Rating 5. Absolutely! The potential use of this tool by domain experts is only limited by their imagination – not their AI programming skills. • 5 • 4 • Yes, it allowed me to be consistent with logical thought.
Do you think that Disciple is a useful tool for problem solving?	• Rating 5. Yes. • 5 (absolutely) • 4 • Yes. As it develops and becomes tailored to the user, it will simplify the tedious tasks.
Were the procedures/processes used in Disciple compatible with Army doctrine and/or decision-making processes?	• Rating 5. As a minimum yes, as a maximum – better! • This again was done very well. • 4 • 4

introduced by Carl von Clausewitz (1832) as "the foundation of capability, the hub of all power and movement, upon which everything depends, the point against which all the energies should be directed." It is currently defined as comprising the source of power that provides freedom of action, physical strength, and will to fight (Joint Chiefs of Staff, 2008, IV–X).

It is recognized that, "Should a combatant eliminate or influence the enemy's strategic center of gravity, the enemy would lose control of its power and resources and eventually fall to defeat. Should a combatant fail to adequately protect his own strategic center of gravity, he invites disaster" (Giles and Galvin, 1996, p. 1). Therefore, the main goal of any force should be to eliminate or influence the enemy's strategic center of gravity while adequately protecting its own.

Correctly identifying the centers of gravity of the opposing forces is of highest importance in any conflict. Therefore, all the U.S. senior military service colleges emphasize center of gravity analysis in the education of strategic leaders (Warden, 1993; Echevarria, 2003; Strange and Iron, 2004a, 2004b; Eikmeier, 2006).

In spite of the apparently simple definition of the center of gravity, its determination requires a wide range of background knowledge, not only from the military domain but also from the economic, geographic, political, demographic, historic, international, and other domains (Giles and Galvin, 1996). In addition, the adversaries involved, their goals, and their capabilities can vary in important ways from one situation to another. When performing this analysis, some experts may rely on their own professional experience and intuitions without following a rigorous approach.

Recognizing these difficulties, the Center for Strategic Leadership of the U.S. Army War College started an effort in 1993 to elicit and formalize the knowledge of a number of experts in center of gravity. This research resulted in a COG monograph (Giles and Galvin, 1996). This monograph made two significant contributions to the theory of center of gravity analysis. The first was a systematic analysis of the various factors (e.g., politic, military, economic, etc.) that have to be taken into account for center of gravity determination. The second significant contribution was the identification of a wide range of center of gravity candidates.

A significant advancement of the theory of center of gravity analysis was the CG-CC-CR-CV model introduced by Strange (1996) and summarized by the following definitions:

Centers of gravity (CG):	Primary sources of moral or physical strength, power, or resistance.
Critical capabilities (CC):	Primary abilities that merit a center of gravity to be identified as such, in the context of a given scenario, situation, or mission.
Critical requirements (CR):	Essential conditions, resources, and means for a critical capability to be fully operative.
Critical vulnerabilities (CV):	Critical requirements or components thereof that are deficient, or vulnerable to neutralization, interdiction, or attack (moral/physical harm), in a manner achieving decisive results – the smaller the resources and effort applied and the smaller the risk and cost, the better.

Building primarily on the work of Strange (1996) and Giles and Galvin (1996), we have developed a computational approach to center of gravity analysis, which is summarized in Figure 12.21.

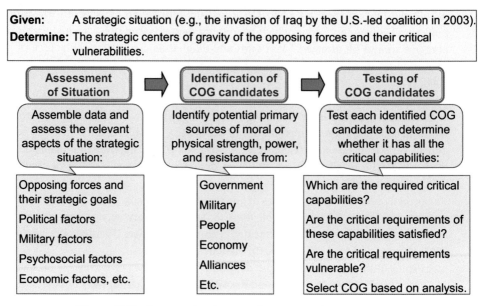

Given: A strategic situation (e.g., the invasion of Iraq by the U.S.-led coalition in 2003).
Determine: The strategic centers of gravity of the opposing forces and their critical vulnerabilities.

Assessment of Situation	Identification of COG candidates	Testing of COG candidates
Assemble data and assess the relevant aspects of the strategic situation:	Identify potential primary sources of moral or physical strength, power, and resistance from:	Test each identified COG candidate to determine whether it has all the critical capabilities:
Opposing forces and their strategic goals Political factors Military factors Psychosocial factors Economic factors, etc.	Government Military People Economy Alliances Etc.	Which are the required critical capabilities? Are the critical requirements of these capabilities satisfied? Are the critical requirements vulnerable? Select COG based on analysis.

Figure 12.21. Computational approach to center of gravity analysis.

This approach consists of three main phases: assessment of the strategic situation, identification of center of gravity candidates, and testing of the identified candidates.

During the *assessment of the situation* (such as the invasion of Iraq by the U.S.-led coalition in 2003), one assembles and assesses data and other relevant aspects of the strategic environment, including the opposing forces (Iraq, on one side, and the U.S.-led coalition, on the other side), their strategic goals, political factors (e.g., type of government, governing bodies), military factors (e.g., leaders, will, and capability), psychosocial factors (e.g., motivation, political activities), economic factors (e.g., type of economy, resources), and so on. This assessment will be used in the next phases of center of gravity analysis.

During the *identification* phase, strategic center of gravity candidates are identified from a belligerent's elements of power, such as its leadership, government, military, people, or economy. For example, a strong leader, such as Saddam Hussein or George W. Bush, could be a center of gravity candidate with respect to the situation at the beginning of the Iraq War in 2003. The result of this phase is the identification of a wide range of candidates.

During the *testing* phase, each candidate is analyzed to determine whether it has all the critical capabilities that are necessary to be the center of gravity. For example, a leader needs to be secure; informed; able to maintain support from the government, the military, and the people; and irreplaceable. For each capability, one needs to determine the existence of the essential conditions, resources, and means that are required by that capability to be fully operative. For example, some of the protection means of Saddam Hussein were the Republican Guard Protection Unit, the Iraqi Military, the Complex of Iraqi Bunkers, and the System of Saddam doubles. Once these means of protection are identified, one needs to determine whether any of them, or any of their components, are vulnerable. For example, the Complex of Iraqi Bunkers is vulnerable because their location and design are known to the U.S.-led coalition and could be destroyed.

Based on the results of the analysis, one can eliminate any center of gravity candidate that does not have all the required critical capabilities, and select the centers of gravity from the remaining candidates. Moreover, the process also identifies the critical vulnerabilities of the selected centers of gravity.

An important characteristic of this approach is that it is both natural for a human and appropriate for automatic processing. By using this approach, we have developed the Disciple-COG agent, briefly described in the following section.

12.4.2 Overview of the Use of Disciple-COG

Disciple-COG is a computer program that guides a military planner in describing a strategic situation and performing a center of gravity analysis following the approach described in the preceding section and summarized in Figure 12.21.

First, Disciple-COG guides the user in identifying, describing, and assessing the aspects of the strategic situation that are relevant to center of gravity analysis. An example of such a situation could be World War II in Europe, at the time of the invasion of the island of Sicily by the Allied Forces, in 1943.

The user–agent interaction is easy and natural for the user, taking place as illustrated in Figures 12.22 and 12.23. The left part of each window is a table of contents whose elements indicate various important aspects of the situation. Initially it contains only "situation." When the user clicks on one such aspect, Disciple-COG asks specific questions intended to acquire a description and/or assessment of that aspect or to update a previously specified description.

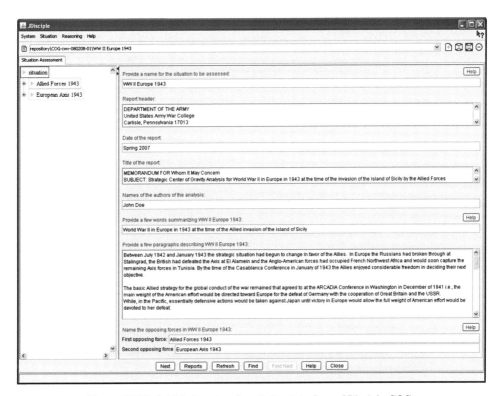

Figure 12.22. Initial situation description interface of Disciple-COG.

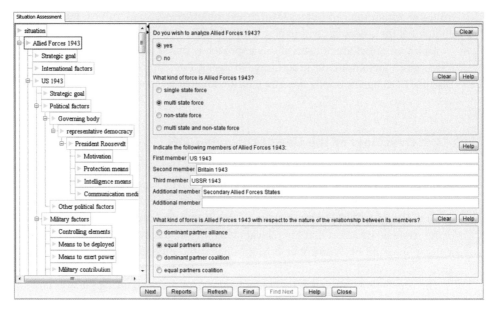

Figure 12.23. Situation description and assessment interface of Disciple-COG.

Figure 12.22 shows the initial interaction screen after the user has clicked on "situation." The right-hand side shows the prompts of Disciple-COG and the information provided by the user, such as:

Provide a name for the situation to be assessed:
WW II Europe 1943

. . .

Name the opposing forces in WW II Europe 1943:
Allied Forces 1943
European Axis 1943

Once the user names the opposing forces (i.e., "Allied Forces 1943" and "European Axis 1943"), Disciple-COG includes them into the table of contents, as shown in the left-hand side of Figure 12.22. Then, when the user clicks on one of the opposing forces (e.g., "Allied Forces 1943"), Disciple-COG asks for its characteristics, as indicated in the right-hand side of Figure 12.23 (e.g., "What kind of force is Allied Forces 1943?"). Because the user characterized "Allied Forces 1943" as a multistate force (by clicking on one of the options offered by the agent), Disciple-COG further asks for its members and extends the table of contents with the provided names (i.e., "US 1943," "Britain 1943," "USSR 1943," etc.) and their relevant aspects (i.e., "Strategic goal," "Political factors," "Military factors," etc.), as shown in the left-hand side of Figure 12.23. The user can now click on any such aspect and will be asked specific questions by Disciple-COG.

Thus, the user's answers lead to the generation of new items in the left-hand side of the window, and trigger new questions from the agent, which depend on the answers provided by the user. Through such context-dependent questions, Disciple-COG guides the user to research, describe, and assess the situation.

As will be discussed in Section 12.4.4, once the user describes various aspects of the situation, Disciple-COG automatically extends its ontology with the corresponding representations. The user is not required to answer all the questions, and Disciple-COG can be asked, at any time, to identify and test the strategic center of gravity candidates for the current description of the situation. The COG analysis process uses the problem reduction and solution synthesis paradigm presented in Section 4.2, following the CG-CC-CR-CV model (Strange, 1996).

Figure 12.24 shows the interface of the Mixed-Initiative Reasoner of Disciple-COG that displays the automatically generated analysis. The left-hand side shows an abstract view of the analysis tree for the problem "Analyze the strategic COG candidates for the WW II Europe 1943 situation."

First, the problem of analyzing the strategic COG candidates for this situation is reduced to analyzing the COG candidates for each of the two opposing forces. Then, because each of the opposing forces is a multimember force, the problem of analyzing the COG candidates for an opposing force is reduced to two other problems: (1) the problem of analyzing the COG candidates for each member of the multimember force (e.g., US 1943 candidates, Britain 1943 candidates, and USSR 1943 candidates, in the case of Allied Forces 1943) and (2) the problem of analyzing the multimember COG candidates.

Continuing, the problem of analyzing the US 1943 candidates is reduced to analyzing the COG candidates with respect to the main elements of power of US 1943, namely people of US 1943, government of US 1943, armed forces of US 1943, and economy of US 1943.

Because the abstract problem "US 1943 candidates" is selected in the left-hand side of the interface of the Mixed-Initiative Reasoner, the right-hand side shows the detailed description of the corresponding reduction tree. Notice that the detailed tree shows both complete problem descriptions and the question/answer pairs that guide their reductions. The leaves of the detailed tree correspond to the abstract subproblems of "US 1943 candidates," such as "Candidates wrt people of US 1943."

The user can browse the entire analysis tree generated by Disciple-COG by clicking on the nodes and the plus (+) and minus (–) signs. For example, Figure 12.25 shows how the

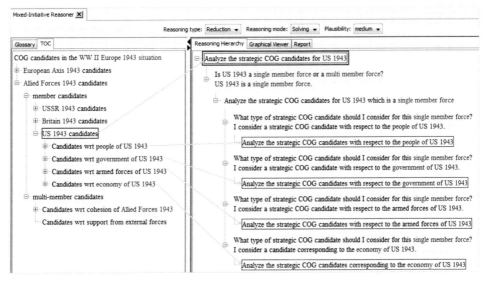

Figure 12.24. Abstract (left) and detailed (right) COG reduction tree.

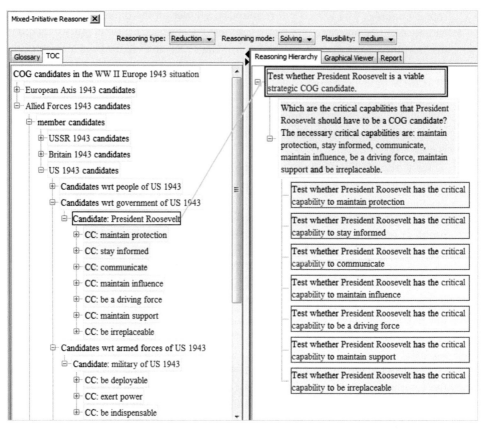

Figure 12.25. Reduction tree for testing a national leader as a COG candidate.

problems of analyzing the COG candidates with respect to the main elements of power of US 1943 (government of US 1943, and armed forces of US 1943) are reduced to identifying and testing specific COG candidates (i.e., President Roosevelt and military of US 1943). Testing each of the identified COG candidates is reduced to the problems of testing whether it has all the necessary critical capabilities. Thus, testing President Roosevelt as a potential COG candidate is reduced to seven problems, each testing whether President Roosevelt has a certain critical capability, as shown in the left side of Figure 12.25.

The left-hand side of Figure 12.26 shows how testing of whether a COG candidate has a certain critical capability is reduced to the testing of whether the corresponding critical requirements are satisfied. In particular, testing of whether President Roosevelt has the critical capability to stay informed is reduced to the problem of testing of whether he has means to receive essential intelligence. These means are identified as US Office of Strategic Services 1943, US Navy Intelligence 1943, and US Army Intelligence 1943. Consequently, the user is asked to assess whether each of them has any significant vulnerability. The user clicks on one of the means (e.g., US Office of Strategic Services 1943 in the left-hand side of Figure 12.26) and the agent displays two alternative solution patterns for its assessment, in the right-hand side of Figure 12.26:

> The US Office of Strategic Services 1943 that provides essential intelligence to President Roosevelt has the following significant vulnerability: . . . .
> Justification: . . .

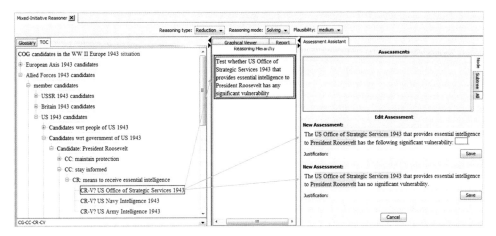

Figure 12.26. Assessing whether a critical requirement has any significant vulnerability.

> The US Office of Strategic Services 1943 that provides essential intelligence to President Roosevelt has no significant vulnerability.
>
> Justification: . . .

The user has to complete the instantiation of one of the two patterns and then click on the corresponding Save button. In this case, the provided solution is the following one:

> The US Office of Strategic Services 1943 that provides essential intelligence to President Roosevelt has the following significant vulnerability: There is a huge amount of information that needs to be collected and analyzed by the US Office of Strategic Services 1943.

Up to this point we have presented the automatic generation of the top-down COG reduction tree and the evaluation of the elementary problems (i.e., potential vulnerabilities) by the user.

The next stage of the COG analysis process is the bottom-up automatic synthesis of the elementary solutions. This will be illustrated in the following, starting with Figure 12.27, which shows how the assessments of the President Roosevelt's individual means to receive essential intelligence (i.e., US Office of Strategic Services 1943, US Navy Intelligence 1943, and US Army Intelligence 1943) are combined to provide an overall assessment of his means to receive essential intelligence:

> President Roosevelt has means to receive essential intelligence (US Office of Strategic Services 1943, US Navy Intelligence 1943, and US Army Intelligence 1943). The US Office of Strategic Services 1943 has the following significant vulnerability: There is a huge amount of information that needs to be collected and analyzed by the US Office of Strategic Services 1943.

The leaf solutions in Figure 12.27 have a yellow background to indicate that they are assessments made by the user. The top-level solution obtained through their combination has a green background to indicate that it was automatically computed by Disciple-COG, based on a previously learned synthesis rule. This rule indicates the pattern of the solution and how it is obtained by combining elements of the patterns of the subsolutions. In particular, notice that the means from individual solutions are gathered into a single list.

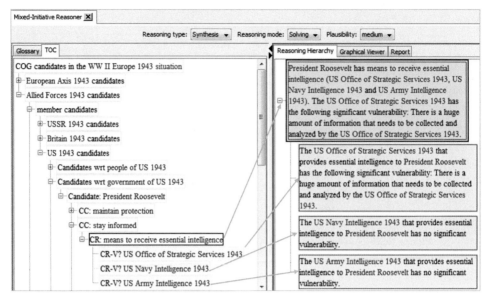

Figure 12.27. Obtaining the overall assessment of a critical requirement by combining individual assessments.

The next bottom-up solution synthesis step is to obtain the assessment of a critical capability by combining the assessments of its critical requirements. Figure 12.28, for instance, shows the assessment of President Roosevelt's critical capability to maintain support, obtained by combining the assessments of the corresponding means (i.e., means to secure support from the government, means to secure support from the military, and means to secure support from the people). This synthesis operation was previously explained in Section 4.2 and illustrated in Figure 4.8 (p. 117).

Next Disciple-COG obtains the assessment of a COG candidate based on the assessments of its critical capabilities, as illustrated in Figure 12.29:

> President Roosevelt is a strategic COG candidate that can be eliminated because President Roosevelt does not have all the necessary critical capabilities (e.g., be irreplaceable).

All the identified COG candidates from the analyzed situation are evaluated in a similar way, and the final solution is a summary of the results of these evaluations, as illustrated in Figure 12.30. In particular, for the WW II Europe 1943 situation, the solution is the following one:

> For European Axis 1943, choose the strategic center of gravity from the following candidates: military of Germany 1943 and industrial capacity of Germany 1943. For Allied Forces 1943, choose the strategic center of gravity from the following candidates: military of USSR 1943, financial capacity of USSR 1943, industrial capacity of USSR 1943, will of the people of Britain 1943, military of Britain 1943, financial capacity of Britain 1943, will of the people of US 1943, military of US 1943, and industrial capacity of US 1943.

The subsolutions of this top-level solution indicate all the COG candidates considered and why several of them have been eliminated.

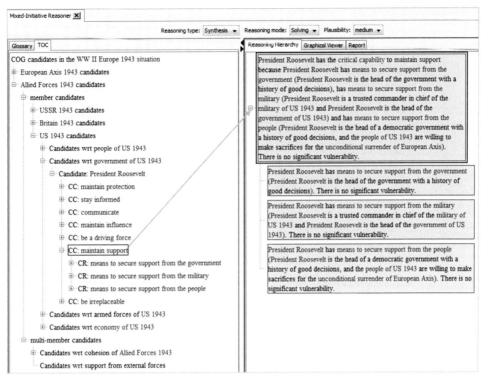

Figure 12.28. Obtaining the overall assessment of a critical capability based on its critical requirements.

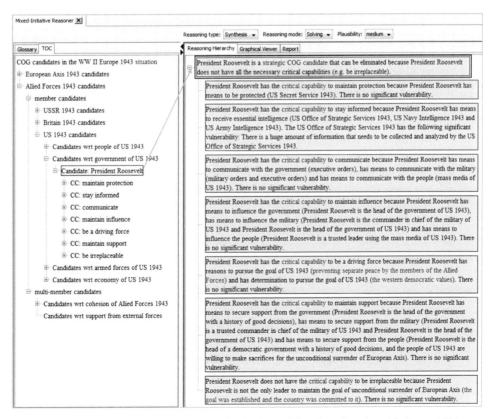

Figure 12.29. Obtaining the assessment of a COG candidate based on its critical capabilities.

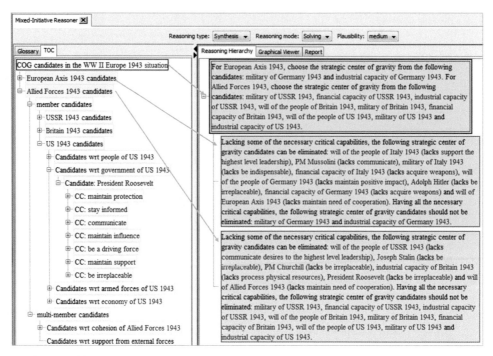

Figure 12.30. Result of the evaluation of the COG candidates corresponding to a situation.

At the end of the analysis, Disciple-COG generates a draft analysis report, a fragment of which is shown in Figure 12.31. The first part of this report contains a description of the strategic situation that is generated from the information provided and assessed by the user, as illustrated in Figures 12.22 and 12.23. The second part of the report includes all the center of gravity candidates identified by Disciple-COG, together with their analyses, as previously discussed. The user may now finalize this report by examining the analysis of each center of gravity candidate and by completing, correcting, or even rejecting it and providing a different analysis.

Successive versions of Disciple-COG have been used for ten years in courses at the U.S. Army War College (Tecuci et al., 2008b). It has also been used at the Air War College and the Joint Forces Staff College. The use of Disciple-COG in such an educational environment is productive for several reasons. First, the user is guided in performing a detailed and systematic assessment of the most important aspects of a strategic situation, which is necessary in order to answer Disciple-COG's questions. Second, the agent generates its solutions by employing a systematic analysis, which was learned from a military expert. Therefore, the user can learn how to perform a similar analysis from Disciple-COG. Third, the details of the analysis and the actual results reflect the personal judgment of the user, who has unique military experiences and biases and has a personal interpretation of certain facts. Thus, the analysis is unique to the user, who can see how his or her understanding of the situation determines the results yielded by Disciple-COG.

It is important to note, however, that the solutions generated by Disciple-COG must be critically analyzed at the end.

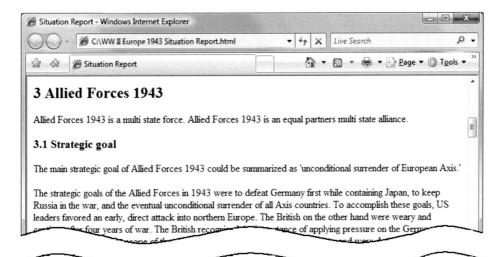

3 Allied Forces 1943

Allied Forces 1943 is a multi state force. Allied Forces 1943 is an equal partners multi state alliance.

3.1 Strategic goal

The main strategic goal of Allied Forces 1943 could be summarized as 'unconditional surrender of European Axis.'

The strategic goals of the Allied Forces in 1943 were to defeat Germany first while containing Japan, to keep Russia in the war, and the eventual unconditional surrender of all Axis countries. To accomplish these goals, US leaders favored an early, direct attack into northern Europe. The British on the other hand were weary and ~~cautious~~ four years of war. The British recognized ~~the importance~~ of applying pressure on the German ~~

COG candidates in the WW II Europe 1943 situation

6.3 US 1943 candidates

6.3.1 Candidate: will of the people of US 1943

The will of the people of US 1943 is a strategic COG candidate that cannot be eliminated because it has all the necessary critical capabilities.

> *CC: receive communication from the highest level leadership*
> The people of US 1943 have the critical capability to receive communication from the highest level leadership because the people of US 1943 have means to receive communication from the highest level leadership (mass media of US 1943). There is no significant vulnerability.

> *CC: communicate desires to the highest level leadership*
> The people of US 1943 have the critical capability to communicate desires to the highest level leadership because the people of US 1943 have means to communicate desires to the highest level leadership (elected representatives of the government of US 1943). There is no significant vulnerability.

> *CC: support the goal of US 1943*
> The people of US 1943 have the critical capability to support the goal of US 1943 because the people of US 1943 have motivation to support the goal (the goal is righteous and the people have confidence in victory). The the goal is righteous and the people have confidence in victory has the following significant vulnerability: The price to pay is very high.

> *CC: support the highest level leadership*
> The people of US 1943 have the critical capability to support the highest level leadership because the people of US 1943 have motivation to support the highest level leadership (the people of US 1943 have elected the government of US 1943). There is no significant vulnerability.

> *CC: maintain positive impact*
> The people of US 1943 have the critical capability to maintain positive impact because the people of US 1943 have means to effectively mobilize labor for war industries and other essential services (volunteering for war industries and services by people of US 1943 and applying for war industry positions by people of US 1943), have means to effectively mobilize manpower for military forces (volunteering by people of US 1943 and conscription of people of US 1943), have means to provide effective financial support (buying bonds of government of US 1943) and have means to perform critical political activities (expressing desires to elected representatives in the government of US 1943). There is no significant vulnerability.

Done   Computer | Protected Mode: Off   100%

Figure 12.31. Fragment of an automatically generated COG analysis report.

12.4.3 Ontology Design and Development

The previous section provided a general overview of the reduction and synthesis process performed by Disciple-COG, which resulted from the modeling of this process by subject matter experts from the U.S. Army War College, primarily Dr. Jerome Comello (Colonel, retired). This modeling process also informed the ontology design and development process, as discussed in Section 6.4. The top part of the resulting ontology is shown in Figure 12.32.

Under the leaf concepts from Figure 12.32 are ontologies for those concepts. For example, Figure 12.33 shows a fragment of the ontology of political factors. Figure 10.22 (p. 323) shows part of the ontology of forces, Figure 10.26 (p. 325) shows part of the ontology of economic factors, and Figure 10.28 (p. 326) shows part of the ontology of resources and infrastructure elements.

The features are also organized hierarchically. Several of the feature ontologies have an almost one-to-one correspondence to a concept ontology. Consider, for example, the ontology of controlling leaders from the middle of Figure 12.33. For each type of controlling leader (e.g., political leader), there is a corresponding feature (i.e., has as political leader), as shown in Figure 12.34. Similarly, the feature ontology from Figure 5.8 (p. 160) corresponds to the ontology of economic factors from Figure 10.26 (p. 325).

12.4.4 Script Development for Scenario Elicitation

Disciple-COG has general knowledge about the center of gravity domain, such as problem reduction and solution syntheses rules (whose applications have been illustrated in Section 12.4.2), as well as ontologies of concepts and features (as discussed in the previous section). However, the agent has no specific knowledge about any particular situation (referred to as *scenario* in this section).

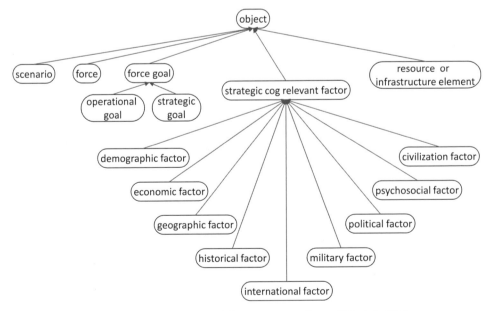

Figure 12.32. The top part of the concept ontology of Disciple-COG.

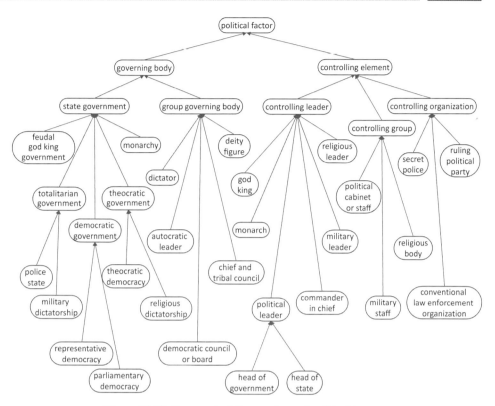

Figure 12.33. Fragment of the ontology of political factors.

When the user starts using the agent, Disciple-COG elicits the description of the situation or scenario to be analyzed, as was illustrated at the beginning of Section 12.4.2 and in Figures 12.22 (p. 367) and 12.23 (p. 368). Scenario elicitation is guided by elicitation scripts that are associated with the concepts and features from the ontology of Disciple-COG. For example, the elicitation script for the feature has as opposing force is shown in Figure 12.35. The script indicates the question to be asked ("Name the opposing forces in <scenario name>:"), the variable that will hold the answer received from the user ("<opposing force>"), the graphical appearance of the interface ("multiple line, height 4"), the way the ontology will be extended with the elicited opposing force ("<opposing force> instance of opposing force," and "<scenario name> has as opposing force <opposing force>"), and the next script to call ("Elicit properties of the instance <opposing force> in new window").

An illustration of the execution of this script was provided at the bottom of Figure 12.22 (p. 367). Figure 12.36 shows the effect of this execution on the ontology of Disciple-COG. Before script execution, the relevant part of the ontology is the one from the top of Figure 12.36. The execution of the script causes Disciple-COG to prompt the user as follows: "Name the opposing forces in WW II Europe 1943." Once the user provides these names ("Allied Forces 1943" and "European Axis 1943"), Disciple-COG introduces them as instances of opposing force, and connects the "WW II Europe 1943" scenario to them, as indicated in the script and illustrated at the bottom part of Figure 12.36.

Disciple-COG contains a Script Editor that allows easy definition of the elicitation scripts by a knowledge engineer (KE). Figure 12.37 shows how the KE has defined the script from Figure 12.35. The are a few differences in the naming of some entities in

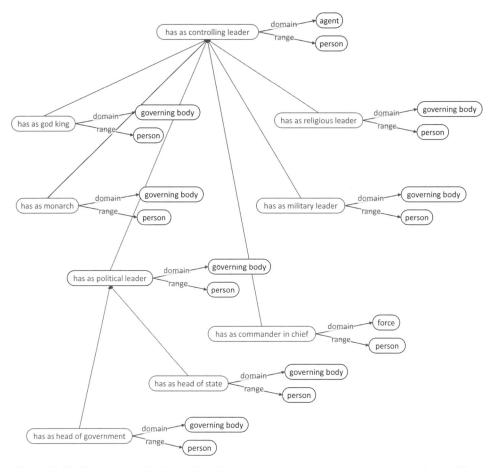

Figure 12.34. Fragment of the hierarchy of features corresponding to the ontology of controlling leaders.

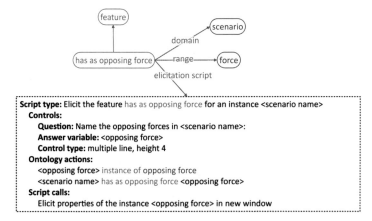

Figure 12.35. Elicitation script for a feature.

Figure 12.37, corresponding to an older version of the Disciple system. In the Feature Hierarchy Browser, the KE has selected the feature has_as_opposing_force, and then has clicked on the Script button. As a result, an editor for the elicitation script was opened, as shown in the right-hand side of Figure 12.37. Then the KE has selected the type of script to

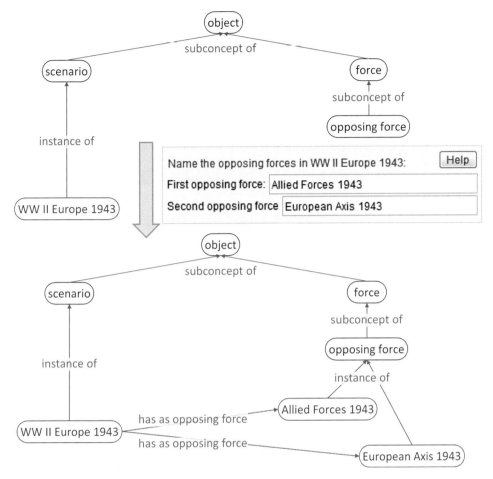

Figure 12.36. The effect of the execution of an elicitation script on the ontology.

be specified: "eliciting the values of has_as_opposing_force for an instance." As a result, the agent has displayed a panel requesting several items of information from the KE:

Control type: multiple-line
Question: Name the opposing forces in <scenario-name>:
Height: 4
Answer variable: <opposing-force-name>
. . .

Next, in the "Ontology actions" panel shown in the middle-right of Figure 12.37, the KE has indicated how the ontology will be extended with the elicited values of the specified variables:

<opposing-force-name>	instance-of	Opposing_force
<scenario-name>	has_as_opposing_force	<opposing-force-name>

Finally, as shown at the bottom-right of Figure 12.37, the KE has indicated the script to be called after the execution of the current script ("elicit properties of an instance"), how will it be displayed (in a new window), and its parameters (<opposing-force-name> and Opposing_force).

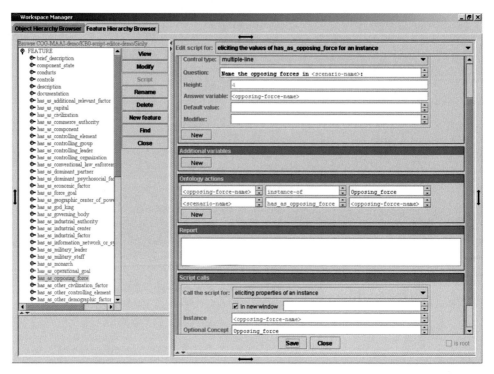

Figure 12.37. Interface of the Script Editor of Disciple-COG.

12.4.5 Agent Teaching and Learning

The teaching and learning of Disciple-COG follow the approach described in the previous sections of this book. Therefore, in this section, we are only going to illustrate them with an example.

The expert formulates an initial problem, such as "Analyze the strategic COG candidates for WWII Europe 1943" (see Figure 12.38), and shows the agent how to solve this problem by using the problem reduction paradigm described in Section 4.2. The expert uses natural language, as if he or she would think aloud. The expert asks a question related to some piece of information that is relevant to solving the current problem. The answer identifies that piece of information and leads the expert to reduce the current problem to a simpler problem (or, in other cases, to several simpler problems): "Analyze the strategic COG candidates for Allied Forces 1943." Figure 12.38 shows a sequence of problem reduction steps.

Each step consists of a problem, a question, its answer, and a subproblem. From each of these steps, Disciple-COG learns a general problem reduction rule by using its ontology as a generalization hierarchy and the methods presented in Chapters 9 and 10. They will be briefly illustrated in the following.

Let us consider the fourth step from the problem reduction tree in Figure 12.38, shown also in the upper-left part of Figure 12.39. As discussed in Chapter 9, rule learning is a mixed-initiative process between the expert (who knows why the reduction is correct and can help the agent to understand this) and the Disciple-COG agent (which is able to generalize the problem reduction example and its explanation into a general rule by using the object ontology as a generalization language).

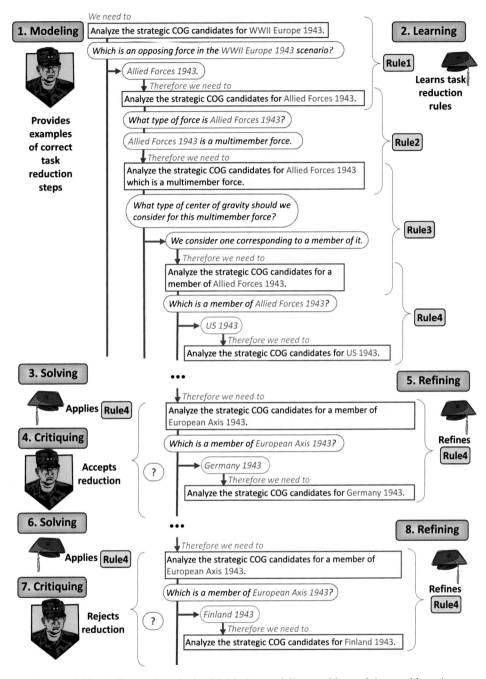

Figure 12.38. An illustration of mixed-initiative modeling, problem solving, and learning.

The question and its answer from the problem reduction step represent the expert's reason (or explanation) for performing that reduction. Because they are in natural language, the expert has to help Disciple-COG "understand" them in terms of the concepts and the features from the object ontology. For instance, the meaning of the question/answer pair from the example in Figure 12.39 (i.e., "Which is a member of Allied Forces 1943? US 1943") is "Allied Forces 1943 has as member US 1943."

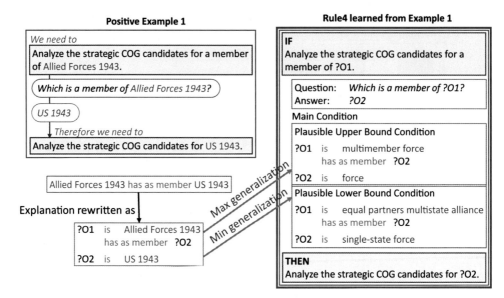

Figure 12.39. Rule learning from an example and its explanation.

Based on the example and its explanation from the left-hand side of Figure 12.39, Disciple-COG learns the rule from the right-hand side of Figure 12.39.

The structure of the rule is generated from the structure of the example where each instance (e.g., Allied Forces 1943) and each constant (if present) is replaced with a variable (e.g., ?O1). The variables are then used to express the explanation of the example as a very specific applicability condition of the rule, as shown in the bottom-left part of Figure 12.39.

Finally, the plausible version space condition of the rule is generated by generalizing the specific applicability condition in two ways.

The plausible lower bound condition is the minimal generalization of the specific condition, which does not contain any specific instance. This generalization is performed in the context of the agent's ontology, in particular the ontology fragment shown in Figure 10.22 (p. 323). The least general concepts from the ontology in Figure 10.22 that cover Allied Forces 1943 are opposing force and equal partners multistate alliance. However, Allied Forces 1943 has the feature has as member, and therefore any of its generalizations should be in the domain of this feature, which happens to be multimember force. As a consequence, the minimal generalization of Allied Forces 1943 is given by the following expression:

$$\{\text{opposing force, equal partners multistate alliance}\} \cap \{\text{multimember force}\}$$
$$= \{\text{equal partners multistate alliance}\}$$

Similarly (but using the range of the has as member feature, which is force), Disciple-COG determines the minimal generalizations of US 1943 as follows:

$$\{\text{single-state force}\} \cap \{\text{force}\} = \{\text{single-state force}\}$$

The reason the lower bound cannot contain any instance is that the learned rule will be used by Disciple-COG in other scenarios (such as Afghanistan 2001–2002), where the instances from WWII Europe 1943 do not exist, and Disciple-COG would not know how to generalize them.

The plausible upper bound condition is the maximal generalization of the specific condition and is generated in a similar way. In particular, the maximal generalization of Allied Forces 1943 is given by the following expression:

$$\{\text{object}\} \cap \{\text{multimember force}\} = \{\text{multimember force}\}$$

Also, the maximal generalization of US 1943 is:

$$\{\text{object}\} \cap \{\text{force}\} = \{\text{force}\}$$

As Disciple-COG learns new rules from the expert, the interaction between the expert and Disciple-COG evolves from a teacher–student interaction toward an interaction where both collaborate in solving a problem. During this mixed-initiative problem-solving phase, Disciple-COG learns not only from the contributions of the expert, but also from its own successful or unsuccessful problem-solving attempts, which lead to the refinement of the learned rules.

As indicated in Figure 12.38, Disciple-COG applied Rule 4 to reduce the task, "Analyze the strategic COG candidates for a member of European Axis 1943," generating an example that is covered by the plausible upper bound condition of the rule. This reduction was accepted by the expert as correct. Therefore, Disciple-COG generalized the plausible lower bound condition to cover it. For instance, European Axis 1943 is a multimember force, but it is not an equal partners multistate alliance. It is a dominant partner multistate alliance dominated by Germany 1943, as can be seen in Figure 10.22 (p. 323). As a consequence, Disciple-COG automatically generalizes the plausible lower bound condition of the rule to cover this example. The refined rule is shown in the left-hand side of Figure 12.40. This refined rule is then generating the task reduction from the bottom part of Figure 12.38. Although this example is covered by the plausible lower bound condition of the rule, the expert rejects the reduction as incorrect. This shows that the plausible lower bound condition is not less general than the concept to be learned, and it would need to be specialized.

This rejection of the reduction proposed by Disciple-COG initiates an explanation generation interaction during which the expert will have to help the agent understand why the reduction step is incorrect. The explanation of this failure is that Finland 1943 has only a minor military contribution to European Axis 1943 and cannot, therefore, provide the center of gravity of this alliance. The actual failure explanation (expressed with the terms from the object ontology) has the form:

Finland 1943 has as military contribution military contribution of Finland 1943 is minor military contribution

Based on this failure explanation, Disciple-COG generates a plausible version space for an Except When condition and adds it to the rule, as indicated on the right-hand side of Figure 12.40. In the future, this rule will apply only to situations where the main condition is satisfied and the Except When condition is not satisfied.

12.4.6 Experimental Results

The most remarkable feature of Disciple-COG is that it was developed to be actually used to teach military personnel and it has been indeed used as a learning and a

Rule4 after Positive Example 2	Rule4 after Negative Example 3

Rule4 after Positive Example 2

IF
Analyze the strategic COG candidates for a member of ?O1.

Question: *Which is a member of ?O1?*
Answer: *?O2*

Main Condition

Plausible Upper Bound Condition

?O1   is   multimember force
           has as member   ?O2

?O2   is   force

Plausible Lower Bound Condition

?O1   is   multistate alliance
           has as member   ?O2

?O2   is   single-state force

THEN
Analyze the strategic COG candidates for ?O2.

Rule4 after Negative Example 3

IF
Analyze the strategic COG candidates for a member of ?O1.

Question: *Which is a member of ?O1?*
Answer: *?O2*

Main Condition

Plausible Upper Bound Condition

?O1   is   multimember force
           has as member   ?O2

?O2   is   force

Plausible Lower Bound Condition

?O1   is   multistate alliance
           has as member   ?O2

?O2   is   single-state force

Except-When Condition

Plausible Upper Bound Condition

?O2   is   force
           has as military contribution   ?O3

?O3   is   minor military contribution

Plausible Lower Bound Condition

?O2   is   single-state force
           has as military contribution   ?O3

?O3   is   minor military contribution

THEN
Analyze the strategic COG candidates for ?O2.

Figure 12.40. Rule refined with additional examples.

decision-support assistant in courses or individual lectures at the U.S. Army War College, Air War College, Joint Forces Staff College, U.S. Army Intelligence Center, and other civilian, military, and intelligence institutions (Tecuci et al., 2002a; 2002b). In particular, successive versions of Disciple-COG have been used for elective courses and have been part of the U.S. Army War College curriculum, uninterruptedly, since 2001, for a decade. The textbook *Agent-Assisted Center of Gravity Analysis* (Tecuci et al., 2008b) provides a detailed presentation of this agent, the embodied theory for COG determination that is consistent with the joint military doctrine, and the use of this agent for the education of strategic leaders. It includes a CD with lecture notes and the last version of the agent (see lac.gmu.edu/cog-book/).

Each year, after being used in one or two courses, Disciple-COG was evaluated by the students. The following, for instance, describes the evaluation results obtained in one of these courses taught at the U.S. Army War College.

Each military student used a copy of the trained Disciple-COG agent as an intelligent assistant that helped him or her to develop a center of gravity analysis of a war scenario. As illustrated in Section 12.4.2, each student interacted with the scenario elicitation module that guided him or her to describe the relevant aspects of the analyzed scenario. Then the student invoked the autonomous problem solver (which used the rules learned by Disciple-COG) and the report generator, obtaining a center of gravity analysis report. This report contained the center of gravity candidates found by Disciple-COG, together with the justifications for their identification as candidates, and the justifications for the results of their testing (i.e., their elimination or their preservation as likely centers of gravity). These justifications are generated based on the rules learned by Disciple-COG and are intended to help the students learn how to identify and test the center of gravity candidates for war scenarios. The students were asked to study and evaluate the justifications generated by Disciple-COG and to finalize the report. Figure 12.41 summarizes the results of their evaluations. For instance, out of the 110 justifications generated for all the analyzed scenarios, 76 were considered correct, 30 acceptable, and only 4 incorrect. Moreover, most of the time the students have found these justifications to be complete and easy to understand.

The use of Disciple-COG extended over four three-hour sessions. At the end, the students were asked to evaluate a wide range of aspects related to the usability and utility of the three Disciple-COG modules used and of Disciple-COG as a whole. The students were presented with statements on various aspects of Disciple-COG and were asked to express their level of agreement with these statements by using a five-point scale (strongly disagree, disagree, neutral, agree, and strongly agree). Figure 12.42 includes some of the global evaluation results, showing that the students considered Disciple-COG easy to learn and use and its use as assignment well suited to the course's learning objectives. Disciple-COG helped them to learn to perform a strategic COG analysis of a scenario and should be used in future versions of this course. Finally, a system such as Disciple-COG could be used in other U.S. Army War College courses.

The evaluation results in Figure 12.42 are consistent with the results obtained in other similar courses. For example, Figure 12.43 presents some of the evaluation results obtained in a course at the Air War College.

This demonstrates that the Disciple approach allowed the development of an agent that has been found to be useful for a complex military domain.

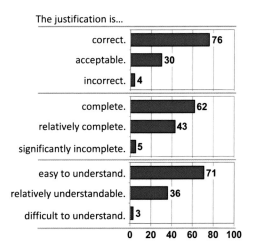

Figure 12.41. Subjective evaluation of the justifications generated by Disciple-COG.

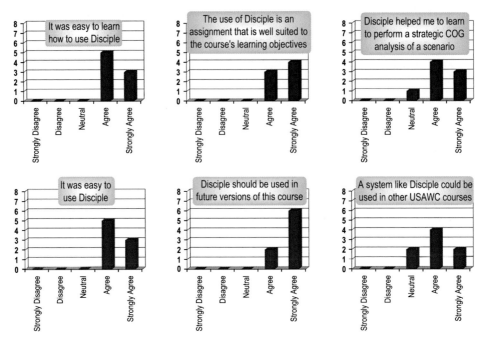

Figure 12.42. Global evaluation results from a COG class experiment at the U.S. Army War College.

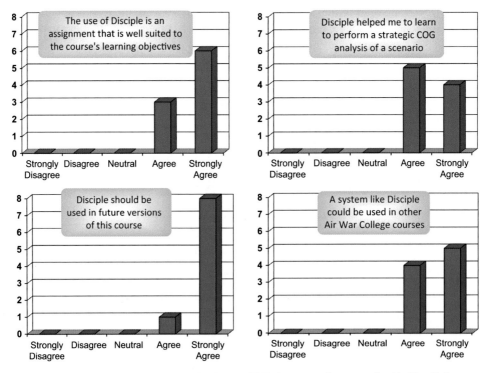

Figure 12.43. Global evaluation results from a COG class experiment at the Air War College.

12.5   DISCIPLE-VPT: MULTI-AGENT COLLABORATIVE PLANNING

12.5.1   Introduction

While most of this book has focused on the development of agents for evidence-based reasoning, the previous sections of this chapter have shown the generality of the knowledge representation, reasoning, and learning methods of the Disciple approach by describing other types of Disciple agents. This section takes a further step in this direction by presenting a different type of Disciple architecture, called Disciple-VPT (virtual planning team). Disciple-VPT (Tecuci et al., 2008c) consists of virtual planning experts that can collaborate to develop plans of actions requiring expertise from multiple domains. It also includes an extensible library of virtual planning experts from different domains. Teams of such virtual experts can be rapidly assembled from the library to generate complex plans of actions that require their joint expertise. The basic component of the Disciple-VPT tool is the Disciple-VE (virtual experts) learning agent shell that can be taught directly by a subject matter expert how to plan, through planning examples and explanations, in a way that is similar to how the expert would teach an apprentice. Copies of the Disciple-VE shell can be used by experts in different domains to rapidly populate the library of virtual experts of Disciple-VPT.

A virtual planning expert is defined as a knowledge-based agent that can rapidly acquire planning expertise from a subject matter expert and can collaborate with other virtual experts to develop plans that are beyond the capabilities of individual virtual experts.

In this section, by *planning*, we mean finding a partially ordered set of elementary actions that perform a complex task (Ghallab et al., 2004).

A representative application of Disciple-VPT is planning the response to emergency situations, such as the following ones: a tanker truck leaking toxic substance near a residential area; a propane truck explosion; a biohazard; an aircraft crash; a natural disaster; or a terrorist attack (Tecuci et al., 2007d). The U.S. National Response Plan (DHS, 2004) identifies fifteen primary emergency support functions performed by federal agencies in emergency situations. Similarly, local and state agencies undertake these functions responding to such emergencies without or before any federal assistance is provided. Each such function defines an expertise domain, such as emergency management; police operations; fire department operations; hazardous materials handling; health and emergency medical services; sheltering, public works, and facilities; and federal law enforcement. In this case, the library of Disciple-VPT will include virtual experts corresponding to these domains.

The next section presents the general architecture of Disciple-VPT and discusses the different possible uses of this general and flexible tool. Section 12.5.3 describes a sample scenario from the emergency response planning area, which is used to present the features of Disciple-VPT. Section 12.5.4 presents the architecture of the Disciple-VE learning agent shell, which is the basis of the capabilities of Disciple-VPT, including its learning-oriented knowledge representation. Section 12.5.5 presents the hierarchical task network (HTN) planning performed by the Disciple virtual experts. After that, Section 12.5.6 presents a modeling language and methodology developed to help a subject matter expert explain to a Disciple-VE agent how to plan, by using the task reduction paradigm. Section 12.5.7 discusses how a Disciple-VE agent can perform complex inferences as part of a planning process. The next two sections, 12.5.8 and 12.5.9, present the teaching and learning methods of Disciple-VE, first for inference tasks and then for planning tasks. Section 12.5.10 presents the organization of the library of virtual experts of Disciple-VPT. After that, Section 12.5.11 presents Disciple-VPT's approach to multi-agent collaboration. Section 12.5.12 discusses the development of two virtual experts, one for fire operations and the other for emergency management. Section 12.5.13 presents some evaluation results, and Section 12.5.14 summarizes our research contributions.

12.5.2 The Architecture of Disciple-VPT

Figure 12.44 presents the end-user's view of the three major components of Disciple-VPT:

- *VE Assistant,* an agent that supports the user in using Disciple-VPT
- *VE Library,* an extensible library of virtual planning experts
- *VE Team,* a dynamically assembled team of virtual experts selected from the VE Library

The user interacts with the VE Assistant to specify a situation and the profiles of several human experts who may collaborate to plan the achievement of various goals in that situation. Next, a team of virtual planning experts with similar profiles is automatically assembled from the VE Library. This VE Team then simulates the planning performed by the human experts, generating plans for achieving various goals in the given situation.

The goal of a system such as Disciple-VPT is to allow the development of collaborative planners for a variety of applications by populating its library with corresponding virtual

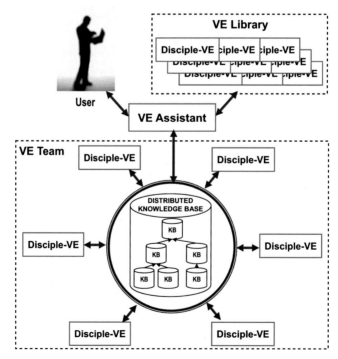

Figure 12.44. Overall architecture of Disciple-VPT.

experts. For instance, planning the response to emergency situations requires virtual experts for emergency management, hazardous materials handling, federal law enforcement, and so on. Other application areas, such as planning of military operations, require a different set of virtual experts in the VE Library. Moreover, for a given type of task and application area, different multidomain planning systems can be created by assembling different teams of virtual experts.

There are many ways in which a fully functional Disciple-VPT system can be used for training or actual planning assistance. For instance, in the context of emergency response planning, it can be used to develop a wide range of training scenarios by guiding the user to select between different scenario characteristics. Disciple-VPT could also be used to assemble teams of virtual planning experts who can demonstrate and teach how people should plan the response to various emergency situations. Another approach is to assemble combined teams that include both people and virtual experts. The team members will then collaborate in planning the response to the generated emergency scenario. In a combined team, human responders can play certain emergency support functions by themselves or can play these functions with the assistance of corresponding virtual experts. During the training exercise, a responder who has a certain emergency support function will learn how to perform that function from a corresponding virtual expert with higher competence. The responder will also learn how to collaborate with the other responders or virtual experts who perform complementary support functions.

The Disciple-VPT approach to expert problem solving extends significantly the applicability of the classical expert systems (Buchanan and Wilkins, 1993; Durkin, 1994; Awad, 1996; Jackson, 1999; Awad and Ghaziri, 2004). Such an expert system is limited to a narrow expertise domain, and its performance decreases dramatically when attempting to solve problems that have elements outside its domain of expertise. On the contrary, a Disciple-VPT type system can efficiently solve such problems by incorporating additional virtual experts. Because many expert tasks actually require collaboration with other experts, a Disciple-VPT–type system is more suitable for solving real-world problems.

The next section introduces in more detail a scenario from the emergency response planning area that informed the development of Disciple-VPT.

12.5.3 The Emergency Response Planning Problem

Emergency response planning was introduced in the previous sections. The following is a sample emergency situation that will be used to present Disciple-VPT:

> Workers at the Propane bulk storage facility in Gainsville, Virginia, have been transferring propane from a train car to fill one of two 30,000 gallon bulk storage tanks. A fire is discovered in the fill pipe at the bulk tank, and a large fire is developing. The time is 15:12 on a Wednesday in the month of May. The temperature is 72 degrees and there is a light breeze out of the west. The roads are dry and traffic volume is moderate. The fire department is summoned to the scene five minutes after the fire started. The facility is located in a rapidly growing area 2,000 feet from an interstate highway and 200 feet from two heavily traveled U.S. highways. New shopping centers have popped up in the area, including grocery stores, large box building supply facilities, and large box retail facilities. As always, these facilities are accompanied by fast food restaurants and smaller retail stores. Residential concentrations include

approximately 2,400 residents. The Local Emergency Operations Plan has all the required components, including public information, communications, and sheltering. Shelters utilize schools managed by the Red Cross. The Virginia Department of Transportation provides highway services.

Planning the appropriate response to this emergency situation requires the collaboration of experts in fire department operations, emergency management, and police operations. The generated plan will consist of hundreds of partially ordered actions.

One group of actions deals with the arrival of resources, such as fire units, emergency management services units, police units, as well as individuals with different areas of expertise (e.g., emergency manager, safety officer, highway supervisor, planning officer, training logistics officer, public information officer).

Another group of actions deals with the establishment of the structure of the Incident Command System (ICS) and the allocation of resources based on the evaluation of the situation. The structure of the ICS follows the standard U.S. National Incident Management System (FEMA, 2007). The National Incident Management System establishes standard incident management processes, protocols, and procedures so that all local, state, federal, and private-sector emergency responders can coordinate their responses, share a common focus, and more effectively resolve events. Its main components are the unified command, the command staff, and the general staff. The structure and organization of these components depend on the current situation. For example, in the case of the preceding scenario, the unified command includes representatives from the fire department, police department, highway department, and propane company. The command staff includes a safety officer, a public information officer, and a liaison officer. The general staff includes an operation section, a planning section, a logistics section, and a finance and administration section. Each of these sections is further structured and staffed.

Yet other groups of actions deal with the various activities performed by the components of the Incident Command System. For instance, in the case of the preceding scenario, the fire management group may perform the cooling of the propane tank with water. The evacuation branch may evacuate the Gainsville hot zone. The emergency manager may arrange for transportation, sheltering, and emergency announcements to support the evacuation. The Gainsville perimeter control branch implements the perimeter control for the Gainsville hot zone. The Gainsville traffic control branch implements the traffic control to facilitate the evacuation of the Gainsville hot zone. The Gainsville command establishes rapid intervention task forces to respond if the propane tank explodes.

One difficulty in generating such a plan, apart from the fact that it involves many actions, is that the actions from the preceding groups are actually performed in parallel. The goal of Disciple-VPT is to provide a capability for rapid and low-cost development of virtual planning experts to be used in this type of multidomain collaborative planning. Moreover, the plans generated by the system should be more comprehensive than those produced by a collaborative team of humans and should be generated much faster and cheaper than currently possible. The next section introduces the Disciple-VE learning agent shell, which is the basis of Disciple-VPT.

12.5.4 The Disciple-VE Learning Agent Shell

The concept of a learning agent shell was introduced in Section 3.2.3. The Disciple-VE learning agent shell is an extension of a Disciple shell that incorporates capabilities of learning for planning to enable rapid development of knowledge-based planners, as will be discussed in the following sections.

As discussed in Chapter 4, the general problem-solving paradigm of a Disciple agent is problem reduction and solution synthesis (Nilsson, 1971; Powell and Schmidt, 1988; Tecuci, 1988; Durham, 2000). In the context of planning, this approach reduces to hierarchical task network (HTN) planning, where an initial complex task is reduced to a partially ordered set of elementary actions (Tate, 1977; Allen et al., 1990; Nau et al., 2003; Ghallab et al., 2004). In the case of Disciple-VE, planning tasks are integrated with inference tasks, which significantly increases the power of HTN planning.

As with other Disciple agents, the knowledge base of Disciple-VE contains two main types of knowledge: an object ontology and a set of reasoning rules. A fragment of the object ontology for emergency response planning is shown in Figure 12.45. For example, the major fire emergency concept represents all the incidents that are major fire emergencies. One such instance is Gainsville incident. As shown in Figure 12.45, this information is represented as "Gainsville incident instance of major fire emergency."

As discussed in Section 5.3, the instances and concepts are organized into generalization hierarchies, as illustrated in Figure 12.45. These structures are not strict hierarchies, meaning that a concept may be a subconcept of several concepts (e.g., propane is both a chemical substance and a hazardous substance).

The instances and concepts may have features representing their properties and relationships, such as "Gainsville incident is caused by fire1," and "fire1 is fueled by gas propane f1." The bottom part of Figure 12.46 shows all the features of fill pipe1 in the interface of the Association Browser of Disciple-VE.

Each feature, such as is fueled by, is characterized by a domain (in this case, fire) and a range (hazardous substance). The features are also organized into a generalization hierarchy. For example, the top part of Figure 12.46 shows (a rotated view of) a fragment of the feature hierarchy, in the interface of the Hierarchical Browser of Disciple-VE. In this hierarchy, the feature has as part (shown in the left-hand side of Figure 12.46) is more general than has as member, which, in turn, is more general than has as supervisor.

Together, the object hierarchy and the feature hierarchy represent the object ontology of a Disciple-VE agent. Thus, *the object ontology is a hierarchical representation of the objects from the application domain, representing the different kinds of objects, the properties of each object, and the relationships existing between objects.*

In general, the object ontology does not contain all the relevant concepts and instances from the application domain and is therefore incomplete. Also, the representation of a given concept or instance may not include all its relevant features, being itself incomplete. Such an object ontology will have to be extended by the agent during the planning and learning process.

As discussed previously, and also illustrated in the following sections, the object ontology plays a crucial role in Disciple, being the basis of knowledge representation, user–agent communication, planning, knowledge acquisition, and learning.

The representation of concepts in Disciple-VE is discussed in Section 7.2. For example, the concept "fire fueled by gas propane" is represented by the pair {?O1, ?O2}, where ?O1 is a fire fueled by ?O2, and ?O2 is gas propane, as indicated by the following expression.

?O1	instance of	fire
	is fueled by	?O2
?O2	instance of	gas propane

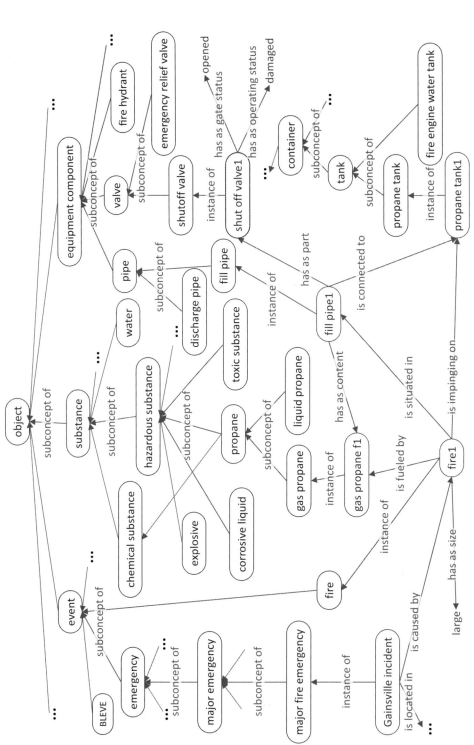

Figure 12.45. Fragment of the object ontology from the emergency planning area.

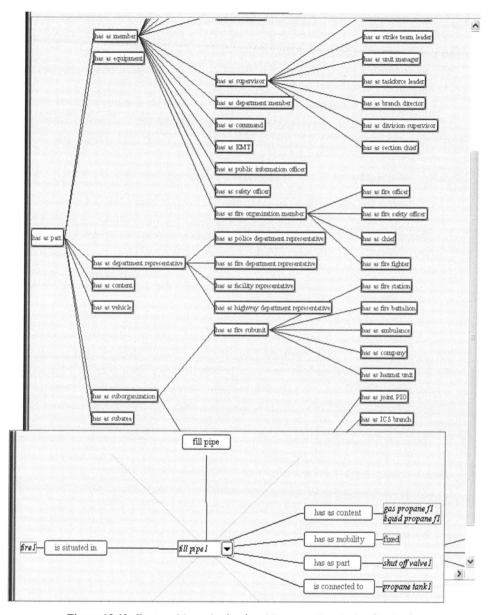

Figure 12.46. Feature hierarchy (top) and instance description (bottom).

In general, a concept may be a conjunctive expression. For example, the following expression represents the concept "fire fueled by gas propane where the fire is not small."

?O1	instance of	fire
	is fueled by	?O2
?O2	instance of	gas propane
Except-When		
?O1	instance of	fire
	has as size	small

The reasoning rules of Disciple-VE are expressed with the elements of the object ontology. *Reduction rules indicate how general planning or inference tasks can be reduced to simpler tasks, actions, or solutions. Synthesis rules indicate how solutions of simpler tasks can be combined into solutions of complex tasks, or how actions can be combined into partially ordered plans for more complex tasks.*

The next section introduces the type of hierarchical task network planning performed by Disciple-VE and the associated elements that are represented into its knowledge base.

12.5.5   Hierarchical Task Network Planning

The planning paradigm used by Disciple-VE is HTN planning (Ghallab et al., 2004), extended to facilitate agent teaching and learning and mixed-initiative planning.

The goal of an HTN planner is to find a partially ordered set of elementary actions that perform a complex task by successively decomposing the task into simpler and simpler tasks, down to the level of elementary actions. HTN planning is the planning approach that has been used for practical applications more than any other approach because it is closer to how human experts think when solving a planning problem.

We will illustrate the HTN planning process performed by a Disciple-VE agent with the abstract example from Figure 12.47. In this example, Planning Task 1 is reduced to Planning Task 2 and Planning Task 3. This means that by performing Planning Task 2 and Planning Task 3, one accomplishes the performance of Planning Task 1. Because Planning Task 2 is reduced to Action 1 and Action 2, and Planning Task 3 is reduced to Action 3, a plan for performing Planning Task 1 consists of Action 1, Action 2, and Action 3.

There are two types of reductions: task decomposition and task specialization. *Task decomposition means breaking a task into a partially ordered set of subtasks and/or actions. Task specialization means reducing a task to a more detailed task or to an action.*

The tasks or actions in a decomposition can be partially ordered. For instance, in Figure 12.47, Action 2 has to be performed after Action 1 has been performed. Notice also

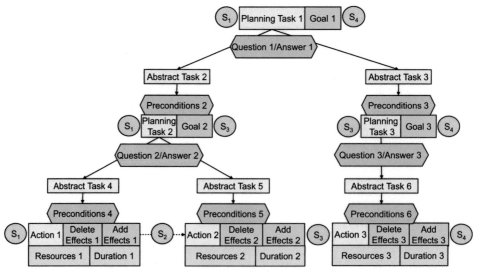

Figure 12.47. Hierarchical task network planning example.

that there is no order relation between Planning Task 2 and Planning Task 3. This means that these tasks may be performed in parallel or in any order. Stating that Planning Task 3 is performed after Planning Task 2 would mean that any subtask or action of Planning Task 3 has to be performed after all subtasks and actions of Planning Task 2. Formulating such order relations between the tasks significantly increases the efficiency of the planning process because it reduces the number of partial orders that it has to consider. On the other hand, it also reduces the number of generated plans if the tasks should not be ordered.

Planning takes place in a given world state. *A world state is represented by all the objects present in the world together with their properties and relationships at a given moment of time.* For instance, the bottom part of Figure 12.45 shows a partial representation of a world state where fire1, which is situated in fill pipe1, is impinging on propane tank1. As will be discussed in more detail in Section 12.5.10, each world state is represented by Disciple-VE as a temporary state knowledge base.

The states are changed by the performance of actions. Abstract representations of actions are shown at the bottom of Figure 12.47. *An action is characterized by name, preconditions, delete effects, add effects, resources, and duration. An action can be performed in a given world state S_i if the action's preconditions are satisfied in that state. The action's execution has a duration and requires the use of certain resources. The resources are objects from the state S_i that are uniquely used by this action during its execution. This means that any other action that would need some of these resources cannot be executed in parallel with it. As a result of the action's execution, the state S_i changes into the state S_j, as specified by the action's effects. The delete effects indicate what facts from the initial state S_i are no longer true in the final state S_j. The add effects indicate what new facts become true in the final state S_j.*

An action from the emergency planning area is shown in Figure 12.48. The action's preconditions, name, delete, and add effects are represented as natural language phrases that contain instances, concepts, and constants from the agent's ontology. The action's duration can be a constant, as in this example, or a function of the other instances from the action's description. Resources are represented as a list of instances from the ontology. The starting time is computed by the planner.

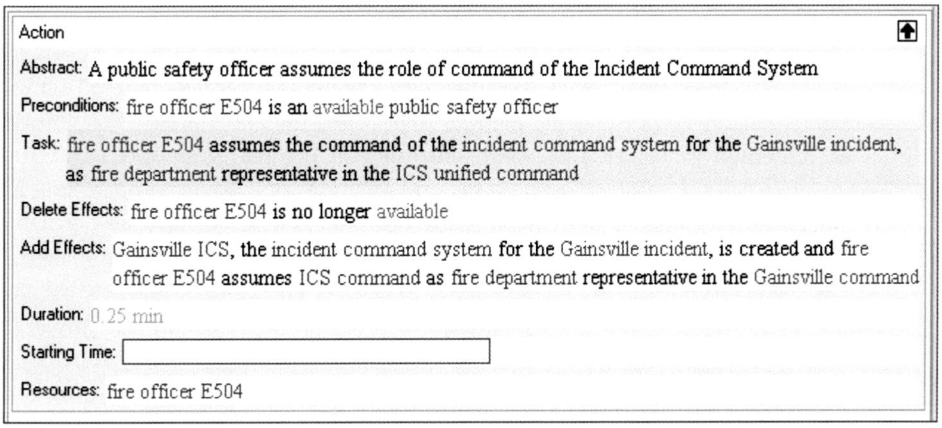

Action ⬆

Abstract: A public safety officer assumes the role of command of the Incident Command System

Preconditions: fire officer E504 is an available public safety officer

Task: fire officer E504 assumes the command of the incident command system for the Gainsville incident, as fire department representative in the ICS unified command

Delete Effects: fire officer E504 is no longer available

Add Effects: Gainsville ICS, the incident command system for the Gainsville incident, is created and fire officer E504 assumes ICS command as fire department representative in the Gainsville command

Duration: 0.25 min

Starting Time: [   ]

Resources: fire officer E504

Figure 12.48. An example of an action.

A goal is a representation of a partial world state. It specifies what facts should be true in a world state so that the goal is achieved. As such, a goal may be achieved in several world states.

A task is characterized by name, preconditions, and goal. A task is considered for execution in a given world state if its preconditions are satisfied in that state. Successful execution of the task leads to a new world state in which the task's goal is achieved. Unlike actions, tasks are not executed directly, but are first reduced to actions that are executed.

Figure 12.49 shows a task reduction tree in the interface of the Reasoning Hierarchy Browser of Disciple-VE. The initial task, "Respond to the Gainsville incident," is reduced to five subtasks. The second of these subtasks (which is outlined in the figure) is successively reduced to simpler subtasks and actions.

Figure 12.50 shows the reduction of the initial task in the interface of the Reasoning Step Editor, which displays more details about each task. As in the case of an action, the task's name, preconditions, and goal are represented as natural language phrases that include instances and concepts from the agent's ontology. Notice that none of the visible "After" boxes is checked, which means that Sub-task (1), Sub-task (2), and Sub-task (3) are not ordered.

The single most difficult agent training activity for the subject matter expert is to make explicit how he or she solves problems by using the task reduction paradigm, an activity that we call modeling an expert's reasoning. To cope with this problem, we have developed an intuitive modeling language, a set of modeling guidelines, and a set of modeling modules that help the subject matter experts to express their reasoning (Bowman, 2002). However, planning introduces additional complexities related to reasoning with different world states and with new types of knowledge elements, such as preconditions, effects, and goals. For these reasons, and to facilitate agent teaching by a subject matter expert, we have extended both the modeling approach of Disciple and the classical HTN planning paradigm (Ghallab et al., 2004), as discussed in the next section.

12.5.6 Guidelines for HTN Planning

To teach the agent how to plan, the expert first has to show the agent an example in the form of a planning tree such as the ones in Figures 12.47 and 12.50. The expert formulates the initial task (e.g., Planning Task 1 in Figure 12.47) and then follows a systematic procedure to develop a detailed plan of actions that perform the initial task. This follows a task reduction paradigm where the initial task is successively reduced to simpler and simpler tasks, down to the level of elementary actions. The partially ordered set of these elementary actions represents the plan for performing the initial task.

As presented in Figure 12.47 and illustrated in Figures 12.49 and 12.50, the task reduction process is guided by questions and answers, as if the expert is asking himself or herself how to reduce the current task. Consider, for instance, a task that may be reduced (i.e., performed) in different ways. Then the question should be related to the factors that determine the reduction strategy to choose. Therefore, the answer will help the expert to choose the strategy and define the reduction. If there is only one way to reduce the current task, then no question/answer pair is necessary.

Thus, to develop a planning tree, follow the modeling guidelines discussed in Section 4.12. The other guidelines, discussed in the previous chapters, are also applicable, but there are additional planning-specific guidelines, which will be discussed in the following.

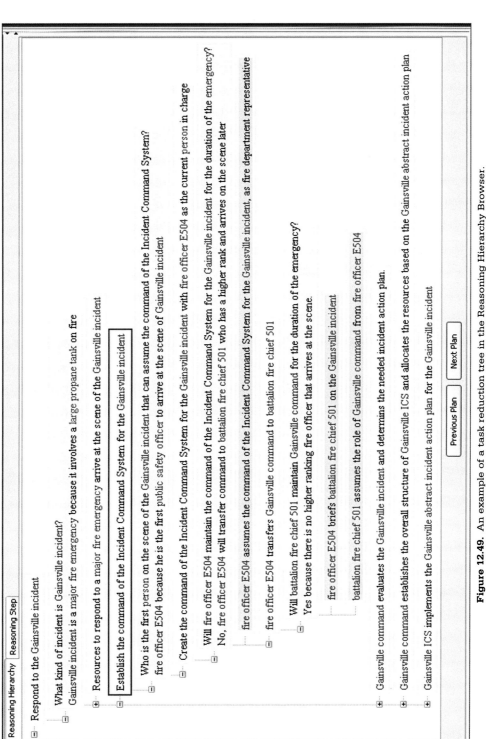

Figure 12.49. An example of a task reduction tree in the Reasoning Hierarchy Browser.

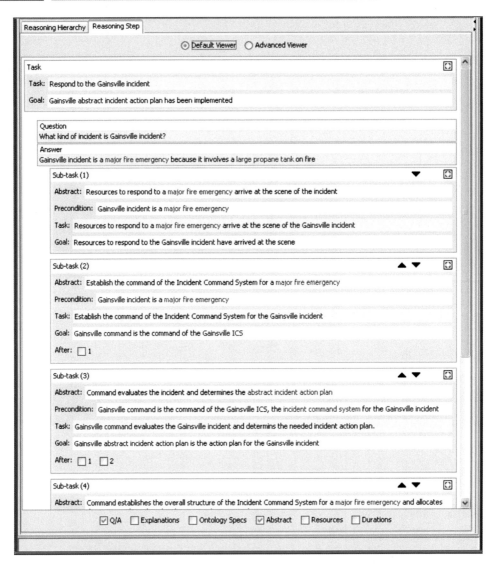

Figure 12.50. An example of a task reduction step in the Reasoning Step Editor.

Guideline 12.1. **Use a plausible task ordering when specifying a task decomposition**

Notice that Planning Task 1 from Figure 12.47 has to be performed in the initial state S_1. Planning Task 2 is also performed in the state S_1 and its preconditions have to be satisfied in that state. Similarly, Action 1 has to be performed in the state S_1. However, this action changes the world state from S_1 to S_2. Therefore, Action 2 has to be performed in the state S_2 and its preconditions have to be satisfied in that state. Moreover, it also changes the world state to S_3.

What is the state in which Planning Task 3 is performed? Because there is no order relationship between Planning Task 2 and Planning Task 3, Planning Task 3 can, in principle, be performed either in the state S_1, or S_2, or S_3. In reality, some order relationships may be determined by the resources used by the elementary actions. For instance, if both Action 2 and Action 3 need the same resource, they cannot be executed in parallel.

When showing a planning example to the agent, the expert does not need to consider all the previously discussed possible ordering relations, which would be very difficult in the case of the complex problems addressed by Disciple-VE. Instead, the expert has to consider one possible order, such as the one in which Planning Task 3 is performed after Action 2, in state S_3. This allows both the expert and the agent to have a precise understanding of the state in which each task is performed, which is necessary in order to check that its preconditions are satisfied. Thus, when specifying a decomposition of a task into subtasks and/or actions, the expert has to describe the subtasks and actions in a plausible order, even though they can also be performed in a different order.

Guideline 12.2. Specify the planning tree in a top-down and left-to-right order

Allowing the process specified by Guideline 12.1 required the extension of the HTN planning paradigm, as discussed in the following. Let us consider the decomposition of Planning Task 1 from Figure 12.47 into Planning Task 2 and Planning Task 3, by following the top-down and left-to-right process. At the time the expert has to specify this decomposition, he or she knows that Planning Task 2 has to be performed in the state S_1, but the expert does not know the state in which Planning Task 3 has to be performed. This state can be determined only after the entire subplan for Task 2 has been specified. In other words, Task 3 can be only specified after the entire subplan for Task 2 has been specified. In order to resolve this contradiction, we have introduced the notion of abstract task.

An abstract task is a simplified specification of a task that does not depend on the actual state in which the task is going to be executed. As such, an abstract task does not have any precondition, and does not refer to any specific objects or their properties.

An abstract task can be reduced to a concrete task if certain preconditions are satisfied. In principle, the same abstract task may be reduced to different concrete tasks. Therefore, the abstract task is not a characteristic of a given concrete task.

Guideline 12.3. Define preconditions when reducing an abstract task to a concrete task

When reducing an abstract task to a concrete task, formulate the preconditions to identify those instances and constants from the current world state that are referred to in the name of the concrete task, but are not referred to in the previous elements of the task reduction step that includes this concretion.

To illustrate this guideline, let us consider again the reduction step from Figure 12.50 and the pane labeled "Sub-task (3)." Notice that the concrete task includes the following instances: "Gainsville command" and "Gainsville incident." Each of these instances appear in the elements listed under Sub-task (2). For example, "Gainsville command" appears in the "Goal" part. Therefore no preconditions are required to make the concretion from the abstract task to the concrete task shown in the pane labeled "Sub-task (3)." However, the expert may still wish (and is allowed) to specify preconditions that identify the instances that appear in the concrete task, as was actually done in this example.

With the introduction of the abstract tasks, the expert can now reduce Planning Task 1 from Figure 12.47 to Abstract Task 2 and Abstract Task 3. Then he or she can continue with the reduction of Abstract Task 2 to Planning Task 2, a reduction performed in state S_1. Precondition 2 represents the facts from the state S_1 that are required in order to make this reduction.

After that, the expert continues with the reduction of Planning Task 2 to Action 1 and Action 2. Thus Planning Task 2 is actually performed by executing Action 1 and Action 2, which changes the world state from S_1 to S_3. At this point, the expert can specify the goal achieved by Planning Task 2. This goal is an expression that depends on the effects of Action 1 and Action 2, but is also unique for Task 2, which is now completely specified. Next the expert can continue with planning for Abstract Task 3 in the state S_3.

Guideline 12.4. Specify the goal of the current task to enable the specification of the follow-on tasks

The goal of a task represents the result obtained if the task is successfully performed. The main purpose of the goal is to identify those instances or facts that have been added by the task's component actions and are needed by its follow-on tasks or actions. Thus, specify this goal to include these instances or facts.

To illustrate this guideline, let us consider the Sub-task (2) pane in Figure 12.50. Notice that the two instances from the "Goal" part ("Gainsville command" and "Gainsville ICS") are used in the follow-on expressions of the reduction from Figure 12.50.

The Reasoning Hierarchy Browser, shown in Figure 12.49, and the Reasoning Step Editor, shown in Figure 12.50, support the modeling process. The Reasoning Hierarchy Browser provides operations to browse the planning tree under development, such as expanding or collapsing it step by step or in its entirety. It also provides the expert with macro editing operations, such as deleting an entire subtree or copying a subtree and pasting it under a different task. Each reduction step of the planning tree is defined by using the Reasoning Step Editor, which includes several editors for specifying the components of a task reduction step. It has completion capabilities that allow easy identification of the names from the object ontology. It also facilitates the viewing of the instances and concepts from the expressions being edited by invoking various ontology viewers.

An important contribution of Disciple-VE is the ability to combine HTN planning with inference, as described in the following section.

12.5.7 Integration of Planning and Inference

As illustrated in Figure 12.47, each planning operation takes place in a given world state, and the actions, through their effects, change this state. The planning process is complex and computationally expensive because one has to keep track of these various world states. However, some operations do not involve the change of the world state, but reasoning about a given state. Let us consider the top-level reasoning steps from Figure 12.49, where the task, "Respond to the Gainsville incident," is reduced to five subtasks. The third of these subtasks, "Gainsville command evaluates the Gainsville incident and determines the needed incident action plan," is further reduced to two inference actions (not shown in Figure 12.49):

Inference: Gainsville command evaluates the situation created by the Gainsville incident.

Inference: Gainsville command determines the incident action plan for overpressure situation with danger of BLEVE.

The first of these inference actions has as result "overpressure situation with danger of BLEVE in propane tank1 caused by fire1." BLEVE is the acronym for boiling liquid expanding vapors explosion.

From the perspective of the planning process, an inference action simulates a complex inference process by representing the result of that process as the add effect of the inference action. An inference action is automatically reduced to an inference task. *The inference task is performed in a given world state to infer new facts about that state.* These facts are represented as the add effects of the corresponding inference action and added into the world state in which the inference action is performed.

The inference process associated with an inference task is also performed by using the task reduction paradigm, but it is much simpler than the planning process because all the reductions take place in the same world state. An abstract example of an inference tree is shown in Figure 12.51.

An inference task is performed by successively reducing it to simpler inference tasks, until the tasks are simple enough to find their solutions. Then the solutions of the simplest tasks are successively combined, from the bottom up, until the solution of the initial task is obtained.

This task reduction and solution synthesis process is also guided by questions and answers, similarly to the planning process (and as discussed in Section 4.2). Figure 12.52 shows the top part of the inference tree corresponding to the following inference task:

Inference: Gainsville command determines the incident action plan for overpressure situation with danger of BLEVE.

This task is first reduced to two simpler inference tasks:

Determine what can be done to prevent the overpressure situation with danger of BLEVE to evolve in a BLEVE1.
Determine how to reduce the effects in case the overpressure situation with danger of BLEVE does evolve in a BLEVE1.

The first of these subtasks is successively reduced to simpler and simpler subtasks, guided by questions and answers, as shown in Figure 12.52.

Notice that an inference tree no longer needs to use elements such as abstract tasks, preconditions, actions, effects, resources, or duration. The teaching process is also much simpler than in the case of the planning process. Therefore, we will first present how the expert can teach Disciple-VE to perform inference tasks. Then we will present how the

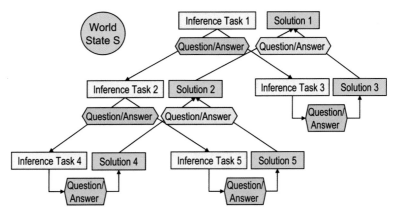

Figure 12.51. Abstract inference tree.

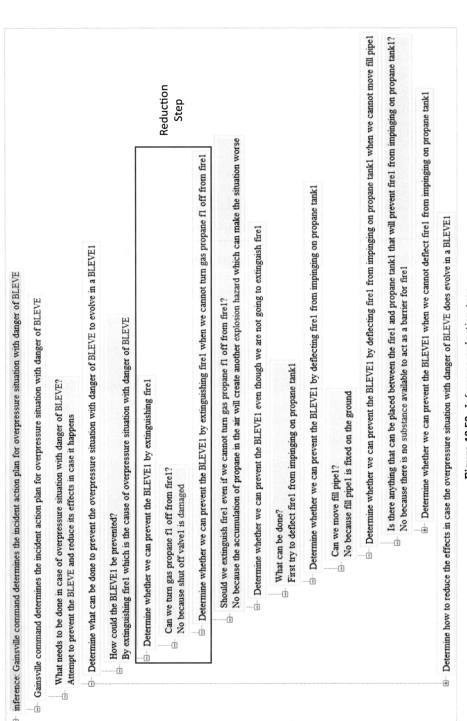

Figure 12.52. Inference reduction tree.

teaching and learning methods for inference tasks have been extended to allow the expert also to teach the agent how to perform planning tasks.

12.5.8 Teaching Disciple-VE to Perform Inference Tasks

Disciple-VE learns inference tasks by employing the methods discussed in Chapters 9 and 10. Therefore, in the following discussion, we will illustrate this process by referring to these chapters.

Let us consider again the fragment of the inference tree shown in Figure 12.52. During the teaching process, the subject matter expert builds this inference tree. Each step in the tree consists of a task, a question, its answer, and one or several subtasks. From each of these steps, the agent learns a general task reduction rule. Table 9.1 defines the problem of learning these rules.

Let us consider the third reduction step from the task reduction tree in Figure 12.52, a step also shown in Figure 12.53. From this task reduction step, Disciple-VE learned the rule shown in Figure 12.54. This is an IF-THEN rule that preserves the structure and natural language patterns from the example. Indeed, the IF task, the question/answer pair, and the THEN task are generalizations of the corresponding elements from the example where the instances and constants have been replaced with variables. In addition, the rule contains a main condition. An instance of the rule is considered a correct reduction if the corresponding variable values satisfy the main condition.

The rule in Figure 12.54 is only partially learned because, instead of a single applicability condition, it contains a plausible version space for it. The plausible lower bound of the applicability condition is the set of the tuples of the rule variable values that are less general than the corresponding elements of the Lower Bound column and satisfy the relationships from the Relationship table. For example, any value of ?O4 should be an instance of shut off valve, which has as operating status ?S1, which should have the value damaged. Moreover, this value of ?O4 should be the value of the relationship has as part of an instance of ?O5, which should be a fill pipe and should have the relationships indicated in the relationship table, and so on. The plausible upper bound of the applicability condition is interpreted in a similar way, using the concepts from the Upper Bound column.

Rule learning is accomplished through a mixed-initiative process between the expert (who knows why the reduction is correct and can help the agent to understand this) and

Figure 12.53. Example of a reduction step for an inference task.

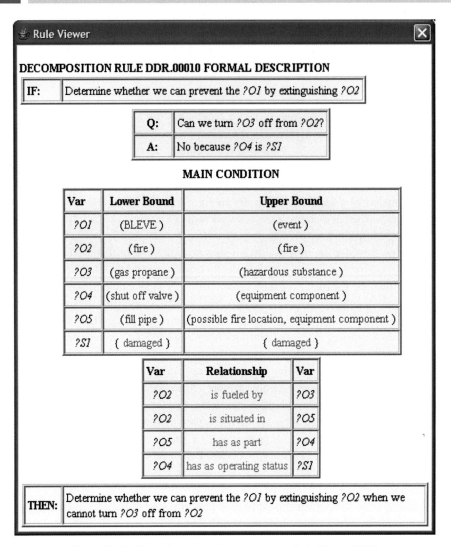

Figure 12.54. The rule learned from the example in Figure 12.53.

the Disciple-VE agent (which is able to generalize the task reduction example and its explanation into a general rule, by using the object ontology as a generalization language). The learning method is the one in Table 9.2 and will be illustrated in the following.

The first step of the learning method is Mixed-Initiative Understanding (explanation generation). The question and its answer from the task reduction step represent the expert's reason (or explanation) for performing that reduction. Therefore, understanding the example by Disciple-VE means understanding the meaning of the question/answer pair in terms of the concepts and features from the agent's ontology. This process is difficult for a learning agent that does not have much knowledge because the experts express themselves informally, using natural language and common sense, and often omit essential details that they consider obvious. The question/answer pair from the example in Figure 12.53 is:

Question: Can we turn gas propane f1 off from fire1?
Answer: No because shut off valve1 is damaged.

We can expect a person to assume, without being told, that the reason we are considering turning the gas propane f1 off from fire1 is because it is fueling fire1. We can also expect the person to assume that we are considering shutting off valve1 because it is part of fill pipe1 with the propane. However, an automated agent is not able to make these assumptions and has to be helped to get an as complete understanding of the example as possible. For instance, a more complete explanation of the example from Figure 12.53 consists of the facts shown in Figure 12.55.

The process of identifying such explanation pieces is the one described in Section 9.5. The quality of the learned rule depends directly on the completeness of the found explanation. However, there is no requirement that the found explanation be complete, and in fact this rarely occurs. The agent will continue to improve the rule while using it in reasoning (as described in Chapter 10), when it will be easier to discover the missing explanation pieces.

The next step of the rule-learning method is Example Reformulation (see Table 9.2), which consists in transforming the example from Figure 12.53 and its explanation from Figure 12.55 into an equivalent IF-THEN rule, by replacing each instance or constant with a variable and restricting the variables to those values, as illustrated in Figure 12.56. This expression is an instance of the general rule to be learned. The goal of the rule-learning process is to determine which values of the variables from the condition lead to correct task reduction steps. That is, Disciple-VE has to learn the concept that represents the set of instances of the rule's variables for which the corresponding instantiation of the rule is correct (i.e., *the applicability condition of the rule*).

First Disciple-VE generalizes the applicability condition from Figure 12.56 to an initial plausible version space condition, as described in Section 9.7 and illustrated in the following.

The plausible upper bound condition is obtained by replacing each variable value with its maximal generalization, based on the object ontology.

Let us consider the value fire1 of the variable ?O2. The most general concept from the object ontology that is more general than fire1 is object. However, the possible values for ?O2 are restricted by the features of fire1 identified as relevant as part of the explanation of the example from Figure 12.55. As indicated in Figure 12.56, ?O2 should have the features is fueled by and is situated in. This means that the values of ?O2 have to be part of the domains of these features. Thus:

$$\text{most general generalization(fire1)} = \text{object} \cap \mathbf{Domain}(\text{is fueled by})$$
$$\cap \mathbf{Domain}(\text{is situated in})$$
$$= \text{object} \cap \text{fire} \cap \text{object} = \text{fire}$$

fire1 is fueled by gas propane f1
fire1 is situated in fill pipe1 has as part shutoff valve1
shutoff valve1 has as operating status damaged
the value is specifically damaged

Figure 12.55. Explanation of the example from Figure 12.53.

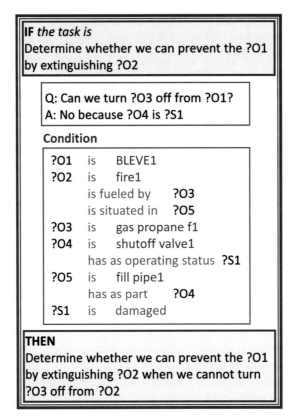

IF *the task is*
Determine whether we can prevent the ?O1
by extinguishing ?O2

Q: Can we turn ?O3 off from ?O1?
A: No because ?O4 is ?S1

Condition

?O1	is	BLEVE1	
?O2	is	fire1	
	is fueled by	?O3	
	is situated in	?O5	
?O3	is	gas propane f1	
?O4	is	shutoff valve1	
	has as operating status	?S1	
?O5	is	fill pipe1	
	has as part	?O4	
?S1	is	damaged	

THEN
Determine whether we can prevent the ?O1
by extinguishing ?O2 when we cannot turn
?O3 off from ?O2

Figure 12.56. Specific inference rule covering only the initial example.

Applying a similar procedure to each variable value from the condition in Figure 12.56 one obtains the plausible upper bound condition shown in Figure 12.57.

The plausible lower bound condition is obtained by replacing each variable value with its minimal generalization that is not an instance, based on the object ontology. The procedure is similar to the one for obtaining the plausible upper bound condition. Therefore:

$$\text{least general generalization(fire1)} =$$

$$\text{fire} \cap \textbf{Domain}(\text{is fueled by}) \cap \textbf{Domain}(\text{is situated in}) =$$

$$\text{fire} \cap \text{fire} \cap \text{object} = \text{fire}$$

The reason the lower bound cannot contain any instance is that the learned rule will be used by Disciple-VE in other scenarios where the instances from the current scenario (such as fire1) do not exist, and Disciple-VE would not know how to generalize them. On the other hand, we also do not claim that the concept to be learned is more general than the lower bound.

Notice that the features from the explanation of the example significantly limit the size of the initial plausible version space condition and thus speed up the rule-learning process. This is a type of explanation-based learning (DeJong and Mooney, 1986; Mitchell

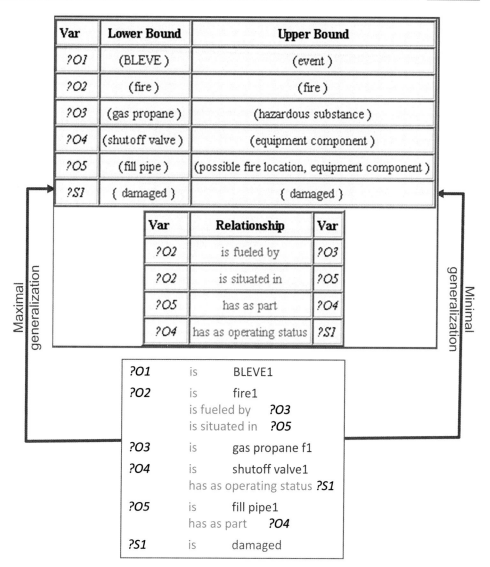

Var	Lower Bound	Upper Bound
?O1	(BLEVE)	(event)
?O2	(fire)	(fire)
?O3	(gas propane)	(hazardous substance)
?O4	(shutoff valve)	(equipment component)
?O5	(fill pipe)	(possible fire location, equipment component)
?S1	{ damaged }	{ damaged }

Var	Relationship	Var
?O2	is fueled by	?O3
?O2	is situated in	?O5
?O5	has as part	?O4
?O4	has as operating status	?S1

Maximal generalization

Minimal generalization

?O1	is	BLEVE1
?O2	is	fire1
	is fueled by	?O3
	is situated in	?O5
?O3	is	gas propane f1
?O4	is	shutoff valve1
	has as operating status	?S1
?O5	is	fill pipe1
	has as part	?O4
?S1	is	damaged

Figure 12.57. Generation of the initial plausible version space condition.

et al., 1986) except that the knowledge base of Disciple-VE is incomplete and therefore rule learning requires additional examples and interaction with the expert.

After the rule was generated, Disciple-VE analyzes it to determine whether it was learned from an incomplete explanation (Boicu et al., 2005). To illustrate, let us consider again the process of understanding the meaning of the question/answer pair from Figure 12.53, in terms of the concepts and features from the agent's ontology. In the preceding, we have assumed that this process has led to the uncovering of implicit explanation pieces. However, this does not always happen. Therefore, let us now assume that, instead of the more complete explanation pieces considered in the preceding, the identified explanation pieces of the example are only those from Figure 12.58. In this case, the learned rule is the one from Figure 12.59.

shutoff valve1 has as operating status damaged
the value is specifically damaged

Figure 12.58. Incomplete explanation of the example from Figure 12.53.

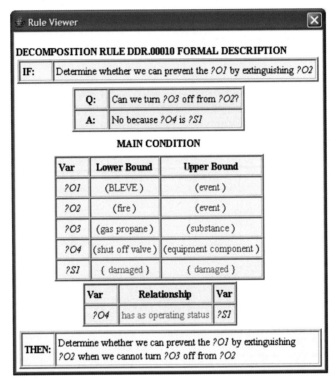

Figure 12.59. Rule learned from the example in Figure 12.53 and the explanation in Figure 12.58.

The variables from the IF task of a rule are called input variables because they are instantiated when the rule is invoked in problem solving. The other variables of the rule are called output variables.

During the problem-solving process, the output variables are instantiated by the agent with specific values that satisfy the rule's applicability condition. In a well-formed rule, the output variables need to be linked through explanation pieces to some of the input variables of the rule. Therefore, one rule analysis method consists of determining whether there is any output variable that is not constrained by the input variables. For instance, in the case of the rule from Figure 12.59, Disciple-VE determined that the variables ?O3, ?O4, and ?S1 are not constrained and asks the expert to guide it to identify additional explanation pieces related to their corresponding values (i.e., gas propane f1, shutoff valve1, and damaged).

If the rule passes the structural analysis test, Disciple-VE determines the number of its instances in the current knowledge base and considers that the rule is incompletely learned if this number is greater than a predefined threshold. In such a case, the agent will attempt to identify which variables are the least constrained and will attempt to constrain them further by interacting with the expert to find additional explanation pieces.

Following such a process, Disciple-VE succeeds in learning a reasonable good rule from only one example and its explanation, a rule that may be used by Disciple-VE in the planning process. The plausible upper bound condition of the rule allows it to apply to situations that are analogous with the one from which the rule was learned. If the expert judges this application to be correct, then this represents a new positive example of the rule, and the plausible lower bound condition is generalized to cover it, as discussed in Section 10.1.3.1. Otherwise, the agent will interact with the expert to find an explanation of why the application is incorrect and will specialize the rule's conditions appropriately, as discussed in Section 10.1.4. Rule refinement could lead to a complex task reduction rule, with Except-When conditions that should not be satisfied in order for the rule to be applicable.

12.5.9 Teaching Disciple-VE to Perform Planning Tasks

12.5.9.1 Why Learning Planning Rules Is Difficult

Figure 12.60 compares the learning of inference rules with the learning of planning rules. The left-hand side of Figure 12.60 shows an inference step and a planning step, while the right-hand side shows the rules that would be learned from these steps. In the case of an inference step, Disciple-VE learns a rule by generalizing the expressions from the examples to patterns and by generating a plausible version space for the applicability condition of the rule.

The learning of the planning rule is much more complex, not just because it involves the learning of several applicability conditions, but mainly because these conditions have to be learned in different states of the world. Indeed, Condition 11g and Condition 2g are learned in the state S_1, but Condition 3g has to be learned in the state S_3. However, the state S_3 is only known after the entire reduction tree for Planning Task 2 has been developed. What this means is that Disciple-VE would start learning the rule in the state S_1, will then continue with the planning and inference corresponding to the subtree of Planning Task 2, and only after that can resume and finalize the learning of the rule. But this is impractical for two main reasons. First, it leads to the starting of learning many complex planning rules, with the associated management of temporary representations for these rule fragments. Second, these incompletely learned rules cannot be used in problem solving. Thus, in the case of a planning tree that contains recursive applications of a task reduction step, Disciple-VE would start learning a new rule for each application, although these rules will end up being identical.

12.5.9.2 Learning a Set of Correlated Planning Rules

The main source of difficulty for learning a planning rule from the planning example in Figure 12.60 is the need first to develop the entire planning tree for Planning Task 2. We have discussed a similar difficulty in Section 12.5.6, in the context of modeling the expert's planning process. In that case, the expert could not specify the reduction of Planning Task 1 into Planning Task 2 and Planning Task 3 before completing the entire planning for Planning Task 2. The solution found to that problem was to introduce the notion of an abstract task. This notion will also help overcome the difficulty of learning planning rules, as will be explained in the following.

Rather than learning a single complex planning rule from a task reduction example, Disciple-VE will learn a set of simpler planning rules that share common variables, as illustrated in the right part of Figure 12.61.

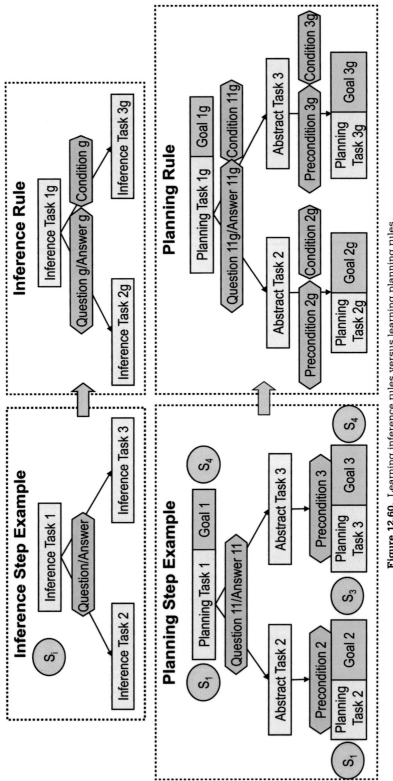

Figure 12.60. Learning inference rules versus learning planning rules.

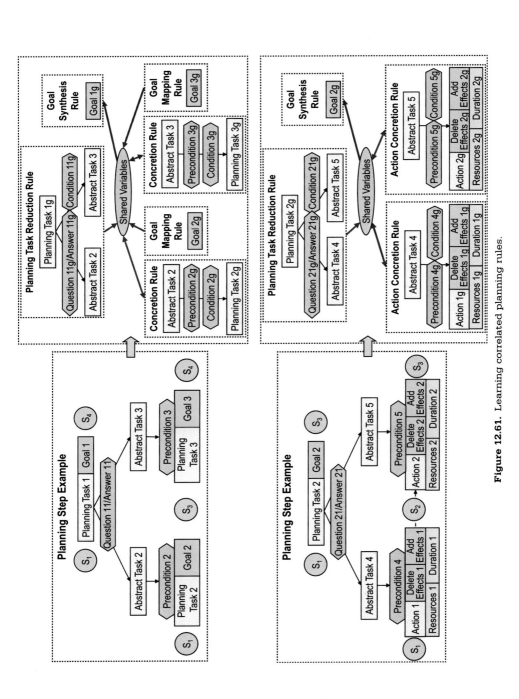

Figure 12.61. Learning correlated planning rules.

These rules will not be learned all at once, but in the sequence indicated in Figure 12.62. This sequence corresponds to the sequence of modeling operations for the subtree of Planning Task 1, as discussed in Section 12.5.6.

First the expert asks himself or herself a question related to how to reduce Planning Task 1. The answer guides the expert to reduce this task to two abstract tasks. From this reduction, the agent learns a planning task reduction rule (see Figure 12.62a), by using the method described in Section 12.5.9.4. Next the expert reduces Abstract Task 2 to Planning Task 2, and the agent learns a task concretion rule (see Figure 12.62b) by using the method described in Section 12.5.9.5. After that, the expert continues specifying the reduction tree corresponding to Planning Task 2, and the agent learns rules from the specified planning step, as indicated previously. During the development of this planning tree, the agent may apply the preceding rules, if their conditions are satisfied, and may refine them based on the expert's feedback. After the entire subtree corresponding to Planning Task 2 is

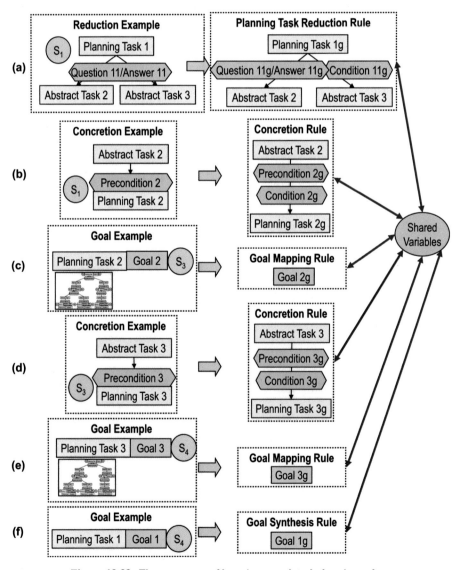

Figure 12.62. The sequence of learning correlated planning rules.

developed, the agent can learn the goal mapping rule corresponding to Goal 2, as described in Section 12.5.9.4. The learning of the concretion rule for Abstract Task 3 and of the goal mapping rule for Goal 3 is done as described previously. After that, Disciple-VE learns the goal synthesis rule corresponding to Goal 1, as described in Section 12.5.9.4.

The preceding illustration corresponds to a reduction of a planning task into planning subtasks. However, a planning task can also be reduced to elementary actions, as illustrated at the bottom part of Figure 12.61. In this case, Disciple-VE will learn more complex action concretion rules instead of task concretion rules, as discussed in Section 12.5.9.6. In the following sections, we will present the aforementioned learning methods.

12.5.9.3 The Learning Problem and Method for a Set of Correlated Planning Rules

The problem of learning a set of correlated planning rules is presented in Table 12.5, and the corresponding learning method is presented in Table 12.6. We will illustrate them by using the top task reduction from Figure 12.49 (shown also in Figure 12.50).

12.5.9.4 Learning Correlated Planning Task Reduction Rules

The method for learning a correlated planning reduction rule is presented in Table 12.7. This method is similar to the method of learning an inference rule presented in Table 9.2 and Section 12.5.8, except for the insertion of Step 3 in Table 12.7, which adds to the set **V** the variables from the learned rule and their values in the example.

To illustrate the method in Table 12.7, let us consider the top reduction in Figure 12.49 (shown also in Figure 12.50). In that reduction, the top-level task is reduced to five abstract tasks. The reduction is justified by the following question/answer pair:

Question: What kind of incident is Gainsville incident?
Answer: Gainsville incident is a major fire emergency because it involves a large propane tank on fire.

Table 12.5 The Learning Problem for Correlated Planning Rules

GIVEN
- A sequence of reduction and synthesis steps called SE that indicate how a specific planning task is reduced to its immediate specific subtasks and/or actions and how its goal is synthesized from their goals/effects.
- A knowledge base that includes an ontology and a set of rules.
- A subject matter expert who understands why the given planning steps are correct and may answer the agent's questions.

DETERMINE
- A set of reduction, concretion, goal, and/or action rules called SR that share a common space of variables, each rule being a generalization of an example step from SE.
- An extended ontology (if needed for example understanding)

Table 12.6 The Learning Method for Correlated Planning Rules

Let **SE** be a sequence of reduction and synthesis steps that indicate how a specific planning task **T** is reduced to its immediate specific subtasks and/or actions, and how its goal is synthesized from their goals/effects.

    1. Initialize the set **V** of shared variables and their values in **SE**: $V \leftarrow \Phi$

    2. Learn a planning task reduction rule from the reduction of **T** to the abstract tasks **AT$_i$** and update the set **V** (by using the method described in Table 12.7 and Section 12.5.9.4).

    3. For each abstract task **AT$_i$** do

        If   **AT$_i$** is reduced to a concrete Task **T$_i$**

        Then 3.1. Learn a planning task concretion rule and update set **V** (using the method from Section 12.5.9.5).

                  3.2. Develop the entire subtree of **T$_i$** (this may lead to the learning of new rules by using the methods from Tables 9.2 and 12.6).

                  3.3. Learn the goal mapping rule for **T$_i$** (using the method from Section 12.5.9.4).

        Else if **AT$_i$** is reduced to an elementary action **A$_i$**

        Then 3.1. Learn an action concretion rule and update the set **V** (using the method from Section 12.5.9.6).

    4. Learn the goal synthesis rule for **T** (by using the method described in Section 12.5.9.4).

As part of example understanding, Disciple-VE will interact with the expert to find the following explanation pieces, which represent an approximation of the meaning of the question/answer pair in the current world state:

Gainsville incident instance of major fire emergency
Gainsville incident is caused by fire1
fire1 is situated in propane tank1 instance of propane tank
propane tank1 has as size large

Continuing with the steps from Table 12.7, Disciple-VE will learn the rule from the left-hand side of the pane in Figure 12.63.

The final list of shared variables is shown in the right-hand side of this pane. The right-hand side of the pane shows also the goal produced by the goal synthesis rule. This rule generalizes the expression representing the goal associated with the IF task by replacing its instances and constants with the corresponding variables from the list of shared variables. Similarly, the goal mapping rule generalizes the goals of the THEN tasks.

12.5.9.5 Learning Correlated Planning Task Concretion Rules

The method of learning a correlated planning task concretion rule is similar to the method of learning a correlated planning reduction rule presented in Table 5.7 and Section 12.5.9.4. To illustrate it, let us consider again the reduction from Figure 12.50. The Sub-Task (3) pane includes a concretion step, which is shown again in Figure 12.64. The rule learned from this concretion example is shown in Figure 12.65.

As part of *Mixed-Initiative Understanding* (see Table 12.7), what needs to be understood are the preconditions of the concretion step. The approximation of their meaning is:

Table 12.7 The Learning Method for a Correlated Planning Task Reduction Rule

Let **E** be a reduction of a specific planning task **T** to one or several abstract tasks **AT$_i$**, reduction taking place in state **S$_k$**, and let **V** be the set of shared variables and their values.

(1) Mixed-Initiative Understanding (Explanation Generation)
Determine the meaning of the question/answer pair from the example **E**, in the context of the agent's ontology from the state **S$_k$**, through mixed-initiative interaction with the subject matter expert. This represents a formal explanation **EX** of why the example **E** is correct. During this process, new objects and features may be elicited from the expert and added to the ontology. This is done in order to better represent the meaning of the question/answer pair in terms of the objects and features from the ontology.

(2) Example Reformulation
Generate a variable for each instance and each constant (i.e., number, string, or symbolic probability) that appears in the example **E** and its explanation **EX**. Then use these variables to create an instance **I** of the concept **C** representing the applicability condition of the rule **R** to be learned. **C** is the concept to be learned as part of rule learning and refinement. Finally, reformulate the example as a very specific IF-THEN rule with **I** as its applicability condition. The elements of the rule are obtained by replacing each instance or constant from the example **E** with the corresponding variable.

(3) Updating of Shared Variables and Values
Add to the set **V** the new variables and their values from the condition **C**.

(4) Analogy-based Generalizations
Generate the plausible upper bound condition of the rule **R** as the maximal generalization of **I** in the context of the agent's ontology.
Generate the plausible lower bound condition of the rule **R** as the minimal generalization of **I** that does not contain any specific instance.

(5) Rule Analysis
If there is any variable from the THEN part of a rule that is not linked to some variable from the IF part of the rule, or if the rule has too many instances in the knowledge base, then interact with the expert to extend the explanation of the example and update the rule if new explanation pieces are found. Otherwise, end the rule-learning process.

Gainsville incident has as ICS Gainsville ICS has as ICS unified command Gainsville command

The *Rule Analysis* step takes the value of the set **V** into account to determine the unlinked output variables. In particular, an output variable from the concrete task does not need to be linked to input variables if it is part of the input value of **V**.

12.5.9.6 Learning a Correlated Action Concretion Rule

If the reduction of a planning task includes actions, then Disciple-VE learns also correlated action concretion rules, as illustrated at the bottom part of Figure 12.61. The learning method is similar to that for learning a correlated task concretion rule, except that the resulting rule has additional action components such as Delete Effects, Add Effects, Resources, and Duration.

Let us consider the abstract task from Figure 12.48 and its concretion. The action concretion rule learned from this example is shown in Figure 12.66.

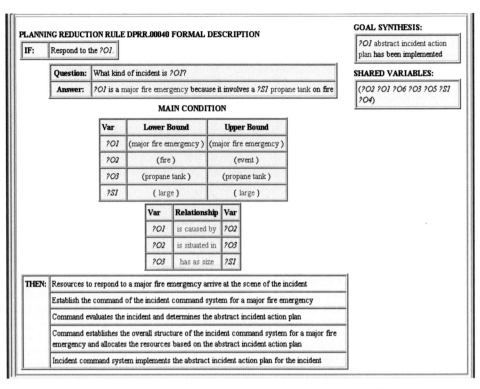

Figure 12.63. Planning reduction rule learned from the reduction in Figure 12.49.

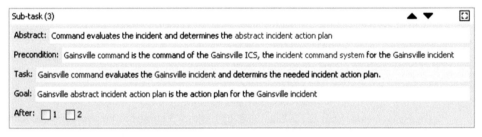

Figure 12.64. A task concretion example.

12.5.10 The Virtual Experts Library

The previous sections have presented the capability of a Disciple-VE agent shell to acquire planning expertise rapidly from a subject matter expert. This capability makes possible the development of a wide range of planning agents that can collaborate in performing complex tasks. These agents are maintained in the VE Library, where their knowledge bases (KBs) are hierarchically organized, as illustrated in Figure 12.67. In this illustration, there are four expertise domains, D1, D2, D3, and D4, and nine virtual experts, each associated with a KB from the bottom of the hierarchy. Each virtual expert agent VE is a customization of the Disciple-VE shell. The three leftmost virtual experts are experts in the

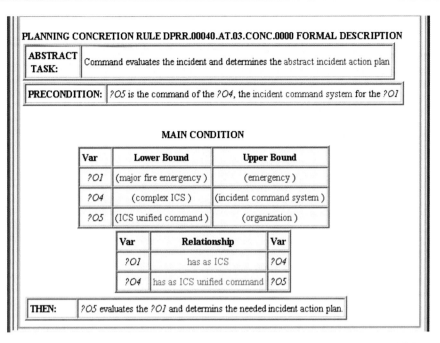

Figure 12.65. The planning concretion rule learned from the example in Figure 12.64.

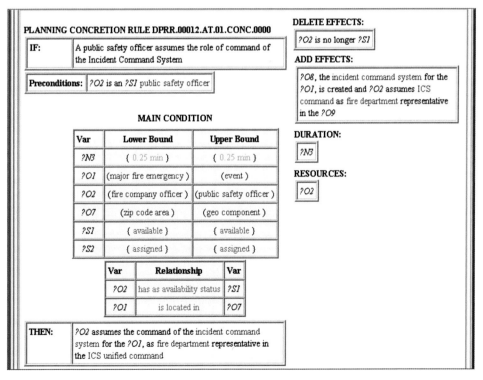

Figure 12.66. The correlated action concretion rule learned from the example in Figure 12.48.

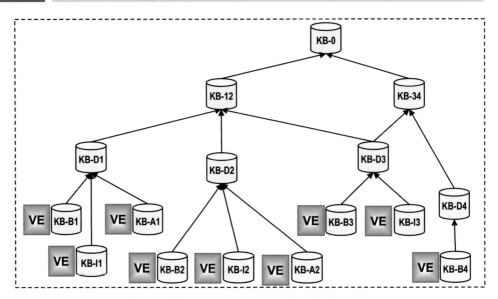

Figure 12.67. The organization of the VE Library.

domain D1 with different levels of expertise: basic, intermediary, and advanced. In addition to receiving their specific KBs (e.g., KB-B1), they all inherit general knowledge about the domain D1, knowledge represented in KB-D1. They also inherit knowledge from the higher-level KBs, KB-12 and KB-0. These higher-level KBs contain general knowledge, useful to many agents, such as ontologies for units of measure, time, and space.

Traditional knowledge engineering practice builds each KB from scratch, with no knowledge reuse, despite the fact that this is a very time-consuming, difficult, and error-prone process (Buchanan and Wilkins, 1993; Durkin, 1994; Awad, 1996; Jackson, 1999; Awad and Ghaziri, 2004). On the contrary, the hierarchy of KBs from the VE Library offers a practical solution to the problem of knowledge reuse, speeding up the process of building a new virtual expert. Consider, for example, developing a new virtual expert for the D3 domain. This expert will already start with a KB composed of KB-D3, KB-34, and KB-0. Thus, the VE Library can also be regarded as a knowledge repository for the new virtual experts to be developed.

The updating of each KB from the hierarchical repository (e.g., KB-12) is the responsibility of a team consisting of a knowledge engineer and one or several subject matter experts. They use the specialized browsers and editors of the Disciple-VE shell. The left-hand side of Figure 12.68 shows the interface of the Object Browser, which displays the objects in a tree structure. The objects that are inherited from an upper-level KB (such as information measure or length measure) are displayed with a gray background. The right-hand side of Figure 12.68 shows the interface of the Object Viewer, which displays additional information about the object selected in the Object Browser (e.g., fire engine company E501), such as its direct superconcepts and its features. The top part of Figure 12.46 shows the interface of the Hierarchical Browser, which displays the hierarchical relationships between objects or features in a graph structure. The bottom part of Figure 12.46 shows the interface of the Association Browser, which displays an object and its relationships with other objects. Additional tools include the Object Editor, the Feature Editor, and the Rule Editor. All these tools have been introduced in Chapters 5 and 6.

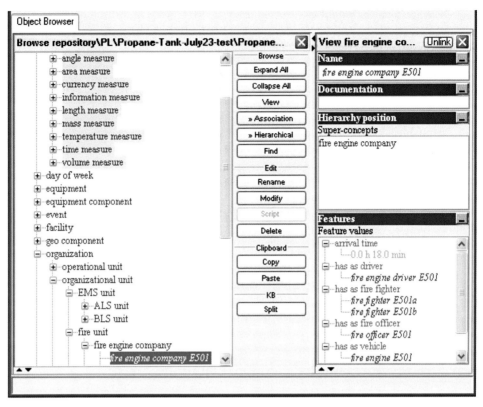

Figure 12.68. The interface of the Object Browser and Object Viewer.

To allow the KBs from the hierarchy to be updated and extended separately, the Disciple-VPT system maintains multiple versions for each KB. Let us assume that each KB from Figure 12.67 has the version 1.0. Let us further assume that the management team for KB-0 decides to make some changes to this KB that contains units of measure. For instance, the team decides to include the metric units, to rename "gallon" as "US gallon," and to add "UK gallon." As a result, the team creates version 2.0 of KB-0. However, the other knowledge bases from the library (e.g., KB-12) still refer to version 1.0 of KB-0. The management team for KB-12 is informed that a higher version of KB-0 is available. At this point, the team can decide whether it wants to create a new version of KB-12 that inherits knowledge from version 2.0 of KB-0. The KB update process uses the KB updating tool of Disciple-VE. This tool creates version 2.0 of KB-12 by importing the knowledge from version 1.0 of KB-12, in the context of version 2.0 of KB-0. Even though the version 2.0 of KB-12 has been created, Disciple-VPT still maintains KB-0 version 1.0 and KB-12 version 1.0, because these versions are used by KB-D1 version 1.0 and by other KBs from the repository. The management team for KB-D1 may now decide whether it wants to upgrade KB-D1 to the new versions of its upper-level KBs, and so on. Because of the version system, each KB from the library maintains, in addition to its version, the versions of the other KBs from which it inherits knowledge.

Another important knowledge management functionality offered by Disciple-VPT is that of splitting a KB into two parts, a more general one and a more specific one. This allows a KB developer first to build a large KB and then to split it and create a hierarchy of KBs.

When a virtual expert is extracted from the VE Library and introduced into a VE Team (see Figure 12.44), all the KBs from which it inherits knowledge are merged into a shared KB in order to increase the performance of the agent. Let us consider the Intermediate agent from the domain D3 (see Figure 12.67). In this case, KB-D3, KB-12, KB-34, and KB-0 are all merged into the Shared KB of this agent. As a consequence, the structure of the KBs of this agent during planning is the one from Figure 12.69. Notice that, in addition to the Shared KB, there are three other types of KBs, Domain KB, Scenario KB, and State KB, all hierarchically organized. Domain KB is the KB of this Intermediate agent from the domain D3, knowledge independent of any particular scenario. Each scenario is represented into a different KB called Scenario KB. For example, there would be a Scenario KB for the propane tank fire scenario described in Section 12.5.3, and a different Scenario KB for a scenario involving red-fuming nitric acid spilling from a truck parked near a residential area (Tecuci et al., 2008c). Moreover, under each scenario KB there is a hierarchy of State KBs. KB-S1 represents the state obtained from SKB-M after the execution of an action which had delete and/or add effects. As additional actions are simulated during planning, their delete and add effects change the state of the world. KB-S11, KB-S12, and KB-S13 are the states corresponding to three alternative actions. The entire description of the state corresponding to KB-S11 is obtained by considering the delete and add effects in the states KB-S11 and KB-S1, and the facts in the scenario SKB-M.

12.5.11 Multidomain Collaborative Planning

Each virtual agent from the VE Library is expert in a certain expertise domain. However, these expertise domains are not disjointed, but overlapping, as illustrated in Figure 12.70.

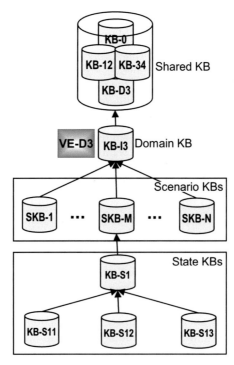

Figure 12.69. The organization of an agent's knowledge base during planning.

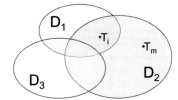

Figure 12.70. Sample coverage of expertise domains.

In this illustration, the planning task T_m belongs only to D_2 and can be performed only by a virtual expert from that domain. T_i is a task common to D_1 and D_2 and can, in principle, be performed either by a virtual expert in D_1 or by a virtual expert in D_2. In general, a virtual expert will cover only a part of a given expertise domain, depending on its level of expertise. For instance, the virtual expert library illustrated in Figure 12.67 includes three virtual experts from the domain D_1, a basic one, an intermediate one, and an advanced one, each covering an increasingly larger portion of the domain. Therefore, whether a specific virtual expert from the domain D_2 can generate a plan for T_m and the quality of the generated plan depend on the expert's level of expertise.

A virtual expert has partial knowledge about its ability to generate plans for a given task, knowledge that is improved through learning. For instance, the virtual expert knows that it may be able to generate plans for a given task instantiation because that task belongs to its expertise domain, or because it was able to solve other instantiations of that task in the past. Similarly, it knows when a task does not belong to its area of expertise. The virtual experts, however, do not have predefined knowledge about the problem-solving capabilities of the other experts from a VE Team or the VE Library. This is a very important feature of Disciple-VPT that facilitates the addition of new agents to the library, or the improvement of the existing agents, because this will not require taking into account the knowledge of the other agents.

The task reduction paradigm facilitates the development of plans by cooperating virtual experts, where plans corresponding to different subtasks of a complex task may be generated by different agents. This multi-agent planning process is driven by an auction mechanism that may apply several strategies. For instance, the agents can compete for solving the current task based on their prior knowledge about their ability to solve that task. Alternatively, the agents may actually attempt to solve the task before they bid on it.

12.5.12 Basic Virtual Planning Experts

We have developed two basic virtual experts: a fire department operations expert and an emergency management expert. The development of these virtual experts was guided by the toxic substance leaking scenario described in Tecuci et al. (2008c) and by the propane tank on fire scenario described in Section 12.5.3.

First we have worked with a subject matter expert to model the plan generation process for these two scenarios by using the task reduction paradigm, as illustrated in Figure 12.50. Besides the development of the reasoning trees, another result of this modeling process was the development of the modeling methodology presented in Section 12.5.6. Yet another result of this modeling process was the identification of the object concepts that need to be present in the ontology of Disciple-VE so that it can perform this type of reasoning. Based on this specification of the object ontology, and by using the ontology development modules of Disciple-VE, we have developed an object ontology consisting of 410 concepts, 172 feature definitions, 319 generic instances, and 944 facts. Fragments of this ontology were presented in Figures 12.45 and 12.46.

Although we have worked with both aforementioned scenarios to develop the modeling trees and the ontology, the teaching of the fire expert and of the emergency management expert was based only on the scenario of the propane tank on fire. As a result of the teaching process, the virtual fire expert learned eighty-one planning rules, and the virtual emergency management expert learned forty-seven planning rules. The two developed virtual experts share the object ontology.

12.5.13 Evaluation of Disciple-VPT

To perform a preliminary evaluation of the Disciple-VPT system, we have developed a *scenario pattern* based on the scenario from Section 12.5.3. Then we have asked a fire department operations expert and an emergency management expert to define a specific scenario based on this pattern, by providing the missing elements. For example, the two experts decided on the day and time of the incident, the position of the fire with respect to the propane tank, the estimated amount of propane in the tank, the available resources (fire engine companies, truck engine companies, hazardous materials [hazmat] units, police personnel, county personnel, etc.), and the time that they are arriving at the scene of the incident. After that, both the team of human experts and Disciple-VPT independently generated plans to respond to this situation.

The plan generated by Disciple-VPT consisted of eighty-nine partially ordered elementary actions. A fragment of this plan is shown in Figure 12.71. This plan was evaluated by the aforementioned experts and by the expert with whom we have developed the agents. Then each expert filled out a questionnaire. The questionnaire included statements about various characteristics of the generated plan and about the Disciple-VPT system. The experts were asked to indicate whether they strongly agree (SA), agree (A), are neutral (N), disagree (D), or strongly disagree (SD) with these statements.

The top part of Table 12.8 presents some of the results of the evaluation of the plan generated by Disciple-VPT, which the human experts considered good and easy to understand. One of the experts disagreed with the way Disciple-VPT ordered some of the actions. However, this reflected a disagreement between the evaluating experts and not a planning error, the generated order being that taught by the expert who instructed Disciple-VPT.

The evaluation of the hierarchical plan generation process (see the middle of Table 12.8) shows that it significantly improves the understandability of this process. Finally the experts agreed or strongly agreed that Disciple-VPT has many potential applications in emergency response planning, from developing exercises for training, to actual training, and to its use as planning assistant.

A limitation of this evaluation is that it is based on the opinion of only three experts. More experts are needed in order for the results to have statistical significance.

12.5.14 Final Remarks

This section presented a major extension of the Disciple theory and methodology for the development of knowledge-based agents by subject matter experts, with limited assistance from knowledge engineers.

Id	Action	Result	Resources	Start Time	Duration
1	Suburbane Propane Company facility manager, a person, arrives at the scene of the Gainsville incident	**Add:** Suburbane Propane Company facility manager arrived at the scene and is available to take required actions	Suburbane Propane Company facility manager	0.0 s	1.0 min 0.0 s
2	ALS unit M504, an ALS unit, arrives at the scene of the Gainsville incident	**Add:** ALS unit M504 arrived at the scene and is available to take required actions	ALS unit M504, paramedic 504a, and paramedic 504b	0.0 s	5.0 min 0.0 s
3	fire engine company E504, a fire engine company, arrives at the scene of the Gainsville incident	**Add:** fire engine company E504 arrived at the scene and is available to take required actions	fire engine driver E504, fire fighter E504b, fire engine company E504, fire engine E504, deluge nozzle E504, water hose E504, fire officer E504, and fire fighter E504a	0.0 s	5.0 min 0.0 s
	...	...	...	...	...
48	fire officer E504 assumes the command of the incident command system for the Gainsville incident, as fire department representative in the ICS unified command	**Delete:** fire officer E504 is no longer available **Add:** Gainsville ICS, the incident command system for the Gainsville incident, is created and fire officer E504 assumes ICS command as fire department representative in the Gainsville command	fire officer E504	5.0 min 0.0 s	15.0 s
49	Gainsville command evaluates the situation created by the Gainsville incident	**Add:** overpressure situation with danger of BLEVE in propane tank1 is caused by fire1	Gainsville command	5.0 min 15.0 s	30.0 s
50	Gainsville command determines the abstract incident action plan for overpressure situation	**Add:** The plan is to apply cooling water, to evacuate people from 1.0 mi around propane tank1, to perform traffic control, perimeter control, and to establish rapid intervention task forces	Gainsville command	5.0 min 45.0 s	30.0 s
	...	...	...	...	...
54	fire engine company E504 sets up water hose E504 to apply water to propane tank1	**Delete:** water hose E504 is available **Add:** water hose E504 is assigned	fire engine company E504, fire engine driver E504, fire fighter E504b, fire fighter E504a, water hose E504, and fire engine E504	8.0 min 30.0 s	3.0 min 0.0 s
55	fire engine company E525 drops off deluge nozzle E525 for fire engine company E504	**Delete:** deluge nozzle E525 that belongs to fire engine E525 is no longer available **Add:** deluge nozzle E525 is assigned	fire fighter E525a, fire officer E525, deluge nozzle E525, fire engine driver E525, and fire fighter E525b	8.0 min 30.0 s	2.0 min 0.0 s
	...	...	...	...	...
63	fire engine company E525 establishes continuous water supply from fire hydrant1 for fire engine company E504	**Add:** fire hydrant1 is assigned to fire engine company E504	fire fighter E525a, fire fighter E525b, fire officer E525, fire engine driver E525, and fire engine company E525	14.0 min 30.0 s	7.0 min 0.0 s
	...	...	...	...	...

Figure 12.71. Fragment of a plan generated by Disciple-VPT.

Table 12.8 Evaluation Results

Generated Plan	SA	A	N	D	SD
The generated plan is easy to understand.		3			
The generated plan consists of a good sequence of actions.		2		1	
The objectives of the actions are clear from the generated plan.		3			
The generated plan has a good management of the resources.	1	1	1		
The level of detail in the plan is appropriate.		3			

Hierarchical Plan Generation Process	SA	A	N	D	SD
The hierarchical task-reduction structure makes the logic of the plan clear.	2	1			
The hierarchical task-reduction structure makes the goals of the plan clear.	1	2			
The questions, the answers, and the preconditions help understand the logic of the plan generation process.	2	1			
The preconditions, effects, duration, and resources make the specification of the plan's actions clear.	1	2			
The hierarchical task-reduction structure may be used to teach new persons how to plan.	3				

Usability of Disciple-VPT	SA	A	N	D	SD
Disciple-VPT could be used in developing and carrying out exercises for emergency response planning.	2	1			
Disciple-VPT could be used for training the personnel for emergency response planning.	2	1			
Disciple-VPT could be used as an assistant to typical users, guiding them how to respond to an emergency situation.		3			

First, we have extended the Disciple approach to allow the development of complex HTN planning agents that can be taught their planning knowledge, rather than having it defined by a knowledge engineer. This is a new and very powerful capability that is not present in other action planning systems (Tate, 1977; Allen et al., 1990; Nau et al., 2003;

Ghallab et al., 2004). This capability was made possible by several major developments of the Disciple approach. For instance, we have significantly extended the knowledge representation and management of a Disciple agent by introducing new types of knowledge that are characteristic of planning systems, such as planning tasks and actions (with preconditions, effects, goal, duration, and resources) and new types of rules (e.g., planning tasks reduction rules, concretion rules, action rules, goal synthesis rules). We have introduced state knowledge bases and have developed the ability to manage the evolution of the states in planning. We have developed a modeling language and a set of guidelines that help subject matter experts express their planning process. We have developed an integrated set of learning methods for planning, allowing the agent to learn general planning knowledge starting from a single planning example formulated by the expert.

A second result is the development of an integrated approach to planning and inference, both processes being based on the task reduction paradigm. This improves the power of the planning systems that can now include complex inference trees. It also improves the efficiency of the planning process because some of the planning operations can be performed as part of a much more efficient inference process that does not require a simulation of the change of the state of the world.

A third result is the development and implementation of the concept of library of virtual experts. This required the development of methods for the management of a hierarchical knowledge repository. The hierarchical organization of the knowledge bases of the virtual experts also serves as a knowledge repository that speeds up the development of new virtual experts that can reuse the knowledge bases from the upper levels of this hierarchy.

A fourth result is the development of the multidomain architecture of Disciple-VPT, which extends the applicability of the expert systems to problems whose solutions require knowledge of more than one domain.

A fifth result is the development of two basic virtual experts, a basic fire expert and a basic emergency management expert, that can collaborate to develop plans of actions that are beyond their individual capabilities.

Finally, a sixth result is the development of an approach and system that has high potential for supporting a wide range of training and planning activities.

13 Design Principles for Cognitive Assistants

This book has presented an advanced approach to developing personal cognitive assistants. Although the emphasis in this book has been on cognitive assistants for evidence-based hypothesis analysis, the Disciple approach is also applicable to other types of tasks, as was illustrated by the agents presented in Chapter 12. Moreover, the Disciple approach illustrates the application of several design principles that are useful in the development of cognitive assistants in general. In this chapter, we review these principles, which have been illustrated throughout this book. Each of the following sections starts with the formulation of a principle and continues with its illustration by referring back to previous sections of the book.

13.1 LEARNING-BASED KNOWLEDGE ENGINEERING

Employ learning technology to simplify and automate the knowledge engineering process.

It is generally accepted that knowledge engineering is very difficult, involving many creative tasks. One way to simplify this process significantly is to automate as much of the knowledge engineering process as possible. As discussed in Section 3.3.6, the approach taken with Disciple is to replace each knowledge base development activity of the knowledge engineer (e.g., modeling the problem-solving process, ontology development, rule learning, rule refinement) with an equivalent activity that can be performed directly by a subject matter expert and the Disciple agent, with limited or no support from the knowledge engineer (see Figure 3.19, p. 107).

Consider, for example, the modeling of the problem-solving process. A knowledge engineer would need to instruct a subject matter expert how to express his or her reasoning in the divide-and-conquer analysis and synthesis framework. Then the expert and the agent can model the solutions of new problems by themselves. In this process, the agent will support the expert in various ways. For example, the agent may employ previously learned rules to suggest likely reductions of the current problem or hypothesis. Or it may learn and reuse reasoning patterns to suggest reductions to the expert.

Now consider the development and testing of the reasoning rules, which the knowledge engineer does through interviews with the subject matter expert, as discussed in Section 3.1.4. This time-consuming and error-prone task is reduced to several tasks that the subject matter expert and the Disciple agent can easily perform, as discussed in Sections 9.4 and 10.1.2. In particular, the expert provides examples and helps the agent to understand them, and the agent generates the reasoning rules. Then the agent employs the rules in problem solving and the expert critiques the reasoning process which, in turn, guides the agent in refining the rules.

13.2 PROBLEM-SOLVING PARADIGM FOR USER–AGENT COLLABORATION

Use a problem-solving paradigm that is both natural for the human user and appropriate for the automated agent.

Cognitive assistants, by their very nature, need to be based on problem-solving paradigms that facilitate user–agent collaboration. On one hand, the employed problem-solving paradigm needs to be natural enough for the human users. On the other hand, it has to be formal enough to be automatically applied by the agents.

As discussed in Chapter 4, Disciple agents employ a divide-and-conquer approach where complex problems or hypotheses, expressed in natural language, are successively reduced to simpler and simpler ones, guided by corresponding questions and answers. The typical questions are those from Rudyard Kipling's well-known poem, "I Keep Six Honest . . .": "What?" "Why?" "When?" "How?" "Where?" and, "Who?"

While the analysis part of the problem-solving strategy is very natural, its synthesis part may be challenging, as pointed out by Toffler (1984), and also experienced by us with the development of many Disciple agents, such as Disciple-COG (see Sections 4.1 and 12.4). Therefore, in Disciple-EBR, we have developed a simplified version of solution synthesis for evidence-based reasoning that is actually very easy to use, as discussed in Sections 4.3 and 4.4.

13.3 MULTI-AGENT AND MULTIDOMAIN PROBLEM SOLVING

Use a problem-solving paradigm for the agent that facilitates both collaboration between users assisted by their agents and the solving of problems requiring multidomain expertise.

Many existing or potential applications of cognitive assistants are cross-domain, requiring the collaboration not only between a user and his or her assistant, but also among several users, each with his or her own area of expertise, as illustrated by the emergency response planning domain addressed by Disciple-VPT (see Section 12.5). The problem reduction strategy employed by the Disciple agents can reduce a multidisciplinary problem to subproblems that may be solved by different experts and their agents. Then, the domain-specific solutions found by individual users may be combined to produce the solution of the multidisciplinary problem. With such an approach, each agent supports its user, not only in problem solving, but also in collaboration and sharing of information with the other users.

13.4 KNOWLEDGE BASE STRUCTURING FOR KNOWLEDGE REUSE

Structure the knowledge base to facilitate knowledge reuse.

Knowledge base development is a very complex activity, and knowledge reuse can significantly simplify it. Moreover, knowledge reuse facilitates the communication with other agents that share the same knowledge.

Disciple agents facilitate the reuse of knowledge through two types of knowledge structuring. First, the agent's knowledge is structured into an ontology that defines the concepts of the application domain and a set of problem-solving rules expressed with these concepts. The ontology is the more general part, being applicable to an entire domain. Therefore, when developing a new application, parts of the ontology can be reused from the previously developed applications in that domain.

A second type of knowledge structuring is the organization of the knowledge repository of the agent as a three-level hierarchy of knowledge bases, as discussed in Section 3.3.5 (see Figure 3.17, p. 104). The top of the knowledge repository is the Shared KB, which contains general knowledge for evidence-based reasoning applicable in all the domains. Under the Shared KB are Domain KBs, each corresponding to a different application domain. Finally, under each Domain KB are Scenario KBs, each corresponding to a different scenario. Therefore, when developing the KB for a new scenario, the agent reuses the corresponding Domain KB and the Shared KB. Similarly, when developing a new Domain KB, the agent reuses the Shared KB.

13.5   INTEGRATED TEACHING AND LEARNING

Use agent teaching and learning methods where the user helps the agent to learn and the agent helps the user to teach it.

Learning the elements of the knowledge base is a very complex process. In the Disciple approach, this process is simplified by a synergistic integration of teaching and learning, as discussed in Chapters 9 and 10. In particular, the user helps the agent to learn by providing representative examples of reasoning steps, as well as hints that guide the agent in understanding these examples. But the agent also helps the user to teach it by presenting attempted solutions to problems for the user to critique, as well as attempted explanations of an example, from which the user can select the correct ones.

13.6   MULTISTRATEGY LEARNING

Use multistrategy learning methods that integrate complementary learning strategies in order to take advantage of their strengths to compensate for each other's weaknesses.

No single learning strategy is powerful enough to learn the complex reasoning rules needed by the agent, but their synergistic combination is, as illustrated by the methods employed by the Disciple agents. In particular, a Disciple agent employs learning from explanations and analogy-based generalization to generate a plausible version space rule from a single problem-solving example and its explanation (see Section 9.4, p. 258, and Figure 9.9, p. 259). It then employs learning by analogy and experimentation to generate additional examples of the learned rules that are to be critiqued by the user, and it employs empirical induction from examples, as well as learning from failure explanations, to refine the rule based on the new examples and explanations (see Section 10.1.2 and Figure 10.1, p. 295). This results in a powerful method that enables the agent to learn very complex rules from only a few examples and their explanations, obtained in a natural dialogue with the user.

13.7   KNOWLEDGE ADAPTATION

Use methods that allow continuous adaptation of agent's knowledge.

Due to the complexity of the real world and to its dynamic nature, an agent's knowledge elements will always be approximate representations of real-world entities. Therefore, improving and even maintaining the utility of a cognitive assistant depends on its capacity to adapt its knowledge continuously to better represent the application domain.

The rule-learning methods of the Disciple agents continually improve the rules based on their failures and successes. But these improvements are done in the context of an existing ontology, which may itself evolve. Therefore, when the ontology undergoes significant changes, the previously learned rules need to be relearned. This process can be done automatically, if each rule maintains minimal generalizations of the examples and the explanations from which it was learned, as was discussed in Section 10.2.

13.8   MIXED-INITIATIVE MODELING, LEARNING, AND PROBLEM SOLVING

Use mixed-initiative methods where modeling, learning, and problem solving mutually support each other to capture the expert's tacit knowledge.

Figure 13.1 illustrates the synergistic integration of modeling, learning, and problem solving as part of the reasoning of a Disciple agent. These activities mutually support each other. For example, problem solving generates examples for learning to refine the rules, and the refined rules lead to better problem solving..

Modeling provides learning with the initial expert example for learning a new rule. But the previously learned rules or patterns also support the modeling process by suggesting possible reductions of a problem or hypothesis, as discussed, for instance, in Section 3.3.2.

Finally, modeling advances the problem-solving process with the creative solutions provided by the user. But problem solving also supports the modeling process by providing the context for such creative solutions, thus facilitating their definition.

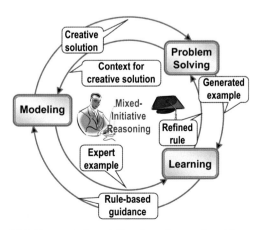

Figure 13.1. Integrated modeling, learning, and problem solving.

13.9   PLAUSIBLE REASONING WITH PARTIALLY LEARNED KNOWLEDGE

Use reasoning methods that enable the use of partially learned knowledge.

As already indicated, an agent's knowledge elements will always be approximate representations of real-world entities. This is more so for a learning agent that incrementally improves its knowledge. Since most of the knowledge of a learning agent is partially learned, the agent should be able to use partially learned knowledge in problem solving. Otherwise, it would not be able to function as an assistant until it is "fully" developed.

A Disciple agent not only uses partially learned knowledge in problem solving, but also assesses the plausibility (or confidence level) of a problem or hypothesis reduction based on its position with respect to the plausible version space conditions of the corresponding reduction rule, as discussed in Section 7.7 (see Figure 7.14, p. 216). The agent can also assess the plausibility of an entire reasoning tree by considering the confidence levels of its component reductions.

13.10   USER TUTORING IN PROBLEM SOLVING

Employ approaches to user tutoring that allow the agent to teach its problem-solving paradigm easily and rapidly to its users, facilitating their collaboration.

A cognitive assistant collaborates with its user in problem solving. This requires the user not only to understand the agent's reasoning but also to contribute to it. A subject matter expert teaches a Disciple agent similarly to how the expert would teach a student, through problem-solving examples and explanations. Then, when a user employs a Disciple agent, he or she can easily learn from its explicit reasoning, as illustrated by the Disciple-COG agent discussed in Section 12.4. Alternatively, the agent can behave as a tutoring system, guiding the student through a series of lessons and exercises, as illustrated by TIACRITIS (Tecuci et al., 2010b).

Personalized learning, which was identified as one of the fourteen Grand Challenges for Engineering in the Twenty-first Century (NAE, 2008), is a very important application of cognitive assistants.

13.11   AGENT ARCHITECTURE FOR RAPID AGENT DEVELOPMENT

Employ learning agent shells that allow rapid agent prototyping, development, and customization.

As discussed in Section 3.2.3, a learning agent shell enables rapid development of an agent because all the reasoning modules already exist. Thus one only needs to customize some of the modules and to develop the knowledge base. For example, the customizations performed to develop Disciple-COG consisted in developing a report generator and a simplified interface for the problem solver.

As discussed in Section 3.2.4, a learning agent shell for evidence-based reasoning further speeds up the development of an agent. First, the agent shell was already customized for evidence-based reasoning. Second, part of the knowledge base is already defined in the shell, namely the Shared KB for evidence-based reasoning (EBR KB).

13.12 DESIGN BASED ON A COMPLETE AGENT LIFE CYCLE

Design the agent by taking into account its complete life cycle, to ensure its usefulness for as long a period of time as possible.

This involves the incorporation of methods that support the various stages in the life cycle of the agent. For example, Figure 13.2 illustrates a possible life cycle of a Disciple agent that was discussed in Section 3.2.4.

The first stage is *shell customization*, where, based on the specification of the type of problems to be solved and the agent to be built, the developer and the knowledge engineer may decide that some customizations or extensions of the Disciple shell may be necessary or useful. The next stage is *agent teaching* by the subject matter expert and the knowledge engineer, supported by the agent itself, which simplifies and speeds up the knowledge base development process. Once an operational agent is developed, it is used for *training* of end-users, possibly in a classroom environment. The next stage is *field use*, where copies

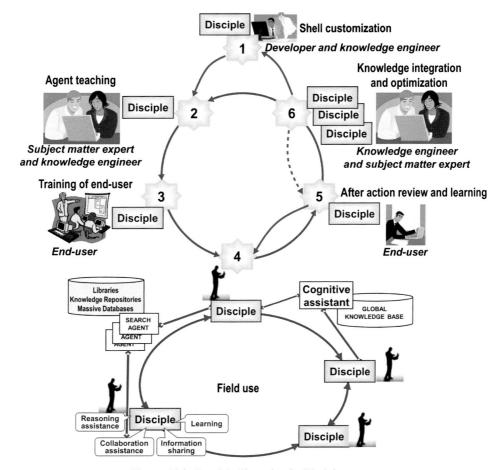

Figure 13.2. Possible life cycle of a Disciple agent.

of the agent support users in their operational environments. At this stage, each agent assists its user both in solving problems and in collaborating with other users and their cognitive assistants. At the same time, the agent continuously learns patterns from this problem-solving experience by employing a form of nondisruptive learning. However, because there is no learning assistance from the user, the learned patterns will not include a formal applicability condition. It is during the next stage of *after action review and learning*, when the user and the agent analyze past problem-solving episodes, that the formal applicability conditions are learned based on the accumulated examples. In time, each cognitive assistant extends its knowledge with additional expertise acquired from its user. This creates the opportunity of developing a more competent agent by integrating the knowledge of all these agents. This can be accomplished by a knowledge engineer, with assistance from a subject matter expert, in the next stage of *knowledge integration and optimization*. The result is an improved agent that may be used in a new iteration of a spiral process of development and use.

References

Allemang, D., and Hendler, J. (2011). *Semantic Web for the Working Ontologist: Effective Modeling in RDFS and Owl*, Morgan Kaufmann, San Mateo, CA.

Allen, J., Hendler, J., and Tate, A., (eds.) (1990). *Readings in Planning*, Morgan Kaufmann, San Mateo, CA.

Anderson, T., Schum, D., and Twining, W. (2005). *Analysis of Evidence*, Cambridge University Press, Cambridge, UK.

Awad, E. M. (1996). *Building Expert Systems: Principles, Procedures, and Applications*, West, New York, NY.

Awad, E. M., and Ghaziri, H. M. (2004). *Knowledge Management*, Pearson Education International, Prentice Hall, Upper Saddle River, NJ, pp. 60–65.

Basic Formal Ontology (BFO) (2012). *Basic Formal Ontology*. www.ifomis.org/bfo (accessed August 31, 2012).

Betham, J. (1810). *An Introductory View of the Rationale of the Law of Evidence for Use by Non-lawyers as Well as Lawyers* (vi works 1–187 (Bowring edition, 1837–43, originally edited by James Mill circa 1810).

Boicu, C. (2006). *An Integrated Approach to Rule Refinement for Instructable Knowledge-Based Agents*. PhD Thesis in Computer Science, Learning Agents Center, Volgenau School of Information Technology and Engineering, George Mason University, Fairfax, VA.

Boicu, C., Tecuci, G., and Boicu, M. (2005). Improving Agent Learning through Rule Analysis, in *Proceedings of the International Conference on Artificial Intelligence*, ICAI-05, Las Vegas, NV, June 27–30. lac.gmu.edu/publications/data/2005/ICAI3196Boicu.pdf (accessed April 12, 2016)

Boicu, M. (2002). *Modeling and Learning with Incomplete Knowledge*, PhD Dissertation in Information Technology, Learning Agents Laboratory, School of Information Technology and Engineering, George Mason University. lac.gmu.edu/publications/2002/BoicuM_PhD_Thesis.pdf (accessed November 25, 2015)

Boicu, M., Tecuci, G., Bowman, M., Marcu, D., Lee, S. W., and Wright, K. (1999). A Problem-Oriented Approach to Ontology Creation and Maintenance, in *Proceedings of the Sixteenth National Conference on Artificial Intelligence Workshop on Ontology Management*, July 18–19, Orlando, Florida, AAAI Press, Menlo Park, CA. lac.gmu.edu/publications/data/1999/ontology-1999.pdf (accessed November 25, 2015)

Boicu, M., Tecuci, G., Marcu, D., Bowman, M., Shyr, P., Ciucu, F., and Levcovici, C. (2000). Disciple-COA: From Agent Programming to Agent Teaching, in *Proceedings of the Seventeenth International Conference on Machine Learning* (ICML), Stanford, CA, Morgan Kaufman, San Mateo, CA, lac.gmu.edu/publications/data/2000/2000_il-final.pdf (accessed November 25, 2015)

Bowman, M. (2002). *A Methodology for Modeling Expert Knowledge That Supports Teaching Based Development of Agents*, PhD Dissertation in Information Technology, George Mason University, Fairfax, VA. lac.gmu.edu/publications/data/2002/Michael%20Bowman-Thesis.pdf (accessed November 25, 2015)

Bresina, J. L., and Morris, P. H. (2007). Mixed-Initiative Planning in Space Mission Operations, *AI Magazine*, vol. 28, no. 1, pp. 75–88.

Breuker, J., and Wielinga, B. (1989). Models of Expertise in Knowledge Acquisition, in Guida, G., and Tasso, C. (eds.), *Topics in Expert Systems Design, Methodologies, and Tools*, North Holland, Amsterdam, Netherlands, pp. 265–295.

Buchanan, B. G., and Feigenbaum, E. A. (1978). DENDRAL and META-DENDRAL: Their Applications Dimensions, *Artificial Intelligence*, vol. 11, pp. 5–24.

Buchanan, B. G., and Shortliffe, E. H. (eds.) (1984). *Rule-Based Expert Systems: The MYCIN Experiments of the Stanford Heuristic Programming Project*, Addison-Wesley, Reading, MA.

Buchanan, B. G., and Wilkins, D. C. (eds.) (1993). *Readings in Knowledge Acquisition and Learning: Automating the Construction and Improvement of Expert Systems*, Morgan Kaufmann, San Mateo, CA.

Buchanan, B. G., Barstow, D., Bechtal, R., Bennett, J., Clancey, W., Kulikowski, C., Mitchell, T., and Waterman, D. A. (1983). Constructing an Expert System, in Hayes-Roth, F., Waterman, D., and Lenat, D. (eds.), *Building Expert Systems*, Addison-Wesley, Reading, MA, pp. 127–168.

Carbonell, J. G. (1983). Learning by Analogy: Formulating and Generalizing Plans from Past Experience, in Michalski, R. S., Carbonell, J. M., and Mitchell, T. M., *Machine Learning: An Artificial Intelligence Approach*, Tioga, Wellsboro, PA, pp. 137–162.

Carbonell, J. G. (1986). Derivational Analogy: A Theory of Reconstructive Problem-Solving and Expertise Acquisition, in Michalski, R. S., Carbonell, J. G., and Mitchell, T. M. (eds.), *Machine Learning: An Artificial Intelligence Approach*, vol. 2, Morgan Kaufmann, San Mateo, CA, pp. 371–392.

Chaudhri, V. K., Farquhar, A., Fikes, R., Park, P. D., and Rice, J. P. (1998). OKBC: A Programmatic Foundation for Knowledge Base Interoperability, in *Proceedings of the Fifteenth National Conference on Artificial Intelligence (AAAI-98)*, AAAI Press, Menlo Park, CA, pp. 600–607.

Clancey, W. (1985). Heuristic Classification, *AI Journal*, vol. 27, pp. 289–350.

Clausewitz, C. von (1832 [1976]). *On War*, translated and edited by Howard, M., and Paret, P. Princeton University Press, Princeton, NJ.

Cohen, L. J. (1977). *The Probable and the Provable*, Clarendon Press, Oxford. UK.

Cohen, L. J. (1989). *An Introduction to the Philosophy of Induction and Probability*, Clarendon Press, Oxford, UK.

Cohen, M. R., and Nagel, E. (1934). *An Introduction to Logic and Scientific Method*, Harcourt, Brace, New York, NY, pp. 274–275.

Cohen, P., Schrag, R., Jones, E., Pease, A., Lin, A., Starr, B., Gunning, D., and Burke, M. (1998). The DARPA High-Performance Knowledge Bases Project, *AI Magazine*, vol. 19, no. 4, pp. 25–49.

Cooper, T., and Wogrin, N. (1988). *Rule-based Programming with OPS5*, Morgan Kaufmann, San Mateo, CA.

Cross, S. E., and Walker, E. (1994). DART: Applying Knowledge-based Planning and Scheduling to Crisis Action Planning, in Zweben, M., and Fox, M. S. (eds.), *Intelligent Scheduling*, Morgan Kaufmann, San Mateo, CA, pp. 711–729.

Cyc (2008). OpenCyc Just Got Better – Much Better! www.opencyc.org (accessed August 22, 2008).

Cyc (2016). The Cyc homepage, www.cyc.com (accessed February 3, 2016).

Dale, A. I. (2003). *Most Honourable Remembrance: The Life and Work of Thomas Bayes*, Springer-Verlag, New York, NY.

David, F. N. (1962). *Games, Gods, and Gambling*, Griffin, London, UK.

David, P. A., and Foray, D. (2003). Economic Fundamentals of the Knowledge Society, *Policy Futures in Education. An e-Journal*, vol. 1, no. 1, Special Issue: Education and the Knowledge Economy, January, pp. 20–49.

Davies, T. R., and Russell, S. J. (1990). A Logical Approach to Reasoning by Analogy, in Shavlik, J., and Dietterich, T. (eds.), *Readings in Machine Learning*, Morgan Kaufmann, San Mateo, CA, pp. 657–663.

DeJong, G., and Mooney, R. (1986). Explanation-based Learning: An Alternative View, *Machine Learning*, vol. 1, pp. 145–176.

Department of Homeland Security (DHS) (2004). *National Response Plan*.

Desai, M. (2009). *Persistent Stare Exploitation and Analysis System (PerSEAS)*, DARPA-BAA-09-55, https://www.fbo.gov/index?s=opportunity&mode=form&id=eb5dd436ac371ce79d91c84ec4e91341&tab=core&_cview=1 (accessed April 13, 2016)

DOLCE (2012). Laboratory for Applied Ontology, www.loa-cnr.it/DOLCE.html (accessed August 31, 2012)

Drucker, P. (1993). *Post-Capitalist Society*, HarperCollins, New York.

Durham, S. (2000). Product-Centered Approach to Information Fusion, *AFOSR Forum on Information Fusion*, Arlington, VA, October 18–20.

Durkin, J. (1994). *Expert Systems: Design and Development*, Prentice Hall, Englewood Cliffs, NJ.

Dybala, T. (1996). *Shared Expertise Model for Building Interactive Learning Agents*, PhD Dissertation, School of Information Technology and Engineering, George Mason University, Fairfax, VA. lac.gmu.edu/publications/data/1996/Dybala-PhD-abs.pdf (accessed April 12, 2016)

Echevarria, A. J. (2003). Reining in the Center of Gravity Concept. *Air & Space Power Journal*, vol. XVII, no. 2, pp. 87–96.

Eco, U., and Sebeok, T. (eds.) (1983). *The Sign of Three: Dupin, Holmes, Peirce*, Indiana University Press: Bloomington.

Eikmeier, D. C. (2006). *Linking Ends, Ways and Means with Center of Gravity Analysis*. Carlisle Barracks, U.S. Army War College, Carlisle, PA.

Einstein, A. (1939). Letter from Albert Einstein to President Franklin D. Roosevelt: 08/02/1939. The letter itself is in the Franklin D. Roosevelt Library in Hyde Park, NY. See the National Archives copy in pdf form at media.nara.gov/Public_Vaults/00762_.pdf (accessed November 16, 2014).

EXPECT (2015). The EXPECT homepage, www.isi.edu/ikcap/expect/ (accessed May 25, 2015).

Farquhar, A., Fikes, R., and Rice, J. (1997). The Ontolingua Server: A Tool for Collaborative Ontology Construction, *International Journal of Human–Computer Studies*, vol. 46, no. 6, pp. 707–727.

Federal Rules of Evidence (2009). 2009–2010 ed. West Publishing, St. Paul, MN.

Feigenbaum, E. A. (1982). Knowledge Engineering for the 1980s, *Research Report*, Stanford University, Stanford, CA.

Feigenbaum, E. A. (1993). Tiger in a Cage: The Applications of Knowledge-based Systems, Invited Talk, *AAAI-93 Proceedings*, www.aaai.org/Papers/AAAI/1993/AAAI93-127.pdf. (accessed April 13, 2016)

Fellbaum, C. (ed.) (1988). *WordNet: An Electronic Lexical Database*. MIT Press, Cambridge, MA.

FEMA (Federal Emergency Management Agency) (2007). National Incident Management System. www.fema.gov/national-incident-management-system (accessed April 13, 2016).

Ferrucci, D., Brown, E., Chu-Caroll, J., Fan, J., Gondek, D., Kalynapur, A. A., Murdoch, J. W., Nyberg, E., Prager, J., Schlaefer, N., and Welty, C. (2010). Building Watson: An Overview of the DeepQA Project, *AI Magazine*, vol. 31, no. 3, pp. 59–79.

Filip, F. G. (1989). Creativity and Decision Support System, *Studies and Researches in Computer and Informatics*, vol. 1, no. 1, pp. 41–49.

Filip, F. G. (ed.) (2001). *Informational Society-Knowledge Society*, Expert, Bucharest.

FM 100-5. (1993). *U.S. Army Field Manual 100-5*, Operations, Headquarters, Department of the Army, Washington, DC.

FOAF (2012). The Friend of a Friend (FOAF) project. www.foaf-project.org/ (accessed August 31, 2012)

Forbes (2013). www.forbes.com/profile/michael-chipman/ (accessed September 2, 2013)

Forbus, K. D., Gentner, D., and Law, K. (1994). MAC/FAC: A Model of Similarity-Based Retrieval, *Cognitive Science*, vol. 19, pp. 141–205.

Friedman-Hill, E. (2003). *Jess in Action*, Manning, Shelter Island, NY.

Gammack, J. G. (1987). Different Techniques and Different Aspects on Declarative Knowledge, in Kidd, A. L. (ed.), *Knowledge Acquisition for Expert Systems: A Practical Handbook*, Plenum Press, New York, NY, and London, UK.

Gentner, D. (1983). Structure Mapping: A Theoretical Framework for Analogy, *Cognitive Science*, vol. 7, pp. 155–170.

Geonames (2012). GeoNames Ontology–Geo Semantic Web. [Online] www.geonames.org/ontology/documentation.html (accessed August 31, 2012)

GFO (2012). General Formal Ontology (GFO). [Online] www.onto-med.de/ontologies/gfo/ (accessed August 31, 2012)

Ghallab, M., Nau, D., and Traverso, P. (2004). *Automatic Planning: Theory and Practice*, Morgan Kaufmann, San Mateo, CA.

Giarratano, J., and Riley, G. (1994). *Expert Systems: Principles and Programming*, PWS, Boston, MA.

Gil, Y., and Paris, C. (1995). Towards model-independent knowledge acquisition, in Tecuci, G., and Kodratoff, Y. (eds.), *Machine Learning and Knowledge Acquisition: Integrated Approaches*, Academic Press, Boston, MA.

Giles, P. K., and Galvin, T. P. (1996). *Center of Gravity: Determination, Analysis and Application*. Carlisle Barracks, U.S. Army War College, Carlisle, PA.

Goodman, D., and Keene, R. (1997). *Man versus Machine: Kasparov versus Deep Blue*, H3 Publications, Cambridge, MA.

Gruber, T. R. (1993). A Translation Approach to Portable Ontology Specification. *Knowledge Acquisition*, vol. 5, pp. 199–220.

Guizzardi, G., and Wagner, G. (2005a). Some Applications of a Unified Foundational Ontology in Business, in Rosemann, M., and Green, P. (eds.), *Ontologies and Business Systems Analysis*, IDEA Group, Hershey, PA.

Guizzardi, G., and Wagner, G. (2005b). Towards Ontological Foundations for Agent Modeling Concepts Using UFO, in *Agent-Oriented Information Systems (AOIS)*, selected revised papers of the Sixth International Bi-Conference Workshop on Agent-Oriented Information Systems. Springer-Verlag, Berlin and Heidelberg, Germany.

Hieb, M. R. (1996). *Training Instructable Agents through Plausible Version Space Learning*, PhD Dissertation, School of Information Technology and Engineering, George Mason University, Fairfax, VA.

Hobbs, J. R., and Pan, F. (2004). An Ontology of Time for the Semantic Web, *CM Transactions on Asian Language Processing (TALIP)*, vol. 3, no. 1 (special issue on temporal information processing), pp. 66–85.

Horvitz, E. (1999). Principles of Mixed-Initiative User Interfaces, in *Proceedings of CHI '99, ACM SIGCHI Conference on Human Factors in Computing Systems*, Pittsburgh, PA, May. ACM Press, New York, NY. research.microsoft.com/~horvitz/uiact.htm (accessed April 13, 2016)

Humphreys, B. L., and Lindberg, D.A.B. (1993). The UMLS Project: Making the Conceptual Connection between Users and the Information They Need, *Bulletin of the Medical Library Association*, vol. 81, no. 2, p. 170.

Jackson, P. (1999). *Introduction to Expert Systems*, Addison-Wesley, Essex, UK.

Jena (2012). Jena tutorial. jena.sourceforge.net/tutorial/index.html (accessed August 4, 2012).

JESS (2016). The rule engine for the JAVA platform, JESS webpage: www.jessrules.com/jess/download.shtml (accessed February 3, 2016)

Joint Chiefs of Staff (2008). *Joint Operations*, Joint Pub 3-0, U.S. Joint Chiefs of Staff, Washington, DC.

Jones, E. (1998). *HPKB Year 1 End-to-End Battlespace Challenge Problem Specification*, Alphatech, Burlington, MA.

Kant, I. (1781). *The Critique of Pure Reason*, Project Gutenberg, www.gutenberg.org/ebooks/4280 (accessed, August 19, 2013)

Keeling, H. (1998). *A Methodology for Building Verified and Validated Intelligent Educational Agents – through an Integration of Machine Learning and Knowledge Acquisition*, PhD Dissertation, School of Information Technology and Engineering, George Mason University, Fairfax, VA.

Kent, S. (1994). Words of Estimated Probability, in Steury, D. P. (ed.), *Sherman Kent and the Board of National Estimates: Collected Essays*, Center for the Study of Intelligence, CIA, Washington, DC.

Kim, J., and Gil, Y. (1999). Deriving Expectations to Guide Knowledge Base Creation, in *Proceedings of AAAI-99/IAAI-99*, AAAI Press, Menlo Park, CA, pp. 235–241.

Kneale, W. (1949). *Probability and Induction*, Clarendon Press, Oxford, UK. pp. 30–37.

Kodratoff, Y., and Ganascia, J-G. (1986). Improving the Generalization Step in Learning, in Michalski, R., Carbonell, J., and Mitchell, T. (eds.), *Machine Learning: An Artificial Intelligence Approach*, vol. 2. Morgan Kaufmann, San Mateo, CA, pp. 215–244.

Kolmogorov, A. N. (1933 [1956]). *Foundations of a Theory of Probability*, 2nd English ed., Chelsea, New York, NY, pp. 3–4.

Kolmogorov, A. N. (1969). The Theory of Probability, in Aleksandrov, A. D., Kolmogorov, A. N., and Lavrentiev, M. A. (eds.), *Mathematics: Its Content, Methods, and Meaning*, vol. 2, MIT Press, Cambridge, MA, pp. 231–264.

Langley, P. W. (2012). The Cognitive Systems Paradigm, *Advances in Cognitive Systems*, vol. 1, pp. 3–13.

Laplace, P. S. (1814). *Théorie Analytique des Probabilités*, 2nd édition, Paris, Ve. Courcier, archive. org/details/thorieanalytiqu01laplgoog (accessed January 28, 2016)

Le, V. (2008). *Abstraction of Reasoning for Problem Solving and Tutoring Assistants*. PhD Dissertation in Information Technology. Learning Agents Center, Volgenau School of IT&E, George Mason University, Fairfax, VA.

Lempert, R. O., Gross, S. R., and Liebman, J. S. (2000). *A Modern Approach to Evidence*, 3rd ed., West Publishing, St. Paul, MN, pp. 1146–1148.

Lenat, D. B. (1995). Cyc: A Large-scale Investment in Knowledge Infrastructure, *Communications of the ACM*, vol. 38, no. 11, pp. 33–38.

Loom (1999). Retrospective on LOOM. www.isi.edu/isd/LOOM/papers/macgregor/Loom_Retrospec tive.html (accessed August 4, 2012)

MacGregor, R. (1991). The Evolving Technology of Classification-Based Knowledge Representation Systems, in Sowa, J. (ed.), *Principles of Semantic Networks: Explorations in the Representations of Knowledge*, Morgan Kaufmann, San Francisco, CA, pp. 385–400.

Marcu, D. (2009). *Learning of Mixed-Initiative Human-Computer Interaction Models*, PhD Dissertation in Computer Science. Learning Agents Center, Volgenau School of IT&E, George Mason University, Fairfax, VA.

Marcus, S. (1988). SALT: A Knowledge-Acquisition Tool for Propose-and-Revise Systems, in Marcus, S. (ed.), *Automating Knowledge Acquisition for Expert Systems*, Kluwer Academic., Norwell, MA, pp. 81–123.

Masolo, C., Vieu, L., Bottazzi, E., Catenacci, C., Ferrario, R., Gangemi, A., and Guarino, N. (2004). Social Roles and Their Descriptions, in Dubois, D., Welty, C., and Williams, M-A. (eds.), *Principles of Knowledge Representation and Reasoning: Proceedings of the Ninth International Conference (KR2004)*, AAAI Press, Menlo Park, CA, pp. 267–277.

McDermott, J. (1982). R1: A Rule-Based Configurer of Computer Systems, *Artificial Intelligence Journal*, vol. 19, no. 1, pp. 39–88.

Meckl, S., Tecuci, G., Boicu, M., and Marcu, D. (2015). Towards an Operational Semantic Theory of Cyber Defense against Advanced Persistent Threats, in Laskey, K. B., Emmons, I., Costa, P. C. G., and Oltramari, A. (eds.), *Proceedings of the Tenth International Conference on Semantic Technologies for Intelligence, Defense, and Security – STIDS 2015*, pp. 58–65, Fairfax, VA, November 18–20. lac.gmu.edu/publications/2015/APT-LAC.pdf (accessed January 12, 2016)

Michalski, R. S. (1986). Understanding the Nature of Learning: Issues and Research Directions, in Michalski, R. S., Carbonell, J. G., and Mitchell T. (eds.), *Machine Learning*, vol. 2, Morgan Kaufmann, Los Altos, CA, pp. 3–25.

Michalski, R. S., and Tecuci, G. (eds.) (1994). *Machine Learning: A Multistrategy Approach*, vol. IV, Morgan Kaufmann, San Mateo, CA. store.elsevier.com/Machine-Learning/isbn-9781558602519/ (accessed May 29, 2015)

Minsky, M. (1986). *The Society of Mind*, Simon and Schuster, New York, NY.

Mitchell, T. M. (1978). *Version Spaces: An Approach to Concept Learning*. PhD Dissertation, Stanford University, Stanford, CA.

Mitchell, T. M. (1997). *Machine Learning*. McGraw-Hill, New York, NY.

Mitchell, T. M., Keller, R. M., and Kedar-Cabelli, S. T. (1986). Explanation-Based Generalization: A Unifying View, *Machine Learning*, vol. 1, pp. 47–80.

Murphy, P. (2003). *Evidence, Proof, and Facts: A Book of Sources*. Oxford University Press, Oxford, UK.

Musen, M. A. (1989). *Automated Generation of Model-based Knowledge Acquisition Tools*, Morgan Kaufmann., San Francisco, CA.

NAE (National Academy of Engineering) (2008). *Grand Challenges for Engineering*. www.engineer ingchallenges.org/cms/challenges.aspx (accessed April 13, 2016)

Nau, D., Au, T., Ilghami, O., Kuter, U., Murdock, J., Wu, D., and Yaman, F. (2003). SHOP2: An HTN Planning System, *Journal of Artificial Intelligence Research*, vol. 20, pp. 379–404.

Negoita, C. V., and Ralescu, D. A. (1975). *Applications of Fuzzy Sets to Systems Analysis*, Wiley, New York, NY.

Nilsson, N. J. (1971). *Problem Solving Methods in Artificial Intelligence*, McGraw-Hill, New York, NY.

Nonaka, I., and Krogh, G. (2009). Tacit Knowledge and Knowledge Conversion: Controversy and Advancement in Organizational Knowledge Creation Theory, *Organization Science*, vol. 20, no. 3

(May–June), pp. 635–652. www.ai.wu.ac.at/~kaiser/birgit/Nonaka-Papers/tacit-knowledge-and-knowledge-conversion-2009.pdf (accessed April 13, 2016)

Noy, N. F., and McGuinness, D. L. (2001). Ontology Development 101: A Guide to Creating Your First Ontology. *Stanford Knowledge Systems Laboratory Technical Report KSL-01-05 and Stanford Medical Informatics Technical Report SMI-2001-0880*, March, Stanford, CA.

NRC (National Research Council) (1996). *National Research Council: National Science Education Standards*. National Academy Press, Washington, DC. www.nap.edu/openbook.php?record_id=4962 (accessed April 13, 2016)

NRC (National Research Council) (2000). *National Research Council: Inquiry and the National Science Education Standards*, National Academy Press, Washington, DC. www.nap.edu/catalog.php?record_id=9596 (accessed April 13, 2016)

NRC (National Research Council) (2010). *Preparing Teachers: Building Evidence for Sound Policy*, National Academies Press, Washington, DC. www.nap.edu/catalog.php?record_id=12882 (accessed April 13, 2016)

NRC (National Research Council) (2011). *A Framework for K-12 Science Education: Practices, Cross-cutting Concepts, and Core Ideas*. www.nap.edu/catalog.php?record_id=13165 (accessed April 13, 2016)

Obrst, L., Chase, P., and Markeloff, R. (2012). Developing an Ontology of the Cyber Security Domain, in *Proceedings of the Seventh International Conference on Semantic Technologies for Intelligence, Defense, and Security – STIDS*, October 23–26, Fairfax, VA.

OKBC (Open Knowledge Based Connectivity) (2008). OKBC homepage. www.ksl.stanford.edu/software/OKBC/ (accessed August 4, 2012)

O'Keefe, R. M., Balci, O., and Smith, E. P. (1987). Validating Expert Systems Performance, *IEEE Expert*, no. 2, vol. 4, pp. 81–90.

Oldroyd, D. (1986). *The Arch of Knowledge: An Introductory Study of the History of the Philosophy and Methodology of Science*, Routledge Kegan & Paul, London, UK.

Ontolingua (1997). *Ontolingua System Reference Manual*. www-ksl-svc.stanford.edu:5915/doc/frame-editor/index.html (accessed August 4, 2012).

Ontolingua (2008). The Ontolingua homepage. www.ksl.stanford.edu/software/ontolingua/ (accessed August 4, 2012).

OWLIM (2012). OWLIM family of semantic repositories, or RDF database management systems. www.ontotext.com/owlim (accessed August 4, 2012).

Pan, F., and Hobbs, J. R. (2004). Time in OWL-S. *Proceedings of the AAAI Spring Symposium on Semantic Web Services*, Stanford University, Stanford, CA, AAAI Press, Palo Alto, CA, pp. 29–36.

Pan, F., and Hobbs, J. R. (2012). A Time Zone Resource in OWL. www.isi.edu/~hobbs/timezonehomepage.html (accessed August 31, 2012)

Pease, A. (2011). *Ontology: A Practical Guide*, Articulate Software Press, Angwin, CA. www.ontologyportal.org/Book.html (accessed April 13, 2016)

Peirce, C. S. (1898 [1992]). *Reasoning and the Logic of Things*, edited by Ketner, K., Harvard University Press, Cambridge, MA.

Peirce, C. S. (1901 [1955]). Abduction and Induction, in *Philosophical Writings of Peirce*, edited by Buchler, J., Dover, New York, NY, pp. 150–156.

Pellet (2012). OWL 2 Reasoner for Java. clarkparsia.com/pellet/ (accessed August 4, 2012).

Plotkin, G. D. (1970). A Note on Inductive Generalization, in Meltzer, B., and Michie, D. (eds.), *Machine Intelligence 5*, Edinburgh University Press, Edinburgh, UK, pp. 165–179.

Pomerol, J. C., and Adam, F. (2006). On the Legacy of Herbert Simon and His Contribution to Decision-making Support Systems and Artificial Intelligence, in Gupta, J. N. D., Forgionne, G. A., and Mora, M. T. (eds.), *Intelligent Decision-Making Support Systems: Foundations, Applications and Challenges*, Springer-Verlag, London, UK, pp. 25–43.

Powell, G. M., and Schmidt, C. F. (1988). *A First-order Computational Model of Human Operational Planning*, CECOM-TR-01-8, U.S. Army CECOM, Fort Monmouth, NJ.

Protégé (2000). *The Protégé Project*. protege.stanford.edu (accessed April 13, 2016)

Protégé (2015). Protégé ontology editor and knowledge base framework, homepage. protege.stanford.edu (accessed May 25, 2015).

Puppe, F. (1993). Problem Classes and Problem Solving Methods, in *Systematic Introduction to Expert Systems: Knowledge Representations and Problem Solving Methods*, Springer Verlag, Berlin and Heidelberg, Germany, pp. 87–112.

Ressler, J., Dean, M., and Kolas, D. (2010). Geospatial Ontology Trade Study, in Janssen, T., Ceuster, W., and Obrst, L. (eds.), *Ontologies and Semantic Technologies for Intelligence*, IOS Press, Amsterdam, Berlin, Tokyo, and Washington, DC, pp. 179–212.

Rooney, D., Hearn, G., and Ninan, A. (2005). *Handbook on the Knowledge Economy*, Edward Elgar, Cheltenham, UK.

Russell, S. J., and Norvig, P. (2010). *Artificial Intelligence: A Modern Approach*, Prentice Hall, Upper Saddle River, NJ, pp. 34–63.

Schneider, L. (2003). How to Build a Foundational Ontology – the Object-centered High-level Reference Ontology OCHRE, in *Proceedings of the 26th Annual German Conference on AI, KI 2003: Advances in Artificial Intelligence*, Springer-Verlag, Heidelberg, Germany, pp. 120–134.

Schreiber, G., Akkermans, H., Anjewierden, A., de Hoog, R., Shadbolt, N., Van de Velde, W., and Wielinga, B. (2000). *Knowledge Engineering and Management: The Common KADS Methodology*, MIT Press, Cambridge, MA.

Schum D. A. (1987). *Evidence and Inference for the Intelligence Analyst* (2 vols), University Press of America, Lanham, MD.

Schum, D. A. (1989). Knowledge, Probability, and Credibility, *Journal of Behavioral Decision Making*, vol. 2, pp. 39–62.

Schum, D. A. (1991). Jonathan Cohen and Thomas Bayes on the Analysis of Chains of Reasoning, in Eells, E., and Maruszewski, T. (eds.), *Probability and Rationality: Studies on L. Jonathan Cohen's Philosophy of Science*, Editions Rodopi, Amsterdam, Netherlands, pp. 99–145.

Schum, D. A. (1999). Marshaling Thoughts and Evidence during Fact Investigation, *South Texas Law Review*, vol. 40, no. 2 (summer), pp. 401–454.

Schum, D. A. (1994 [2001a]). *The Evidential Foundations of Probabilistic Reasoning*, Northwestern University Press, Evanston, IL.

Schum, D. A. (2001b). Species of Abductive Reasoning in Fact Investigation in Law, *Cardozo Law Review*, vol. 22, nos. 5–6, pp. 1645–1681.

Schum, D. A. (2011). Classifying Forms and Combinations of Evidence: Necessary in a Science of Evidence, in Dawid, P., Twining, W., and Vasilaki. M. (eds.), *Evidence, Inference and Inquiry*, British Academy, Oxford University Press, Oxford, UK, pp. 11–36.

Schum, D. A., and Morris, J. (2007). Assessing the Competence and Credibility of Human Sources of Evidence: Contributions from Law and Probability, *Law, Probability and Risk*, vol. 6, pp. 247–274.

Schum, D. A., Tecuci, G., and Boicu, M. (2009). Analyzing Evidence and Its Chain of Custody: A Mixed-Initiative Computational Approach, *International Journal of Intelligence and Counterintelligence*, vol. 22, pp. 298–319. lac.gmu.edu/publications/2009/Schum%20et%20al%20-%20Chain%20of%20Custody.pdf (accessed April 13, 2016)

Shafer, G. (1976). *A Mathematical Theory of Evidence*, Princeton University Press, Princeton, NJ.

Shafer, G. (1988). Combining AI and OR, *University of Kansas School of Business Working Paper No. 195*, April.

Simon, H. (1983). Why Should Machines Learn? in Michalski, R. S., Carbonell, J. G., and Mitchell, T.M. (eds.), *Machine Learning*, vol. 1, Morgan Kaufmann, Los Altos, CA, pp. 25–38.

Simonite, T. (2013). Bill Gates: Software Assistants Could Help Solve Global Problems, *MIT Technology Review*, July 16. www.technologyreview.com/news/517171/bill-gates-software-assistants-could-help-solve-global-problems/ (accessed April 13, 2016)

Siri (2011). Apple's Siri homepage. www.apple.com/ios/siri/ (accessed April 12, 2016)

Strange, J. (1996). *Centers of Gravity & Critical Vulnerabilities: Building on the Clausewitzian Foundation so That We Can All Speak the Same Language*, Marine Corps University Foundation, Quantico, VA.

Strange, J., and Iron, R. (2004a). Understanding Centers of Gravity and Critical Vulnerabilities, Part 1: What Clausewitz (Really) Meant by Center of Gravity. www.au.af.mil/au/awc/awcgate/usmc/cog1.pdf (accessed May 25, 2015)

Strange, J., and Iron, R. (2004b). Understanding Centers of Gravity and Critical Vulnerabilities, Part 2: The CG-CC-CR-CV Construct: A Useful Tool to Understand and Analyze the Relationship between

Centers of Gravity and Their Critical Vulnerabilities. www.au.af.mil/au/awc/awcgate/usmc/cog2.pdf (accessed May 25, 2015)

Tate, A. (1977). Generating Project Networks, in *Proceedings of IJCAI-77*, Boston, MA, Morgan Kaufmann, San Francisco, CA, pp. 888–893.

Tecuci, G. (1988). *Disciple: A Theory, Methodology and System for Learning Expert Knowledge*, Thèse de Docteur en Science, University of Paris-South. lac.gmu.edu/publications/1988/TecuciG_PhD_Thesis.pdf (accessed April 13, 2016)

Tecuci, G. (1992). Automating Knowledge Acquisition as Extending, Updating, and Improving a Knowledge Base, *IEEE Transactions on Systems, Man and Cybernetics*, vol. 22, pp. 1444–1460. lac.gmu.edu/publications/1992/TecuciG_Automating_Knowledge_Acquisition.pdf (accessed April 13, 2016)

Tecuci, G. (1993). Plausible Justification Trees: A Framework for the Deep and Dynamic Integration of Learning Strategies, *Machine Learning Journal*, vol. 11, pp. 237–261. lac.gmu.edu/publications/1993/TecuciG_Plausible_Justification_Trees.pdf (accessed April 13, 2016)

Tecuci, G. (1998). *Building Intelligent Agents: An Apprenticeship Multistrategy Learning Theory, Methodology, Tool and Case Studies*, Academic Press, London, UK. lac.gmu.edu/publications/1998/TecuciG_Building_Intelligent_Agents/default.htm (accessed April 13, 2016)

Tecuci, G., and Keeling, H. (1999). Developing an Intelligent Educational Agent with Disciple, *International Journal of Artificial Intelligence in Education*, vol. 10, no. 3-4. lac.gmu.edu/publications/1999/TecuciG_Intelliget_Educational_Agent.pdf (accessed April 13, 2016)

Tecuci, G., and Kodratoff, Y. (1990). Apprenticeship Learning in Imperfect Theory Domains, in Kodratoff, Y., and Michalski, R. S. (eds.), *Machine Learning: An Artificial Intelligence Approach*, vol. 3, Morgan Kaufmann, San Mateo, CA, pp. 514–551. lac.gmu.edu/publications/data/1990/apprenticeship_1990.pdf (accessed April 13, 2016)

Tecuci, G., and Kodratoff, Y. (eds.) (1995). *Machine Learning and Knowledge Acquisition: Integrated Approaches*, Academic Press, London, UK. lac.gmu.edu/publications/1995/TecuciG_MLKA_Integrated_Approaches.pdf (accessed April 13, 2016)

Tecuci, G., and Michalski, R. S. (1991). A Method for Multistrategy Task-Adaptive Learning Based on Plausible Justifications, in Birnbaum, L., and Collins, G. (eds.), *Machine Learning: Proceedings of the Eighth International Conference*, June, Chicago, IL, Morgan Kaufmann, San Mateo, CA, pp. 549–553. lac.gmu.edu/publications/1991/TecuciG_Multistrategy_Learning_Method.pdf (accessed April 13, 2016)

Tecuci, G., Kedar, S., and Kodratoff, Y. (guest eds.) (1994). *Knowledge Acquisition Journal*, vol. 6, no. 2 (special issue on the integration of machine learning and knowledge acquisition), pp. 89–214.

Tecuci, G., Boicu, M., Wright, K., Lee, S. W., Marcu, D., and Bowman, M. (1999). An Integrated Shell and Methodology for Rapid Development of Knowledge-based Agents, in *Proceedings of the Sixteenth National Conference on Artificial Intelligence* (AAAI-99), July 18–22, Orlando, FL, AAAI Press, Menlo Park, CA, pp. 250–257. lac.gmu.edu/publications/data/1999/ismrdkba.pdf (accessed April 13, 2016)

Tecuci, G., Boicu, M., Wright, K., Lee, S. W., Marcu, D. and Bowman, M. (2000). A Tutoring Based Approach to the Development of Intelligent Agents, in Teodorescu, H. N., Mlynek, D., Kandel, A., and Zimmermann, H. J. (eds.), *Intelligent Systems and Interfaces*, Kluwer Academic Press, Boston, MA. lac.gmu.edu/publications/data/2000/2000_Disciple-Planning.pdf (accessed April 13, 2016)

Tecuci, G., Boicu, M., Bowman, M., and Marcu, D., with commentary by Burke, M. (2001). An Innovative Application from the DARPA Knowledge Bases Programs: Rapid Development of a Course of Action Critiquer, *AI Magazine*, vol. 22, no. 2, pp. 43–61. lac.gmu.edu/publications/2001/TecuciG_Disciple_COA_IAAI.pdf (accessed April 13, 2016)

Tecuci, G., Boicu, M., Marcu, D., Stanescu, B., Boicu, C., Comello, J., Lopez, A., Donlon, J., and Cleckner, W. (2002a). Development and Deployment of a Disciple Agent for Center of Gravity Analysis, in *Proceedings of the Eighteenth National Conference of Artificial Intelligence and the Fourteenth Conference on Innovative Applications of Artificial Intelligence*, AAAI-02/IAAI-02, Edmonton, Alberta, Canada, AAAI Press/MIT Press, New York, NY, and Cambridge, MA, pp. 853–860. lac.gmu.edu/publications/data/2002/dddacga.pdf (accessed April 13, 2016)

Tecuci, G., Boicu, M., Marcu, D., Stanescu, B., Boicu, C., and Comello, J. (2002b). Training and Using Disciple Agents: A Case Study in the Military Center of Gravity Analysis Domain, *AI Magazine*, vol. 24, no. 4, pp. 51–68. lac.gmu.edu/publications/2002/TecuciG_Disciple_COG_IAAI.pdf (accessed April 13, 2016)

Tecuci, G., Boicu, M., Ayers, C., and Cammons, D. (2005a). Personal Cognitive Assistants for Military Intelligence Analysis: Mixed-Initiative Learning, Tutoring, and Problem Solving, in *Proceedings of the First International Conference on Intelligence Analysis*, May 2–6, McLean, VA, MITRE Corporation, Bedford, MA. lac.gmu.edu/publications/data/2005/Tecuci-Disciple-LTA.pdf (accessed April 13, 2016)

Tecuci, G., Boicu, M., Boicu, C., Marcu, D., Stanescu, B., and Barbulescu, M. (2005b). The Disciple-RKF Learning and Reasoning Agent, *Computational Intelligence*, vol. 21, no. 4, pp. 462–479. lac.gmu.edu/publications/2005/TecuciG_Disciple_RKF_CI.pdf (accessed April 13, 2016)

Tecuci, G., Boicu, M., and Cox, M. T. (guest eds.) (2007a). *AI Magazine*, vol. 28, no. 2 (special issue on mixed-initiative assistants). www.aaai.org/ojs/index.php/aimagazine/issue/view/174/showToc (accessed May 29, 2015)

Tecuci, G., Boicu, M., and Cox, M. T. (2007b). Seven Aspects of Mixed-Initiative Reasoning: An Introduction to the Special Issue on Mixed-Initiative Assistants, *AI Magazine*, vol. 28, no. 2 (special issue on mixed-initiative assistants), pp. 11–18. lac.gmu.edu/publications/2007/BoicuM_AIMagazine_Intro.pdf (accessed April 13, 2016)

Tecuci, G., Boicu, M., Marcu, D., Boicu, C., Barbulescu, M., Ayers, C., and Cammons, D. (2007c). Cognitive Assistants for Analysts, *Journal of Intelligence Community Research and Development (JICRD)*. Also published in Auger, J., and Wimbish, W. (eds.) (2007). *Proteus Futures Digest: A Compilation of Selected Works Derived from the 2006 Proteus Workshop*, 1st ed., Proteus Management Group, Carlisle Barracks, PA, pp. 303–329. lac.gmu.edu/publications/2007/TecuciG_Cognitive_Assistants.pdf (accessed April 13, 2016)

Tecuci, G., Boicu, M., Hajduk, T., Marcu, D., Barbulescu, M., Boicu, C., and Le, V. (2007d). A Tool for Training and Assistance in Emergency Response Planning, in *Proceedings of the Hawaii International Conference on System Sciences*, HICSS40, January 3–6, Hawaii, IEEE Computer Society Press. lac.gmu.edu/publications/2007/Disciple-VPT%20Hawaii.pdf (accessed April 13, 2016)

Tecuci, G., Boicu, M., Marcu, D., Boicu, C., and Barbulescu, M. (2008a). Disciple-LTA: Learning, Tutoring and Analytic Assistance, *Journal of Intelligence Community Research and Development (JICRD)*, July. lac.gmu.edu/publications/2008/Disciple-LTA08.pdf (accessed April 13, 2016)

Tecuci, G., Boicu, M., and Comello, J. (2008b). *Agent-Assisted Center of Gravity Analysis*, CD with Disciple-COG and Lecture Notes used in courses at the U.S. Army War College and Air War College. George Mason University Press, Fairfax, VA. lac.gmu.edu/cog-book/ (accessed April 13, 2016)

Tecuci, G., Boicu, M., Marcu, D., Barbulescu, M., Boicu, C., Le, V., and Hajduk, T. (2008c). Teaching Virtual Experts for Multi-Domain Collaborative Planning, *Journal of Software*, vol. 3, no. 3 (March), pp. 38–59. lac.gmu.edu/publications/2008/TecuciG_Disciple_VE_JS.pdf (accessed April 13, 2016)

Tecuci, G., Schum, D. A., Boicu, M., Marcu, D., and Hamilton, B. (2010a). Intelligence Analysis as Agent-Assisted Discovery of Evidence, Hypotheses and Arguments, in Phillips-Wren, G., Jain, L.C., Nakamatsu, K., and Howlett, R.J., (eds.), *Advances in Intelligent Decision Technologies*, SIST 4, Springer-Verlag, Berlin and Heidelberg Germany, pp. 1–10. lac.gmu.edu/publications/2010/Tecuci-Discovery-in-motion-imagery.pdf (accessed April 13, 2016)

Tecuci, G., Schum, D. A., Boicu, M., Marcu, D., Hamilton, B., and Wible, B. (2010b). Teaching Intelligence Analysis with TIACRITIS, *American Intelligence Journal*, vol. 28, no. 2 (December), pp. 50–65. lac.gmu.edu/publications/2010/Tiacritis-AIJ.pdf (accessed April 13, 2016)

Tecuci, G., Marcu, D., Boicu, M., Schum, D. A., and Russell, K. (2011a). Computational Theory and Cognitive Assistant for Intelligence Analysis, in *Proceedings of the Sixth International Conference on Semantic Technologies for Intelligence, Defense, and Security – STIDS*, November 16–18, Fairfax, VA, pp. 68–75. ceur-ws.org/Vol-808/STIDS2011_CR_T9_TecuciEtAl.pdf (accessed May 29, 2015)

Tecuci, G., Schum, D. A., Boicu, M., and Marcu, D. (2011b). *Introduction to Intelligence Analysis: A Hands-on Approach with TIACRITIS*, 2nd ed., Learning Agents Center, George Mason University, Fairfax, VA (1st ed., 2010).

Tecuci, G., Schum, D. A., Marcu, D., and Boicu, M. (2014). Computational Approach and Cognitive Assistant for Evidence-based Reasoning in Intelligence Analysis, *International Journal of Intelligent*

Defence Support Systems, vol. 5, no. 2, pp. 146–172. lac.gmu.edu/publications/2014/Disciple-CD-IJIDSS.pdf (accessed April 13, 2016)

Tecuci, G., Marcu, D., Boicu, M., and Schum, D. A. (2015). COGENT: Cognitive Agent for Cogent Analysis, *Proceedings of the 2015 AAAI Fall Symposium "Cognitive Assistance in Government and Public Sector Applications*, pp. 58–65, Arlington, VA, November 12–14. lac.gmu.edu/publications/2015/Cogent-overview.pdf (accessed January 31, 2016)

Tecuci, G., Schum, D. A., Marcu, D., and Boicu, M. (2016). *Intelligence Analysis as Discovery of Evidence, Hypotheses, and Arguments: Connecting the Dots*, Cambridge University Press, New York, NY.

Toffler, A. (1984). Science and Change, foreword to Prigogine, Ilya, and Stengers, Isabelle, *Order out of Chaos: Man's New Dialogue with Nature*, Bantam, New York, NY, pp. xi–xxvi.

TopBraid Composer (2012). TopBraid Composer Ontology Development Tool. www.topquadrant.com/products/TB_Composer.html (accessed August 4, 2012).

Toulmin, S. E. (1963). *The Uses of Argument*, Cambridge University Press, Cambridge, UK.

Turing, A. (1950). Computing Machinery and Intelligence, *Mind*, vol. 59, pp. 433–460.

Turoff, M. (2007). Design of Interactive Systems, in *Emergency Management Information Systems Tutorial, 40th Hawaii International Conference on System Sciences*, HICSS-40, Hawaii, January 3.

UMLS (2012). Unified Medical Language System, U.S. National Library of Medicine. www.nlm.nih.gov/research/umls/ (accessed August 4, 2012)

UNESCO (2005). Toward Knowledge Societies, unesdoc.unesco.org/images/0014/001418/141843e.pdf (accessed October 1, 2011)

Van Gelder, T. J. (2007). The Rationale for Rationale, *Law, Probability and Risk*, vol. 6, pp. 23–42.

Van Melle, W., Scott, A. C., Bennett, J. S., and Peairs, M. (1981). *The EMYCIN Manual, Report No. HPP-81-16*, Computer Science Department, Stanford University, Stanford, CA.

Veloso, M. (1994). *Planning and Learning by Analogical Reasoning*, Springer Verlag, Berlin, Germany.

W3C (2015). Semantic Web. www.w3.org/standards/semanticweb/ (accessed April 13, 2016)

Walton, D. (2004). *Abductive Reasoning*, University of Alabama Press, Tuscaloosa, AL.

Warden, J. A. III. (1993). Strategic Warfare: The Enemy as a System, in Mitchum, A. U. (ed.), *Concepts in Airpower for the Campaign Planner*, Air Command and Staff College, Maxwell AFB, AL.

Waterman, D. A., and Hayes-Roth, F. (eds.) (1978). *Pattern-Directed Inference Systems*, Academic Press, Orlando, FL.

Wigmore, J. H. (1913). The Problem of Proof, *Illinois Law Review*, vol. 8, no. 2, pp. 77–103.

Wigmore, J. H. (1937). *The Science of Judicial Proof: As Given by Logic, Psychology, and General Experience and Illustrated in Judicial Trials*, 3rd ed., Little, Brown, Boston, MA.

Winston, P. H. (1980). Learning and Reasoning by Analogy, *Communications of the ACM*, vol. 23, pp. 689–703.

WordNet (2012). *WordNet: A Database for English*, Princeton University, Princeton, NJ. wordnet.princeton.edu/ (accessed August 4, 2012)

Zadeh, L. (1983). The Role of Fuzzy Logic in the Management of Uncertainty in Expert Systems, *Fuzzy Sets and Systems*, vol. 11, pp. 199–227.

Appendixes

SUMMARY: KNOWLEDGE ENGINEERING GUIDELINES

Knowledge Base Guidelines

Guideline 3.1. Work with only one knowledge base loaded in memory (p. 111)
Guideline 3.2. Create a knowledge base and save successive versions (p. 111)

Modeling Guidelines

Guideline 4.1. Structure the modeling process based on the agent's specification (p. 147)
Guideline 4.2. Define reduction trees in natural language using simple questions (p. 148)
Guideline 4.3. Identify the specific instances, the generic instances, and the constants (p. 148)
Guideline 4.4. Guide the reduction by the possible need of future changes (p. 149)
Guideline 4.5. Learn and reuse reduction patterns (p. 149)

Ontology Development Guidelines

Guideline 6.1. Define similar siblings (p. 186)
Guideline 6.2. Group similar siblings under natural concepts (p. 187)
Guideline 6.3. Recognize that a single subconcept may indicate ontology incompleteness or error (p. 187)
Guideline 6.4. Adopt and follow a naming convention (p. 188)
Guideline 6.5. Name subconcepts based on superconcepts (p. 189)
Guideline 6.6. Represent well-established categories from the real world as concepts (p. 195)
Guideline 6.7. Define concepts and instances to represent knowledge corresponding to n-ary relations (p. 196)
Guideline 6.8. Define feature names that distinguish them from concept names (p. 196)

Guidelines for Rule and Hypothesis Learning

Guideline 9.1. Properly identify all the entities in the example before starting rule learning (p. 285)
Guideline 9.2. Avoid learning from examples that are too specific (p. 286)

Guidelines for Rule Refinement

Abstraction Guideline

Planning Guidelines

SUMMARY: OPERATIONS WITH DISCIPLE-EBR

Evidence-based Reasoning: Connecting the Dots

Methodologies and Tools for Agent Design and Development

Modeling the Problem-Solving Process

Ontologies

Ontology Design and Development

Rule Learning

Rule Refinement

Operation 10.1. Refine rule with positive example (p. 319)
Operation 10.2. Refine rule with negative example (p. 320)
Operation 10.3. Replace a generated reasoning step with a modeling step (p. 320)
Operation 10.4. View a rule with the Rule Browser (p. 320)
Operation 10.5. Delete a rule with the Rule Browser (p. 321)

Abstraction of Reasoning

Operation 11.1. Introduce a hypothesis into the abstract reasoning tree (p. 334)
Operation 11.2. Modify the abstraction of a hypothesis (p. 334)
Operation 11.3. Remove a hypothesis from the abstract reasoning tree (p. 334)

SUMMARY: HANDS-ON EXERCISES

2.4   Hands On: Browsing an Argumentation (p. 76)
       Knowledge Base: 01-Browse-Argumentation
3.4   Hands On: Loading, Saving, and Closing Knowledge Bases (p. 107)
4.5   Hands On: Was the Cesium Stolen? (p. 124)
       Knowledge Base: 02-Evidence-based-Analysis
4.6   Hands On: Hypothesis Analysis and Evidence Search and Representation (p. 130)
       Knowledge Base: 03-Evidence-Search
4.8   Hands On: Believability Analysis (p. 140)
       Knowledge Base: 04-Believability-Analysis
4.10   Hands On: Modeling, Formalization, and Pattern Learning (p. 144)
       Knowledge Base: 05-Modeling-Learning
4.11   Hands On: Analysis Based on Learned Patterns (p. 146)
       Knowledge Base: 06-Analysis-Reuse
5.11   Hands On: Browsing an Ontology (p. 165)
       Knowledge Base: 07-Ontology-Browsing
6.5   Hands On: Developing a Hierarchy of Concepts and Instances (p. 180)
       Knowledge Base: 08-Ontology-Development-Objects
6.7   Hands On: Developing a Hierarchy of Features (p. 189)
       Knowledge Base: 09-Ontology-Development-Features
6.8   Hands On: Defining Instances and Their Features (p. 192)
       Knowledge Base: 10-Ontology-Development-Facts
9.11   Hands On: Rule and Hypotheses Learning (p. 275)
       Knowledge Base: 11-Rule-Learning
                      11-Rule-Learning-short
9.12.5 Hands On: Explanations with Functions and Comparisons (p. 285)
       Knowledge Base: 12-Explanations
10.5   Hands On: Rule Refinement (p. 319)
       Knowledge Base: 13-Rule-Refinement
                      13-Rule-Refinement-short
11.4   Hands On: Abstraction of Reasoning (p. 331)
       Knowledge Base: 14-Abstractions

Index

Printed in the United States
by Baker & Taylor Publisher Services